Dao Companions to Chin

Volume 17

While "philosophy" is a Western term, philosophy is not something exclusively Western. In this increasingly globalized world, the importance of non-Western philosophy is becoming more and more obvious. Among all the non-Western traditions, Chinese philosophy is certainly one of the richest. In a history of more than 2500 years, many extremely important classics, philosophers, and schools have emerged. As China is becoming an economic power today, it is only natural that more and more people are interested in learning about the cultural traditions, including the philosophical tradition, of China.

The Dao Companions to Chinese Philosophy series aims to provide the most comprehensive and most up-to-date introduction to various aspects of Chinese philosophy as well as philosophical traditions heavily influenced by it. Each volume in this series focuses on an individual school, text, or person.

All books to be published in this Series will be fully peer-reviewed before final acceptance.

Thierry Meynard • Philippe Major
Editors

Dao Companion to Liang Shuming's Philosophy

Editors
Thierry Meynard
Sun Yat-sen University
Guangzhou, China

Philippe Major
University of Basel
Basel, Switzerland

ISSN 2211-0275 ISSN 2542-8780 (electronic)
Dao Companions to Chinese Philosophy
ISBN 978-3-031-18004-0 ISBN 978-3-031-18002-6 (eBook)
https://doi.org/10.1007/978-3-031-18002-6

This Springer imprint is published by the registered company Springer Nature Switzerland AG
The registered company address is: Gewerbestrasse 11, 6330 Cham, Switzerland

Acknowledgements

We would like to thank all the contributors to this volume who have managed to work on their contribution despite many disruptions caused by the Covid-19 epidemic in their own personal life as well as in their academic institutions with restricted access to library resources and personal contacts. We also appreciate their willingness to adapt their contribution to our many comments and suggestions. We learned a lot from their work as well as from the debates we had on our understandings of LIANG Shuming's philosophy.

In 2019, Professor HUANG Yong invited us to edit this volume before the outbreak of the pandemic, and we are thankful for his flexibility with the schedule. We contacted most contributors by the end of 2019, and the chapters were written in 2020 and in the first half of 2021, during a period in which many of us had to work in on-and-off quarantine.

Finally, we would like to thank Christopher Coughlin, Shanthini Kamaraj, and all the staff at Springer who have been working for the production and promotion of the work.

Contents

Contributors

Guy S. Alitto University of Chicago, Chicago, IL, USA

Yanming An Clemson University, Clemson, SC, USA

Yim Fong Chan University of Basel, Basel, Switzerland

Joseph Ciaudo University of Orléans, Orléans, France

Hung-Yok Ip Oregon State University, Corvallis, OR, USA

Jingjing Li Leiden University, Leiden, Netherlands

Philippe Major University of Basel, Basel, Switzerland

Milan Matthiesen University of Basel, Basel, Switzerland

Thierry Meynard Sun Yat-sen University, Guangzhou, China

Ady Van den Stock Ghent University, Ghent, Belgium

Zbigniew Wesołowski SVD Monumenta Serica, Sankt Augustin Institute, Germany

Chan-Iiang Wu National Taiwan University, Taipei, Taiwan

James Zhixiang Yang BNU-HKBU United International College, Zhuhai, China

Huajun Zhang Beijing Normal University, Beijing, China

Chapter 1
Introduction

Thierry Meynard and Philippe Major

The aim of this volume is to provide an exhaustive and updated analysis and discussion of the philosophy of LIANG Shuming 梁漱溟 (1893–1988), one of the most contested figures of modern Chinese intellectual history. For the last 100 years, his thought has been interpreted in such contrasting and contradictory ways—as Buddhist, Confucian, and Marxist, as conservative and modernist—that it seems at times difficult to grasp who the "real" Liang was. Confronted with the many faces of the man and his thought, researchers can either attempt to discern the one identity that ties them all together or allow for the multifaceted nature of his thought to remain open and focus on the diversity and tensions inherent in it. The present volume opts for the latter option.

A self-educated man who never felt at home in the academic milieu, Liang held a complex relationship with philosophy. On the one hand, from his early years as a so-called "utilitarian" onwards, Liang was eager to deepen his understanding of Euro-American philosophies. On the other hand, he remained, throughout his life, skeptical of the figure of the armchair philosopher who never felt the need to put their thought into practice. Thinking, for Liang, was the first step in a process that remained incomplete unless it led to praxis. Like Marx, Liang thought the goal was to change the world, and not merely interpret it. As such, he regarded himself as a man of action and a problem-solver rather than a philosopher. As Guy Alitto notes in his biography, "Liang continually protested that he had neither the qualifications not the inclinations of a scholar or a philosopher; he was instead simply

T. Meynard
Sun Yat-sen University, Guangzhou, China
e-mail: meiqianl@mail.sysu.edu.cn

P. Major (✉)
University of Basel, Basel, Switzerland
e-mail: philippe.major@unibas.ch

T. Meynard, P. Major (eds.), *Dao Companion to Liang Shuming's Philosophy*, Dao Companions to Chinese Philosophy 17,
https://doi.org/10.1007/978-3-031-18002-6_1

'conscientious about solving problems,' and this was regarded by others as scholarship or philosophy" (Alitto 1979: 144n21).

To those familiar with Liang's ambivalent rapport to abstract thinking, the irony involved in devoting a volume to his philosophy will not go unnoticed. Yet as pointed out above, Liang was not *against* philosophy—he simply saw it as a means to an end. And he himself lived his life following his conviction that the goal was to change the world. It is this conviction that brought him to actively engage in rural reconstruction and politics, serving as a mediator between the Guomindang and the Chinese Communist Party (hereafter CCP) during the Civil War. It might in fact very well be his reticence to see himself as a "pure" philosopher that made Liang an original thinker whose contribution to the emerging philosophical field in Republican China should not be underestimated.

Liang's first contribution to the philosophical field came in the form of articles in which he discussed Buddhism, often putting it in parallel with the thought of Western philosophers such as Henri Bergson (1859–1941). Soon after, Liang was to become the first modern Chinese intellectual to publish a widely read treatise of philosophy of culture; a genre which has proven to be much more prominent in twentieth-century China than it has been in the West. Philosophy of culture became an important means through which Chinese philosophers understood China's place in a new world, and no Chinese philosopher of culture can avoid the towering influence Liang's *Eastern and Western Cultures and Their Philosophies* (*Dong-Xi wenhua ji qi zhexue* 東西文化及其哲學; 1921; hereafter DXWH) has had on the field.

From the 1930s onwards, social concerns moved to the fore of Liang's thought, but such concerns remained rooted in his philosophy of culture of the 1920s. In his works on rural reconstruction, for example, he laid out the particulars of his plan for nation-building from the rural ground up, but he did so on the basis of his philosophical understanding of moral reason (*lixing* 理性) as the core of Chinese culture. Published in 1949, *The Substance of Chinese Culture* (*Zhongguo wenhua yaoyi* 中國文化要義; hereafter ZGWH) built on his rural construction work in order to offer a path-breaking inquiry into the field of social philosophy. Although Liang admitted the value of Marxist class analysis for the study of some societies, he rejected its application to Chinese society historically, thus providing an interesting alternative interpretation of history that challenged what would become the established party line. Many of Liang's analyses are still of interest to this day.

Liang would later return to social philosophy in his last work *Human Mind and Human Life* (*Renxin yu rensheng* 人心與人生; hereafter RXYRS), published in 1984, in which he adopted Marxist terminologies to argue for a teleological historical model at the end of which stood a Buddhist enlightenment of humanity. Social concerns, in this book as in his previous work, were closely tied to a number of philosophical issues related to human suffering, interpersonal relations, and the metaphysical ground of morality, for example. While it is fair to say that Liang was not *only* or *simply* a philosopher, it is hard to deny the philosophical tenor and value of his oeuvre.

Moreover, Liang's influence on his contemporaries, and specifically on philosophers, cannot be underestimated. Although Xiong Shili 熊十力 (1885–1968) is often portrayed as the founder of what is now known as "New Confucianism" (better known as *Dangdai xin rujia* 當代新儒家 in Chinese), LIANG Shuming was in effect the first to argue for Confucianism's universal relevance in the modern period in reaction to the New Culture Movement and its vehement critique of the Confucian tradition. Although the retrospective association of Liang with the "New Confucian" group is certainly debatable, his influence on other members retrospectively classified as "New Confucian" cannot be denied. Liang's epistemological positions, as laid out in his DXWH, became a mainstay of modern Confucian discourses regarding the distinction between Western and Confucian/Chinese philosophies, notably through the medium of the 1923–1924 debate on philosophy of life and scientism. Finally, Liang was also the first of a long list of modern Chinese thinkers to integrate both Buddhist and Confucian terminologies in their philosophy—regardless of whether this was ultimately done, in Liang's case, for Buddhist or Confucian purposes (something on which scholars disagree).

Finally, as noted above, Liang's philosophy remained, throughout his life, closely related to his actions and the socio-historical context within which such actions were undertaken. Liang thus provides a practical example of a modern philosopher not only conceptualizing philosophy as a way of life, to use Pierre Hadot's (1922–2010) expression, but also shaping his life around it. This can also be viewed as an implementation of the Confucian ideal of the "union of thought and action" (*zhixing heyi* 知行合一) that was central to the Taizhou school (*Taizhou xuepai* 泰州學派) that influenced Liang's thought deeply, although it can also be interpreted as the outcome of a Boddhisatva pledge to help fellow sentient beings escape from suffering. Liang's philosophy, when put in relation to his life and the historical context, can therefore help us think through the meaning such union of thought and action can acquire for a modern philosopher.

1 A Mosaic of Liang's Thought

LIANG Shuming's philosophy has been the subject of an important number of monographs and articles published in the Chinese language: WANG Zongyu (1992), ZHENG Dahua (1993, 1999), and GUO Qiyong (1996)—among others—have published monographs on his thought, while to name but a few, WU Chan-liang (2000), CHEN Lai (2001, 2006, 2009a, b), WANG Yuanyi (2002), JING Haifeng (2005), PENG Guoxiang (2007), GU Hongliang (2008), LIN Anwu (2009), and YANG Zhende (2009) have published important chapters and articles dedicated to Liang's philosophy. Biographical accounts of Liang's life have been provided by LIANG Peishu (2001), MA Yong (2008), and LI Yuanting and YAN Binghua (2009).

The relatively high interest with which Liang's philosophy has been studied in the Chinese language has not, however, translated itself into wider interest in Western languages. Only three Anglophone monographs have been devoted to Liang thus far. Guy Alitto's biographical monograph (1979) on Liang is still unsurpassed to this day, although the fact that it was published more than 40 years ago in itself goes to show that more studies on Liang are needed. More recently, the main reference on Liang's thought in English has been the monograph of Thierry Meynard (2011), whose analysis of Liang's thought focuses on his discussion of religions. Another monograph authored in English by the late Catherine Lynch (2018) was published, focusing on the populist strands in Liang's work. In other European languages, only one monograph devoted to Liang exists, to our knowledge: the German-language work of Zbigniew Wesołowski (1997). A restrained number of articles have also been published in English, either on the question of whether Liang was a Buddhist or Confucian (Hanafin 2003; Meynard 2007), on his most important work DXWH (An 2002; Wesołowski 2005; Major 2017a, b, 2018; Lin 2009), on his relation with the philosophy of Bergson (An 1997), on his understanding of religions (Meynard 2008, 2012, 2014, 2015), his rural reconstruction project (Thøgersen 1998, 2002; Wu and Tong 2009), and on the question of democracy in his thought (Ip 1991).

Given that Alitto's work is biographical and Meynard's and Lynch's monographs focus on particular aspects of his thought, an English-language book-length introduction to Liang's philosophy represents an important addition to the European-language literature available on Liang. As such, this *Dao Companion* fills an important gap in the research on Liang, by bringing together research on the different aspects of his philosophy (Buddhism, Confucianism, Democracy, Religion, Rural Reconstruction, etc.), including aspects that have thus far not been covered by the extent literature in English, such as his work after 1949 and the reception of his thought in the Chinese-speaking world and in the West.

In European-language scholarship, one of the most debated issues has been whether Liang should be considered a Buddhist or a Confucian thinker. Another concern has been that of assessing whether Liang should be regarded as a conservative or progressive thinker, as a traditionalist or modernist. Our goal, in this volume, is to not to provide final answers to these questions, but rather bring to light the complexity and pluralism inherent in Liang's thought itself. In an interview with Guy Alitto, Liang in fact portrayed himself as both Confucian and Buddhist,[1] and he vehemently rejected the idea that he was a conservative or traditionalist—despite his appreciation of *certain* Chinese traditions.[2] Liang saw himself as a modern intellectual—only one that did not see tradition as an antithesis to all things modern.

The time has come, we suggest, to study Liang's thought in all its complexity. In order to achieve this goal, the chapters of this volume, apart from the biographical one and those devoted to the reception of his philosophy, center on one of the many aspects of his thought: Liang the Buddhist, Liang the Bergsonian, Liang the philosopher of culture, etc. Our hope is that such an approach will contribute to

[1] Liang stated: "You can say that I am a Confucian, a follower of Confucius, and you can say that I am a follower of Siddhartha, because there is no conflict or contradiction [between the two]." Liang and Alitto 2013: 21.

[2] In answer to Alitto's question as to whether he accepted "the designation 'conservative' that some Chinese and foreigners have applied" to him, Liang replied: "Of course I'm not conservative. From what I just said a moment ago, you can see that I'm not conservative." Liang and Allito 2013: 201.

revealing the many resources and identities of Liang's multi-faceted and multi-layered philosophy. What emerges from the present volume is therefore a mosaic of Liang's thought—one that does not shy away from the tensions and multidimensionality that inhere in it.

This approach also leaves enough room for the contributors to disagree with one another in their interpretation of Liang's thought. While some of the contributors view him as the founder of New Confucianism, others emphasize his Buddhist commitments, while others highlight his counter-enlightenment engagement, his entanglement with Marxism and Western philosophy, his ambivalence toward the Confucian tradition, the nationalist verve that stood at the core of his rural reconstruction thought, and his political commitment that oscillated between democracy and meritocratic minority leadership. Yet although the contributors to this volume offer at times divergent and opposing interpretations of the man and his thought, and although the editors do not always share the points of view of the contributors, we nevertheless have in common a commitment to the diversity of perspectives offered in the present volume.

The authors of each chapter reflect on some of the central themes that run through the entire body of work Liang has produced. One of the themes that runs through each chapter is that of the "union of thought and action" which characterizes his legacy. As such, Liang's philosophy is placed in parallel with his life and the socio-historical context in which his thought is inscribed. This provides a fascinating account of how philosophy is of this world. For example, the historical metanarrative Liang deploys in DXWH was informed by the context of the New Culture Movement and by his own intellectual journey, which Liang himself divided into three phases: utilitarianism, Buddhism, and Confucianism. It is not a coincidence that Liang's understanding of history is shaped by three cultures characterized by these three schools of thought.

Another theme of importance in the majority of chapters is the question of Liang's commitments to both Buddhism and Confucianism. While we felt the necessity to devote an entire chapter to Liang's engagement with Buddhism in his earlier writings, as some of the views expressed in them were not as fully elaborated upon after Liang's supposed "conversion" to Confucianism, we did not see the necessity to dedicate a single chapter to Liang's Confucianism, as the topic is recurrent in Liang's entire oeuvre from the 1920s onwards, and as such it is repeatedly addressed through the present volume by the majority of the chapters.

A third theme that marks Liang's entire oeuvre and that provides a thread that binds the following chapters together is that of the tension between his interests in existential and national or social issues, which in turn are closely related to Liang's own ambivalence toward the options of participating in social life (*rushi* 入世) or retreating from it (*chushi* 出世). This tension is moreover closely tied to Liang's dual identity as Confucian (*rushi*) and Buddhist (*chushi*). This tension is reflected upon by the authors of this volume in its manifestation at both levels of Liang's thought and actions.

2 Overview

The volume begins with a chapter by Guy S. Alitto, who revisits, more than 40 years after the publication of his influential biography, the complex and eventful life of LIANG Shuming. Alitto's account—which draws resources from extremely valuable conversations he had with Liang in the 1980s—offers a complex overview of Liang's entanglements with the major events and public figures of his times. The biographical chapter starts—in good Confucian fashion—with his family background and the tremendous impact his father had on Liang, notably on his penchant for activism and moral perfectionism. The picture Alitto draws of Liang's youth—that of an independent thinker and contrarian who did not hesitate to join the revolution that ousted the Qing dynasty—could not be further removed from the paradigmatic image of conservatism and traditionalism with which Liang came to be associated during much of the twentieth century. But Liang's early involvements in the tumultuous political world of the young Republic would leave him disillusioned—and looking for answers to his existential angst in Buddhism before becoming an outspoken advocate of Confucianism in 1920. Alitto then goes on to describe in great details Liang's gradual transition toward rural reconstruction, laying particular emphasis on the complex social networks in which the philosopher evolved: his commune-like style of living with disciples and friends, his close contacts with military commanders, his ties to the intellectual elite, etc. Apart from the fact that he never saw himself as a scholar, Alitto suggests that the key to understand Liang's willingness to give up his prestigious position at Peking University and engage in rural reconstruction efforts lies in his lifelong concern for the unity of theory and practice. It is this commitment to practice that would later compel him to engage in politics during the Second Sino-Japanese War, act as a mediating political figure during the 1940s, join the Chinese People's Political Consultative Conference at Mao's request in 1950, and engage in numerous private discussions on the fate of China with the chairman until their falling out in 1953. The chapter then closes with an assessment of Liang's experiences during and after the Cultural Revolution, up until his last days in June 1988.

The following chapters delve into the philosophical thought of Liang. Jingjing LI begins by analyzing the philosophical evolution of Liang in his early period (1913–1921). This period is dominated by Buddhism, which Liang sees as providing a better access to authentic transcendence compared to Immanuel Kant (1724–1804), Henri Bergson, and other Western philosophers. From 1913 to 1917, Liang adopted a metaphysical version of Buddhism which establishes a transcendental realm over the mundane realm, and in this period he criticized Yogācāra (known as Consciousness-Only or *weishilun* 唯識論 in Chinese) as being too attached to mundane reality. However, in 1917, he shifted to an epistemological version of Buddhism, and especially the interpretation of Yogācāra by Xuanzang 玄奘 (602–664), which establishes the transcendental and mundane realms not as distinct but as correlative. Xuanzang indeed proposes a deep reshaping of the relationship between the mind and mundane reality: it is not so much that the mind should overcome the duality between itself and reality by positing a transcendental realm over the mind and the world, but that our process of cognition should be transformed such that the mundane reality of the world is affirmed but without creating any attachment to it. Jingjing Li describes this position as "correlative non-dualism," and shows also its societal implications because the individual mind cannot be enclosed into solipsism but needs to work with the minds of all the other sentient beings to bring about a transformation of consciousness at the collective level. Liang's efforts in understanding the complex history of Yogācāra are nourished by his reading of the great Buddhist scholar Ouyang Jingwu 歐陽竟無 (1871–1943), the most powerful voice at that time against the idealist interpretation of Buddhism. But while Ouyang was mostly speaking within the Buddhist intellectual tradition, Liang was also engaging the discussion with Western philosophy, especially Kant, stressing that Yogācāra is superior to Western philosophy because it gives access to ultimate reality, a position which greatly influenced Mou Zongsan 牟宗三 (1909–1995). Liang's efforts culminated with the publication of *Outline of Indian Philosophy* (*Yindu zhexue gailun* 印度哲學概論) in 1919. Liang's intellectual shift had important consequences for his own personal life. While he was a devout practitioner of Buddhism in this eight-year period, he initially had the idea of leaving the mundane world and becoming a monk, but with his discovery of the correlation between the transcendental and mundane realms he gradually took distance from his project of monastic life and was then aiming at living out his Buddhist faith within the world. Also, in 1918, his father committed suicide as a martyr of a Confucian world in the process of disappearing. Already in his *Manual of Yogācāra* (*Weishi shuyi* 唯識述義; 1920), Liang shows his shift toward this-worldly life, stressing the transformation from ignorance to the wisdom of emptiness. But it is with his DXWH that Liang completes his return to this-worldly life through a systematic articulation of Western philosophy, Confucianism, and Indian philosophy (Yogācāra). In this new synthesis, Buddhism does not only represent the final historical stage of humankind, but as often overlooked, it provides also the overarching conceptual framework by which the endless human will expresses itself through material achievements and then moral insights before the will negates itself. By assigning to Confucianism alone the responsibility for ethical and political issues in the present world, Liang undermines the moral and political dimensions of Buddhism which were promoted at that time by Taixu 太虛 (1890–1947), the reformer of modern Buddhism in China. But Liang did not abandon completely Buddhism for the present age, because his advocacy of Confucianism can be read as a Bodhisattava's compassionate practice toward the ultimate liberation that Buddhism alone can give.

At the same time Liang was investigating Yogācāra, he received a strong influence from French philosopher Henri Bergson since 1915, and he declared at the end of his life, in 1980, his admiration for Bergson. Joseph Ciaudo therefore has some ground to call his chapter "Liang the Bergsonian." China at that time was experiencing indeed a rushing flow of new ideas, and same as Yogācāra, Bergson could provide a frame to understand the flow of consciousness. Bergson's ideas about evolution and life bear strong similarities with Yogācāra, as Zhang Taiyan 章太炎

(1869–1936) had noticed very early on. Liang paid more specifically attention to the concept of intuition in Bergson since he read it as an integral experience, which unlike Kant, opened to metaphysical truth. Yet the Bergsonian influence over DXWH is not so much to be found in the concept of intuition, which serves very different purposes, but mostly in the metaphysical method of Bergson as opposed to the method of science. This way, Liang could reappropriate the Asian traditions of Buddhism and Confucianism as metaphysical—but not necessarily anti-scientific—experiences. In the dispute between metaphysics and science in the early 1920s, Liang was an advocate for metaphysics, that is, for Bergson. Same as for Yogācāra, Liang made a creative use of Bergson to serve his own philosophical agenda. For example, Liang's notion of intuition has a moral import which is not present in Bergson, stressing its importance as a moral insight in the nature of humanity and society, something MOU Zongsan would develop decades later. Also, while Bergson had explained how the *élan vital* faces different obstacles which have been overcome differently in the animal world and among human beings, Liang investigates the different responses to the problem of life at the level of the three world cultures of the West, India, and China. Liang's interest in Bergsonian evolution resurfaced at the end of his life, in RXYRS, a work finished in 1975 and published in 1984.

The two previous chapters investigate the creative use, in Liang's philosophy, of two major sources: Yogācāra and Bergson. The following chapters takes a more thematic approach to Liang's philosophy. First, Zbigniew Wesołowski looks at his philosophy of culture which can be understood as Sinodicy or justification for Chinese culture against the background of the anti-Chinese cultural movement at that time. Liang defines three different cultural directions or orientations to solve the three basic problems of life, material and social survival, moral existence, and transcendence beyond life itself. While the West, China, and India had each developed their own culture to address specifically each of those three problems, Liang considered that the short-cuts initiated early on by Confucius and Buddha revealed themselves too premature since the first issue of material and social survival had not been adequately solved. Therefore, like the movement of New Culture, Liang stresses the need for China to develop the intellect (*lizhi* 理智) like in the West. But China needs also to uphold its emphasis on moral reason as represented by the Confucian sages. The first culture represented by the West had become in the modern age a necessity for any particular culture unless it disappears, and similarly Confucianism also acquires a universal necessity. But for Liang, the time for Buddhist direct perception (*xianliang* 現量) has not yet arrived. Liang does not oppose monks who take this path, but this would be counterproductive at the collective level of society since it was not yet prepared for this. Because the driving force in China at the time was coming not from India but from the West, Liang turned his attention to explicate the cultural differences between China and the West as they play out within social structures, and this led him to understand Chinese traditional culture as alive at the level of the village. In *The Final Awakening of the Self-Salvation Movement of the Chinese People* (*Zhongguo minzu zijiuyundong zhi zuihou juewu* 中國民族自救運動之最後覺悟; 1930), Liang stresses that the problems of Chinese culture should be first addressed at the level of the village, and in *A General Idea of Rural*

Reconstruction (*Xiangcun jianshe dayi* 鄉村建設大意; hereafter XCJS), published in 1936, he stresses the need to reinforce communal organization by schooling the entire village. Liang's analysis of Chinese culture and society reaches its mature stage with ZGWH, where he describes 14 characteristics of Chinese culture in a short chapter which has become a reference in sinological studies. While Western culture is based on intellect, Chinese culture is based on moral reason (*lixing*) and on moral feelings devoid of any selfishness.

While Wesołowski's chapter focuses on Liang's understanding of culture(s) in his work up until the establishment of the People's Republic of China (hereafter PRC), the following chapter by Thierry Meynard touches on the same period, but looks at another central theme of Liang's work: religion. While many contemporaries of Liang were eager to condemn religion as a pre-modern, feudal phenomenon that would soon recede into the horizon of the past as China would modernize, Liang held a much more nuanced and complex view of the role religion could play in a modern context. This does not entail he was not influenced in many ways by the various discourses on religion that took place in Republican China. Meynard describes, for example, how the Jesuit assumption that China had substituted religion with morality and was thus able to create a secular order was reintroduced into China in the Republican period, notably thanks to Bertrand Russell's (1872–1970) influential visit to China at the beginning of the 1920s. Liang's construal of Confucianism as what Meynard calls "an apparent religion" was thus greatly indebted to Russell and the Jesuit apprehension of the Chinese socio-political order as non-religious. A man of his time, Liang nevertheless held views that were sharply contrasting those of his contemporaries. Against the relegation of religion to premodern history that was rooted in Auguste Comte's positivist reading of history, which was highly popular in China at the time, Liang proposed the opposite view, according to which the future of humanity would in fact be characterized by a religious revival. Liang's take on religion was therefore built on the foundation of the three phases of his historical metanarrative, on the basis of which he distinguished three religions and assigned to each of them a different role and task. Christianity, under Liang's pen, is depicted as a highly organized social religion that lacks reflexivity and prevents the development of a true morality that emanates from within the individual, as opposed to laws imposed by an external God. Liang was indeed opposed to institutionalized forms of religion, including those promoted at the time by influential thinkers such as KANG Youwei 康有為 (1858–1927) or Taixu. As mentioned above, according to Liang Confucianism was not properly speaking a religion, although it could perform the moral and spiritual functions traditionally ascribed to religions, thanks to the Duke of Zhou and Confucius, who played a central role in the gradual transition of Chinese culture from religion to the ritualization of human life. Finally, Buddhism—purified from its institutional manifestations—represents for Liang *the* religion *par excellence*, insofar as it is expected to enable humanity, at the end of history, to achieve a radical form of transcendence from this world. The chapter closes with a short discussion of Liang's views on spirits before addressing the relevance of Liang's ideas on religion to us who live in the twenty-first century.

In the following chapter, Chan-liang Wu draws on the distinction between being and becoming in order to put forth the argument that Liang proposed, in the 1920s, a philosophy of living (*shengsheng sixiang* 生生思想) that offered a counterbalance and critique to the philosophy of being inherent in Enlightenment rationality. Insofar as it drew its inspiration from a variety of Chinese sources, however, Liang's philosophy of living cannot be conceived as a mere reproduction of German Romantic or philosophy of life (*Lebensphilosophie*) critiques of the Enlightenment. Indeed, Wu reviews the metaphysical, epistemological, ethical, and social commitments of Liang, highlighting the many origins of each. His metaphysics, for example, drew both from a Buddhist voluntarist emphasis on human will as well as an organic and dynamic view of life that was shared by Confucianism, Daoism, and Chinese medicine. Epistemologically, although Liang's framework remained Buddhist in nature, it also incorporated influences stemming from the shared language of Chinese metaphysics, and his comparison between Western and Chinese epistemologies was greatly indebted to his understanding of the distinction between Chinese and Western medicine. Liang also heavily criticized the processes of reification and alienation in capitalism from a perspective that Wu calls "an amalgamation of Confucian and socialist utopias." Wu concludes by arguing that although Liang's critique of rationalism, utilitarianism, and alienation bears striking similarities with German romanticism, expressivism, and *Lebensphilosophie*, it significantly differs from them in terms of the local resources from which it drew, and in terms of its greater emphasis on living as an active and organic cosmic process, on the need to break down the barrier between self and non-self, and on the limitations of law in achieving social order. Although Wu does not deny the influence of Western philosophers on Liang, he departs from readings of Liang that emphasize the centrality of the influence of Bergson in the development of his thought, rather perceiving this influence mainly as one of "confirmation" of ideas Liang inherited from the many strains of thought inscribed in Chinese traditions.

Ady Van den Stock presents next Liang the Rural reformer. In DXWH, Liang had advocated for China a dual path of Westernization and revival of Confucian culture, and because he believed that the countryside had better retained traditional culture, he decided to leave the capital Beijing and to start his program of national salvation in the provinces at the village level. However, he discovered that even the peasant culture was short of his own ideal and started to promote the need for a self-awakening and the recovery of the fundamental spirit of the nation. This spirit was not anymore defined in abstract terms but was articulated in XCJS in social, economic, and political terms. While Marxism explained society in terms of class conflicts, Liang presented Chinese traditional culture as free from class division, and yet the conciliatory nature of Chinese culture has prevented society to develop. The solution for Liang is not to return to the past as a conservatist would argue, but to build a nation by rejuvenating the culture through human emotions and moral reason expressed in Confucian rituals and customs. The true goal of rural reconstruction is not, in fact, the countryside as such, but the nation, with the creation of a new form of collective life where the individuals are awakened to their moral responsibility toward the local community to be built. For Liang, national salvation does not rely on politics nor on the state, but on the moral resources of the society.

In the following chapter, Yanming AN provides an interpretation of Liang's 1949 publication ZGWH, focusing particularly on the moral and social philosophies inscribed in the work. An shows that this work was meant as the first in a two-step process whereby the problems of old China would first be outlined before appropriate solutions could be proposed. Although Liang had the intention of completing the work with a study of contemporary political issues in China—which would lead him to propose solutions—he never managed do so after the establishment of the PRC in 1949. An's analysis centers on three aspects of ZGWH. First, Liang's redefinition of "the premature birth of culture" as one that involves the discovery of "reason" (*lixing*) was an important departure from his previous emphasis on intuition in DXWH; a departure An ascribes to the influence of Bertrand Russell, and particularly the distinction the latter makes between instinct, mind, and spirit. Second, Liang argued that in ancient times China had already experienced a departure from religion (pace Marcel Gauchet, who saw such departure as intrinsically Christian). Indeed, as Thierry Meynard's chapter also makes clear, religion had been replaced by morality in the Chinese setting, due to the influence of the Duke of Zhou and Confucius and through the adoption of a system of ritual-custom closely tied to the cultivation of "reason," understood by Liang in moral terms. Finally, Liang drew two sets of distinction between Western and Chinese societies. On the one hand, the role played by corporate life in Western society is contrasted to the ethic-based nature of Chinese society, which refers to the strong emphasis placed on ethical relationships between individuals within that society. On the other hand, while Liang acknowledged that class antagonism stood at the core of Western society, he rejected the application of the concept of class to Chinese history on the grounds that Chinese society was structured around *professional* (rather than class) distinctions between scholar, peasant, artisan, and merchant.

Hung-Yok IP investigates the political thought of LIANG Shuming during the Republican era first by situating it in the recent debates on the relevance of Western-type democracy in China (Daniel Bell, TAN Sor-Hoon, KIM Sungmoon). Ip shows how the young Liang enthusiastically adopted Western democracy in his first important work, with the belief that democracy will be beneficial to moral individual development, and also to the economic and social development of China. However, in the 1930s and 1940s he grew more skeptical about participatory democracy for China, and advocated a meritocratic minority leadership, though he did not support a one-party dictatorship, either of the Guomindang or the CCP. Despite his hesitations toward the political system that China should adopt, he believed that Western democracy could foster moral growth if individuals did not strive only for their own individual rights but also for those of others through political participation. Ip returns at the end of her paper to comparing Liang and Bell's views on Confucian meritocracy, as well as Liang and Tan's views on participatory democracy.

While for the most part the previous chapters deal with Liang's philosophy prior to the establishment of the PRC, Yim Fong CHAN addresses the under-researched topic of Liang's thought after 1949, focusing particularly on the last major work of

Liang: RXYRS. While the image of Liang in the Chinese-speaking world outside the mainland has been built around reports of his standing up to Mao in 1953, so much so that Liang came to represent the Confucian detractor *par excellence*, Chan demonstrates that in his last work, Liang shows signs of approval of Marxist ideology. Terminologies borrowed from Marxist sources and from Mao are in fact interspersed throughout Liang's text. This does not mean, however, that Liang had renounced his life-long Buddhist and Confucian commitments. On the contrary, Liang found intricate ways to reconcile the last two with Marxist ideology, notably by recycling significant elements of the three-tier view of history he had presented in DXWH. In RXYRS, however, socialism was to satisfy basic human needs during the first phase of his reworked historical model, while the transition to communism would see a rebirth of Confucianism. This would then lead to the full realization of communism, which Liang associates with Buddhist enlightenment. This goes to show the extent to which Liang felt free to entirely rethink the basic tenets of Marxism, rejecting not only the religion-as-opium-of-the-people thesis, but also—and more importantly—materialist conceptions of history. Indeed, for Liang, the driving force behind historical development was to be found in the human heart-mind, and more specifically in its capacity to achieve what Liang terms *zijue* 自覺 or self-awareness, which he explains by drawing from Yogācāran understandings of consciousness. At the core of self-awareness stands a sense of selflessness—closely associated with the all-important notion of moral reason or *lixing*—that allows humanity to transcend the limiting conditions of selfhood, first by forgetting the self and achieving "genuine morality" in the mundane realm during the Confucian period and second by breaking free of all attachment to the self in order to achieve supramundane enlightenment, as taught by the "genuine religion," i.e., Buddhism. Although all human beings are endowed with self-awareness and moral reason, the majority has until recently been unable to properly activate them, since the emergence of social classes led to the contamination of the originally pure nature of human beings. Indeed, departing from Marxist orthodoxy, Liang regards class conflict as the byproduct of the selfish identity that comes with class membership and that clouds the selfless heart-mind human beings share. The gradual fulfillment of basic human needs followed by the realization of classless society—along with the abolition of national borders—would thus come hand in hand with the slow but inexorable rediscovery of the purity of the heart-mind, which would in turn allow human beings to reach new levels of autonomy in order to then "make history."

The last three chapters deal specifically with the reception of Liang's work. After the founding of the PRC in 1949, Liang decided to stay in the Mainland and support the new regime, perhaps because he was hoping that his ideas could somehow influence the new regime. In fact, his ideas exerted most of their influence outside, in Hong Kong and Taiwan, and in his chapter James Zhixiang Yang looks at Liang's legacy, especially through the figure of Tang Junyi 唐君毅 (1909–1978). Both Liang and Tang lost their fathers in tragic circumstances, and the untimely death of their fathers was for both of them a moral awakening to uphold the memory of their father, to be filial through their own personal conduct and dedication to a Confucian way of life. Another common experience is that both were shocked by the radicalism of the May Fourth Movement. Tang had read Liang's works already while he was on the mainland, and while in Hong Kong, he made great efforts to promote Liang as the founder of what would later be known as "New Confucianism." He referred to Liang in his own teaching at the New Asia College, and arranged the publication of Liang's works in Hong Kong and Taiwan. The influence of Liang is also apparent in Tang's own works. Same as Liang, Tang recognizes the plurality of cultures, the universal value of Confucianism, the role of moral rationality in human cultural consciousness, etc. The influence of Liang is found also in the New Confucian Manifesto of 1958, with Tang being considered as its main drafter. The Manifesto represents the reaction of Tang against the anti-traditionalism which arose from the May Fourth Movement, and addresses key issues from Liang, like the vitality of Confucianism, the relation between China and the West, and the function of democracy and science in the Confucian tradition. On the issue whether Confucianism is a religion, Liang had advocated that Confucianism was not in fact a religion, but a substitute for it. However, Tang is more sympathetic to religion and tries to show the religious spirit of Confucian humanism. On the question of democracy, Liang had expressed its incompatibly with Confucianism, but Tang on the contrary demonstrates the compatibility between the two, on the grounds that the Confucian tradition contains seeds from which democracy can grow.

Huajun ZHANG looks at the broad reception of Liang in Mainland China since the 1980s from diverse academic disciplines, including philosophy, history, political science, sociology, education, etc. The study of Liang answers to the current questions about the modernization of the Chinese nation and about peaceful living within a modernized nation. Arising from those two questions, the first issue is about Liang's idea of Chinese cultural modernization. Scholars have moved away from simplistic characterizations of Liang as a conservatist or multiculturalist, as a Buddhist or Confucian, and instead are interpreting his philosophy of Chinese culture as expressing the customs and rituals of China and also spiritual values and attitudes with universal bearing, like the idea of *gang* 剛 (resoluteness). A second issue is Liang's ideas on philosophy of life. Scholars have increasingly acknowledged the importance of Buddhism in Liang's philosophy of life, while the basic framework of understanding still remains Confucian, not so much as an exclusive focus on reading classical texts, but more importantly as a focus on developing and realizing the individual human mind through practical cultivation. Scholars also paid attention to a concept of Liang developed since the 1930s, namely "ethical rationality" (*lixing*). This rationality is distinguished from calculative reason and underlines the selfless feeling toward others. The understanding of this important concept in Liang's philosophy of life has led to a better appreciation of Liang's late works, like RXYRS, which were previously largely ignored. The third issue is the relevance of the rural reconstruction movement for China. For contemporary scholars, Liang is not a conservatist, but he embraces modern social progress and calls upon the need of developing new moral relations in the modern world through the cultivation of the individual's ethical rationality.

Philippe Major and Milan Matthiesen provide for the first time an exhaustive analysis of the reception of Liang's thought in European languages, with a focus on philosophy but dealing also with politics and sociology. Are presented the first discussions on Liang from the early 1920s to the 1940s in English, French and German, discussions which are little known but set the stage for different interpretations in the decades which follow. Also, little known is the literature in European languages during the Mao years which deal with the failure of Liang's Rural Reconstruction and Liang's political thought. After the opening of China, Alitto presented his influential study of Liang as the last Confucian, which has set the ground for researchers to investigate his relation to Mao, the Rural Reconstruction, democracy, and his conservatism. Liang is also presented as a Modern Populist by Catherine Lynch. But the most influential view of Liang in the last 30 years was to present him as a New Confucian, though this was challenged by scholars who have read Liang's philosophy as based on Buddhism. In the last decade, new approaches have emerged, like an attention to Liang's production of discourse, to his social history, or to his cosmopolitanism. The diversity of views on Liang's thought in European languages reflects in fact the diversity of Liang's own thought.

We hope that this volume will deepen the understanding and appreciation for modern Chinese philosophy, and especially Liang's philosophy, in the English-speaking world, and foster more philosophical dialogues at a time when they are urgently needed.

References

DXWH *Dong-Xi wenhua ji qi zhexue* 東西文化及其哲學 [*Eastern and Western Cultures and Their Philosophies*; 1921], *LSMQJ*, 1989, vol. 1: 319–547.

LSMQJ *Liang Shuming quanji* 梁漱溟全集 [*Complete Works of Liang Shuming*, vols. I to VIII]. Jinan: Shandong Remin Chubanshe, 1989–1993.

RXYRS *Renxin yu rensheng* 人心與人生 [*Human Spirit and Human Life*; 1984], *LSMQJ*, 1990, vol. 3: 523–760.

WSSY *Weishi shuyi* 唯識述義 [*Manual of Yogācāra*; 1920], *LSMQJ*, 1989, vol. 1: 251–320.

XCJS *Xiangcun jianshe dayi* 鄉村建設大意 [*A General Idea of Rural Reconstruction*; 1936], *LSMQJ*, 1989, vol. 1: 599–720.

YDZX *Yindu zhexue gailun* 印度哲學概論 [*Outline of Indian Philosophy*; 1919–1922], *LSMQJ*, 1989, vol. 1: 23–250.

ZGMZ *Zhongguo minzu zijiu yundong zhi zuihou juewu* 中國民族自救運動之最後覺悟 ["The Final Awakening of the Self-Saving Movement of Chinese Nation"; 1930], *LSMQJ*, 1992, vol. 5: 44–118.

ZGWH *Zhongguo wenhua yaoyi* 中國文化要義 [*Substance of Chinese Culture*; 1949], *LSMQJ*, 1990, vol. 3: 1–316.

Alitto, Guy. 1979. *The Last Confucian: Liang Shu-ming and the Chinese Dilemma of Modernity*. Chicago: Chicago University Press.

An, Yanming. 1997. Liang Shuming and Henri Bergson on Intuition: Cultural Context and the Evolution of Terms. *Philosophy East and West* 47 (3): 337–362.

———. 2002. Liang Shuming: Eastern and Western Cultures and Confucianism. In *Contemporary Chinese Philosophy*, ed. Chung-Ying Cheng and Nicholas Bunnin. Boston: Blackwell Publishers.

Chen, Lai 陳來. 2001. Liang Shuming's *Eastern and Western Cultures and Their Philosophies* and Its Cultural Pluralism 梁漱溟的《東西文化及其哲學》與其文化多元主義. In *The*

Search for Modern Chinese Philosophy: New Cheng-Zhu Studies and New Lu-Wang Studies 現代中國哲學的追尋—新理學與新心學. Beijing: Renmin.
———. 2006. *Tradition and Modernity: A Humanist View* 傳統與現代:人文主義的視界. Beijing: Beijing daxue chubanshi.
———. 2009a. *Tradition and Modernity: A Humanist View*. Leiden-Boston: Brill.
———. 2009b. LIANG Shuming and Tantric Buddhism 梁漱溟與密宗. *Hebei Academic Journal* 河北學刊 29 (6): 30–38.
Gu, Hongliang 顧紅亮. 2008. *The Confucian Lifeworld* 儒家生活世界. Shanghai: Shanghai Renmin Chubanshe.
Guo, Qiyong 郭齊勇 and Gong, Jianping 龔建平. 1996. *The Philosophical Thought of LIANG Shuming* 梁漱溟哲學思想. Wuhan: Hubei People Press.
Hanafin, John. 2003. The 'Last Buddhist': The Philosophy of LIANG Shuming. In *New Confucianism: A Critical Examination*, ed. John Makeham. New York: Palgrave.
Ip, Hung-Yok. 1991. LIANG Shuming and the Idea of Democracy in Modern China. *Modern China* 17 (4): 469–508.
Jing, Haifeng 景海峰. 2005. *New Confucianism and Twentieth Century Chinese Thought* 新儒學與二十世紀中國思想. Zhengzhou: Zhongzhou guji chubanshe.
Li, Yuanting 李淵庭 and Yan Binghua 閻秉華. 2009. *LIANG Shuming* 梁漱溟. Beijing: Qunyan chubanshe.
Liang, Shuming, and Guy Alitto. 2013. *Has Man a Future? Dialogues with the Last Confucian.* Heidelberg: Springer.
Liang, Peishu 梁培恕. 2001. *Biography of LIANG Shuming* 梁漱溟傳. Beijing: Mingbao chubanshe.
Lin, Anwu 林安梧. 2009. LIANG Shuming and His Theory of the Reappearance of Three Cultural Periods. In LIANG Shuming's Thought and Its Reception, ed. Thierry Meynard. Special Issue, *Contemporary Chinese Thought* 40(3): 16–38.
Lynch, Catherine. 2018. *LIANG Shuming and the Populist Alternative in China*. Leiden-Boston: Brill.
Ma Yong 馬勇, ed. 2008. *LIANG Shuming, an Extraordinary Thinker* 梁漱溟思想奇人. Beijing: Peking University Press.
Major, Philippe. 2017a. Rethinking the Temporalization of Space in Early Republican China: LIANG Shuming's *Eastern and Western Cultures and Their Philosophies*. *International Communication of Chinese Culture* 4 (2): 171–185.
———. 2017b. Textual Authority and Its Naturalization in LIANG Shuming's *Dong-Xi wenhua ji qi zhexue*. *Monumenta Serica: Journal of Oriental Studies* 65 (1): 123–145.
———. 2018. Tradition and Modernity in LIANG Shuming's *Eastern and Western Cultures and Their Philosophies*. *Philosophy East & West* 68 (2): 460–476.
Meynard, Thierry. 2007. Is LIANG Shuming Ultimately a Confucian or Buddhist? *Dao: A Journal of Comparative Philosophy* 6 (2): 131–147.
———. 2008. Intellectuels chinois contemporains en débat avec les esprits : Le cas de LIANG Shuming (1893–1988). In *Le Sacré en Chine*, ed. Michel Masson. Brépols: Bruxelles.
———. 2011. *The Religious Philosophy of LIANG Shuming: The Hidden Buddhist*. Leiden-Boston: Brill.
———. 2012. Introducing Buddhism as Philosophy: The cases of LIANG Shuming, XIONG Shili and TANG Yongtong. In *Learning to Emulate the Wise: The Genesis of Chinese Philosophy as an Academic Discipline in Twentieth-century China*, ed. John Makeham. Hong Kong: Chinese University Press.
———. 2014. LIANG Shuming and His Confucianized Version of Yogācāra. In *Transforming Consciousness: The Intellectual Reception of Yogācāra Thought in Modern China*, ed. John Makeham. Oxford: Oxford University Press.
———. 2015. Confucianism as the Religion for Our Present Time: The Religious Dimension of Confucianism in LIANG Shuming's Thought. In *Contemporary Confucianism in Thought and Action*, ed. Guy Alitto. Heidelberg: Springer.
Peng, Guoxiang 彭國翔. 2007. *Confucian Tradition: Between Religion and Humanism* 儒家傳統—宗教與人文主義之間. Beijing: Peking University Press.

Thøgersen, Stig. 1998. Reconstructing Society: Liang Shuming and the Rural Reconstruction Movement in Shandong. In *Reconstructing Twentieth-Century China: State Control, Civil Society, and National Identity*, ed. Kjeld Erik Brodsgaard and David Strand. Oxford: Clarendon Press.

———. 2002. *A County of Culture: Twentieth Century China Seen from the Village Schools of Zouping, Shandong*. Ann Arbor: University of Michigan Press.

Wang, Yuanyi 王遠義. 2002. Confucianism and Marxism: An Analysis of Liang Shuming's View of History 儒學與馬克思主義:析論梁漱溟的歷史觀. *Humanitas Taiwanica* 臺大文史哲學報 56: 145–195.

Wang, Zongyu 王宗昱. 1992. *Liang Shuming* 梁漱溟. Taipei: Dongda.

Wesołowski, Zbigniew. 1997. *Lebens und Kulturbegriff von Liang Shuming (1893–1988): dargestellt anhand seines Werkes "Dong-Xi wenhua ji qi zhexue."* Sankt Augustin: Institut Monumenta Serica.

———. 2005. Understanding the Foreign (the West) as a Remedy for Regaining One's Own Cultural Identity (China): Liang Shuming's (1893–1988) Cultural Thought. *Monumenta Serica* 53: 361–399.

Wu Chan-liang [Zhanliang] 吳展良. 2000. "Liang Shuming's Generative Thought and Its Critique of Western Rationalism (1915–1923) 梁漱溟的生生思想及其對西方理性主義的批判 (1915–1923)." In *A Collection of Articles on the Academic Nature and Mode of Thinking of Modern Chinese Scholars* 中國現代學人的學術性格與思維方式論集. Taipei: Wunan.

Wu, Shugang, and Binchang Tong. 2009. Liang Shuming's Rural Reconstruction Experiment and Its Relevance for Building the New Socialist Countryside. In *Liang Shuming's Thought and his Reception*, ed. Thierry Meynard. M.E Sharpe: Armonk, NY.

Yang, Zhende 楊貞德. 2009. "Human Heart-Mind and History: The Evolutionary Discourse in Liang Shuming's Conservatism" 人心與歷史—梁漱溟保守主義中的進化論述. In *Turning toward the Self: The Individual in Modern Chinese Political Thought* 轉向自我: 近代中國政治思想上的個人. Taipei: Institute of Chinese Literature and Philosophy, Academia Sinica.

Zheng, Dahua 鄭大華. 1993. *Liang Shuming and Modern New Confucianism* 梁漱溟與現代新儒學. Taipei: Wenjin.

———. 1999. *Evaluation of the Academic Thought of Liang Shuming* 梁漱溟學術思想評傳. Beijing: Beijing Tushuguan.

Chapter 2
Liang Shuming: A Life

Guy S. Alitto

To sum up: I am not a scholar! I am someone who goes all out to do things! I've been in action for all that I am worth my entire life! (總結一句 我不是一個書生。我是一個拼命幹的人。我一生都是拼命幹的).*

1 Introduction

LIANG Shuming 梁漱溟 (1893–1988) was unique in many ways. He was the only twentieth-century Chinese philosopher who joined his thought with actual practice and created a concrete program of social reform and cultural revival. Throughout his life, he was the only consistent and persuasive voice in defense of traditional culture. He was the only major intellectual who was more of an activist than a scholar. He was the only major intellectual on the mainland of China who preserved his independence of thought even after 1949. Throughout his life he abided by his maxim "Unity of thought and action; independent thought" (表里如一； 獨立思考).

His life was singular also in something of an uncanny way: from 1900 through to 1953 (and again in the 1980s), his life ran like a thread through most of the major events, thought currents and personalities in twentieth-century Chinese history from the 1900 Boxer Rebellion through the 1989 Tiananmen Incident. Following Liang's life is like viewing twentieth century Chinese history unfold.

G. S. Alitto (✉)
University of Chicago, Chicago, IL, USA
e-mail: galitto@uchicago.edu

*Liang rendered in public this concluding appraisal of his life shortly before his death. Captured on video, he delivered these lines in an extremely vigorous, animated, almost desperate fashion (http://ny.zdline.cn/h5/article/detail.do?artId=8130; https://www.bilibili.com/video/BV1Zg4y1z7kW?spm_id_from=333.905.b_7570566964656f.2)

T. Meynard, P. Major (eds.), *Dao Companion to Liang Shuming's Philosophy*, Dao Companions to Chinese Philosophy 17,
https://doi.org/10.1007/978-3-031-18002-6_2

2 Family Background

Liang's family was distinctive, its bloodlines more non-Han than Han. Founded by the fifth son of Kublai Khan, the family occupied high-ranking official posts through the Yuan Dynasty (1271–1368) until its overthrow, when the family changed its surname to a Han one. The sixth generation went over to the Ming dynasty (1368–1644), and the family held high rank and offices throughout the dynasty. With the establishment of the Qing Dynasty in 1644, it started producing officials through the examination system down to Shuming's father.

Shuming's great grandfather Baoshu 梁寶書 moved the family to Guilin 桂林, which then became their official "native town." Although Baoshu had an outstandingly successful official career, censors accused him of disobedience to his immediate superior in his last post and so he was dismissed from office. That event placed the family into heavy debt from which it never fully recovered. Liang's grandfather LIANG Chengguang 梁承光 (1829–1864) although a highly successful official, was something of a spendthrift; he maintained several horses simply because he was fond of riding. He died in office at the age of 35 when Liang's father, LIANG Ji 梁濟 (1858–1918), was only seven. His mother's family was an elite member of the Bai minority people (*baizu* 白族) in Yunnan 雲南. LIANG Shuming's Bai maternal grandfather won a *Jinshi* (進士) degree and served as an official. LIANG Ji, however, inherited the family debt and not much else; he lived his entire life under the constant threat of insolvency. He maintained his family in shabby gentility by selling his wife's trousseau and his own calligraphy to supplement his salary as a tutor and later his meager official salary (Liang Ji 2008: 5–27; Li and Yan 2009: 1–2; WDZX: 1–2).

3 Father and Son

LIANG Ji's own childhood was close to what might be considered "poverty" for a scholar official class family. After Baoshu's sudden death, the family took refuge in the house of in-laws, suffering years of crowded quarters and penny-wise frugality, while his formal (ritual) mother, a highly educated woman, took in students and his natural mother (secondary wife) took in washing (Liang Ji 2008: 5–12, 127–128, 130–141).[1]

What a father says to his children is not heard by the world but will be heard by posterity; Shuming's father LIANG Ji was indisputably the most significant influence on him. Indeed, LIANG Ji's personality and character foreshadowed Shuming's in almost every aspect. LIANG Ji's own scrupulous Confucian conscience evolved no

[1] LIANG Ji's "formal" mother refers to his father's principal wife. She seems to have been something of a Confucian zealot when it came to principles of behavior and the responsibilities of the elite toward society.

doubt from his mother's vigorous oversight of his education and moral development. In turn, LIANG Ji passed on this heightened moral scrupulousness to Shuming.

LIANG Ji was a constant contrarian who stressed results, solutions, and action in the real world, an approach also evident in Shuming's lifelong efforts. An independent thinker and committed activist LIANG Ji devoted most of his efforts to raising the levels of both patriotism and public morals. He was a true radical in the vein of his contemporary KANG Youwei 康有為 (1858–1927), but unlike Kang, he addressed his efforts to the urban masses through popular opera and colloquial language newspapers. In 1902, he and his friend PENG Yisun 彭詒孫 (1864–1921) founded *Beijing Daily* (*Jinghua ribao* 京華日報), the first Chinese newspaper aimed at promoting nationalism and reform among the common people. To reach a broader audience they took another revolutionary step and published the paper in the colloquial language. He and Peng also established one of China's first children's magazines, *Enlightenment Pictorial* (*Qimeng huabao* 啟蒙畫報) (Liang Ji 2008: 27–29; WDZX: 16–18). As soon as he had an official position, he launched reform programs of various sorts aimed at relieving the poor.

Another like-father like-son trait was a persistent and scrupulous pursuit of moral perfection. This enterprise of forging oneself into an ethical paragon of inner spiritual perfection and outward propriety was a lifelong obsession with LIANG Ji. He set the most stringent standards of proper conduct for himself. The nickname LIANG Ji gave his son—"my replica"—was totally apt (SMSH: 98). Shuming followed suit, earning the nickname that his friends gave him "the proud" (*ao* 傲).

LIANG Ji inspired such filial emulation precisely because he did not compel it. Again, manifesting his own independent nature, LIANG Ji consciously cultivated a friendly, spontaneous relationship with his children, urged them to talk freely with him, and actively sought out their opinions. He purposefully encouraged them to develop a spirit of independence and taught them to hold their own opinions even in the face of parental opposition. Unlike most fathers of this generation, LIANG Ji refused to beat or bully his son, thus providing him with no firm authority against which to struggle. Thus, LIANG Shuming was forced to act as his own authority figure, critic and punisher (Alitto 1986: 5–9).

In 1899 at age 7, in keeping with his father's radical politics and unorthodox child-rearing, Liang began his formal education at Beijing's first Western-style school, the Sino-Western Primary school (*ZhongXi xiaoxuetang* 中西小學堂) (SMSQ: 57–64; WDZX: 10–12).

The parallel of LIANG Shuming's life with important events, trends and personalities of Chinese history began here. In June of 1900, thousands of "Boxers" arrived in Beijing looking to destroy all foreign influence. This obviously included the Sino-Western Primary school, which they burned to the ground. As a protective measure, the Liang family also burnt Shuming's schoolbooks. Unlike most officials, LIANG Ji remained in Beijing during the Eight-Nation Allied Armies occupation (1900–1901). Shuming continued his education in three other private Western-style schools and two Liang family schools (LSMQJ: II, 667–668). During this period, no doubt under the influence of his father, he developed his lifetime practice of voracious reading of newspapers and periodicals (WDZX: 10–12; SMSQ: 57–64). He also became a passionate nationalist who looked to the West for solutions to China's problems.

The next historical trend in which LIANG Shuming was embroiled was growing nationalism and anti-imperialism. At age 12 he took to the streets to participate in the 1905 anti-American boycott, searching Beijing shops for the reprehensible American goods. Here he also demonstrated his lifelong penchant for action and the unity of theory and practice. In the autumn of the next year, LIANG Shuming entered Shuntian Middle School (*Shuntian zhongxuetang* 順天中學堂), an elite Western-style institution. Many of his classmates also became historical figures, such as ZHANG Shenfu 張申府 (1893–1986), a founder of the Chinese Communist Party who introduced ZHOU Enlai 周恩來 (1898–1976) to it, and eminent Buddhist scholar TANG Yongtong 湯用彤 (1893–1964). Liang entered school considering himself and his ideas quite exceptional but he was soon humbled by classmates with more sophisticated philosophical views.

Liang's contrarian streak also began manifesting itself at this time. He developed a flair for controverting the generally accepted and was vocal in his criticisms of most established opinions, which elicited an evaluation from his teacher that he was someone "who delights in maliciously opposing others." Following his father again, Shuming was obstinately unappreciative of any of the treasures of China's literary heritage. "There was not one I did not despise" (WDZX: 27). He especially disliked China's traditional philosophical greats such as Laozi and Zhuangzi.

Politically Liang was also his father's clone as an enthusiastic supporter of constitutionalism, party government, and rule by law. In 1911, however, Liang departed significantly from his father's path. He joined the Revolutionary Alliance (*Tongmenghui* 同盟會) and was soon engaged in "pistol and bomb tricks," smuggling such items into Beijing in a mule cart in preparation for Republican terrorist activities (Alitto and Liang 2013: 26).

With the abdication of the Manchu court on February 12, 1912, all Revolutionary Alliance activities ceased. Liang and friends immediately founded the newspaper *Republican News* (*Minguobao* 民國報), where he served as field reporter and editor. He proceeded to Nanjing, the capital of the new Chinese Republic, where he had access to clandestine and secret proceedings within the National Assembly, the State Council and the reorganization of the Revolutionary Alliance party. Confronted directly with the nasty crudeness of actual politics, Liang became hugely disillusioned with the revolution. At the same time, he suddenly awakened to the viciousness of everyday life and experienced an intense existential crisis; he became acutely depressed, even going so far as attempting suicide twice.

In the early spring of 1913, when *Minguobao* was taken over by the Revolutionary Alliance, Liang and his friends left the newspaper. Liang also left the successor to the Revolutionary Alliance, the Nationalist Party (Guomindang 國民黨) (SMSQ: 1–2; WDZX: 38–40; WNLD: 3–4; LSMQJ: III, 3–7).

4 Buddhism

The previous year, Liang had become seriously interested in *Weishi* 唯識 (Yogācāra) Buddhism and began his lifelong vegetarian diet. From the latter part of 1913 through the middle of 1916, he devoted himself to Buddhist study and self-cultivation. He planned to become a monk but in 1915 published a short article and involved himself in a project with the influential journalist HUANG Yuansheng 黃遠生 (1885–1915) (SMSQ: 21–26; Alitto and Liang 2013: 27–29, 126).

His relationship with his father changed dramatically at this time. Not only were both parents vehemently opposed to his plan to become a monk (and so remain childless), but LIANG Ji and his son began passionate verbal clashes on politics. Although LIANG Shuming had become totally disillusioned with the Republican Revolution, he still saw republican institutions such as representative bodies and political parties as the only viable path for China's national salvation. LIANG Ji, on the other hand, viewed the Republic as a political and cultural catastrophe, and became anxious about complete eradication of China's moral system and values. LIANG Ji decided that he would eventually make himself a martyr for them (Alitto 1986: 41–50).

The year 1916 began a cascade of extraordinary events that changed Shuming's life completely. Although still planning a monkish future, he again manifested his unrelenting inclination for action, even amid his other-worldly contemplations. In June the would-be new emperor of China, YUAN Shikai 袁世凱 (1859–1916), died and the national assembly was restored, together with the formation of the "Good Person" cabinet. Liang's maternal cousin ZHANG Yaozeng 張耀曾 (1885–1938) became Minister of Justice and immediately engaged Shuming as personal secretary for handling secret correspondence (Alitto 1986: 51–52; Alitto and Liang 2013: 28, 167–168).

Also around this time Liang's published a long essay reflecting on the nature of human suffering and put forth Buddhism as solution (SMSQ: 1–20; LSMQJ: I, 1–22). Revealing a sophisticated grasp of Western philosophical thought as well as profound knowledge of *Weishi* Buddhism, it brought Liang overnight fame in both academic and lay Buddhist circles (SMSQ: 1–20). Precisely at this time Peking University's new president CAI Yuanpei 蔡元培 (1868–1940) was assembling his faculty for a completely recast institution. Upon reading Liang's work, he immediately appointed him instructor of Indian Philosophy (Alitto 1986: 52). Thus, at age 24, Liang became a teacher at China's premier institution of higher learning without ever attending a university himself.

Upon arriving at Peking University in November of 1917, it is significant that Liang distributed to the faculty not an academic tome but a pamphlet he had just finished that was a call for political action (Alitto 1986: 53–54; Alitto and Liang 2013: 83, 176). A year later in November of 1918, LIANG Ji made good on his decision to launch himself into eternity for the sake of traditional Chinese moral values. His suicide provoked vigorous public discussion (Alitto 1986: 17, 19, 54–59).

About a year and a half later, Liang Shuming shifted his advocacy of Buddhism to championing Confucian moral values. Naturally this has led to the speculative conclusion that his father's suicide had a decisive and definitive impact on his intellectual and personal development. In this author's opinion, however, this would be a gross oversimplification. Long before his father's suicide, Liang had often expressed approval of and advocacy for traditional Confucian values despite his personal commitment to Buddhism. Indeed, upon meeting with President Cai Yuanpei and Dean of Letters Chen Duxiu 陳獨秀 (1879–1942) when he arrived at Peking University, he boldly and vigorously stated his intention to advocate both Buddhism *and* Confucianism (LSMQJ: I, 344). A year after his father's death, Liang announced a radical shift in his public persona as well as personal life—from advocate of Buddhism to champion of Confucianism (Alitto 1986: 5–6, 21–25, 51–52, 94, 96, 210).[2]

It was in 1920, however, that this shift became public in a series of lectures entitled "Eastern and Western Cultures and their Philosophies" (*DongXi wenhua ji qi zhexue* 東西文化及其哲學). The book version of these lectures, published in 1921, created a national sensation and attracted an unprecedently large audience for a scholarly work; it also catapulted Liang into national prominence. He even appeared in public opinion polls on "The Greatest Living Chinese" (Zhu 1924; Weekly Review: 223–226). His regular lectures at the university suddenly drew such numbers of students and outside auditors that he was forced to give his courses in the main hall of the school. His outside lectures became major events worthy of press coverage (Alitto 1986: 75).

Liang's basic defense of Confucian culture was that its fundamentals would become the dominant world culture and so should not be abandoned. Although he admitted that China urgently required adoption of the then dominant Western cultural values of science and democracy, he argued that because the West itself would inevitably take up Confucian culture, a return to the "true" Confucian culture was essential. So, his prescription might be summed up in his words: "Completely accept Western culture while fundamentally amending its mistakes" and "Critically reappraise and bring forth anew China's original attitude" (DXWH: 202).

But Liang's major concern was still unity of theory and practice. Herein lies the key to his lifelong quest for a popular revival of Confucian values. How was this to be accomplished? At the end of the book, he clearly stated that although he did not have a concrete plan with specific content, "It should not become an enterprise just of small coteries; it should be widespread [throughout society]… We can make Confucius' path broad and universal" (DXWH: 202). He promised to follow up later with details about how to approach the masses and organize them. "Confucianism is not a kind of thought, but rather a way of life. I am still estranged from this way of life; allow me to try it a bit and I will have something to say later" (DXWH: 213). The next years of his life would be devoted to finding a specific concrete practice for his theory.

---

[2]It is important to note that what Liang abandoned was his public advocacy of Buddhism, not Buddhism itself. He devoted his life to the popular revival of Confucian moral values, but personally remained committed to Buddhism.

5 Quest for a Program of Revival

During his tenure at Peking University, Liang became close friends with Li Dazhao, co-founder of the Chinese Communist Party (*Conversations* 1984). Ironically, Liang also seemed to be appealing to the contemporary military elite, who often sought him out. Such men as Feng Yuxiang 馮玉祥 (1882–1948), Yan Xishan 閻錫山 (1883–1960), Jiang Baili 蔣百里 (1882–1938), Chen Mingshu 陳銘樞 (1889–1965) and Wu Gongbo 伍庸伯 (1886–1952) all sought him out.[3]

It was in fact Wu who introduced Liang to his wife's younger sister, a pure-blooded Manchu widow surnamed Huang 黃, whom Liang married in December of 1921 (LSMQJ: IV, 175–195). Liang married her "out of love of virtue, not sexual desire." Belatedly he was performing his filial duty. "I led my bride to pay obeisance before my father's picture and wept" (Alitto 1986: 73).

Despite his personal and professional success while at Peking University, Liang felt unqualified in his role as professor. As he maintained throughout his life, he was "no scholar," even in his specialty of Buddhism. As a self-taught lay Buddhist, he felt he lacked a thorough knowledge of the complex Buddhist terminology. Unlike most of his contemporary fellow intellectuals, he had never earnestly read the Confucian classics, much less memorized them.[4] He never developed a knowledge of or taste for traditional literature or art. Not surprisingly Liang attempted to resign his university post several times between 1921 and 1924. In late 1922, he did arrange to have Xiong Shili 熊十力 (1885–1968) invited to Peking University to teach *Weishi* Buddhism. Xiong had received some training at Nanjing, at the China Buddhist Institute (*Zhina neixueyuan* 支那內學院). Upon arrival, Xiong lived in the Liang family home, joining many Liang's students who resided there in a commune cum academy. Most of his life Liang followed this pattern. Until the Cultural Revolution he always lived with or near several of his disciples.

In the summer of 1924, Liang finally succeeded in resigning, ostensibly to go to Shandong to create a university in Qufu 曲阜, Confucius' birthplace. He had been invited to do so by a new Shandongese friend Wang Hongyi 王鴻一 (1874–1930). This plan fell through, but in Caozhou 曹州, Shandong province, Wang had a plan to create Chonghua Academy (*Chonghua xueyuan* 重華學院), in which Liang involved himself (Li and Yan 2009: 62–63).[5]

Back in Beijing in 1925, Liang resumed his commune cum academy lifestyle. During 1925 through 1926, however, Liang was somewhat depressed. He had been frustrated in his search for a concrete method for realizing his goals. Throughout

[3] Wu was a major military figure in the Republic. In 1916 he was put in charge of building China's first air force. He remained Liang's close friend until his death.

[4] Liang stated dozens of times in his writing throughout his life, and repeatedly told me that he was no scholar (*xuezhe* 學者).

[5] One of the applying students, Li Yuanting 李淵庭 accompanied Liang as a fervent disciple for the following 60 years and in the 1980s compiled Liang's *Chronicles* (*Nianpu* 年譜). Chonghua 重華 was the legendary sage emperor Shun's name.

this period, he refused several teaching posts. Meanwhile in Guangzhou the reorganized Nationalist Party, together with its ally the Chinese Communist Party, began preparing for the Northern Expedition, with the aim of reuniting China through military means. Several of Liang's militarist friends were now involved, and wrote to him repeatedly urging him to go to join in the effort. Liang was hesitant but sent three of his students to investigate the situation (Alitto 1986: 147, 154).

At the beginning of the next year, 1926, XIONG Shili and several students joined Liang. Included in the group this time was Liang's only foreign friend, the German Alfred Westharp (1882–?), whom he had met at a conference on education in Taiyuan 太原, Shanxi province, in 1921 (SMSH: 105–112, 121–143).[6] A Montessorian educator and passionate musician, Westharp was running a foreign language school in Taiyuan but moved to Beijing at Liang's invitation.

During this year Liang often met with WANG Hongyi who was urging Liang toward rural reform, an interest that Liang seems to have been exploring at least a year before. He claimed that the "sprouts" of rural reconstruction germinated in 1922. In early 1923, he gave a lecture in Caozhou (again at the behest of WANG Hongyi) titled "Nation-building relying on the rural villages" (*nongcun liguo* 農村立國), but still feared the idea was just a "subjective Utopia" (ZGMZ: 13).

In September 1926, the Northern Expedition was launched. At the urging of friends and students Liang did get as far as Shanghai and Nanjing, but never went to Guangzhou before returning home to Beijing.

In April of 1927, LI Dazhao was arrested and executed by the warlord ZHANG Zuolin 張作霖 (1875–1928) who had seized control of Beijing. Liang and ZHANG Taiyan's 章太炎 (1869–1936) attempts to save him failed, but got the family released from jail. A fund was raised for the family. Among the friends and colleagues who donated to the fund for the family, Liang contributed the largest amount.[7]

[6]A fascinating and mysterious character, Westharp (Chinese names WEI Xiqin 衛西琴 and WEI Zhong 衛中; Japanese name Furono Chūichi 古野忠) went to Japan during the war where he settled and had a long and prolific career as a writer. His name at birth was Victor Egon Friedlaender. His father Abraham (Adolf) Friedlaender, of Jewish origin, converted to Christianity in 1892 and changed his name to Adolf Frensdorf and the name of his wife and his four children. He arrived in China in 1913, and because European hostilities soon commenced, was unable to receive money from his wealthy family. At that point he got in touch with the famous translator YAN Fu 嚴復 (1854–1921) who translated some of his writings and also gave him high level Chinese connections. Westharp was indeed an odd duck. He studied music with Debussy, followed Montessori in pedagogy, and created his own psychological and pedagogical theories. He was an accomplished pianist who sometimes was given to such bizarre behavior as performing piano sonatas nude in a dark, heated room, his theory being that when performing no other sensations should be allowed to interfere with the music. Understandably he was viewed by some Chinese as a charlatan or a mad man, but because he was an unabashed Sinophile, and because his educational theories coincided with Liang's own, he and Liang became fast friends. Mr. Erhard Neckermann, a German Sinologist, gave me information in correspondence on Westharp's various names.

[7]Liang's grandson, LIANG Qinning 梁欽寧 (1964–), showed me the document listing contributions.

6 Emergence of Rural Reconstruction

In this year Liang committed himself to a project of local self-government and rural reconstruction. He had an abrupt and dramatic "awakening" to the unsuitability of Western "cheap tricks" for China. This event was primarily an awakening of confidence in China's ability to survive with modified forms of its own institutions (LSMQJ: V, 13; ZS: 12).[8]

In May, Liang took a second trip to the South to Guangzhou, together with two of his students. Li Jishen 李濟深 (1885–1959), the general in charge of the Guangdong provincial government had been urging him to go for over a year. At first, Liang resided in the home village of his student, but Li pressed him to go to Guangzhou. Liang did go, and as representative for Li, chaired the provincial Reconstruction Commission, where he first presented his rural reform ideas. Unbeknownst to Liang, Li also had requested approval from the central government to appoint Liang to a Guangdong provincial government post. As soon as Liang heard about this, he begged off (LSMQJ: V, 18–20; Alitto and Liang 2013: V, 17).

Liang's ideas on rural reconstruction and local self-government programs "matured" during his Guangdong province sojourn. The Guangdong government political committee sent his detailed proposals for approval to Nanjing, but the process descended into a tangle of bureaucratic red tape. Liang grew impatient with the slow turning of bureaucratic wheels and so concluded that "the opportune time had not yet arrived."

During the summer Liang travelled to Shanghai and Nanjing where he twice visited Tao Xingzhi's 陶行知 (1891–1946) famous Xiaozhuang Experimental Rural Normal School (*Xiaozhuang shiyan xiangcun shifan xuexiao* 曉莊實驗鄉村師範學校) outside Nanjing. Tao's was the only rural reform program that ever elicited Liang's unqualified praise and approval. It achieved this rare distinction, of course, by happening to coincide with Liang's own ideas about the nature of knowledge and his inclinations toward action rather than theorizing. Tao had reacted in much the same way as Liang to the urban-oriented "book education" system of the early Republic. A disciple of John Dewey, he had worked out a more practical alternative based on the Deweyan concepts of "education is life" and "education is society." Tao's philosophical roots, like Liang's, were anchored in Wang Yangming 王陽明 (1472–1529) and his doctrine of "the unity of action and knowledge" (Kong 1934: 319–320).

---

[8] It appeared as though he was now abandoning science and democracy, which he had previously held to be crucial for China. In fact, however, he was no less insistent than he had always been that China desperately needed to learn science and democracy. Yet there was a decided difference: he no longer believed that certain *specific* Western social, political, or economic institutions—such as industrialized cities and representative assemblies—should or could be imported into China. After 1927, he sometimes substituted the words "technology," "development of intellect," or even "economic development," for what he had previously termed "science." He denounced Western political institutions, but now he stressed "organization" (*zuzhi* 組織 or *tuanti* 團體) and implied the involvement and influence of the ordinary person in the affairs of the commonweal, as well as the guarantee of minimal civil rights. Examples from Liang's writings are numerous.

Liang also visited Ding County (*Ding Xian* 定縣) in Hebei province. During the time he had been in Guangdong, the China Mass Education Movement Association (*Zhonghua pingmin jiaoyu cujinhui* 中華平民教育促進會) led by YAN Yangchu 晏陽初 ("Jimmy" Yen 1890–1990) had moved into the county with generous American financial backing. Yan had expanded the old urban mass-literacy campaigns of the past into a broader program of general rural reconstruction, which included village self-government and agricultural improvement (SMSH: 224–232; Kong 1934: 67–75). From Ding County, Liang went to Shanxi Province. As soon as he arrived "Model" Governor YAN Xishan immediately invited Liang to a discussion of rural reform. Liang proceeded through the province, visiting some of the successful village governments and talking with the provincial officials who administered the village self-government program. After Shanxi, Liang originally had intended to return to Guangzhou, but at the end of 1928, Guangdong descended into political chaos, so instead he returned to his hometown, now named Beiping 北平. Overall, Liang was quite dissatisfied with the rural reconstruction projects he visited. Although he admired the efforts of the workers, he felt basically that the model-village method was hopelessly inadequate. "The problem of China will not be solved by education or by any kind of social service enterprise" (SMSH: 265–266). Ding County's project received a provincial government subsidy as well as funds and personnel from the Mass Education Association. Liang saw two harmful effects in such arrangements. First, the whole program was maintained artificially; once the outside source of trained staff and money was cut off, the projects would cease to exist. Second, they did not sufficiently involve the peasants. "The villagers see public property—either from the government or another outside source—as something that has nothing to do with them. And because the expenses do not come from their own pockets, they are ignorant of and apathetic toward public affairs" (SMSH: 234).

Liang's general conclusion was that unless the rural reconstruction and village self-government movement was a mass mobilization of the people by themselves from the grassroots upward, it would inevitably fail. Moreover, any governmental or official role in the rural movement would inevitably have a deleterious effect. Extending provincial or *xian* bureaucracy downward into the lower levels of rural society was not local self-government, but its exact opposite: bureaucratization, which was, in Liang's view, incompatible with mass mobilization (SMSH: 262–263).

Upon arriving back in Beiping, WANG Hongyi introduced him to two reform-minded young intellectuals from Henan province, PENG Yuting 彭禹庭 (1893–1933) and LIANG Zhonghua 梁仲華 (1897–1968), who had the backing of the "Christian General" FENG Yuxiang and his subordinate HAN Fuju 韓復榘 (1890–1938), who administered Henan province, to set up an institute devoted to research of rural problems and the training of rural reconstruction workers. Liang readily joined them and in October 1929, opened the Henan Village Government Academy (*Henan cunzhi xueyuan* 河南村治學院) and wrote its mission statement. The funds for the academy did not come from the provincial government but were raised by a member of the group (Alitto and Liang 2013: 160). Liang seems to have spent little time at the academy itself. He was in Beiping during most of 1929–30 managing and writing for the academy's public organ, *Village Government Monthly* (*Cunzhi yuekan* 村治月刊) (ZGMZ: 17; ZS: 34; XCJS: 106, 321).

In the spring and summer of 1930, CHIANG Kai-shek's 蔣介石 (1887–1975) Nanjing government went to war with FENG Yuxiang. Because his erstwhile subordinate HAN Fuqu went over to Chiang, Feng was defeated. Chiang's troops occupied Henan in October, and one of their first acts was to shut down the Village Government Academy (Village 1930 Oct 1.9). All was not lost, however, because Chiang rewarded Han with the governorship of Han's home province, Shandong. Han promptly invited the Village Government Academy group to establish a similar institution in Shandong and offered to give them control of an entire county. Liang immediately went to Shandong's capital, Jinan, to discuss the matter. Liang wanted a county that was "not too big and not too small, not too rich and not too poor," as well as near a train station so he could quickly go to the provincial capital (Alitto, *Conversations* 1980, 1984). Liang decided on Zouping 鄒平 county as the site for what would be titled the Shandong Rural Reconstruction Institute (*Shandong xiangcun jianshe yanjiuyuan* 山東省鄉村建設研究院) (Zhang and Xu 1938: I, 31–38; ZGMZ: 224; Alitto and Liang 2013: 153–155). For the following 7 years, Liang and his Institute would be paramount among several attempts to find a non-Communist alternative non-Nationalist blueprint for China.

Unlike the other attempts, however, Liang's was based upon a cultural solution to the problems of government. After visiting Shanxi province local self-government sites, Liang used a striking metaphor to describe what he had seen:

> The Chinese people may well be compared to bean curd, and the strength of the officials likened to an iron hook. One may take the iron hook and with the best of intentions come to help the bean curd. But no help at all is better [than this kind of help], because once helped, the bean curd will certainly be damaged. (SMSH: 272–273)

Any official government in the rural movement would inevitably have a deleterious effect. Liang's program would be based upon the traditional Village Compact (*xiangyue* 鄉約), in his vision a spontaneously generated and voluntarily maintained social group through which villagers would cooperate to meet their common economic, educational, and military needs. There was no need for statutes and mechanistic laws. Ethically based propriety and decorum (*li* 禮) would provide moral standards. The organs of government were termed "schools," with the "students" (the general public) electing a "wise and virtuous" person to serve as "school director." The director's chief function was to mediate disputes between students. All schools would be organizationally linked at the *xiang* (鄉), *xian* (縣) and provincial administrative levels ultimately to form one great nationwide social-educational-cultural system (XCJS: 205–207, 213–214, 262–263, 296–297, 312–314, 319, 364–365, 398–399, 400–410; ZS: 63–65).

The institute introduced new organizations, such as coops, new technologies, such as advanced types of crops, and new public mobilization campaigns (anti-opium, anti-gambling, anti-early marriage, and so on). It achieved almost universal literacy in the county. It revived traditional Confucian values and non-traditional new values, such as modern hygiene and medicines. All these measures were for the most part successful.[9]

During his years at Zouping, Liang developed a national association of rural reconstructors and made international contacts with rural workers in Europe and Japan. The Zouping militia system, modeled partly on the Swiss model of citizen soldiers, was notably effective; by 1937, 70 of Shandong's 107 counties had instituted it.

7 War Years

Liang's efforts in Shandong came to an end in mid-1937 when the Japanese invaded. For the following decade he was almost continually on the road, devoting himself primarily to the twin enterprises of winning the war against Japan and avoiding civil war. Liang did attempt to further the rural reconstruction cause during the war to some degree working within governmental advisory bodies, but most of his energies were taken up with political activities to keep the country united (Alitto 1986: 279–281, 288–292).

His travels really started a month before the war. Repeatedly invited to Chongqing 重慶 and Chengdu 成都, he finally went at the end of May. Lingering for a month, he gave over 30 lectures on rural reconstruction. War clouds had been gathering for months and both Liang and his audiences knew that the Japanese would continue to goad the Nanjing government into war. Liang's June 13 lecture, titled "How to Resist," stated outright that the only way China could win such a war was by mobilization of the rural areas. He argued that the war would not be won with military means, but only through expanding rural reconstruction work (LSMQJ: V, 1023–1032).

After returning to Shandong from his lectures in Sichuan in July, Liang spent the month rushing between Zouping, Jinan and Nanjing. Of his many urgent tasks, the most urgent was to persuade Han Fuju to remain in Shandong to fight the Japanese. In this he ultimately failed, so he had no choice but to pull his Zouping cadre and some of the militia out of the province. From that point on, Liang continued dashing about working for national unity until the end of 1947. He left the province just a few days ahead of the advancing Japanese. After arriving in the new temporary national capital at Hankou 漢口, he personally and in tears reported to Chiang what

[9]From 1986 to 1993, I interviewed several hundred Zouping residents who were young adults or children in the 1930s. They uniformly expressed great respect for the rural cadre of the institute. What they remembered best were measures that benefitted their own families. For example, if the family grew cotton, they were grateful for the introduction of Trice cotton and the Cotton Transport and Marketing Coop that the institute organized. If they raised livestock, they remembered the superior breeds that were introduced by the Institute. Of the hundreds of interviews, the one that struck me most was with a lady in her 80s who remembered her life according to "food quality periods." She put early 1930s into the highest level, along with the mid-1980s.

had transpired in Shandong. Chiang merely smiled, saying, "I already know about it all" (GXCGZ).

Until the middle of December, Liang was continuously on the move. He went to Wuhan, the temporary capital, as a member of the National Defense Council and to Xuzhou as consultant to general Li Zongren 李宗仁 (1891–1969). Stress from 6 months of travel probably brought on his illness in December. As soon as he recovered, however, as a member of the Council he was off to Shaanxi and Henan provinces for an inspection tour. His actual purpose was to go to Yan'an to see Mao Zedong. Liang had met Mao in 1918 at the house of his Peking University colleague Yang Changji 楊昌濟 (LSMQJ: VI, 198).[10] Liang spent over 2 weeks in Yan'an conferring with Party leaders and touring Party and government institutions. He met privately with Mao in his home eight times. Sometimes their conversations would continue through the night into morning. Liang was not altogether happy with Mao's attitude, as Mao would often lie in bed with his face away from Liang (*Conversations* 1980). Naturally, Liang emphasized China's unique qualities, while Mao, the Marxist, argued that all societies share certain features (LSMQJ: VI, 198–205). The week-long Liang-Mao debates ended with Liang concluding: "The reason China is China lies precisely in these special features. You overemphasize its common qualities and neglect its special qualities. How can that be right?' My debate with Mr. Mao ended here" (LSMQJ: VI, 205).

Continuing his tour, Liang entered Shandong in February. Once again Li Zongren invited him to consult, this time for the defense of Xuzhou 徐州. Liang spent about a month consulting with Li and communicating with some of his rural reconstruction followers. Throughout March, April and May, Liang scurried about trying to hold together his rural reconstructors. Li Zongren had scored a major victory at Taierzhuang 台兒莊 but the Japanese soon recovered and continued their march westward. By June, Liang was in Chongqing, now the wartime capital, and through the summer performed as a member of the Standing Committee of the newly created People's Political Consultative Conference (*Zhongguo renmin zhengzhi xieshang huiyi* 中國人民政治協商會議; hereafter PPCC). He put forward many rural reform measures, but ultimately nothing came of them. His militia plan, based on the Zouping model, did result in some action, but in early 1940, Chiang Kai-shek heard "rumors" about these activities and ordered Liang's Military Service Association disbanded. Disabused of his hopes for effective action through the PPCC, he left the Southwest rear area. Instead, he wanted to go to the North China war zone to see for himself what the actual conditions were behind enemy lines, to reestablish contact with his followers in Shandong, and to find out how the detachment of Zouping militia and cadre—a guerilla war military unit called the Third Political Corps (*Disan zhengzhi dadui* 第三政治大隊)—was faring.

---

[10]When they met, Mao immediately asked Liang two questions: "Are you from Beijing or one of us Hunanese?" (Why are you here in a gathering of Hunan natives?) and "When were you born?" (to ascertain who was "senior").

After a Communist New Fourth Army unit helped him cross into Shandong, the Eighth Route 115th Division took over as his escort. Twice the timely intervention of New Fourth and Eighth Route troops rescued Liang and his party from the Japanese.

In early June 1939 his party was in Shandong's mountainous Mengyin 蒙陰 county when the Japanese launched a "mopping up" campaign. During the resulting chaos, Liang and a few followers were separated from the main body (Alitto 1986: 292–295). The Japanese launched a second attack and so they fled without sleep in a pouring rain, marched along a rough, precipitous mountain trail "in pitch blackness (torches would attract the enemy's attention) … holding on to each other's clothing and not… speaking. Twice people slipped and fell into the crevasses, and we had no way of knowing if they survived or not…. [Wet, cold], hungry, and tired, we marched on… to daybreak." In the morning "I found my way down the mountainside and met up with two or three others. We went in search of a place to dry off and eat…. [When] one of the staff reported that the enemy was approaching… we ran for cover… [and eventually] hid .. in a big cave…. Outside the cave the Third Political Coups and other Chinese troops "battled [the Japanese]… At dusk, the firing died down, and by night had stopped altogether…. The next morning the battle resumed as furiously as the day before. A Japanese patrol passed by the mouth of the cave, but it did not search inside." In midafternoon, both armies withdrew, and Liang, together with one rural reconstuctor student, made their way out of the county (LSMQJ: VI, 243–244).

Even more troubling to Liang than witnessing the destruction of the Third Political Corps (and almost losing his own life), was the discovery of a hidden but ferocious Nationalist- Communist civil war raging behind enemy lines.

In the early fall of 1939, Liang arrived in Chengdu with a plan for national unity already in mind. After reporting to CHIANG Kai-shek on his trip, he met with other rural reconstruction and liberal political leaders. Encouraged by the initial reception of his plan, Liang proceeded to Chongqing to contact other minor political party leaders. On the evening of November 29, he had a formal audience with Chiang to request official permission to establish his Association of Comrades for National Unity and Construction (*tongyi jianguo tongzhihui* 統一建國同志會). Although Chiang was less than pleased, he did give the Association his public blessing. Thus the "third force" in Chinese politics was born. It was destined for an exciting but foredoomed life of 8 years.

By the end of 1940, however, Liang concluded that only an independent, democratic political party could save the deteriorating situation. He hoped that a third political party would signal the beginning of an entirely new political system. In March, when word came of a serious, large-scale Nationalist-Communist military clash in Hupei, Liang immediately proposed that his Comrades Association mediate the dispute. Both CHIANG Kai-shek and the Chinese Communist Party initially responded positively, but in the end, nothing came of it. Consequently, on March 25, he and his colleagues founded an actual political party, the "League of Chinese Democratic Political Groups" (*Zhongguo minzhu zhengtuan datongmeng* 中國民主政團大同盟). It brought together Liang's Rural Reconstruction group, the Chinese

Youth Party, the National Socialist Party, the Third Party, the Vocational Education Group, and the National Salvation Association. Liang secretly decamped to the sanctuary of Hong Kong where he created the party's newspaper, *Light* (*Guangmingbao* 光明報).

The Nationalist Party's reaction was quick and hostile: just 2 days later, SUN Ke 孫科 (1891–1973)—son of SUN Yat-sen and president of the legislative *yuan*—was in Hong Kong making speeches against the league program; the pro-Nationalist party Hong Kong newspaper, *Liangxinhua* (良心話), opened a barrage of vitriolic attacks on Liang and the league; at the request of the Nationalist Party, the British authorities searched Liang's house; and some league members were dismissed from the PPCC (Alitto 1986: 295–298).

On Christmas day of 1941 the Japanese army stormed into Hong Kong and so terminated *Light*. After a narrow escape from the invaders, Liang made his way to his ancestral home of Guilin, where for 2 years he wrote quite a lot and, his first wife having died in 1934, remarried.

On September 19 of 1944, the "League of Chinese Democratic Political Groups" reorganized and formed the "Democratic League." Quite naturally, they elected Liang to the standing committee of the executive council and director of the Domestic Relations Committee. He did manage to avoid the chairmanship of the league by nominating ZHANG Lan 張瀾 (1872–1955), which allowed Liang to remain in Guilin rather than moving to Chongqing.

During his Guilin sojourn, Liang continued to participate in political debates and made a start on what would become his penultimate book, *The Essence of Chinese Culture* (*Zhongguo wenhua yaoyi* 中國文化要義).

When the Japanese half-million man offensive Operation Ichigo reached Guilin in November, however, the Liangs ran for cover in the Guangxi province countryside where he remained until the Japanese surrender in August 1945. With the collapse of the Nationalist-Communist agreement on coalition government in November, Liang moved to Chongqing. Upon his arrival, ZHOU Enlai called on him.

On Christmas Day, 1945, the U.S. Marshall Mission arrived to mediate the increasingly severe conflict between Nationalist and Communist troops in North China. To work out a permanent political solution, a Political Consultative Conference was convened in January 1946. For 3 weeks the representatives of the Nationalist and Communist Parties, together with the Democratic League leaders hammered away at an agreement to serve as the basis for a democratic postwar China. In his fervor Liang seems to have spoken more than any other delegate at the conference (Qin and Wu 1946).

By March, however, this agreement too broke down. In April Liang reluctantly accepted the post of General Secretary of the Democratic League and in that capacity scurried from meeting to meeting in an effort to avert full-scale civil war. In the middle of July, amid his frantic activities, two Yunnan League leaders—WEN Yiduo 聞一多 (1899–1946) and LI Gongpu 李公樸 (1902–1946)—were assassinated in Kunming 昆明. In his role of Democratic League General Secretary, Liang immediately flew to Kunming to investigate. In his public report, Liang straightforwardly concluded that the assassinations were the work of Yunnan Nationalist Party secret agents. On July 18, Liang publicly issued his report which he read aloud at a press conference. At the end, he ad-libbed "You secret agents! Do you have a bullet number three? I'm here waiting for it!" (Li and Yan 2009: 403).

Liang played his final act in the negotiations drama at the end of October. Without consulting Liang, ZHOU Enlai, or Marshall, CHIANG Kai-shek suddenly announced a National Assembly for November 12, an action which in effect would shut down negotiations. Zhou was on the verge of returning to Yan'an when Liang, out of desperation, wrote a proposal that would satisfy both sides. League leaders were enthusiastic, so on October 28 Liang sent it to Chiang and Marshall, and went personally to Zhou's house to present it to him. Zhou, however, was outraged that the proposal had been sent to Chiang and Marshall without consulting him first. Dumbfounded, Liang left, and then withdrew from the League altogether (Chang 1952: 182; Zuo 1952: 106). He returned to his school outside of Chongqing, planning to devote the rest of his life to writing and teaching (LSMQJ: VI, 612–620).

In 1949, Liang published *The Essence of Chinese Culture* and continued to publish articles commenting upon current events (LSMQJ: VI, 786–832). Some young leftists commenced prophetically ominous attacks on Liang in the Hong Kong press. (Rightists had been excoriating him all along.) They criticized and parodied his role in the peace negotiations, his withdrawal from politics, his nonpartisan independence, his praise of Marshall, his "Confucian spirit," his writings on public issues since retirement, and even his marriage (*Dagongbao* Feb. 13, 1969, Chang 1952). Liang did publish an answer to them stating that they did not understand him or the dramatic "misunderstanding" he had had with ZHOU Enlai (LSMQJ: VI, 796–799).

8 Liang and Mao: Final Chapter

Liang had planned to spend the rest of his days pondering Chinese culture and the problems of human life in his small town. His old friend MAO Zedong, however, was not willing to allow him to cultivate his Sichuan garden. He was named as a delegate to the first People's Political Consultative Conference (PPCC), the representative body in Mao's "New Democracy." Liang wrote to Mao trying to beg off, but eventually acquiesced, arriving in Beijing in January 1950. As Mao was in Moscow, Liang did not meet with the Chairman until the evening of March 12. They began their reunion meeting at 7:00 PM and continued to talk until after midnight, when they were served dinner, after which they continued their discussion, in the same pattern as their talks in Yan'an. The conversations went well, with Liang agreeing to inspect land-reform in various places and Mao agreeing to arrange for some of Liang's students to join him in Beijing. Based on his formula "In order to build a new China, old China must be understood," Liang proposed creation of an institute devoted to researching Chinese culture; Mao agreed in principle (Li and Yan 2009: 217–222; *Conversations* 1984). An enormous fly, however, was lurking in the meeting ointment. Mao had planned to have Liang join the new government in an official capacity. When he replied to the invitation with "Wouldn't it be good if I stayed outside?," Mao "looked quite annoyed" (*hen bu gaoxing* 很不高興) (*Conversations* 1980, 1984).[11]

Beginning in March Liang did spend 6 months traveling through North China inspecting local governments, factories and land-reform. In October, he returned to Beijing reporting directly to Mao on his experiences. He was satisfied enough with the Communists and their programs to issue a public statement of approval (LSMQJ: VI, 840–889). In 1951 Liang went to Sichuan to inspect land reform, and again reported personally to Mao (Li and Yan 2009: 223–224).

From March 1950 through to September 1953, Mao often sent a car to bring Liang to his residence for private discussions (Alitto and Liang 2013: 172). They were a continuation of their 1938 talks in Yan'an. Their close personal relationship ended dramatically in September 1953 at a meeting of the Central People's Government Council (*Zhongyang renmin zhengzhi* 中央人民政治).[12] To put the "clash" in the simplest terms, Liang criticized the Party's plan to build up urban heavy industry at the expense of the rural areas in the manner of the 1930s Soviet Union. Urban workers were "in the ninth level of heaven," while the peasants were "in the ninth level of hell." This provoked Mao into a unique series of passionately ferocious rants against Liang (Mao 1977 107–115).[13]

What would explain his curiously inappropriate vehemence and exaggerated denigration of Liang? First, Mao undoubtedly felt that he was the champion of the peasantry and was outraged that Liang would dare assume such a role. Second, Mao had treated Liang especially well, had continued to take his ideas seriously and had established a solid friendship with him, so he felt that this "betrayal" showed downright ingratitude. Third, given his subsequent actions, Mao himself must have had secret deep misgivings about the Soviet Model of forced-draft industrialization. No matter what the cause, this ended their remarkable private relationship. Mao still treated Liang cordially in public, and Liang remained a member of the PPCC's standing committee and would be a member of the National Assembly.

---

[11] Liang explained to me that at the time he feared that although the Communists had won the civil war by early 1950, he saw signs that it might continue and so wanted to preserve his status as a middleman in future negotiations with the Nationalists. He was quite proud of the fact that he never had been a government official.

[12] This body had been elected by the much larger People's Political Consultative Conference and served as a central government body until 1954. The forerunner of the National People's Congress, it in effect was also a constitutional convention which passed the "Common Program" (*gongtong gangling* 共同綱領), the fundamental plan of the government.

[13] The tirades took place over several days, the actual unfolding of events was extremely complex and would require several pages to unravel. This was the only time that Mao utterly lost his temper in public.

In 1955, however, a national criticism campaign was launched against him (*Criticism* 1955).[14] The campaign touched off a larger wave of support and praise for him in anti-Communist Hong Kong and Taiwan, where he was hailed as the embodiment of the traditional scholar of moral rectitude who refused to compromise his principles for the sake of expediency (Qin 1955; Shu 1955). In the following years, Liang did occasionally make statements or publish small essays, but he was, in effect, silenced.

9 The Cultural Revolution

On August 24th, 1966, Liang and his wife were assaulted by the local junior high students ("Red Guards"). They threw many paintings, calligraphy scrolls, books and furniture into a pile in the courtyard and burnt them. Included in the bonfire were family heirlooms from Liang's great grandfather, grandfather and father. They occupied the Liangs' house, beat up Mrs. Liang so that blood from her wounds soaked through her clothing. They then threw the couple into a broom closet room at first without any bedding and with only their light summer clothes (Alitto and Liang 2013: 70–72, 109–112). The Liangs were ordered to sweep the streets and clean the toilet daily. Mrs. Liang was forced to eat raw loofah off the ground. At ages 70 and 74, the Liangs worried about survival. Liang wrote Mao and Zhou twice, describing their living conditions, but received no reply (Alitto and Liang 2013: 70–72, 109–112; Li and Yan 2009: 261–264). Yet years later, when asked if this treatment made him angry, Liang replied, "These were children. How could one be angry with them?"[15]

For over a decade following, the Liangs were relegated to small rooms around the city. Over time their living conditions gradually improved. The years of mistreatment took a greater toll on Mrs. Liang. She died in 1979 after months of being comatose. Liang personally kept the death vigil and recited Buddhist scripture. Shortly thereafter in early 1980 the PPCC moved Liang to an apartment in building no. 22, the "ministers' building" (*buzhanglou* 部長樓). Built in 1979, this was a modern apartment building on Beijing's major East-West boulevard in the Muxidi 木樨地 neighborhood. Liang lived there from 1980 to his death in June 1988. It housed famous cultural and political figures. Liang's neighbor across the hall, for instance, was the famous writer, DING Ling 丁玲 (1904–1986). LIU Shaoqi's 劉少奇 (1898–1969) widow and LU Xun's 魯迅 (1881–1936) son also lived there. After

[14] Simultaneously a criticism campaign was started against HU Shi 胡適 (1891–1962), the model Western-oriented liberal and Liang's opposite number. Critics referred to Liang as the "feudal" counterpart of Hu's bourgeois thought. Interestingly, Liang told me that "someone" surreptitiously visited him to counsel that he should not take the criticism campaign "personally," as its purpose had little to do with him as an individual (*Conversations* 1980, 1984).

[15] His grandson Liang Qinning 梁欽寧 posed the question. He told me of the incident many times.

this move to more comfortable and presentable quarters, Liang could receive foreign visitors.[16]

10 Resurrection and Concluding Mortality

With the relaxation of the political atmosphere, Liang once more came into the public eye. He seems to have become an underground hero to dissenting-minded students because of his 1953 confrontation with MAO Zedong. During the 1980s, the "Cultures Question" once again became the focus of many intellectuals and so Liang, as a major figure, was once more the center of attention. The "Chinese Culture Academy" (*Zhongguo wenhua shuyuan* 中國文化書院) that Liang had intreated Mao for in 1950 was created in October 1984 (Figs. 2.1 and 2.2).

His last book *The Human Heart/mind and Human Life* (*Renxin yu rensheng* 人心與人生) finally came out in 1984. From 1980 through 1987, he continued to write and publish and was quite active as a member of the Democratic League and the PPCC Standing Committee. When I last visited Liang in the summer of 1986, he seemed in good spirits and quite vigorous for a 94-year-old. Although somewhat frail physically, his mental acuity remained unimpaired.

In July of 1986 his old colleague in rural reconstruction YAN Yangchu visited him at his home where they had a spirited and lengthy reunion. In October he participated in congratulatory observances of his 95th birthday. On October 31, the leadership of the Democratic League presented him with a birthday cake at a celebratory banquet at the Fragrant Hills Hotel. Over six hundred people attended. In early November the Academy of Chinese Culture held a symposium on Liang's thought where he made his last public address. In December, he met with famous Russian and Japanese Sinologists. He conducted conversations with a Taiwanese scholar on the importance of rural reconstruction. The same year nine of his books were republished.

This happy situation totally changed the next year, however, in a rather curious way. The year began auspiciously enough. In February Liang was invited to attend an academic symposium in Hong Kong. He declined to attend physically, but at FEI Xiaotong's 費孝通 (1910–2005) suggestion, he did record a video reading his short essay. Fei then brought the video to the meeting. As late as April 10, Liang seemed quite exuberant and energetic, as he had an animated two-hour conversation with the daughter of an old friend. Then, on the 13th, Liang suddenly voiced a desire to

[16] The June 4 Tiananmen Incident started with the army firing into a civilian crowd gathered in front of this building on the evening of June 3 as they were blocking the entrance to the traffic overpass at *Fuxingmenwai* (復興門外). The building itself was raked with machine gun fire, killing one inhabitant. Liu Shaoqi's widow's apartment was destroyed in the action. Liang's family members were still in his apartment and some were in the crowd fired upon. Although Liang had died almost a year before, it is interesting to note that even posthumously, he remained at the center of historical action, as he was from the 1900 Boxer Rebellion onward.

Fig. 2.1 Liang Shuming and Guy Alitto discussing *The Last Confucian* in August 1980

Fig. 2.2 Liang Shuming ca. 1984

pay his respects at the ancestral tombs in Liangxiang 良鄉, about 25 km from his home. It was a windy unseasonably cool day and Liang began to feel unwell (Li and Yan 2009: 346–351).[17] This was the commencement of a cascade of afflictions that culminated in his death. Just 2 days later Liang had so much difficulty breathing that he was brought to the Peking Union Hospital, where he was diagnosed with uremia. Although he spoke to visitors and family members after this, he became progressively weaker. In the middle of May, he sudden called out that he had something to say. When his son Peikuan 培寬 was at his bedside he said haltingly but tranquilly: "YUE Meizhong[18] 嶽美中 [1900–1982] said 'A doctor can cure illness, but cannot cure life.' A human's life span is limited. My allotted life span has been reached. Don't force me to stay. Let things take their own course" (Li and Yan 2009: 349). He thereupon refused medications to treat his uremia.

By June he had difficulty eating and repeatedly entreated to be released from the hospital and to return home. On June 20, oddly, he seemed to agree with the physician's recommendation that he undergo artificial kidney surgery on the 24th. On the morning of the 23rd, however, he suddenly developed tachycardia and began to spit up blood. When asked by the physician how he felt, he haltingly uttered his last words: "I'm very weary; I want to rest" and immediately expired (Li and Yan 2009: 346–351). Thus ended a remarkable life.

Liang's "posthumous career" blossomed after his death, with innumerable books and articles about him published first on paper and then on the internet. An internet search of his name results in over a million hits.

As stated at the outset, this was a unique life in many ways. Even given its considerable intellectual achievements, it was a life of action more than of a closeted thinker. Despite his huge writing productivity, it is clear enough from this biographical sketch that from age 12 onward, he devoted his life largely to action. Although he did not have the same political success, he might well be remembered historically as a Chinese Gandhi.

Explanation of Oral History Sources

I visited LIANG Shuming four times, in 1980, 1982, 1984, 1986. During the 1980 and 1984 visits, we talked every morning for about 4 h for a period of 2 weeks. In

[17] Liang's son, Peishu 培恕, described the event as his father "suddenly" expressing this desire. The actual "Grave Sweeping day" (*Qingmingjie* 清明節) had been on April 4th in the previous week. It was the first time in many years that Liang had travelled so far. This journey was a conclusive performance of a filial duty. I have my suspicions that Liang, at some level, had decided that it was time to make his way into eternity. Liang told me that he had had his fortune told three times. He said that two of the three fortunes he mentioned predicted that he would die at age 94, the third fortune stopped at 1966 but did not actually predict death. Liang argued that that fortune, although misleading, was not entirely wrong because in 1966 the Cultural Revolution did enormous damage, although it did not kill him. Liang had reached the chronological age of 94 in 1986. The way Liang described these incidents to me in 1980 certainly convinced me that he truly believed in them. In fact, he did mention the predictions to his sons, who urged him to forget about them.

[18] Famous physician of Chinese traditional medicine whom Liang had known (and was treated by) for most of his life. He was attacked at the outset of the Cultural Revolution but was protected and supported by ZHOU Enlai.

1982 and 1986, most of those conversations were recorded and transcribed in the two books listed below. Before, during and after recordings, I had unrecorded conversations with Mr. Liang. Some of the unrecorded conversations I vividly remember to this day. I took notes on others afterwards.

I translated and annotated the 1980 recorded conversations in *Has Mankind a Future?* For the convenience of readers who do not know Chinese well, I cite the translation in this book rather than the Chinese original, *Zhege shijie hui hao ma* 這個世界會好嗎 (Will this World Get Better?). The second book of recorded conversations is *Wucao buchu ru cangshen he?* 吾曹不出如苍生何? (If we do not set forth, what will happen to the people?), published in 2010 at Beijing Teaching and Research Press (Liang and Alitto 2010). In this chapter I refer to all unrecorded conversations simply as "Conversations."

References

DXWH *Dong-Xi wenhua ji qi zhexue* 東西文化及其哲學 [*Eastern and Western Cultures and Their Philosophies*; 1921]. Shanghai: Pacific Ocean Library, 1922.

GXCGZ *Gao xiangcun gongzuo tongren tongxue shu* 告鄉村工作同人同學書 [*Letter to My Shandong Rural Work Colleagues and Students*]. Pamphlet, 1938, n.p.

LSMQJ *Liang Shuming quanji* 梁漱溟全集 [*Complete Works of Liang Shuming*, vols. I to VIII]. Jinan: Shandong Remin Chubanshe, 1989–1993.

SMSH *Shuming sahou wenlu* 漱溟卅後文錄 [*Writings of Liang Shuming after the Age of Thirty*]. Shanghai: Shanghai shuduan, 1930.

SMSQ *Shuming saqian wenlu* 漱溟卅前文錄 [*Writings of Liang Shuming before the Age of Thirty*]. Shanghai: Shanghai shuduan, 1924.

WDZX *Wo de zixue xiaoshi* 我的自學小史 [*Short Account of My Self-education*]. Shanghai, Huahua shudian, 1947.

WNLD *Wo nuli de shi shenma?* 我努力的是什麼? ["My Endeavors"]. *Light* 光明報 [Hong Kong], September 18 to November 3, 1941.

XCJS *Xiangcun jianshe lilun* 鄉村建設理論 [*The Theory of Rural Reconstruction*; 1937]. Zouping: Xiangcun shudian, 1937.

ZGMZ *Zhongguo minzu zijiu yundong zhizuihou juewu* 中國民族自救運動之最后覺悟 [*The Final Awakening of the Chinese People's Self-salvation Movement*]. Beiping: Village Government Monthly Press, 1932.

ZS *Zishu* 自述 ["Autobiographical Statement"; 1934], *Xiangcun jianshe lunwenji diyiji* 鄉村建設論文集第一集 [*Collection of Writings on Rural Reconstruction, First Series*]. Zouping: Shandong xiangcun jianshe yanjiuyuan, 1934.

Alitto, Guy S. 1986. *The Last Confucian: Liang Shu-ming and the Chinese Dilemma of Modernity*. Berkeley: University of California Press.

Alitto, Guy S., and Shu Ming Liang. 2013. *Has Man a Future: Dialogues with the Last Confucian*. New York: Springer.

Central Daily News 中央日報. Nanjing, 1930–1936, 1946–1947; Chongqing, 1940–1947.

Chang, Carsun [Zhang Junmai 張君勱]. 1952. *The Third Force in China*. New York: Bookman Associates.

Criticism of Liang Shu-ming's Thought 梁漱溟思想批判. 1955. Beijing: Sanlian shudian, 2 vols.

Kong, Xuexiong 孔雪雄. 1934. *The Present-day Chinese Rural Movement* 中國今日之農村運動. Shanghai: Zhongshan wenhua jiaoyuguan.

Li, Yuanting 李淵庭 and Yan, Binghua 閻秉華. 2009. *A Chronological Biography of Liang Shuming* 梁漱溟年譜. Beijing: Qunyan Press.

Liang, Ji 梁濟. 2008. *Posthumous Writings of Liang Juchuan* 梁巨川遺書. Edited by Huang Shuhui 黄曙輝. Shanghai: East China Normal University Press.

Liang, Shuming 梁漱溟, Alitto, Guy 艾恺. 2010. *If We Don't Go Forth, What Will Happen to the People?: Interview with Liang Shuming in Old Age* 吾曹不出如蒼生何:梁漱溟晚年口述. Beijing: Beijing Teaching and Research Press.

Mao, Zedong 毛澤東. 1977. *Selected Works of Mao Zedong* 毛澤東選集. Vol. V. Beijing: People's Press.

Qin, Huanzhang 秦綏章, Wu Boqing 吴伯卿. 1946. *Complete Record of the Political Consultative Conference* 政治協商會議始末記. Zhongxin chubanshe: Changsha.

Qin, Jing 秦鏡. 1955. Settling Accounts Again with Liang Shuming 梁漱溟再遭清. *Democratic Critic* 民主評論 6: 11.

Shu, Ying 樹瑩. 1955, October 14. Liang Shu-ming Becomes the Target of Public Attacks 梁漱溟成眾矢之的. *Observatory Journal* 天文台報. Hong Kong.

The China Weekly Review. 1923, January 6. Shanghai.

Village Government Monthly 村治月刊. 1929–1930. Beiping: Village Government Monthly Press.

Zhang, Yuanshan 章元善, Xu Shilian 許仕廉, eds. 1936–1938. *Experiments in Rural Reconstruction* 鄉村建設實驗. Shanghai: Zhonghua shuju, 3 vol.

Zhu, Wushan 朱悟禪. 1924. Analysis of the Peking University's Twenty-fifth Anniversary Public Opinion Survey 北大二十五週年紀念日「民意測量」之分析. *New Republic* 新民國 1: 5.

Zuo, Shunsheng 左舜生. 1952. *Random Recollections of the Past Thirty Years* 近三十年見聞雜記. Hong Kong: Ziyou chubanshe.

Chapter 3
Liang the Buddhist

Jingjing Li

1 Introduction

This chapter focuses on the early writings of Liang Shuming 梁漱溟 (1893–1988). I speak of Liang as a "Buddhist" to capture the profound influence of Buddhism, especially that of the Yogācāra doctrine of "consciousness-only" (*weishi* 唯識, *vijñaptimātra*), on this phase of his thought. The term "Buddhist" is used in three overlapping ways. First, it highlights how Liang openly presented himself as a practicing Buddhist from 1913 to 1921. Second, it pinpoints the source of inspiration for his philosophical thinking. Third, it indicates the significance of Buddhism in his worldview.

The first sense in which Liang is a Buddhist stems from a narrative popularized by Liang himself. Since the 1930s, Liang described how he was an advocate of Western utilitarianism and pragmatism before 1913, a devout Buddhist from 1913 to 1921, and eventually a family-centered Confucian from 1921 onwards. In light of this narrative, Liang has been perceived as a proponent of Confucianism.[1] Nevertheless, his engage-

[1]Due to Liang's promotion of Confucianism, he was first recognized as a cultural conservative (Alitto 1976, 1979). Later on, scholars, championed by Chang Hao, argued for classifying Liang as a "contemporary New Confucian" (*dangdai xinrujia* 當代新儒家) because of Liang's contribution to the modern reform of this tradition (Chang 1976; Wei 1984; Cao 1995; Lin 1996; Zheng 1999; Yang 2003; Wesołowski 2003; Gu 2008; Ma 2008; Guo and Gong 2011; Chen 2014). While many acknowledge Liang's engagement with Buddhism and Confucianism (Wang 1986; Gong 1996), the foundational role of Buddhism in Liang's philosophy has been rediscovered recently (Zhang 2001; Hanafin 2003; Meynard 2007, 2011, 2014; Lee 2015). To highlight the multifaceted nature of Liang's thought, scholars have gone beyond the Buddhist-Confucian binary to read Liang as an advocate of voluntarism (Gao 1991) or populism (Lynch 2018).

J. Li (✉)
Leiden University, Leiden, The Netherlands
e-mail: j.li@phil.leidenuniv.nl

T. Meynard, P. Major (eds.), *Dao Companion to Liang Shuming's Philosophy*, Dao Companions to Chinese Philosophy 17,
https://doi.org/10.1007/978-3-031-18002-6_3

ment with Buddhism is admittedly more nuanced than his narrative makes it appear. During the mid-1960s, he expressed in "On the Problem of My Thought" (談我的思想問題, henceforth TWDSX) that he had always been a Buddhist since the 1910s (TWDSX: 119). In understanding Liang's standpoint, it is crucial to situate him within the socio-political climate of the early Republican era. As Liang stressed in "The Changes and Differences in My Understanding of Human Psychology" (我對人類心理認識前後轉變不同, henceforth WDRL), he dedicated his life to two problems: the "problem of China" (*zhongguo wenti* 中國問題) and the "problem of human life" (*rensheng wenti* 人生問題) (WDRL: 130). While the former centers on the particular place of China in the modern world, the latter concerns an existential crisis universally experienced by humans. Striving to develop a proposal for resolving these problems, Liang negotiated the tensions between East and West, traditional and modern, local and global, as well as personal and national.

In this process, Buddhism—especially the Yogācāra doctrine of consciousness-only—provided Liang with a set of vocabulary that allowed him to enter into these negotiations. Therefore, the second sense in which Liang is a Buddhist indicates how Yogācāra served as a source of inspiration for his articulation of epistemology and metaphysics from a non-Western perspective. For Liang, the rearticulated Eastern philosophies are not only compatible with but also complementary to their Western counterparts: they remedy the existential crisis exacerbated by a version of social Darwinism inherent in Euro-American modernity. He continued to enquire into how China could deploy the Eastern wisdom preserved in Buddhism and Confucianism to draw up a modernization plan beyond Westernization. Innovatively incorporating the Yogācāra doctrine of consciousness-only into his thought, Liang took a first step in rejuvenating Eastern philosophies for the universal well-being of humans and the modernization of China.

While Liang appreciated the insights of Yogācāra, he discerned a lack of systematic moral theories that made Yogācāra limited in its applicability to "this-worldly" (*shijian* 世間) matters.[2] In an effort to overcome this limitation, Liang rediscovered Confucianism. Specifically, he conceived of Confucian moral cultivation in this-worldly life as the starting point for resolving the said existential crisis. In this manner, this-worldly cultivation becomes a preparatory practice for the Buddhist pursuit of the "other-worldly" (*chushijian* 出世間) awakening. He borrowed the Bodhisattvas' vow "not to leave behind any sentient being in *saṃsāra* and thus not enter *nirvāṇa*" (不捨眾生, 不入涅槃) to illustrate non-duality as the fluid transformation of this-worldly cultivation and other-worldly liberation (DMGXZ: 1139).

[2] I use the pair of "this-worldly" and "other-worldly" to paraphrase a plethora of terms in Liang's work. For example, he writes *shunshijian* 順世間 (following the this-worldly) and *chushijian* 出世間 (the other-worldly) in "On Finding the Foundations and Resolving the Doubt" (究元決議論, henceforth JYJYL) (JYJYL: 19); *shijian* 世間 (this-worldly) and *fofa* 佛法 (Buddhist dharma) in "Buddhist Dharma and This-Worldly Realm" (佛法與世間, henceforth FFYSJ) (FFYSJ: 454); *shijian* 世間 (this-worldly) and *chushijian* 出世間 (other-worldly) in "On the Difference Between Confucianism and Buddhism" (儒佛異同論, henceforth RFYT) (RFYT: 153); and *shengsi* 生死 (*saṃsāra*) and *niepan* 涅槃 (*nirvāṇa*) in "Summary of the Recorded Interview with American Scholar Guy Alitto" (答美國學者艾愷先生訪談記錄摘要, henceforth DMGXZ) (DMGXZ: 1139).

For Liang, the Buddhist view of non-duality is not merely a theoretical project but also his life principle. In light of this principle, he moved freely from Confucian practices to Buddhist aspirations, which corresponds to the last definition of him being a Buddhist.

As this chapter argues, these three senses in which Liang is a Buddhist are not only interconnected but also mutually reinforced in his early work. Previous studies have presented the intellectual history of Liang's engagement with Buddhism in every phase of his thought (Zhang 2001; Lee 2015) and further traced the combined influence of Confucianism and Buddhism on his thinking (Wang 1986; Gong 1996; Hanafin 2003). Drawing upon these studies, I will explore the philosophical motivation behind Liang's explicit turn to Confucianism, his consistent reliance on Buddhism, and his free movements between these two traditions. In particular, I follow Thierry Meynard's outline of how Yogācāra provided Liang with the resources to redefine the notion of transcendence and rethink the interplay between this-worldly flourishing and other-worldly awakening (Meynard 2007, 2011, 2014).

This argument will unfold in three sections. Section 1 contextualizes Liang's engagement with multiple Buddhist ideas during the Yogācāra revival movement of the early Republican period and explores how the early-later distinction in Yogācāra informed his system of thought. Section 2 analyzes his philosophical thinking between 1913 and 1916. When Liang started to develop an interest in Buddhism, he was attracted to the Yogācāra-*tathāgatagarbha* syncretism in early Yogācāra texts.[3] Espousing a Buddhist version of metaphysical idealism, Liang subordinated this-worldly matters—part of the illusory conventional reality—to the ultimate goal of eradicating suffering for the recuperation of the awakened mind. He continued to conceive of various intellectual traditions in the East and West as studies of conventional reality secondary to the Buddhist teaching of emptiness. Section 3 details Liang's turn to later Yogācāra from 1917 to 1921. Under the guidance of OUYANG Jingwu 歐陽竟無 (1871–1943), Liang prioritized later Yogācāra treatises composed by Xuanzang 玄奘 (c. 602–664) and his disciple Kuiji 窺基 (632–682). Gradually, Liang distanced himself from metaphysical idealism. Instead, he promoted a version of correlative non-dualism that stresses the correlation of ideality and reality as the ground for the fluid transformation of ignorance and awakening. As such, this-worldly life is no longer deemed to be a non-existent illusion: it is reaffirmed as the target to be criticized, reformed, and transformed. In recognizing the value of this-worldly life, Liang discerned how Yogācāra centers on personal liberation, which gave him an incentive to promote Confucianism for a detailed account of morality at the interpersonal level. Eventually, he incorporated Yogācāra epistemology in his reformulation of the Confucian philosophy of life, from which he derived a modernization plan for China and a preparatory practice for the Buddhist pursuit of universal awakening.

---

[3] KENG Ching differentiates the stronger meaning of *tathāgatagarbha* as an innate quality synonymous with suchness, from the weaker meaning as a state of mind other than ignorance (Keng 2009). In this chapter, *tathāgatagarbha* is used mainly in the stronger sense, whereas the weaker one is generally referred to as "Buddha-nature."

2 The Diversity of Viewpoints in Yogācāra

In a 1980 interview about his study of Buddhism, Liang contended that he did not completely understand Yogācāra until 1917 (DMGXZ: 1149). He specified that his work prior to that year was indebted to the "old tradition of consciousness-only" (*jiu weishipai* 舊唯識派) and not the authentic teachings of consciousness established by Xuanzang's "new tradition" (*xinpai* 新派) (DMGXZ: 1149). As suggested by this interview, Liang was fully aware of how his early thinking was influenced by diverse viewpoints within Yogācāra.

As one of the major Mahāyāna traditions, Yogācāra uses the study of consciousness to argue for emptiness. The tradition is said to be founded by Maitreya in South Asia and further developed by Asaṅga and Vasubandhu toward the end of the 300 s CE. It was then transmitted to East Asia by scholar-monks, such as Bodhiruci 菩提流支 (?–537) and Paramārtha 真諦 (499–569), who translated its numerous texts into Chinese.[4] Yogācāra kept developing in South Asia. During the 500 s, Dignāga systemized Yogācāra thought through Buddhist logic and inspired another generation of Yogācāra commentators. These newly developed ideas continued to be introduced to China. Growing up in this intellectual climate, Xuanzang found it impossible to reconcile the disputes among his fellow Yogācārins. Therefore, he traveled to India to study Yogācāra. Upon his return to the Tang Empire (618–907) in 645, Xuanzang translated Sanskrit texts into Chinese under the auspices of Emperor Taizong (598–649). He had hoped that these new translations would end the multiple disputes among his fellow Yogācārins, but instead, supporters of the older translations criticized him for being disrespectful to his predecessors. Inheriting these tensions between "early preaching" (*gushuo* 古說) and "later texts" (*jinwen* 今文), Xuanzang's disciple, Kuiji, composed commentaries to defend his master (T45N1861, P247a15-16). Toward the end of the Tang dynasty, the study of Yogācāra gradually subsided. It resurged during the Ming dynasty (1368–1644), which in turn set the stage for the Yogācāra revival movement in the early Republican era. During this period, lost Buddhist scriptures were brought back to China, and new treatises were translated into Chinese. Acknowledging the above flow of ideas, scholars have recognized the diversity present within the interpretations of the Yogācāra doctrine of consciousness-only.

Developing his interest in Buddhism during the Yogācāra revival, Liang familiarized himself with the distinction between early and later Yogācāra, which he referred to as the old-new differentiation.[5] As for early Yogācāra, its proponents were Sthiramati and Nanda in South Asia, and Paramārtha in East Asia. In contrast, the

[4] John Makeham describes the translations of Bodhiruci, Paramārtha, and Xuanzang as three consecutive waves of Yogācāra transmission in East Asia (Makeham 2014: 5–10).

[5] Contemporary scholars describe this distinction as one between early Yogācāra's "mind being truly pure" (*zhenxin* 真心) and later Yogācāra's "mind being falsely deluded" (*wangxin* 妄心). Discussions on the early-later distinction started in the early Republican era, as shown in Lü Cheng 1986 (1924); Taixu 2005 (1931); Mei Guangxi 2014 (1931); and Ouyang Jingwu 1995 (1938).

promoters of later Yogācāra were Dignāga and Dharmapāla in South Asia, and Xuanzang in East Asia. To better understand the Buddhist roots in Liang's early thinking, especially his reaffirmation of this-worldly life, I center the following discussion on how the approaches to consciousness in Yogācāra allow for dissimilar interpretations of emptiness and awakening.

Liang was first drawn to the early Yogācāra theory of consciousness. According to Paramārtha, who is considered a proponent of early Yogācāra in East Asia,[6] consciousness can be understood as a "two-part" (*erfen* 二分) relationship between the "seeing part" (*jianfen* 見分, *darśanabhāga*) *qua* the act of perceiving and the "image part" (*xiangfen* 相分, *nimittabhāga*) *qua* the perceived phenomenon (T43N1830, P320c21).[7] That is to say, consciousness is that which comes to know a phenomenon by directing itself towards it. Paramārtha proceeds to depict the interactions between the eight types of consciousness constituting the mind of a sentient being. Among them, the first five consciousnesses are the five senses that offer sense data to be processed and synthesized by the sixth consciousness. While this sixth consciousness, named *manovijñāna*, is productive in conceptual thinking, it can be interrupted in extreme states such as deep sleep, which indicates the existence of a seventh consciousness, called *manas*, which sustains the coherent self-identity of sentient beings. *Manas* further relies on the eighth *ālaya* consciousness to ensure the continuity of death and rebirth. In Paramārtha's model, *ālaya* functions in accordance with the two-part structure to bring forward the subject-object duality (T31N1587, P61c11). The subjective aspect of experience then gives rise to *manas* as the ego-producer, and the objective aspect brings about the other six consciousnesses that produce the sense of unchanging objects/*dharmas* (T31N1587, P62a-b). The subject-object duality underpins the illusion that causes sentient beings to become ignorant of the impermanent nature of things in their experiences and develop attachment to them (T31N1587, P62b20-21). In turn, these attachments animate feelings and emotions through which sentient beings internalize ignorance as a habitual way of living. Paramārtha evokes the notion of "seed" (*zhongzi* 種子, *bīja*) to capture such a habitual tendency of perceiving and living (T31N1587, P62c20-21). Described in this manner, previous ignorant views and deeds do not vanish but leave karmic imprints on the mind and remain in *ālaya* as polluted seeds that cultivate more wrongdoings and trap sentient beings in *saṃsāra*. Due to its preservation of seeds, *ālaya* is also known as the "storehouse consciousness."

Thus, if sentient beings wish to liberate themselves from ignorance, they should eradicate duality, recuperate the non-dual state of mind, and attain awakening

[6] Scholars have argued that Paramārtha incorporated his own understanding into his translations, which made them representative of his Yogācāra-*tathāgatagarbha* syncretism (Takasaki 1975; Yinshun 1988; Lai 2006; Zhou 2006). Recently, KENG Ching argued that Paramārtha's position was closer to Xuanzang's (Keng 2009). Nevertheless, without access to Keng's insight, most intellectuals in the early Republican era followed the popular understanding of Paramārtha as the exponent of Yogācāra-*tathāgatagarbha* syncretism.

[7] When referring to Buddhist scriptures from the *Taishō Shinshū Daizōkyō*, I put the volume number, sequence number, page number, and section number inside brackets.

(T31N1587, P62b22-24). Since regular consciousness is "dualist" (*fenbie* 分別) by nature, the non-dual state of mind evolves into the ninth *amalavijñāna* (the spotless consciousness) as the "immaculate mind" (*qingjingxin* 清淨心) (T31N1616, P864a26-28). Paramārtha turns to the Yogācāra theory of three natures to associate the phenomena produced by the dualist consciousnesses with the "imagined nature" (*fenbie xing* 分別性, *parikalpitasvabhāva*), the producing consciousnesses with the "other-dependent nature" (*yita xing* 依他性, *paratantrasvabhāva*), and the non-dual state of mind with the "absolute nature" (*zhenshi xing* 真實性, *pariniṣpannasvabhāva*) (T31N1587, P63b). In this manner, *ālaya* becomes synonymous with *tathāgatagarbha* (*rulaizang* 如來藏, Buddha-matrix) as the Buddha-nature innate to all sentient beings (T30N1584, P1018c6). That is to say, the mind of all sentient beings is originally immaculate, only to then be temporarily polluted by ignorance. In its polluted state, *ālaya* serves as the origin of illusions to sustain *saṃsāra*. When the duality is removed and *nirvāṇa* is acquired, the purified *ālaya* reveals itself as the originally immaculate mind that is subsequently equated with emptiness, "suchness" (*zhenru* 真如, *tathatā*), and the pure dharma realm (T31N1616, P864c12-13). This is how the Yogācāra theory of consciousness is harmonized with the doctrine of *tathāgatagarbha* in Buddhist scriptures attributed to Paramārtha, which include *The Awakening of Faith in the Mahāyāna* (*Dasheng qixin lun* 大乘起信論), *The Summary of Mahāyāna* (*She dasheng lun* 攝大乘論), *The Treatise on Three Non-Existent Natures* (*Sanwuxing lun* 三無性論), and *The Treatise on the Transforming Consciousness* (*Zhuanshi lun* 轉識論). As to be seen shortly, these texts shaped Liang's initial understanding of Yogācāra.

In early Yogācāra, nothing truly exists outside of this non-dual state of mind. Paramārtha, thus, expounds on the view that the mind is exhaustive of everything in the cosmos, which yields a version of metaphysical idealism. His Yogācāra-*tathāgatagarbha* syncretism exerted a profound influence on the intelligentsia since the revitalization of Yogācāra in the Ming period. For example, interpreting the Daoist concept of "equalizing things" (*qiwu* 齊物), ZHANG Taiyan 章太炎 (1869–1936) draws upon the theory of consciousness from Buddhist treatises, such as *The Awakening of Faith in the Mahāyāna* and *The Summary of Mahāyāna*. Applauding the Yogācāra-*tathāgatagarbha* syncretism, Zhang criticizes Xuanzang and Kuiji's refutation of the mind as originally immaculate (Zhang 1985: 50). However, his contemporary OUYANG Jingwu—an adamant advocate of later Yogācāra and an admirable teacher for Liang—deems the harmonization of Yogācāra and *tathāgatagarbha* to be a deviation from Mahāyāna teachings.[8]

Unlike Paramārtha, Xuanzang follows the later Yogācāra master, Dharmapāla, to explain the functionality of consciousness through a "four-part" (*sifen* 四分) structure—the seeing part, the image part, the part of "self-awareness" (*zizhengfen* 自證分, *svasaṃvittibhāga*), and the "reflexive awareness of self-awareness"

[8] Their disputes fueled the debates over the authenticity of *The Awakening of Faith in the Mahāyāna* (Meynard 2014; Lin 2014; Aviv 2020).

(*zhengzizheng* 證自證) (T31N1585, P10b).[9] As such, consciousness is portrayed as an underlying flow of self-awareness that gives rise to the act of perceiving and the perceived phenomenon constantly; and, in this process, consciousness is always reflexively aware of its functionality. In light of this four-part structure, Xuanzang refuses to assimilate all consciousnesses into a meta-consciousness but underscores their distinctive cognitive capacities (T31N1587, P1a16). Following the four-part structure, *ālaya* gives rise to the image part of three types of phenomena: the entire "material cosmos" (*qishijian* 器世間), the "corporeal body" (*yougenshen* 有根身), and seeds. As to the seeing part, it is described as a holistic act of perceiving that constitutes the primordial bodily experience of a sentient being in every moment of *saṃsāra* (T31N1585, P10a13-19).

Directing itself toward the seeing part of *ālaya*, the seventh consciousness (*manas*) misperceives it as an unchanging *ego* and becomes attached to this immutable self-in-itself habitually (T31N1585, P22a8-10). At the same time, the other six consciousnesses direct themselves toward *ālaya*'s image part, and the sixth consciousness (*manovijñāna*) habitually objectifies the sense-data collected by the five senses. Together, *manas* and *manovijñāna* misperceive phenomena as immutable self and *dharma* and habitually become attached to them, which shows how habitual misperception animates innate (*jusheng* 俱生) attachments (T31N1585, P22a13; P7a1). Based on these habitual misperceptions, the sixth consciousness conceptually differentiates the self from other *dharmas* to produce discriminative (*fenbie*分別) attachments (T31N1585, P2a21; P7a6). These habitual and conceptual misperceptions continue to be consolidated by the "mental factors" (*xinsuo* 心所, *caitta*)—namely, the affective mental states of feeling, emotion, affliction, etc.—that entrap sentient beings in *saṃsāra*.

In Xuanzang's view, ignorance does not stem from consciousness *per se*. Rather, the functionality of consciousness furnishes each sentient being with an open possibility: misperceiving things as immutable entities or seeing things as interdependent and empty. Xuanzang uses the three natures to detail this open possibility. The imagined nature (*bianjisuozhi xing* 遍計所執性) describes misperceptions generated by *manas* and *manovijñāna*, both habitually and conceptually. As such, the existence of the imagined nature becomes "fictitiously real" (*jiayou* 假有) (T31N1585, P47a10). The absolute nature (*yuanchengshi xing* 圓成實性), which has "real existence" (*shiyou* 實有), captures the mindset of sentient beings when they are awake (T31N1585, P47c12). The other-dependent nature (*yitaqi xing* 依他起性), whose "seemingly real existence" (*xushi* 虛實) Xuanzang acknowledges (T31N1585, P46c8-9), characterizes the functionality of consciousness that makes it possible for ignorance to transform into awakening. As such, consciousness-only suggests that the mind, as a system of eight consciousnesses, serves as the condition for the possibility of various phenomena. Each mind further reaches out to other

[9] *Svasaṃvitti* is also translated as self-realization, self-cognition, or self-authenticating (Yao 2005; Meynard 2014). I am opting for self-awareness to underscore how *zizheng* is also a type of nondual, pure sensation known as *xianliang*.

minds to mutually constitute a larger shared world, a mutual constitution that is compared to how "when the lamps are on, they illuminate each other as if they were a whole" (如眾燈明，各遍似一) (T31N1585, P10c15-16).[10] Sentient beings, as subjects of knowledge and as agents, can navigate the shared world *qua* an intersubjectively accessible reality in two opposite ways: by perpetuating ignorance or by perceiving things as they are. Instead of depicting the mind as the cosmic origin, Xuanzang expresses a version of correlative non-dualism that stresses how the transcendental ideality of (inter-)subjectivity is always correlated with conventional/empirical reality, a correlation that ensures the non-duality of ignorance and awakening.

Acknowledging intersubjective agency, Xuanzang perceives awakening as a collaborative realization of insight that corrects conceptual misperceptions and changes the habitual way of living. Far from being an innate quality, Buddha-nature becomes an ideal state to be achieved through a collaborative effort (T31N1585, P9a5-7). Only when all minds are purified from ignorance will consciousness "transform" (*zhuanyi* 轉依, *āśrayaparivṛtti*) into wisdom.[11] Thierry Meynard speaks of this transformation as the realization of "a universal Buddhist awakening" (Meynard 2011: 70). By then, the realm of suffering evolves into the pure *dharma* realm—an ideal world free from mental defilement (T45N1861, P372b). Emptiness is not tantamount to, but becomes the true nature of, the purified mind and the pure *dharma* realm (T43N1830, P546a3-5). Later Yogācāra's depiction of *zhuanyi* proposes a more nuanced view of transcendence than that in early Yogācāra. While this-worldly *saṃsāra* and other-worldly *nirvāṇa* remain different in quality, later Yogācārins acknowledge the value and worth of this-worldly life. *Saṃsāra* is not renounced as an undesirably nonexistent illusion but retains as a fictitiously real world to be criticized, reformed, and transformed for the realization of *nirvāṇa*. The way in which *nirvāṇa* and *saṃsāra* complement, not contradict, each other suggests their non-duality.

Envisioning Buddha-nature as an ideal, Xuanzang problematizes the view of the mind as both originally immaculate and temporarily polluted. If the mind is originally immaculate, *ālaya* will store only pure seeds that generate correct views and actions to ensure this sentient being's awakening, which makes it impossible for an originally pure mind to be polluted (T31N1585, P8c24). Conversely, if the mind is already polluted, a sentient being will have only impure seeds in *ālaya* and remain incapable of correcting misperceptions (T31N1585, P8c26). As explicated by Kuiji, for sentient beings who have no pure seeds in their minds, the compassionate

[10] Liang relays this quote to make a case for reading Yogācāra as a philosophy that centers on personal experience (WSSY: 304). Since the late-Ming dynasty, scholar-monks have focussed on this quote in their debate on whether Yogācāra thought is solipsist (Chien 2017).

[11] For Xuanzang, such transformation is realized through the "five stages of consciousness-only" (*weishi wuwei* 唯識五位) (T31N1585, P48b15-20). While the Yogācāra formulation of the Bodhisattvas' practice does not seem to capture Liang's attention, Liang turns to Confucianism to derive a proposal for eradicating misperceptions as the preparation for the Buddhist pursuit of universal awakening.

Bodhisattvas will help them regain the capacity of removing misperception (T45N1831, P610c2-8). Known as the first ones who have acquired wisdom, the Bodhisattvas comprehend the interconnectedness of all minds and thus find it imperative to collaborate with others for realizing universal awakening. It is in line with this understanding of the mind that OUYANG Jingwu places grave doubt on the Yogācāra-*tathāgatagarbha* harmonization (Aviv 2020: 89–90).[12] Following Ouyang's promotion of later Yogācāra, Liang is convinced of the importance of the Bodhisattvas' practice. Nevertheless, he does not locate the mechanics of such compassionate practice inside Yogācāra, insofar as he turns to Confucianism for a systematic account of morality, a process which I will examine in the next two sections.

3 The First Period (1913–1916): "Other-Worldly Teaching for Saving All Sentient Beings"

Liang grew up in a time when people from all walks of life were concerned with rebuilding China into a prosperous modern nation. Prior to his turn to Buddhism, he actively engaged in discussion on China's modernization. As documented in "The Short History of My Self-Learning" (我的自學小史, henceforth WDZX), Liang followed Western utilitarianism and pragmatism piously, in the conviction that the natural human desire for happiness should function as the engine of social progress (WDZX: 680). Like many of his contemporaries, Liang perceived social Darwinism as the gist of Westernization that would facilitate China's nation-building. However, the Beiyang government's unsuccessful reforms smashed his faith (WDZX: 680). Reflecting on the limitation of Westernization, he elucidated the impossibility of social Darwinism to guarantee universal happiness and prosperity (WDZX: 689). Indeed, the natural human desire nourished social progress and injustice alike—while humans were instinctively motivated to ameliorate their life through competition, they were also inclined to exploit others, exacerbating egocentrism and aggregating suffering (WDZX: 689). Temporarily, Liang endorsed socialism in order to bring about a prosperous society without private ownership of property (WDZX: 691). Yet, he soon changed his mind. Suffering was an integral part of an overall existential crisis inherently experienced by sentient beings, which could not be cured through the abundance of material goods or anything from the exterior world (WDZX: 691). Hence, he decided to take refuge in Buddhism.

At that time, the revival of Yogācāra garnered a growing level of intellectual attention. With access to numerous Buddhist texts and secondary literature, Liang credited ZHANG Taiyan as a major source of inspiration (WDZX: 695). Stemming from the viewpoint that nothing exists but the non-dual state of mind, Liang advocated the "other-worldly teaching for saving all sentient beings" (出世間法, 救拔一

[12] It should be noted, as detailed by Eyal Aviv, that Ouyang revised his critique of Yogācāra-*tathāgatagarbha* harmonization later on (Aviv 2020: 145–150).

切眾生) in a 1914 letter entitled "On Buddhism" (談佛, henceforth TF) (TF: 489). This pronouncement encapsulates Liang's twofold project. On the explicative level, the "other-worldly teaching" of emptiness expounds on the nature of reality and the cause of suffering; and on the prescriptive level, "saving all sentient beings" is the goal of prescribing a remedy for universal suffering and a plan for China's modernization.

Liang's project matured in his 1916 article entitled "On Finding the Foundations and Resolving the Doubt." Liang first explains how emptiness epitomizes the ultimate nature of reality. In his 1914 letter, he had borrowed the Buddhist vocabulary of the "conventional" (*quan* 權) and the "ultimate" (*shi* 實) to outline the interplay between the illusory this-worldly life and the other-worldly emptiness (TF: 489). The prioritization of emptiness is systematized by Liang in his 1916 article, with extensive reference to Buddhist scriptures, especially those in favor of Yogācāra-*tathāgatagarbha* syncretism, like *The Awakening of Faith in the Mahāyāna* and *The Treatise on Three Non-Existent Natures*. In parallel with his previous juxtaposition of ultimate emptiness with conventional illusions, he introduces the distinction between "the school of nature" (*xingzong* 性宗) and "the school of characteristics" (*xiangzong* 相宗) (JYJYL: 4). This distinction was popularized by masters of the Huayan (華嚴) school of Buddhism who enriched Paramārtha's viewpoint.[13] While schools of nature, such as Huayan and Tiantai (天台), explain how emptiness serves as the origin of illusory phenomena, the school of characteristics, like Yogācāra, focuses on illusions to elucidate how characteristics are manifestations of the ultimate nature of reality *qua* emptiness. Following Huayan masters, Liang ranks the school of characteristics below the school of nature (JYJYL: 9).

In unpacking his viewpoint, Liang presents *ālaya*—the eighth consciousness—as synonymous with the *tathāgatagarbha* (JYJYL: 6). Drawing upon *The Awakening of Faith in the Mahāyāna*, Liang relays the view that the mind is originally pure and only polluted temporarily by ignorance. As the "mind being truly pure" (*zhenxin* 真心), *ālaya* amounts to emptiness that is not determined by this-worldly laws of causality (JYJYL: 7). Then, in its polluted state, *ālaya* becomes dichotomized and gives rise to illusions in the material cosmos under the causal chain (JYJYL: 7). Upon declaring emptiness as the ultimate nature of reality, Liang uses the three non-existent natures to explain how illusions manifest emptiness: the so-called immutable self and *dharmas* are nothing but false imaginations. The imagined nature of illusion reveals the "non-existent nature of manifested images" (*xiang wuxing* 相無性) (JYJYL: 8). Indeed, illusory images arise on the basis of subject-object duality as the result of the functionality of consciousness. This then illustrates the other-dependent nature and suggests the "non-existent nature of arising" (*sheng wuxing* 生無性) (JYJYL: 8). The underlying *ālaya*, once purified from illusion and misperception, returns to its originally pure state as the non-dual state of mind

[13] Incorporating Yogācāra theories into their own systems of thought, Huayan masters approached early and later Yogācāra quite differently (Lü 1986: 2584–2962; Keng 2009: 81–85).

characterized by the absolute nature. Thus, the immaculate mind *qua* emptiness conveys the "absolute non-existent nature" (*shengyi wuxing* 勝義無性) (JYJYL: 8).

Combining the teachings of absolute emptiness and illusory manifestation, Liang specifies that the ultimate nature of reality is "the mind being exhaustive of everything, as pure suchness devoid of false illusions" (全物皆心, 純真無妄) (JYJYL: 8)—which later becomes his formulation of metaphysical idealism. Liang's reservation about Yogācāra stems from his endorsement of Paramārthian Yogācāra-*tathāgatagarbha* syncretism. As such, he confines his analysis to early Yogācārins' theories of consciousness and extensively quotes their texts, a limitation he acknowledged in the 1980s (DMGXZ: 1149). Liang goes on to trace the cause of suffering. Inclined to perceive the world in terms of a subject-object duality, sentient beings are prone to treat things as immutable entities which generate "desires and cravings" (*yunian* 慾念) (JYJYL: 16). In their ignorance of emptiness, they experience "feelings" (*ganshou* 感受) of "pleasure" (*le* 樂) when desires are satisfied and endure "suffering" (*ku* 苦) when cravings are unfulfilled (JYJYL: 16). Since desires never cease to emerge and cannot always be fulfilled, it is certain that the amount of suffering exceeds that of pleasure (JYJYL: 16–17). As such, sentient beings are entrapped in the insurmountable existential crisis of this-worldly life due to ignorance of the ultimate nature of reality *qua* emptiness (JYJYL: 15).

Hence, this existential crisis can be resolved once sentient beings renounce this-worldly ignorance and recuperate other-worldly emptiness (JYJYL: 19). At the prescriptive level of this project, Liang casts doubt on the promise of various proposals oriented toward this-worldly life (JYJYL: 17–18). Earlier in his 1914 letter, he had deemed several intellectual traditions in the East and the West as secondary to Buddhism, because they were not apt for the ultimate eradication of human suffering (TF: 489). His own proposal comes to fruition in 1916. Juxtaposing the this-worldly realm of causality with the other-worldly realm of emptiness, he uses Buddhist vocabulary to translate Western philosophy. For instance, Liang equates "ether" (*yitai* 以太)—which is identified by Gustave Le Bon (1841–1931) as the metaphysical origin of physical matter—with *ālaya* (JYJYL: 6). In doing so, he regrets that Le Bon fails to connect the immaterial origin with absolute emptiness (JYJYL: 6). Similarly, even though Liang appreciates Kant's position—as he understands it—that "thing-in-itself" (*wuru* 物如) is beyond the scope of dualistic thinking, he does not believe that humans can attain "free-will" (*ziyou* 自由) in this-worldly life (JYJYL: 10–12). As for social Darwinist Herbert Spencer and his critic Henri Bergson, although they comprehend the illusory nature of this-worldly matters, they remain unaware of the ultimate nature of reality *qua* the other-worldly emptiness (JYJYL: 13–14). In a comparative framework, Liang brings to light how Buddhism preserves the ultimate truth in contrast to other systems of thought across time and place.

It follows that a world devoid of suffering can never be realized by proposals oriented toward this-worldly life. Humans can use these proposals to increase the chance of fulfilling desires (JYJYL: 17), but suffering will also mount as pleasure grows (JYJYL: 18). Under the influence of Zhang Taiyan, Liang reveals how social Darwinism presents only one side of the story and glosses over the evolution of evil

(JYJYL: 18). He thus concludes that these this-worldly centered proposals could temporarily promote human flourishing. Eventually, humans should move beyond this-worldly life to eradicate the cause of suffering, which necessitates the Buddhist path. In Liang's terms, "socialism, anarchism, Kant's democracy, and Nietzsche's *übermensch* … as I anticipate, are not unattainable" (JYJYL: 18), yet "those who follow this-worldly life to promote social progress shall also facilitate the success of Buddhism" (JYJYL: 20). Liang's position at the prescriptive level resonates with his prioritization of absolute emptiness as the ultimate nature of reality at the explicative level. In its ability to resolve human suffering, Buddhism promises China a modernization that starts with a Western style of socialism and ends with a non-Western Buddhist future (JYJYL: 20).

Such a promise, in turn, consolidates Liang's determination to become a Buddhist practitioner (JYJYL: 20). After the release of his 1916 article, Liang's talent was recognized by the president of Peking University, CAI Yuanpei 蔡元培 (1868–1940), who invited Liang to teach Indian philosophy at this institute. Through his interaction with colleagues and students, Liang deepened his study of Buddhism. As recounted in "In Memory of Mr. Xiong Shili" (憶熊十力先生, henceforth YXSL), Liang particularly admired the work of OUYANG Jingwu at the China Institute of Inner Learning (*Zhina neixue yuan* 支那內學院) (YXSL: 522). Influenced by Ouyang's approach, Liang dedicated more time to later Yogācāra, especially the writings of Xuanzang and his disciples. As a result, he came to scrutinize his previous interpretations of Buddhism. In the 1923 appendix to JYJYL, Liang expressed his critique of ZHANG Taiyan (JYJYL: 21–22).[14] As he specified in remorse, his argumentation in the 1916 article was premised on a false proposition that downplayed the value and worth of this-worldly life (JYJYL: 22; WDZX: 698). In the next section, I will examine how his study of later Yogācāra—especially Yogācāra epistemology—from 1917 to 1921 led to his reassessment of this-worldly life.

4 The Second Period (1917–1921): "Return to the This-Worldly Realm"

Liang's "return to the this-worldly realm" (*huidao shijian lai* 回到世間來) was accomplished in three steps (WDZX: 698). He initiated this process upon advancing his study of Yogācāra epistemology in *Outline of Indian Philosophy* (印度哲學概論, henceforth YDZX), substantialized his reaffirmation of the value of this-worldly life in *Manual of Yogācāra* (唯識述義, henceforth WSSY), and finalized his turn to

[14] Respecting Ouyang as the only authority in Yogācāra studies, Liang became critical of his previous colleagues, such as ZHANG Kecheng 張克誠 (1865–1922) and JIANG Weiqiao 蔣維喬 (1873–1958) (Meynard 2014: 202–205). In contrast, he spoke very highly of LÜ Cheng who was acknowledged by Liang as Ouyang's protégé (YXSL: 523).

this-worldly Confucian duties in *Eastern and Western Cultures and Their Philosophies* (東西文化及其哲學, henceforth DXWH).

The *Outline of Indian Philosophy* is a textbook Liang authored for teaching Indian philosophy at Peking University (YDZX: 26). In this work, Liang expands his previous twofold project into a threefold one by introducing a detailed investigation of "epistemology" (*renshilun* 認識論) along with "ontology" (*bentilun* 本體論) on the explicative level and the "doctrine of the this-worldly realm" (*shijianlun* 世間論) on the prescriptive level (LSMQJ 1/3–4). As an initial effort, this textbook does not fully depart from metaphysical idealism. In the first section on ontology, Liang perpetuates the view that the *ālaya* consciousness is the "utmost cosmic origin" (*yuzhou zhi dagenben* 宇宙之大根本), both pure as absolute emptiness and impure as the totality of illusory dharmas (YDZX: 104). Referencing *The Awakening of Faith in the Mahāyāna*, Liang prescribes the solution to suffering as leaving this-worldly realm for the other-worldly emptiness (YDZX: 247). Indeed, although Liang strives to position Buddhism as neither monist nor dualist, neither materialist nor idealist, he does not make a case for this claim until he shifts his focus from speculative philosophy to the acquisition of knowledge in the second section on epistemology.

The second section starts with the theory of Buddhist logic as presented in the later Yogācāra theory of *liang* 量 (*pramāṇa*, measurement), where measuring is an analogy for knowing (YDZX: 144). According to later Yogācārins, there are three modes of knowledge: *xianliang* 現量 (*pratyakṣapramāṇa*), *biliang* 比量 (*anumānapramāṇa*), and *feiliang* 非量 (*apramāṇa*), which Liang interprets as pure sensation, abstract concept, and concrete idea respectively (YDZX: 148). Liang speaks of *xianliang*—a mode of knowing purely devoid of any "duality" (*fenbie* 分別)—as "pure sensation" (*danchun ganjue* 單純感覺) to specify how it does not need the mediation of concepts (YDZX: 148–153). Among the eight types of consciousness, the first five, *qua* the five senses, are targeted toward the "particular characteristics" (*zixiang* 自相) of an object, thus furnishing a person with pure sensation (YDZX: 153). To be more specific, when a person comes to perceive a white porcelain bottle, for example, the eye-consciousness provides the pure sensation of white (YDZX: 153). A pure sensation does not involve any abstract thinking of whiteness, nor does it transform into a coherent "perception" (*zhijue* 知覺) of the bottle as a unity of color, shape, texture, etc. (YDZX: 153). Once abstract thinking is evoked, such a mode of knowing becomes *biliang*, an inference that is able to conceptualize the "common characteristics" (*gongxiang* 共相) shared by various objects of cognition (YDZX: 153). Nevertheless, if this person mixes pure sensation with inference, the mode of knowing becomes *feiliang* (YDZX: 153). The previous example of perceiving an object as a coherent unity of various types of sensations with an unchanging identity—the perception of the white porcelain bottle as the specific one in front of this person—illustrates *feiliang* as "concrete idea" (*juti zhi guannian* 具體之觀念) (YDZX: 161).[15] Indeed, Liang considers the coherent perception of this specific white porcelain bottle in front of a person as a type of concrete idea in contrast to *biliang* as the "abstract concept" (*chouxiang zhi gainian* 抽象之概念) of whiteness in general (YDZX: 161).

Thereafter, Liang associates these modes of knowing with the three natures. Both concrete idea and abstract concept thrive by means of conceptualization, which enables a person to falsely imagine phenomena in experience as immutable and unchanging (YDZX: 163). As such, concrete idea and abstract concept are associated with the imagined nature (YDZX: 163). Conceptualization is founded on the non-dual cognition of particular characteristics—namely, on pure sensation in the this-worldly realm—which shows the other-dependent nature (YDZX: 163). "This-worldly sensation" (*shijian xianliang* 世間現量) further opens the door to the "sensation at the level of the Buddha" (*fowei xianliang* 佛位現量) through which a person sees things as they are in both the this-worldly and other-worldly realms (YDZX: 164). As such, the sensation at the level of the Buddha entails the absolute nature (YDZX: 164). At this point, Liang pinpoints the limitations of "Western dogmatism" (*duduanlun* 獨斷論) and "skepticism" (*huaiyilun* 懷疑論) (YDZX: 166–167). Against dogmatism, Yogācārins prove that the ultimate nature of reality is beyond the grasp of conceptual thinking; and *contra* skepticism, Yogācārins contend that truth is immediately presented through pure sensation (YDZX: 167). Closing the rift between dogmatism and skepticism, the Yogācāra theory of *pramāṇa* enriches Kant's critical philosophy for its affirmation of the knowability of "noumena" (*benti* 本體) through the non-dual insight of *xianliang* (YDZX: 167).

In parallel with the three natures, Liang continues to depict how consciousness serves as the condition for the possibility of various "cognitive objects" (*jing* 境) in one's experience (YDZX: 168). When *ālaya* and the five senses function, they direct themselves toward objects that present things as they are, in pure sensation (YDZX: 169). These objects are referred to as *xingjing* 性境 (objects as such) (YDZX: 169). As mentioned in Sect. 1, the sixth and the seventh consciousnesses aim at *ālaya* to produce concrete ideas that habitually misperceive *ālaya*'s seeing part and image part as immutable self and *dharma* respectively. Based on this habitual misperception, the sixth consciousness produces abstract concepts to reinforce ignorance. Relevant to this discussion, Liang comes to describe the object in the habitual misperception as *daizhijing* 帶質境 (objects expressing the basic stuff) insofar as these objects present various types of "basic stuff" (*zhi* 質) of real existence under false imagination, such as the seemingly real seeing and image parts of *ālaya*

[15] From the Yogācāra perspective, *feiliang* is erroneous knowledge, which Liang specifies as non-knowledge (*feizhishi* 非知識) (YDZX: 160–161). For Yogācārins, it is a mistake to impose a concept on sense manifold, a mistake that is exemplified by how the seventh consciousness superimposes an unchanging ego on the seeing part of *ālaya* and misperceives it as a self-in-itself. Erroneous knowing can also come from fallacious inference, which does not seem to be fully unpacked by Liang (YDZX: 160). Kuiji's example of fallacious inference is that if someone perceives smoke and infers fire, but it turns out that what this person has seen is just mist over a huge waterfall, then the misinference of fire on the basis of the misinference of smoke becomes fallacious inference (T44N1840, P140a9).

(YDZX: 169). Objects in conceptual misperception are referred to as *duyingjing* 獨影境 (objects as merely illusory representations), for they are not straightforwardly presented but merely amount to "illusory representations" (*yingxiang* 影像) of the basic stuff (YDZX: 170).[16]

In his discussions on the three modes of knowing, the three natures, and the three types of cognitive objects, Liang describes this-worldly sensation as that which connects abstract concept and concrete idea in an ignorant mindset, with awakening *qua* sensation at the Buddha level. As such, Liang no longer deems the functionality of consciousness in the this-worldly realm to be illusorily non-existent. Rather, it allows for the open possibility between misperception and insight. The open possibility is determined by the mind of each person. As suggested by the analysis of cognitive objects, the mind does not passively receive external stimuli. Rather, it actively reaches out to constitute a meaningful perceptual-field full of illusory representations, the basic stuff under false imagination, or things as they actually are. In other words, the transcendental ideality of the mind is correlated with conventional/empirical reality to ensure the non-duality and the fluid transformation of ignorance and awakening. Liang expresses the correlative non-duality of these two realms as "non-duality of the oneness of all *dharmas*" (*yiqiefa yixing fei-er* 一切法一性非二) (YDZX: 72). Turning to Western philosophy, he concludes that epistemic realism fails to explain the origin of illusory representations in its affirmation of mind-independent reality, while epistemic idealism cannot attest to the objective existence of the basic stuff (YDZX: 169). For Liang, even Kant fails to demarcate how things actually are from the basic stuff of real existence and illusory representations (YDZX: 169).

Liang's conception of correlative non-dualism matured in his 1920 *Manual of Yogācāra*. A major breakthrough of this manual consists in Liang's recognition of epistemology as the first philosophy that provides a methodological foundation for metaphysical enquiries (WSSY: 271). In light of his stress on epistemology, Liang no longer perceives the school of characteristics as inferior to the school of nature. Rather, he identifies later Yogācāra as representative of all Buddhist teachings (WSSY: 269).

For Liang, later Yogācāra's doctrine of consciousness-only directs one's attention back to everyday, this-worldly experience (WSSY: 282). This is why Liang opens his interpretation of consciousness-only by describing how a person comes to know a white porcelain bottle (WSSY: 282). This person first acquires pure sensations as various types of immediate awareness of the white color or the hard texture, etc. (WSSY: 283). Pure sensations then serve as the ground for two types of mediated knowledge. From synthesizing immediate awareness, the person can derive *feiliang* as a concrete idea of a white porcelain bottle instantaneously, and *biliang* as the inference of an abstract concept of "white porcelain bottle" (WSSY: 283). Since

[16] Here, Liang does not refer to Kuiji's treatise on consciousness-only (T43N1831, P620a19-b27), but cites Yongming Yanshou 永明延壽 (904–976) (T48N2016) for elucidating these three types of cognitive objects.

both abstract concept and concrete idea are founded upon sensation, it is through sensation that various objects appear in a person's experience. As such, Liang contends that consciousness-only is *ipso facto* "sensation-only" (*weiyou ganjue* 唯有感覺) (WSSY: 286). Sensation unfolds through the four-part structure of the seeing part, the image part, the self-awareness, and the reflexive awareness of self-awareness, as an indication of how mental acts and perceived phenomena arise from the underlying flow of consciousness that is reflectively aware of its functionality (WSSY: 287).

Thus, the mind—the system of eight types of consciousness—should not be reduced to a collection of mental acts as a unity of psychological activities. Nor is it the same as an absolute idea *qua* the underlying self-awareness. In Liang's terms, the mind in the Yogācāra sense is a "thing" (*dongxi* 東西), not an "activity" (*zuoyong* 作用), a "whole" (*zhengge* 整個), not a "half" (*banbian* 半邊) (WSSY: 288). This is how Liang demarcates later Yogācāra's position from strands of idealism that perceive the mind as a unity of psychological activities or an absolute idea. He then moves on to the Yogācāra critique of realism. The term "*ālambanapratyaya*" (*suoyuanyuan* 所緣緣) is introduced to describe the "condition" (*yuan* 緣, *pratyaya*) of that "which can be perceived" (*suoyuan* 所緣, *ālambana*) (WSSY: 297). By definition, an *ālambanapratyaya* must fulfil two requirements: it should have real existence to be a condition, and it should be perceivable. Some realists inside the Buddhist community conceive of atom-like *paramāṇu* (*jiwei* 極微) as *ālambanapratyaya*, without being mindful of how such objects are too small to be perceivable (WSSY: 298). Others depict a combination of atom-like *paramāṇu* as *ālambanapratyaya*, subsequently overlooking that certain fictional combinations have no real existence (WSSY: 299). For instance, if a person hallucinates and sees two moons, the existence of the second moon is hardly real (WSSY: 299). Thus, it is not the case that there are mind-independent real objects serving as external stimuli to affect the mind and produce knowledge (WSSY: 296). Rather, the mind actively serves as the condition for the possibility of these objects to appear in one's experience. As such, objects depend on consciousness to be cognized (WSSY: 301). Through its description of knowledge, Liang follows later Yogācāra to explain how transcendental ideality is correlated with empirical reality—a correlation that secures the transformability from this-worldly ignorance to other-worldly awakening.

Upon using the Yogācāra doctrine of consciousness as the methodological foundation for metaphysical enquiries, Liang attributes the origin of suffering to knowledge, given that the cognition of consciousness serves as the ground for the rise of mental factors, including the affective mental states of feeling, emotion, and affliction (WSSY: 309–318). While he speaks of Yogācāra epistemology as the unique contribution of Indian culture, he reads this tradition with a focus on personal experience and liberation to underscore how the perceptual-field, as a "world of sense for each individual," is inaccessible to others (WSSY: 304). Recall the discussion on Bodhisattva in Sect. 1. If Liang centers on the personal level of experience, he probably will need other resources outside the Buddhist tradition to furnish people with a moral theory at the interpersonal level and finalize the mechanics for the Bodhisattvas' compassionate practice. Meanwhile, in 1918, Liang's father committed suicide in defense of Confucianism, which led him to rediscover this tradition in grief. According to a "Speech Delivered at the First Seminar on Confucius' Philosophy" (在孔子哲學第一次研究會上的演講, henceforth KZZX), Liang locates the moral teaching of *jiaohua* 教化 (education and transformation) in Confucianism as a skillful means to be used by Buddhists as an integral part of their Bodhisattva practice in this-worldly life that prepares them for realizing otherworldly emptiness (KZZX: 550).

These deliberations led to his 1921 monograph on *Eastern and Western Cultures and Their Philosophies* (東西文化及其哲學, henceforth DXWH). Together with the 1920 manual, it shows how Liang demarcates "Indian culture" (*yinduhua* 印度化) and "Chinese culture" (*zhonguohua* 中國化) from "Western culture" (*xihua* 西化) (WSSY: 259). In his investigation of these cultures, he starts by defining culture as a way of life that unfolds through moment-by-moment arising "events" (*shi* 事) of a seeing part and an image part (DXWH: 376). Explicitly utilizing Yogācāra vocabulary, Liang innovatively incorporates the doctrine of consciousness-only into his philosophical framework. He continues to detail that life by nature is an endless "will" (*yiyu* 意欲) (DXWH: 352). The three forms of will characterize Western culture, Chinese culture, and Indian Culture, respectively: "forward-moving" (*xiangqian* 向前) in its stress on conquering things in the world, "self-reconciliating" (*ziweitiaohe* 自為調和) in its emphasis on the harmonious co-existence of a person and the world, and "backward-moving" (*xianghou* 向後) in its negation of any form of duality (DXWH: 381–395).

In the 1921 work, Liang continues to make a case for his analysis of will through epistemology (DXWH: 396). Advancing the epistemic theory in *Outline of Indian Philosophy*, he connects more explicitly the three modes of knowing with the three types of cognitive objects (DXWH: 397). First, pure sensation *qua xianliang* is the immediate awareness of *xingjing*—namely, objects that present things as they are (DXWH: 397). For instance, pure sensation furnishes a person with an immediate awareness of tea flavor when this person tastes tea, with a straightforward awareness of white when seeing a white cloth (DXWH: 397). From pure sensations, a person can derive abstract concepts of black tea, green tea, strong tea, or light tea and distinguish them from the concepts of non-tea beverages such as water or wine, even when this person has never tasted any one of them (DXWH: 398). Abstract thinking produces inference *qua biliang* that is directed toward a specific type of cognitive objects called *duyingjing*, as merely mental representations without reference to any basic stuff in everyday experience (DXWH: 399).

The most ingenious part of this discussion can be found in Liang's delineation of concrete ideas or *feiliang*. Here, Liang refashions the definition of concrete ideas to remove the negative connotation the concept of *feiliang* held in its original Buddhist context. He reinterprets this mode of knowing as "intuition" (*zhijue* 直覺)—a state between immediate awareness and abstract thinking (DXWH: 399). As such, intuition arises on the basis of sensation and paves the way for inference, which furnishes a person with a concrete understanding of the self and other things in everyday experience (DXWH: 399). Intuition is the basis for several mental factors, such as "aesthetic feelings" (*yiwei* 意味) (DXWH: 400). Its cognitive object amounts to *daizhijing,* which is characterized by Liang as partly objective due to its reference to the basic stuff of real existence and partly subjective due to the meaning bestowed by a subject (DXWH: 400). Although Yogācārins ascribe *feiliang* as the epistemic origin of habitual misperceptions and innate attachments, Liang appreciates it as intuition that indicates the individual creativity needed to flourish in the this-worldly realm.

In this epistemic framework, Liang portrays Western culture as that which uses inference on the basis of pure sensation for empowering the forward-moving will and enabling social progress (DXWH: 485). Nonetheless, due to the epistemic limitation of inference, Western culture cannot realize the ultimate truth of emptiness but only reinforces the self-other confrontation, which determines its inability to resolve the existential crisis (DXWH: 518). Turning to Chinese culture, Liang reworks Confucianism into a way of life that prioritizes intuition over inference (DXWH: 486). Confucianism proposes to overcome dualist thinking by immersing the microcosmic individual "I" into the macrocosmic universal "I" (DXWH: 448). Such an immersion can be realized through moral cultivation, which will terminate conceptual misperceptions and discriminative attachments (DXWH: 486). By virtue of Confucianism, a person is able, together with other people, to initiate the purification of consciousness in this-worldly life, as preparation for removing the habitual misperceptions and innate attachments to realize the utmost transformation of the mind(s). While Confucianism furnishes Chinese culture with the self-reconciliating will, only Indian Buddhism can bring about universal awakening (DXWH: 487). Subordinating inference to pure sensation, Buddhism enables a person to perceive emptiness in terms of this-worldly sensation (DXWH: 411). Eventually, this person goes beyond cognition to become one with emptiness as the "realization of suchness in ultimate wisdom" (*genbenzhi zheng zhengru* 根本智證真如) (DXWH: 411). The backward-moving will in Indian culture, thus, finalizes the transformation of the this-worldly society into the other-worldly pure dharma realm (DXWH: 411–413).

Now that Chinese and Indian cultures play their distinctive yet complementary and indispensable roles in the realization of universal awakening, Liang concludes that the world is in the process of accepting first Western science for social progress and then Chinese Confucianism for moral cultivation, before finally embracing Indian Buddhism for liberation (DXWH: 526–528). Remarking on how Indian and Chinese cultures are premature, Liang perceives the modernization of China not as Westernization but as Sinicization—namely, a rejuvenation of Confucianism (DXWH: 539). Upon acquiring this viewpoint, Liang confidently returns to this-worldly life.

5 Conclusion

Since Liang embraced the Yogācāra idea of non-duality as a life principle, he was able to engage in the Confucian moral cultivation in this-worldly life as the beginning of purifying consciousness for the Buddhist pursuit of other-worldly emptiness and universal awakening. As previously mentioned, Liang read Yogācāra with a focus on personal liberation and was subsequently convinced that Buddhism as a teaching of other-worldly emptiness is limited in providing sufficient resources to remedy this-worldly problems (DXWH: 529). In his terms, Buddhism preserved only the "method" (*fangfa* 方法), not the mechanism for "self-aware" (*zijue* 自覺) and "self-disciplined" (*zilü* 自律) moral actions (RFYT: 169). It was this conviction that made him question the potential of humanistic Buddhism (DXWH: 528).[17]

Nonetheless, the Buddhist pursuit of other-worldly emptiness remained an aspiration for those who cultivate themselves in compliance with Confucian morality. That explains why Liang disapproved of Xiong Shili's critique of Buddhism, insofar as Liang considered Xiong to be oblivious to the Bodhisattva spirit of staying in this-worldly life to save all sentient beings without being entrapped in *saṃsāra* (DXSH: 773). It can be inferred that Liang located a concrete mechanism of the Bodhisattvas' compassionate practice in Confucian moral theories. As such, he was able to move freely between being this-worldly Confucian in practice and other-worldly Buddhist in aspiration.

References

DMGXZ *Da meiguo xuezhe aikai xiansheng fantanjilu zhaiyao* 答美國學者艾愷先生訪談記錄摘要 ["Summary of the Recorded Interview with American Scholar Guy Alitto"; 1980], *LSMQJ*, 1993, vol. 8: 1137–1178.

DXWH *Dong-Xi wenhua ji qi zhexue* 東西文化及其哲學 [*Eastern and Western Cultures and Their Philosophies*; 1921], *LSMQJ*, 1989, vol. 1: 319–547.

FFYSJ *Fofa yu shijian* 佛法與世間 ["Buddhist Dharma and This-Worldly Realm"; 1978], *LSMQJ*, 1993, vol. 7: 454.

JYJYL *Jiuyuan jueyi lun* 究元決議論 [*On Finding the Foundations and Resolving the Doubt*; 1916], *LSMQJ*, 1989, vol. 1: 1–22.

LSMQJ *Liang Shuming quanji* 梁漱溟全集 [*Complete Works of Liang Shuming*, vols. I to VIII]. Jinan: Shandong People Press, 1989–1993.

RFYT *Ru-Fo yitong lun* 儒佛異同論 ["On the Difference Between Confucianism and Buddhism"; 1966], *LSMQJ*, 1993, vol. 7: 152–169.

TF *Tan fo* 談佛 ["On Buddhism"; 1914], *LSMQJ*, 1991, vol. 4: 487–492.

TWDSX *Tan wode sixiang wenti* 談我的思想問題 ["On the Problem of My Thought"; 1964], *LSMQJ*, 1993, vol. 7: 117–124.

WDRL *Wo dui renlei xinli renshi qianhou zhuanbian butong* 我對人類心理認識前後轉變不同 ["The Changes and Differences in My Understanding of Human Psychology"; 1965], *LSMQJ*, 1993, vol. 7: 130–143.

[17] For a more detailed analysis of Liang's exchange with Taixu, see Cheng 2002; Meynard 2011.

WDZX *Wo de zixue xiaoshi* 我的自學小史 [*The Short History of My Self-Learning*; 1942], *LSMQJ*, 1989, vol. 2: 661–699.

WSSY *Weishi shuyi* 唯識述義 [*Manual of Yogācāra*; 1920], *LSMQJ*, 1989, vol. 1: 251–320.

YDZX *Yindu zhexue gailun* 印度哲學概論 [*Outline of Indian Philosophy*; 1919–1922], *LSMQJ*, 1989, vol. 1: 23–250.

YXSL *Yi Xiong Shili xiansheng* 憶熊十力先生 ["In Memory of Mr. Xiong Shili"; 1983], *LSMQJ*, 1993, vol. 7: 522–523.

ZKZZX *Zai kongzizhexue diyici yanjiuhui shang de yanjiang* 在孔子哲學第一次研究 會上的演講 ["Speech Delivered at the First Seminar on Confucius Philosophy; 1918"], *LSMQJ*, 1991, vol. 4: 549–550.

Alitto, Guy. 1976. The Conservative as Sage: Liang Shu-ming. In *The Limits of Change: Essays on Conservative Alternatives in Republican China*, ed. Charlotte Furth. Cambridge: Harvard University Press.

———. 1979. *The Last Confucian: Liang Shu-ming and the Chinese Dilemma of Modernity*. Berkeley: University of California Press.

Aviv, Eyal. 2020. *Differentiating the Pearl from the Fish-Eye: Ouyang Jingwu and the Revival of Scholastic Buddhism*. Leiden: Brill.

Cao, Yueming 曹躍明. 1995. *A Study of the Philosophical Thinking of Liang Shuming* 梁漱溟哲學思想研究. Tianjin: Tianjin Renmin Chubanshe.

Chang, Hao. 1976. New Confucianism and the Intellectual Crisis of Contemporary China. In *The Limits of Change: Essays on Conservative Alternatives in Republican China*, ed. Charlotte Furth. Cambridge: Harvard University Press.

Chen, Lai 陳來. 2014. *The Ontology of Ren* 仁學本體論. Beijing: Sanlian Shudian.

Cheng, Gongrang 程恭讓. 2002. Theoretical Issues with Humanistic Buddhism Examined from the Debate between Taixu and Liang Shuming 太虛與梁漱溟的一場爭辯看人生佛教的理論難題. *Philosophical Investigations* 哲學研究 5: 71–77.

Chien, Kai-Ting 簡凱廷. 2017. Scrutinizing Kongyin Zhencheng's Interpretation of Faxiang Theories 空印鎮澄對相宗學說之商榷. *Chung-Hwa Buddhist Studies* 中華佛學研究 18: 1–39.

Gao, Ruiquan 高瑞泉. 1991. *The Decline of the Mandate of Heaven* 天命的沒落. Shanghai: Shanghai Renmin Chubanshe.

Gong, Jianping 龔建平. 1996. On the Syncretism of Confucianism and Buddhism in Liang Shuming's Philosophy of Life 略論梁漱溟人生哲學中的儒佛雙重性. *Academic Journal of Shaanxi Normal University* 陝西師範大學學報 3: 96–102.

Gu, Hongliang 顧紅亮. 2008. *The Confucian Lifeworld* 儒家生活世界. Shanghai: Shanghai Renmin Chubanshe.

Guo, Qiyong 郭齊勇 and Gong Jianping 龔建平. 2011. *The Philosophical Thinking of Liang Shuming* 梁漱溟哲學思想. Beijing: Beijing Daxue Chubanshe.

Hanafin, John. 2003. The 'Last Buddhist': The Philosophy of Liang Shuming. In *New Confucianism: A Critical Examination*, ed. John Makeham. New York: Palgrave.

Keng, Ching. 2009. *Yogācāra Buddhism Transmitted or Transformed?* Ph.D. Dissertation. Harvard University.

Kuiji 窺基. *Commentary of the Treatise on the Perfection of Consciousness-only* 成唯識論述記. T.43, No. 1830. (see Takakusu et al.)

Kuiji 窺基. *Handbook to the Treatise on the Perfection of Consciousness-only* 成唯識論掌中樞要. T.43, No. 1831. (see Takakusu et al.)

Kuiji 窺基. *Commentary of the Treatise on the Entering the Correct Principles of Hetuvidyā* 因明入正理論疏. T.44, No. 1840. (see Takakusu et al.)

Lai, Shen-Chon 賴賢宗. 2006. *The Exchange between Tathāgatagarbha and the Yogācāra Doctrine of Consciousness-only* 如來藏說與唯識思想的交涉. Taipei: Xinwenfeng Chuban.

Lee, Hing-Yu 李慶餘. 2015. *Between This World and Other World* 在出世與入世之間. Taipei: Xuesheng Shuju.

Lin, Chen-Kuo. 2014. The Uncompromising Quest for Genuine Buddhism. In *Transforming Consciousness: Yogācāra Thought in Modern China*, ed. John Makeham. Oxford: Oxford University Press.

Lin, An-Wu 林安梧. 1996. *History of Contemporary New Confucian Philosophy* 當代新儒家哲學史論. Taipei: Mingwen Shuju.

Lü, Cheng 呂澂. 1986. *The Collected Writings of Lü Cheng on Buddhism* 呂澂佛學論著選集. Jinan: Qilu Shushe.

Lynch, Catherine. 2018. *Liang Shuming and the Populist Alternative in China*. Leiden: Brill.

Ma, Yong 馬勇. 2008. *The Legendary Thinker, Liang Shuming* 思想奇人梁漱溟. Beijing: Beijing Daxue chubanshe.

Makeham, John. 2014. Introduction. In *Transforming Consciousness: Yogācāra Thought in Modern China*, ed. John Makeham. Oxford: Oxford University Press.

Mei, Guangxi 梅光羲. 2014. *The Selected Writings of Mei Guangxi* 梅光羲著述集. Shanghai: Dongfang Chubangshe.

Meynard, Thierry. 2007. Is Liang Shuming Ultimately a Confucian or Buddhist? *Dao: A Journal of Comparative Philosophy* 6: 131–147.

———. 2011. *The Religious Philosophy of Liang Shuming: The Hidden Buddhist*. Leiden: Brill.

———. 2014. Liang Shuming and His Confucianized Version of Yogācāra. In *Transforming Consciousness: Yogācāra Thought in Modern China*, ed. John Makeham. Oxford: Oxford University Press.

Ouyang, Jingwu 歐陽竟無. 1995. *The Selected Writings of Ouyang Jingwu* 歐陽竟無集. Beijing: Zhongguo Shehuikexue Chubanshe.

Paramārtha 真諦. *The Treatise on the Matrix of Determination* 決定藏論. T.30, No. 1584. (see Takakusu et al.)

Paramārtha 真諦. *The Treatise on the Transforming Consciousness* 轉識論. T.31, No. 1587. (see Takakusu et al.)

Paramārtha 真諦. *Eighteen Verses on the Empty* 十八空論. T.31, No. 1616. (see Takakusu et al.)

Taixu 太虛. 2005. *The Collected Writings of Master Taixu Vol. 10* 太虛大師全書第十卷. Beijing: Zongjiao Wenhua Chubanshe.

Takakusu, Jinjirō 高楠順次郎, Watanabe, Kaikyoku 渡辺海旭, and Ono, Genmyō 小野玄妙. eds. 1924–1932. *Taishō Shinshū Daizōkyō* 大正新脩大藏經. Tokyo: Taishō Issaikyō Kankōkai. https://21dzk.l.u-tokyo.ac.jp/SAT/index_en.html. Accessed 27 Feb 2021.

Takasaki, Jikidō 高崎直道. 1975. *The Formation of Tathāgatagarbha Thinking* 如来蔵思想の形成. Tokyo: Shunjusha.

Wang, Zongyu 王宗昱. 1986. A Confucian or A Buddhism: An Interview with Liang Shuming 是儒家，還是佛家 — 訪梁漱溟先生. In *Chinese Culture and Chinese Philosophy* 中國文化與中國哲學, ed. Center for National Studies at Shenzhen University. Shanghai: Dongfang Chubanshe.

Wei, Chen-Tung 韋政通. 1984. *Confucianism and Modern China* 儒家與現代中國. Taipei: Dongda Tushu.

Wesołowski, Zbigniew 魏思齊. 2003. *The View on Culture of Liang Shuming* 梁漱溟 *(1893–1988)* 的文化觀. Taipei: Fujen Daxue Chubanshe.

Xuanzang 玄奘. *Treatise on the Perfection of Consciousness-only* 成唯識論. T.31, No. 1585. (see Takakusu et al.)

Yang, Guorong 楊國榮. 2003. *On the Confucian Doctrine of Mind-Nature* 王學通論. Shanghai: Huadong Shifan Daxue Chubanshe.

Yao, Zhihua. 2005. *The Buddhist Theory of Self-Cognition*. New York: Routledge.

Yinshun 印順. 1988. *The Study of Tathāgatagarbha* 如來藏之研究. Taipei: Zhengwen Chubanshe.

Yongming Yanshou 永明延壽. *Records of the Mirror of Orthodoxy* 宗鏡錄. T.48, No. 2016. (see Takakusu et al.)

Zhang, Taiyan 章太炎. 1985. *The Collected Writings of Zhang Taiyan Vol. 4* 章太炎全集第四卷. Shanghai: Shanghai Renmin Chubanshe.

Zhang, Wenru 張文儒. 2001. Liang Shuming and Buddhism 梁漱溟與佛學. *Journal of Xiangtan Normal University* 湘潭師範學院學報 23 (2): 5–11.
Zheng, Dahua 鄭大華. 1999. *On the Scholarly Thought of Liang Shuming* 梁漱溟學術思想評傳. Beijing: Beijing Daxue Chubanshe.
Zhou, Guihua 周貴華. 2006. *Consciousness-only, Mind-nature, and Tathāgatagarbha* 唯識心性與如來藏. Beijing: Zongjiao Wenhua Chubanshe.

Chapter 4
Liang the Bergsonian

Joseph Ciaudo

1 Introduction: LIANG Shuming and Bergsonism

LIANG Shuming was a Bergsonian. This is a statement difficult to challenge. Although Liang did not openly identify himself as a "disciple" of the French philosopher, he clearly acknowledged having read Henri Bergson (1859–1941) in his youth and taking into account several dimensions of his philosophy. Liang did not accept the whole philosophical system of Bergson, but he produced several positive evaluations of the man in a time when New culture advocates tended to criticize him (See e.g. Hu 1923: 293–296). Several pieces of scholarship have already documented this (e.g. Alitto 1986: 98–101; Cao 1995: 98–100; Weng 1995; An 1997; Wesolowski 1997: 83–86; Meynard 2010: 82–83). But it is also worth underlining that Liang was also a Bergsonian in the eyes of his contemporaries. For instance, he was invited by LI Shicen 李石岑 (1892–1934) to serve as one of the main contributors to the special issue of the journal *People Bell* (*Minduo* 民鐸) dedicated to Bergson in 1921, while people who disliked Bergson's philosophy tended to resent Liang for reusing some of its main concepts.

Hence, stating that Liang was a Bergsonian entails saying nothing unconventional or of much profundity, lest one investigates into what "being a Bergsonian" meant at that time and in that place. As a consequence, the present chapter will have to address several questions to clarify this label. Among others, one could ask: Was

The author would like to warmly thank Philippe Major, Thierry Meynard, Ady Van den Stock, Bart Dessein, Dan Lusthaus and the two anonymous reviewers for their valuable comments and insights on earlier versions of this text or elements discussed in this text.

J. Ciaudo (✉)
University of Orléans, Orléans, France
e-mail: joseph.ciaudo@univ-orleans.fr

T. Meynard, P. Major (eds.), *Dao Companion to Liang Shuming's Philosophy*, Dao Companions to Chinese Philosophy 17,
https://doi.org/10.1007/978-3-031-18002-6_4

Liang Bergsonian because he had read the philosopher, agreed with him on certain issues and gave a positive evaluation of his work? Was Liang a specialist of Bergson, or did he contribute to his introduction in China? Was he a Bergsonian because contemporaneous thinkers regarded him as such? Did Liang elaborate his own philosophy or thought in discussion with Bergsonism—a term to be understood in this chapter in a very encompassing sense covering both the philosophy of Bergson and its more general intellectual orientation—or by employing some of its key concepts?

But to tackle all these possible interrogations, engaging in a ground-clearing exercise is first needed. Liang took interest in Bergson's philosophy during what could be denominated "the Bergsonian moment," a period characterized by a form of global Bergsonism. Henri Bergson's impact and celebrity went far beyond the frontiers of France and Western Europe, in which he already played a role in what Frederic Worms has called the "the 1900 moment" in philosophy—a moment notably characterized by the emergence of a new series of common issues regarding psychology, life and more generally epistemology (Worms 2006, 2009). Bergson was a living superstar (Azouvi 2007) whose works were translated all around the world, providing a decisive shock and stirring heated discussions across many intellectual traditions.[1] Everywhere Bergson's books arrived, they were received with either much enthusiasm or skepticism. Often introduced in an order that did not follow the writing chronology, his *oeuvre* was usually read without a clear idea of the general reflection Bergson had wished to build book by book, essay by essay, since his seminal *Essai sur les données immédiates de la connaissance* (1889), translated into English as *Time and Free Will*. However, notions and images taken from here and there served local scholars in their debates. In the case of China, being in favor or against Bergson, invoking his concept of intuition, endorsing his idea of a "creative evolution," mimicking or rejecting his distinction between "science" and "metaphysics" became dividing lines between intellectual factions, and questions of critical importance for the nascent academic field of "philosophy" (Shino 2009). Admiring Bergson in the young Chinese Republic was for many a sign of being in the camp of the neoconservatives and the Confucian thinkers. Most of the people who presented Bergson in Chinese were, indeed, infatuated with Confucian thought, or had defended the legitimacy of Confucianism in modern China.[2] Moreover for many Chinese of the time, there was a "flavor of Chinese philosophy" in Bergson's prose (He Lin, quoted in An 1997: 343).

---

[1] Many academic works have now been dedicated to the reception of Bergson in Germany (Zanfi 2013), Russia (Nethercott 1995; Fink 1999), the Ottoman Empire and then Turkey (Sarmis 2016), Japan (Miyayama 2005; Ebersolt 2012), and of course China (Lai 1993; Wu and 吳先伍. 2005; Ciaudo 2016).

[2] The main protagonists in the introduction of Bergson in China notably include Qian Zhixiu 錢智修 (1883–1947), Zhang Dongsun 張東蓀 (1886–1973), Liu Shuya 劉叔雅 (1889–1958), Liang Qichao 梁啟超 (1873–1929), Zhang Junmai 張君勱 (1887–1969), and Lin Zaiping 林宰平 (1879–1960). Some scholars have even defended that Bergsonism played a huge role in the formation of New Confucianism (Jing 2005).

It would therefore be easy to reduce Liang's Bergsonian identity to these other labels. After all, Liang was extolling in the 1920s a pro-Confucian message and was clearly one of the main actors of what Kevin CHANG has called Chinese "domestic vitalism" (Chang 2017). Yet, as this chapter will make clear, Liang did not dwell in Bergson's philosophy merely because he was a New Confucian—which would be an anachronistic assessment. Liang was a Bergsonian in the sense that he read his works diligently. Thanks to a pretty acute, albeit uncomplete, understanding of his philosophy, he evaluated Bergson's contribution in a general history of European philosophy and in a general framework of cultural comparison. Bergson's reflection gave inspiration to LIANG Shuming, and probably helped him clarify his own thoughts. But he did not accept Bergsonism as a whole nor did he use Bergson solely to defend Confucius.

To explore the topic at hand, we will approach LIANG Shuming mainly as a reader of Bergson. But as will soon become unmistakable, one could read the French philosopher with different objectives in mind, such as questioning the validity of Yogācāra (*weishi* 唯識 in Chinese), or underlining the modernity of Confucianism. To begin with, let us thus first clarify what LIANG Shuming knew concretely of Bergson's philosophy, or more precisely which books were on his shelves.

2 LIANG Shuming: A Reader of Bergson

> I think that the vitalist school of philosophy, of which Bergson was the main representative, stirred in me the most vibrant and profound interest. I remember that some twenty years ago, I bought Bergson's works, and read them very slowly. At that moment, I had the following wishes: I yearned to be given enough time undisturbed so I could peruse all his books. Reading him was a great pleasure in life.
>
> 覺得最為發揮盡致使我深感興趣的是生命派哲學，其主要代表者為柏格森。記得二十年前，余購讀柏格森著，讀時甚慢，當時嘗有愿心，愿有從容時間儘讀柏氏書，是人生一大樂事。(ZH: 126)

These lines, written in 1935, showcase that Liang's encounter with Bergson was an important event in his life. In 1980, he also told Guy Alitto that "at least about philosophical thinkers, the person I like the most and whom I most revere, is Henri Bergson" (Liang and Ai 2010: 135). Yet, one needs to admit that references to the French philosopher are very scarce in Liang's other autobiographical writings. He hardly ever expounded on his youthful infatuation with Bergson's philosophy. The little evidence available can nonetheless help us draw the following picture.

LIANG Shuming seems to have discovered Bergson in 1915, thanks to the recommendation of a friend, ZHANG Shenfu 張申府, alias Songnian 崧年 (1893–1986), who also recommended him Schopenhauer, Gustave Lebon and Nietzsche—authors who occupy an important place in his early quotations of Western philosophers. Zhang, with whom Liang had been classmate at the Shuntian 順天 school, was at that time studying philosophy at Peking University and soon became a teacher there. Though Zhang introduced Liang to many names of Western philosophy, it is also worth noting that Liang's evaluation of Bergson ran counter to Zhang's, and it became a recurrent subject of discussion and then conflict between the two (DYLS: 656).[3]

Liang probably read some texts of Bergson as early as 1915, but it seems that he really entered in the works of the French philosopher in 1916 as one finds several references to him in his *Treatise on Finding the Foundation and Resolving the Doubt* (*Jiuyuan jueyilun* 究元決疑論) published that very year. It is, furthermore, obvious that Liang later read *An Introduction to Metaphysics* in English (Bergson 1913a) for, in 1920, he does not quote Chinese translations of the text, but the British edition (*e.g.* WSSY: 276).[4] He may also have read *Creative Evolution* in the language of Shakespeare, for when he does refer his readers to this work in the 1920s, he translated the title as *Chuangzao Jinhua* 創造進化, and did not follow Zhang Dongsun who had published a complete Chinese translation under the title *Chuanghua lun* 創化論 in 1919 (Bergson 1919). He also read what American and British scholars had written about the French philosopher; he quoted Lindsay's *Philosophy of Bergson* (Lindsay 1911) and Herbert Wildon Carr's *The Philosophy of Change* (Carr 1911). He was additionally aware of what Russell thought of Bergson, as he quoted him (WSSY: 277) and redacted an article to denounce the British philosopher's caricatural presentation of Bergson's positions (DYLS). One can also surmise that he was familiar with the presentation of Bergson that had been given in Chinese periodicals by his intellectual contemporaries, notably Qian Zhixiu (Qian 1913), for Liang associated Henri Bergson to Rudolf Eucken in the same manner as the editor of the *Eastern Miscellany* Journal (*Dongfang zazhi* 東方雜志). In his 1980 interview, Liang Shuming also mentioned having read in English *Time and Free Will* as well as *Matter and Memory* (Liang and Ai 2010: 162), but it is not clear whether he studied those books as early as the 1920s or later in his life. I would suspect the second possibility is the correct one.

These few remarks are of particular interest because it means that Liang Shuming gained a certain understanding of Bergson through his own effort while dabbling in Anglo-Saxon translations of and literature about the French philosopher.[5] He was not misled by inexact or problematic Chinese translation of the texts.[6] He engaged with Bergson despite the fact that "his books are not easy to read" (Liang and Ai 2010: 162).

Furthermore, Liang's professed admiration for Bergson in 1980 may indicate that reading the French philosopher had a very powerful impact on him throughout his life, and he may have perused his books several times through the passing years. Yet one also needs to reckon that Liang's references to Bergson are mostly confined to his early works, and some specialists of Liang Shuming have even spoken of a

[3] On Zhang Songnian's harsh and politically motivated criticism of Bergson cf. Zhang 1921a.

[4] At that time, only Liu Shuya's 劉叔雅 uncomplete translation of *Introduction to Metaphysics* was available to the Chinese readership: Liu 1918. A partial translation by Cai Yuanpei 蔡元培 (Cai 1921) and a complete one by Yang Zhengyu 楊正宇 (Yang 1921) would follow in 1921.

[5] One should remark here that at that time no Chinese intellectual read Bergson in French.

[6] For an exploration of the difficulties raised when translating Bergson into Chinese, see notably Lai 1993: 146–184; and Ciaudo 2013.

"Bergsonian moment" in his life (notably Meynard 2010, 2014). Mentions of the philosopher of duration after the mid-twenties are indeed quite rare, and these occurrences have long been neglected by the researchers working on Liang. Bergson was notably discussed in the following texts: *Outline of Yogācāra* (*Weishi shuyi* 唯識述義) (WSSY), *Eastern and Western Cultures and Their Philosophies* (*Dongxi wenhua jiqi zhexue* 中西文化及其哲學) (DXWH), as well as in two articles, one regarding the proximity of Bergson's philosophy and Yogācāra (WSJY) and one about Russell's criticism of the French philosopher (DYLS). "LIANG Shuming the Bergsonian" may therefore simply look as a stage in Liang's intellectual development, an important stage nonetheless for his discussion of Bergson could be regarded as a common element in his early works as HU Yuanling 胡元玲 recently argued (Hu 2019).

3 LIANG Shuming: A Buddhist Reader of Bergson?

In his *Treatise on Finding the Foundation and Resolving the Doubt*, LIANG Shuming revealed, for the first time, his intellectual interest for Bergson with the following sentence:

> What Bergson shed light upon brings me extreme surprise and pleasure. I would therefore like to integrate his ideas in my discussion of the world.
> 柏格森之所明，尤極可驚可喜。今欲說世間者，因取以入吾論。(JYJY: 13)

A discussion of several comments by Wildon Carr on Bergson's philosophy followed the remark. In this early work, Liang did not merely give a positive evaluation of Bergson, he also reproduced several of his ideas regarding the nature of the universe and evolution, notably that everything is movement, or that instinct and intelligence as two modes of living in the world are the results of an evolutionary process. The text was, furthermore, not devoid of parallels between Bergson's philosophy and Buddhism. He, for instance, wrote that "the intellect of living things in Bergson's philosophy corresponds to the eight forms of cognition or *parijñāna*" (JYJY: 14). Liang also wrote that "the incessantly changing movement of life (*bu xi zhuan bian* 不息轉變) is not different from how Buddhism explains that no phenomenon has a nature of its own (*yita xing* 依他性, skt. *paratantra-svabhāva*)" (JYJY: 14).[7]

This connection drawn between the two systems of thought is of significance in the history of the reception of Bergson in China. Very soon after Bergsonism had been introduced into China, several scholars, notably ZHANG Taiyan 章太炎 (1869–1936), defended the idea that it presented much resemblance with Buddhism and most specifically Yogācāra philosophy. As soon as he arrived on Chinese shores, Bergson was enrolled in a discussion of comparative philosophy in which Liang played a critical role. In 1921, at the occasion of the publication of the *People Bell*

[7] For an analysis of Liang's first presentation of Bergson within this text and its Buddhism background cf. Han 2020.

special issue on Bergson, a real debate was put into print.[8] The apple of discord was notably whether the notion of "intuition" in Bergson's works could be associated with some notions of the Buddhist school. Some claimed that it was similar to the "storehouse consciousness" (*zangshi* 藏識, Skt. *ālayavijñāna*), others to "direct perception" (*xianliang* 現量, Skt. *pratyakṣa*) or "intellection/inferential reasoning" (*biliang* 比量, Skt. *anumāna*). LIANG Shuming took part in the discussions and rejected these ideas. His judgment was final:

> As such, this thing called "intuition" cannot be recognized by Yogācāra. As we can see, Bergson and the intuitionist clique speak, for instance, of "duration," "movement," "real self," many notions that a scholar from the Yogācāra tradition cannot admit. These are all "fallacies" (*feiliang* 非量, Skt. *apramāṇa*) and should be opposed with the strongest force. One could almost say that the two schools are sworn enemies; how could one be confounded with the other!?
>
> 所以直覺這個東西是唯識所不承認的。因此我們看：　像柏格森一直覺派一所說的種種，如“綿延”，“流動”，“真我”……都是唯識家所不承認的，都是指為“非量”的，所極力反對的。差不多兩家正式仇敵了，怎好認成一家人呢　　！(DXWH: 652)

One could be tempted to say that LIANG Shuming had completely changed his mind on this topic. Read out of context, he could even sound anti-Bergsonian. But one needs to be precise, for Liang's early association of Bergson to Yogācāra was concerned with intellect and not intuition—a word that is absent from his 1916 text. As a matter of fact, his 1921 article on Yogācāra and Bergson as well as other elements in his books show that Liang later became an increasingly attentive reader regarding the question of intuition. Unlike most of his contemporaries', his texts displayed a genuine understanding of this notion. He clearly identified Bergson in the history of western philosophy, as someone who tried to restore metaphysics after its Kantian condemnation. Intuition, to the contrary of sensation and conceptual inference, was able to furnish access to the Universe as an absolute. Quoting *An Introduction to Metaphysics*, Liang accepted the idea that it was an "integral experience" (*quanzheng de ganyan* 全整的感驗) (WSSY: 276). He reproduced the idea that to philosophize "is to invert the habitual direction of the work of thought" (Bergson 1913a: 59). He also pointed at the fact that there are two types of intuition for the French philosopher: "An intuition that relates to the senses" and one "that surpasses the intellect" (WSJY: 650), which is a clear reference to the passage of *Creative Evolution* where Bergson had wrestled with the Kantian position (Bergson 1913b: 360). Liang's writing also pointed at the fact that he was aware of the proximity between intuition and instinct in Bergson's works (WSJY: 651).[9] Liang understood what Bergson used intuition for, and could regard it as a method to suppress the delimitation between subject and object, and to access life as a continuum. But in

[8] For a general presentation of this debate, cf. Yao 2014.

[9] Bergson notably wrote that "by intuition I mean instinct that has become disinterested, self-conscious, capable of reflecting upon its object and of enlarging it definitely" (Bergson 1913b: 176). Liang even confused the two notions when dealing with elements of Mozi's philosophy, but rectified this point in the preface of the third edition of *Eastern and Western Cultures* dated from 1922 (DXWH: 322).

the end, he doubted (*keyi* 可疑) of its concrete result (DXWH: 409) for Bergson's philosophy presented, in his opinion, important defects related to ontology and epistemology. He notably denounced Bergson's understanding of "intuition" as too subjective, emanating entirely from the individual, which impeded it to attain truth (DXWH: 406). This more critical stance toward Bergson's philosophy could be explained by two main factors: first, since 1916 Liang had gained a stronger foothold in Yogācāra[10] and more generally Indian philosophical schools; secondly, he also moved away from Carr's sympathetic reading of Bergson and took interest in Lindsay's more critical book. To understand what Liang reproached Bergsonism for, it is useful here to see how Liang indirectly replied to Bergson by using his very own metaphor when dealing with epistemology: cinema.

In the fourth chapter of *Creative Evolution*, Bergson had explained that "the mechanism of our ordinary knowledge is of a cinematographical kind" (Bergson 1913b: 306). For Bergson the mind "behaves in much the same way as the movement (…) of the cinematographical film, a movement hidden in the apparatus and whose function it is to superpose the successive pictures on one another in order to imitate the movement of the real object" (Bergson 1913b: 313). The problem lies in the fact that "there is *more* in a movement than in the successive positions attributed to the moving object, *more* in a becoming than in the forms passed through in turn, *more* in the evolution of form than the forms assumed one after another" (Bergson 1913b: 316). The intellect offers but a diminution of reality, for it operates on the premise that reality is motionless—time has been spatialized. Furthermore, Bergson laid out the idea that "Modern, like ancient, science proceeds according to the cinematographical method. It cannot do otherwise; all science is subject to this law. For it is of the essence of science to handle signs, which it substitutes for the objects themselves" (Bergson 1913b: 329). Science is for that matter no invention of men; it is simply how our mind works. However, according to Bergson, science is not the only method to know the world or the self: there is also metaphysics. Bergson had clearly drawn the line between science and metaphysics in his *Introduction to Metaphysics*: the former proceeds through an outside analysis of objects, while the latter invites us to enter inside the objects by the means of intuition. "By intuition is meant the kind of *intellectual sympathy* by which one places oneself within an object in order to coincide with what is unique in it and consequently inexpressible" (Bergson 1913a: 6). Therefore, when Bergson spoke of "giving up," "escaping," or "setting aside" the cinematographical habits of our intellect (Bergson 1913b: 312, 313, 342), he wished to develop:

> another faculty, complementary to the intellect, (…). For, as soon as we are confronted with true duration, we see that it means creation, and that if that which is being unmade endures, it can only be because it is inseparably bound to what is making itself. Thus, will appear the necessity of a continual growth of the universe, I should say of a life of the real. And thus will be seen in a new light the life which we find on the surface of our planet, a life directed the same way as that of the universe, and inverse of materiality. To intellect, in short, there will be added intuition. (Bergson 1913b: 343)

[10] Cf. Meynard 2014: notably 203–205 and the chapter by Li Jingjing in this book.

Intuition was therefore conceived as another means of knowledge, a supplement to intelligence, which according with what was quoted by Liang (and reproduced above) provided access to Life in its "duration," and "movement," or to the "real self". It was a means to access both the inner and outer worlds of the subject. In *Eastern and Western Cultures,* Liang discussed "intuition" within the framework of Yogācāra epistemology and denoted it as *feiliang*, that I translate as "fallacy" or "fallacies" (DXWH: 399–401, notably p. 401: 直覺就是"非量"). Several pieces of secondary scholarship have defended the idea that Liang had given a new meaning to *feiliang* by identifying it with *zhijue* (e.g. An 1997 or Hanafin 2003) and therefore my translation here could be contested. However, this particular point should merit an ample discussion that would go far beyond the argument I would like to make here[11]—for the question of whether *zhijue* is a "revised *feiliang*" or not doesn't affect the issue of Liang's attitude towards Bergson's understanding of intuition that is here at hand. This remark regarding translation being said, let us now see what

[11] The problem of how to understand the connection between *zhijue* and *feiliang* in *Eastern and Western Cultures* lies in how one reads this particular section (DXWH: 399–401). Here, Liang indeed writes "直覺就是'非量'" which could be translated as "*zhijue* is in fact '*feiliang*.'" But we are in fact facing two difficulties: one semantic and one grammatical. What does "非量" mean? And what does "是" mean? In the same section, Liang explains rejecting the term *feiliang* because it is a negative term—negative in two senses: in terms of value (*xiaoji* 消極) but also in a verbal sense (*fouding* 否定)—*feijiang* 非量 is a negation of *liang* 量. And it is true that from an Yogācāra perspective "intuition" is no *liang* 量 or *pramāna*, that is a "proper means of knowledge." By the way, in his *Outline of Yogācāra*, Liang had written that *feiliang* was no knowledge (*feilaing ji fei zhishi* 非量即非知識) (WSSY: 158). Although one could argue that Liang has his own idiosyncratic definition of *feiliang*, it seems to me that he was in fact following a Buddhist reading of *feiliang*. Still in this section, Liang writes that "When they speak of things in relation to *feiliang* (*feiliang xi* "非量"係), they include elements that could be regarded as close or similar to *xianliang* and *biliang*" (唯識家所謂"非量"係包括"似現量""似比量"而言). An often neglected, but key term is *xi* 係: it could suggest that *feiliang* is a category including many means of knowledge, an idea incidentally present in the *Commentary on Gate to Logic* (*Nyāyamukha*) (*Yinming ru zhengli lunshu* 因明入正理論疏), a text to which Liang's sentence is a direct reference, if not a quotation: "everything that looks like *xiliang or biliang* [without being it properly] should be included in *feiliang*" (似現似比，總入非量) (T1840-95c). The character *zong* 總 clearly indicates that there is not only one *feiliang*; many things could be denoted as *feiliang*: it is a general category. When reading Liang's sentence "*zhijue* is in fact '*feiliang*'" (直覺就是"非量"), one therefore has to be very careful. *Shi* 是 does not mean "to be" as a verb; it is no synonym of "to equate" or "to correspond to"; it is but a copula. The reverse sentence "'非量'是直覺" "'*feiliang*' is in fact *zhijue*" would probably not be acceptable for Liang. *Feiliang* is, in a sense, an attribute. *Zhijue* is but one type or form of *feiliang*, and one could add here that it is a type that Liang wishes to save from Buddhist denigration. *Zhijue* is therefore not only read positively, it is also much more appropriate (*wei dang* 為當) because it refers to something precise unlike *feiliang* which is but a generic term to say "not a proper means of knowledge," and that explains why Liang would drop the term *feiliang* and prefer *zhijue*. In Buddhist terms, and in Liang Shuming's epistemology, *zhijue* is still a fallacy, but a fallacy that could work to grasp Life in a Confucian setting. Therefore, though I denote *zhijue* as a fallacy, my meaning is not to say that *zhijue* could not be a useful mode of thinking in and of itself. Another possibility of translation could have been to render it as "non-*pramāna*," but giving to the anglophone readers a term in half-Sanskrit lacks elegancy.

Liang wrote in *Eastern and Western Cultures* about the example of cinema in the section about epistemology, and notably the primacy of "direct perception":

> For example, when the first step of direct perception (*xianliang*) occurs, intellection (*biliang*) or fallacies (*feiliang*) that come from the selfish interest have not arisen yet. Thus, when something flies before our eyes, one simply sees the flight. Flight is solely a form of movement, a signification and a direction. It is not a concrete thing, and it can therefore not be recognized by direct perception. Because direct perception, that is sensation, only captures an image[12] (*yingxiang* 影像, Skt. *pratibimba*) of the thing—be it a bird or a flag—, it could be compared to a photograph. When the thing that flies before my eyes do so for a hundred instants, I experience accordingly a hundred sensations that succeed one another; there are a hundred pictures that reveal themselves in sequences. Each of these pictures is in a state of immobility, and as such, even with a hundred pictures I cannot see the flight from beginning to end. Simultaneously it is necessary that intuition (*zhijue*) and other faculties come into play to thread all these pictures together; it is only then that the movement of flight is seen. It works according to the very same principle as the cinematographer. As a consequence, if one does not see the flight, that means that intuition did not take place, and that we are only in presence of direct perception. Arriving at this step of direct perception is possible only when one has been totally liberated. Then, not only does the void movement of flight disappears, but also the very continuity of photographs, and as such one accesses complete emptiness and non-being. Since photographs stem from sensations, one could compare the sensation to a question, to which the photograph is but a possible answer. If you do not ask any question, there will be no answer. When one presumptuously formulates inquiries, the sensory organs are tools for interrogating. When the bare form of an object [or raw substance] (*benzhi* 本質, Skt. *bimba*) encounters the mental changes of the eight forms of consciousness (*ba shi bian* 八識變), it produces images (*yingxiang*). [But] when one attains the great liberation, there are no more inquiries nor questions, raw substances and images fade away; thus the direct perception offers direct realization of "thusness" (*zhenru* 真如, Skt. *tathātā*)—*i.e.* the fundamental reality.
>
> 譬如頭一步的現量就是私利的比非量都不起了，所以看飛動的東西不見飛動。飛動是一種形勢、意味、傾向而已，並不是具體的東西，現量無從認識他。因為現量即感覺中隻現那東西——或鳥或幡——的影像，這影像隻是一張相片。當那東西在我眼前飛動假為一百刹那，我也就一百感覺相續而有一百影片相續現起。在每一影片其東西本是靜的，那麼，一百影片仍隻有靜的東西，其飛動始終不可見。必要同時有直覺等作用把這些影片貫串起來，飛動之勢乃見，這與活動電影一理。所以不見飛動，為直覺不起獨有現量之証。到次一步的現量是解放到家的時候才有的，那時不但虛的飛動形勢沒了，乃至連實的影片也沒了，所以才空無所見。因為影片本是感覺所自現，感覺譬如一問，影片即其所自為之一答，你如不問，自沒有答。當我們妄求時，感官為探問之具，遇到八識變的本質就生此影像；乃至得到大解放，無求即無問，什麼本質影像也就沒了，於是現量直証"真如"——即本體。(DXWH: 413)

After reading this long quotation, Liang's criticism of Bergson appears in all its clarity. To him, intuition does not enable us to escape the cinematographical habits of our mind. In this sense, the word "*zhijue*" that appears in the quoted paragraph

---

[12] One should note in passing that Liang's definition of "image" is completely different from Bergson's. In *Matter and Memory*, Bergson called "image" "a certain existence which is more than that which the idealist calls *a representation*" (Bergson 1911b: xi); it is "an objective reality" (Bergson 1911b: 28) independent from perception. On the contrary, "images" are the result of a direct perception or sensation for Liang; they reside within the mind.

doesn't mean "intuition" in a Bergsonian sense; it is a more generic concept, or "intuition" as understood personally by Liang—and one should keep in mind that when Liang uses "*zhijue*" without clearly mentioning the name of Bergson in the very same text, it is much probable that he doesn't use the term in a Bergsonian sense. If Liang followed the French thinker in the idea that it is through intuition that one can seize movement, it is however irrelevant because intuition creates movement in the mind, and does not give access to something in reality: "Motion is an illusion for Liang" (Hanafin 2003, 216). As such, intuition works within the cinematographer; it is not a means to access reality in its "thusness" (*tathātā* or *zhenru* 真如) or as the noumenal world. In order to establish a proper and more robust metaphysics, attention should therefore not be accorded to this "fallacy"—fallacy in the sense that it helps us only to grasp an illusion—but to "direct perception"; and "people who think that Bergson's intuition is similar to the direct perception of Buddhism are simply uttering nonsensical phrases and wrong guesses" (WSSY: 279–280). In a sense, Bergson's intuition was either regarded as completely foreign to the Yogācāra tradition,[13] or simply as one more mental activity that the Buddhist practitioner should discard in his *via negativa* work. At the same time however, that does not mean that it was useless on a philosophical level. On the contrary, as already stated by Thierry Meynard, "Liang's Bergsonian moment was crucial for the development of his own thought, since it helped him to understand how a sound Buddhist epistemology could lead to a correct Buddhist metaphysics" (Meynard 2010: 83). Liang had learned from the supposed failure of Bergson's intuition,[14] and one can even wonder whether his later uses of the concept of intuition, notably in his discussion of Confucianism had much to do with Bergsonism. Employing the same word did not necessarily mean that they denote the same concept: *zhijue* could be discussed as the Bergsonian concept of intuition, or as a concept employed by Liang to connote a form of intuitive thought in the Confucian tradition. It is however possible that Liang willingly played on this proximity of words, to reauthorize Confucius within a discursive context in which everything European is simply regarded as more "scientific."

Two ideas should additionally be stressed here: first, LIANG Shuming understood Bergson as a philosopher of method. Bergson had sketched out a methodological principle—"intuition"—to conduct inquiries in metaphysics. This was probably linked to the fact that his two main references were *An Introduction to Metaphysics* and *Creative Evolution*, the latter being a book that according to its author "does not aim at resolving at once the greatest problems [, but] (…) simply desires to define the method" (Bergson 1913b:xiv). Liang took over Bergson's famous distinction: "The experimental method is scientific; for now, I call metaphysics the intuitive method" (DXWH: 357). Yet, he was not completely satisfied with this second

[13] At least of how Liang regarded this tradition, for as some scholars already noted Liang had "a very plastic understanding of Yogācāra" (Meynard 2014: 210).

[14] But he had also learned much from comparing Yogācāra to the philosophies of Karl Pearson or Bertrand Russell, see e.g. Meynard 2014: 218.

method in terms of epistemology. He was to his core a Buddhist of the Yogācāra tradition. As such, Bergson's philosophical positions could make sense as logical arguments but not as soteriological and ontological truths. Liang rightly noted that Bergson had dealt with the problems of "duration," "movement" and "real self." However, these points were precisely elements that he could not accept. For Bergson there was one reality that we can all intuitively access: "our personality in its flowing through time—our self which endures" (Bergson 1913a: 8). But for Liang anyone who "wants to lift the veil and to directly attain the one true absolute reality, must discard the double attachment (*erzhi* 二執) [to the self (*wozhi* 我執) and to the *dharmas* or the world (*fazhi* 法執)]" (DXWH: 412). Hence, the self that Bergson accesses with intuition was regarded as an illusion to be lifted. John Hanafin has argued that "Liang [found] in Western and Chinese philosophy themes that corresponded to, and therefore reinforced his fundamentally *Weishi* beliefs (…) because Liang subscribed to the *Weishi* view that everything was in a state of continuous change, the more readily he focused on this same theme in the process philosophy of Bergson or in the *Book of Changes*" (Hanafin 2003, 195), but a precise reading also shows that Liang was quite selective in his reading of the word "change," for it did not mean exactly the same thing in the philosophy of Bergson, the *Book of Changes* or Yogācāra epistemology. Liang read in the Bergsonian incessantly changing movement of life, or the *élan vital*, something associated to the problem of phenomena not having a nature of their own and being codependent—which is obviously not what Bergson intended to state. Now, we should also add that Liang completely disregarded "duration," which is, in fact, the very foundation of Bergson's philosophy.[15] He never discussed this key notion, and simply remarked that considering life and duration as inseparable was merely following a "commonplace" (*changjian* 常見) (DXWH: 414).[16] Therefore, Liang could not completely accept Bergson's intuition which was primarily the intuition of duration. Gilles Deleuze wrote accordingly that "intuition, as [Bergson] understands it methodologically, already presupposes *duration*" (Deleuze 1991: 13). As such, there was here something lost in translation. Had Bergson been able to read Chinese, he could have replied that Yogācāra epistemology epitomized what he had denounced as a "spatialization of time." But it is not here the place to open this discussion.

[15] This key idea was in truth neglected by most of the Chinese readers of Bergson, and one may wonder whether the late introduction of *Time and Free Will* (only translated into Chinese in 1927)—the book in which Bergson defended the philosophical pertinence of this notion—is not to be imputed here.

[16] In fact, one could wonder whether he did really understand it because he sometimes had weird formulations. In *Eastern and Western Cultures* for instance, he wrote that according to Bergson "the fundamental reality of the universe is not a fixed and immobile body, it is 'living' (*shengming* 生命) and 'enduring' (*mianyan* 綿延)". Two lines below he adds that "to have a direct intuitive access to duration means living the duration" (*zhijue shi ji shenghuo shi* 直覺時即生活時), but he used at this occasion the character *shi* 時 or "time," as if he did not really see the difference between time and duration (DXWH: 406).

The second important idea is that Liang accepted intuition as a method and a possible means of knowledge—despite its being irrelevant for Yogācāra. It was a pertinent concept to approach intellectual practices in a cross-cultural framework. Although the intuition—and most notably intuition as Liang believed Bergson had understood it—was not the best way to grasp reality, it was nonetheless a worthy attempt that could find parallels in other intellectual traditions, notably in Confucianism. In fact, in his discovery of intuition as the method of metaphysics, Bergson had formulated a philosophy long put into practice by the Chinese. This is the reason why Bergson was regarded as an anomaly in the Western cultural path. Liang even took Bergson as an illustration of the transformation taking place in the West, as the West was reorienting itself toward a new trajectory that corresponded to the very mode of life characterizing Chinese culture: he was applying the intellect to intuition.[17] He was part of an ongoing trend in which Liang also included people such as Rudolf Eucken, William James or Peter Kropotkin.

4 Liang Shuming: A Confucian Reader of Bergson?

Guy Alitto once wrote that "Liang interpreted Chinese metaphysics with the aid of the Frenchman" (Alitto 1986: 96), and this was perhaps one of the best use Liang made of Bergsonism: it helped him to characterize the Chinese intellectual tradition, or at least what he considered to be Chinese intellectual orthodoxy as an intuitionist tradition. However, one needs to be cautious here, for when Liang Shuming spoke of "intuition" (*zhijue* 直覺) to denote Confucianism, he did not mean "intuition" in the Bergsonian sense.[18] Furthermore, when one speaks of intuition in the Chinese context one needs to be very careful with the vocabulary used. Aside from *zhijue* which can refer both to intuition as an undifferentiated and general concept and Bergsonian intuition in particular, notions such *liangzhi* 良知, *liangxin* 良心, and *ren* 仁 were at some point assimilated to intuition by Liang. He also used the term *zhiguan* 直觀 to a lesser extent (e.g. DXWH: 357 & 393), but this rendering had

[17] On this issue cf. the chapter by Zbigniew Wesolowski in this book.

[18] Two types of arguments can support this position: firstly, in terms of conceptual articulation, both concepts do not overlap—one word refers to two different things; secondly, and most importantly, when Liang discussed intuition in Confucianism, he did not draw precise parallels with Bergsonian intuition as he had done in his discussion of Yogācāra. The discussion always remained at a very general level. When Liang spoke of intuition when dealing with Confucianism, he was using intuition in a more general sense. Afterall, Henri Bergson is not the only philosopher to have ever written on intuition.

actually the same meaning as *zhijue*.[19] In a seminal article on the topic, AN Yanming has written that Liang "actually uses it [the term intuition] in three senses without always realizing or identifying the change in meaning. They are *zhijue* as a method of knowledge, *zhijue* as an equivalent of *benneng* [本能 "instinct, or intrinsic abilities"], and *zhijue* as an equivalent of *liangzhi*" (An 1997: 347). However, before investigating the Confucianization of intuition, it is worth taking into account the bigger picture:

The reference to Bergson in dealing with Chinese philosophy seems to be clear-cut for Liang, since he believed that "Chinese metaphysics is concerned with the question of change (*bianhua* 變化)" (DXWH: 442 & 443), and that most of the Chinese notions are intuitive (*zhijue de* 直覺的) (DXWH: 444). LIANG Shuming clearly stated in *Eastern and Western Cultures* that Bergson's philosophy could bring something to Chinese philosophy:

> Bergson's philosophy was of great help to approach Indian thought; similarly it can trace a new path for Chinese thought. For example, the Chinese manipulate notions whose meaning is acquired by intuition and experiences; what they denote is very fluid and cannot be included in a scientific form of reasoning. Thus, in a world where science dominates, they are necessarily cast aside. But nowadays, Bergson has lambasted as too fixed the concepts of science. He believes that metaphysics should oppose scientific reasoning with conceptions that are more mobile and flexible. Does it not sound like opening a path to the Chinese mode of thinking?
>
> 柏格森的哲學固與印度思想大有幫忙，似也有為中國思想開其先路的地方。譬如中國人所用這出於直覺體會之意味的觀念，意有所指而非常流動不定，與科學的思路扞格不入，若在科學思路佔唯一絕對勢力的世界就要被排斥不容存留。而今則有柏格森將科學上明確固定的概念大加指摘，他以為形而上學應當一反科學思路要求一種柔順、活動的觀念來用。這不是很像替中國式思想開其先路嗎?(DXWH: 445)

As a matter of fact, Liang's concrete association of Bergson with Confucianism did not start with the notion of intuition, but with that of "Life."[20] For after having stated that most of Chinese philosophical notions are intuitive, he expanded on the centrality of "Life" in the writing of Confucius. LIANG Shuming considered that Confucius' metaphysics discoursed on "the life of the universe, which is characterized by being

[19] It is, in fact, highly probable that these occurrences are located in segments of the text edited or noted down by someone different from the biggest part of the book, for in these passages "metaphysics" is also not rendered as usual *xing er shang xue* 形而上學 but by *xuanxue* 玄學. The presence of the term *zhiguan* 直觀 in *Culture of East and West* also adds more weight to the textual argument in the previous footnote. As was rightly pointed out by An Yanming "from the beginning", the term *zhijue* "has borne the apparent imprint of Henri Bergson's Vitalism" (An 1997: 337), but this is not the case with *zhiguan* which is closer to the term *Anschaaung* in German philosophy. In Japan, *zhiguan* was more often used in the translation of German philosophy, while *zhijue* was used for English texts (Ishizuka and Shibata 2003: 206). Liang could thus use a concept of intuition without associating it with Bergson.

[20] I should insist here on the word "association" and not "comparison" here. Liang never compared precisely "intuition" or "Life" in Confucianism and Bergson's philosophy, he simply suggested that they could look alike, or that Bergson could serve as an inspiration. When Liang presented Bergson as someone who epitomized the gradual "Sinicization" of the West, he simply remarked that Bergson's and Confucius' thought shared some similarities. One could argue that it is here a classic case of "family resemblance" (*Familienähnlichkeit*) in the sense of Wittgenstein.

in 'perpetual transformation' (*shengsheng zhi suo yi* 生生之所易)" (DXWH: 448). This foundational idea was supposed to be drawn from Chinese original metaphysics, that is the *Book of Change* (DXWH: 447). As already outlined by some reviewers of Liang's book in the 1920s, this was an original insight into early Confucian philosophy. Stating that "Life (*sheng* 生) was the most important concept, and that by understanding it, one could understand the sayings of Confucius" (DXWH: 448) was indeed reading the Master through the lenses of vitalism—a perspective corroborated at that time by WU Jianzhai's 吳檢齋 (1884–1939) research on WANG Yangming 王陽明 (1472–1529). Hence, the scholar WENG Zhiguang 翁芝光 has described Liang's uses of Bergson as a "Confucianization of Western philosophy of life" (Weng 1995: 66), but one could also say that it was a vitalization of Confucianism. While Buddhism was life negating, Confucianism—which Liang understood through the spectacles of the Taizhou school and Wang Gen's 王艮 (1483–1541) writing—was life-affirming. And this was also a feature of Bergsonism. They also shared a form of optimism. Liang had commented as early as 1916 that the optimism of Bergson found its source in his understanding of life's incessant changes being at the source of creativity and all phenomena (JYJY: 14). The resemblance between these descriptions is hard to miss. Liang portrayed Confucius as someone who lived his life without asking to himself too many questions or one could say without too much intellection. He simply went with the flow of life by following his intuition (*ren ta de zhijue* 任他的直覺) (DXWH: 451). This sympathetic description of the Sage and his behavior, though backed by many quotations of the *Classics*, calls to mind what Bergson had written of the artist:

> Could reality come into direct contact with sense and consciousness, could we enter into immediate communion with things and with ourselves, probably art would be useless, or rather we should all be artists, for then our soul would continually vibrate in perfect accord with nature. (Bergson 1911a: 150)

There is no textual evidence for the fact that Liang had read the *Laughter* from which is taken the above quotation, but one must reckon that changing the word "artist" for "noblemen" (*junzi* 君子) or "sage" (*xianren* 賢人 or *shengren* 聖人), could turn this sentence into something that Liang could have written when characterizing Confucius. While Bergson regarded the artist as the embodiment of intuition, LIANG Shuming thought that the genuine intuitive practice was deployed by the sage.[21] And he called this deployment: humaneness (*ren* 仁). Here, in order to show that this was a shared characteristic of humanity that needs to be realized in actuality, LIANG Shuming tried to equate several notions from the Confucian classics. To him, the innate knowledge (*liangzhi* 良知) or original heart (*liangxin* 良心)

[21] This reading that partially presages what Bergson will develop in 1932 in *The Two Sources of Morality and Religion* was typical of the moralization of Bergson's intuition within the Chinese intelligentsia cf. Ciaudo 2016. One should also note that despite art being a topic hardly expanded upon in Liang's work, he reckoned that "intuition" was necessary to attain aesthetic emotions (DXWH: 462).

from *Mencius* and even the formula "following one's nature" (*shuaixing* 率性) from the *Zhongyong* could "be called in the parlance of today, intuition" (DXWH: 452).

However, in delineating this "incisive intuition" (*minrui de zhijue* 敏銳的直覺) of how to behave in concord with life and nature and affirming that this was what "Confucius called humanness" (*Kongzi suo wei ren* 孔子所謂仁) (DXWH: 453), Liang was engaging himself in what could be regarded from Bergson's perspective as two small confusions. Firstly, intuition became an ethical or moral notion, that could help "to maintain a harmonious social network, or social organization" (An 1997: 350), something that was absolutely not in Bergson's original works. Intuition became the key to unlock a happier future for "all the evils arise from the paralysis of intuition" and "all the virtues find their source in intuition" (DXWH: 454). Secondly, and more importantly, Liang got confused in his own philosophical apparatus,[22] for *ren* is not "intuition" proper, as intuition is the path to follow in order to get access to *ren*, which is a state of mind (*xinli zhuangtai* 心理狀態) (DXWH: 453). This transition from intuition as a *ren*, to *ren* as a state of mind is of importance because it also shows that Liang tried to grasp the notion of intuition not merely as a term to be used in philosophical discourses but also as a concrete practice to be implemented in everyday life. Opening the door of intuition could have a concrete effect: by mastering intuition, one could be like Confucius who had lived happily (DXWH: 464–465).[23] Practicing intuition could produce social and personal benefit. All in all, Bergson's intuition did not correspond to the intuitionist trends present in the Chinese intellectual tradition—at that time Bergson had no interest in self-cultivation—, but reading Bergson had helped Liang to identify this trend, and shed light on its value for the modern world.

Though Bergson facilitated this positive evaluation of Confucianism, one should nonetheless not forget the big picture.

> I sometimes tell myself that it was a great chance for the Chinese academic world that Dewey and Russell came to lecture in China these last two years, and not Bergson or Eucken. Had it been the latter and not the former, do you think that anything could have been done about our chronic illness?
>
> 我嘗嘆這兩年杜威、羅素先到中國來，而柏格森、倭鏗不曾來，是我們學術思想界的大幸；如果杜威、羅素不曾來，而柏格森、倭鏗先來了，你試想於自己從來的痼疾對症否？(DXWH：533)

Despite his interest for Bergson, Liang thought that his philosophy was not what China needed. At that time, his homeland needed science, that is "intellect" (*lizhi* 理智) and not intuition. This remark finds its justification in Liang's philosophy of culture, that is presented in detail in the next chapter. Without encroaching upon Zbigniew Wesolowski's text, it is, however, noteworthy to raise a paradox regarding the inability of Bergson to save the Chinese from their predicament. Liang's

[22] Notably when he wrote that "humanness is instinct (*benneng* 本能), natural impulses (*qinggan* 情感) and intuition" (DXWH: 455).

[23] Around the same time, Zhang Junmai met with Bergson in Paris and bluntly asked him "whether one should meditate to cultivate intuition" or if it was something that could be taught (Zhang 1921b: 12).

philosophy of culture, and therefore its conclusion regarding the fact that Western culture should be imported critically and Indian culture dismissed (DXWH: 528), was partially based on an adaptation of Bergson's *élan vital*.

When LIANG Shuming wrote that one can find at the core of every culture a "*Will*" (*yiyu* 意欲), he explained having taken this formulation from Schopenhauer (DXWH: 352).[24] But as it has rightly been pointed at by Weng Zhiguang (Weng 1995: 68), this term could also be read as a synonym for *élan vital*. As a matter of fact, there is an important connection between the theory of Will in Schopenhauer's works and Bergson's conception of this notion (François 2008). And in his *Treatise* of 1916, Liang had himself suggested that Schopenhauer's "Will to live" (*Wille zum Leben*, *qiu sheng zhi yu* 求生之慾) was akin to Bergson's notion of life and creative evolution (JYJY: 13). A Bergsonian tonality is also noticeable when Liang denounced the theories of culture by Henri Thomas Buckle (1821–1862), KANEKO Umaji 金子馬治 (1870–1930) and CHEN Duxiu 陳獨秀 (1879–1942) and said that they "did not recognize the creative activity (*chuangzao de huodong* 創造的活動) and the direction of will (*yizhi de quwang* 意志的趨往)" (DXWH: 372).

But this is of secondary importance in comparison to how Liang presented this "Will" and how it expresses itself through history. In *Creative Evolution*, Bergson had showcased how the *élan vital* had enfolded within the living world by encountering obstacles. By addressing life problems with different methods and solutions, different species had taken different paths. Insects specialized in instincts, and human beings in intelligence. But with his notion of Will, Liang suggested that this *élan vital* could take different paths in different cultures. Similar to organisms that have to face challenges and expand therein their vital impetus so do societies. Different groups of men have traced their own paths: in the West, intuition applied to intellect; in China, the intellect applied to intuition; and in India, the intellect applied to sensation (DXWH: 485).[25] As such, for Liang all men were not similar *Homo faber*, for the creations produced by men could take many forms, and in a sense, Bergson had only given a general description of the evolution of humankind from the standpoint of western civilization. It was time to provincialize his theory, and show that India and China had addressed the problem of life and had given way to other outcomes. Although he did not state it so, one may therefore wonder whether Liang was not trying to question the unilinear conception of man's evolution extolled by Bergson.

In speaking of LIANG Shuming as a Bergsonian, we should therefore not simply consider him as someone who liked and introduced elements of Bergson's philosophy in China, but as someone who wrestled with his texts. Reading Bergson was critical for Liang not because he took over some of his concepts but because it made him a better philosopher who critically think about the world he lives in. It is perhaps a point that has been neglected so far—for most of the research regarding

[24] It is, however, quite suspicious that Liang does not take back the Chinese translation provided by CHEN Daqi as *yizhi* 意志 though most of Liang's understanding of the history of Western philosophy seems to be informed by his *Outline of Philosophy* (Chen 1919).

[25] On this matter cf. Wesolowski 2005 and the following chapter.

Liang's connection to Bergson has been focused on the question of concepts—; however, it seems that Liang partially learn to philosophize and to write philosophy through Bergson. This is a statement valuable not only in the realm of ideas, but also in the manner to express them. Like the Frenchman, Liang sow in his texts many images, metaphors and examples to clarify abstruse or complex notions—as shown above with the case of the cinematograph. Even when he did not make reference to Bergson or quote him, the impression left by *Creative Evolution* and *Introduction to metaphysics* on his expression is obvious for the reader familiar with these texts.

As such, and as a partial conclusion, it appears that Bergson's most decisive impact on LIANG Shuming was located in its conception of life as a flow, and in the notion of "life impetus" or *élan vital* that moves us forward. These notions, as well as Bergson's prose and to a lesser extent his "intuition" as a means to grasp the continuum of life, resonated in Liang's mind: he developed his philosophical thinking in dialogue with them.

5 Liang Shuming: A Lifelong Reader of Bergson?

In her dissertation about the Chinese's reception of Bergson, LAI Huei-Yun has documented how "Chinese interest for Bergson faded away after the mid-1920s" (Lai 1993: 303). Bergson was a philosopher whose works were on everyone's mind before the controversy over science and metaphysics in 1923–1924, but, except for several political reuses, this debate almost condemned him to oblivion within Chinese philosophical discussions. However, as suggested above in the quotation of his interviews with Guy Alitto, Liang kept a lifelong interest for the French philosopher. It is therefore worth having a look into his later writings to understand or at least highlight the profound impact the Frenchman had had on the Chinese thinker. Of course, this chapter would not be the ideal place to expand extensively on the reference to Bergson in an *oeuvre* that spans over 70 years, but several remarks can be made on the topic, for Liang's later usage of Bergson confirms the general picture we have sketched so far.

A first set of allusions to Bergson can be found in *Morning words* (*Zhaohua* 朝話, 1937). Aside the brief autobiographical remarks that were quoted in the first pages of this chapter, Liang made reference to the French philosopher in several little texts that dealt with "life" and "creation"—two notions that were coalesced in Bergson's most famous work. In those texts, Liang extolled the idea that there was a continuity of life, and that "the universe was a big living continuum" (ZH: 94) retaining a general theme that he shared with the French philosopher, but he did not dwell in the details nor give any concrete quotations of Bergson. The second passage is to be found in a sub-section dealing with "remarrying" (*zaihun* 再婚). Here was Bergson's name clearly brought forth, and so was his division of memory into "real memory" (*zhen jiyi* 真記憶) "and 'habit-memory' (*zhun jiyi* 準記憶), but nothing more was added (ZH: 118).[26] From these very small elements one can simply deduce that in the 1930s LIANG Shuming still displayed a conception of life as a continuum that was close to Bergson's, and that he had read *Matter and Memory*. Nothing more.

Many specialists of LIANG Shuming have investigated the evolution of Liang's vocabulary over the years, notably regarding intuition. It is now beyond doubt that his notion of *zhijue*, with its Bergsonian flavor, evolved progressively into 'reason' (*lixing* 理性).[27] Yet it is interesting to note that even in the chapter 'Reason—a characteristic of mankind' (*lixing—renlei de tezheng* 理性—人類的特徵) of *The Fundamentals of Chinese Culture* (*Zhongguo wenhua yaoyi* 中國文化要義), Liang followed almost word for word Bergson's description of the evolutionary process of life. His distinction between the anthropoids specialized in the use of instincts and the vertebrates who master intellect (ZGWH: 123–124) echoes similar developments in Bergson's *Creative Evolution* or even in Wildon Carr's book.[28] Despite not properly quoting Bergson, his outline of evolution and life remained a key reference for LIANG Shuming.

Last but not least, there is a multiplication of references to Bergson in Liang's late writings. Hints toward or quotations of Bergson and his conception of creative evolution can be found in small texts published in magazines (*e.g.* TLTZM: 497), in lectures,[29] but also in one of his most important works: the book *Human Mind and Human Life* (*renxin yu rensheng* 人心與人生). Without entering in a minute analysis of these texts and how they mobilized the philosopher of duration, several elements need to be stressed: Firstly, they clearly show that Liang had moved away from Bergson's intuition, as remarks concerning this notion become almost inexistent. On the contrary, Bergson's insights on evolution, and his conception of life remained a key reference for the Chinese thinker. In *Human Mind and Human life*—finished in 1975 and published in 1984—Liang still convoked Bergson's theory of evolution, notably in regard to the evolutionary divergence between instinct and intellect (RXYRS: 571–581). In several sections, he even quoted *Creative Evolution* directly from the English translation (RXYRS: 577, 653–654 & 669)—which means that the *magnum opus* from Bergson followed him throughout his intellectual odyssey. Besides, one should note that Liang's knowledge of Bergson's works included much more texts, for he mentioned an article taken from *Mind Energy* (RXYRS*: 981, also quoted from the Chinese translation in RXYRS: 581) or from *Time and Free Will* (RXYRS*: 991). Liang's response to Guy Alitto was therefore not a lie: around 1980, Liang was really working on Bergson's books, and he discussed parts of his work that he had ignored in his early years, like Bergson's

[26] It seems to be a reference to one idea defended in the subsection "Two forms of memory" in Chap. 2 of *Matter and Memory*.

[27] See notably An 1997, and the chapter by An in the present book.

[28] See for example Bergson 1913b: 34; & Carr 1911: 31–44.

[29] There are for instance many direct references to Bergson in the lecture "Human mind and Human life" (*renxin yu rensheng* 人心與人生) (RXYRS*)—not to be confused with the book of the same title.

reflection on liberty or the problem of mind-matter dualism. His remarks regarding the inability of the intellect to grasp the real time (*i.e.* duration) and the need it has to spatialize time (RXYRS: 576) also show that by the end of his life, he had grasped much more of what Bergson originally wanted to say. LIANG Shuming was therefore a life-long Bergsonian. He gained through the passing year an ever-greater understanding of the French philosopher. It is as if Bergson kept enticing his own cogitation.

In conclusion, LIANG Shuming's 'Bergsonian moment' endured an entire lifetime. Most of Liang's references to and discussion of Henri Bergson were chronologically located in his earliest and latest texts. It is as if a loop was closed. Reading Bergson in his youth was an entry gate to question Yogācāra's epistemology and metaphysics. Unlike many contemporaries, Liang did not inquire into Yogācāra in order to find a substitute for Western thinking. He noted that more and more Western philosophers—including Bergson—had a vested interest in the question of consciousness and wished to see whether the manner through which they tackled the issue was of relevance to think critically about the main tenets of the Yogācāra texts. In this regard, Bergson and his *Creative Evolution* could not come close to texts such as the *Demonstration of Nothing but Consciousness* (*Cheng weishi lun* 成唯識論), but it always stirred in him new reflections. It also helped him to reevaluate Confucianism, and present it as an intuitionist tradition, in which the concept of Life occupies a very important role.

All in all, by exploring Liang's comments on Bergson's philosophy, as well as his borrowings, one cannot help but identify a form of ambivalence. Liang praised the French philosopher, but simultaneously criticized his metaphysics. He used 'intuition' to put forward the core ideas of Confucianism, but soon abandoned it for the concept of 'Reason' (*lixing*). And one could be tempted to say that the problem of Bergson's place within LIANG Shuming's life and thought is in fact interlaced with the issue of his dual identity as a Confucian and a Buddhist. From a Buddhist point of view, Bergsonism was not enough: it failed at establishing a proper metaphysics. But from the point of view of a Confucian, it was bringing water to the mill by giving emphasis to the idea of life being in perpetual transformation and that intuitive modes of cognition and actions should be privileged. It is as if Liang's evaluation and uses of Bergson could be understood as a form of *upāya* (*fangbian* 方便), an 'expedient means.' Bergsonism was not a truth, but it raised the awareness towards important elements in both the Chinese and the Indian intellectual traditions. It helped Liang to characterize both of them. Bergson was located at a crossroad for him.

Many scholars have suggested that it is sometimes difficult to unravel whether the shared ideas of Bergson and LIANG Shuming on the question of life were the product of an influence coming from Bergson, or whether Liang found in Bergson's confirmation to support a conception. The crux of the issue is in fact the possible correlation of multiple concepts stemming from different traditions. When Liang affirmed that 'life is a continuum' (DXWH : 376), he for instance used the Buddhist term *xiangxu* 相續 (Skt. *saṃtāna*), and it is through this concept that he read the *mouvement* in Bergson's text, but also 'change' as *bian* 變 in Confucianism. Taken out of their respective systems these terminologies could be regarded as amputated of their core meaning, but simultaneously it is also this flexibility that enabled a productive dialogue between different cultures, and an affirmation of the importance of life. The present chapter has therefore shown that one should understand the label 'LIANG Shuming the Bergsonian' mainly in the sense that Liang was an attentive reader of Bergson. However, it has also hinted at the idea that 'Life' was a concept that pervaded all his works, so one should maybe speak of 'LIANG Shuming the Vitalist.'

Acknowledgement Part of the research presented in this chapter was conducted thanks to the support of the Chiang Ching-kuo foundation, project number RG007-P-21.

References

DXWH *Dong-Xi wenhua ji qi zhexue* 東西文化及其哲學 [*Eastern and Western Cultures and Their Philosophies*; 1921], *LSMQJ*, 1989, vol. 1: 319–547.

DYLS *Duiyu Luosuo zhi bu man* 對於羅索之不滿 ["My unsatisfaction with Russell"; 1921], *LSMQJ*, 1991, vol. 4: 656–659.

JYJYL *Jiuyuan jueyi lun* 究元決議論 [*Treatise on Finding the Foundation and Resolving the Doubt*; 1916], *LSMQJ*, 1989, vol. 1: 1–22.

LSMQJ *LIANG Shuming quanji* 梁漱溟全集 [*Complete Works of LIANG Shuming*, vols. I to VIII]. Jinan: Shandong People Press, 1989–1993.

TLTZM *Tan letian zhiming* 談樂天知命 ["Discussions about enjoying Heaven and understanding its mandate"; 1979], *LSMQJ*, 1993, vol. 7: 496–497.

RXYRS *Renxin yu rensheng* 人心與人生 [*Human Spirit and Human Life*; 1984], *LSMQJ*, 1990, vol. 3: 523–760.

*RXYRS** *Renxin yu rensheng* 人心與人生 ["Human Spirit and Human Life"; 1979] *LSMQJ*, 1993, vol. 7: 979–1012.

WSJY *Weishijia yu Bogesen* 唯識家與柏格森 ["Yogācāra and Bergson"; 1921], *LSMQJ*, 1991, vol. 4: 656–659.

WSSY *Weishi shuyi* 唯識述義 [*Outline of Yogācāra*; 1920], *LSMQJ*, 1989, vol. 1: 249–318.

YDZX *Yindu zhexue gailun* 印度哲學概論 [*Outline of Indian Philosophy*; 1919], *LSMQJ*, 1989, vol. 1: 23–248.

ZGWH *Zhongguo wenhua yaoyi* 中國文化要義 [*The Fundamentals of Chinese Culture*; 1949], *LSMQJ*, 1990, vol. 3: 1–316.

ZH *Zhaohua* 朝話 [*Morning Talks*; 1935], *LSMQJ*, 1989, vol. 2: 35–140.

Alitto, Guy S. 1986. *The Last Confucian: LIANG Shu-ming and the Chinese Dilemma of Modernity*. Berkeley: University of California Press.

An, Yanming. 1997. LIANG Shuming and Henri Bergson on Intuition: Cultural Context and the Evolution of Terms. *Philosophy East and West* 47 (3): 337–362.

Azouvi, François. 2007. *La gloire de Bergson: Essai sur le magistère philosophique*. Paris: Gallimard.

Bergson, Henri. 1911a. *Laughter: An Essay on the Meaning of the Comic*. Trans. Brereton Cloudesley & Rothwell Fred. London: Macmillan

———. 1911b. *Matter and Memory*. Trans. Nancy Margaret Paul and W. Scott Palmer. London: George Allen & Unwin Ltd.

———. 1913a. *An Introduction to Metaphysics*. Trans. Hulme T. E. London: Macmillan

———. 1913b. *Creative Evolution*. Trans. Mitchell Arthur. New York: Henry Holt and Company.

———. 1919. *Creative Evolution* 創化論. Trans. ZHANG Dongsun 張東蓀. Shanghai: Shangwu Yinshuguan.

Cai, Yuanpei 蔡元培. 1921. Abbreviated Translation of Bergson's *Introduction to Metaphysics* 節譯柏格森玄學導論." *Minduo* 民鐸 3.1.

Cao, Yueming 曹躍明. 1995. *Studies on LIANG Shuming's Thought* 梁漱溟思想研究. Tianjin: Tianjin Renmin Chubanshe.

Carr, Wildon H. 1911. *Henri Bergson: The Philosophy of Change*. London: T. C. & E. C. Jack.

Chang, Ku-Ming (Kevin). 2017. 'Ceaseless Generation': Republican China's Rediscovery and Expansion of Domestic Vitalism. *Asia Major* 30.2: 101–131.

Chen, Daqi 陳大齊. 1919. *Introduction to Philosophy* 哲學概論. Beijing: Beijing Daxue.

Ciaudo, Joseph. 2013. Introduction à la métaphysique bergsonienne en Chine: échos philosophiques et moralisation de l'intuition. *Noesis* 22: 293–328.

———. 2016. Bergson's 'Intuition' in China and Its Confucian Fate (1915–1921): Some Remarks on *Zhijue* in Modern Chinese Philosophy. *Problemos* Supplement 2016: 35–50

Deleuze, Gilles. 1991. *Bergsonism*. New York: Zone Books.

Ebersolt, Simon. 2012. Le Japon et la philosophie française du milieu XIXe au milieu du XXe siècle. *Revue philosophique* 137 (3): 371–383.

Fink, Hilary L. 1999. *Bergson and Russian Modernism, 1900–1930*. Evanston: Northwestern University Press.

François, Arnaud. 2008. *Bergson, Schopenhauer, Nietzsche. Volonté et réalité*. Paris: PUF.

Han, Li 韓 莉. 2020. LIANG Shuming and Buddhism: On the *Treatise on Finding the Foundation and Resolving the Doubt* 梁漱溟と仏教:「究元決疑論」をめぐって. *Journal of East Asian Cultural Interaction Studies* 東アジア文化交渉研究 13: 489–507.

Hanafin, John J. 2003. The 'Last Buddhist': The Philosophy of LIANG Shuming. In *John Makeham, New Confucianism: A Critical Examination*. New York: Palgrave Macmillan.

Hu, Shi 胡適. 1923. World Philosophy of the Last Fifty Years 五十年來之世界哲學. Reproduced in *Hu Shi Wenji* 胡適文集3: 266–310. Beijing: Beijing daxue chubanshe, 1998.

Hu, Yuanling 胡元玲. 2019. LIANG Shuming's Discussion of the Crisis of Eastern and Western Philosophies and the Way to Solve Them: A Common Thread in *Eastern and Western Cultures and Their Philosophies* and *Outline of Yogācāra* 梁漱溟論東西哲學危機及解決之道—《東西文化及其哲學》及《唯識述義》二書中的一個思想脈絡. *Journal of National Taiwan Normal University* 師大學報 64.1: 55–82.

Ishizuka, Masahide 石塚正英, and Takayuki Shibata 柴田隆行, eds. 2003. *Dictionary of Translated Terms Regarding Philosophy and Thought* 哲学・思想翻訳語事典. Tōkyō: Ronsōsha.

Jing, Haifeng. 2005. On the Influence of Bergson on Modern New Confucianism 論柏格森對現代新儒學思潮. *Modern Philosophy* 現代哲學 3: 76–82.

Lai, Huei-Yun. 1993. *Les études sur Henri Bergson en Chine (1913–1941)*. Phd Dissertation. Paris: École des Hautes Études en Sciences Sociales.

Liang, Shuming 梁漱溟, and Ai, Kai 艾愷 (Guy Alitto). 2010. *Has Man a Future? Dialogues with the Last Confucian* 這個世界會好嗎?梁漱溟晚年口述. Beijing: Foreign Language Teaching and Research Press.

Lindsay, A.D. 1911. *The Philosophy of Bergson*. London: Dent.

Liu, Shuya 劉叔雅. 1918. The Philosophy of Bergson 柏格森之哲學. *New Youth* 新青年 4.2.

Meynard, Thiery. 2014. LIANG Shuming and his Confucianized Version of Yogācāra. In *Transforming Consciousness: Yogācāra Thought in Modern China*, ed. John Makeham. Oxford: Oxford University Press.

———. 2010. *The Religious Philosophy of LIANG Shuming: The Hidden Buddhist*. Leiden: Brill.

Miyayama, Masaharu 宮山 昌治. 2005. The Reception of Bergson's Philosophy During the Taishō Era 大正期におけるベルクソン哲学の受容. *Jinbun* 人文 4: 83–104.

Nethercott, Frances. 1995. *Une rencontre philosophique: Bergson en Russie, 1907–1917*. Paris: L'Harmattan.

Qian, Zhixiu 錢智修. 1913. Outines of the Theories of Two Great Contemporary Philosophers 現今兩大哲學家學說概論. *Eastern Miscellaneous* 東方雜志 10.1.

Sarmis, Dilek. 2016. *La pensée de Bergson dans la genèse de la Turquie moderne: un prisme des transitions lexicales, institutionnelles et politiques de la fin de l'Empire ottoman à la Turquie républicaine*. Phd Dissertation. Paris: EHESS.

Shino, Yoshinobu 志野好伸. 2009. Delineating the Limits of Philosophy: Case Study of the Reception of Henri Bergson in Modern China 哲学の境界画定: 近代中国におけるベルクソン受容の一例. *Chuugoku testugaku kenkyuu* 中国哲学研究 24: 146–162.

Yao, Binbin 姚彬彬. 2014. The Debates Over the Connections Between Bergson's Philosophy and Buddhism Around 1921 1921年前後關於柏格森哲學與佛學關係論辯之始末. *Journal of East China Normal University: Humanities and Social Sciences* 華東師範大學學報(哲學社會科學版) 3: 84–88.

Wesolowski, Zbigniew. 1997. *Lebens- und Kulturbegriff von Liang Shuming (1893–1988): Dargestellt anhand seines Werkes Dong-Xi wenhua ji qi zhe-xue*. Sankt Augustin: Institut Monumenta Serica.

———. 2005. Understanding the Foreign (the West) as a Remedy for Regaining One's Cultural Identity (China): Liang Shuming's (1893–1988) Cultural Thought. *Monumenta Serica* 53: 361–399.

Weng, Zhiguang 翁芝光. 1995. The Influence of Bergson's Philosophy of Life on the New Confucian Thought of Liang Shuming 論柏格森生命哲學對梁漱溟新儒學思想的影響. *Jianghan Tribune* 江漢論壇 11: 66–72.

Worms, Frédéric. 2006. L'idée de moment 1900: Un problème philosophique et historique. *Le Débat* 140 (3): 172–192.

———. 2009. *La Philosophie en France au XXe siècle*. Paris: Gallimard.

Wu, Xianwu 吳先伍. 2005. *Searching and Criticizing Modernity: Bergson and Chinese Modern Philosophy* 現代性追求與批評:柏格森與中國近代哲學. Hefei: Anhui renmin chubanshe.

Yang, Zhengyu 楊正宇. 1921. *Introduction to Metaphysics* 形而上學序論. Shanghai: Shangwu yinshuguan.

Zanfi, Caterina. 2013. *Bergson et la philosophie allemande: 1907–1932*. Paris: A. Colin.

Zhang, Songnian 張崧年. 1921a. The Communist Parties in England and France 英法共產黨. *New Youth* 新青年 9.6.

Zhang, Junmai 張君勱. 1921b. Notes of an Interview with the French Philosopher Henri Bergson 法國哲學家柏格森談話記. *Minduo* 民鐸 3.1.

Chapter 5
Liang the Philosopher of Culture

Zbigniew Wesołowski SVD

1 Introduction: The Crisis of Chinese Culture in the Nineteenth–Twentieth Centuries

The first Opium War (1840–1842) and the Nanjing peace treaty which finished it, through which the English dictated their conditions and required from the Chinese absolute obedience, started a colonial invasion of Western powers in China. The Chinese had until then lived in a Sinocentric and self-sufficient world (as the Westerners had lived in a Eurocentric, colonialist and imperialistic one), and now were forced to look outside their own borders and face the Western challenge with its military superiority. Deep changes due to this Western encroachment and clash between China and the West left the Chinese in the long run with no other choice than to try to understand—not without opposition and hesitation—Western culture and civilization. From that time on, Chinese culture itself became a problem, and understanding it was no longer an easy task.

As though this challenge from the West—and also from Japan and Russia—was not formidable enough, domestic problems also arose within China. Here we only mention the Taiping Uprising (1851–1864), a confrontation between the Chinese Empire under the declining Qing Dynasty (1644–1911) and the Taiping Movement. The self-proclaimed younger brother of Jesus Christ, Hong Xiuquan 洪秀全 (1814–1864), founded this religious and increasingly political movement after contacts with Christian missionaries and after experiencing his own illness-related visions. The movement started its rebellion in the Jintian 金田 village (Guangdong) and was named the *Taiping tianguo* 太平天國 (the Celestial Kingdom of Great

Z. Wesołowski SVD (✉)
Monumenta Serica Institute, Sankt Augustin, Germany
e-mail: wesolowski@monumenta-serica.de

T. Meynard, P. Major (eds.), *Dao Companion to Liang Shuming's Philosophy*, Dao Companions to Chinese Philosophy 17,
https://doi.org/10.1007/978-3-031-18002-6_5

Peace), described as the "most gigantic man-made disaster" (Kuhn 1977: 350) of the nineteenth century, with estimates of its death toll ranging from 10 to 30 million.

As LIANG Shuming 梁漱溟 (1893–1988) was born in 1893, there appeared two bigger cultural movements which aimed at helping China recover from crisis. First there was a movement of Westernization (*yangwu yundong* 洋務運動), then that of the Self-Strengthening Movement (*ziqiang* 自強). As he was 5 years old, the Constitutional Reform and Modernization of 1898 (*wuxu weixin* 戊戌維新; also called *bianfa weixin* 變法維新) was severely suppressed by empress dowager Cixi 慈禧 (1835–1908). The main figures of this movement were KANG Youwei 康有為 (1852–1927) and his disciples—LIANG Qichao 梁啟超 (1873–1929) and TAN Sitong 譚嗣同 (1866–1898). Tan became the first martyr for the sake of the Chinese revolution which eventually succeeded in the Revolution of 1911 (*xinhai geming* 辛亥革命). There was also a movement of transforming Confucianism into a state religion, the most prominent promoter of which was the above-mentioned KANG Youwei. This movement was superseded by a tremendous cultural movement in China—the May Fourth Movement of 1919 (*wusi yundong* 五四運動). The May Fourth Movement was an anti-imperialist, anti-feudal (anti-traditional), political and cultural movement triggered by the Versailles treaty after the World War I, led mostly by intellectuals based on the rudiments of communist ideology, like CHEN Duxiu 陳獨秀 (1879–1942) or LI Dazhao 李大釗 (1889–1927). Then as a reaction to this development, conservatism emerged. At the beginning of the 20th century, the movement of Communism entered China, which gave rise to the People's Republic of China in 1949 and is still in power in Mainland China. The facts just stated are the historical context of LIANG Shuming's cultural thought, in which a tension between culture and politics dominated.[1]

2 Liang's *Dong-Xi wenhua ji qi zhexue* 東西文化及其哲學 (1921) as an Answer to His Quest for Solving the Problem of Chinese Culture[2]

It seems that the best way to understand LIANG Shuming is in terms of his search for authentic existence. To put it shortly, in every form of authentic existence, we have a tension between ontology and axiology through the lenses of an epistemological dimension, that is, the relation of subject and object in knowing reality.[3] Liang is

[1] Cf. Alitto 1979 and 2005; cf. also Wesołowski 2005: 363–366.

[2] Cf. Wesołowski (Wei Siqi) 2003: 25–125 and Major 2017: 123–145.

[3] In 1982, Frederick J. Streng (1933–1993) published a remarkable contribution with the title "Three Approaches to Authentic Existence: Christian, Confucian, and Buddhist" (371–392). Although his main concern was the comparison of thought among three 20th-century thinkers, that is, Paul Tillich (1886–1965), a Christian, TANG Junyi 唐君毅 (1909–1978), a Confucian, and NISHITANI Keiji 西谷啓治 (1900–1990), a Buddhist, he also explicated the concept of authentic existence: "To live authentically human being must know and actualize the 'the nature of things'"

really a multi-faceted personality which reveals itself in his thought and action.[4] His thinking was predominantly gained from his life-world, and this world was submerged into a threefold crisis, i.e., his individual (Liang as a particular human being), national (Liang as a Chinese, a human being belonging to a particular human culture) and universal (Liang as a part of the whole humankind).[5]

Before formulating the definition of Chinese and Indian cultures, Liang inserted into his cultural discourse three important theoretical parts concerning his understanding of life: 1. "Explanation of life" (DXWH: 376–379); 2. "Three kinds of problem in human life" (379–381), and 3. "Three directions of human life" (381–383). Liang's concept of life could be generally understood as a teaching on human orientation in the world.[6] Each human wisdom contains necessarily certain conceptual determinations, differentiations, and divisions. His assertion of the lack of difference between life and the living is a kind of Buddhist notion of participation in which the self-identity of a particular living being is not acknowledged—that is Liang's application of the Buddhist concept of non-self (*wuwo* 無我). His whole concept of life is Buddhist, and, as such, it is a soteriological one: How to get rid of suffering in the world.

According to LIANG Shuming's *Eastern and Western Cultures and Their Philosophies* (*Dong-Xi wenhua ji qi zhexue* 東西文化及其哲學; henceforth DXWH), human life[7] in its realization and concretization is a process of principally dealing with a threefold problem. First is a material problem: a domain of in principle limitless growth of human power over matter enabled by causality,[8] understood as an influence by which one event, process, state or object, i.e., a cause, within the inorganic and physical world (matter) contributes to the production of another event, process, state or object, i.e., an effect where the cause is partly responsible for the effect, and the effect is partly dependent on the cause. That is for Liang the realm of a material problem. Second is a social problem: a domain of a

(Streng 1982: 371). Cf. also Wesołowski 2005: 366–374 and TU Weiming 1976: 242–273, 396–400.

[4] Cf. Alitto 1979 and 2005.

[5] Cf. Wesołowski 2005: 368–369.

[6] Cf. Wesołowski 1997: 111–160.

[7] Cf. Wesołowski 1997: 118–125.

[8] Causality as the relation between cause and effect is the fabric of the dynamic world in which we human beings live. We all make frequent attempts to reason causation relationships of everyday events (e.g., the cause of my headache or any other cause of my suffering). Even the greatest scientific discoveries are about causality (e.g., Newton's discovery of the cause for an apple's fall, i.e. gravity, and Darwin's natural selection as the cause of evolution). Human causal thinking has become detached from space and time so that instead of just reacting to perceptual input, our minds can simulate actions and forces and their causal consequences. This finds its way in human development of technologies which in turn enable us to make observations and carry out experiments in an unprecedented scale. A fundamental Buddhist teaching on causality or causation and the ontological status of all phenomena is the doctrine of *pratītyasamutpāda* (dependent origination). The doctrine teaches that all phenomena arise in dependence on causes and conditions and lack intrinsic being.

conditional availability (or conditional non-availability) of the object of desire, that is of another mind or the will of another person. This domain is a realm of human relationships or a social problem. The act of loving in return (redamancy) is an example of such a conditional availability or conditional non-availability (the phenomenon of unrequited love or one-sided love). Finally is an individual-spiritual problem: a domain of the absolute non-availability within the power of causality, especially in view of the necessity of aging and death in the life process. Besides this threefold problem, there is according to Liang also a domain of neutrality—a kind of indifference towards desires being satisfied or not, a kind of Stoic adiaphora, i.e., actions that morality neither mandates nor forbids. For LIANG Shuming, it is a realm of natural feelings and esthetical-artist life in which natural spontaneity is more at work, like in singing or dancing.

According to Liang, human life as such is a process of dealing with the above-mentioned three basic problems –material, social, and individual-spiritual. In view of this understanding, the meaning and the timeline of human history is outlined. Human history is nothing else than a process through which the three problems of life are being resolved one at a time, following the progressive difficulty of the problems faced. A relatively easy problem is that of dealing with matter, which according to Liang the first period of human history is devoted to resolving. However, this period was coming—slowly but surely—to a close during Liang's lifetime. Afterwards the second problem of social relationship will come to the fore, and humanity is already on the threshold of this problem. The third problem of the individual-spiritual, which is the most difficult one, will become the most formidable challenge in the distant future.

Besides, fundamental for Liang was the understanding of life as a continuum of the organismic-volitional self-movement of the question-answer affairs, i.e. a constant, uninterrupted need to deal with problems (questions) that require an answer. The will-driven human life as a process of questions being followed by answers (that is actually a struggle, not only and totally suffering like in Buddhist faith) can assume within the scope of its threefold problem three basic attitudes: (1) to demand and to go forward; (2) to adjust one's own intentions, to hold the golden mean; and (3) to turn back and to move backwards. This explanation is very important to Liang. He says: "The three directions are of great importance, because our whole explanation of culture is based upon them." (DXWH: 382)

After this elucidation of Liang's basic conceptual grasp of life and will, we are better prepared to understand his definitions of Western, Chinese, and Indian cultures.

> Western culture is [such a culture] the basic spirit of which is to demand and go forward (*xiang qian yaoqiu* 向前要求) or [to put it in other words:] Western culture is a culture which, based upon the spirit possessing [the attitude] to demand and go forward, produced science (*sai'ensi* 塞恩斯) and democracy (*demokelaxi* 德謨克拉西)—these two specific characteristics.
>
> 西方化是以意欲向前要求為其根本精神的。或說:西方化是由意欲向前要求的精神產生「賽恩斯」與「德謨克拉西」兩大異彩的文化。(DXWH: 353)

> Chinese culture is [such a culture] the basic spirit of which consists in the will-itself [tending to] harmony and holding the golden mean.
> 中國文化是以意欲自為、調和、持中為其根本精神的。(DXWH: 383)

> Indian culture is [such a culture] the basic spirit of which is to turn back and move backwards.
> 印度文化是以意欲返身向後要求為其根本精神的。(DXWH: 383)

Against the background of what has been already said, we can easily discover the main strains of Liang's cultural thought. First, his typology of the three basic human cultures, i.e., Western, Chinese, and Indian, conforms to his typology of the individual awareness of three types of men, i.e., that of the man in the street (Mozi 墨子 [ca. 468–ca. 367 BC] or modern Westerners), Confucius (551–479 BC), and Buddha (ca. 480–400 BC), the last two whom Liang regarded as precocious geniuses who foresaw the cultures of the future. Second, Liang's typology of the tree basic cultures directly derives from the three basic directions of the will, i.e., to demand and to go forward is tantamount to Western-pragmatic culture, to adjust one's own intentions and to hold the golden mean is related to Sino-Confucian culture, and to turn back and to move backwards is identified with Indo-Buddhist culture. As we see, each of these directions allows humanity to resolve one of the three problems.

Liang's notion of precocity of Chinese culture, i.e., his key theorem of the premature character of Chinese culture articulated in the DXWH, was the quintessence of his cultural thought which was put into practice in his manifold activities of rural reconstruction during the period of 1928–1937. In order to connect Liang's DXWH to the next period in the development of his cultural philosophy, we will cite from "The Final Awakening of the Self-Saving Movement of Chinese Nation" (*Zhongguo minzu zijiu yundong zhi zuihou juewu* 中國民族自救運動之最後覺; 1930; henceforth ZGMZ) an interesting comparison as to the prematurity of Chinese culture:

> China is like an intelligent child whose body has not yet fully grown, [but at the same time] he/she has prematurely developed her/his intelligence. Because of the prematurity of her/his intelligence, the growth of the body was [again] hindered. This obstacle [in turn] impeded [further] proper development of her/his intelligence. To say it pithily, China is not infantile but mature; although we say "mature," her form [however] sometimes displays infantile traits. That is what I said before—'It was not in accordance with the normal process of nature'
> 而中國則彷彿一個聰明的孩子, 身體發育未全, 而智慧早開了; 即由其智慧之早開, 轉而抑阻其身體的發育, 復由其身體發育之不健全, 而智慧遂亦不得發育圓滿良好。質言之, 中國不是幼稚而是成熟; 雖云成熟, 而形態間又時顯露幼稚, 即我前說的「非循夫自然之常」是已。(ZGMZ: 100).

In the DXWH, Liang's concept of culture reached another philosophical pinnacle, because he used the Buddhist epistemological approach to grasp the essence of human culture. We can call it a "Buddhist epistemological turn." This turn occurs in the short passage "*Sanfang shenghuo zhi zhenjie*" 三方生活之真解 (A True Interpretation of the Life in the Three Regions: DXWH: 485–487). This time Liang defines the three cultures as follows:

1. The life of the West consists in that intuition (*zhijue* 直覺) applies to intellect (*lizhi* 理智);
2. The life of China consists in the intellect applying to intuition;

3. The life of India consists in the intellect as it applies to sensation (*xianliang* 現量).
   (一)西洋生活是直覺運用理智的;
   (二)中國生活是理智運用直覺的;
   (三)印度生活是理智運用現量的。(DXWH: 485)

These three definitions of human life, and implicitly of human culture, lead us to Liang's *Weishi* 唯識–Buddhist thought.[9] In this Buddhist-soteriological perspective the three cultures can be roughly construed as follows:

1. Western-pragmatic culture is a culture whose direction of the will is a primordial one, i.e., to demand and go forward. The epistemological emphasis of this culture lies in the condition in which the intuition of the will-oriented and differentiated self (the intuition of I; grammatically: the first-person singular nominative case personal pronoun) avails itself of the intellect. This culture—according to Liang—was reaching at the time its culmination, which means that the material problem would in principle soon be solved. The rise of this culture is due to the fact that an intellect-using I-intuition of the self based on the primordial direction of the will leads to a pronounced knowledge of itself which results in an overdue stress on the self. This constitutes the experience of a basic double duality, i.e., that of subject and object and that of one self and another self or other selves. This way of life means in the Buddhist perspective a dual attachment. The proper product of such a culture is "the matter of the outer world" (*waijie wuzhi* 外界物質, DXWH: 504). The prototypes of this cultural attitude were ancient Greek thinkers and Mozi in China. The culmination of this type was epitomized by John Dewey (1859–1952) and William James (1842–1910).
2. Sino-(Taizhou泰州[10]-)Confucian culture is a culture whose basic direction of the will is harmony. The epistemological stress of this culture lies in the claim that intellect applies the intuition which especially wants to know life as such (life-intuition). The epistemic identity is in this case the awareness of the inborn and intuitive self.[11] This culture has already reached its individual culmination in the life of Confucius (Confucius' self-finding as true harmony).[12] According to

[9]Cf. Wesołowski 1997:199–210.

[10]In Liang Shuming's understanding of the Taizhou scholars, and especially that of their founder Wang Gen 王艮 (1483–1541), the precious point was that they were not only thinkers, but also activists. To be a scholar-activist was an ideal for Liang Shuming as a Confucian. Cf. Cheng 2009:45–65, Alitto 1979, and Yan 2009: 173–188.

[11]Here is required the knowledge of Buddhism: Liang believed in a double attachment (*erzhi* 二執), i.e., *fazhi* 法執 (world attachment) and *wozhi* 我執 (self-attachment), the latter of which has two kinds: *jusheng wo* 具生我 and *fenbie wo* 分別我. *Jusheng wo* is for him the inborn, life-oriented, and intuitive self and *fenbei wo* is a differentiated, egocentric, and egoistic self which is at work in Western-pragmatic culture. Cf. Wesołowski 1997: 115.

[12]DXWH 480–481: "Only the attitude of Confucius was anything but 'to be tolerant and [merely] indulgent' and 'to deal with something carelessly.' He 'never got into a position in which he did not find himself.' Only [on the basis of] this self-finding [*zide* 自得] [one can] [completely] take the second way [of human culture]. Only then is there a positive appearance [of such a culture]. Self-finding is the only appropriate direction of the second way which is the will, which is only harmony [*tiaohe* 調和] and keeping the golden mean [*chizhong* 持中]. All compliance, patience

Liang, this kind of culture is on the brink of becoming the dominant cultural attitude of the world in the near future. Its rise is due to the fact that an intellect-oriented intuition (or: an intellect based on the cognition through the life-intuition) with the help of harmony as the basic direction of the will achieves a pronounced knowledge of life and its truth as self-finding or self-accepting. The proper product of this cultural attitude is a "life of the inner world" (*neijie sheng-ming* 內界生命, DXWH: 504), i.e., Confucian spirituality as a life of just inborn, intuitive self-attachment. This is tantamount to the solving of the second, i.e., social problem of human life. Liang saw a kind of Confucianizing of world culture starting to take place at the time.

3. Indo-(*weishi-*)Buddhist culture is a culture whose basic direction of the will is to negate itself, i.e., to turn back and to move backwards towards a renunciation of the world (ascetic attitude). The epistemological emphasis of this culture is based on the notion that intellect only applies sensation (*xianliang* 現量[13]). The epistemic moment of identification is the highest awareness, i.e., the *ālāya*-consciousness.[14] According to Liang, this cultural attitude has already been individually realized in the life of Buddha. It will be universally extended in the long run as the third and last stage of human history. The rise of this culture is due to the fact that intellect bound to the backward-oriented will avails itself of sensation. The proper product of it is the "primordial being of non-life" (*wusheng benti* 無生本體, DXWH: 504), i.e., a unity with the only true reality as the entrance into Nirvana.

What for us is here of special interest is the conviction of LIANG Shuming that the imminent future mode of world culture will be that of the Sino-Confucian cultural attitude. He even prophesied that in the nearest future the emotion of love in its

---

and careless handling are considered harmony that has become natural. But only self-finding is true harmony [*zhen tiaohe* 真調和]." This spiritual ideal of life, which Liang saw realized in Confucius, is an authentic human existence (to be oneself and to show oneself whom he is) within the second cultural way, i.e., Sino-(Taizhou-)Confucian culture.

[13] This epistemic attitude leads a total renunciation of the world, which consists in a radical attempt to completely destroy the dual attachment (i.e., world-attachment and double self-attachment as an innate and a differentiated self-attachment). Here one could cite the whole section "*Fojiao de xing'er shangxue fangfa*" 佛教的形而上學方法 (The metaphysical method of Buddhism; DXWH: 409–414) and especially the words: a radical attempt to completely destroy [*xianliang*] lead unswervingly to: Silence! Cessation! Liberation!" (DXWH: 412–413).

[14] The classification of so-called "Eight Consciousnesses" is a teaching of the *weishi*-Buddhism (Yogācāra). According to this teaching, there are five sense consciousnesses (eyes, ears, nose, tongue, body), which are supplemented by the sixth awareness, i.e., the mental consciousness (thoughts / ideation) and the seventh known as the defiled mental consciousness (also called: deluded awareness; posited on the basis of straightforward cognition in combination with inferential cognition; its form of physical phenomenon is, e.g., self-attachment: with Liang, a specificity of Western culture), and finally the fundamental store-house consciousness (all-encompassing foundation consciousness), which is the basis of the other seven. This eighth consciousness is understood as the one to collect and store away the impressions of previous experiences, which form the seeds of future karma in this life and in the next after rebirth. Cf. Wesołowski 1997: 196.

particular form as a love between man and woman[15] will be the greatest and the most formidable problem of this period, i.e., the period of the second domain of a conditional availability or non-availability of the object of desire (see above), that is of another mind or the will of another person (Wesołowski 1997: 145). This domain is called by LIANG Shuming a realm of human relationships or a social problem for the solution of which Sino-(Taizhou-)Confucian culture is responsible.

The concept of culture presented in the DXWH is a universalistic and in the end an "absolutistic" concept based on the universality of the above-mentioned three problems of human life and the universality of the three directions of the will representing life itself. Thus, Liang's concept of culture is also rooted in voluntaristic vitalism.[16] The absolutistic dimension of his concept of culture relies predominantly on the use of *weishi*-Buddhist epistemology. This viewpoint is also Liang's theoretical summit, because in his reflection on human faculties of knowledge, we simultaneously reach the limits of human wisdom and cognition. Besides, Liang's *weishi* theory of culture is unfalsifiable because there is no way that it can be empirically proven false. In analytic philosophy, there is a general conviction that most religious language is unfalsifiable (Flew: 1951).

Besides, LIANG Shuming's mode of thinking, which he displayed in his DXWH, can be called "monocausalism," i.e., searching for the one and only one root cause for the explanation of human culture, in his case—the Chinese one. Thus, the prematurity of Chinese culture (*wenhua zaoshou* 文化早熟) was the ultimate diagnosis in LIANG Shuming's DXWH. Liang's cultural thought, as applied to Chinese culture, is also a manifestation of classical "Sinodicy"[17]—a theory of the justification of the weaknesses of Chinese culture. This cultural theory is a kind of apology and argumentation for the greatness, the premature character of Chinese culture with

---

[15] How true it sounds today! The sexual revolution (1960–1980) as a time of sexual liberation was a social movement throughout the United States of America that challenged traditional codes of behavior related to sexuality and interpersonal relationships. Later it spread in the wider world, especially in Europe. Such sexual liberation included increased acceptance of sex outside of traditional heterosexual, monogamous relationships (primarily marriage). This crisis of love between man and woman, which in the present-day is connected with sexual liberation and the crisis of sexual identity, sexual orientation, gender identity, and LGBT ideology should have been for Liang the most formidable problem at the beginning of the second social problem of humanity which is already under way. Of course, he himself must have believed that all these phenomena will be ultimately overcome because of his faith in Sino-Confucian familism, in which (traditional) family means the only suitable and adequate locus of nascency, development and cultivation of human feelings. The beginning of these basic familial feelings are instinctive faculties in *xiao* (filial piety) and *ti* 悌 (brotherly obedience). *Xiao* and *ti* as originally instinctive faculties have to be developed first into feelings, and then cultivated as virtues in family relations. Cf. Wesołowski 1997: 141, 145, 146, 272f., 290, 315, 386, and 391.

[16] Cf. Chap. 4: Liang the Bergsonian.

[17] This neologism of mine was built following words such as theodicy (Leibniz: an attempt to answer the question of why a good God permits the manifestation of evil) and anthropodicy (Nietzsche: arguments attempting to justify the existence of humanity as good in view of evils done by concrete men and women).

regard to its many different shortcomings which are actually a part of each human culture.

3 Cultural Thought of Liang's Rural Reconstruction Program

As this chapter takes on LIANG Shuming as Philosopher of culture, we will not describe Liang's manifold activities of rural reconstruction during the period of 1928–1937. Below we will present an exposition of ZGMZ (from 1930) and the small book *A General Idea of Rural Reconstruction* (*Xiangcun jianshe dayi* 鄉村建設大意; 1936; henceforth XCJS) in order to better understand the development of Liang's cultural thought being put into action.

In the article ZGMZ, Liang again sets out to more concretely solve the riddle of Chinese culture and its present predicament. Similar to the approach found in DXWH, he holds on to a comparative method in his cultural studies. What is important for us is the fact that Liang narrowed down the scope of his cultural comparison to China and the West. For him it is in comparison with Western culture that peculiar features of Chinese culture can be better grasped. On the side of his cultural thought there is one concept which prevails, i.e., *rensheng taidu* 人生態度 (attitude of human life). This concept is already present in DXWH, and there from a systematic and conceptual framework, it occupied a third place, after the concept of life and culture. The idea of attitude of life, which has an intimate relationship with Liang's doctrine of the will and its three basic directions, not only allows him to explain the changes in cultural attitudes of nations and individuals, but also provides him with the possibility of conscious changes in life-styles brought about by educational efforts.

Let us have a closer look at the content of the ZGMZ. In the DXWH Liang described the deep structure of Western culture as: (1) nature-conquering, (2) scientific spirit (with critical dimension), and (3) democracy. In the ZGMZ he started with three points about the West: (1) "Westerners are a newly advanced people. Western culture is a phenomenon that comes from modern time"; (2) "Western culture progressed very rapidly. It developed within a very short period"; (3) "Western culture possesses a very aggressive conquering power and a voracious and devouring disposition" (ZGMZ: 47). Next to it there is another "trinity" (*san wei yi ti* 三為一體) of modern culture—"capitalistic economy, democratic rule of the newly advanced middle class, and modern nation-state" (ZGMZ: 50). This description is far reaching, because it includes all important factors and phenomena of modern European culture—capitalism even gave rise to socialism, a national/nationalistic state entails imperialism and colonialism, and democratic reign has to do with the history of European revolutions. One organizational factor, which Liang mentioned in this context, i.e., Christianity, will play a full role first in *The Essential Meaning of Chinese Culture* (*Zhongguo wenhua yaoyi* 中國文化要義; 1949; henceforth ZGWH).

Below we give an example of Liang's explanation of the tremendous leap of Western society, i.e., from the medieval to its modern form. He used the above-mentioned concept of attitude of human life, which is also intimately connected with his theory of the universal reappearance of each of the three basic cultures, realized individually in John Dewey and William James (Western), Confucius (China) and Buddha (India). Thus, for him the change of Western culture from its medieval to its modern form is a change from the third attitude of human life (i.e., a religious one[18] in the form of Christianity) to the first one, the prototype of which are the ancient Greeks and also, in China, Mozi. This process in the history of Europe is normally called secularization, which means a liberalization of the individual and society at large from the control and domination of religious authority. The rise of modern Europe proper happened in Liang's understanding in even a shorter period of time, i.e., within the 18th and 19th centuries in the wake of industrialization.

Without going into the details of his understanding of European history, we have to stress a slight shift in his comparative approach—the abstract and philosophical skeleton of his cultural thought takes on more flesh, i.e., rich historical material is selected by him to corroborate his theories.

Against this background Liang started his discourse about Chinese culture which all in all includes six short passages: (1). "Awakening Has Arrived" (already inserted in the part about Western culture; ZGMZ: 44); (2). "What about the Chinese?" (ZGMZ: 63–73); (3). "Solving the Riddle of China Step by Step" (ZGMZ: 73–102); (4). "The Mistakes We Have Committed until Now" (ZGMZ: 102–110); (5). "Our New Direction after Today" (ZGMZ: 110–116), and (6). "Supplementary Notes" (ZGMZ: 116–118).

Our starting point is Liang's twofold riddle of Chinese culture: "One pertains to the society of long history without changes, a stagnated culture without progress. The second one [points to] human life almost without religion" (ZGMZ: 64). The first riddle is well-known and acknowledged, and forms an important component of the negative image of China in the Western Sinological world, especially popular through Georg W.F. Hegel's (1770–1831) lectures on philosophy of history. The second one seems to have been a special contribution of Bertrand Russell (1872–1970), an outspoken atheist, to Liang. Russell in his book *The Problem of China* (London 1922) mentioned three features of Chinese culture, the second of which was: "the ethics of Confucius replaced religion in China" (ZGMZ: 69). This conviction was already present in the DXWH. There Liang considered the Chinese as those who are "the most indifferent people [in the world] towards religion" (DXWH: 524).

[18] According to Liang, the only true religious attitude is that of Buddhism, i.e., the third attitude of human life, and only this will have a universal revival in the furthest future of human history. Cf. Wesołowski 1996: 241–267 and Meynard 2011.

The display of shortcomings of the Chinese in their history was connected with their efforts and movements to save China from her predicament. There seems to be one great mistake with two levels. The mistake consists principally in "renouncing one's own [Chinese] intrinsic spirit, and in looking outside for one's own future" (ZGMZ: 106), and a deeper level of this mistake is that "we [Chinese] want to make China a 'modern state'" (ZGMZ: 108). From this background, it is not difficult to think about the content of Liang's "final awakening." (Liang's "final awakening" refers to the title of ZGMZ.) This awakening has two parts—one negative and another affirmative. With regard to the negative part, Liang says:

1. Our first impracticable way in politics is that of modern democracy in Europe;
2. the second impracticable way in politics is that opened by the communist party in Russia;
3. our first impracticable way in economy is that of modern capitalism in Europe;
4. our second impracticable way in economy is the one the communist party in Russia wants to go.

   一, 我們政治上的第一個不通的路——歐洲近代民主政治的路;
   二, 我們政治上的第二個不通的路——俄國共產黨發明的路;
   三, 我們經濟上的第一個不通的路——歐洲近代資本主義的路;
   四, 我們經濟上的第二個不通的路——俄國共產黨要走的路。(ZGMZ: 111)

The affirmative part outlines his program of rural reconstruction. Its content includes the following:

1. The significance of village government (*cunzhi* 村治)[19] in solving the political problem of China;
2. The significance of village government in solving the economic problem of China;
3. The significance of village government in solving the problem of Chinese culture;
4. The significance of village government in solving the problem of education in China;
5. The propagation and realization of the method of village government.

   一, 村治在解決中國政治問題上的意義。
   二, 村治在解決中國經濟問題上的意義。
   三, 村治在解決中國文化問題上的意義。
   四, 村治在解決中國教育及其他問題上的意義。
   五, 倡行村治的方法。(ZGMZ: 115)

On the theoretical level, Liang realized the formidable goal of rural reconstruction in his work *Xiangcun jianshe lilun* 鄉村建設理論 (*Theory of Rural Reconstruction*; another title of this work is *Zhongguo minzu zhi qiantu* 中國民族之前途 [*The Future Way of the Chinese People]*; LSMQJ, vol. II: 141–585) from 1937, but it is at the same time that the implementation of his program came to an end because of the aggressive war of Japan (1937–1945). In the last part of the ZGMZ, Liang proclaimed that "the great revival of Chinese culture" has to become the "future world culture" (ZGMZ: 115).

Liang's XCJS is the transmission of his idea of rural reconstruction to the primary-school teachers of Zouping 鄒平 County in Shandong, where he attempted to realize his program. Because most teachers were countrymen, Liang used plain Chinese to conduct his presentation, but it does not depreciate the expressive power

[19] The term *cunzhi* (village government) was Liang's original name for his reconstruction of the Chinese village. From 1933 on there was a common agreement in China to call these efforts generally *xiangcun jianshe* (rural reconstruction).

of his talks. The XCJS can be likened to a four-part symphony: (1). "What is rural reconstruction?" (XCJS: 602–615); (2). "What is the most important in rural reconstruction?" (XCJS: 616–625); (3). "Village organization" (XCJS: 626–665); and (4). "Concrete method of rural reconstruction—hamlet and village schools" (XCJS: 666–710). The members of his philharmonic orchestra should eventually be all the peasants of China. In Liang's understanding the movement of rural reconstruction was primarily a cultural one with the purpose of creating a new world culture, starting with the village as a traditional focal point of Chinese society. The comparison with Western culture remained until then an indispensable part of his cultural thought. Since her encounter with the West, China was trying to change herself and to learn from the West, but with a detrimental effect on culture and economy, for China was learning "a kind of urban civilization"[20] (XCJS: 608). Chinese culture, however, was "an originally village-based and -oriented society" (XCJS: 608). As to Chinese cities, they are not places of production, but only "consumer-cities" (XCJS: 608). Liang was afraid that this tendency would make China a "purely westernized modern state" (XCJS: 608) at the cost of the enormous suffering of the Chinese peasants.

The main concerns of the XCJS were, of course, the transmission of his understanding of this problem and, in accordance with it, the outline of an educational program of village organization. In his comparison with the West, Liang discovered four main reasons for the lack of communal organization in traditional Chinese society: (1). China lacked a pedagogue in the form of the Church in the West (XCJS: 635); (2). The small scale of the farming system and handicraft in traditional China;[21] (3). A lack of international competition and a tendency to be passive and inactive—Liang said: "The Chinese have no concept of state (*guojia* 國家)—this is known by everybody" (XCJS: 638)—(4). The fourth reason is a well-accepted fact in the Sinological world—the Chinese emperor and his administrative apparatus did not allow the Chinese to build up any communal/community organizations. Such organizational structures tended to be seen as a potential for rebellion. That is why the Chinese in the past had no chance to develop their organizational habits and talents.

The consequence of this comparative cultural analysis is to start an educational program for Chinese peasants in order to learn village organization. The key element of this village organization is hamlet and village schools (*cunxue xiangxue* 村學鄉學). The term "school" actually stands for a total schooling, the educational

[20] In this context Liang used the word *wenming* 文明 (civilization). Actually, in ZGWH he distinguished between culture and civilization: "So-called civilization is [the totality] of products of achievements we have in our life … The stereotyped and concrete artifices of life are civilization, and an abstract way of life is culture. However, culture and civilization can be considered as one thing with two sides, for example a system of government can be regarded as the artifice of a nation, that is civilization, or as the way of life of a nation—culture" (ZGWH: 380–381).

[21] In this context, Liang made another definition of culture: "So-called culture is the means (*fangfa* 方法) of getting along (*guo rizi* 過日子) of a society. A given society has its way of living (Westerners have their own way of life, and the Chinese, too, have their own way of life). Their ways to live are a culture" (XJD: 611).

process of the whole village, beginning almost with infants and ending with the most aged, inclusive of both sexes, who are taught separately. Each inhabitant of a village had a role to play—that is Liang's fundamental content of rural reconstruction.[22]

This educational program had its basic spirit. This spirit was the old teaching of China—the invisible treasure of the Chinese in which he differentiated two parts—"shallow points," such as the imperial system or different rites, and "deep and fine points," which Liang demonstrated with the help of two attitudes of the Confucian spirit: "The one is reciprocal human and friendly feelings which make the other party important (*hu yi duifang wei zhong de lunli qingyi* 互以對方為重的倫理情誼), and the other is edification of human life based on mending one's way and pursuing the good (*gaiguo qianshan de rensheng xiangshang* 改過遷善的人生向上). According to this true Confucian spirit, discovered by Liang, the communal organization of village government should be run by three principles: (1). "Hamlet and village schools will not speak of decisions by the vote of majority" (XCJS: 698–701); (2). "[These schools] will not speak of the right of freedom" (XCJS: 701–703); (3). "[They] will not use methods and means which do not consider human feelings" (XCJS: 703–707).

In the explanation of the old Chinese teaching (*lao daoli* 老道理; XCJS: 613), we already discover the concept *lixing* 理性 (reason), which became the key concept in Liang's comparative cultural thought in ZGWH.

4 Liang's *Zhongguo wenhua yaoyi* 中國文化要義 as a Quintessence of His Understanding of Chinese Culture[23]

With ZGWH, Liang Shuming reached the peak of his cultural thought. Liang started to write this work in 1942, and finished it in 1949. The historical framework of his intellectual endeavor was a very peculiar one—World War II raged in China with the Japanese invasion, the beginning of which thwarted his rural reconstruction program. The completion of this work happened just a few months before the rise of Communist China (1 October 1949). In the ZGWH, Liang presented his theory of the peculiar characteristics of Chinese culture (*Zhongguo wenhua tezheng* 中國文化特徵) and discussed the national character of the Chinese (*Zhongguo minzuxing* 中國民族性). His research method displays more or less the same mode of thinking of the DXWH which we called "monocausalism," i.e., searching for the one and only cause for the ultimate explanation of Chinese culture. In this line of thinking,

[22] In this concept of rural reconstruction, Liang argued against other alternative concepts such as that of local autonomy (*difang zizhi* 地方自治) and self-defense organization (*ziwei zuzhi* 自衛組織). His concept has some prototype in Song dynasty, called *xiangyue* 鄉約—a village covenant (cf. XJD: 669–671).

[23] Wesołowski (Wei Siqi) 2003: 127–194.

Liang's theory of peculiar characteristics of Chinese culture leads to just one overall characteristic, the old name of which was the prematurity of Chinese culture.

In this theory, Liang enumerated fourteen items which according to him do not exhaust the variety and fullness of Chinese culture, but are its representative character. These peculiar characteristics are the following:

1. China is a vast land and populous people (ZGWH: 14);
2. She displays the assimilating and fusing capacity of such a big nation (ZGWH: 14);
3. She has a long history (ZGWH: 14)—these are to Liang "the three great characteristics" of China;
4. Chinese culture embodies great power despite different weaknesses, such as those in acquiring knowledge, in economy (China remained an agrarian society throughout history), military and politics—the last two weaknesses resulting from the lack of organizational structure (ZGWH: 14–15). In the final analysis (ZGWH: 289–305), the second and fourth characteristics fall more or less into the same category, but are regarded from different perspectives;
5. China is a society which did not change for a long time and a stagnated culture without progress, so it is too difficult to judge what kind of society it is (ZGWH: 15, 16–19);
6. Chinese culture displays a human form of life which almost does not have religion (ZGWH: 15–16: the fifth and sixth characteristic are to be found in ZGMZ);
7. A deep-rooted family system of utmost importance (ZGWH: 19–21; already in XCJS: 599–720, this became the basis of the old Chinese teaching, i.e., human-familial relationships);
8. The academic standard has not tended towards the advancement of science (ZGWH: 21–22), ("… although China from early times made many discoveries and inventions");
9. Chinese culture did not strive for democracy, freedom, and equality. The legal system was not (fully) formulated (ZGWH: 22–26; according to Liang this does not go beyond the fifth characteristic);
10. In Chinese culture, the ethical climate is of special importance (ZGWH: 26) (according to Liang this characteristic is intimately connected with the sixth as "one mode with its positive and negative aspect");
11. China is not like a state—the Chinese have substituted the concept of state with that of *tianxia* 天下 as "all under heaven" (ZGWH: 26–28) (this idea was already present in XCJS);
12. (Since the Eastern Han Dynasty) China was regarded as a culture without a proper army (soldiers) (ZGWH: 28);
13. The special importance of filial piety (*xiao* 孝[24])—Chinese culture is a kind of *xiao*-culture (ZGWH: 28–29);
14. Recluses/hermits (*yinshi* 隱士) were the conspicuous expression of Chinese culture.

[24] Poškaitė 2014: 99–114, Qi 2015: 141–161, and Whyte 2004: 106–127.

In the conclusion of ZGWH (289–306), Liang made a nine-part recapitulation of his investigation of Chinese culture with the help of peculiar characteristics. Without going into the details of this recapitulation, we want to state that an overall peculiar characteristic of Chinese culture that permeated the whole ZGWH is the early manifestation of reason (*lixing zao qi* 理性早啟), which was another name for the prematurity of Chinese culture (*wenhua zaoshu* 文化早熟) of the DXWH. The premature character of Chinese culture, however, implies for Liang a kind of serious disease (cf. "Five Big Diseases of Chinese culture," ZGWH: 284–289). The five manifestations of this disease are as follows:

1. Infantile disorder (*youzhi* 幼稚);
2. decrepit condition (*lao shuai* 老衰);
3. impracticality (*bu luoshi* 不落實);
4. having fallen into the negative passivity without a future (*luo yu xiaoji yi zai mei you qiantu* 落于消極亦再沒有前途);
5. ambiguity without straightforwardness (*aimei er bu mingshuang* 曖昧而不明爽).

The following diagram depicts the main content of Liang's theory of the peculiar characteristics of Chinese culture (Chart 1):

The Latin numerals (I–V) depict as follows:

I : the essence of Chinese culture: Prematurity of culture (DXWH) / early manifestation of reason (ZGWH);
II : the modus operandi of early manifestation of reason: *wudui* 無對 (deconstruction of objects) done by reason; self-consciousness, autonomy and the setting out from mind (further explication see below);
III : attitudes of Chinese life as results of realization of early manifestation of reason: inwardly directed effort, familial-ethical human relations;
IV : a basic and conspicuous characteristic of Chinese culture displayed in history—sinification;

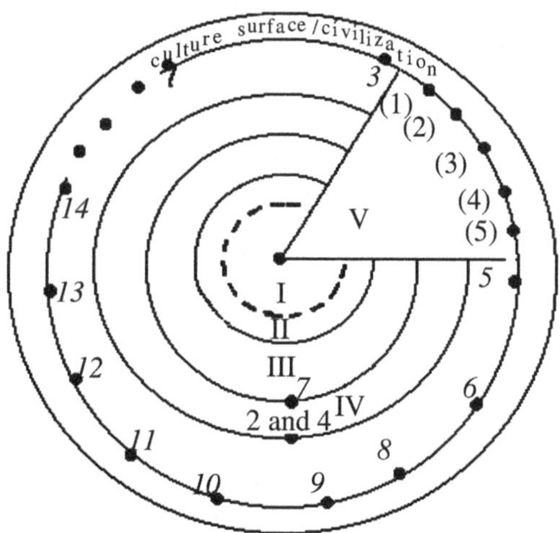

Chart 1 Liang's theory of Chinese culture with all characteristics and layers. (Taken from Wesołowski 2005: 391)

V : five manifestations of the disease of cultural precocity (as a part of historically developed Chinese culture; here on the right side).

The most salient point of Liang's theory of the peculiar characteristics of Chinese culture comes from his concept of lack, with the meaning of not having at all or not enough. This concept implies its dialectical counter-part, i.e., fullness or over-fullness, plenitude or over-plenitude and so on. Thus the lack on one side makes the fullness on the other side. The mode of substitution (*yi* 以 … *dai* [*ti*] 代[替] …) in Liang's way of thinking is the simplest result of this dialectic. Thus, according to Liang, in China (1) morality was substituted for religion (ZGWH: 95–122), (2) the concept *tianxia* was substituted for the state (ZGWH: 26), (3) customs (*lisu* 禮俗) were substituted for law (ZGWH: 198), (4) feelings were substituted for force (*yi qing dai shi* 以情代勢), and (5) the individual was substituted for organization (ZGWH: 205). Among Liang's fourteen peculiar characteristics of Chinese culture, there are six which display the mode of lack (5, 6, 8, 9, 11, and 12). As mentioned above, the opposite is plenitude, and this is especially seen in number 10 (moral atmosphere) and 7 (a deep-rooted familism). According to Liang, morality has a direct relationship with reason, and the concept of reason is a key one in the ZGWH, especially in view of Chinese culture as the early manifestation of reason.

As clearly outlined above, the most important concept of ZGWH is that of reason (*lixing*). According to Liang, this reason is a characteristic of humankind and the emotive dimension of human mentality (*renlei xinsi zuoyong de qing yi mian* 人類心思作用的情一面), whereas intellect (*lizhi* 理智) is an epistemic dimension of human mentality (*xinsi zuoyong de zhi yi mian* 心思作用的知一面; cf. ZGWH: 125–126). The essence of reason lies in "impersonal feeling" (無所私的感情—feelings devoid of any selfishness: ZGWH: 125). In view of comparison with the Western tradition, we could straightforwardly call Liang's concept of reason "moral reason." Such moral reason, emotive dimension of human mentality or impersonal feeling is manifested in sobriety and calmness, peace and harmony (*qingming anhe* 清明安和). The opposite of this feeling is a feeling of foolish hiding (*yubi* 愚蔽), one-sided stubbornness, violence or selfishness (cf. ZGWH: 112). The human heart-mind (*renxin* 人心) is where reason plays its important role. Thus within human mind and reason, Liang discovered the particularity of human life as such (Chart. 2). In line with his vitalism and neo-evolutionary theory of development of human faculties (desire, instinct, sensation, feeling, intellect and reason), which was not systematically developed in ZGWH, Liang expounded their function, meaning and relations, as far as they were of help to express his cultural thought. For example, human intellect was seen by him "only as a developmental tendency within the instinct itself which consisted in reducing the use of the instinct and advancing the use of intellect" (ZGWH: 124).

Within human life and psyche, filled with its different faculties, there are many dialectical tensions which for Liang have culture-generating implications. The main tension exists between body/corporeality (*shen* 身) and mind/mentality (*xin* 心). According to Liang, Chinese culture directly set out from the mind (that is another version of the early manifestation of reason therein), whereas Western culture only

dimensions of human life	Different faculties	"external" cognitive faculties: understanding of material principle (*wuli zhi li* 物理之理) (scientific knowledge/ tools of life)	"internal" cognitive faculties: understanding of reasonability (*qingli zhi li* 情理之理) (moral behavior, human life as such)
Body/corporeality (*you suowei* 有所為) (*youdui* 有對)	Instinct desire sensation feeling**	sensation*	(feeling of instinct) ↑ human feelings |
	intellect	intellect*** epistemological dimension of reason	| ↓
mind (*wu suowei* 無所謂) (*wudui* 無對)	reason		reason (feeling of reason) emotive dimension of reason (self-conscious)

(function of mentality: intellect and mind rows)

* According to Liang, there must be two kinds of sensation: 1) a common, original, natural sensation; 2) a special, epistemological, scientific sensation.

** Feeling and sensation should have the same origin. As a matter of fact, a part of sensation derives from family life, and they are, as in the case of Chinese family, especially ethicized.

*** Intellect is beyond the scope of selfish/unselfish (in the DXWH, for Liang Sino-Confucian life-intuition [*feiliang* 非量, *zhijue* 直覺] was the only human faculty which was unselfish).

Chart 2 Dimensions of human life with its various faculties and the place of reason. (Taken from Wesołowski 2005: 396)

set from the body, and then slowly developed reason. Another differentiation among Liang's faculties of human life was done with the help of the pair master / tools (*zhuren* 主人 / *gongju* 工具). Only moral reason should become the master of human life, and not other faculties such as desire, instinct, sensation, human feelings, or intellect. Liang characterizes the usurpation and change of the place of the master and its tools as a "moral mistake" (*cuowu* 錯誤) in human life, which is much more serious than mistakes committed in the epistemological dimension within the realm of intellect.

The opposition body/mind corresponds to that of *you suowei* 有所為 (already present in DXWH), which can be translated as "purpose- and calculation-bound actions," and *wu suowei* 無所為—"purpose- and calculation-free actions." This opposition received a new name in ZGWH—*youdui* 有對 (lit: having an opposite or encountering an obstacle) which entails constructing and dependence on objects (or in other words, human intentionality is the necessity of fulfilling biological needs, of feelings having its objects, or of minds to be about, to represent, or to stand for something else). *Youdui* especially characterizes all non-human organisms with their scope of utility (*liyong* 利用) and resistance (*fankang* 反抗). Its counterpart is *wudui* 無對 which I translate as "deconstruction of objects" or even better: "beyond the realm of intentionality." This pair of terms comes from Buddhist soteriology.[25] Liang used it to compare Chinese and Western cultures: "The original intention was to use *youdui* and *wudui* to compare China with the West, that is, to speak about mind, and that means to only point to reason [as the difference between them]" (ZGWH: 259; see also ZGWH: 100, 132, 135).

Against this background, Liang expounded the relationship between reason and Chinese culture, i.e., the early manifestation of reason. As above already mentioned, this early manifestation of reason brought about within Chinese culture—and especially in comparison with Western culture—some cultural shifts, i.e., (1) morality was substituted for religion, (2) familial-ethical human relations were substituted for feudalism, (3) ceremonies (customs) were substituted for law, (4) feelings were substituted for force, (5) and diversity in occupations (*zhiwu fentu* 職務分途) were substituted for social classes etc.

Liang's discourse on the national character of the Chinese has only a corroborative function in proving his main theorem of ZGWH, i.e., the prematurity of Chinese culture as its early manifestation of reason. He also enumerated 10 national characteristics of the Chinese (ZGWH: 30–31):

1. selfish and self-profit-oriented, regarding one's own family as the priority (*zisi zili—yi ziji jiating wei zhu* 自私自利—以自己家庭為主);
2. hardworking and thrifty (*qinjian* 勤儉);
3. inclined to talk about courtesy (*aijiang limao* 愛講禮貌);
4. peaceful, gentle and frail-looking (*heping wenruo* 和平文弱);
5. content with one's lot and self-satisfied (*zhizu zide* 知足自得);
6. conservative (*shou jiu* 守舊);
7. careless (obscure) (*mahu* 馬虎 [*mohu* 模糊]);

[25] On the one hand, this pair is primarily about the outer pole of consciousness as object or world-relatedness (in general intentionality, Buddhist *fazhi* 法執—world attachment). On the other hand, it is also concerned with the inner pole of consciousness as self-centeredness, self-consciousness or general reflexivity (Buddhist *wozhi* 我執—the twofold self-attachment). Confucius, according to Liang, destroyed the second aspect of double self-attachment, i.e., *fenbei wo* is a differentiated, egocentric, and egoistic self which is at work in Western-pragmatic culture. The Buddha destroyed both, i.e., the first aspect *jusheng wo* which is for him the inborn, life-oriented, and intuitive self and the second—*fenbei wo*. Buddha's enlightenment meant, of course, the destruction of world attachment. Cf. fn. 19.

8. steadfast, persevering, and cruel (*jianren canren* 堅忍殘忍);
9. tenacious and resilient (*renxing ji tanxing* 韌性及彈性);
10. skillful and very experienced (*yuanshu laodao* 圓熟老到).

Within the national traits of the Chinese, Liang made a distinction between the primary (innate, inborn or genetic factors) and the secondary ones (social or time-acquired factors). According to him, the national characteristics of the Chinese are embodied in the Confucian tradition, and are only a remote reflection of what was expressed in the corresponding life-forms of Dan Duke of Zhou (Zhou *gong* Dan 周公旦, r. 1042 BC – 1035 BC), Confucius, Mencius (372–289), or Wang Yangming (1472–1529).

The scope of comparison in ZGWH was also narrowed down, and principally restricted to China and the West, as it was already in his ZGMZ and XCJS. Liang said: "The present book takes only the comparison between China and the West as its subject matter, and India is not discussed here" (ZGWH: 260). The crux of this comparison became the question of religion. Liang made some general comments on the difference between China and the West. He said: "The difference between China and the West is only relative, not absolute … The community life of the Westerners is exceptionally strong, and with the Chinese—family life. This is exactly a difference of these two places. Through this we have two opposite cultures" (ZGWH: 76). At the end of ZGWH, Liang used a very special formulation to talk about the difference between China and the West:

> To summarize what has been said, the problem [of selfishness and orientation towards self-profit] comes only from the structure of society and the needs of the times, and the Chinese and Westerners are basically not any different. If there is any difference, it is in this point: The Westerners set out from the body (*shenti* 身體) and the Chinese [partake of] the early manifestation of reason.
>
> 綜核以上所論, 問題只在社會結構與時勢需要上, 中國人西洋人根本沒有什麼不同。如其有之, 那就是西洋人從身體出發而中國人理性早起這一點。(ZGWH: 315)

Against the background of ZGWH, this is the biggest difference possible! In his comparison of China with the West, Liang was searching to show the individuality (*gexing* 個性) of Chinese culture, i.e., to interpret it as a product of the early manifestation of reason within humankind. The problem of religion in ZGWH became "the watershed between Chinese and Western cultures" (cf. *Zhongguo wenhua de fenshuiling* 中國文化的分水岭, ZGWH: 52–55). The main function and contribution of religion (Christianity) in the West was for Liang its being a pedagogue of community life and organized life-style. It is this aspect of human life that—according to Liang—Chinese culture badly needed. Although China lacked this kind of pedagogue, there was, however, another one: morality based on radical familial-ethical human relations. This morality replaced religion. The Confucian tradition became the teacher of old China.

In the ZGWH, Liang Shuming demonstrated his "ultimate" understanding of Chinese culture. However, all human cultures, including Chinese and Western cultures, are in fact a manifestation of the human spirit, mind or mentality, especially embodied in human reason.

5 Conclusion

Liang, as a philosopher of culture, was in this chapter explored by means of four works, i.e., DXWH (1921), the ZGMZ (1930), the XCJS (1936) and the ZGWH (1949). These works echo the tremendous predicament of Chinese culture which started its new unprecedented phase with the foreign intrusion in China after the unequal treaty in Nanjing of 1842 in the wake of the First Opium War (1839–1842). Since then, Chinese culture has lost its own "transparency" and "non-questionability." "The hundred years of national humiliation" (*bainian chiru* 百年耻辱: 1839–1949) began as the period of intervention and subjugation of China by Western powers, Russia and Japan (Adcock Kaufman 2010: 1–33). In comparison with other modern Chinese thinkers, such as Hu Shi 胡適 (1891–1962), representing a kind of scientific liberalism of Western style, or Chen Duxiu, as promoter of Marxist thought in China, Liang Shuming displayed a neo-traditional or conservative approach in solving the dilemma of Chinese culture.[26]

Liang's cultural thought is understood here as a manifestation of "Sinodicy," as a philosophical theory of the justification of Chinese culture. This cultural theory is a kind of apology and argumentation for the greatness of Chinese culture in the face of its many different shortcomings which are actually part of each human culture. From the outset, Liang's cultural theory was worked out against the background of Western culture, which existentially threatened and posed a real challenge to the identity of Chinese culture. Liang is the first Chinese thinker who through a comparison of Chinese culture with Western and Indian cultures attempted to find for Chinese culture its place and meaning in the system of world cultures. The direction and result of this cultural exploration were to present an "absolutistic" conception of culture. In the DXWH, Liang's cultural thought was grounded in vitalism and epistemology of the Buddhist Consciousness-Only (*weishi-*) School. His vitalism, though in connection with Bergson and the Confucian Lu-Wang tradition,[27] expressed principally a Buddhist understanding of life through the concept of the

[26] Here I understand conservatism (from Latin "conservare," "to preserve," or also "to preserve something in its original context") as a collective term for intellectual and political movements that aim at the preservation of the existing order or the restoration of former aspects of social order and culture. Conservatism is based on the idea of a political and intellectual continuity designed for peaceful evolution and an orientation towards proven, historically grown traditions. "Conservative" in this sense was often used in the cultural discourse on modern China and Liang, especially by Guy S. Alitto (1979).

The concept of neo-traditionalism is more my own choice to characterize Liang Shuming's cultural thought, by which I mean his attempt to make the deliberate revival and reworking of old Chinese culture with its practices and institutions in new political-social contexts for the future China.

[27] The Lu-Wang tradition refers to the learning of Lu Xiangshan 陸象山 (also known as Lu Jiuyuan 陸九淵, 1139–1192) and Wang Yangming 王陽明 (also known as Wang Shouren 王守仁, 1472–1529). Because both stressed the role of the mind (*xin* 心) as the proper focus of practice, posterity came to call their learning the "Lu-Wang tradition" or *xinxue* 心學, as a mind-based learning. The culmination of this tradition, Liang saw it in Wang Gen—the founder of the

will with its three basic directions (i.e., a primordial one—to demand and go forward; the negation of it—to turn back and move backwards, and the harmonizing one—to adjust one's own intention and hold the golden mean). Thus, human culture is—in a Buddhist manner of speaking—a life process of coping with dual attachment (i.e., with world-attachment and double self-attachment as an innate and a differentiated self-attachment). The concept of culture presented in the DXWH is a universal-philosophical one based on the great breadth of the three directions of the will and the universality of the three problems of human life (i.e., material, social and that of the individual mind).

Through Liang's understanding of Western culture as a pragmatic culture whose peculiar contribution lies in solving the material problems of humankind and whose culmination was taking place during Liang's life, he was able to show the universality of Chinese culture as a Sino-Confucian culture, pointing to its legitimate place in the realm of world culture as a second period of universal human history dealing with the solution of problems connected with human relationships. This thought stands in connection with the idea of the prematurity of Chinese culture—a topic which is actually the central one of the ZGWH, and which Liang never gave up in his cultural thought. The above-mentioned theoretical-philosophical framework of the claim for the universality of his cultural thought has another source, i.e., in his psychogenesis as a history of Liang's thinking.[28] He claimed to have gone in his psyche through the three periods of human history as different kinds of culture.

> The third period [of the evolution of my views on human life] is the transition from Buddhist to Confucian thinking since I was 28 and 29 years old, i.e., the time of the publication of DXWH. In these three periods—which is very strange—it is like this: the first period can be called Western thinking, the second Indian and the third Chinese. It seems as if the three great systems of world culture have gone round in my thinking.
>
> 第三時期由佛家思想轉入於儒家思想，從二十八九以後，即發表《東西文化及其哲學》一書之際。在此三個時期中，令人感覺奇巧者，即是第一個時期可謂為西洋的思想，第二個時期可謂為印度的思想，第三個時期可謂為中國的思想。彷彿世界文化中三大流派，皆在我腦海中巡迴了一次。(ZS: 9)

The timeline of his psychogenesis ran through Western-pragmatic (14/15–19 years old), Indo-Buddhist (20–28/29 years old), and Sino-Confucian cultures (from 29 years old onwards and the timeline of the history of humankind, which he presented in his DXWH, was a sequence of Western-pragmatic, Sino-Confucian and Indo-Buddhist cultures. This understanding goes beyond the rational structure of the human mind. Probably Liang saw himself implicitly as a Boddhisattva.[29] It, however, underlines Liang's basic concept of culture as manifestation of human spirit, mind or mentality, especially embodied in moral reason.

In the ZGWH, Liang moved from a Buddhist vitalistic and epistemological position to a neo-evolutionistic vitalism and epistemology (i.e., crypto-Buddhist

---

Confucian Taizhou School. Cf. YAN Xiaomei 2009: 173–188. On Liang and Bergson, see Chap. 4 in the present volume.

[28] Wesołowski 1997: 95–96.

[29] Wesołowski 1997: 95, fn. 3.

position). The concept of the will with its three basic directions from the DXWH was shortened to the formulation of "the three attitudes of human life." The cognitive faculties, such as sensation, intuition, intellect and reason, were perceived in their evolutionary development. The concept of intuition, which in the DXWH was so crucial for a proper understanding of Chinese culture, disappeared completely and was replaced by Liang's key concept of reason. According to him, this reason is a characteristic of human mind—the emotive dimension of human mentality, whereas intellect is the epistemological dimension of human mentality. This human mentality is actually the motor behind the evolution of human culture. The essence of reason lies according to Liang in impersonal feeling, i.e. in unselfish feeling. In the DXWH, intuition was only of unselfish character (Wesołowski 1997: 128). The seat of selflessness in the ZGWH became human reason (*lixing*). In view of these theoretical-conceptual readjustments, Liang expounded the relationship between reason and Chinese culture. The concept of prematurity from the DXWH was articulated in the ZGWH as an early manifestation of reason. According to him, reason displayed within Chinese culture a function of substitution, i.e., morality was substituted for religion, familial-ethical human relations were substituted for feudalism, customs were substituted for law, diversity in occupations was substituted for social classes and so on.

Liang's cultural thought leads us not only to see Chinese culture in its individuality, but also almost in its insuperable uniqueness which is beyond any comparison. However, all human cultures, including Chinese and Western cultures, are in fact a manifestation of human spirit, mind or mentality, especially embodied in human reason. Liang saw Chinese culture as an early manifestation of reason, but actually according to his logic of cultural thought, Indo-Buddhist culture should be an even earlier manifestation of human reason! In fact, the present humankind has already started its second axial period (extending the thought of Karl Jaspers [1883–1969]) as an age of globalization. We human beings of various and different cultures are getting closer together and creating kind of a new world culture. However, the roots of this world civilization are of Christian Western provenience.

All in all, Liang Shuming was a man of pithy but in-depth insights and of prophetic intuitions. However, the present economic and international rise of communist China does not seem to go into the direction of his great vision of Chinese culture.

References

DXWH *Dong-Xi wenhua ji qi zhexue* 東西文化及其哲學 [*Eastern and Western Cultures and Their Philosophies*; 1921], *LSMQJ*, 1989, vol. I: 319–547.

LSMQJ *Liang Shuming quanji* 梁漱溟全集 [*Complete Works of Liang Shuming*, vols. I to VIII]. Jinan: Shandong Remin Chubanshe, 1989–1993.

XCJS *Xiangcun jianshe dayi* 鄉村建設大意 [*A General Idea of Rural Reconstruction*; 1936], *LSMQJ*, 1989, vol. I: 599–720.

ZGMZ *Zhongguo minzu zijiu yundong zhi zuihou juewu* 中國民族自救運動之最後覺悟 ["The Final Awakening of the Self-Saving Movement of Chinese Nation"; 1930], *LSMQJ*, 1992, vol. V: 44–118.

ZGWH *Zhongguo wenhua yaoyi* 中國文化要義 [*Essential Meaning of Chinese Culture*; 1949], *LSMQJ*, 1990, vol. III: 1–316.

ZS *Zishu* 自述 ["Autobiography"; 1934], *LSMQJ*, 1989, vol. II: 1–34.

Adcock Kaufman, Alison. 2010. The 'Century of Humiliation,' Then and Now: Chinese Perceptions of the International Order. *Pacific Focus* 25 (1): 1–33.

Alitto, Guy S. 1979. *The Last Confucian. Liang Shu-ming and the Chinese Dilemma of Modernity*. Berkeley\Los Angeles\London: University of California Press.

———. 2005. The Conservative as Sage: Liang Shu-ming. In *The Limits of Change. Essays on Conservative Alternatives in Republican China*, ed. Charlotte Furth. Cambridge, MA\London: Harvard University.

Cheng, Yu-Yin. 2009. The Taizhou School (*Taizhou Xuepai* 泰州學派) and the Popularization of *Liangzhi* 良知 (Innate Knowledge). *Ming Studies* 60: 45–65.

Flew, Antony G.N., ed. 1951. *Logic and Language*. Oxford: Basil Blackwell.

Kuhn, Philip A. 1977. Origins of the Taiping Vision: Cross-Cultural Dimensions of a Chinese Rebellion. *Comparative Studies in Society and History* 19 (3): 350–366.

Major, Philippe. 2017. Textual Authority and Its Naturalization in Liang Shuming's *Dong-Xi wenhua ji qi zhexue*. *Monumenta Serica* LXV.1: 123–145.

Meynard, Thierry. 2011. *The Religious Philosophy of Liang Shuming: The Hidden Buddhist*. Leiden: Brill.

Poškaitė, Loreta. 2014. Filial Piety (*xiao* 孝) in the Contemporary and Global World: A View from the Western and Chinese Perspectives. *Asian Studies II* XVIII.1: 99–114.

Qi, Xiaoying. 2015. Filial Obligation in Contemporary China: Evolution of the Culture-system. *Journal for the Theory of Social Behaviour* 45 (1): 141–161.

Streng, Frederick J. 1982. Three Approaches to Authentic Existence: Christian, Confucian, and Buddhist. *Philosophy East and West* 32 (4): 371–392.

Tu Wei-ming. 1998. Hsiung Shih-li's Quest for Authentic Existence. In Charlotte Furth, ed., *The Limits of Change: Essays on Conservative Alternatives in Republican China*. Cambridge: Harvard University Press, 1976. Also in: Tu Wei-ming, *Humanity and Self-Cultivation: Essays in Confucian Thought*. Boston: Cheng & Tsui Company, 1998.

Wesołowski, Zbigniew. 1996. Liang Shumings (1893–1988) Religionsbegriff. In *"Fallbeispiel" China. Ökumenische Beiträge zu Religion, Theologie und Kirche im chinesischen Kontext (China – Model Case. Ecumenical Contributions on Religion, Theology, and Church within the Chinese Context)*, ed. Roman Malek. Sankt Augustin\Nettetal: Steyler Verlag.

———. 1997. *Lebens- und Kulturbegriff von Liang Shuming (1893–1988). Dargestellt anhand seines Werkes* Dong-Xi wenhua ji qi zhexue 東西文化及其哲學 (Liang Shuming's [1893–1988] Concepts of Life and Culture Based on his Work *Dong–Xi wenhua ji qi zhexue*). Sankt Augustin: Institut Monumenta Serica.

———. (Wei Siqi 魏思齊). 2003. *Liang Shuming (1893–1988) de wenhua guan: genju* Dong–Xi wenhua ji qi zhexue *yu* Zhongguo wenhua yaoyi *jieshuo* 梁漱溟(1893–1988)的文化觀-根據《東西文化及其哲學》與《中國文化要義》解說 (Liang Shuming's [1893–1988] Concept of Culture Based on his Works: *Dong–Xi wenhua ji qi zhexue* and *Zhongguo wenhua yaoyi*). Taibei: Furen daxue chubanshe.

———. 2005. Understanding the Foreign (the West) as a Remedy for Regaining One's Own Cultural Identity (China): Liang Shuming's (1893–1988) Cultural Thought. *Monumenta Serica* 53: 361–399.

Whyte, Martin. 2004. Filial Obligations in Chinese Families: Paradoxes of Modernization. In *Filial Piety: Practice and Discourse in Contemporary East Asia*, ed. Charlotte Ikels. Stanford: Stanford University Press.

Yan, Xiaomei. 2009. How to Make Sense of the Claim 'True Knowledge Is What Constitutes Action': A New Interpretation of Wang Yangming's Doctrine of Unity of Knowledge and Action. *Dao: A Journal of Comparative Philosophy* 8 (2): 173–188.

Chapter 6
Liang the Philosopher of Religion

Thierry Meynard

1 Introduction

Religion or religiosity, what matters the most? Liang would certainly answer the latter as he seems to share the concerns of many of our contemporaries on the negative impacts of religion as an institutional organization. However, his critiques need to be contextualized not in the post-Christian society of the West, but in early Twentieth-century China as a cultural resistance to the West, and notably to Christianity. Liang's understanding of Christianity was certainly influenced by his uneasiness regarding Western colonialism, but this did not preclude him to see also some advantages in religious organizations like Christianity, and he came to reach a quite balanced view on religion, in comparison to more radical stances at that time. Beyond his meaningful critiques of religion as institution, what makes Liang an even more interesting philosopher of religion is that he could articulate religion as a personal religious quest. As we shall explain, this quest plays out within Confucian ethical relationships (especially at the level of family and friendly relations) on a model very different from the church model. However, the moral transformation of the self points out towards something beyond, a transcendental realm which could be qualified as mystical.

As Zbigniew Wesołowski has shown in the previous chapter, Liang's philosophy of culture articulated three types of culture (Western, Chinese, Indian). In those three cultures, religion functions at different levels. At the most basic level, religious organizations enable society to develop, filling the social need for efficient cooperation. For Liang, Christianity represents this level at its best, and he examines in his later works how Confucianism and Marxism could also remedy to the lack of

T. Meynard (✉)
Sun Yat-sen University, Guangzhou, China
e-mail: meiqianl@mail.sysu.edu.cn

T. Meynard, P. Major (eds.), *Dao Companion to Liang Shuming's Philosophy*, Dao Companions to Chinese Philosophy 17,
https://doi.org/10.1007/978-3-031-18002-6_6

collective life in China. On a second level, exemplified by Confucianism, religion provides consolation to the individual faced with existential questions, as well as fostering a spiritual harmony within the individual and within the group. Finally, in its highest meaning, religion addresses the transcendental quest for meaning through a radical renunciation to the world. This transcendence is best expressed by Buddhism. Those three functions of religion—social, psychological and transcendental—correspond to three different stages in the development of humanity facing specific problems. Christianity first helps to solve the question of collective survival by organizing society under one God and one Church. Then, Confucianism finds the spiritual balance between the individual and the group, allowing the individual greater freedom. Finally, Buddhism helps to solve the ultimate questions of the meaning of life, by asserting a radical transcendence. We should make it clear at first that these three religions, Christianity, Confucianism, Buddhism, serve mostly as illustrations of three different stages or types and should not be narrowly understood as concrete historical religions.

2 Concept of Religion

It is often said that the concept of religion was introduced into China through Japan around 1900, but in fact, it was introduced in details some 260 years before. This fact is usually overlooked, but was exposed recently by TAN Jie 譚杰 in his analysis of the *Western Learning on Personal Cultivation* 修身西學 (1636) by the Italian Jesuit Alfonso Vagnone (1566–1640). Based on the meaning of the word by Cicero (106–43 BC), Thomas Aquinas (1225–1274), and Leonard Lessius (1554–1623), Vagnone explained that religion is a virtue belonging to the moral virtue of justice since religion is something that we owe to God. He translated it phonetically as *leliruo* 肋里若 and semantically as *qinchong* 欽崇, a semantic loan from the *Book of Documents* or *Shangshu* 尚書 (Tan 2018: 105). This virtue implies a set of ritual acts due to God like devotion, prayer, sacrificial offering or mass, etc. (Gao 2019: 273).

The Jesuit missionaries applied this meaning of religion as virtue to understand Buddhist and Daoist rituals, which they considered as idolatrous worships addressed to false gods. However, the nature of Confucian rituals is more elusive, and the Jesuits could not describe it according to the traditional meaning of religion, either as correct or false virtue, but they were somehow forced to describe it with the neutral category of civic or political rituals. The Jesuit writings therefore describe China as a society with a high degree of morality, but without religion. By doing so, the Jesuits "created a space devoid of religiosity and transcendence, which they refer to as civil and which later became the secular" (Meynard 2011: 8). In the perspective of the Jesuits, the a-religious space of Confucianism was to be converted sooner or later to Christianity, but ironically the Enlightenment thinkers adopted in a positive sense the separation between religious and secular spheres, and from then on, religion took the modern meaning of a particular system of beliefs attached to a particular social organization. In Nineteenth-century Europe, religion was constituted as a specific object following its own principles, quite different from the ordinary society.

When Liang and other intellectuals discussed religion around 1920, they may have been aware that the Chinese neologism for religion (*zongjiao* 宗教) was a product of secular modernity, but they completely ignored that the concept took its root from the Jesuit understanding of China. However, this concept was still very foreign to Chinese traditional religion, described by the sociologist C.K. Yang (1911–1999) as "diffused religion," that is encompassing all the aspects of the social life, without a rigid division between the religious and secular spheres. Because religion was conceived as a particular set of beliefs and an organization, the three traditional teachings (*jiao* 教) of Confucianism, Buddhism and Daoism were construed as three opposing religions, rather than "three dimensions of Chinese heritage or indeed three aspects of Chinese life" (Yao and Zhao 2010: 14–15). Also, the image of China as moral but without religion, which was built in the West for more than 200 years, eventually came back to China, and many Chinese intellectuals adopted this view and strived to find further historical evidence in their own tradition.

To understand Liang's philosophy of religion, it is important to contextualize his discourse within the vivid debates on religion at that time. The pressing issue was the salvation of the country in face of immense internal and external difficulties. The issues of education, science, democracy, feminism, etc., were all determined by the question of national survival, and the issue of religion was no exception. Therefore, the debates on religion focused on the social and political functions of religion, under the forms of two related questions: Did China have a religion or not? If China does not have a religion, does it need one or not?

Three main positions were elaborated. First, a minority (especially the Chinese Christians) held that China did not have a religion but urgently needed one. Second, reformists like KANG Youwei 康有為 (1858–1927) considered that China did have a religion, but this native religion needed to be more clearly defined and institutionalized, and thus Kang promoted the foundation of a State religion, the Church of Confucius 孔教會. Kang's disciple, LIANG Qichao 梁啟超 (1873–1929), promoted Buddhism instead, but without pretending to establish it as a State religion.

However, a third opinion prevailed among the intellectuals: regardless of whether China had a religion or not, it was not needed, neither then nor in the future. Thinkers associated with the New Culture Movement agreed that scientific progress was making religion obsolete and that religion would—or should—not exist in modern China. In 1921, CHEN Duxiu 陳獨秀 (1879–1942) declared that religions obstruct individual rationality and national progress and should be discarded. But while Chen advocated purely and simply the eradication of all religions, other intellectuals were searching for substitutes to religion. In 1917, CAI Yuanpei 蔡元培 (1868–1940) had proposed that religion could be replaced by atheistic education which addressed the affective needs of the people (Bastid-Bruguière 2002: 83–85).

In a paper written in Chinese in 1928 and published in English in 1931, "The Confucianist Theory of Mourning Sacrificial and Wedding Rites" 儒家對於婚喪祭禮之理論, FENG Youlan 馮友蘭 (1895–1990) adopted an historical perspective and explained that the religious rituals of early China had been progressively transformed into moral rituals. Feng reproduced his view in his *History of Chinese Philosophy* (中國哲學史, 1934), and Wang Zhixin 王治心 (1881–1968) made further developments of Feng Youlan's view in his own groundbreaking work *Outline of the History of Chinese Religious Thought* (中國宗教思想史大綱, 1933). Liang adopted the views of Feng and Wang on the transformation of ancient Chinese religion to morality (ZGWH: 417), and this view is still today very influential in Chinese academic circles. This view can be understood as the continuation of the Jesuit reading of China as moral but non-religious, and as suggests Zbigniew Wesołowski in the previous chapter, Bertrand Russell (1872–1970) seems an important link, since he came to China in 1920 and 1921 and gave very influential conferences. Russell characterizes traditional Chinese civilization with three features, the second being "the substitution of the Confucian ethic for religion among the educated classes" (Russell 1922: 30). Most likely, FENG Youlan, WANG Zhixin and LIANG Shuming adopted directly or indirectly this view from Russell. In fact, among the 14 characteristics of Chinese culture enumerated by Liang at the beginning of *Substance of Chinese Culture*, Liang mentions as the sixth characteristic that China practically lacks religion, and there he mentioned the view of Russell (ZGWH: 16). It seems that Feng, Wang and Liang later added historical evidences in support of Russell's view. While the Jesuits considered that the ancient monotheism held by Confucius disappeared during the Han dynasty, attributing the change to an external factor (the entry of Buddhism in China), Feng and the others placed the shift from religion to morality during the Zhou dynasty, and attributed it to the Duke of Zhou and Confucius.

The opposition of the intellectuals to religion was due mostly to the perception that religion in the West, being irrational and unscientific, was in decline and that it may disappear quickly. Such a view was deeply influenced by the positivism of Auguste Comte (1787–1857) who had placed religion in the infancy of humanity, which was to be substituted by the "positivistic age." Liang knew and mentioned in his works the theory of Comte, but he took the opposite view, holding that religion constitutes, in fact, the horizon and the future of humanity.

The Republican government adopted the concept of religions and recognized five religions (Buddhism, Daoism, Islam, Catholicism and Christianity) which were to be organized according to the modern model of religious organizations. This allowed the government to circumscribe and limit their influence within Chinese society, unlike the pervasive influence Chinese religions had under the traditional model of diffused religion. It has often been noticed that the most pervasive form of Chinese religious life, which constituted the actual practice of the vast majority of the people, that is, the local popular religions, did not hold any legal status and their existence was threatened to disappear. As many governments in Europe at that time, the Republican government was pursuing a secular policy against religion.

Liang was familiar with the governmental discourse on religion and with the discourse of the reformists and of the New Culture Movement, but he may have been dissatisfied with their ideological takes on religion, and he himself went on to develop an approach based on religious attitude and behavior, or what we could call human religiosity. He discusses abundantly religion in all his writings, but more especially in the fourth chapter of *Outline of Indian Philosophy* (YDZX: 58–66), in the third chapter of *Eastern and Western Cultures and their Philosophies* in the following sections: "Definition of religion" (DXWH: 416–421), "Its true necessity" (DXWH: 421–433), "Its true possibility" (DXWH: 433–440), "The religion of Confucius" (DXWH: 466–476), in the sixth chapter of *Substance of Chinese Culture*: "Morality as substitute of religion" (ZGWH: 95–122), and finally in the eleventh chapter of *Human Mind and Human Life* (RXRS: 688–725). Liang's discourse on religion deals with the history of religion, sociology of religion, psychology of religion, but Liang was not an historian, sociologist or psychologist, and because religion for him essentially addresses the question of the ultimate meaning of our human existence, it is better to understand it as a philosophy of religion, a branch of philosophy which was already discussed in China at least since the work *Philosophy of Religion* by Tu Xiaoshi 屠孝實 (1898–1932) in 1927.

Liang adopted the Western concept of religion, but he radically transformed it. First, while most intellectuals marginalized the role of religion, Liang placed religiosity or spirituality at the heart of the three orientations of the will, and of the three cultures, as Zbigniew Wesołowski shows in Chap. 5 of this volume, and this pervasive role of religion is illustrated by Liang's first general definition of religion: "What we call religion is thought with a special attitude and leading to a certain behavior" (DXWH: 395). A second characteristic of Liang's understanding of religion is to ground religion in the attitude and behavior of concrete individuals, and not in the needs of society, with the great advantage of distinguishing the issue of religion from the issue of national salvation which dominated the discourse of the reformists like KANG Youwei and LIANG Qichao, and of the promoters of the New Culture Movement like CHEN Duxiu. This led Liang to propose a more precise definition of religion based on individual aspirations: "To seek the consolation and encouragement of our desires through a transcendent knowledge" (DXWH: 420). Liang would repeat a similar definition in his other works (ZGWH: 98; RXRS: 693). This second definition of religion with its two elements of human aspirations and faith beyond reason is quite precise and also broad enough to encompass many types of religion. Finally, Liang modified further the concept of religion because he categorized three types or degrees of religion, with Christianity representing conventional religion, Confucianism an apparent religion, and Buddhism the true religion since it aims effectively at the supramundane (*chushijian* 出世間), as we shall see next.

3 Critiques of Religion as Institution

Liang considers religion as the most powerful activity in social life, but he holds that the social impact of religion can be best observed in Western society. Even though Liang acknowledges that Christianity has lost most of its hold on the whole of society with the advent of modernity, he still considers that modern Western society has inherited the cultural patterns of this sociological religion. In ZGWH, Liang analyses the strengths of Western culture based on Christianity, which can be categorized under five headings: social cohesiveness, social dynamism, universality, social progress and group psychology (Meynard 2007: 132). Those elements explain how Christianity has shaped a strongly structured society. Religion surely brings a lot of divisions and tensions between the world and God, orthodoxy and heresy, body and spirit, instinct and reason, but it is precisely through and by those divisions and tensions that a densely complex and unified social body is constantly being shaped. On the contrary, China had the insight of moral reason (*lixing* 理性) very early, but, lacking the structure to sustain it, the nation has been stopped in its social progress.

While Liang recognizes the positive aspects of Christianity in terms of social development, he measures basic flaws compared to the two other models of religion, the moral religion of Confucianism and the transcendental religion of Buddhism. The major criticisms Liang addresses to this social religion are a mechanical collective life, an exaggerated exclusivity, and an external seeking. First, the frame of religious institutions does not help the development of a reflexive morality: "The psychology of the gathering of masses entails a great mechanicity, blindness, impulse, and difficulty to reflect" (ZGWH: 200). Religion as a social body holds some rigid and immutable truths that are enforced upon the lives of the individuals; but life itself, especially the moral life of the individuals, is seen as a continuous process of changes upon which rigid truths are irrelevant. By holding onto those sedimented truths, people set themselves apart from the reality of life, which is an ever-changing reality. They create attachments to false ideologies, preventing themselves from developing a true morality. The second major defect of this kind of social religion is an exaggerated exclusivity. While the spirit of religion goes in the direction of universality, believers unconsciously adhere to a social organization, developing "a feeling of stupidity and crankiness" and "a spirit of violence and impulse" (ZGWH: 111). Christians proselytize as if the same truth could apply to all regardless of their own personal questioning and of their different degrees of spiritual maturity. Third, Liang criticizes Christianity's lack of a true introspection: the faithful checks his moral life against the external standards of sins decreed by God, preventing him from developing a true morality. For Liang, this externality of Christian morality has developed in the modern West into another externality: morality based on external profits or advantages, as exemplified in the utilitarian traditions where the standard of the good is measured quantitatively, mostly in material terms. The problem is to seek for something outside, be it divine, political or economic.

Even though Christianity was able to concretely shape a society where moral reason was enhanced, yet it cannot fully develop the inner essence of humanity, but rather leads to a partisan and mechanical attitude which fails to fully understand the inner heart. Christianity is ultimately unable to answer the deep quest of meaning of the individuals and to provide peace of mind. Religion may present itself as an absolute truth, setting an ultimate standard of meaning, but this truth is soon or later being questioned, creating more doubt and frustration for the disillusioned individual.

It is important to point out that Liang understood Christianity mostly as a social organization, as a church. He had little insight into the personal faith of the Chinese Christians, and furthermore he seems to ignore the mystical literature of Christianity—it was not available in Chinese language at that time. Also, like many intellectuals at his time, Liang considered the terms "religion" and "morality" to be mutually exclusive and he was himself quite opposed to conventional religions. Even though he clearly understood the positive role of Christianity in the historical genesis of Western societies and in promoting good morals, yet he wanted people to focus on their true interiority, instead of relying on religious beliefs. Probably Liang's thought was a bit constrained in this dichotomy between religion and morality, which was so influential then.

It would be wrong to assume that Liang targeted exclusively Christianity. While many intellectuals embraced the new concept of religion with the Christian church as institutional model, Liang on the contrary resisted attempts to look at religion essentially as a social institution. We can see this in his relation to Confucianism and Buddhism. In order to strengthen China, Kang Youwei had advocated to transform Confucianism as a Church, as mentioned above. However, Liang expressed his disgust towards such a move which he sees founded upon an utilitarian mind. Liang was especially shocked by the subscription campaign to build temples to Confucius where the financial contribution of the donators will be advertised; for Liang this was a complete ignorance of the Confucian *ren* 仁 (DXWH: 464). Kang's attempt to transform Confucianism as a State religion did not find much support, and Liang's opposition to transform Buddhism as a social religion was more sustained and systematic. He was especially opposed to the projects of the Buddhist monk Taixu 太虛 (1890–1947) to promote social Buddhism, and those following words of Liang seem to target Taixu: "If someone wishes to walk the Buddhist path for himself, I can accept; but if he promotes it for society, then I am forced to oppose it" (DXWH: 534). For Liang indeed, the social and moral problems of society should be actively addressed, but this was not the role of Buddhism because the real objective of Buddhism is not to improve our present world, to make it a better place—which ultimately are an illusion—, but to find liberation from the present world. Liang's critiques ultimately pushed Taixu to develop at a deeper level his vision of Humanistic Buddhism, but Liang never adhered to it (Meynard 2011: 127–146).

As we can see, Liang was very cautious about any institutional form of religion, may it be in Christianity, in Confucianism, or even in Buddhism. Religion as institution may be good at certain levels for society, but ultimately it represents an hindrance to the authentic religious quest of individuals which should be free from any attachment to a sectarian group and to any idea of competition for power, influence or prestige. As we shall see below, Liang considered Confucianism as an apparent religion, and Buddhism as the authentic religion, but this does mean that he was personally committed to any set of dogma and to any religious affiliation. He could recognize many good values and insights in Buddhism, Confucianism, Christianity, Daoism, Marxism, etc., but he was a free thinker, and his thought was syncretic.

4 Confucianism: Not a Religion But Like a Religion

Liang affirmed that religion is common to all humanity, and yet he held that Confucianism "is not a religion, but like a religion" (非宗教而似乎宗教, DXWH: 417). It is not a religion in the conventional sense (Christianity) because Confucius does not request any allegiance to a set of beliefs or organization, but Confucius invites each one to return to his own self-nature through introspection and through the practice of rituals, especially to the ancestors, and thus Confucianism fulfills the moral function of religion (DXWH: 468).

By returning to moral reason, people experience a fundamental unity with the moral life of the cosmos, and obtain consolation and peace from this. In this way, Confucian morality performs the psychological function of providing consolation, which Liang had assigned to religion (a constituting element in the second definition above). Here, Liang drew mostly from the Song and Ming Neo-Confucians for whom the personal inner heart is enlarged to the dimensions of the moral cosmos, enabling humans to achieve real freedom within the world. Through moral reason, individuals apprehend the movements of the cosmic life, and embrace its flux. By balancing their inner moral feelings with reason, they are associated with the pace of the cosmos, and they derive consolation from this.

For Liang, Confucius gave Chinese culture an orientation completely different to that of all other civilizations in regard to religion. In *Substance of Chinese Culture*, he discussed further the religion of Confucius, stating that for him, the root problem of religion was not its irrationality, but its immorality. The worship of deities destroys benevolence (*ren*仁) because people crave for external things and thus wrongly believe in the existence of deities who could fulfill their requests. People first deviate from correct moral attitudes and then develop wrong ideas, rather than the reverse.

We have mentioned above the influential thesis of 1928 by FENG Youlan about an historical shift from religion to morality in ancient China. In *Substance of Chinese Culture*, Liang fully embraced Feng's view, and added his own elaborations (ZGWH: 113). According to him, with the Duke of Zhou and Confucius, the center of Chinese culture shifted from religion to non-religion. The worship of heaven and ancestors became only one aspect of education. In this new setting, attention shifted from the temple to family. Liang therefore contrasted the community-centered life of Christianity in the West with the family-centered life of China. This created two different cultures—one of religion and one of non-religion. While religion calls for all believers to observe certain religious tenets, Confucianism emphasizes self-examination and does not set a universal standard, with the conviction that everyone has moral reason, a "sense of what is right and wrong" (*shifei zhixin* 是非之心, ZGWH: 108). While Feng talks about a transformation of religion towards morality, Liang radicalized the theory, talking about a "replacement of religion with morality" (*yi daode dai zongjiao* 以道德代宗教, ZGWH: 95), meaning that the Confucian path makes traditional religion obsolete.

While *Eastern and Western Cultures and their Philosophies* looks at culture, *Substance of Chinese Culture* pays attention to society, and in respect to the religion of Confucius, Liang developed his theory of "rituals without rituals" (*wuli zhi li* 無禮之禮) and "music without sound" (*wusheng zhi yue* 無聲之樂, ZGWH: 131). We have shown above that Liang called people to turn to their inner self. But this turn to the self was concretely made through rituals, and Liang showed how Confucius gave to rituals a new meaning. In traditional rites, the worshipper and the object of worship stand in clear and distant opposition. On the contrary, Confucian rituals bridge this gap so that the worshipper is introduced into a fundamental harmony between oneself and the cosmos. Fully participating to the cosmic life, he/she becomes united with heaven and earth. Solemn rituals at temples can realize this, but for Liang, the whole of human life is to be ritualized, becoming a great liturgy, including relations with parents and siblings, with teachers and students, etc. Most importantly, rites do not express division, but rather a harmony which embraces the self and the cosmos (Meynard 2015: 120).

Liang's interpretation of the Confucian rites is deeply influenced by the cosmological language of Neo-Confucianism, and yet it perfectly reflects Confucius' understanding of rituals, not as religious sacrifices paid to some deities or supernatural forces, but as the moral and esthetical expression of a fundamental harmony among human beings and beyond. Liang notices that it is also the meaning expressed by Xunzi 荀子 who points out that common people are mistaken in thinking that rituals are addressed to deities, while the *junzi* 君子 understands rituals as ornaments (*wen* 文)—that is, the refined expression of an inner attitude of respect (ZGWH: 113). Therefore, rituals do not stress the objective presence of divinity, but rather the state of mind of the worshiper.

For Liang, rituals are operative because they change the usual way of thinking and behaving of the people. Through rituals, the mind recognizes distinctions for what they are, and refrain from creating rigid divisions, or as Liang said, "the mind can become an entity that is one with everything, allowing the cosmos to communicate without separation, despite its vastness" (RFYT: 159). This idea finds its roots in the thoughts of Confucius, about whom it is reported in *Lunyu* 論語 9.4: "There were four things from which the Master was entirely free: he had no foregone conclusions, no arbitrary predeterminations, no obstinacy, and no egoism." Precisely because Confucius realized the ontological unity between the human mind and the cosmos, he could overcome the mundane distinctions arising from self-centeredness and egoism.

Liang expressed Confucian ethics by using the Buddhist concept of cutting attachments. Accordingly, Confucianism can effectively overcome the discriminating mind's attachment to the mistaken ideas of the self (分別我執) and of the world (分別法執), and thereby people can find spiritual harmony in the world and ultimately reach the essence of the cosmic life in its state of flux (RXRS: 660). Yet, because Confucianism wants us to be actively engaged into our concrete world, we should not cut the inborn attachments to the self (俱生我執) and to the world (俱生法執), that is, we should not cut the objective conditions in which our own existence is founded. This is reserved to the Buddhist stage, when people will discard their own existence and thereby reach the essence of the cosmic life in its state of tranquility and unconditionality, neither arising nor ceasing. As he said in *Human Mind and Human Life*, "we cannot but distinguish between two aspects: the essence of the cosmic life in state of flux and its essence in the state of tranquility, of unconditionality, without arising and ceasing. The two aspects are not identical, neither distinct, two but still one, one but still two. And the way of Confucianism deals mainly with the first and Buddhism with the second" (RXRS 1984: 660).

Therefore, Liang envisioned the modern age not as shaped by religion (neither the religion of the West nor the religion of India), but as being shaped by Confucian morality. Confucianism provides the modern age with an alternative to conventional religion, by developing self-reflection, introspection and the inner life. With the individual always in danger of being swallowed by the artificiality and superficiality of modern society, in Confucianism one can find a moral quest and an ethical practice. By fulfilling our moral duties towards one another, one penetrates further into the true meaning of life. Not only does an individual thus uplift his moral life, he also enters into an aesthetic and spiritual experience. For Liang, humanity was entering into the ethical age.

While history is marching towards the final Buddhist awakening, Confucianism is the best way for the present since it can positively prepare the path for the transcendental question to arise, first by rejecting the impasse of too worldly religions, and second by insisting on the cultivation of the mind.

5 Religious Quest Aiming at Buddhist Liberation

According to Liang, the first type of religion (Christianity) is flawed because of its irrational beliefs and constraining social organizations, while the second type of religion (Confucianism) cannot overcome the inborn attachment and cut off the fundamental support on which the natural and mental life relies to develop. The Buddhism that Liang promotes as the third and perfect type of religion is not evidently the institutional or popular forms of Chinese Buddhism, but rather a radical form which has historically flourished in India but has been walked elsewhere only by a very few people.

Liang's religious quest is grounded on the pervasive perception of human suffering, a reality which is unavoidable in one's personal life but also in the life of people around. In facing suffering, many people have recourse to religious beliefs, betraying their fear for their own existence. Their faith makes them believe they can change the events of this world to their advantage, or find a realm of happiness and bliss after this life, imagined in analogical terms with this world. But by doing so, they exert pressure on their human nature, consigning their existence to a narrow egoistical sphere. For Liang, facing the question of suffering, only Indian people, and especially Indian Buddhists, have found the correct attitude; they are not concerned about their life, enclosed by their suffering, but display the highest courage: "In other regions, most of the people are coward and they necessarily deform their nature. Most Indians do not seek support to preserve their life, but they usually and normally seek to leave the world—they call it *nirvana*" (DXWH: 437).

Liang expresses the idea of radical transcendence with the word *chaojue* 超絕 which means "to surpass" (*chao* 超) by "cutting through" (*jue* 絕, DXWH: 419). This concept differs from *chaoyue* 超越 which means "to surpass" by "going beyond" (*yue* 越). This second notion of transcendence is understood in analogy with the present world, and betrays an existence still imprisoned in *samsara*. A religion resting on this kind of soft transcendence is unable to achieve final liberation: "Though religion leaves this world, it yet establishes that world, and it is still unable to be a religion truly leaving the world" (YDZX: 60). While Liang acknowledges that all historical religions deal with the transcendence or the supernatural, however, most of them keep being attached to this world. The popular religions expect from the supernatural some concrete benefits for this worldly life. Even more elaborate religions such as Christianity establish an ultimate reality or an after-life that they model after the world: God is thought of in the analogical category of being, person, will, etc.; paradise is thought of in terms of a space. Also, as we have shown above, Christianity engages in the world to transform it, to make it a better place, thereby creating more attachments to it.

In *Outline of Indian philosophy*, Liang analyzed the Indian schools as "philosophical religions" (哲學的宗教, YDZX: 60). He maintained that they sought a transcendent and cosmic reality which is reached through the dialectical method of negation. Therefore, Indian schools are essentially religious, but they use a special kind of philosophy as a method, not the ordinary kind to obtain a positive knowledge on oneself and on the world, but a negative philosophy to achieve a higher reality—a wisdom beyond Western rationality and Confucian moral intuition. Liang concisely described the Buddhist philosophical method as "canceling understanding through understanding" (以理解取消理解, YDZX: 158). The mind can access ultimate reality only when reason has systematically destroyed all conceptual attachments that reason had itself created. Then, the mind can identify completely with ultimate reality, without any distinction between the inner and outer worlds. In the mind, there cannot be any self-reflective activity, or a space for self-awareness, but only pure and spontaneous activity. Therefore, Indians have adopted the right attitude and the right philosophy which enable them to understand ontological reality (DXWH: 416). Also, their understanding did not remain at the level of the individual; by destroying the mind's conceptual constructions concerning the absolute, Indians had successfully united with it.

At the normative level, only Buddhism can be called a true religion since its essence is "leaving this world" (*chushi* 出世). It is therefore Liang's understanding of Buddhism which gives ultimately the normative definition of religion. Liang looks at the *via negativa* as the only solution: "The Indians fundamentally reject the worldly life. Therefore their renouncing is not only about this life, but they consider all the life and reject it all; that is what means to cut and to extinguish" (YDZX: 60).

In *Human Mind and Human Life*, Liang develops his idea of the relation between the mundane and the supramundane, speaking of them in ontological terms: "The mundane and the supramundane are what the philosophers call the phenomena (*xianxiang* 現象) and the noumenon" (*benti* 本體, RSYRS: 705). The supramundane is the permanent ontological foundation of the physical and mental world, which is in constant flux and always changing. While primitive Buddhism interpreted the mutual interaction between *saṃsāra* and *nirvāna* in terms of an epistemic difference (delusion-enlightenment), Liang, following Chinese Buddhism, interpreted it in terms of an ontological difference (potentiality-actuality). The epistemic difference between *saṃsāra* and *nirvāna* in classical Yogācāra is transformed here in different degrees of Being. As Liang said, "if we acknowledge that *saṃsāra* is real, then *nirvāna* is even more real" (RSYRS: 706). Liang went to describe ultimate reality using a Neo-Confucian term: the "mind of the cosmos" (*yuzhou zhixin* 宇宙之心).

However, Liang did not eliminate the tension between the mundane and the supramundane, as if fusing them into one metaphysical entity, but he stated that "*saṃsāra* and *nirvāna* are neither identical, nor distinct" (RSYRS: 705). Even though "*nirvāna* is the basis of *saṃsāra*," (RFYT: 157), there is still a real dissymmetry between the two. Only *nirvāna* is the transcendent reality which encompasses all of reality, human and physic, and which is eternally tranquil (Meynard 2011: 123).

6 Discourse on the Spirits and the *Shentong*

The spirits (*guishen* 鬼神) held an important position in Chinese thought before the Qin dynasty and during the Han dynasty. Much later, Zhu Xi (1130–1200) provided a rational interpretation based on *qi* and the two polarities of *yin* and *yang*. One of the first books of "philosophy" introduced from Japan was a translation by Cai Yuanpei of *Lectures on Demons* 妖怪學講義 by the founder of the Institute of Philosophy in Japan, the Buddhist Inoue Enryō 井上圓了 (1858–1919), motivated by a desire to criticize and debunk popular superstitions, which was also the reason behind Cai's effort to translate this work into Chinese. In 1939, Feng Youlan himself devoted one chapter of *New Principle Learning* 新理學 to the spirits, mostly based on Zhang Zai 張載 (1020–1077).

Liang was opposed to the superstitious practices connected to the spirits because he considered the manipulation of the spirits for private interests to be immoral. He did not have definitive proofs of the existence of spirits, but held that there were many signs which indicated their existence. He believed that some people could obtain supernatural knowledge about the past, the present and the future. In his first essay, written in 1916, Liang referred to the example of the lay Buddhist Yang Wenhui 楊文會 (1837–1911) who had predicted before his death the revolution and the fall of the Chinese empire (JYJY: 15). At the end of his life, Liang himself said that he was the reincarnation of a Chan monk (Meynard 2011: 186).

Liang did not accept limiting his worldview to what is known by the science of his day, and he held that "in the future, with the progress of knowledge, we shall know more about the spirits little by little" (*RSYRS*: 698). He believed that the human mind, when liberated from worldly illusions, could communicate freely with the deepest level of reality, up to the point of knowing events in the past and future. These phenomena were not irrational, and a science of the mind would one day explain them.

Liang's belief in the spirits is founded on Buddhism and Confucianism, for both of which death is not seen as an ultimate end, but as a passage or transformation into a new reality which has a strong connection with the world of the living. In ancient China, it was believed that the temporary vital forces (*hunpo* 魂魄) were unbound at death, but still remained, reconstituting under new forms. Buddhism introduced the idea of transmigration, especially the idea that between two lives there is an "intermediary *yin* body" (*zhong yin shen* 中陰身) which possesses supernormal abilities (*shentong* 神通), notably a higher degree of communication with the other forms of life. This ability is determined by previous lives, and especially by the individual practice in the most recent life. This practice for Liang could be Daoist, Buddhist or Hindu, with the fruits of Buddhahood (*foguo* 佛果) being released at the moment of death. Those spirits could see or hear things which are not seen or heard anywhere else, and mental communication could allow them to know the thoughts of others. Also, trans-sensorial communication allowed the five senses to communicate with one another, so that the five senses know what each sense knows individually (*RSYRS*: 699). Thus, one who reaped the fruits of Buddhahood could access absolute freedom in which all barriers between himself and the external world disappear.

The Buddhist *shentong* does not function in *nirvāna*, but within *saṃsāra*, and so Liang applies it to the moral realm of Confucian metaphysics. Drawing from the vitalism of Bergson, Liang sees life as an ever-expanding reality which overcomes the obstacles met through an unceasing creativity: "The essence of life, demanding communication and unification, goes forward progressively, expands everywhere, and increases its capacity for action" (*RSYRS*: 698). This vitalism allows Liang to affirm his belief in the existence of spirits, especially in their ability to communicate. Through the Buddhist notion of *shentong* and Bergsonian vitalism, Liang expresses his Confucian belief in the human mind's moral and spiritual communication with the cosmos.

7 Relevance of Liang's Philosophy of Religion

For some, the thought and life of Liang would appear too eclectic and too extremist. However, despite appearances, he was not an eclectic, but a real syncretist. Even though some issues may still remain unsolved in his thinking, he has shown a remarkable coherence in his understanding of Christianity as a social religion, Confucianism as an ethical religion, and Buddhism as transcendental religion. The three types of religions are needed to bring the final awakening to its term.

Surely Liang held an elitist view on religion since he considered the mass of the people in the modern age not yet ready to face the ultimate question of the meaning of existence and unprepared to embrace the radical form of Buddhist enlightenment. Liang's philosophy of religion can only be understood as an individual quest for meaning where each one faces his own questions in due time, and therefore Liang was very sceptic about religious dogma which pretend to give answers available to all and valid for all times. For Liang, there was no need to transmit any religion to anyone because each one faces his own questions in due time. This philosophy of religion as personal quest calls upon each one's aspiration, inner freedom and responsibility. Perhaps Liang would have felt sorry for people desiring only a comfortable life in this world and unwilling to address the ultimate question of meaning, but he would have probably refrained from judging them.

Despite Liang's particular attention to individual freedom and responsibility in the religious quest, he attempted mapping a road for the final liberation for all by integrating positive elements of Christianity and Confucianism that could effectively prepare society and culture towards it. This theory of stages should not strike us as unfamiliar. After all, in the Nineteenth and Twentieth centuries in the West, many like Kierkegaard and Freud have expounded similar theories. But we may still touch here on more problematic aspects of Liang's thought.

First, the theory of stages goes against the more holistic approach we are now familiar with, emphasizing the interconnectedness of the different aspects of economy, politics, society, culture and spirituality, which need to be addressed not sequentially but at the same time.

Also, by keeping silent on the transcendental orientation of his worldly action, Liang may have deprived it from the spiritual energy that would have appealed to many. But precisely, Liang consciously kept his social engagement distinguished from his private religious quest. In his thought, the question of religion is eminently important, but is not imposed in all the fields of human thought and action. The question of religion stays constantly in tension with the engagement in the world, and Liang rejects the temptation to absorb society and morality within religion. In the other direction, religion is a constant reminder about something beyond society and ethics, so that no reality of the world, may it be a particular country, culture, language, or religion, and even human intellect or morality should be absolutized. In his interview with Guy Alitto at the end of his life, Liang accepted to be called a Buddhist, a Confucian, a Marxist, etc. This is to say that he recognized good things in all those, that he did not strictly identify himself with any thought, because none is absolute.

Thanks to Liang, many Chinese scholars were able to go beyond the narrow concept of religion promoted by the New Culture Movement and by Chinese Marxism. They were able to rediscover the true religious bearings of Confucianism. Liang's ideas concerning religion have greatly influenced contemporary New Confucian philosophers, helping them to reclaim Confucianism's spiritual tradition (Bresciani 2001: 83). In the past 50 years, philosophers belonging to this movement have reassessed the question of religion with greater openness. In his analysis of Chinese culture as being without religion, Liang has followed the lead of Feng Youlan as we mentioned, but Liang's specific contribution was to underline the spiritual dimension of Confucianism. Liang's influence can be felt in the "Declaration on Behalf of Chinese Culture Respectfully Announced to the People of the World" by ZHANG Junmai 張君勱 (1886–1969), TANG Junyi 唐君毅 (1909–1978), XU Fuguan 徐複觀 (1903–1982) and MOU Zongsan 牟宗三 (1909–1995), and proclaimed on January 1, 1958. The four authors emphasized that Confucianism was not a purely intellectual theory, but a life commitment which held that the supreme ideal of sagehood was to be in communion with Heaven. Though Confucianism did not develop into an organized religion, it still contained a deep religiosity. The Declaration, drafted by TANG Junyi, went beyond the artificial dichotomy established by Liang between religion and morality, stating that, for Confucianism, "human existence is simultaneously moral and religious," and it did not shy away from using the term "religion," and qualified Confucianism as a "humanistic religion" (*renwen zongjiao* 人文宗教) or an "ethical religion" (*daode de zongjiao* 道德的宗教; Bresciani 2001: 54). More recently, TU Weiming 杜维明 (b. 1940), following the idea of "philosophy as way of life" of Pierre Hadot (1922–2010), has developed the concept of "Confucian spirituality" as a way of life (Tu 2003). Some scholars have also attempted to go beyond the misrepresentation of Chinese culture as one of immanence opposed to the Western culture of transcendence. TANG Yijie 湯一介 (1927–2014) has developed the idea of an "immanent transcendence" (*neizai chaoyue* 内在超越) in Chinese culture or Confucianism (Tang 1991), and YU Yingshi 余英時 (b. 1930) of inward transcendance (*neixiang chaoyue* 内向超越) opposed to outward transcendance (*waixiang chaoyue* 外向超越; Yu 1984).

In this beginning of the Twenty-first century, humanity is confronted by religious extremism that is endangering peace in many parts of the world. As Liang shows, Confucianism can be an ethical resource for all of humanity because of its strong universalism, going beyond the barriers that religion often raises between people. In the context of a worldwide culture torn apart by religious conflicts, Confucianism can provide a secular foundation to society and to the world, since it calls each individual to make the self-conscious experience of a moral and spiritual transformation by which particular attachments to ideologies, religions and cultures are discarded, in order to create a unity assumed as an individual and collective responsibility. The idea of a social bound not grounded on religion, or on God, but grounded on the awareness that people are the masters of their own destiny has been described by the French historian and philosopher Marcel Gauchet (b. 1946), in the context of Western societies, as the "coming out of religion" (Gauchet 1985). Gauchet reads in Christianity a principle which was leading to the "coming out of religion," but which happened only in modern times. In China, according to Feng and Liang, the passage from the religious sphere to secular morality and politics would have happened at the time of Confucius and this would mean that China had accomplished secularization 2000 years before the West. On this account, Christianity is not the unique case of a religion that brings about the coming out of religion.

But the crux of the matter is not the unanswerable question of whether Confucianism or Christianity was the first to inaugurate the passage from religion to secularization. What is far more important is the kind of secularization we are talking about. Here, Liang reminds us that secularization cannot be based only on a set of values, principles and institutions, but should imply, above all, the moral and spiritual transformation of the individuals in an ethical community. It is only at this deep level of humanity that an individual can find their spiritual needs being addressed. It is precisely here that Western secularization departs from the Confucian one, since the former considers individuals as prior to society, with individual needs radically distinguished from collective needs. In other words, the Confucian secularization challenges the Western categories in which its own secularization is founded, like the dichotomy between individuals and state, or the distinction between the religious and the secular.

More importantly, Liang suggests that we should move beyond the modern split between the religious and the secular, and understand Confucianism as precisely an inner principle which should be present in all particular traditions, that is the articulation of particular beliefs to our common human nature. This articulation should not be done by eradicating all religious and cultural differences. As we all know, when differences are not allowed to be expressed in the public space, it is often for the profit of a certain class representing the dominant order, and then, the exclusion of differences provokes frustration, violence and radicalism. Therefore, what is needed is for each particular tradition and culture to appropriate something from Confucian ethics and spirituality, expressing its passage from particular beliefs to our common nature through introspection and ethics. Understood this way, Confucianism may not need to be against religions, but can be their ally.

Finally, Liang's philosophy of religion tackles the question of the ultimate meaning of existence, which is the core question of religion. Liang does not give any positive answer to the question, because there is no immediate and direct answer to it. Instead of letting aside this impossible question, the philosopher of religion upholds it constantly as long as he/she lives. The question of religion is constantly present, but somehow hidden in his/her own consciousness; it may induce a unique way of being in the world and some concrete decisions, deeds and commitments, and yet it can never be reduced to those; it may give insight and consolation, but the quest is always open-ended. This philosophy of religion expresses a very subjective experience to the question of ultimate meaning. It could be criticized as ending into solipsism and subjectivism, and somehow making the question of religion disappear from the public social sphere, but Liang's own writings are a testimony of the importance of the question for anyone.

References

DXWH *Dong-Xi wenhua ji qi zhexue* 東西文化及其哲學 [*Eastern and Western Cultures and Their Philosophies*; 1921], *LSMQJ*, 1989, vol. 1: 319–547.

JYJY *Jiuyuan jueyi lun* [*Treatise on Finding the Foundation and Resolving the Doubt*, 1916], *LSMQJ*, 1989, vol. 1: 3–22.

LSMQJ *Liang Shuming quanji* 梁漱溟全集 [*Complete Works of Liang Shuming*, vols. I to VIII], Jinan: Shandong People Press, 1989–1993.

RFYT *RuFo yitong lun* 儒佛異同論 [*Treatise on Differences and Similarities*], *LSMQJ*, 1993, vol. 7: 152–169.

RXYRS *Renxin yu rensheng* 人心與人生 [*Human Spirit and Human Life*], *LSMQJ*, 1990, vol. 3: 523–760.

YDZX *Yindu zhexue gailun* 印度哲學概論 [*Outline of Indian Philosophy*; 1919], *LSMQJ*, 1989, vol. 1: 23–247.

ZGWH *Zhongguo wenhua yaoyi* 中國文化要義 [*Substance of Chinese Culture*; 1949], *LSMQJ*, 1990, vol. 3: 1–316.

Alitto, Guy. 1979. *The Last Confucian: Liang Shu-ming and the Chinese Dilemma of Modernity*. Berkeley: University of California Press.

Bastid-Bruguière, Marianne. 2002. La campagne antireligieuse de 1922. *Extrême-Orient Extrême-Occident* 24: 77–93.

Bresciani, Umberto. 2001. *Reinventing Confucianism: The New Confucian Movement*. Taipei: Ricci Institute.

Gauchet, Marcel. 1985. *Le désenchantement du monde*. Paris: Gallimard.

Gao Yizhi 高一志 [Alfonso Vagnone). 2019. *Western Learning on Personal Cultivation* 修身西學今注. Edited by Thierry Meynard 梅謙立, Tan Jie 譚杰 and Tian Shufeng 田書峰. Beijing: Commercial Press.

Meynard, Thierry. 2007. Is Liang Shuming ultimately a Confucian or Buddhist? *Dao: A Journal of Comparative Philosophy* 6: 131–147.

———. 2011. *The Religious Philosophy of Liang Shuming*. Boston: Brill.

———. 2015. Confucianism as the Religion for our Present Time: The Religious Dimension of Confucianism in Liang Shuming's Thought. In *Contemporary Confucianism in Thought and Action*, ed. Guy Alitto. Heidelberg: Springer.

Russell, Bertrand. 1922. *The Problem of China*. New York: The Century.

Tan Jie 譚杰. 2018. Prehistory of the Concept of *zongjiao*: Introduction of the Concept of Religion in Late Ming Early Qing '宗教'概念之前史: RELIGIO 概念在明末清初的譯介. *Modern Philosophy* 現代哲學 5: 102–108.

Tang Yijie 湯一介. 1991. *Confucianism, Daoism, Buddhism and the Question of Immanent Transcendence* 儒道釋與內在超越問題. Nanchang: Jiangxi renmin chubanshe.

The Analects. 1893. Translation James Legge. Oxford: Clarendon Press.

Tu, Weiming, and Mary Evelyn Tucker, eds. 2003. *Confucian Spirituality*. New York: Crossroads.

Yao, Xinzhong, and Yanxia Zhao. 2010. *Chinese Religion: A Contextual Approach*. London: Continuum.

Yu Yingshi 余英時. 1984. *Looking at the Modern Meaning of Chinese Tradition from the System ofValues* 從價值系統看中國文化的現代意義. Taipei: Shibao wenhua chubangongsi.

Chapter 7
Liang the Philosopher of Living: On the Counter-Enlightenment Thought of Liang Shuming During the 1920s

Chan-liang Wu

1 Introduction

The popularity of counter-Enlightenment thought, or namely the critiques towards Enlightenment rationalism and universalism, during and following the May Fourth period (1915–1927) is a remarkably influential phenomenon within modern Chinese history, albeit one which is seldom studied or even mentioned.[1] To illustrate the prevalence of counter-Enlightenment thought throughout this period, let us first quote from two famous contemporaries. In 1927, Hu Shi (胡適; 1891–1962) wrote:

> In recent years, scholars in our country have a strong tendency to follow Lu-Wang Neo-Confucianism. Some advocate "inner life"; some elevate the "philosophy of moral consciousness" [*liangzhi* 良知]; some promote Yogācāra Buddhism; some interpret the Confucian *ren* (仁) as intuition; and some champion "philosophy of feeling." [Rudolf Christoph] Eucken [1846–1926] and [Henri] Bergson [1859–1941] have become supporters of the Lu-Wang school. [...] For those who care about the future of Chinese thought, we are now confronting a turning point and must make a decision. (Hu 1927: 196; quoted from Yu 1984: 73)

[1] Isaiah Berlin, the seminal writer on this subject, used Counter-Enlightenment to refer to a movement that arose primarily in late eighteenth- and early nineteenth-century Germany against the rationalism and universalism of the French Enlightenment (Berlin 1981). In this chapter, I choose to define Counter-Enlightenment, following Berlin's example, as critique or protest toward rationalism and universalism.

C. Wu (✉)
National Taiwan University, Taipei, Taiwan
e-mail: wuwei@ntu.edu.tw

T. Meynard, P. Major (eds.), *Dao Companion to Liang Shuming's Philosophy*, Dao Companions to Chinese Philosophy 17,
https://doi.org/10.1007/978-3-031-18002-6_7

For Hu Shi, this decision entails the adoption of the Western scientific method and a logical mode of thinking, both of which were acutely challenged by contemporary counter-Enlightenment thought. Following these remarks, well-known Marxist Ai Siqi (艾思奇; 1910–1966) wrote in 1933:

> The [science and philosophy (views) of life] debate concluded with Mr. Wu Zhihui's [吳稚暉; 1865–1953] "dark" cosmology and view of life, and it seems that science has won. In fact, the scientific view of life is still completely dark and it cannot suppress the fierce growth of the metaphysicians. [...] The study of Indian philosophy, Daoism, and Confucianism has dominated. Tagore has been invited to China. People such as [Buddhist] Tang Dayuan [唐大圓; 1885–1941] and Abbot Taixu [太虛; 1890–1947] have been celebrated. [...] End-of-the-century European philosophers, from [Arthur] Schopenhauer [1788–1860], [Friedrich] Nietzsche [1844–1900], Eucken and Bergson, to [Wilhelm] Dilthey [1833–1911], all took the study of man as central to philosophical questions.[2] (Ai 1988: 516)

Hu's and Ai's anxieties confirm the strength of the Chinese counter-Enlightenment around the May Fourth period, and precisely as they had noticed, this influential current was being supported by powerful Chinese, Indian, and Western sources.

Chinese counter-Enlightenment thought is a very complex phenomenon that consists of myriads of schools and was influenced by various Eastern and Western modes of thinking and sources.[3] Of the different schools, the present study will focus primarily on the "philosophy of living" (*shengsheng sixiang* 生生思想) school for two reasons: first, it was—stated simply—the most influential school of counter-Enlightenment thought, and second, it may best represent the contentions between Western rationalism and the traditional Chinese mind.[4] To deepen our grasp of the often very intricate counter-Enlightenment content of the philosophy of living, I will concentrate predominately on a close analysis of Liang Shuming's (梁漱溟; 1893–1988) Neo-Confucian philosophy. Liang is not only a major founder of modern China's New Confucianism and cultural conservatism, but also a truly original thinker in his own right. Seeing that Liang was immersed in Chinese medicine as well as Buddhist, Daoist, and Confucian traditions, an analysis of his philosophy of living is able to demonstrate a modernized traditional type of Chinese worldview

[2] Ai maintained that the rise of philosophy of living, whether formed domestically or imported, was a symptom of the declining struggle of national and world capitalism, as well as a resurgence of feudalism.

[3] See Wu 1993.

[4] Originally, I had used "philosophy of life" to characterize Liang's thought in this paper, albeit with an emphasis that his "philosophy of life" differs from German *Lebensphilosophie* (philosophy of life) in that the former accentuates the cosmic process of "becoming," whereas the latter remains beholden to the idea of life as "being." However, Dr. Philippe Major, the co-editor of this volume, reminded and persuaded me that it is more accurate to use "philosophy of living" to describe Liang's thought since "living" can better express the "process of becoming." Later on, Dr. Major also introduced to me the work by French philosopher François Jullien titled *Philosophie du vivre* (*The Philosophy of Living*, Calcutta: Seagull Books, 2016), in which Jullien himself makes this distinction and emphasizes Chinese philosophy as a philosophy of living. I cannot thank Dr. Major enough for this invaluable suggestion.

as well as the conflicts between the Chinese tradition and a modern Western worldview steeped in rationalism.

In this article, I focus on the metaphysics, epistemology, and ethics as well as the social aspects of Liang's philosophy of living, while paying particular attention to the Confucian, Buddhist, and Daoist sources of his views. Beyond what has been mentioned above, one of the major goals of the present work is to indicate that Liang's philosophy of living, being a response to Enlightenment rationalism, is not another form of Romantic or Neo-Romantic philosophy, or even of German *Lebensphilosophie* (often translated as "philosophy of life"), since it draws mainly from Yogācāra Buddhism, Chinese medicine, Neo-Confucianism, and Daoism, sources which differ significantly from those of Romanticism or post-Romantic Western philosophies. Historically, Liang's "philosophy of living" is also not associated with the similarly named "philosophy of life" (*renshengguan* 人生觀) camp represented by ZHANG Junmai (張君勱; 1886–1969), a follower of the Neo-Romantic philosophy of Rudolf Eucken, within the 1923 debate on science and philosophy of life.

2 The Sources of Liang's Counter-Enlightenment Thought

Liang's ingenious reinterpretation of the Chinese intellectual tradition along Neo-Confucian lines and his critique of modernity exercised a great influence on contemporary and future generations of Chinese intellectuals, especially in the conservative camp. Moreover, his insights into Chinese and Western philosophies and cultures enabled him to see some fundamental distinctions between these two great intellectual traditions on issues ranging from metaphysics, epistemology to ethics and social problems. And this might be the most valuable and interesting part of his thought.

Liang's critique of Western rationalism bears a striking resemblance to the stance of a number of post-Enlightenment thinkers, including Johann Gottfried Herder (1744–1803), Karl Marx (1818–1883), Nietzsche, Martin Heidegger (1889–1976), and Max Weber (1864–1920). He had no opportunity to examine most of their works, however, and his failure to mention Herder, Weber, or Heidegger in his writings suggests that in all probability he had never heard of them. Although the anti-intellectual tenor of Nietzsche's worldview resonated with Liang, Nietzsche had little use for his broader philosophical system.[5] Yet Liang had read the Chinese translation of works by Schopenhauer, Peter Kropotkin (1842–1921), Bergson, John Dewey (1859–1952), Bertrand Russell (1872–1970) and several socialist

[5] Liang acquired a cursory familiarity with the Marxist critique of capitalism by reading a number of socialist works. He was, of course, unacquainted with the young Marx's theory of alienation and reification, which he developed as early as 1844, but which appeared in print only in 1932. Liang's criticism of these phenomena characteristic of the capitalist order rested on a Buddhist and Neo-Confucian philosophical foundation.

thinkers, and had learned much from their writings. He thus incorporated important components of their philosophical frameworks into a Chinese worldview critical of the mainstream of the Western intellectual tradition.

Many readers overlooked Liang's originality and profundity because he adopted a simple colloquial style to examine many of the most fundamental issues of philosophy and human civilizations. His limited knowledge of the West and frequent factual errors prompted some scholars to dismiss his work as irrelevant, while others questioned the research methodology he had applied to his grand cultural theory (Alitto 1979: ch. V). The similarity between Liang's thought and that of several Western thinkers has also led some commentators to conclude that he borrowed heavily from European works.[6] All of them failed to see that Liang's worldview evolved through an integration of Buddhist and Chinese philosophical elements, and that the fundamental distinction between China and the West assured Liang a penetrating grasp of basic issues. There are, for sure, many important differences between the intellectual resources from which Liang drew. However, as a great thinker, he managed to integrate some of the most fundamental principles of the major Chinese resources, used them to examine Western sources, and brought them to light to his contemporaries. To many, Liang was probably the first modern Chinese to articulate many of the most fundamental differences between the Western and Chinese worldviews and mindsets successfully.[7] We shall conduct a systematic review of the basic structure of his theory before assessing his contribution to the development of modern Chinese thought.

3 The Meeting of the Chinese and Western Worldviews and Attitudes Towards Life

The New Culture Movement raised some pressing questions for contemporary Chinese. What are the essences of Chinese and Western cultures? What are China's basic cultural values? Should China Westernize, and, if so, to what extent?

In his *Dong Xi wenhua ji qi zhexue* (東西文化及其哲學; *Eastern and Western Cultures and Philosophies*; hereafter DXWH), Liang attempted to answer these questions. Beginning with the problem of "cultural essence," he formulated a view

[6] For example, see Alitto 1979: 107–17. Since Liang sought to define a number of modern concepts and encourage a dialogue between Chinese and Western thoughts, he often identified those particular ideas he borrowed from the West. This was the case even when he engaged in a systematic analysis of the basic themes of his own thought (E.g.: RXYRS: 75–89). Although this has led some readers to conclude that he derived much of his thought from the West, Liang's interpretation remained inseparable from his Buddhist, Confucian, and Daoist worldview.

[7] Although there was a series of Debates between Eastern and Western Cultures (*Dong Xi wenhua lunzhan* 東西文化論戰) between progressive and relatively conservative Chinese intellectuals ever since 1915, probably none of them had reached the depth of understanding of this issue, as will be discussed in this paper, as Liang.

of culture as an organic whole that had developed from a unifying theme and suggested that China, the West, and India represented three distinct cultural templates defined by different attitudes towards life, namely, outwardly in the West, inwardly in India, and in the middle in China. According to Liang, each corresponded to an emphasis on a different mental faculty—reason and/or understanding (*lizhi* 理智) in the West, intuition (*zhijue* 直覺) in China, and "immediate sense" (*xianliang* 現量) in India (DXWH: 177).

The meeting of China and the West, therefore, meant the encounter between distinct lifestyles, patterns of cognition, mental attitudes, and the worldviews that had evolved from these attitudes. In other words, the dialogue between rationalism and Chinese thought symbolized the interaction of the "spirits" and philosophies of the Chinese and Western traditions. Liang characterized the Westerner as an individualist intent on manipulating the external world through reason, "the highest form of self-regarding emotion."[8] This use of the rational faculty stemmed from a desire to conquer the natural environment and to acquire material possessions through dispassionate analysis and calculation (DXWH: 158). Liang identified science, democracy, and this relentless drive for mastery of nature as the three most distinctive achievements of the West and argued that they arose from its basic cultural style (DXWH: 54–55).

Yet to conquer nature means to change the "original harmony [between humans and nature]" and to fight with nature ruthlessly. To study things scientifically, on the other hand, means to alter the harmonious relationship between man and the environment, and to break, analyze, separate and cut the world into pieces in order to understand it. As for democracy, it means struggling with other people and with the authorities to reach a consensus among ambitious and contending individuals. One must be highly motivated and rational, which also means to be indifferent and calm to the not-me-world, in order to achieve those objectives (DXWH: 104).

Using the same logic, Liang characterized the modern West's attitude towards life as a utilitarianism rooted in "rational calculation, knowledge, and rational management" (DXWH: 155). Competitive capitalism and the ruthless struggle between individuals marked a Western economic system in which workers "are used by machines" and for "tedious and uninteresting" labor (DXWH: 162–65). Even people of high position must "devote [themselves] to the management and pursuit of merchandise, be calculative all the time, and suppress their feelings and emotions" (DXWH: 165–66). Similarly, Liang maintained that laws based on human reason rather than mutual good will ensured the cohesion of the Western social order. The Western world appeared to Liang as a "fragmented" entity divided by human reason into innumerable categories, elements, interest groups, regulations, and laws.

Liang offered a harsh criticism of the Western rational worldview, although European thinkers of the period formulated an equally scathing critique of the

[8] Liang's definition of reason as the highest form of "self-regarding emotion" comes from sociologist Benjamin Kidd (1858–1916), an influential socialist thinker in China during the New Culture Movement (DXWH: 174–75).

Western Enlightenment tradition.[9] In certain respects, Liang's assessment of modernity resembles the Weberian vision of an "iron cage" and rests on a similar assumption that rationalism, with its focus on instrumental reason rather than value rationality in Liang's view, lies at the heart of modern Western thought.

In contrast, Liang argues that Chinese culture attempted to harmonize the individual's relationship with the natural environment and the human community through the use of intuition. He suggests that this critical faculty facilitated the exchange of emotions between human beings and ensured an affection for the natural world that was absent in the Western tradition. At the same time, Chinese attitudes towards life cultivated human desires within a carefully defined set of constraints instead of suppressing or wantonly indulging them (DXWH: 159). In his view, Chinese value life more than reason, art more than science, ethics and education more than law and punishment, natural community more than rational organization, sharing more than acquisition, internal satisfaction more than worldly achievement (DXWH: 151–52, 194, 195). This basic style, he explained, limited Chinese achievements in science and technology, slowed institutional and economic growth, and hindered progress towards individual rights, freedom, and democracy (DXWH: 65–66). Yet Chinese cherished family life, friendship, and "healthy and affectionate relations" with community, country, and nature more deeply than other cultural groups; and, most importantly, the Chinese knew how to attain mental balance and emotional satisfaction without religion.

Two distinct philosophical strains dominated Liang's worldview while he was writing DXWH: a voluntarism that originated in Mahāyāna Buddhism and a "philosophy of living" derived from Confucianism, Daoism, and traditional Chinese medicine. Buddhist voluntarism played a critical role in his systematic analysis of world cultures and his critique of Western rationalism. His long-standing belief in a Chinese philosophy of living, in the meantime, served as the basis of his interpretation of the traditional Chinese worldview. These two philosophies, then, offer the keys to understanding Liang's mental universe.

Like their ideological counterparts in Western intellectual history, Liang's voluntarism and philosophy of living were both at odds with rationalism and thus by their very nature offered an alternative to Enlightenment thought. His philosophy exalted human instinct, sentiment, will, and intuition, and valued concepts such as holism, monism, process, dynamism, moral subjectivity, mutual affection, tradition, custom, natural community, and "becoming." In contrast, he sought to criticize reason, analytical methodology, knowledge, science, technology, technocracy, order, law, structure, atomism, pluralism, social engineering, contract theory, utilitarianism, modern society, and the mechanistic worldview based on the idea of "being." Although Liang did not explore each of these topics in detail, his philosophical talent and broad interests still led him to engage with most of the topics. Given its resulting complexity, it is impossible to unveil his grand scheme all at once. In the

[9] Liang possessed some basic knowledge of the history of Western philosophy and a certain measure of familiarity with contemporary Western thinkers introduced in China. But he never used the Mandarin terms for Enlightenment, Romanticism, or post-Enlightenment.

following section, therefore, I will start with matters pertaining to the first principles, the "metaphysical issues."

4 Conflicts in Metaphysics: Becoming Rather Than Being

Past researchers have failed to fully analyze Liang's complex discussion of the metaphysical principles of the Chinese and Western worldviews. Liang's voluntarism and philosophy of living rest on similar conceptions of eternal change and the organic unity of the universe, placing special emphasis on the idea of a dynamic, life-like cosmic process. In contrast to what he perceives as the essence of the Chinese worldview, the metaphysics of Western culture and rationalism emphasize the concepts of substance, order, and form. In sum, according to my analysis, Liang suggests that a worldview of "becoming" marks Indian and Chinese culture, while Westerners have fashioned a philosophical framework rooted in the concept of "being."[10]

Although many thinkers underscored the importance of change during the twentieth century, Liang's integration of the principle of "becoming" into a comprehensive philosophical system distinguished his work from that of his contemporaries. The writings of philosophers such as ZHANG Junmai, ZHANG Dongsun (張東蓀; 1886–1973) and LI Dazhao (李大釗; 1889–1927) resemble Liang's philosophy in important ways, but none grasped the enormous implications of a worldview of "becoming." In contrast, this idea served as the philosophical basis of Liang's system of thought. While many anticipated the crucial significance of a dynamic worldview, then, only Liang used the fundamental distinction between "being" and "becoming" to explain the basic differences between Chinese and Western cultures.[11]

4.1 From Buddhist Voluntarism to Philosophy of Living

LIANG Shuming was not interested in pure philosophical questions and he seldom presented his thought in a Western philosophical way. He was the kind of thinker who consistently attempted to inquire into the most fundamental principles of existence in order to solve the endless contradictions and sufferings in real life. Only with this intense drive, Liang said, can one become a true thinker (SMSH: 197,

[10] It is wrong to assume that Liang had little interest in metaphysics and cosmology. For example, He 1945: 9.

[11] Liang himself noted that the Confucian tradition highly valued order and rationality (*li*). Nevertheless, in his eagerness to discover the essence of Chinese thought, he tended to criticize these concepts. He did discuss the relationship between "Confucian rationalism" and "Confucian intuitionism," but acknowledged that his comments were vague and misleading (DXWH: 1–4).

200).[12] However, being a good thinker, he also brought forth that any true "philosophy" must have a core that is a prerequisite for real understanding. Although his major concern was ethical and moral, we will find that the core of his philosophy ultimately lies in his metaphysical and cosmological views.

Although Liang began to write DXWH after his conversion to Confucianism in 1921, Mahāyāna Buddhism continued to dominate his worldview. In DXWH, he observed, "I am applying only a Buddhist view to judge everything. The method I employed to observe a culture came exclusively from Buddhism" (DXWH: 48). Although this statement ignores his other intellectual influences, it highlights the central importance of Buddhism to his philosophical system. The Yogācāra Buddhism embraced by Liang posits that "the essence of living is will" and "there is no universe apart from living." Elsewhere he defines "living" as the "continuation of things," and a "thing" as the exercise of will. In his view, our sensation and consciousness represent different forms of will. Their use gives rises to seemingly objective phenomena, but in fact external events have no independent reality. In short, Liang argues for the fundamental identity of object and subject, and suggests that the self, life, the universe, and will each constitute part of an indivisible whole.[13] While he asserts that the cosmos embodies what he refers to as the "great will" (*da yiyu* 大意欲), he rejects the concept of transcendence and claims that reality does not exist apart from the process of living (DXWH: 48–50).[14]

Liang's concepts of "living" and "will" represent the cornerstones of his system of metaphysics. Theoretically the two are said to be one, and there should not be any difference between reality and process, substance and phenomena; however, we still find that the concept of living refers more to the process, whereas that of will refers more to the substance in his writings. Although in principle he claimed that the two were ultimately one and the same, in reality, he often emphasized that the essence of things is will. That shows Liang derived his belief that "the essence of living is will" from the voluntarism inherent in the Buddhist tradition rather than from a Confucian "philosophy of living."[15]

This distinction is significant because voluntarism is essential to Buddhism, while philosophy of living is crucial to Confucianism. The emphasis on will reveals a strong idealist tendency and the influence of the concept of substance (*benti* 本體): both are attacked by orthodox Confucians. The stress on living, by itself, is not too much concerned with the specific substance of existence, whether it is will,

[12] Liang maintained that he never intended to be a scholar or philosopher, but he was someone who liked to think thoroughly about the nature of things (Ibid).

[13] According to Thierry Meynard, although the identity of subject and object in Yogācāra is ultimately meant as an epistemological claim, in China it was soon associated with an ontological one. Thus, the tradition which Liang borrowed from is the latter, a Chinese form of Yogācāra that is metaphysical in orientation. See Meynard 2014.

[14] Liang's emphasis on process resembles the basic argument of A. Whitehead's most important work: *Process and Reality*.

[15] Here "voluntarism" means that will plays a central role in life, but not to the extent that the individual is able to decide with radical freedom their destiny.

spirit, God, matter, or energy. Philosophy of living is a philosophy of process, of becoming, and is central to the traditional Chinese worldview. While Liang was writing DXWH, he employed Buddhist voluntarism to picture the essence of the entirety of existence and human civilizations. Philosophy of living, not yet fully developed, was reserved for Chinese tradition only. Only after he acquired a better understanding of Confucianism in later years, did his worldview shift from voluntarism to philosophy of living.

4.2 Philosophy of Living and the Chinese Tradition

After Liang's conversion to Confucianism, "philosophy of living" gradually supplanted voluntarism as his central belief.[16] In this section, I will demonstrate that the idea of life dominated Liang's Confucian framework, that this "philosophy of living" stemmed primarily from the Buddhist and Chinese traditions, and that it played a crucial role in determining his attitude towards Western rationalism.

Guy Alitto has suggested that Liang derived his philosophy and interpretation of Confucianism from Bergsonian anti-scientific intuitionism, activism, and vitalism, and many Chinese scholars have accepted this view (Alitto 1979: 109).[17] Alitto remarks that

> Bergson's central epistemological idea was that intuition could catch the flux of reality "on the wing" so to speak (instead of congealing it by intellectual analysis into fixed, inflexible categories), and to reach absolute knowledge and truth. Liang, in effect, fashioned his own theory of the Chinese Mind and of Confucianism with this and other Bergsonian concepts. (Alitto 1979: 96)

Although Alitto misuses the Hegelian term "absolute knowledge" to describe Liang's attitude toward the capacity of intuition, his claim that Bergson's intuitionism and "metaphysics of flux" closely resembles Liang's stance appears accurate. The problem with Alitto's assertion lies in its failure to identify the origins of Liang's theory in Buddhism, Chinese medicine, and Song-Ming Confucianism

---

[16]Although Liang wrote DXWH after his adoption of Confucianism, he still adhered to Buddhist philosophical ideas. As illustrated above, however, Liang's Yogācāra Buddhist worldview contained both the elements of voluntarism and philosophy of living, and he often failed to draw a clear distinction between Buddhist and Confucian beliefs. While writing DXWH, the Buddhist perspective continued to dominate his worldview, and Liang tended to identify "living" with "will." Only in his later years did Liang place greater emphasis on the former and begin to ignore the latter. This suggests that the influence of idealist Buddhist metaphysics weakened over time and that his worldview came to more closely resemble that of an orthodox Confucian.

[17]Also see Feng 1989: 800; Wang 1982: 301–02; and Lu and Wang 1984: 81–82.

rather than Bergson's ideas. Bergson's influence, or the "confirmation" from the West, came later, and contained many things that differed from the above sources.[18]

As mentioned earlier, Liang's Confucian philosophy of living developed from a Buddhist metaphysics of will and living. Yet in a broader sense, he derived his ideological framework not simply from the Yogācāra School but from his diverse intellectual background. Liang thus discovered the basic themes of his grand philosophical system in Chinese medicine, Daoism, and Confucianism, its metaphysical and cosmological structure in Yogācāra Buddhism, and its modernist components from Western physical and biological science, philosophy of life, and Vitalism. Behind it lay Liang's inquiry into the human condition and his search for a humane worldview.

While discussing the origins and importance of his philosophy of living, Liang stated

> *Ziran* [自然; nature, (things)-from-themselves] and life [*shengming* 生命] are the two essential concepts of my thought. I view this universe as alive, and take *ziran* as the canon of everything. It seems that I emphasize the natural more than the artificial. This is the Chinese way. Both Daoism and Confucianism, the two (most) important Chinese schools, take life as their basic concept. The *Four Books* say: "What says Heaven? Four seasons proceed, and all things grow;" and "Be proper and keep harmony, the universe will be in order, and everything will flourish." They express fully the meaning of life and *ziran*. [...] For a certain period, I intensely studied Buddhism, and then turned to Confucianism. In initiating this change, the Ming Confucian WANG Xinzhai 王心齋 [WANG Gen 王艮; 1483–1541] provided the greatest inspiration and led me to the gate of Confucianism. He honored *ziran* the most, and from this I began to understand the meaning of Confucianism. [...] Later, comparing [the two concepts] with Western thought, I was deeply attracted by philosophy of life as represented by Bergson, who elucidates it the best. Moreover, studying Chinese medicine has benefitted my philosophy. Medical texts inspired me to [examine the nature of] life; [...] Confucianism, the Western philosophy of life, and Chinese medicine are the source of my thought. (ZH: 123–24)

We can see from Liang's self-analysis that *ziran* and "life" had eventually become his most important philosophical concepts. In the same article, he attributed these ideas to the influence of Confucianism, Daoism, the Western philosophy of life, biology, and Chinese medicine and argued that they offer "a method or view which can be used everywhere" (ZH: 123–24). Yet Liang passed over the Mahāyāna Buddhism that had played so crucial a part in his early intellectual development because its spirit and metaphysical assumptions differ from a philosophy centered on the concepts of "life" and *ziran*.

The idea of *ziran* and life represent Liang's life-long central belief that the essence of existence is a life-like, dynamic cosmic process that is unceasingly

[18]To support his theory of "Bergsonian Confucianism," Alitto asserted that "Liang had read Bergson by at least 1915, while he did not seriously study Chinese philosophy until late in the summer of 1916." (Ibid.) In fact, Liang paid great attention to Confucian moral teaching and began to study the classics, later writings in the Confucian tradition, and contemporary commentaries on these earlier works by 1907 (*LSQJ*, pp. 681–684). Moreover, we should not forget that Liang grew up in a Confucian society.

growing and changing.[19] Liang's thought underwent many modifications in later years. However, the emphasis on the process, instead of on the end or result, never changed.[20] To him, the process is the only end, the only reality. Only thing-from-itself is *ziran*, and it is much more valuable than things from a calculative basis other than itself. This attitude not only served as the foundation of his Confucian philosophy but characterized the broader New Confucian movement as well (ZH: 123).

Liang identified nature with this cosmic process, which he viewed as a growing, active, interconnected, responsive, and organic whole like life itself. To a certain extent, then, Liang used life and nature interchangeably to explain his philosophy. Yet since Liang had a greater interest in human affairs than nature and viewed humankind as the center of the cosmic process, the concept of "life" looms larger in his writings. Liang used this philosophy of living to define Dao (道), the highest principle of existence, by asking "What is Dao? Dao is the great life of the universe. To be one with Dao is to be one with the great life of the universe" (ZH: 127).

Liang often alluded to the *Analects* (*Lunyu* 論語) and the *Doctrine of the Mean* (*Zhongyong* 中庸) to demonstrate that his philosophy of living captured the spirit of Confucianism, noting that:

> The word *sheng* [living] is the most important concept. Knowing this is to understand all the words of Confucianism. Confucianism is nothing other than following the way of *ziran*, [so as] to live and develop vigorously and smoothly. He [Confucius] maintains that the universe is perpetually flourishing and developing. Everything desires to live, so [we should] let it grow without artifice. It will match the universe itself and fill the whole universe with the fragrance of spring and the tenor of life. (DXWH: 121)

This quotation expresses the traditional Confucian and Daoist ideal of the "unity of the universe and man" (*tian ren he yi* 天人合一) and also restates the Confucian conviction that "providing life is the greatest virtue of heaven and earth" (*tiandi zhi da de yue sheng* 天地之大德曰生). It suggests that Liang viewed the world as an integrated and life-like cosmic process and held "natural" life as the key to human existence and ultimate good.[21] Following this basic principle would lead to the discovery of the highest virtue, art, and truth.

Chinese medicine guided Liang to similar conclusions. He had begun to study medicine, both Chinese and Western, in 1914 and found that the "logic" and methodology of Chinese and Western medicine differed at a fundamental level (WDNL: 44). He argued that "Chinese medicine is thoroughly [embodied by] the concept of

---

[19] Liang's worldview could be called a kind of "philosophy of organicism," or philosophy of process, and thus had no need of a creator or supreme being. Alluding to Joseph Needham, Frederick W. Mote claims that the early Chinese saw the world as an "organismic, spontaneously self-generated cosmos" (Mote 1972: 8). Mote believes that these characteristics distinguished Chinese cosmology from that of other ancient traditions (Ibid., 7–8).

[20] In this respect, he was influenced by many modern Western thinkers such as Darwin, Spencer, Schopenhauer, Le Bon, and Bergson (JYJY: 17–33, 43).

[21] Liang believed that Confucianism and Daoism basically shared a common metaphysical and cosmological view. (DXWH: 116–18).

life," which he understood as the overall vitality of the individual. Chinese physicians could not assess one's health by examining specific parts of the human body, and thus when a Chinese doctor "measured the pulse," he focused on the "strength of the entire life-force." In contrast, the "object of contemporary Western medicine is not life but the body;" it "emphasizes only a part of the mechanism [of the body]," but does not pay enough attention to the "change, growth, and decline of life" (ZH: 125–26).[22] To Liang, life is an organic whole that we cannot reduce to the sum of its parts. In short, this holistic concept of human existence that Liang found in Chinese medicine exercised an important influence on his interpretation of the Chinese worldview.

This dynamic and organic worldview, although seemingly subjective and perhaps even mystical by Western standards, is basically a naturalistic one, and can be traced to Daoism. Liang's shift from the Buddhist, idealist worldview to a more "naturalistic" worldview is best illustrated by his new emphasis on the concept of *ziran*. *Ziran* served as the central concept of Daoism, and commentators around the late Warring States or Qin period integrated this idea into the study of the Confucian classics to establish the cosmological and metaphysical foundation of their philosophical system.[23] The term means "from itself" and provides the ideological underpinning for the Daoist belief that the world arose spontaneously rather than from the creative work of a divine being. Both Daoist and Confucian traditions reject the doctrine of transcendence, the idea of the thing-in-itself, and the teleological perspective common to Western thought (Grant 1989: 147). In the mind of the Daoist, the world simply exists and simply "is." The search for ideal forms or divine origins will inevitably end in frustration. In contrast, Dao implies the spontaneous creation and flows of all phenomena and suggests that the natural "way" created by the interplay of things should govern. Things should be from and for themselves. Human interference in the natural development of the universe thus produces mischief and disorder. I suggest that we identify this naturalistic view of the cosmic process not as mysticism but as a form of Daoist "rationalism." The rationalist component of this philosophical system rejects the efficacy of mystic power and defines the meaning of existence in universal terms (Weber 1951: 226–27, Qian 1971). Yet the Daoist emphasis on the limitations of human knowledge undermines its capacity to present a rigorous and systematic knowledge system. Daoism thus remains a compelling interpretation of the world but differs markedly from the systematic rationalism developed in the West.

The writings of the late-Ming Neo-Confucian scholar WANG Gen first inspired Liang to examine the concept of *ziran* and encouraged him to transit from the Buddhist to the Confucian way of life.[24] Liang's preoccupation with professional ambitions and sexual desire during this period ensured that he defined the concept

[22] Yet Liang acknowledged the efficacy of Western medicine and the many shortcomings of its Chinese counterpart.

[23] See Qian 1977.

[24] WANG Gen belonged to the Left Wing of the popular but radical WANG Yangming school (de Bary 1970: 125–26, 157, 165–66).

in terms of the natural flow of instinctive human aspirations. In addition, during his years at Beijing University Liang identified the vitality of life rather than human progress or individual salvation as the meaning of the cosmic process. Later in DXWH, he returned to the *Yi Zhuan* (易傳), *The Doctrine of Mean*, and other pre-Qin classics as the basis of his interpretation of the Chinese worldview. This shift from the teachings of the late-Ming Lu-Wang school to pre-Han Confucianism is not coincidental, but stems from the "dynamic worldview" they held in common. During an age of political and intellectual revolution, Liang and many of his contemporaries felt China had to revive the creativity of the classical period that had declined after the Song dynasty. Led by LIANG Qichao (梁啟超; 1873–1929), these intellectuals believed the rise of Song Neo-Confucianism had resulted in centuries of intellectual malaise in China. LIANG Shuming critiqued the Song Neo-Confucian emphasis on principle and "reason" (*li* 理) and instead preferred the dynamic worldview of the late-Ming Taizhou (泰州) school and of the pre-Qin classics (DXWH: 150). Like many contemporary scholars, Liang hoped to rediscover the original spirit of Chinese culture and emancipate his nation from the stultifying traditions that had come to impede social development over the centuries. The stress on unbounded vitality, life force, and spirit in Liang's writings ensured an almost instinctive dislike of a Western rationalism he viewed as rigid and over-determined.

5 Epistemology of the Philosophy of Living and of the Chinese Language and Learning

Buddhist epistemology had a profound influence on Liang's philosophy. Considering Confucianism's and Daoism's paucity of a systematic analysis of the knowing process, Buddhist epistemology remains rooted as the basis of his theory of knowledge even after orienting himself towards Confucianism. Following his conversion, however, he substantially modified Yogācāra epistemology by situating intuition—a source of false knowledge according to the Buddhist view—as a major factor in the formation of valuable knowledge (DXWH: 69, 72–74).

5.1 The Nature and Functions of Intuition

According to his new theory, our knowledge of the world is based on sensation, an element that is disparate, however, by its very nature: only through intuition do immediate sense data begin to possess meaning. When staring at a white cloth, for instance, the eye is unable to directly detect the whiteness, as only "discrete" dots of color are perceived; impressions or feelings of whiteness are grasped by intuition from the discrete sense data (DXWH: 70–72). After encountering numerous intuitive impressions of whiteness, reason—accompanied by its abstractive capacity—then extracts the "concept" of whiteness from the individual impressions.

The above epistemology is founded on Liang's cosmology of becoming, and in view of the essence of the world being change, the transient, disparate and immediate sense data are the entirety of what our senses have been postulated to detect. Beyond that, any impressions or discerned meanings are artificial interpretations of an essentially transient reality. Intuition is thus a person's first step towards meaning and reason follows, the two marching in step.

Intuition thus refers to the mental function that is able to deduce the scent or flavor of a cluster of raw empirical data. Borrowing from this conception, Liang attributed other complex forms of intuitive knowledge to intuition, namely the holistic feeling one experiences while gazing at a work of calligraphy or a painting and while reading a text. He regarded the former as "intuition attached to sensation" and the latter as "intuition attached to reason," seeing that reading is unable to be separated from reasoning (DXWH: 70–72).

Despite assigning a new status to intuition in his theory of knowledge and then, as we will see, awarding prominence to intuition within both ethics and metaphysics, Liang acutely criticized its application in the empirical sphere. Here we shall begin with an analysis of Liang's rather ingenious interpretations of several basic characteristics of the Chinese language as well as their relationship with a worldview of becoming. Liang asserted:

> Since Chinese metaphysics addresses the question of change, the method it adopts is certainly different from that of the West and India because the static and rigid concepts used in describing the substantial questions is completely unsuited to the discussion of change. The terms it [Chinese metaphysics] uses are abstract. […] In order to recognize this kind of abstract scent or tendency, we must rely entirely on our intuition so as to experience and appreciate [it]. The so-called *yin* (陰; the passive, negative, feminine principle), *yang* (陽; the active, positive, masculine principle), *qian* (乾; heaven, active principle), *kun* (坤; earth, passive principle); all of these are terms from the *Yijing* [易經; *Book of Changes*] and could not be derived from sensations or reason. The concepts formed by reason are explicit and fixed, but these [Chinese concepts] are dynamic and holistic. (DXWH: 116)

He further maintained that this form of abstract, dynamic and holistic "metaphysical language," embedded with its emphasis on intuition, was commonly employed in the Chinese language, whether in academic settings or in more quotidian existence. Traditional Chinese medicine, for example, is teeming with terminology, such as "air, blood, phlegm, heart, liver, spleen, lung, [and] kidney," which does not merely refer to substances or organs, but also signifies the complex functions related to them: "[They are] not concrete things, but some meaningful phenomena that cannot be defined" (DXWH: 30). Moreover, from the perspective of Chinese medicine, "*yin*, *yang*, and the 'five phases/elements' [*wuxing* 五行], these elastic and abstract metaphysical symbols, are fundamental principles; therefore, all other concepts, by extension, are elastic." Providing his audience with a summation, Liang proffered that since "the Chinese love to use *yin* and *yang* to describe everything, everything is metaphysics, but not science" (DXWH: 30–31).

Since fixed and well-defined concepts for ordinary use are simply unable to describe the "one and changing essence" of the world properly, Liang contended Chinese metaphysical language inclines towards the indefinable and the abstract in correspondence to the changing essence of the world (DXWH: 31). This language has a basic characteristic: "no-expression" (*wu biaoshi* 無表示), because the ultimate surpasses words (or expression). Any description of the ultimate is limited, partial, and even self-contradictory (DXWH: 119). This assertion is precisely a renewed expression of the greatest Daoist, Laozi (老子), who had remarked: "The speakable Dao is not the ultimate Dao." Dao is beyond *logos*.

Liang characterized the pursuit for the unspeakable essence of things, or the "Dao beyond *logos*," as prompting the Chinese to "not only lack logical reasoning but fill them with an 'illogical spirit,'" and he continued: "When the Chinese engage in scholarship and thinking, they must reach the unspeakable and indefinable realm to finish the job." Due to this spirit and employment of "indefinable language," the Chinese strongly favor correlative thinking and causal analogies (DXWH: 29–31).[25] To then conclude, Liang propounded: "The Chinese concept that has its indication but lacks a fixed and solid content is [the consequence of] a metaphysical attitude; the clear and definite concept used by the Westerners is [result of] the scientific method" (DXWH: 31).

5.2 *Art, Holism, and the Non-logical Spirit*

From the above propositions, it is not difficult to imagine that for Liang, this kind of intuitive and metaphysical attitude inhibits Chinese scholarship; that is, it is a kind of art rather than a form of science. Liang maintained that in Chinese medicine, and in other spheres of Chinese scholarship as well, individual genius, wisdom, art and intuition assume a superior position to "objective standards and rules." In a direct comparison to Western science, Chinese learning is consequently unsystematic, unorganized, subjective, speculative, full of discrepancies and divided into different schools. The "artistic" approach also compels Chinese scholars to worship the geniuses of a bygone era and to undervalue objective standards. Furthermore, since it emphasizes personal wisdom and acumen, it is pragmatic and, more specifically, merely attuned to practical methods but not basic principles, thus lacking a rigorous and systematic theory or knowledge to—stated simply—aid people in dealing with what surrounds them (DXWH: 26–27).

The major differences between intuitive and rational attitudes as well as between artistic and scientific scholarships are fundamentally linked to people's different visions of "causality." Compared to the emphasis placed on the rigorous and rigid verification of the cause of a well-defined disease in Western medicine, Liang

[25] This argument offers a new perspective for the interpretation of Chinese correlative thinking. Cf. Needham 1962: 279–90.

highlighted that "a Chinese doctor would not look for the exact pathogen of a patient's illness because he considers that the [ill] man is unhealthy as a whole" (DXWH: 29). From the perspective of Chinese medicine, the causes of a disease are multiple, related to the well-being of one's physical condition in its entirety, and are unable to be reduced to one-to-one causal relationships. It is the rational attitude that compels Westerners to devote themselves to the rigorous understanding of the definite causal relationships between "the substances of things," whereas a holistic view towards the same subject matter leads the Chinese to an intuitive grasp of the overall state or well-being of the object of observation. The fundamental difference in their methodologies is reflected in their differing views of causality and reality. In this way, Liang asserted that Chinese medicine could not be "blended" or "integrated" with Western medicine; the same was true for Chinese and Western scholarships (WDNL: 44–45).

Liang's argument is highly original and perceptive, but also controversial for his time. It is no doubt that he highlighted, even exaggerating, the characteristic differences between China and the West, and simultaneously neglected the rigorous, and relatively "positivist" and "systematic" facets of traditional Chinese scholarship, especially in the areas of textual, classical and historical studies. However, these "positivist" and "systematic" sides of traditional Chinese scholarship are still not entirely "positivist" nor "systematic" from a Western point of view, namely because they fail to be fully "logical." This fact alone also helps to illustrate the effectiveness of Liang's observations.

It is also worth noting Liang's evaluations of Chinese medicine and "empirical Chinese scholarship" varied with time. During the New Culture Movement, for example, Liang, while only just beginning to know how to describe the basic characteristics of Chinese medicine, was influenced by other commentators' acute censures of traditional scholarship and thus maintained that the holistic, intuitive, and speculative method of Chinese scholarship should be limited to the subjects of metaphysics and ethics—both dealing with the question of reality itself. He insisted it should be left outside of the empirical arena, an area belonging to science, saying: "All the mistakes of Chinese learning are caused by the lack of scrutiny in method—applying the abstract and metaphysical 'logic' to the substantial questions of empirical knowledge" (DXWH: 117).[26] Within the empirical arena, he said, the metaphysical and intuitive attitude wields loose and even false analogies, and lacks the support of authentic knowledge of the causal relationship between things. It is also marked by the lack of a clear and dependable methodology, deflects interest in pure knowledge, and is ultimately bereft of methods in dealing with practical affairs. Liang was thus forced to conclude: "What is obtained from the scientific method is

[26] This reminds us of Kant's distinction between the study of the phenomenal world and the noumenal world, and both Kant and Liang questioned the limit of human understanding, knowledge, and empirical study. Kant, with a worldview of being, left the study of ethics, metaphysics, "thing in itself," or the noumenal world not to human understanding (*Verstand*) but to pure reason (*Vernunft*). Liang, on the other hand, with a metaphysics of becoming, left the comprehension of reality to pure, or immediate, sense.

knowledge; what is obtained from the metaphysical method is not knowledge, but subjective opinions" (DXWH: 29).

In his later years, however, despite still maintaining a great respect for the scientific method and the rigorous, systematized and well-defined knowledge system it produced, Liang possessed a more sympathetic and deeper understanding of Chinese scholarship. He summarized in 1940 the basic difference between Chinese and Western scholarship: "On the one [Western] side, the basic method and view is static, scientific, mathematical, and analytical; on the other [Chinese] side, the basic method and view is dynamic, metaphysical, evolutionary, and undivided" (ZH: 129). The Chinese method is particularly adept at perceiving phenomena, especially those concerning life, as a whole; Chinese learning, however, is not progressive. In juxtaposition, while the Western method excels in procuring precise knowledge, given its analytic tendency, it fails to view things as a vital whole. The concepts conceived by Western medicine, for example, no matter how precise and advanced, "are imaginary, [and do] not [represent] life as a whole" (ZH: 129), a problem which, he claimed, had led to the death of his eldest son who had been receiving Western medical treatment during his last days (ZH: 125–26). With this tragedy in mind, however, he still held Western medicine in high esteem and predicted that Chinese medicine would be understood and interpreted by Western medicine in the long run. Chinese medicine, on the other hand, lacks the capacity of self-reflection and self-improvement, and is thus unable to interpret Western medicine in kind (ZH: 125).

Considering Liang's repeated emphasis that Chinese learning and medicine are holistic in their way of thinking, to study a thing in its context is thus the only way to fully understand it. This holistic approach is antithetical to Immanuel Kant's (1724–1804) illuminating view on the basic qualification of science:

> If it becomes desirable to present any cognition as science, it will be necessary first to determine exactly its differentia, which no other science has in common with it and which constitutes its peculiarity; otherwise the boundaries of all sciences become confused, and none of them can be treated thoroughly according to its nature. (Kant 1977: 11)

For a similar reason, the holistic approach championed by Liang could also be severely criticized by Karl Popper (1902–1994) as the enemy of science and reason. But based on Liang's premise, namely the essence of the world is one, undivided, and intertwined, one cannot stick to a particular idea or method in order to reach reality and the highest or absolute truth. It is precisely this attitude which helps to elucidate why Liang, similar to his traditional Chinese counterparts, refused to specialize in any one given area of studies while in pursuit of the fundamental and the ultimate: the Dao.

With Liang's interpretation and criticism of the Chinese way of knowing, we can notice that reason is not fully confirmed in, or by, his theory of knowledge. Reason is regarded as useful in supplying us knowledge in the sphere of experience, but is unable to bring us to reality, especially in the field of ethics. On the other hand, despite the abundance of criticisms being placed on Chinese scholarship and its associated way of thinking, Liang himself still wielded a very Chinese way of thinking and language; he made holistic and impressionist observations rather than theoretical analyses; and he employed intuition and correlative thinking rather than reason and argument. The way in which DXWH had been composed and the manner in which his cultural theory had been established are testimonies to Liang's "method." The dialogue between reason and intuition found within his works remains complex and full of contentions, and it is a dialogue, which assists us in defining his ultimate philosophy as well as his actions.

6 Ethical and Social Philosophy

6.1 Buddhist and Confucian Legacies

The difference between Chinese, Indian, and Western systems of ethics, according to Liang, originates in their different mental attitudes towards the world. Resembling his conceptions concerning metaphysics and epistemology, the ethics purported by Liang also possesses a Buddhist origin. Influenced by Mahāyāna Buddhism, Liang understood reality as an ever-changing cosmic process and thus considered any concrete ideas regarding things, including the idea of ego and the self, as illusory. Both reason and intuition lead to illusions; the only reliable mental faculty is immediate sense. From a Buddhist perspective, human suffering is fundamentally linked to the illusions of people, and only by rejecting erroneous conceptions, rigid distinctions, illusionary emotions, and wanton desires created by reason and intuition are we able to free ourselves from various predicaments (ZH: 81–86). This "undifferentiated attitude" of Buddhist metaphysics and ethics assisted Liang in sensitizing himself to an extraordinary degree to the phenomena of alienation, reification, and fragmentation as well as the split between subject and object caused by the processes of rationalization and industrialization in the West.[27]

Following his conversion to Confucianism, the central tenets of his thought revolved around the promotion of the natural flowing of inner feelings and intuition. This attitude stems directly from a worldview of becoming and vitality, and from a metaphysics which situates the universal "process of living" as the only reality.[28] According to this view, human beings are only part of this cosmic process; therefore, the meaning of life is found in our union with it, not by the means of analytical reason, but through an intuitive grasp of this ubiquitous process.

The type of intuition advocated by Liang is by no means a collective or vague label for all sorts of direct feelings. Rather, it is a highly cultivated and purified

[27] Liang did not know the terms of alienation, reification, and fragmentation, but developed his penetrating criticism independently.

[28] With regard to the central importance of this metaphysics of living, Liang said: "The Confucian philosophy of living derives entirely from this kind of metaphysics. There are no words of Confucius that do not speak of this. From the beginning to the end, it has always been this message" (DXWH: 120–21).

mental state. In order to unite with the undifferentiated universal process, one has to rid oneself of personal (*si* 私) desire, prejudiced knowledge and convictions, detrimental deliberation, and calculation. He positioned Confucius as the highest model: Confucius's mind is always flexible; Confucius adheres to no finite rationales, rules, or doctrines, and never goes to extremes; Confucius refrains from calculation and acts only according to the immediate intuition which leads to natural beauty, harmony, and goodness.[29] Aside from his Neo-Confucian interpretation of Confucius, Liang followed the Neo-Confucian tradition by frequently alluding to the *Mencius* (*Mengzi* 孟子), the *Doctrine of the Mean*, the *Great Learning* (*Daxue* 大學), and the *Yijing*. It was the Ming Neo-Confucian CHEN Baisha 陳白沙 (1428–1500) as well as WANG Yangming's 王陽明 (1472–1529) disciples NIE Shuangjiang 聶雙江 (1487–1563) and LUO Nian'an 羅念庵 (1504–1564), however, who offered him the crucial teaching on cultivating intuition.[30] Significant emphasis is placed in these Neo-Confucians on achieving serenity and placidness (*ji* 寂) before responding (*gan* 感), and one has to release one's inner self from desires and prejudice before one can truly be responsive. Only then is one able to "accommodate the changes of the universe itself" and achieve "natural fitness" (DXWH: 128–30).

In addition, by reuniting oneself with the undifferentiated universal principle, one can transcend the barriers between things and become compassionate towards the world. This is due to intuition that—unlike reason—does not draw a clear distinction between the subject and object as well as the self and the world, thus not alienating itself from the world. Since the ubiquitous process of living is one, the ego always feels at home with itself, and with the rise of the feelings of harmony and affection, alienation and reification no longer occur. People are then highly responsive to each other's feelings and situations, mutual understanding is achieved, and warm sentiment is further fostered. Liang employed this concept of "keen intuition" to interpret the central doctrine of Confucius—benevolence (*ren* 仁)—as well as Mencius's (孟子; 372–289 BC) and WANG Yangming's innate conscience (*liangzhi*) (DXWH: 125–26, 135–40). He also maintained that "all the virtues of human beings originally come from this intuition" (DXWH: 127). By arriving at this level, one is only then able to proclaim that one understands the universal Dao, or the ultimate truth of everything. Liang's metaphysics, epistemology, and ethics thus become one within this highest union.

Being the central doctrine of his philosophy, Liang incessantly gave prominence to the conception that intuition is the only channel to our true life. Furthermore, he established reason and intuition as being antithetical within ethics, asserting that "Confucians always use intuition; they seldom use reason." "The single most important attitude of Confucius," Liang added, "is not to calculate. This is the most distinctive attitude of Confucianism" (DXWH: 121, 131). According to Liang, the

---

[29] Liang did, rather appropriately, allude to the *Analects* and *Mencius* to refute the assertion offered by HU Shi that early Confucians, dissimilar to later Neo-Confucians who were influenced by Buddhism, paid scarce attention to the study of the mind (DXWH: 125–128).

[30] Similar to Liang, Chen was also reputed for emphasizing a worldview centered on the concept of life (*sheng*). See Chan 1965.

Confucian conception of "benevolence [*ren*] is human instinct, compassion, and intuition; [...] when compassion is elevated, reason subsides" and vice versa. Man is essentially dominated by intuition and instinct; will and feeling are more essential than knowledge (DXWH: 124, 131, 140–41). The art of life can only be achieved through intuition—not reason—and in the process of creating an ideal attitude towards life; free choice stemming from our intuition should be the only moral basis (DXWH: 134, 140).

6.2 *Critique of Utilitarianism and the Western Lifestyle*

In contrast to the Chinese attitude towards life, Liang felt that the Western counterpart is characterized by a robust self-consciousness and internal desires while using reason and knowledge to achieve goals (DXWH: 159). He credited this attitude with power, efficiency, organizational ability, and the subduing of nature, but simultaneously criticized it, describing the ethical attitude of the West as utilitarian—which would become the major target of his criticism (DXWH: 133–34, 158). But he also highlighted utilitarianism was primarily dominant within the Anglo-American sphere; that is, continental thinkers had established a different tradition. Nevertheless, in Liang's view, the two parties' common emphasis on reason and knowledge make it plain that they are descendants of the same Greek tradition initiated by Socrates (DXWH: 155–58, 169).

Liang's criticism of utilitarianism, advanced within the context of his theories on metaphysics and epistemology, can be seen as a portion of an overall acute critique of what—borrowing today's terminology—has been labeled objectification, alienation, and reification. To begin, his criticism of the phenomena of alienation and reification within Western culture penetrates to the very core. Since the cosmic process itself is beyond conceptualization, in Liang's view, the Western mind starts to alienate itself from the essence of the world by "objectivizing" the world. The will to move forward, while desiring a specific goal, objectifies the goal for its own need and severs the subject from both the object and rest of the world. Reason, according to Liang, as the highest form of this self-regarding emotion (attitude), is the tool employed by the will to objectify and manipulate all things. Finally, the conceptualization of the "I," or ego, together with individualism, is also a product of this process (DXWH: 104).[31]

Liang, as Heidegger, traced this mode of thinking to the origin of Western civilization—Greece. "Objectification" on the metaphysical and epistemological level is

[31] This reminds us of Hegel, Heidegger, Habermas, and their respective followers' critique of the "subject-centered reason" and "modern subjectivism" initiated by Descartes. Habermas 1987: 132–33.

the prelude to alienation and edification on the ethical level.[32] Clear demarcations between people and between things via the process of objectification are a prerequisite for a utilitarian-style careful reckoning of gain and loss. The embodiment of this rational and objectivizing attitude towards things in ethics is necessarily utilitarian, which differs fundamentally from Confucian, Daoist, and Buddhist emphases on an immediate, natural response. At the same time, Liang was also averse to Western intellectualism and what he understood as the main principle of life in the West since the time of Socrates: "taking knowledge as virtue" (*yi zhishi wei daode* 以知識為道德).[33] In Liang's mind, knowledge is the tool and result of reckoning, not necessarily virtue (DXWH: 169–170).[34]

Operating within reality, reasoning and calculation prohibit the natural representation of the life force and create internal conflicts—or what we may call "internal alienation." Liang stated:

> Confucius always followed his intuition without inner conflict. The common people, however, always try to use reason. In fact, their reasoning stops midway and they have to eventually depend on intuition. Our behavior is dominated by intuition; reason cannot manipulate it. (DXWH: 124)

Calculative reason or understanding is unable to categorically direct our behavior; therefore, if one wants to use it to control oneself, they will inevitably be mired in the inner conflicts between reason and emotion as well as between competing rationales (DXWH: 123). Moreover, calculation induces the cruelty of people onto others and prompts others to be treated as if they are lifeless objects, breeding alienation within society. Desire, accompanied by calculative and often dogged reasoning process, assails its counterpart—the keen and compassionate intuition (DXWH: 123, 130). On the whole, Liang's criticism of utilitarianism is an attack on its rationalism, intellectualism, and self-regarding desire.[35]

[32] Guy Alitto has already indicated that Liang's "various anti-capitalist animadversions" are criticisms concerning alienation, the machine, and rationalism (Alitto 1979: 95). However, he did not see Liang's reproach of alienation as a part of Liang's criticism of the phenomenon of objectification.

[33] Socrates maintained that "virtue is knowledge," which means "seeing virtue for what it is means that one will choose it over any alternative if one is acting rationally." The knowledge of virtue, to Socrates, has either a utilitarian, eudaemonist or heroic nature (Pangle 2014: 32–33). Liang misunderstood him as having taken the knowledge of gain and loss in life, which is utilitarian and calculative, to decide what is virtue.

[34] This also resembles Zhuangzi's famous saying: "Knowledge comes from contention." See Qian 1969: 27.

[35] Liang's insistence on the unification of thought and action is well illustrated by Guy Alitto (1979: 135).

6.3 Reification and Alienation in Capitalism

In DXWH, Liang Shuming's rebuke of capitalism focuses on the reification and alienation prevalent in a rationalized capitalist society. In contrast to modern mechanized society, his ideal is characterized by an emphasis on social instincts, mutual affection, voluntary action, and harmony, in which one acts not according to reckoning but according to intuition so as to freely express one's emotions. In short, it is an amalgamation of Confucian and socialist utopias.

The persistent prominence Liang granted to compassion and harmony within human life naturally led him to his socialist economic philosophy. He was highly attracted by the "guild socialism" newly advocated by Russell, which is characterized by a form of communitarianism and consumption-oriented economy, and then combined this socialist critique of capitalism with his rebuff of the alienation found in a rationalized economic system. For Liang, reason—along with the will to conquer—objectifies and reifies the world. Machines represent the objectification of material, while individualism can be regarded as the objectification of humanity. Capitalism (branded by the conquering of nature by calculation) prohibits people's natural affection towards the world, and people are also treated like objects within the system. Competitiveness and efficiency thus become the primary, if not the only, concern (DXWH: 166–67, 174). Economic fluctuations bring about recessions and unemployment. The poverty-stricken and machine-enslaved underclass is tortured by hard work, a tasteless life, and broken families, whereas the upper class is bound by endless calculation. Humankind no longer has real feelings. Thus, Adam Smith's (1723–1790) and Herbert Spencer's (1820–1903) advocacy of free competition, mechanization, division of labor, and production-oriented economy is also to blame (DXWH: 161–66).

Liang hoped that the individualistic and production-oriented economy could be converted into a socialist, guild economy oriented towards distribution and consumption. He also asserted, seeing that the matter of subsistence had gradually been solved by the economic and social institutions created by the aggressive Western culture, that the energy of the people would ultimately shift towards social and emotional concerns (DXWH: 166–67). However, our insatiable desire for goods, the pressures of endless domestic and international competition, changes forced by technological innovations, and a myriad of other factors which have accelerated and intensified modern economic activities were all underestimated by Liang. In this tremendously competitive world of modern capitalism, one naturally had serious doubts regarding whether a humanized, and less rationalized, guild economic system would be able to survive (DXWH: 166–67). Nevertheless, intellectuals throughout the world who operated during the period between the two world wars were haunted by the inhumane aspects of capitalism and dreamed of different kinds of socialism—a trend which Liang found himself wrapped up into.

6.4 Confucian Utopia Versus a Legal Society

LIANG Shuming held that voluntary action is the basis of an ideal society and disapproved of law imposed by state. Fully understanding the need for law in a chaotic China, however, Liang regarded law and regulation as a sort of necessary second choice, or compromise, during his early years (SMSQ, 57–58, 63). In DXWH, his criticism of Western law being a calculated social convention was nevertheless aroused by his bitter distaste for rationalism and utilitarianism. He wrote:

> Nowadays, everything depends on law. Social life under this kind of law is very much coerced by force. […] The basis of law is to utilize the people's reckoning to control. […] This kind of mandatory law just cannot exist in the future. (DXWH: 194)

By "the basis of law is to utilize the people's reckoning to control," Liang implies that people obey the law not because they like to do so, but because after calculation they conclude that obedience is in their best interests. It is not voluntary, but rather mandatory. Liang was not aware, however, that aside from the utilitarian aspect of modern Western law—the social contract championed since the time of Thomas Hobbes (1588–1679)—other non-utilitarian elements of modern Western law had been conceptualized, namely natural law as well as Christian law. The criticism presented above is thus a rebuke of any form of superimposed law—whether rule by law or rule of law. His criticism of law as rule by both force and punishment is targeted not only at the West but also at Chinese Legalism (*Fajia* 法家), which promoted rule by law. In this sense, it is a continuation of the age-old debate of "morality or law" waged between Confucians and Legalists (DXWH: 194–95).

Liang's ideal society was a Confucian society in which social order is maintained primarily by education and self-cultivation. He specifically argued that "only by improving people's character and by depending on man's social instincts, compassion, and non-calculative, congenial psychology," are we able to create an ideal society (DXWH: 195). Rule by award and punishment as well as reckoning ultimately leads to the deterioration of the people's character. The most critical facet is thus cultivating will and feelings. Teaching by reason and knowledge, Socrates' ideal, is unable to achieve this goal, as it cannot attain true life–our feelings. Art without religion cannot likewise culminate in an effect capable of changing, or improving, society; religion is powerful but creates problems and unreasonable situations. Only Confucian rites and music (*liyue* 禮樂), which are designed to foster people's feelings of harmony, joy, and peace, are thus able to forge an ideal society (DXWH: 133, 141–43, 194–196).

Within his writings in DXWH, Liang did not discuss politics to a great extent and failed to really see how democracy, as a social institution, builds upon Enlightenment rationalism. Concerning his thoughts on democracy, he did, however, emphasize that it originates from the people's struggle for their own rights against authority (DXWH: 55, 61–62). The Chinese, while burdened with a diminishing will to acquire, lack the will to struggle for their rights. In a country plagued by warlords and irresponsible authorities, Liang was aware that "personal rights and social order are the most important." But they would not come peacefully and had to be fought for. From this perspective, he further asserted that "the democratic spirit is completely right" (DXWH: 204, 206, 208).

Moreover, Liang understood the characteristics of democracy as "the advancement of individuality and the development of social character" (DXWH: 41). People with a strong sense of individuality are inclined to fight. Therefore, in order to maintain power and unity, the people must organize themselves through law. Despite not clearly illustrating this point in his writings, logically, Liang—like Hobbes before him—almost certainly believed that this form of organization derives from the people's reckoning (DXWH: 37–41, 152, 161–62).

From an ethical perspective, Liang detested regulation, law, reckoning, and the so-called will to acquire, and longed for the social order of a Confucian society achieved by embracing the cultivation of people via rites and music. However, practical needs prompted him to embrace a Western-style political struggle for human rights and order. This rift between his ethical and political thought would widen in his later years, leading him to abandon Western democracy eventually. While authoring DXWH, nevertheless, Liang retained the hope that a dialogue between Confucianism and democracy as well as one between Chinese and Western cultures in general could be achieved.

7 German Romanticism, Expressivism, and Philosophy of Life: A Comparison

As illustrated above, LIANG Shuming's theory in many ways resembles modern Western criticism of Greek and, especially, Enlightenment rationalism. He alluded to a number of post-Enlightenment Western thinkers to further strengthen his argument that a rational worldview has numerous complications and that the West had been undergoing a fundamental change in an attempt to remedy and even break away from its rationalist tradition. In light of these similarities, one last inquiry persists; that is, can we categorize him with these post-Enlightenment thinkers? A typological comparison is necessary to answer this question.

Guy Alitto has argued that Liang, like a great many non-Western conservatives throughout the world, reacted towards modernity in much the same way as German Romantic thinkers had first reacted to the French Enlightenment (Alitto 1986: 18–40, 112–18, 183–204). In regards to several facets of Liang's thought, Alitto's argument is undoubtedly valid; however, due to the tremendously different traditions involved and the influences of post-Darwin Western science and philosophy, Liang and the philosophy of German Romanticism still diverge concerning many basic aspects.

One major factor overlooked by Alitto is that German Romanticism is inseparable from German idealism, the latter of which is embedded in a rationalist tradition. The works of early German rationalists such as Gottfried Wilhelm Leibniz (1646–1716) and Christian Wolff (1679–1754) were the source of inspiration and wisdom for almost all the German thinkers of the Romantic period. Kant's assertion that the noumenal world cannot be reached through understanding (*Verstand*) but only through practical reason (*praktischen Vernunft*) in the realm of moral law, for example, set the philosophical foundation for the German idealist and Romantic movements. As Nietzsche's later criticism of German Romanticism has shown, Romanticism is also inseparable from the rationalist and idealist tradition established by Socrates and Plato—a tradition that Nietzsche, a son of Romanticism, eagerly desired to transcend. Liang clearly did not emerge from such a rationalist tradition, and even lesser did he inherit another paramount element of Romanticism—Christianity. It is thus hard to believe that his response to Western rationalism, as the core of both modernization and Enlightenment, would be essentially the same as that of the above Romantic thinkers.

Liang's adverse reaction towards Western rationalism is indeed remarkably similar to a major trend, namely Expressivism, in German thought of that period. Expressivism, a term used by Isaiah Berlin and Charles Taylor to describe a trend of thought that sprang forwards from *Sturm und Drang*, was most impressively formulated by Herder and later became a major element of Romanticism and modern Western culture. Its philosophy can be regarded "as a protest against the mainstream Enlightenment view of man—as both subject of and object of an objectifying scientific analysis" (Taylor 1979: 1). Against the atomistic view of the Enlightenment, German Expressivists view human life, community, history, culture, and Volk "as having a unity rather analogous to that of a work of art, where every part or aspect only found its proper meaning in relation with all the others" (Taylor 1979: 1–2). Their conviction that "it is just because men were seen as reaching their highest realization in expressive activity, that their lives could themselves be seen as expressive unities," has earned them the title of Expressivism (Taylor 1979: 2). Liang did not grant art such a high position in life and culture, as his major concern rested not in art or literature, but in ethics. But he clearly wished to treat human life, community, history, and people as a artistic unity. Moreover, his belief in the Confucian teaching of benevolence—the natural affection in human relationships and between man and nature—forms the core of his philosophy, which is not only moral but also artistic, even being religious. From this unified and harmonic worldview, he criticized the modern Western world for being fragmented and objectified, as did the Expressivists before him.

However, it remains true that Liang's philosophy also conflicts with Romanticism and Expressivism in a number of notable ways. To begin, Expressivism is deeply rooted in Greek and Christian traditions, whereas Liang's thought derived predominantly from Confucianism, Buddhism, Chinese Medicine and Daoism. The emphasis placed on an artistic and organic entity, or holism, by Expressivism shares commonalities with Liang, but the prominence given to the achievement of an art form possesses a very strong idealistic tint. The philosophy proffered by Liang, without such an ideal form in mind, is more similar to twentieth-century philosophies of becoming and of process. In other words, Expressivists maintained that an art form that could and should be achieved exists; in contrast, Liang was essentially against any kind of form and strictly emphasized the original vitality of life.

Analogous to Zen Buddhism, for Liang, the fulfillment of life is at this moment, not in distant ideals.

Among twentieth-century thinkers, Liang's philosophy—as he admitted—is most similar to Bergson's philosophy of life. Both magnified becoming and the concept of life, and were averse to machinism, materialism, and rationalism. Bergson's philosophy of life, however, is characterized by vitalism as well as his pantheistic and dynamic vision of the universe, and was strongly influenced by the Christian, especially Roman Catholic, tradition. The vitalist life-drive he emphasized is a modern representation of the Holy Spirit, whereas his theory of creative evolution is modeled on a reverse process of the Christian tradition of a divine creation (Lovejoy 1976: 317). In juxtaposition, Liang's philosophy of living, which is derivative of Daoist and Neo-Confucian traditions, is a form of naturalism rather than a kind of spiritualism.

A similar situation can be observed when comparing Liang with *Lebensphilosophie* thinkers. The latter, including Hans Driesch (1867–1941) and Ludwig Klages (1872–1956)—similar to Bergson and Liang—openly condemned intellectualism within the Western tradition and praised the forces of life in the years immediately preceding and following World War I (Liebert 1926: 207–08). However, with a substantialist mode of thinking, they held an essentialist idea of "life" which emphasizes entirely an abstract and often unnecessary understanding of life-affirming and life-denying principles (Spaulding 1906: 518–27; Lebovic 2006: 25–27). Liang's philosophy of living, in contrast, views the universe as a living process rather than stressing the essence of the universe as "life." Moreover, *Lebensphilosophie* thinkers, just as Bergson had, usually shared a kind of vitalism. Driesch, for example, believed that the secret of life which he deduced from the persistence of embryological development despite interferences like dissection come from his so-called "entelechy," or a mind-like life creating force in an Aristotelian sense (Jenkinson 1911: 548–549). Ludwig Klages also maintained a kind of vitalism that "endowed the soul with mystical powers," and openly and radically challenged reason to the extent that he possessed a willingness to go to battle for his beliefs (Lebovic 2006: 27–28). Liang was not a vitalist, and despite openly criticizing reason, he did not have the desire or penchant to go to war with reason.

In essence, Liang's reflections on Western rationalism and Chinese tradition cannot simply be classified as a Romantic, Expressivist, or *Lebensphilosophie* reaction towards Enlightenment rationalism. Although Liang shares with the three parties a rather similar critique of rationalism and machinism, after closer analysis we discover that his solutions to these matters differ in important ways from them. That is, his solutions were derived from Confucian, Buddhist, and Daoist sources as well as from Chinese medicine. More specifically, the form of fusion with a universe in constant change found within Liang's philosophy is brought about by the dissolution of the boundary between self and non-self, a facet which is seemingly not emphasized in Romanticism and Expressivism, or at least not in the same manner. At the same time, Liang's social philosophy, rooted in Confucian ethics and a critique of law that would later lead him to his rural reform project, is also apparently absent within Romanticism and *Lebensphilosophie*.[36]

In the West, Enlightenment and Romanticism, Expressivism, or Philosophy of Life, acting as mutual antitheses, form various kinds of dialectical relationships; however, in modern China, even noted conservative Chinese intellectuals attempted in a variety of ways to make rationalism and science compatible with Chinese culture. The tension between Enlightenment rationality and the Chinese intellectual tradition was often neglected or even suppressed, as is illustrated by the ambiguities and contradictions in Liang's own attitudes towards Western rationalism. For example, he composed an overall criticism of Western rationalism, but simultaneously emphasized the necessity for science, logic, and the subjugation of nature, all of which—in his mind—are related to Western rationalism. The differences and ambiguities between Enlightenment rationality and Chinese culture described above have yet to be fully explored by scholars.

The dialogue between Western rationalism and Chinese modes of thinking is far from complete, but at the same time, the call for the rationalization of China has hardly met any powerful opposition in the open. Regardless, considering Liang's penetrating critique towards Western rationalism and keen observation of the fundamental differences between Chinese and Western traditions, the reality is it would be very difficult for Western rationalism to take root in the Chinese modes of thinking. A study of the often-neglected counter-Enlightenment thought within modern Chinese intellectual history can thus shed more light on this issue.

References

DXWH *Dong-Xi wenhua ji qi zhexue* 東西文化及其哲學 [*Eastern and Western Cultures and Their Philosophies*; 1921]. Taipei: Wenxue Chubanshe reprint, 1968.

JYJY *Jiuyuan jueyilun* 究元決疑論 [*A Treatise on Inquiring into the Ultimate Origin and Solving Doubts*; 1916]. Shanghai: Shangwu Yinshuguan, 1924.

LSMQJ *Liang Shuming quanji* 梁漱溟全集 [*The Anthology of Liang Shuming*]. Jinan: Shandong People's Press, 1990.

RXYRS *Renxin yu rensheng* 人心與人生 [*Human Spirit and Human Life*; 1984]. Shanghai: Shanghai People's Press, 2011.

SMSH *Shuming sahou wenlu* 漱溟卅後文錄 [*Collected Writings of Liang Shuming After 30 [Years Old]*; 1930]. Shanghai: Shangwu Yinshuguan; Taipei: Dipingxian Chubanshe reprint, 1971.

SMSQ *Shuming saqian wenlu* 漱溟卅前文錄 [*Collected Writings of Liang Shuming Before 30 [Years Old]*; 1923]. Shanghai: Shangwu Yinshuguan, 1923.

WDNL *Wo de nuli yu fanxing* 我的努力與反省 [*My Efforts and Reflections*]. Guilin: Lijiang Chubanshe, 1987.

ZH *Zhaohua* 朝話 [*Morning Speeches*; 1932–1935]. Changsha: Shangwu Chubanshe, 1940.

[36] Here I would like to express my gratitude to Dr. Philippe Major as his comments concerning the present article aided many sections and this paragraph in particular.

Ai, Siqi 艾思奇. 1988. Chinese Philosophy and Thought from the Last Twenty-Two Years 二十二年來之中國哲學思潮. In *A Collection of Resources for Teaching the History of Modern Chinese Philosophy* 中國現代哲學史教學資料選輯. Beijing: Peking University Press.

Alitto, Guy. 1979. *The Last Confucian: Liang Shu-ming and the Chinese Dilemma of Modernity*. Berkeley: University of California Press.

———. 1986. *On Cultural Conservatism* 文化守成主義論. Taipei: Shibao Chuban Gongsi.

Berlin, Isaiah. 1981. The Counter-Enlightenment. In *Against the Current: Essays in the History of Ideas*. Oxford: Oxford University Press.

Chan, Wing-tsit 陳榮捷. 1965. The Creativity and Dynamic Philosophy of [Chen] Baisha 白沙之動的哲學與創作. *Guangdong Documents* 廣東文獻 2 (4): 38–39.

De Bary, William Theodore. 1970. *Self and Society in Ming Thought*. New York: Columbia University Press.

Feng, Qi 馮契. 1989. *History of Modern Chinese Philosophy* 中國近代哲學史. Shanghai: Shanghai People's Press.

Grant, Michael. 1989. *The Classical Greeks*. New York: Charles Scribner's Sons.

Habermas, Jürgen. 1987. *The Philosophical Discourse of Modernity*. Cambridge, MA: MIT Press.

He, Lin 賀麟. 1945. *Contemporary Chinese Philosophy* 當代中國哲學. Chongqing: Shengli Chubanshe; Taipei Reprint.

Hu, Shi 胡適. 1927. *The Philosophy of Dai Dongyuan* 戴東原的哲學. Shanghai: Shangwu Yinshuguan.

Jenkinson, J.W. 1911. Vitalism. *The Hibbert Journal* 9: 545–559.

Kant, Immanuel. 1977. *Prolegomena to Any Future Metaphysics*. Trans. P. Carus. Indianapolis: Hackett Publishing Company.

Lebovic, Nitzan. 2006. The Beauty and Terror of 'Lebensphilosophie': Ludwig Klages, Walter Benjamin, and Alfred Baeumler. *South Central Review* 23 (1): 23–39.

Liebert, Arthur. 1926. Contemporary Metaphysics in Germany. *The Monist* 36 (2): 198–221.

Lovejoy, Arthur O. 1976. *The Great Chain of Being*. Cambridge: Harvard University Press.

Lu, Xichen 呂希晨 and Wang, Yumin 王育民. 1984. *History of Contemporary Chinese Philosophy* 中國當代哲學史. Zhangchun: Jilin Renmin Chubanshe.

Meynard, Thierry. 2014. Liang Shuming and his Confucianized Version of Yogācāra. In *Transforming Consciousness: Yogācāra Thought in Modern China*, ed. John Makeham. Oxford: Oxford University Press.

Mote, Frederick W. 1972. The Cosmological Gulf Between China and the West. In *Transition and Permanence: Chinese History and Culture*, ed. David C. Buxbaum and Frederick W. Mote. Hong Kong: Cathay Press.

Needham, Joseph. 1962. *Science and Civilization in China*. Vol. 2. Cambridge: Cambridge University Press.

Pangle, Lorraine Smith. 2014. *Virtue Is Knowledge: The Moral Foundations of Socratic Political Philosophy*. Chicago: University of Chicago Press.

Qian, Mu 錢穆. 1969. *A Collection of Studies on the Zhuangzi* 莊子纂箋. Taipei: Sanmin Shuju.

———. 1971. The Cosmology of Zhuangzi and Laozi 莊老的宇宙論. In *A General Analysis of Zhuangzi and Laozi* 莊老通辨. Taipei: Sanmin Shuju.

Qian, Mu 錢穆. 1977. "Yizhuan yu Xiaodailiji zhong zhi yuzhoulun 《易傳》與《小戴禮記》中之宇宙論." In Zhongguo xueshu sixiangshi luncong 中國學術思想史論叢 V. 2. Taipei: Sanmin Shuju三民書局.

Spaulding, E.G. 1906. Driesch's Theory of Vitalism. *The Philosophical Review* 15 (5): 518–527.

Taylor, Charles. 1979. *Hegel and Modern Society*. Cambridge: Cambridge University Press.

Wang, Zongyu 王宗昱. 1982. *Liang Shuming* 梁漱溟. Taipei: Dongda Chuban.

Weber, Max. 1951. *The Religion of China*. Trans. H. H. Gerth. New York: The Free Press.

Wu, Chan-liang 吳展良. 1993. *Western Rationalism and the Chinese Mind: Counter-Enlightenment and Philosophy of Life in China, 1915–27*. Yale University PhD Dissertation, Michigan University Microfilm.

Yu, Yingshi 余英時. 1984. *Hu Shi in Modern Chinese Intellectual History* 中國近代思想史上的胡適. Taipei: Linking Publishing Company.

Chapter 8
Liang the Rural Reformer

Ady Van den Stock

1 Introduction

LIANG Shuming's 梁漱溟 (1893–1988) involvement with the movement for "rural reconstruction (*xiangcun jianshe* 鄉村建設)," which came into full swing during the Nanjing Decade (1927–1937), is a fascinating and relatively little-known episode in the history of the twentieth-century reinvention of the Confucian tradition.[1] It is not in the least due to his theoretical as well as practical contributions to rural reform in modern China that Liang stands out among other "New Confucian" thinkers as, in the words of Guy Alitto, a "lifelong activist" (Alitto 2015). Indeed, Liang did not so much identify himself as a "philosopher" (he was by all accounts an autodidact in the newly established academic discipline of philosophy), but rather as someone whose thought is fundamentally aimed at resolving pressing social and political issues (van Slyke 1959: 462; Lin 1990: 38; Gu 2016: 6–7). This activist orientation is also reflected in the structural division of his *Theory of Rural Reconstruction* (*Xiangcun jianshe lilun* 鄉村建設理論) (references hereafter abbreviated to XCJSL) from 1937 into two main parts: "understanding the problem" and

[1] Alitto 1976a, Lin 1990, Zhu 1996, Lu 2010, Lynch 2010, and Cui 2013 offer detailed accounts of Liang's theory and practice of rural reconstruction, a topic which also plays an important role in the following book-length studies: Alitto 1979, Zheng 2000, Thøgersen 2002, Han 2005, Gu 2016, Merkel-Hess 2016, and Lynch 2018. It is worth noting that Liang laid claim to the invention of the term "rural reconstruction." See Liang [1936a]: 602, cf. Zheng 2000: 78. James Yen appears to have already begun using the term in 1927 (Hayford 1990: 57).

A. Van den Stock (✉)
Ghent University, Ghent, Belgium
e-mail: Ady.VandenStock@UGent.be

T. Meynard, P. Major (eds.), *Dao Companion to Liang Shuming's Philosophy*, Dao Companions to Chinese Philosophy 17,
https://doi.org/10.1007/978-3-031-18002-6_8

"resolving the problem." Rather tellingly, the latter far surpasses the former in length.[2]

Needless to say, LIANG Shuming's praxis-oriented outlook does not necessarily imply that the relation between his philosophical writings and his concrete actions as a rural and educational reformer is one of seamless continuity. Additionally, it is hardly self-evident to which extent Liang's efforts in the domain of rural reconstruction can be seen as straightforwardly consistent or continuous with his commitment to reactualizing the Confucian teachings, the precise content and meaning of which had become fraught with ambiguity and indeterminacy due to the collapse of their institutional, social, and ritual frame of reference with the downfall of the Qing empire (1644–1911). That said, it is clear that understanding Liang's turn to rural reconstruction requires us to closely examine his conception of the nature and role of Confucianism and of traditional Chinese society in the search for a new social and cultural order able to withstand what he took to be the disastrous tide of Westernization. In the words of Philip A. Kuhn, Liang was at the same time "the most explicitly nativist and socially radical" (Kuhn 1986: 356) of the many proponents of rural reconstruction during the 1930s, something which should already warn us against pigeonholing him as a "conservative" without further ado (see Lynch 2018: 39), his personal "delusion of sagehood" (Alitto 1976b: 224)[3] notwithstanding.

While some contemporary commentators discern a venerable tradition of "rural Confucianism (*xiangcun ruxue* 鄉村儒學)" reaching back as far as Confucius and Mencius (see Yan 2020)[4] and thus interpret Liang's concern for the countryside and the peasantry as being a more or less logical consequence of his commitment to Confucian values (Gu 2016: 27), such a perspective risks distracting us from the historical specificity of his endeavors as well as some of the complexities and ambiguities in his own attitude toward the relation between the Confucian tradition and rural reconstruction as an alternative project of nation-building and modernization, which we will explore in more detail in the following pages.[5] To be sure, Liang did

[2] These two parts respectively take up around 130 and 300 pages in the edition of the text in the second volume of *LSMQJ* from 1990.

[3] Consider Liang's following pronouncement: "I cannot die now, for if I do, heaven and earth will change color and history will change its course . . . Not only would China perish, but the world itself would perhaps be on the edge of extinction" (quoted in Alitto 1976b: 224).

[4] A conference on the topic of "Rural Confucianism and Rural Civilization (鄉村儒學與鄉土文明)" was held a couple of years ago in Beijing from 14 to 16 October 2015, organized by the Chinese Academy of Social Sciences, the International Confucian Association, Nishan Shengyuan Academy 尼山聖源書院, and Yunshen Academy 雲深書院. For a brief report on this event, see Zhao 2016.

[5] In this respect, it is interesting to note that Liang did not perceive any contradiction between his activities as a rural reformer and his continued commitment to Buddhism, as is evident from the fact that he spoke of "engaging in rural work in the spirit of a Buddhist renunciant (以出家的精神做鄉村工作)" (Liang [1933a], also see Meynard 2010: 198–200). For a study of Liang's attempt to reconcile Confucian and communist visions of society and human emancipation after the establishment of the People's Republic, see Van den Stock 2020b.

explicitly appeal to the tradition of the "village covenant (*xiangyue* 鄉約)" put forward by Neo-Confucian thinkers such as Lü Dajun 呂大鈞 (1029–1080) and Lu Futing 陸桴亭 (1611–1672) (see XCJSL: 171–172, 180–186), originally intended as a system of community organization, social integration and solidarity, moral encouragement, and local self-administration which increasingly became a tool for administrative and ideological control by the imperial state during the Qing period (see Übelhör 1989; Hauf 1996). However, the examples of these distant predecessors actually only played a minor role in the articulation of his own project of rural reform. One of the main reasons for this is the fact that Liang believed a renewed version of the "village covenant" would have to emerge out of "society" and the peasant population itself, instead of being imposed from above by the state (XCJSL: 132, 184–185).

While appeals to the Confucian tradition abound throughout the *Theory of Rural Reconstruction*, Liang clearly saw himself as a "creator" rather than a mere "transmitter," with the duty (if not mission) of actively responding to the historically specific conditions of modernity. The idea of *jianshe* 建設 (literally: "construction" rather than "*re*-construction") does not so much refer to the recovery of a past reality, but rather to a complete overhaul of a given state of affairs. That such an overhaul must be accomplished on the basis of a national identity imagined to have "always already" been what it is, even if this identity must now be actively "revived" (see below), or in other words, the fact that "construction" must assume the form of "*re*construction," is indicative of the paradoxical nature of modern nationalism more generally speaking. As such, before we begin analyzing Liang Shuming's philosophical vision of rural reconstruction (Sect. 3) and a new rural-based form of social organization for China (Sect. 4), it is important to first give an idea of the historical background of this vision and its roots in the broader socio-economic and political context of the Republican era (Sect. 2).

2 Liang Shuming and Rural Reconstruction During the 1930s

The period from the late 1920s to the first half of the 1930s in Republican China saw the emergence of an enormous diversity of movements varying in scale, goals, methods, and political outlook that became known under the umbrella term of "rural reconstruction" (Gransow 1994: 6). During this period, no less than 600 organizations and institutions and over 1000 experimental zones aimed at some form of rural reform were set up across China (Chen 1999: 104; Pan et al. 2017: 120). Proponents of rural reconstruction advocated a reorientation of social, political, and economic energies from the more heavily urbanized and industrialized eastern coastal areas to China's vast rural hinterland located "far from the treaty ports" (Zanasi 2004), the latter serving as gateways for the influx of Western modernity. The intellectual and popular interest in the countryside was of such intensity that between 1933 and

1935, 218 journals appeared which were devoted to the issue of land ownership alone (Lynch 2010: 155).

There does not seem to be a definitive consensus concerning the extent to which the Chinese countryside was really, as many leading figures of the rural reconstruction movement proclaimed, on the brink of total collapse (see Bianco 1971: 104–106; Han 2005: 45–50; Merkel-Hess 2016: 17).[6] Whereas the intellectual historian and LIANG Shuming biographer ZHENG Dahua 鄭大華 describes the situation of Chinese peasants during the 1930s as one of "absolute impoverishment" (see Zheng 2000: 24–30), other economic studies point to an overall improvement in farmers' living conditions between 1870 and 1930, interrupted by the global effects of the Great Depression (see Dikötter 2008: 87–88). In any case, there was certainly no lack of abject suffering in rural China due to growing demographic pressure, increasingly scarce arable land, natural calamities, heavy tax and rent burdens, and decades of social and political conflict, leading to the widespread perception of a deep crisis in the Chinese countryside among contemporary observers. In LIANG Shuming's view, the combination of natural disasters (*tianzai* 天災) such as floods, droughts, and earthquakes with manmade catastrophes (*renhuo* 人禍) had resulted in the fact that "the last century of Chinese history can be described as a history of the destruction of the countryside" (XCJSL: 11, 317; cf. Liang [1933b]: 364).

While some rural reform programs were focused on specific goals such as setting up economic cooperatives, tackling banditry, opium addiction, prostitution, gambling, foot binding, child marriages, and illiteracy, or improving irrigation techniques and agricultural production in general, others aimed at a much more comprehensive and far-reaching transformation of Chinese society as a whole (Alitto 1976a: 213; b: 239; Day 2008: 60). Y.C. James Yen's (YAN Yangchu 晏陽初, aka "Jimmy") (1893–1990) YMCA-inspired "mass-education movement (*pingmin jiaoyu yundong* 平民教育運動)," which was carried out in the county of Ding 定 in central Hebei 河北 (see Hayford 1990),[7] and LIANG Shuming's own efforts in Shandong 山東 province are undoubtedly the most famous and influential examples

[6]According to Albert Feuerwerker for instance, "in the vast area of rural China the traditional market structure was flourishing with few signs of decay right down to 1949, a strong indication that the rural economy had not been substantially transformed. The peasant household in the mid twentieth century probably depended more on commodities not produced by itself or by its neighbours than was the case 50 years earlier. But, because there was little real improvement in transportation at the local level, the primary marketing area was not enlarged so as to bring about a radical replacement of standard markets by modern commercial channels organized around larger regional marketing complexes" (Feuerwerker 1983: 32).

[7]James Yen's movement is still the source of inspiration behind the "International Institute of Rural Reconstruction" (IIRR) which he established in 1960. The Institute has its headquarters in the James Yen Center in the Philippines and has offices in 8 other countries. Part of its credo and mission statement reads as follows: "Go to the people, live among them, learn from them, plan with them, work with them […] Not piecemeal, but integrated approach; not to conform, but to transform; not relief, but release" (IRRR 2020).

of the latter type (Alitto 1976b: 239; Pan et al. 2017: 125).[8] One of the misconceptions Liang repeatedly felt the need to dispel was the idea that rural reconstruction is merely concerned with small-scale and narrowly economic projects aimed at increasing agricultural productivity, efforts which would at best be complementary with state-building efforts on a national level (Liang [1933f]: 373–374, [1936a]: 603). Instead, for him, rural reform was nothing less than a path toward "national revival (*minzu fuxing* 民族復興)" and "cultural reconstruction (*wenhua chongxin jianzao* 文化重新建造)" (Liang [1933c]: 419).

A common element in the wide variety of rural reconstruction projects of the 1930s is the fact that its advocates emphasized the importance of local self-government (*difang zizhi* 地方自治)[9] and the social and political mobilization of the peasants (Alitto 1976a: 213), or, in other words, what Kate Merkel-Hess has summarily described as "a people-led approach to modernization" (Merkel-Hess 2016: 10) markedly different from the Leninist conception of political tutelage shared by both the Guomindang (GMD) and the Chinese Communist Party (CCP). Under the influence of the historical and social conditions which led to the growth of the rural reconstruction movement, both the GMD and the CCP had been forced to adjust their initial "urban bias" (Lynch 2010: 154) and, with varying degrees of success, increasingly shifted their attention to developments in the countryside and to the peasantry, which after all still accounted for 79% of China's working population around 1933 (Feuerwerker 1983: 35). The rise of communist peasant associations in places such as Hunan 湖南 and Guangdong 廣東 province in the middle of the 1920s might also have influenced the relatively sudden flourishing of rural reconstruction initiatives in this period (Alitto 1979: 228–229; cf. Zanasi 2004: 142).[10]

The "populist" outlook of most leaders of this movement, however, did not entail a straightforward affirmation and celebration of the revolutionary or emancipatory

---

[8] In what is one of the most comprehensive studies of the rural reconstruction movement available, ZHENG Dahua (Zheng 2000) provides extensive discussions of Yen's and Liang's projects, while also devoting considerable attention to lesser-known experimental areas such as Wuxi 無錫 (Jiangsu), Xu Gongqiao 徐公橋 (Jiangsu), Wujiang 烏江 (Anhui), Zhenping 鎮平 (Henan), and Jiangning 江寧 (Nanjing).

[9] This concept and ideal already played an important role among reformers of the late Qing period (see Lee 1998), during which time the notion of *fengjian* 封建 (later used to translate the term "feudal") also became a central element in reformist discourse (see Murthy 2008).

[10] Interestingly enough, there are indications for an indirect link between some of the most important figures in the early Chinese communist movement and the figure of MUSHANOKŌJI Saneatsu 武者小路 実篤 (1885–1976), a member of the Shirakaba 白樺 ("White Birch") literary society who had founded a community called "New Village" (*Atarashiki mura* 新しき村) in the mountains of Miyazaki Prefecture (Kyūshū), inspired by the ideas of Kropotkin and Tolstoy. The example of Mushanokōji's "New Village" led to a short-lived call for "New Village-ism (*xincunzhuyi* 新村主義)" on the part of ZHOU Zuoren 周作人 (1885–1967) during the New Culture Movement, with Zhou establishing a branch of Mushanokōji's commune in his home in Beijing, attracting the attention of CHEN Duxiu 陳獨秀 (1879–1942), LI Dazhao 李大釗 (1889–1927) and MAO Zedong among others. See Ou 2017: 40–41. Rural reconstruction in China was thus perhaps not simply a reaction against communist activism, but rather very much part of a broader (if not global) utopian concern for the countryside in the late nineteenth and early twentieth century.

potential of the rural population. Instead, reformers such as James Yen and LIANG Shuming shared the assumption that the majority of peasants were mired in ignorance and at most capable of "intuitively feel[ing] their own sufferings," all while remaining "unable to understand the causes of their problems, not to mention find their solutions" (Han 2005: 22, see for example XCJSL: 170, 199), something which would require the intercession of the intelligentsia and massive efforts to increase the level of education in the countryside.[11] Liang clearly believed that the peasants were in desperate need of "spiritual guidance" by intellectuals such as himself (Liang [1936b]: 808) who could serve as "teachers to the masses (衆人之師)" (XJCSL: 317). As Laurence A. Schneider points out in his analysis of the "Folkstudies Movement" initiated by GU Jiegang 顧頡剛 (1893–1980) in the 1920s, academic interest in popular culture and the common people in general was often marked by a combination of reverence for the masses and a paternalistic insistence on the role of an educated elite in guiding the people toward "awakening" and socio-political emancipation (Schneider 1971: 123).[12]

Accordingly, for Liang as well, the rural reconstruction movement was to a large extent synonymous with popular education (Liang [1934b]: 479), the envisaged result being a veritable "schoolification" of both government and society (Alitto 1979: 248; cf. van Slyke 1959: 466). As Alitto emphasizes, "the common focus of both his educational and rural reform was not the masses but the young intelligentsia," who were ideally "both Confucian and expert" (Alitto 1976b: 233), even if he did imagine that the peasants themselves would come to play an ever greater role as the rural reconstruction movement progressed (Lynch 2011: 36) and intellectuals would gradually gain an increasing sense of solidarity with the common people in the countryside (Merkel-Hess 2016: 57).[13] The twentieth-century Confucian philosopher MOU Zongsan 牟宗三 (1909–1995) was thus not completely off the mark when he described the vision espoused by Liang as that of "the path of the nobleman (*junzi* 君子)" (Mou [1934]: 741),[14] given the importance Liang attached to leading by moral example as well as practices of "spiritual cultivation (*jingshen taolian* 精神陶煉)" and "self-cultivation (*xiuyang* 修養)" in carrying out rural reconstruction work (see Liang [1934a], [1936b]). Differentiating between "rule by humanity (*renzhi* 人治)" and "rule by the people (*minzhi* 民治)" (i.e. representative democracy), Liang claimed a central role for "worthy and wise scholars (*xianzhi zhi shi* 賢智之

[11] In a text from 1922, James Yen declared that "if the great majority of the people, because of their social habits and knowledge, consider themselves to be dregs (*hsia-liu* [下流]), they will by that very act transform the world's oldest culture, largest population, the great Chinese nation, into a nation of dregs! Our only hope is to uplift our illiterate brothers and sisters." (Hayford 1990: 39).

[12] For a more recent and comprehensive (though largely descriptive) monograph on the Folkstudies Movement, see Gao 2019.

[13] Similarly, James Yen saw the "transformation of the peasants (*hua nongmin* 化農民)" as being predicated on a process of "peasantization (*nongminhua* 農民化)" on the part of the intellectuals as leaders of the rural reform movement (Zheng 2000: 157–159).

[14] On Mou's own perception of the peasant as an incarnation of "life in itself (*shengming zhi zai qi ziji* 生命之在其自己)" in relation to his critique of communist ideology, see Van den Stock 2020a: 50–55.

士)" (XCJSL: 145) as privileged representatives of "humanity" equipped with the necessary moral as well as intellectual capacities to lead the peasant population toward social self-determination.

A related, if seemingly contrary, assumption among many rural reformers was the idea that, provided they would receive the necessary guidance by more educated elements of society, the peasants could serve as agents of effective social change precisely "because their lives had not been penetrated and contaminated by modern foreign civilization" (Han 2005: 25). The figure of the peasant we find in the writings of rural reformers such as Liang is thus deeply ambiguous, at the same time appearing as the only subject capable of transforming Chinese society because of its supposed "natural" or "untainted" quality and as a blind, indomitable force requiring a prior process of transformation (perhaps one could say "subjectification") in order to be successfully "inducted" into political life (Han 2005: 12) and begin functioning as a self-conscious agent of change and emancipation (see Sect. 4).[15] Social change through rural reconstruction thus first and foremost still required, to use the influential reformer LIANG Qichao's 梁啓超 (1873–1929) famous phrasing culled from the canonical text of the *Great Learning* (*Daxue* 大學), a process of "renewing the people (*xin min* 新民)" leading to the creation of "new citizens (*xinmin* 新民)."[16]

The beginning of LIANG Shuming's involvement with the rural reconstruction movement can be situated around the middle of the 1920s. After abandoning his position as a lecturer at Peking University in 1924, where he had taught Indian philosophy at the invitation of CAI Yuanpei 蔡元培 (1868–1940) since 1917, Liang became interested in educational reform and continued his acquired habit of living in a commune-like fashion, surrounded by students with whom he maintained a close relation centered around a mutual moral scrutiny and collective self-improvement (Alitto 1979: 137–138). The figure of the Shandong educator WANG Hongyi 王鴻一 (1874–1930) played a crucial role in converting Liang to the cause of what Wang called "rural governance (*xiangzhi* 鄉治)" (see Alitto 1979: 145–147; Zheng 2000: 181–184; Gu 2016: 90–91; Merkel-Hess 2016: 63; Lynch 2018: 137–138) and the ideal of "establishing the state through agriculture (*yi nong li guo* 以農立國)" (Zhu 1996: 57–60; Zheng 2000: 179–180).

Liang witnessed various ongoing experiments with rural reform and rural education in Guangzhou 廣州, Nanjing 南京 (TAO Xingzhi's 陶行知 (1891–1946) Xiaozhuang Experimental Rural Normal School, see Yao 2002: 96–100), Jiangsu 江

---

[15] As Kate Merkel-Hess notes, the rural reconstruction movement was preceded by a "social survey movement" in the 1920s and 1930s, "which sought to collect and aggregate information about China's new national subjects and particularly, as the 1920s wore on, those in rural areas" (Merkel-Hess 2016: 2). In other words, "the people" (or segments seen as representative of the population such as "the peasant") were not a known quantity, but rather something to be discursively constructed and subsequently "discovered" (see Hayford 1990: xiii, 62).

[16] The distinction LIANG Qichao's mentor KANG Youwei 康有爲 (1858–1927) drew between morally and politically responsible "citizens (*gongmin* 公民)" as opposed to mere "people (*renmin* 人民)" is also worth considering in this respect (see Lee 1998: 40–42).

蘇, Hebei (James Yen's mass education movement in Ding county), and Shanxi 山西 (the reformist warlord YAN Xishan's 閻錫山 (1883–1960) experiments with "village government," *cunzheng* 村政), all of which left him rather unimpressed and dissatisfied (see Alitto 1979: 167, for the case of Shanxi, see XCJSL: 178–179).[17] Still, soon afterward he became personally involved with the management of the short-lived "Academy of Village Governance" (*Cunzhi shuyuan* 村治書院) in Henan 河南 province (see Liang [1929]) at the request of WANG Hongyi's acquaintance LIANG Zhonghua 梁仲華 (1898–1968) in 1929 (Zhu 1996: 64), an institute that was shut down on Chiang Kai-shek's orders the following year (Thøgersen 2002: 91). The journal *Village Governance Monthly* (*Cunzhi yuekan* 村治月刊) which Wang had founded in Beijing in 1929 served as a first major outlet for LIANG Shuming's ideas on rural reform (see Liang [1937]: 1010). Liang took over as editor from Wang due to the latter's deteriorating health and eventual death in 1930 and went on to create his own journal entitled *Rural Reconstruction* (*Xiangcun jianshe* 鄉村建設) in 1931 (Alitto 1979: 173; Zhu 1996: 154–155; Lynch 2018: 142).

In June 1931, with the support of the GMD military governor of Shandong HAN Fuju 韓復榘 (1890–1938) (previously governor of Henan, where he had also backed the "Academy of Village Governance"), LIANG Shuming, LIANG Zhonghua, and a number of likeminded reformers established the Shandong Rural Reconstruction Institute (*Shandong xiancun jianshe yanjiuyuan* 山東鄉村建設研究院) in the county of Zouping 鄒平 in central Shandong (Alitto 1976a: 214–215). The Institute, which LIANG Shuming conceived of as the "central nervous system" for the revival of Chinese culture and the transformation of Chinese society as a whole (XCJSL: 350–352), initially functioned as an advising body to the county government. During this phase (1931–1933), the organization's focus lay on training students and staff for carrying out rural reform work and dispatching them to different rural areas to found and manage peasant schools. These schools were intended to serve as "the social, political, and economic heart of the village" (Merkel-Hess 2016: 126).

Starting from July 1933, the Nanjing government officially designated Zouping, as well as the county of Heze 菏澤 in western Shandong, as an "experimental county (*shiyanxian* 實驗縣)" (Zhu 1996: 141–142; Merkel-Hess 2016: 112), so that the Rural Reconstruction Institute was effectively merged with the government in these areas and began to act both as an administrative and an educational organization directly answerable to the provincial level.[18] The existing administrative divisions into districts, towns and villages was replaced by a network of rural schools, which in the case of Zouping was further subdivided into rural subdistrict schools (*xiangxue* 鄉學) and village schools (*cunxue* 村學) (see Liang 1935; van Slyke 1959: 468; Alitto 1976a: 222; Wu and Tong 2009: 43–45). In turn, the village schools were divided into four subtypes, respectively catering to (1) school-aged

[17] For a record of some of Liang's observations on the experiments in Jiangsu, Hebei, and Shanxi during his travels, see Liang [1932].

[18] The Institute was divided into three departments: the Research and Training Department, the Rural Service Guidance Office, and the Experimental Farm. See XCJSL: 353–356, Alitto 1976a: 218–221, 1979: 242–246, and Zheng 2000: 94–95.

children, (2) women, (3) adult male peasants (through evening and winter classes), and (4) young adults who had already received primary education (Thøgersen 2002: 108).

Following a national conference organized in Zouping—in the same month the latter was declared an "experimental county" falling under the jurisdiction of the Institute—Liang joined forces with other prominent rural reformers such as James Yen in establishing the "Chinese Association for Rural Reconstruction (*Zhongguo xiangcun jianshe xuehui* 中國鄉村建設學會)" in order to bring the various individuals and organizations involved in rural reform throughout China together (Zhu 1996: 67; Cui 2013: 48). His own Institute continued to expand its activities until the Japanese invasion of Shandong in December 1937, at which point it had already incorporated 70 of the 107 counties in the whole province (Alitto 1976a: 216). Between 1931 and 1936, Liang's Institute managed to train a total of over 2600 teachers and staff members (Chen 1999: 138). Throughout the entire Zouping experiment, the number of "village schools" as well as the overall enrollment numbers, especially in the field of primary education, remained relatively modest (Thøgersen 2002: 97).[19]

In line with Liang's comprehensive vision of rural reconstruction, his reform programs in Shandong were not merely focused on increasing agricultural productivity, but also involved battling opium addiction (see XCJSL: 240–244), encouraging family planning and birth control, setting up hospitals and libraries, establishing economic cooperative societies (*hezuo she* 合作社) (see Alitto 1976a: 227–231; Zhu 1996: 145–150) as well as credit and loan mechanisms (Zhu 1996: 150–152), and organizing local self-defense forces to combat the endemic problem of banditry in the countryside (see XCJSL: 245–250; Alitto 1976a: 231–235).[20] At the center of all these endeavors, however, was the idea of education as a means of creating "peasant self-consciousness (*nongmin zijue* 農民自覺)," a form of consciousness that is simultaneously the precondition for, and something to be further reinforced by, "rural organization (*xiangcun zuzhi* 鄉村組織)" (Liang [1936a]: 616). The entire population in the counties falling under the jurisdiction of the Institute, including the teachers and administrators themselves, was seen as a collective body

[19] "In quantitative terms the village schools were no big success. In 1933 there were 54 village schools in Tsoup'ing [Zouping] with 214 female students in the women's section and 5781 male students in the adult section. By 1936 the RRM [Rural Reconstruction Movement] had been forced to concentrate their efforts in only 28 schools enrolling just 181 female and 1515 male students. Tsoup'ing had around 250 villages and a population of more than 165,000 at this time, so the new type of schooling reached only a small and even declining part of the villagers" (Thøgersen 2002: 111). Cui Xiaohui 崔效輝 puts the total number of educational facilities and students in Zouping around the time of the Japanese invasion at 566 and 27,257 respectively (Cui 2013: 49).

[20] The attempt to recruit peasants into local militia was initially met with distrust and resistance on the part of the population of Zouping due to their recent experiences with warlords who had used similar tactics for drafting peasants into their own private armies. See Thøgersen 2002: 112.

of "students (*xuezhong* 學衆)" (see Liang 1935: 2),[21] thus embodying what Liang called the "unity of government and teaching (*zheng jiao heyi* 政教合一)" (XCJSL: 138) and the "transformation of administrative into educational organizations (行政機關教育機關化)" (Lin 1990: 27). The rural subdistrict and village schools at the center of Liang's rural reconstruction movement were thus not simply conceived of as centers of learning, but rather as bases for the creation of a new form of culture and a new type of society (Liang [1936a]: 666–667). For Liang, such a society would have to be grounded in the "old principles" of Confucianism as well as village life itself, respectively counting as the "formless (*wuxing* 無形)" and "tangible (*youxing* 有形)" roots of Chinese culture (Liang [1936a]: 611–613; cf. XCJSL: 171).

In LIANG Shuming's own retrospective analysis, his movement for rural reconstruction ended in failure. Even as his experiments in Shandong were still ongoing, he already expressed frustration at the inability of his reform programs to disentangle themselves from existing structures of political power and effectively mobilize the peasant population by transforming them into self-conscious and self-determining subjects of social change (see Thøgersen 2009: 12). However, he would eventually attribute the failure of the rural reconstruction movement to the fact that it had come "too soon" (Liang [1977]: 428; Wu 2005: 228), an assessment obviously reflecting his idea of the "precocious" nature of Chinese culture as a whole, thus meting out praise and blame at the same time. After his experiments in Shandong were prematurely ended by the Japanese invasion, Liang continued to defend the theoretical analysis of the nature of Chinese society underlying his concrete proposals for rural reform against an increasingly vocal contingent of historical materialist detractors (see Liang [1941]). However, following the founding of the People's Republic, he eventually became convinced that the CCP's revolutionary mobilization of the peasant population effectively managed to realize many of the goals Liang had set for the rural reconstruction movement (Alitto 1979: 344; Liang and Alitto 2013: 195–196). Not in the least, Liang came to credit the CCP for the successful creation of a new rural-oriented society and new form of collective life (see Liang [1950–1951]), an endeavor his own *Theory of Rural Reconstruction* had still envisaged in terms of allowing for the emergence of "new shoots from the old root (老根新芽)" of the Chinese tradition, as we will see in more detail in the following two sections of this chapter.

[21] That said, Liang distinguished between (1) "students (*xuezhong*)" in a more literal sense, (2) "teachers (*jiaoyuan* 教員)," "school directors (*xuedong* 學董)," and the "school principal (*xuezhang* 學長)," the latter being a morally exemplary person of a certain seniority capable of moral as well as practical supervision who would occupy a "transcendent position (超然地位)" (XCJS: 216, 223) within the school organization, in the sense of not being in charge of administrative affairs, but rather being responsible for impartially mediating between different parties in the case of conflict. For more details on the concrete organizational structure of the village and rural subdistrict schools, see Liang 1935 and Lin 1990: 26–30.

3 *Theory of Rural Reconstruction* (1937): Cultural, Historical, Social, Political, and Economic Elements of a Philosophical Analysis

By his own account, LIANG Shuming's turn toward rural reconstruction coincided with a transformative experience of "awakening (*juewu* 覺悟)," more precisely a realization that China would need to chart its own course in the modern world and abandon its frustrated desire to emulate the West, an impulse he saw as having guided reformist as well as revolutionary discourse and political action ever since the late Qing period (see Liang [1930b]: 109; XCJSL: 320–321; van Slyke 1959: 461; Zheng 2000: 162; Lynch 2011: 45). According to Catherine Lynch, this "awakening" was triggered by the breakdown of the First United Front between the GMD and the CCP in 1927 which plunged the Republic into civil war, leading Liang to abandon most if not all faith in party politics (Lynch 2011: 35).[22] Crucially, Liang now discarded the idea that all cultures follow a fixed evolutionary trajectory put forward in his own *Eastern and Western Cultures and Their Philosophies* (*Dong xi wenhua ji qi zhexue* 東西文化及其哲學) from 1921, which in the case of China would have necessitated, even if only temporarily, a full-scale adoption of Western political institutions, science, and technology, eventually somehow paving the way for the rebirth of Chinese culture (more specifically, Confucianism) in the future (Liang [1921]: 525). Instead, he came to argue that "the genuine life of a nation (民族真生命) lies in its fundamental spirit (根本精神). Abandoning our own fundamental spirit means ruining our own chances of moving forward" (Liang [1930b]: 109–110).

For Liang, this meant that the movement for the "*self*-salvation of the Chinese people (*Zhongguo minzu zijiu yundong* 中國民族自救運動)" (Liang [1930b]: 113, emphasis added) would have to become true to its name in firmly rejecting the path of Westernization and basing itself in a form of "national self-consciousness (*minzu zijue* 民族自覺)" able to endow China with the self-confidence that "*our nation has truly been entrusted with the mission to open up a path for the future of world culture*" (Liang [1930b]: 113, emphasis in the original, cf. Liang [1934a]: 504). While this remark indicates that Liang's notion of "awakening" also had a globally oriented dimension, there can be little doubt that the central concern in his post-1927 writings was that of the "self-salvation" of China, which has its exact correlate in his description of rural reconstruction as a "movement for rural self-salvation (*xiangcun zijiu yundong* 鄉村自救運動)" (XCJSL: 13, Liang [1933b]: 365). In short, Liang's call for "self-salvation," as something to be accomplished by rediscovering the Chinese nation's own "fundamental spirit," coincided with his discovery of the countryside as the true locus of China's "self." National and rural "self-salvation"

[22] That said, in the draft table of contents from 1928 for the manuscript that would later become his *Theory of Rural Reconstruction*, the two last chapters are devoted to describing a possible future direction for the GMD as the party that would have to take up the task of "national revival" (see Zhu 1996: 63).

were thus mutually implicative, if not identical, undertakings for him (see Liang [1933b]: 367).

Propelled by this insight into the need for "self-salvation" through "national awakening (*minzu juewu* 民族覺悟)" (Liang [1930b]: 112), Liang's embrace of rural reform was accompanied by a stronger focus on socio-historical analysis and empirical history in his philosophical writings (Lynch 2011: 45, 49).[23] In other words, the supposed "fundamental spirit" of the Chinese nation was no longer defined in largely abstract terms as embodying a particular orientation of the human "will (*yiyu* 意欲)," as had been the case in his highly influential 1921 lecture series, but came to be articulated in more concrete social, historical, economic, and political terms. This is perhaps nowhere as clear as in the text of his 1937 *Theory of Rural Reconstruction*, in which Liang, as the "only real philosopher" of the rural reconstruction movement, offers "a systematic all-encompassing theory" (Alitto 1976a: 240) underlying the reforms he had been pursuing in Shandong province.[24] As such, in defending the idea that China is a nation rooted in the countryside and the agricultural economy, in sharp contrast to the urban orientation of the industrialized West, Liang's *Theory of Rural Reconstruction* at the same time mobilizes a detailed, empirically informed (if on many accounts highly disputable) analysis of what he takes to be the most fundamental characteristics of traditional Chinese society as well as the main social problems resulting from modernization (XCJSL: 25–47), one which he would further elaborate and expand upon in *The Fundamentals of Chinese Culture* (*Zhongguo wenhua yaoyi* 中國文化要義) published in 1949. Additionally, in thinking through the dire fate of Chinese society in the modern era, Liang made sure to set his own analysis apart from historical materialist visions of socio-economic organization and societal evolution. This was of crucial importance for him, seeing how rural reconstruction was explicitly conceived as an alternative to communist strategies of peasant mobilization, communism ultimately counting as the product of a Western culture of strife and conflict for him (see Liang [1930b]: 109; XCJSL: 250–253; Lin 1990: 22; Lu 2010: 243).

As is well-known, Liang believed that while imperial China had hardly been free of hierarchical and unequal social relations between individuals, it had never been divided into distinct classes in the Marxist sense. In his own words, "there were rulers, but no ruling classes" (XCJSL: 38, 70). Instead, he characterized premodern China as "a society grounded in ethical relations (*lunli benwei de shehui* 倫理本位的社會)," that is to say, ties of affection (*qingyi guanxi* 情誼關係) and moral responsibility (*yiwu guanxi* 義務關係) (as opposed to legally defined "rights")

[23] Nevertheless, Liang still continued to conceive of the relatively recent transformation of the West into a system of industrialized modern nation-states as being grounded in "a changed attitude toward human existence" (Liang [1930b]: 59), that is to say, a rediscovery of the "humanist" and "this-worldly" outlook of Greek antiquity leading to a liberation from the religiosity of the Middle Ages. As such, Liang never ceased to attribute a significant causal force to cultural difference as the ultimate basis for differing trajectories of social, political, and economic development.

[24] A wealth of shorter texts related to rural reconstruction published between 1930 and 1937 can be found in volume 5 of *LSMQJ*.

between family members, as well as teachers and students, neighbors, and friends (XCJSL: 25–28, 147). The only form of social stratification, or rather differentiation, Liang recognized was that of "differing occupational paths (*zhiye fentu* 職業分途)" (XCJSL: 28–30 cf. Liang [1949]: 79–94, 139–156), albeit one with no clear equivalent in rigid class oppositions. He argued that because of the absence of feudal rules of land ownership, primogeniture, and mechanized farming, the Chinese countryside had remained relatively free of the monopolization of land, capital, and political power by one particular class. Instead, the countryside at the basis of traditional Chinese society had essentially been a "natural economy" serving to fulling the need for subsistence of small-scale rural communities centered around the "ethical relations" of family life, a system that had remained more or less structurally stable until the second half of the nineteenth century (XCJSL: 18). For Liang, traditional rural China counts "a social order that simply managed to spontaneously preserve itself" (XCJSL: 38, cf. 396) in the absence of an interventionist state apparatus. Due to the considerable extent of social mobility exemplified by the imperial examination system, which was in principle open to all individuals, or rather men, regardless of their social and economic standing, Chinese society had been characterized by a high degree of "adjustability (*tiaohexing* 調和性)" precluding the emergence of major social antagonisms, let alone class struggle (XCJSL: 22). In terms of the relation between traditional China and the outside world, Liang credited the "assimilative power (*tonghuali* 同化力)" of the Middle Kingdom's "extensive sphere of cultural influence" with having precluded major interstate conflicts (see XCJSL: 22, 42, 52; Liang [1936a]: 606, 637; Van den Stock 2020b).[25]

At the same time, however, Liang faulted this very same virtue of reconciliatory "adjustability" for the stagnation and eventual collapse of Chinese culture and society following its dramatic confrontation with the military supremacy of the West as symbolized by the Opium Wars, without which China would have remained trapped inside a "cyclical alternation of order and chaos devoid of any revolutions" (XCJSL: 32–38).[26] This much makes it clear that Liang did not conceive of rural reconstruction as a conservative or reactionary project aimed at restoring an idealized past. Instead, as he constantly emphasizes in his 1937 book, rural reconstruction aims at "the construction of a new society" and counts as nothing less than a "nation-building movement (*jianguo yundong* 建國運動)" (XCJSL: 20, 48, Liang [1933b]: 368). As Liang explains, "Chinese history has reached a point where it must go through a major transformation in which society is drastically changed, which is

[25] For Liang's contemporary FENG Youlan 馮友蘭 (1895–1990), in whose 1940 *New Treatise on Practical Affairs* (*Xin shilun* 新事論) the distinction between the rural and the urban is treated as coinciding with that between tradition and modernity as such (see Van den Stock 2016: 144–146), the "assimilative power" of Chinese civilization had essentially been the result of China's "urban" status vis-à-vis its "barbarian" neighbors. See Feng [1940]: 47–48.

[26] At one point, Liang claims that the decay of Chinese culture had already set in with the transition from the Ming (1368–1644) to the Qing dynasty and proposes that the confrontation with the West would not have been quite as destructive of the Chinese tradition if the latter had not already turned into a "hollow shell (僵殼)" under the Manchu Qing rule (see XCJSL: 128).

exactly why it is necessary to resolve the problems with which we are faced by pursuing the most lofty of ideals" (XCJSL: 24, cf. 161). Such a drastic change is needed precisely because the Chinese countryside has experienced decades of "absolute destruction." In contrast to the West, such destruction has failed to usher in an economically successful turn toward industrialization and urbanization (CXJSL: 12–13).[27] Instead of giving birth to distinct social classes, China's entry into the modern world had created a deep and sterile divide between the city and the countryside, leading to an increasing alienation of urban elites from the only true basis for national "self-salvation" (see XCJSL: 295; Liang [1930a]: 216–217; van Slyke 1959: 463–464).

As a consequence, Liang believes China finds itself in a kind of limbo state, not yet having embarked on the path toward Western modernization, while at the same time witnessing the total collapse and active discrediting of the inherited social order as well as its traditional culture (XCJSL: 69). More precisely, Liang is convinced that the crisis faced by the Chinese nation is ultimately due to its "loss of cultural balance (*wenhua shitiao* 文化失調)," that is say, the loss of its own "rituals and customs (*lisu* 禮俗)" (XCJSL: 21) as a normative framework for the organization of social, political, and economic life as grounded in "ethical relations." In Liang's view, in traditional Chinese society, the "rituals and customs" of the Confucian tradition effectively extended over the entire social spectrum, so that, as we read in the classical text of the *Great Learning*, "every single person, from the Son of Heaven down to the common people, takes cultivating oneself as the foundation (自天子以至於庶人, 壹是皆以修身為本)" (quoted in XCJSL: 38, 46).[28] The Confucian system of human-centered "rituals and customs" was based on an affirmation of "reason (*lixing* 理性)," a term Liang uses to designate an affective and immersive form of knowledge oriented toward the "ethical relations" between human beings in the here and now, ideally allowing them to attain a form of "self-mastery (*zili* 自力)" in relation to both the natural world and their social environment (XCJSL: 35, 38–39). As he put it summarily: "rituals [*li* 禮] are by necessity grounded in human emotions [*renqing* 人情], human emotions are identical to reason [*lixing* 理性]. This is why it is said [in the *Book of Rites*, *Liji* 禮記] that 'rituals are patterns [*li* 理] [of human relations]' (禮必本于人情; 人情即是理性。故曰:禮者理也)" (XCJSL: 38–39).

By contrast, the recent focus on acquiring the instrumental "rationality (*lizhi* 理智)" characteristic of Western culture, a form of knowledge geared toward distinguishing instead of reconciling subject and object and self and other which lies at the basis of scientific reasoning and technological advancement, has been

---

[27] Despite Liang's staunchly anti-Western stance, he admitted being inspired by similar movements toward economic and educational reform in Europe, most notably agricultural cooperatives and "folk high schools" in Denmark, which he quotes as a source of inspiration and even an example for China on multiple occasions (see Thøgersen 1995).

[28] Liang believed the social stratum of the *shi* 士 (scholar-officials), as privileged representatives of "reason," to have occupied a mediating position between the ruler and the common people in imperial China (XCJSL: 44).

accompanied by a disastrous adoption of the individualistic outlook of the West serving only to undermine the basis of collective life (XCJSL: 63). As Liang puts it, "the sort of public commonality (*gong* 公) found in the West is merely a form of selfishness on a large scale (大範圍的自私) and not genuine commonality" (XCJSL: 52, cf. 135). For Liang, the triumph of disinterested "rationality" over affective "reason" has further corroded the remnants of the traditional Chinese social order, as something rooted in interpersonal relations of affection and responsibility.[29]

In this respect, it is highly significant that LIANG Shuming's focus on the rural hinterland as the only possible site for the "self-salvation" of the Chinese nation as a whole is motivated by the idea that at least some traces of the traditional system of ethical relations have been preserved in the countryside and village life. At one point, he approvingly invokes a saying attributed to Confucius in the *History of the Former Han Dynasty* (*Hanshu* 漢書) according to which "when rituals are lost, we must seek them in the open country (禮失而求諸野)" (quoted in XCJSL: 168), a statement that seems to run counter to his own observation that the countryside has been marked by "absolute destruction" in the recent past. While Liang generally eschews a naïve idealization of bucolic existence, he does at times claim that peasant life is more natural and "at ease" than the hectic and rushed routine of city dwellers, the farming population still maintaining a close relation to the natural environment instead of being caught up in the mechanical manipulation of "dead matter" characteristic of industrial labor (XCJSL: 166–167). Peasants continue to be situated in a close web of family relations, in stark contrast to the increasingly anonymous and atomized lives of urban residents.

Indeed, Liang even describes the countryside as the "root (*ben* 本)" of society and the "home of humanity" as such (XCJSL: 169), that is to say, a place where an ethically oriented form of interpersonal "reason," as corresponding to the "formless root" of Chinese culture (see XCJSL: 170), has managed to stand its ground against the wave of an objectifying "rationality" structurally embodied in the social phenomena of urbanization and industrialization. While cities are indispensable as centers (*zhongxin* 中心) of political and economic life, high culture, and education, they can never displace the villages as the true "core" or "center of gravity (*zhongxin* 重心)" of Chinese society (XCJSL: 169). Interestingly enough, this leads Liang to claim that the economic imperialism of Western colonial powers which China fell prey to in the middle of the nineteenth century with the imposition of various "unequal treaties" has had the paradoxical advantage of precluding the industrialization of China and the latter's entry into the capitalist mode of production and distribution, thus to some extent sheltering China's "inner bones (骨子裏邊)," that is to say, the countryside, from being completely overrun by the forces of marketization, or, as Liang puts it, "Shanghainized (*Shanghaihua* 上海化)" (XCJSL: 334). Liang has no doubt that the global trend of history involves a decisive turn away

[29] When Liang asserts in intentionally paradoxical terms that "relativism is the truth (相對論是真理)," what he means is precisely that the fundamental interrelatedness of human existence is both ontologically and socially prior to the perspective of individualism (see XCJSL: 159–160).

from capitalism as a model of economic development (XCJSL: 16; Liang [1933b]: 366), a position consistent with his youthful attraction to socialism.[30]

Perhaps somewhat surprisingly, there is also a strongly pragmatic and deeply ambiguous dimension to LIANG Shuming's focus on the countryside and the rural economy, in the sense that he does not, as one might expect, categorically reject industrialization as a necessary component of the process of modernization and nation-building. As he himself writes, the economic outlook of the rural reconstruction movement can be summarized as "promoting agriculture in order to stimulate the industry" (XCJSL: 17), not in the least because agriculture is quite simply the only viable sector of the Chinese economy. Additionally, Liang makes it quite clear that increasing agricultural productivity cannot be accomplished if agriculture is not first "scientificized (*kexuehua* 科學化)" and "industrialized (*gongyehua* 工業化)" (XCJSL: 342), the term "industrialized" specifically referring to a systematic, rationally coordinated, and large-scale form of production for him. Invoking historical materialist rhetoric, he stresses that the rural reconstruction movement seeks to accomplish a veritable "socialization of economic production and distribution" (XCJSL: 254). In more concrete terms, Liang notes that surplus rural labor will still have to be deployed in urban industries, specifically during the off-season when farmers are mostly idle (XCJSL: 344), instead of simply being put to better use in the countryside itself. Somewhat ironically then, precisely in order to create the economic basis for a new society oriented toward the countryside and prevent the means of production from becoming monopolized by a handful of individual economic agents, Liang discerns an urgent need for the adoption of advanced productive technologies ("ingenuity," *qiao* 巧) and a transition to large-scale, industrialized production ("magnitude," *da* 大) in the hope of creating sufficient material wealth, arriving at an equitable distribution of goods, and overcoming the divide between urban and rural areas (XCJSL: 257–258). Indeed, he envisions an elusive future in which "agriculture and industry are united (農業工業相結合)" and the "ruralization of the cities (都市的鄉村化)" will somehow go hand in hand with the "urbanization of the countryside (鄉村的都市化)" (XCJSL: 344, cf. 389).

LIANG Shuming's belief in the interdependence between rural reconstruction and industrialization is not easy to reconcile with the idea of "rural *self*-salvation," since the latter ultimately appears to be predicated on successful nationwide industrialization instead of the self-sufficiency of local rural communities, even if the kind of agriculture-centered industrialization he envisages would be focused on producing essential goods and resources necessary for self-subsistence and the satisfaction of immediate human needs instead of benefitting the self-reinforcing growth of

[30]During his teens, Liang already read the Japanese anarchist KŌTOKU Shūsui's 幸徳 秋水 (1871–1911) 1903 book *The Quintessence of Socialism* (*Shakaishugi shinzu* 社會主義神髓) in ZHANG Puquan's 張溥泉 (ZHANG Ji 張繼, 1882–1947) translation (see XCJSL: 255).

capital.[31] His "nativism" was thus hardly tantamount to an unambiguously anti-modern stance. In any case, Liang's surprisingly instrumental approach to the countryside as a basis for "national awakening" and "self-salvation" indicates that the true goal and subject of his rural reconstruction project is not the countryside as such, but rather the Chinese nation. As he himself declares: "We are of course not taking the position of industrial capital, *but neither are we simply adopting the position of the countryside*, rather, *what we are doing is establishing a fundamental course of action for Chinese society*" (XCJSL: 348, emphasis added). This revealing statement points to the necessity of having a closer look at what Liang means when he speaks of "society," which is not as self-evident as the prevalence of this concept in everyday language as well as academic discourse may lead one to believe.

4 "Collective Life" and "Rural Organization": Society Beyond the State

As we have seen above, LIANG Shuming's analysis of the condition of rural China and Chinese society as a whole is not straightforwardly "Utopian," at least not in the specific sense of portraying the countryside as an accomplished ideal society or a "non-place" (*ou topos*) free from the incursions of global as well as national political and economic developments. Quite to the contrary, the latent presence of the "formless root" of the Confucian culture of "reason" in the countryside notwithstanding, Liang makes it clear that this "root" remains without a clear correlate in the institutional and social structure of the Chinese nation. As he never tires of repeating, rural China must first be "united into a great vital force (大生命力量)" (XCJSL: 263), a force stemming from the unity between intellectuals and the peasant population (XCJSL: 289). Over and against the Marxist notion that China will need to go through a proletarian revolution and engage in class struggle in order for society to liberate itself from relations of political domination and economic

---

[31] In Liang's *Theory of Rural Reconstruction*, the distinction between industry and agriculture appears to be of secondary importance in relation to the conceptual difference between the two sides of what Marx called the "commodity form" (*Warenform*): Liang stresses that China should refrain from emulating the "Western" capitalist tendency to produce for the sake of production, that is to say, in order to accumulate *exchange value*, but should rather focus on producing actual *use value* aimed at consumption (XCJSL: 155, 325). This plea for reorienting economic activity toward the production of use value ("consumption") (which can be found in the writings of other "New Confucians" as well, see Van den Stock 2016: 163–164) is also expressed in Liang's insistence on the fact that the "subject of the economy (*jingji zhuti* 經濟主體)" is the human being itself, and that the rural reconstruction movement must try to "keep the economy from slipping from our hands" (XCJSL: 187), that is to say, degenerating into a form of commodity production that is no longer aimed at the satisfaction of real human needs but rather at the self-valorization of exchange value. As such, he is convinced that achieving industrialization by means of the development of agriculture will lead to a renewed focus on production for the sake of consumption and restore human beings to their rightful place as self-determining "subjects" of society (XCJSL: 391).

exploitation, Liang maintains that "it is not that we have an unequal [social] order (不平等的秩序), but rather that there is no order [whatsoever]" (XCJSL: 68, cf. 90, 323). For Liang, the same applies to approaches which single out the warlord system as the main culprit for the ongoing chaos, since the ceaseless conflicts between warlords actually do not denote a "system" at all, which might at least function as a clear and unified target of critique and revolutionary action, but rather point toward a total absence of order (XCJSL: 91–94). As a result of the fact that various political forces continue to battle for supremacy, the Chinese nation remains completely "divided at the upper stratum (分於上)" (XCJSL: 298, 300), thus leaving potential revolutionaries with nothing to overthrow in the first place. Accordingly, in Liang's analysis, the central goal of the rural reconstruction movement is not to topple an exploitative social order, but to "seek for unity from below (求統於下)" (XCJSL: 302) precisely in order to usher in a new type of social organization that will, perhaps for the first time in Chinese history, give birth to a self-conscious and active form of "collective life (*tuanti shenghuo* 團體生活)."

For LIANG Shuming, the emergence of "collective life" in China would be a truly revolutionary event simply because the traditional Chinese social order had relied on passive acceptance and acquiescence (XCJSL: 136–137), rather than being grounded in the sort of active "self-consciousness" and "national awakening" he sees as the precondition for genuine "self-salvation" (see XCJSL: 200–201).[32] As Liang puts it at one point, the traditional "five relations (*wu lun* 五倫)" (between ruler and servant, husband and wife, father and son, older and younger brothers, and between friends) urgently have to be supplemented by an entirely novel relation, namely the properly *social* relation between the individual and the collective (XCJSL: 160; Liang [1936c]: 537). The persistence of "ethical relations" in village life constitutes an increasingly threatened and brittle but still viable basis for the active construction of such a relation, as the true hallmark of a "society" in the proper sense of the word. Moreover, Liang expects "collective life" as a network of bonds between individuals in society to emerge from "ethical relations" themselves, or in other words, from "reason" itself. In his view, the creation of "collective life" cannot be accomplished by means of top-down, state-enforced measures which would at most be capable of forging an artificial type of solidarity and togetherness (XCJSL: 161–162). The lack of "collective life" and social order in China cannot be remedied by designing a political system with the intention of changing society from above. As Liang writes, "we must *turn back to seek it in society* (反求於社會) instead of expecting help from politics" (XCJSL: 279, emphasis added). Social cohesion based in "reason" is thus explicitly contrasted to the kind of unity resulting from political intervention and military force (XCJSL: 73, 395). "Collective life"

[32] Tellingly, instead of interpreting a famous passage from the 80 th chapter of the *Daodejing* 道德經 ("people can hear the sound of each other's chickens and dogs, but they will die of old age without ever having gone to visit each other," 雞犬之聲相聞, 民至老死, 不相往來) as a description of a utopian state, Liang reads it as reflecting a pathological lack of concern for a form of collective existence beyond the immediacy of the "ethical relations" between family members in traditional China (see Liang [1936a]: 628, 634).

must emerge from "self-awareness (*zijue* 自覺)" (XCJSL: 135), from the innate human capacity for "reason," and not from external coercion by the state.

In his understanding, the reason behind the failure of efforts toward "local self-government" starting from the late Qing period lies in the fact that *self*-government must be grounded in the active construction of collective life on the local level by developing a "collective organization (*tuanti zuzhi* 團體組織)" distinct from the bureaucratic apparatus of the state (Liang [1933e]: 311). The "self (*zi* 自)" of "self-government (*zizhi* 自治)" designates the collective life of the population as a society, not a mere conglomerate of individuals, let alone a hierarchical subordination of the many to the few. "Self-government" can therefore only be achieved by first constructing such a "self" (Liang [1933e]: 312–314, [1936c]: 535–536; XCJSL: 131–132). In Liang's view, echoing Sun Yat-sen's famous observation, the "disorganized (*sanman* 散漫)" Chinese people were still very much "a sheet of loose sand (一盤散沙)," a society without a clear organizational structure (Liang [1933e]: 318), or in other words, not a society at all. The ethical relations of Confucianism which had dominated the "fundamental spirit" of the Chinese people for millennia were ultimately relations between individuals, not between members of a form of "collective life" transcending the level of the family (Liang [1933e]: 319).

By contrast, the strength of the West lies precisely in its "organizational capacity" (Liang [1933e]: 320), which Liang believes to have been buttressed by religious beliefs as well as institutions (XCJSL: 135). In China, the emergence of religion had quickly been superseded by the "preciousness" or "early maturity (*zaoshu* 早熟)" and "early enlightenment (*zaoqi* 早啓)" of Chinese culture due to the Confucian celebration of human-centered "reason" (XCJSL: 39–41). As such, he sees the transition to "self-government" in the proper sense of the word as involving a fundamental psychological transformation of the entire Chinese population (Liang [1933e]: 323), all while appealing to China's "fundamental spirit" instead of the individualistic orientation of the West (Liang [1933e]: 325), the combination of "reason" and "organizational capacity" embodying a "concrete fusion of the Chinese and Western spirit (中西精神具體的融合)" (XCJSL: 133). In other words, Liang calls for the construction of "new rituals and customs (*xin lisu* 新禮俗)" (XCJSL: 131) capable of transferring the traditional focus on ethical relations to a properly revolutionary bound between individual and society as a form of "collective life." Before all else, there is a need for "increasing social relations" within China as a society in becoming (XCJSL: 347). While it is thus hardly inaccurate to state that Liang's rural reconstruction movement aimed at a transformation *of* Chinese society, we should bear in mind that it was first and foremost conceived as an attempt to transform China *into* a society by means of the rural reconstruction movement. In his own words, "our rural organization (鄉村組織) actually contains the sprouts for all [social] systems (一切制度的端倪), which simply need to be cultivated, grown, developed, and realized more fully" (XCJSL: 264).

The prevalent characterization of Liang Shuming's view of rural reconstruction as drawing on a conceptual equivalent to the classical sociological distinction between "community" (*Gemeinschaft*) and "society" (*Gesellschaft*) found in the work of Ferdinand Tönnies (1855–1936) (see for example Alitto 1979: 248; Gu 2016: 59, 67–69), misses the point that he clearly does not assume rural China to be a pregiven "community" at all. Rather, China still lacks the sort of "collective life" which he believes to be at the basis of any "society" (both in its "communal" and "social" forms of appearance), even if the latter would merely amount to a type of what Durkheim called "mechanical solidarity" (i.e. the type of solidarity found in "society" as *Gesellschaft*). Such "mechanical solidarity" is institutionalized in externally imposed state apparatuses and legal procedures that lack a proper basis in a determinate "self" capable of active "awakening," self-awareness, and spontaneous collective organization (i.e. the transhistorical *Gemeinschaft* of the Chinese nation). Moreover, Liang's *Theory of Rural Reconstruction* makes it quite clear that rural China cannot function as a "community" without the mediation of what he calls a "great system (大系統)" (XCJSL: 205) or "a big net (一個大的網)" (XCJSL: 328) serving to unite the remnants of the immediacy of "ethical relations" stemming from "reason" into a functional organizational structure, that is to say, without the Institute of Rural Reconstruction as the "central nervous system" of the network of rural subdistrict and village schools it manages through a combination of "teaching and government." As such, Liang envisaged a "system of education *grounded in society* (社會本位的教育系統)" (Liang [1933d], emphasis added). Rather than appealing to the self-sufficient immediacy of "communal" relations then, Liang's detailed proposal for the organization and transformation of the Chinese countryside into an emancipatory "vital force" hinges on the introduction of new structures of mediation, presented as a product of "reason" itself, without which he thinks China cannot arrive at a veritable "socialization" of "ethical relations." In the absence of rural reconstruction as a "system" or "web" of socialization allowing for the emergence of communal life, the rural population would be left to its own devices, delivered over to "blind action" (XCJSL: 210, 212), and remain incapable of reuniting the "formless" and "tangible" roots of Chinese culture in order to save the Chinese nation from its imminent downfall. Liang's philosophy of rural reconstruction thus not only involved a search for social change and "self-salvation," but also, and perhaps before all else, the search for a society and the construction of a self that is up to the task of saving the Chinese nation without relying on the state.

5 Concluding Remarks

While LIANG Shuming's vision of rural reconstruction is rare, if not unique, in modern Confucianist philosophical discourse for its insistence on a non-state centered approach to nation-building, his *Theory of Rural Reconstruction* still testifies to the problem of how to reconcile a particular concept of the nation, as a transhistorical subject supposedly capable of "self-awakening," to the empirical subjects expected to take on the task of restoring China's "fundamental spirit" in the face of their factical "blindness." In other words, in theoretical terms at least, one of the main issues which speaks to the enduring relevance of Liang's philosophy of rural reconstruction in the contemporary Chinese context is that of the problematic relation between the rediscovery of cultural tradition and the possibility of enacting social change under conditions where "we must turn back to seek it in society instead of expecting help from politics," seeing how the Party-State continues to tighten its grip on historical, cultural, and national identity in the present-day People's Republic. In this sense, Liang's notion of rural reconstruction contains unexplored possibilities for rethinking the terms of agreement between society and state within a specific horizon of historical experience and rapid social change. More specifically, the divide between urban and rural areas has hardly vanished from the social landscape of twentieth-first century China (see Rozelle and Hell 2020), let alone from the globe as a whole. As such, whatever its conceptual and historical defects and merits may be, at the very least, Liang's project of rural reform enjoins us to think through the relevance of paying attention to the fate of people such as the rural "migrant workers (*mingong* 民工)"—who currently make up around one third of the Chinese working population, which in turn provides 29% of the global labor force (Ngai 2016: 6)—for engaging in a form of philosophical reflection sensitive to the condition of the modern world.[33]

[33] Liang's vision of rural reform as a precondition for finding, as the subtitle of his *Theory of Rural Reconstruction* reads, "a path forward for the Chinese nation (中國民族之前途)" has continued to inspire intellectuals and activists in contemporary mainland China (see Day 2008, Thøgersen 2009, Ma and Xu 2012, Ou 2017). The late 1990s saw the rise of a veritable "New Rural Reconstruction Movement," even if the "Confucian" inspiration and credentials of the diverse projects seen as belonging to this movement are not always clear-cut (Billioud and Thoraval 2015: 29, footnote 33). This contemporary incarnation of rural reconstruction is aimed at what one of its leading figures, WEN Tiejun 温鉄軍 (b. 1951), famously described as the "three rural problems (*san nong wenti* 三農問題)" (i.e. agriculture, the countryside, and the peasants), which became an important policy issue under the Hu-Wen administration and was explicitly highlighted at the tenth National People's Congress in 2006 (Sit and Wong 2013: 56) in its call for the creation of a "new socialist countryside" (Wu and Tong 2009). While Wen initially traced back his motivations to the figure of James Yen, founding the James Yen Rural Reconstruction Institute in Hebei in 2003 (shut down in 2006 by local authorities, ostensibly over an issue with building permits, see Ou 2017: 45), he later shifted his allegiance to Liang as a source of inspiration (Lu 2010: 235). Although most of the figures associated with the "New Rural Reconstruction Movement" are not dissidents, but rather "have an entangled relation with the state" (Day 2008: 51), it is clear that this movement aims to offer a "powerful critique" (Day 208: 51) of the uneven development between urban and rural areas which has continued under the economic reforms following the end of the Maoist period. WEN Tiejun is not alone in discerning a strong continuity between the pre- and post-Maoist periods, in the sense that an unequal relation between city and countryside inherited from the revolutionary era still characterizes the process of industrialization and economic development in contemporary China (see Day 2008: 53). From this perspective, in the words of Tsui Sit and Tak Hing Wong, "rural collectivization was less an ideological maneuver than an institutional strategy to systematically extract rural surplus at a lower transaction cost," the socialist state effectively engaging in a form of "internal colonialism" (Sit and Wong 2013: 46) or, according to another observer, downright "Apartheid" (Qin [2010]) institutionally buttressed by the "household registration system (*hukou* 戶口)" which binds peasant to their land while at the same time using them as a reserve army of proletarian labor in their capacity as "migrant workers" (see Ngai 2016).

References

LSMQJ *Liang Shuming quanji* 梁漱溟全集 [*The Complete Works of Liang Shuming*, 7 vols.]. Ji'nan: Shandong People Press, 1989–1993.

XCJSL *Xiangxun jianshe lilun* 鄉村建設理論 [*Theory of Rural Reconstruction*; 1937]. Shanghai: Shanghai Renmin Chubanshe, 2011.

Alitto, Guy S. 1976a. Rural Reconstruction During the Nanking Decade: Confucian Collectivism in Shantung. *The China Quarterly* 66: 213–246.

———. 1976b. The Conservative as Sage: Liang Shu-ming. In *The Limits of Change: Essays on Conservative Alternatives in Republican China*, ed. Charlotte Furth. Cambridge, MA: Harvard University Press.

———. 1979. *The Last Confucian: Liang Shu-ming and the Chinese Dilemma of Modernity*. Berkeley: University of California Press.

———. 2015. Liang Shuming: A Lifelong Activist. In *Contemporary Confucianism in Thought and Action*, ed. Guy Alitto. Berlin and Heidelberg: Springer.

Bianco, Lucien. 1971. *Origins of the Chinese Revolution, 1915–1949*. Stanford: Stanford University Press.

Billioud, Sébastien, and Joël Thoraval. 2015. *The Sage and the People: The Confucian Revival in China*. Oxford: Oxford University Press.

Chen, Xianguang 陳憲光. 1999. A Study of Liang Shuming's Movement of Rural Reconstruction and the Chinese Road Toward Modernization 梁漱溟的鄉村建設運動與中國現代化之路的探索. *Journal of Huaqiao University* 華僑大學學報 2: 103–108.

Cui, Xiaohui 崔效輝. 2013. *Liang Shuming's Theory of Rural Reconstruction in the Context of Modernization* 現代化視野中的梁漱溟鄉村建設理論. Hangzhou: Zhejiang Daxue Chubanshe.

Day, Alexander. 2008. The End of the Peasant? New Rural Reconstruction in China. *boundary 2* 35 (2): 49–73.

Dikötter, Frank. 2008. *The Age of Openness: China Before Mao*. Berkeley: University of California Press.

Feng, Youlan 馮友蘭. [1940] 2014. *New Treatise on Practical Affairs* 新事論. Beijing: Beijing Daxue Chubanshe.

Feuerwerker, Albert. 1983. Economic Trends, 1912–1949. In *The Cambridge History of China. Volume 13: Republican China 1912–1949, Part 1*, ed. John K. Fairbank. Cambridge: Cambridge University Press.

Gao, Jie. 2019. *Saving the Nation Through Culture: The Folklore Movement in Republican China*. Vancouver and Toronto: UBC Press.

Gransow, Bettina. 1994. Ein Wegbereiter 'konfuzianischer Modernisierung'. Liang Shuming und die ländliche Aufbaubewegung der dreißiger Jahre. In *Bochumer Jahrbuch Zur Ostasienforschung 18*. München: Iudicium.

Gu, Hongliang 顧紅亮. 2016. *The Confucian Life-World* 儒家生活世界. Shanghai: Shanghai Renmin Chubanshe.

Han, Xiaorong. 2005. *Chinese Discourses on the Peasant, 1900–1949*. Albany: State University of New York Press.

Hauf, Kandice. 1996. The Community Covenant in Sixteenth Century Ji'an Prefecture, Jiangxi. *Late Imperial China* 17 (2): 1–50.

Hayford, Charles W. 1990. *To the People: James Yen and Village China*. New York: Columbia University Press.

IRRR (International Institute of Rural Reconstruction). 2020. Organization website, https://iirr.org/. Last accessed 15 Oct 2020.

Kuhn, Philip A. 1986. The Development of Local Government. In *The Cambridge History of China. Volume 13: Republican China 1912–1949, Part 2*, ed. John K. Fairbank and Albert Feuerwerker. Cambridge: Cambridge University Press.

Lee, Theresa Man Ling. 1998. Local Self-Government in Late Qing: Political Discourse and Moral Reform. *The Review of Politics* 60 (1): 31–53.

Liang, Shuming 梁漱溟. [1921] 1989. *Eastern and Western Cultures and Their Philosophies* 東西文化及其哲學. *LSMQJ* 1: 319–547.

——— 梁漱溟. [1929] 1991. On the Goals of the Henan Academy of Village Governance 河南村治書院旨趣書. *LSMQJ* 4: 905–913.

——— 梁漱溟. [1930a] 1992. Solving the Problem of China 中國問題之解決. *LSMQJ* 5: 206–220.

——— 梁漱溟. [1930b] 1992. The Final Awakening of the Self-Salvation Movement of the Chinese People 中國民族自救運動之最後覺悟. *LSMQJ* 5: 44–118.

——— 梁漱溟. [1932] 1991. Brief Record of Observations from My Journeys in the North 北游所見計略. *LSMQJ* 4: 874–904.

——— 梁漱溟. [1933a] 1992. Engaging in Rural Work in the Spirit of a Buddhist Renunciant 以出家的精神做鄉村工作. *LSMQJ* 5: 425–426.

——— 梁漱溟. [1933b] 1992. Outline for a Theory of Rural Reconstruction 鄉村建設理論提綱. *LSMQJ* 5: 364–372.

——— 梁漱溟. [1933c] 1992. Plan for Reviving the Nation through Rural Reconstruction 由鄉村建設以復興民族案. *LSMQJ* 5: 419–420.

——— 梁漱溟. [1933d] 1992. Plan for a System of Education Grounded in Society 社會本位的教育系統草案. *LSMQJ* 5: 393–409.

——— 梁漱溟. [1933e] 1992. The Problem of Local Self-Government in China 中國之地方自治問題. *LSMQJ* 5: 309–346.

——— 梁漱溟. [1933f] 1992. What Is Rural Reconstruction? 鄉村建設是什麼? *LSMQJ* 5: 373–377.

——— 梁漱溟. [1934a] 1992. Essentials of Spiritual Cultivation 精神陶煉要旨. *LSMQJ* 5: 492–519.

——— 梁漱溟. [1934b] 1992. How Can Mass Education Save China? 民衆教育何以能救中國? *LSMQJ* 5: 479–487.

——— 梁漱溟. 1935. *Essentials of Village and Rural Subdistrict Schools* 村學鄉學須知. Zouping: Shandong Xiangcun Jiaoyu Yuanjiuyuan (reprinted in *LSMQJ* 5: 448–465).

——— 梁漱溟. [1936a] 1989. *The Idea of Rural Reconstruction* 鄉村建設大意. *LSMQJ* 1: 599–720.

——— 梁漱溟. [1936b] 1989. The Method of Self-Cultivation for Rural Workers 鄉村工作人員修養法. *LSMQJ* 5: 804–810.

——— 梁漱溟. [1936c] 1989. Something That Has Been on My Mind 我的一段心事. *LSMQJ* 5: 532–540.

——— 梁漱溟. [1937] 1989. Our Work in Shandong Province 我們在山東的工作. *LSMQJ* 5: 1010–1022.

——— 梁漱溟. [1941] 1990. *Response to Critiques of Rural Reconstruction* 答鄉村建設批判. *LSMQJ* 2: 587–658.

——— 梁漱溟. [1949] 1990. *The Fundamentals of Chinese Culture* 中國文化要義. *LSMQJ* 3: 1–316.

——— 梁漱溟. [1950–1951] 1990. *The Path to the Establishment of the Chinese Nation* 中國建國之路. *LSMQJ* 3: 317–414.

——— 梁漱溟. [1977] 1992. Memories and Reflections on My Involvement in the Rural [Reconstruction] Movement 我致力於鄉村運動的回憶和反省. *LSMQJ* 7: 424–428.

Liang, Shuming, and Guy S. Alitto. 2013. *Has Man a Future? Dialogues with the Last Confucian*. Berlin and Heidelberg: Springer.

Lin, Alfred H.Y. 1990. Confucianism in Action: A Study of Liang Shuming's Theory and Practice of Rural Reconstruction in the 1930s. *Journal of Oriental Studies* 28 (1): 21–43.

Lu, Xinyu. 2010. Rural Reconstruction, the Nation-State and China's Modernity Problem: Reflections on Liang Shuming's Rural Reconstruction Theory and Its Practice. In *Cultural and Social Transformations in Reform Era China*, ed. Cao Tianyu, Zhong Xueping, and Kebin Liao. Brill: Leiden and Boston.

Lynch, Catherine. 2010. The Country, the City, and Visions of Modernity in 1930s China. *Rural History* 21 (2): 151–163.

———. 2011. Radical Visions of Time in Modern China: The Utopianism of Mao Zedong and Liang Shuming. In *Radicalism, Revolution, and Reform in Modern China: Essays in Honor of Maurice Meisner*, ed. Catherine Lynch, Robert B. Marks, and Paul G. Pickowicz. Lanham: Lexington Books.

———. 2018. *Liang Shuming and the Populist Alternative in China*. Leiden and Boston: Brill.

Ma, Hua, and Yong Xu. 2012. Reorganizing Rural China from the Bottom: A Discussion of Recent Experiments with Rural Reconstruction. In *Organizing Rural China, Rural China Organizing*, ed. Ane Bislev and Stig Thøgersen. Lanham: Lexington Books.

Merkel-Hess, Kate. 2016. *The Rural Modern: Reconstructing the Self and State in Republican China*. Chicago: The University of Chicago Press.

Meynard, Thierry. 2010. *The Religious Philosophy of Liang Shuming: The Hidden Buddhist*. Leiden and Boston: Brill.

Mou, Zongsan 牟宗三. [1934] 2003. Where Is the Path to the Revival of the Countryside? 復興農村的出路何在? In *Early Essays 2* 早期文集—下, *The Complete Works of Mou Zongsan* 牟宗三先生全集. Taibei: Lianjing.

Murthy, Viren. 2008. The Politics of *Fengjian* in Late Qing and Early Republican China. In *Beyond the May Fourth Paradigm: In Search of Chinese Modernity*, ed. Kai-wing Chow, Tze-ki Hon, Hung-yok Ip, and Don C. Price. Lanham: Lexington Books.

Ngai, Pun. 2016. *Migrant Labor in China*. Cambridge: Polity Press.

Ou, Ning. 2017. Social Change and Rediscovering Rural Reconstruction in China. In *New Worlds from Below: Informal Life Politics and Grassroots Action in Twenty-First-Century Northeast Asia*, ed. Tessa Morris-Suzuki and Eun Jeong Soh. Canberra: ANU Press.

Pan, Jiaen, Chia-Ling Luo, and Tiejun Wen. 2017. Three 'Centuries': The Context and Development of Rural Construction in China. *Inter-Asia Cultural Studies* 18 (1): 120–130.

Rozelle, Scott, and Nathalie Hell. 2020. *Invisible China: How the Urban-Rural Divide Threatens China's Rise*. Chicago: The University of Chicago Press.

Qin, Hui. [2010] 2019. *Looking at China from South Africa*. Trans. David Ownby. https://www.readingthechinadream.com/qin-hui-looking-at-china-from-south-africa.html#. Last accessed 15 Oct 2020.

Schneider, Laurence A. 1971. *Ku Chieh-Kang and China's New History: Nationalism and the Quest for Alternative Traditions*. Berkeley: University of California Press.

Sit, Tsui, and Tak Hing Wong. 2013. Rural China: From Modernization to Reconstruction. *Asian Studies: Journal of Critical Perspectives on Asia* 49 (1): 43–68.

Thøgersen, Stig. 1995. Liang Shuming and the Danish Model. In *Cultural Encounters: China, Japan, and the West*, ed. Søren Clausen, Roy Starrs, and Anne Wedell-Wedellsborg. Aarhus: Aarhus University Press.

———. 2002. *A County of Culture: Twentieth-Century China Seen from the Village Schools of Zouping, Shandong*. Ann Arbor: The University of Michigan Press.

———. 2009. Revisiting a Dramatic Triangle: The State, Villagers, and Social Activists in Chinese Rural Reconstruction Projects. *Journal of Current Chinese Affairs* 38 (4): 9–33.

Übelhör, Monika. 1989. The Community Compact (*Hsiang-yüeh*) of the Sung and Its Educational Significance. In *Neo-Confucian Education: The Formative Stage*, ed. Wm. Theodore de Bary and John W. Chaffee. Berkeley: University of California Press.

Van den Stock, Ady. 2016. *The Horizon of Modernity: Subjectivity and Social Structure in New Confucian Philosophy*. Leiden and Boston: Brill.

———. 2020a. The 'Learning of Life': On Some Motifs in Mou Zongsan's *Autobiography at Fifty*. *Asian Studies* 8 (3): 35–61.

———. 2020b. Liang Shuming's *China: The Country of Reason*: Revolution, Religion, and Ethnicity in the Reinvention of the Confucian Tradition. *International Communication of Chinese Culture* 7 (4): 603–620.

van Slyke, Lyman P. 1959. Liang Sou-ming and the Rural Reconstruction Movement. *The Journal of Asian Studies* 18 (4): 457–474.

Wu, Fei 吳飛. 2005. Liang Shuming's 'New Rituals and Customs': A Reading of Liang Shuming's *Theory of Rural Reconstruction* 梁漱溟的'新禮俗'—讀梁漱溟的《鄉村建設理論》. *Sociological Research* 社會學研究 5: 228–233.

Wu, Shugang, and Binchang Tong. 2009. Liang Shuming's Rural Reconstruction Experiment and Its Relevance for Building the New Socialist Countryside. *Contemporary Chinese Thought* 40 (3): 39–51.

Yan, Binggang 顏炳罡. 2020. The Origin of 'Rural Confucianism' and the Reconstruction of Rural Civilization 鄉村儒學'的由來與鄉村文明重建. *Journal of Shenzhen University* 深圳大學學報 37(1): 5–13.

Yao, Yusheng. 2002. Rediscovering Tao Xingzhi as an Educational and Social Revolutionary. *Twentieth-Century China* 27 (2): 79–120.

Zanasi, Margherita. 2004. Far from the Treaty Ports: Fang Xianting and the Idea of Rural Modernity in 1930s China. *Modern China* 30 (1): 113–146.

Zhao, Fasheng 趙法生. 2016. Report on the Conference 'Rural Confucianism and Rural Civilization' '鄉村儒學與鄉土文明'學術研討會綜述. *Trends in Philosophy* 哲學動態 4: 107–108.

Zheng, Dahua 鄭大華. 2000. *The Rural Reconstruction Movement during the Republican Era* 民國鄉村建設運動. Beijing: Zhongguo Shehuikexue Wenxian Chubanshe.

Zhu, Hanguo 朱漢國. 1996. *A Study of Liang Shuming's Rural Reconstruction* 梁漱溟鄉村建設研究. Taiyuan: Shanxi Jiaoyu Chubanshe.

Chapter 9
Liang the Moral and Social Philosopher

Yanming An

1 Introduction

Liang Shuming's *The Fundamentals of Chinese Culture* (*Zhongguo wenhua yaoyi* 中國文化要義; henceforth ZGWH) appeared in October 1949, when the People's Republic of China was just established. This is his fourth major work after *Eastern and Western Cultures and Their Philosophies* (*Dongxi wenhua jiqi zhexue* 東西文化及其哲學; henceforth DXWH) (1921), *The Final Awakening of the Chinese People's Self-Salvation Movement* (*Zhongguo minzu zijiu yundong zhi zuihou juewu* 中國民族自救運動之最後覺悟) (1931), and *Theory of Rural Reconstruction* (*Xiangcun jianshe lilun* 鄉村建設理論) (1936). Its preparation and writing underwent 9 years due to military and political interruptions, such as the Japanese invasion and Liang's political activities aimed at domestic peace after World War II.

The third work aforementioned is also entitled *The Future of the Chinese Nation* (*Zhongguo minzu zhi qiantu* 中國民族之前途). It consists of two sections, dealing respectively with the problems in China and their solution. Liang claims that due to the development of worldwide communication and exchange since the last century, Western culture expanded its power on China, resulting in a series of social problems. "In order to know the problems in China, we need to comprehend the change in Chinese society in the last hundred years, as well as the domestic and international causes leading to the change. Meanwhile, a correct grip on the essence of old Chinese society before the change conditions any clear understanding of the change" (ZGWH: 3–4). He begins to examine the old China in *The Future of the Chinese*

Y. An (✉)
Clemson University, Clemson, SC, USA
e-mail: yanming@clemson.edu

T. Meynard, P. Major (eds.), *Dao Companion to Liang Shuming's Philosophy*, Dao Companions to Chinese Philosophy 17,
https://doi.org/10.1007/978-3-031-18002-6_9

Nation and furthers this effort in width and depth in ZGWH. Liang reminds his readers that what is discussed in ZGWH is not modern China, but the old, traditional, and pre-modern one.

It was Liang's plan to work on the solution of Chinese problems after ZGWH. "'Knowing old China and constructing new China,' these are the two slogans of mine. Having completed this book [ZGWH], I will write another one, *A Study on the Issue of Modern Chinese Politics* [*Xiandai Zhongguo zhengzhi wenti yanjiu* 現代中國政治問題研究]." As for Liang, the miserable reality of China in the past decades resulted mainly from political disorder, therefore "the construction of new China must start with a finding of new method in politics" (ZGWH: 7). However, as witnessed by history, after October 1949, the political exploration and discovery have been literally monopolized by the Communist Party and its theorists, including Mao himself. They became a forbidden zone in which Liang and his intellectual friends were not allowed to step. Consequently, *A Study on the Issue of Modern Chinese Politics* was never completed, although some related manuscripts were published after Liang's passing away.

2 Intellect and Reason

Liang was a self-educated scholar of Buddhism, as well as a serious researcher of Confucian doctrines. Meanwhile, he was an eager student of Western scholarship, tending to seek for the solution of Chinese problems in reference to Western methods. The combination of these two sides characterizes his major works, including ZGWH, as a comparative study between China and the West. As Guy Alitto remarks, in this book "Liang systematically compared Chinese and Western social development," and as such it "might be dubbed 'Chinese and Western Cultures and Their Societies'" (Alitto 1986: 177–178).

2.1 The Premature Birth of Chinese Culture

In his visit to Yan'an in 1938, Liang argued with Mao that "the old Chinese society had its special structure. It was not the same as that in the medieval and modern European societies. The Chinese revolution was introduced from outside, not naturally originating from inside. Its particularity [*teshuxing* 特殊性] came from the special structure of old society" (WNLD: 205). Later he concretized this "particularity" with 14 features and further concluded that "when linking them together, we find that all of them originate from a single general trait [*zong tezheng* 總特徵]; herein we get home. Chinese culture appears completely comprehensible; *its fundamentals become understandable*" (ZGWH: 13). Liang defines this "general trait" as "the premature enlightenment of reason [*lixing zaoqi* 理性早啟] and premature birth of culture [*wenhua zaoshu* 文化早熟]" (ZGWH: 334). Put differently, these two are the final account for the existence of all the 14 features.[1]

Liang views the idea of "the premature birth of Chinese culture," which first appeared in DXWH, as one of his major findings. In ZGWH he writes that, despite the big gap of time between the two works, his "opinion about it is almost the same; what changes is just certain expressions" (ZGWH: 300). However, another statement from the same work may cause people to doubt the truthfulness of this self-estimation. It reads that "twenty-seven years ago [when writing DXWH] I did not know [the importance of] reason [*lixing* 理性] yet" (ZGWH: 301). In my opinion, the introduction of "reason" into his system and the replacement of "intuition" with "reason" is not a little change in "expression," but a crucial alteration in Liang's position on Chinese culture.

Since the time of writing his *Theory of Rural Reconstruction*, Liang often defined "the premature birth of culture" by referring to "the premature enlightenment of reason." He writes, "the premature enlightenment of reason and the premature birth of culture may be viewed as synonyms" (ZGWH: 299); "more accurately, the 'premature birth of culture' means that human reason developed too early" (XCJS: 44). In Liang's view, there are three kinds of problem in human life. The first refers to the basic needs for food, clothing, shelter, and procreation. The second refers to the needs of emotional life, including the maintenance of harmonious relationships in family and society and the acquisition of inner contentment even in hardship. The third refers to the needs of attaining the transcendent realm and understanding the ultimate meaning of life. He summarizes the first two problems and the two attitudes toward their solutions as saying that,

> The first kind of problem is about humans' stance toward things; the first attitude is to go straight toward things outside. It may be roughly described as an action starting from the body. The second kind of problem is about humans' stance toward each other; the second attitude is to focus on what is inside. It may be roughly described as an action starting from the heart (reason). (ZGWH: 300)

> Western culture encourages people to start from the body and then move steadily to the heart. Chinese culture encourages people to start from the heart and move to the fields outside. The former is a gradual advancement in a proper order [*xunxu jianjin* 循序漸進], whereas the latter is "premature." This is the exact meaning of the "prematurity of culture." (ZGWH: 298)

Here Liang treats "heart" and "reason" as interchangeable and defines "the prematurity of culture" as a state in which people jump over the phase of the body, acting directly from their heart/reason. This leads to two questions: what is "reason" in Liang, and what inspires Liang's shift from intuition to reason?

---

[1] To know more about Liang's description of the "fourteen features," readers may refer to the Chap. 5 of this volume.

2.2 *Reason and Spirit (*Lingxing *靈性)*

In DXWH, Liang underscored the distinction between Western and Chinese cultures with the two concepts of "intellect" (*lizhi* 理智) and "intuition" (*zhijue* 直覺). The Western source that directly inspired his articulation was Henri Bergson. In ZGWH, however, Liang conceived of a new model concerning human mind, as well as a new look on the relationship between Western and Chinese cultures. Now Bertrand Russell played the major role as inspirer for his new vision.

From October 1920 to July 1921, Russell visited China, giving lectures across the country. In 1920, the Chinese translation of his *Principles of Social Reconstruction*, rendered by YU Jiaju 余家菊 (1898–1976), was published. Liang studied carefully both the Chinese and English versions.

According to Russell, human activities may be derived from three sources, namely instinct, mind, and spirit. For him, "the life of instinct includes all that man shares with the lower animals, all that is concerned with self-preservation and reproduction and the desires and impulses derivative from these." Meanwhile, "the life of the mind is the life of pursuit of knowledge, from mere childish curiosity up to the greatest efforts of thought." It "centers round impersonal thought," meaning that "it concerns itself with objects on their own account, and not merely on account of their bearing upon our instinctive life." Finally, "the life of spirit centers round impersonal feeling." Thanks to this feeling, we are able "to feel the same interest in the joys and sorrows of others as in our own, to love and hate independently of all relation to ourselves, to care about the destiny of man and the development of the universe without a thought that we are personally involved." "All art belongs to the life of spirit," and all "religion starts from the spirit and endeavors to dominate and inform the life of instinct" (Russell 1971: 142–144).

Russell argues that "instinct, mind, and spirit are all essential to a full life; each has its own excellence and its own corruption." Different kinds of people may particularly and one-sidedly develop one of them. "Among uncivilized men instinct is supreme, and mind and spirit hardly exist. Among educated men… mind is developed, as a rule, at the expense of both instinct and spirit." In contrast, "among ascetics and most of those who would be called saints, the life of spirit has been developed at the expense of instinct and mind, producing an outlook which is impossible to those who have a healthy animal life and to those who have a love of active thought" (Russell 1971: 144).

Russell believes that "it is not in any of these one-sided developments that we can find wisdom or a philosophy which will bring new life to the civilized world" (Russell 1971: 145). He describes an ideal relationship among the three as saying that "it is instinct that gives force, mind that gives the means of directing force to desired ends, and spirit that suggests impersonal uses for force of a kind that thought cannot discredit by criticism. This is an outline of the parts that instinct, mind, and spirit would play in a harmonious life" (Russell 1971: 146).

In ZGWH, Liang reports his encounter with Russel's "spirt" and explains its relationship with his "reason."

> Twenty-seven years ago, I did not have a clear knowledge of "reason" yet. I favored Kropotkin's doctrine of morality coming from instinct, but disagreed with Russell's division of instinct, mind [*lizhi* 理智; literally "intellect"] and spirit [*lingxing* 靈性]. After realizing the necessity of differentiating "reason" from "intellect" later, I concluded that Russell's division was an irrefutable truth. Russell's "spirit" was just like what I meant by "reason." (ZGWH: 353)

In addition, Liang borrows Russell's description of "spirit" to define his own "reason." He holds that "reason" may have difficulty in making a uniform decision applicable to all situations. However, it always "centers around impersonal feeling." In a footnote on the same page, he further clarifies that "'impersonal feeling' was mentioned by Russell in his *Principles of Social Reconstruction*. My usage here means almost the same as his" (ZGWH: 148).

On this issue, Gu Hongliang 顧紅亮, a contemporary Chinese scholar, makes a comment that,

> The Chinese translator Yu Jiaju rendered 'spirit' as '*lingxing*' [靈性] and 'impersonal feeling' as '*wusi de ganqing*' [無私的感情]. Liang approved of his translation of 'impersonal feeling," but felt discontented with that of "*lingxing*," thinking that "it may be inappropriate." In his later writing, he replaced "*lingxing*" with "*lixing*" 理性 [reason] and explained "*lixing*" also as "impersonal feeling" or "feeling with no personal involvement" [*wu suo si de ganqing* 無所私的感情]. (Gu 2015: 45)

It should be added that "reason" in Liang, as will be shown in this chapter later, also means an interpersonal feeling, or "feeling-reason" (*qingli* 情理). It promotes one keeping a warm relationship with people in his/her family and community, and even caring about all humans in the world.

Under Russell's guidance, Liang develops a new mode concerning the relations among instinct, intellect ("mind" in Russell), and reason ("spirit" in Russell). Here "instinct" is defined as an innate ability that is passed to human individuals through biological inheritance. It can be neither eliminated from one's life nor acquired through conscious efforts. Since the life of animals particularly depends on instinct, their instinct should be viewed as its typical form. In contrast, both intellect and reason characterize human life. They are "the two aspects of the operation of mind."

> The aspect of knowing is "intellect," while the aspect of feeling is "reason." In actuality, these two are connected closely and inseparably. For example, in mathematics, the mind that does the calculation is the intellect, while the mind that seeks accuracy is the reason. (ZGWH: 147)

Differing from DXWH, this statement abandons the concept of intuition, as well as its position as the indicator of Chinese culture. Moreover, it forges a new term, "operation of mind," to designate an integral unity of intellect and reason. These two components of the same unity are not antagonistic to each other, but complementary for the full practice of human mind.

Nevertheless, despite his affirmation of their "integral unity," Liang does not forget mentioning the different roles which intellect and reason respectively play in Chinese and Western cultures.

> The operation of mind is unique to humans. It is just from here that human cultures originated. The great cultures, such as the ancient Chinese or the modern Western, both developed it to a remarkable level. However, they might lay special emphasis on different aspects. The Westerner is strong in intellect, but weak in reason; whereas the Chinese is strong in reason, but weak in intellect." (ZGWH: 149)

As will be shown below, Liang's idea about "reason," his coinage of "operation of mind," and his stress on the different states of intellect and reason in the two cultures all affect his understanding of traditional Chinese society.

3 Religion and Morality

According to Liang, the Western path was opened through Christianity, whereas the Chinese one started with "the Ethical Teaching of the Duke of Zhou and Confucius" (*zhoukong jiaohua* 周孔教化; henceforth the Ethical Teaching). The issue of religion was the real watershed separating Chinese culture from the Western one (ZGWH: 112–113). To know the nature of the Chinese path, according to Liang, we need to analyze the Ethical Teaching and its distinction from Christianity.[2]

3.1 *The Ethical Teaching as Morality*

Liang writes that "Human cultures all started with religion and all centered round religion. The order and politics of human society originated from religion; human thought, knowledge, and various scholarships all came with religion" (ZGWH: 113). This is a universal rule to which Chinese culture is not an exception. Plenty of evidence proves that religious activities, such as totem worship, commonwealth worship, and gods worship had existed in China since remote antiquity. However, after the rise of the Ethical Teaching the significance of these primitive religions gradually diminished.

The Duke of Zhou 周公 and Confucius are the two greatest names for the formation of the Ethical Teaching. Concretely, "the Duke of Zhou represented the contributors before him, while Confucius represented the contributors after him." The former created political order, as well as the system of ritual and music. The latter studied the order and system, derived from them a philosophical doctrine, and taught people about his findings. "The invention and promotion of philosophical doctrine is more fundamental; it has enlightened people until today. Therefore, Confucius is more influential than the Duke of Zhou in over two thousand years" (ZGWH: 121).

[2] To know more about Liang's analysis of Christianity, readers may refer to Chap. 6 in this volume.

Liang claims that Confucius never seriously discussed the matters of life and death, ghosts, gods, etc., although these are the typical topics with which all religions must deal. "This is sufficient evidence that the Confucian doctrine is not a religion." In other words, "some necessary elements of religion are absent in Confucius. Meanwhile, the Confucian doctrine contains a spiritual tendency foreign to any religion" (ZGWH: 122). Moreover, despite the fact that Confucius did not bluntly refute or criticize religion, he stood actually as its most formidable challenger. It is because he always encouraged people to examine their own heart, to ponder over everything with their own reason, and to develop their ability of differentiating the right from the wrong. Liang further argues:

> May I ask what this is? This is morality, not religion. Morality is about reason; it exists in people's self-consciousness and self-discipline. In contrast, religion is about faith; it depends on believers' compliance with religious commandments. Since the time of Confucius, the Chinese nation, because of his influence, *has taken the path of replacing religion with morality*. (ZGWH: 126)

The Ethical Teaching functions as "the unifier of Chinese culture" or "the center of [Chinese] spirit." It was trusted and embraced by Chinese people and affected other nations around China (ZGWH: 120). On the other hand, however, it signified the premature birth of culture or the premature enlightenment of reason. It is Liang's account that:

> In the history of human culture, the emergence of morality was much later than that of religion. Humans are animals with reason, but the development of their reason must undergo a process with certain phases [*jianci yi kaifa* 漸次以開發]. In the life of an individual person, [his reason] can only become mature along with his growth in age and body. In the life of a society, its thorough development must be founded upon the great progress in social economy and culture. Nevertheless, it is truly surprising that ancient China took one step earlier, *accomplishing this extremely difficult task* [of jumping over the phase of religion and reaching that of morality directly]. (ZGWH: 126)

Now we need question further how religion was replaced by morality in China, or what made this replacement possible?

3.2 *The Replacement of Religion with Morality*

To account for the replacement of religion with morality in China, Liang introduces the Confucian concept of "ritual" (*li* 禮) into his discussion. "What replaced religion in China is simply 'the Ritual of the Duke of Zhou and Confucius' [*zhoukong zhi li* 周孔之禮]." It accomplished the replacement through two social programs, namely "arranging the ethical standings to organize society" [*anpai lunli mingfen yi zuzhi shehui* 安排倫理名分以組織社會] and "setting [a system of] ritual-music and respect-reverence to foster reason [*shewei liyue yirang yi hanyang lixing* 設爲禮樂揖讓以涵養理性]" (ZGWH: 129).

As stated before, both Russell and Liang define "spirit" or "reason" with the same phrase of "impersonal feeling." However, Russell's "spirit" is mainly a psychological-philosophical concept which accounts for the appearance and acceptance of religion in human society. In contrast, Liang's "reason" is both a psychological-philosophical concept and a sociological-anthropological one. Liang follows Russell, employing it in the former sense to highlight the psychological source for the prevalence of "the ritual of the Duke of Zhou and Confucius" in China. Meanwhile, he applies it in the latter sense, defining it as a principle of social organization, and even characterizing it as a particular trait of Chinese culture. We need keep these two uses in mind when thinking about Liang's "reason" and its connection to "ritual." It is his analysis that,

> Confucius deeply loved reason and deeply trusted reason. He inspired people to manifest their own reason; he wanted to materialize "a society in which people totally rationalized their lives." His way [to reach this goal] lied in the ritual-music system. It is true that human reason starts with thinking and language. However, the inspiration and manifestation of reason can hardly be realized simply through thinking and language alone. Abstract logic is much less efficient than concrete ritual and music. *The concrete ritual and music directly affect people's body, affect their blood and breath. Along with the performance and practice of ritual-music, people's psychological state* [*xinli qingzhi* 心理情致] *spontaneously changes without their awareness. Consequently, reason naturally arises in their lives.* (ZGWH: 129)

Fostering reason in people is the first contribution which "ritual" makes for the replacement of religion with morality. It aims to create an atmosphere of "clearness, brilliance, peace, and harmony" (*qing, ming, an, he* 清明安和) in which people naturally and gradually attain a psychic state of tranquility, a warm feeling toward other people and themselves. In fact, the same "clearness, brilliance, peace, and harmony" are also applied by Liang on many occasions to characterize the psychological state in which "reason" prevails. This identical usage underlies a close connection between the system of ritual-music and reason (ZGWH: 130, 154).

Reason manifests itself in two ways. One is "a mind tending to go upward" (*xiangshang zhi xin* 向上之心). It directs people to differentiate the right from the wrong, to feel ashamed of being lazy and negligent in personal life, and to pursue fairness and justice in society (ZGWH: 156). Another is "a feeling of caring for others" (*xiangyu zhi qing* 相與之情). People with this feeling extend the love coming from their family life to people out of their family, to animal, grass, and rock, and therefore have the chance to enjoy supreme harmony in their community and in the universe (ZGWH: 159). Liang proudly claims, "I often said that if the Chinese have not lived in vain in the past thousands of years, and if the Chinese have made any contribution at all, then it is that they first understood why humankind is human" (ZGWH: 153). In other words, it is a great accomplishment of the Chinese culture that its sages discovered reason in a rather early period, and that the Chinese followed the sages' direction to practice reason in their daily life.

The second contribution of "ritual" to the replacement of religion with morality lies in its ability to organize society by arranging ethical standings among people. "Ritual" in this context is defined by Liang as "ritual-custom" (*lisu* 禮俗). It is his opinion about "ritual-custom" and its relation to law and morality that,

> *The ritual-custom presents people with an ideal goal. Because of its performance, people are encouraged to improve themselves for its attainment.* Law presents people with solid facts. A state enforces its people to act as the law requires. … Law does not punish people with moral reason; what punishes people with moral reason is outside the category of law. In contrast, the ritual-custom just sets expectations for people with moral standard. When morality becomes popularized, it develops into the ritual-custom. (ZGWH: 141–142)

What primarily prevailed in traditional China is not law and its application, but the ritual-custom. It set a moral criterion by which people regulated their behaviors in order to be viewed as "good" members of a community. It ensured that each individual's words and deeds tallied to their ethical standings (*mingfen* 名分), making a prince kind and a subject loyal, and a father caring and a son filial, etc.

The institutionalization of the ritual-custom system mainly resulted from Confucius' endeavor. "First, he enlightened people to develop their reason, encouraging them to make decisions in terms of their own 'feeling-reason.' This meant a rejection of old customs and ideas which had been thought as great dogmas with undeniable and unquestionable truthfulness." "Secondly, he taught people to practice sincerely filiality and brotherly fraternity [*xiaoti* 孝悌] and cultivate a passionate affection among family members [*jiaren fuzi* 家人父子]. He advised people to extend this family affection from the near to the far, and finally build up a societal relationship with warm familial affection and friendship [*qingyi* 情誼]" (ZGWH: 138).

Liang explains Confucius' first contribution with following examples. The first refers to a contrast of social institutions between India and China. According to Liang, there exists in India a caste system, even a social group of "untouchable" people. But this social reality, as well as its philosophical support, is absolutely incomprehensible, even unthinkable to the Chinese mind. Religion in India has been extremely flourishing, whereas in China it is not really popular. "Due to the impact of religion, there are a great number of obstinate and irrational ideas prevailing in India. On the contrary, thanks to the rise of reason, the Chinese mind is open and rational" (ZGWH: 136).

Liang's second example refers to a difference between Japan and China. A Japanese Samurai is loyal to his master for the sake of loyalty, without thinking about the master's attitude toward him. In contrast, a Chinese gentleman serves for his ruler in accordance with what the ruler does to him. As Mencius said, "If a prince treats his subjects as his hands and feet, they will treat him as their belly and heart. If he treats them as his horses and hounds, they will treat him as a mere fellow countryman. If he treats him as mud and weeds, they will treat him as an enemy" (Lau 2003: IV. B3). This is a loyalty originating from "feeling-reason" and from a clear recognition of the responsibilities which the two sides have to bear. (ZGWH: 137).

The third example is even more dramatic. Despite the "hierarchy between the elders and the youths" (*zhangyou youxu* 長幼有序) which the Chinese people have sincerely cherished, they still value a stance expressed by the idiom that "old age doesn't [necessarily] make people more reasonable" (*renzhang li buchang* 人長理

不長). The wide acceptance of the idiom and the idea it conveys show the profundity of reason's influence in Chinese folk society. (ZGWH: 137).

Confucius' second contribution is about familial affection and its extension. It profoundly impacted, among other things, Chinese economic life. The primogeniture that had been enforced by law and supported by custom in Japan and Europe was basically absent in Chinese society. When parents died, their property was often equally distributed among their sons. "It is not a small matter; it doesn't come out occasionally. *This is an effort to melt away the unnaturalness of the feudal order with the naturalness of human feeling-reason*" (ZGWH: 139). With the operation of "equal distribution," the love and care of parents are transmitted to all of their sons. It supplies each of them not only with the means for livelihood, but also with a warm reminder that they are all parts of the same family body.

The system of "ritual-custom" is closely connected with that of "ritual-music." In brief, "ritual-music" creates a favorable social atmosphere in which people actively cultivate and naturally develop their "reason," while "ritual-custom" provides people with an ethical standard based on "feeling-reason" by which people make their moral judgements. It should be noted that, according to Liang, they both center around the same "reason." Ultimately it is the full development of "reason" that ensures the Ethical Teaching to function as a quasi-religion, and to annihilate the necessity of religion for the majority of Chinese people.

How could reason constantly sustain its vitality in Chinese society? Put differently, how could the Chinese people tend to follow the guidance of reason for several thousand years? Liang answers,

> It is because there existed in Chinese society a [physical] representative of reason—the scholar [*shiren* 士人]. Old Chinese society consisted of four ranks: scholar, peasant, artisan, and merchant [*shi, nong, gong, shang* 士農工商]. The scholars were the leader of all the other three. They played an extremely important role in the society, although they themselves did not undertake any physical work. This is because they represented reason, managed Ethical Teaching, and maintained social order and stability. (XCJS: 48)

In actuality, the scholars may be viewed as "personalized reason," or "reason's personalization." They are the pilar of old Chinese social structure and the guardian for the prevalence of reason in China.

4 The Features of Chinese Society

Liang claims that "the social structure of a certain time and place is the backbone of entire culture in that time and place" (ZGWH: 57). The Chinese social structure since the Qin-Han period (third century BCE–third Century CE) was characterized by Liang as the "ethic-based" and "profession-differentiated." A comparison with Western society may shed a light on their meanings.

4.1 The Ethic-Based Society

According to Liang, in medieval Europe, people lived a "corporate life" (*jituan shenghuo* 集團生活) in Christian organizations. Because of religious asceticism and restriction, society left little room for individual development. This eventually induced a strong reaction of individualism and liberalism which characterized modern Western history since the Renaissance and Reformation. Nevertheless, especially from the time of World War I more and more people in the West realized the negative consequence of the excessive advocacy of individual interest and began to return to the idea of "corporate life." "From the middle ages to the modern times, from the modern to the contemporary, Westerners perpetually oscillated between the corporate and individual life" (ZGWH: 58). In contrast, the Chinese social structure features differently,

> As for the relationship between society and individual, [a doctrine] which puts its emphasis on the individual is called "individual-based." As for the same relationship, [a doctrine] which puts its emphasis on the society is called "society-based." It is true that Chinese ethics just focuses on the mutual relationship between this and that individual and neglects that between society and individual. This is an unavoidable defect, coming from the absence of "corporate life." However, it developed a principle of mutual respect [among individuals]. This is a great contribution. It is that *no emphasis on any side is fixed. It may change in accordance with [the change within a] relationship. The emphasis is actually placed on the relationship itself.*[3] What is called the ethic-based is just the relationship-based." (ZGWH: 110)

The Chinese word for "ethics" is composed of two characters, *lun* 倫 and *li* 理. The word itself was created as a neologism in Japan and borrowed back to China at the end of the nineteenth century. The first character originally denoted social order or hierarchy among the members of a kinship. Later, its application extended to human relationships in general. The second designates cause or principle regulating movements in human society and in Nature. Together, the word *lunli* 倫理 signifies a theory or doctrine concerning cause or principle in human relationships. Liang holds that the relationship among family members, such as that of parents and children are naturally formed and the most fundamental. Hence ethics primarily emphasizes the importance of family. After growing up, a person gets involved in various social relationships, such as husband and wife in family, teacher and student at school, master and apprentice in business, and prince and subject in politics. "Along with the unfolding of his life, one continuously develops various kinds of connections with people near and far, familiar and strange. These are all relationships, and all relate to ethics. Ethics starts with family but does not end with it" (ZGWH: 95).

---

[3] Liang's principle may be derived from Mencius' argument mentioned before (Lau: IV B3). It insists that my attitude toward you depends on yours toward me. I am loyal to you under the condition that you have played your role as a good master to me. There is no such thing as "fixed loyalty." Our attitude toward each other, as well as the relationship between us is always changeable. What needs to be emphasized is not the positions which we occupied or the names with which we are entitled, but the attitude and changeable relationship.

Liang argues that ethical relationships simply mean "relationships of affection and friendship [*qingyi guanxi* 情誼關係]; they are also relationships of duty [*yiwu guanxi* 義務關係] between two sides." (ZGWH: 95) For instance, a father needs to be kind and a son filial; an elder brother needs to be friendly and a younger brother submissive. In the same vein, the husband and wife, the mutual friends all need to fulfill their duty to each other. Furthermore, there exists in China a general tendency of extending family relationships to the whole society, which is reflected in many popular names. For example, an apprentice calls his master "master-father" (*shifu* 師父), people call their officials "parents-official" (*fumuguan* 父母官), and an emperor calls his people "children-people" (*zimin* 子民), etc. Liang summarizes, "This ensures that *everyone in the society shoulders relevant duties to various people with whom he has ethical relationships*. Meanwhile, *the people who stay with him in certain ethical relationships also shoulder relevant duties to him. As a result, all the people in the society are unintentionally linked together, constructing a formless social network*" (ZGWH: 95).

Liang characterizes the economy in the ethic-based society with three points. The first is "the rightness of common-possessed wealth" (*gongcai zhi yi* 共財之義). In an ethic-based society, the members of a family function as various parts of the same body. When parents are still alive, the wealth should not be divided among their sons; when the grandparents are still alive, the wealth should not be divided among the three generations. Any division of wealth in these situations would be viewed as "a move against reason" (*beili* 背理). The second is "the rightness of distributing wealth" (*fencai zhiyi* 分財之義). In certain situations, it is more convenient for family members to divide their property. The division of property often happens when brothers start to live apart. However, it is not unusual that later, a rich brother shares some of his wealth with a poor one or other relatives. The third is "the rightness of sharing wealth" (*tongcai zhi yi* 通財之義). Theoretically, what is lent to others needs to be paid back. However, it is quite common that the lender would not push the borrower to do so since the money lent is provided as a help to relieve people in need. Occasionally, giving in charity is also seen as a duty. In brief, people in an ethic-based society need to care about each other and take it as their obligation to ensure the well-being of each other. Whoever fails to do so would be regarded as "unrighteous." In addition, a kinship often possesses common property, such as land for worship, village for righteousness, school for righteousness, etc. Some villages also possess their common property, such as community barns, garners for righteousness, and land for schooling. "These are mainly planned for people who live in poverty and for kids' education. They are all derived from the idea of ethical responsibility" (ZGWH: 97).

Ethical relationships exist also in Chinese political life. Traditionally, Chinese people "knew only the ethical duty between prince and subject, official and masses. They had no idea about the corporate relationship between citizen and state" (ZGWH: 99). In their mind, the political structure looked like a huge family in which the emperor stood as "the eldest son of the family" (*da zongzi* 大宗子) and he needed to treat his people "as carefully as protecting babies" (*ru bao chizi* 如保赤子). The political ideal in China was not "wealth and progress," as seen in the

West, but a "grand peace in the world" (*tianxia taiping* 天下太平) in which "everybody benefits from their ethical relationships; a father acts as a good father, and a son acts as a good son. Everybody is nice to each other and protects each other." Similarly, the most efficient method of governance in China was "managing the world through filiality" (*yi xiao zhi tianxia* 以孝治天下) (ZGWH: 99). It requires a ruler establishing himself as a model of filiality first and therewith attracting the whole society on the same path.

4.2 Class and Profession

Since the 1920s, as Arif Dirlik states, "Intense Marxist historiographical activity [...] disseminated Marxist sociohistorical concepts widely so that the materialist conception of history came to shape the views on the past, the present, and the future of significant numbers of Chinese intellectuals" (Dirlik 1978: 3). In this context, Liang became aware of Marxist doctrines and, through his discussion and disputation with the mainstream Chinese interpreters of Marx and Engels, he formulated his idea about the second feature of Chinese society, namely its social differentiation based on the division of professions. Herewith he called Chinese society a "profession-differentiated society" (*zhiye fentu de shehui* 職業分途的社會).

Liang outlines three phases in the history of world cultures. In the first one, due to overwhelming restrictions in people's physiology and psychology, as well as in their external environment, "human cultures in various parts of the earth contained certain similarities, even commonalities. Afterwards, each culture displayed its particular traits, starting to take its own path. Meanwhile, thanks to the contact between each other and to the guidance of great cultural heroes, they gradually fused into a few major paths. Finally, the great communication paved a way for the fusion of these major cultures and will lead to the realization of world culture" (ZGWH: 54).

Liang's description about the first phase is a common knowledge shared by almost all thinkers, including Marx himself. His idea about the third phase also has little contradiction to the well-known description in the *Manifesto of the Communist Party*. "In place of the old local and national seclusion and self-sufficiency, we have intercourse in every direction, universal inter-dependence of nations. And as in material, so also in intellectual production. The intellectual creations of individual nations become common property. National one-sidedness and narrow-mindedness become more and more impossible, and from the numerous national and local literatures, there arises a world literature" (Marx and Engels 1978: 476–477).

However, Liang's divergence from what Marx and Engels stated emerges when he starts to talk about the second phase. Two doctrines from Marx and Engels were especially influential in China then. One is about "class struggle" which Marx and Engels summarized as that,

> The history of all hitherto existing society is the history of class struggles. Freeman and slave, patrician and plebeian, lord and serf, guild-master and journeyman, in a word,

> oppressor and oppressed, stood in constant opposition to one another, carried on an uninterrupted, now hidden, now open fight, a fight that each time ended, either in a revolutionary re-constitution of society at large, or in the common ruin of contending classes. (Marx and Engels 1978: 473–474)

The second doctrine was about the epochs of human history that Marx formulated in his Preface to *A Contribution to the Critique of Political Economy*. "In broad outlines Asiatic, ancient, feudal, and modern bourgeois modes of production can be designated as progressive epochs in the economic formation of society" (Marx and Engels 1978: 5). A great number of Chinese thinkers, within and without the Communist Party, understood these two doctrines as universal truths, applicable everywhere in the world, including China.

In contrast to their interpretation, Liang argues that, although these two doctrines accurately revealed the essence of the Western world, they are not fitting the reality of Chinese history and society. Put differently, the fault does not lie with Marx and Engels, but in the improper universalization which their Chinese interpreters undertook. Liang comments that "People with superficial minds [*qianshi zhiren* 淺識之人], when hearing the materialist conception of history, claimed that there must be the same class struggle and unchangeable historical epochs in the entire Chinese history from the three dynasties in the remote antiquity to the end of the Qing dynasty" (ZGWH: 170). Refusing to accept their interpretation, Liang writes that,

> In Western society, there has been class antagonism [*jieji duili* 階級對立] between feudal lords and serfs in the medieval age and between capitalists and workers in modern times. However, Chinese society resembled neither of them. If Western society could be named "a society of class antagonism," the Chinese one should be named "a profession-differentiated society." (ZGWH: 163)

The "particularity" of Chinese profession-differentiation is rooted in the Chinese social structure. According to Liang, the condition of class antagonism, as seen in the West, is the monopoly of the means of production by a single class (feudal lords or capitalists). In contrast, there was no such monopoly in China because of three economic reasons. First, land could be freely bought and sold, therefore everyone had the chance to acquire or lose land. Consequently, the ownership of land was not the privilege of a small social group (ZGWH: 171). Secondly, inheritance from parents, as stated before, was equally allotted among all sons. This avoided a situation in which the elder son accumulated a large tract of land and property through primogeniture (ZGWH: 173). Thirdly, Chinese industry and commerce in the past one thousand and two hundred years since the Tang dynasty had not experienced any substantial development. For instance, there was no invention of steam engine, electrical engine, or other powerful machines. Hence it was not easy for any small group to manipulate the multitude through controlling these formidable means of production (ZGWH: 177).

Traditionally, what the four ranks of scholar, peasant, artisan, and merchant represented was not four social classes, but four social professions.

> In China, the two professions of ploughing and reading, and the two ranks of peasant and scholar were naturally interconnected to each other, having no segregation between them

> [*qijian qimai hunran xiangtong er buge* 其間氣脉渾然相通而不隔]. If there was no segregation between the scholar and peasant, how was possible to have any segregation between the scholar and the artisan or merchant? Scholar, peasant, artisan, and merchant originally designated people in different professions. Together they formed this broad society. They needed each other and complemented to each other. Segregation means class antagonism, while interconnection [*tong* 通] signifies the complementarity and mutual dependency among the professions. (ZGWH: 179)

This interconnection was materialized and strengthened politically through the system of National Civil Service Examination. In most of Chinese history, it was open to all the four ranks. Any individual man, if interested in gaining a governmental position, was allowed, even encouraged to take the examination. In other words, theoretically there was no legal or hereditary barriers to block any individual man from any rank to realize his dream of social and political mobility.

Moreover, the Chinese emperor, according to Liang, was actually a "single and isolated person" (*gujia guaren* 孤家寡人), as what he usually called himself, although he looked like an absolute lord over all people in the four ranks (ZGWH: 179). This was caused by three reasons. First, although the emperor did have royal relatives working as his assistants, they mostly served in the central government, having no direct control of people and land. Secondly, he co-managed the empire with a group of bureaucratic officials who came from folk society and would go back there eventually. Therefore, they did not really share a common interest and destiny with the emperor. Thirdly, most of governmental officials were chosen from scholars. Since their family members, relatives and friends were all ordinary people, it was natural for them to think from the point of view of people and avoid any conflict with them. Finally, the officials were required to be loyal to the emperor. However, "loyalty" here simply meant "caring about people as if they were one's children" (*aimin ruzi* 愛民如子) and "blunt admonition" (*zhiyan jijian* 直言極諫) against the emperor in extreme situations. In other words, they had an obligation to stand for the interest of the four ranks, even if that might be contradictory to what the emperor wished. It is Liang's conclusion that in medieval Europe, the feudal lords were united together, forming a ruling class over the oppressed serfs. In China, however, the ruling class of hereditary aristocracy had vanished from the political stage after the Qin-Han period. Therewith the emperor had no position to function as its representative or as a symbol of class oppression.

Regarding the origin of and relationship between the ethic-based system and profession-differentiation, Liang writes that "the ethical order became apparent after the disintegration of the feudal system [of the Zhou dynasty], and the profession-differentiation came with the dissolution of classes. These two were complementary to each other and interacted with each other, leading to the formation of this Chinese society" (ZGWH: 220). At the family level, due to the absence of large-scale monopolies of land and means of production, small families, as the basic units of society, were able to function efficiently in agriculture, handicraft, and commerce. Since there were no legal or hereditary barriers to social mobility, the members of a family could work together, accumulating resources and committing their time and energy for the promotion of one or more members in social hierarchy.

Meanwhile the one who acquired social promotion through family support would return to support economically and politically those members staying in the original profession. Doubtlessly, this interaction among family members would solidify the ethical relationship in a family. At the country level, due to the absence of a unified class of feudal lord as his supporter, an emperor might face a number of difficulties in his political governance. As a solution, he had to take an ethical approach to deal with officials around him and the people in general. It is Liang's observation that,

> Since there was no class-division, Chinese politics had to be ethicized [*lunli hua* 倫理化]. Due to the ethicization in politics, society became more professionalized [*zhiye hua* 職業化]. In turn, the professionalization enhanced the ethicization. Therewith ethics and profession, politics and economy interacted to complete each other. They linked together in a cycle and became more and more interdependent." (ZGWH: 224)

With a social structure having no class antagonism, but profession differentiation, China "did not look like a state [*guojia* 國家]" (ZGWH: 184). As for domestic affairs, it was short of certain functions which a regular state possessed. Chinese rulers always showed a kind of "passivity and non-action" (*xiaoji wuwei* 消極無爲] in their political performance. They "took 'no disturbance to people' [*bu rao min* 不擾民] as the most important principle and 'simple governance and light punishment' [*zhengjian xingqing* 政簡刑清] as the highest ideal" (ZGWH: 184). In international affairs, Chinese rulers always tried to avoid confrontation with other nations. "The Chinese national power was not weak. Yet its international confrontation was always light" (ZGWH: 186). History witnessed that the Chinese were often lazy in managing national census concerning land and population and negligent in preparing for national defense, although the former is crucial for knowing the extent of one's power, while the latter for exercising it. In addition, Chinese people, as a matter of fact, had lacked a clear notion of country (*guo* 國). As GU Yanwu 顧炎武 stressed, "there is the fall of a country [*guo* 國] and there is the fall of the world [*tianxia* 天下]. … The matter concerning the defense of country is what 'the meat-eaters' [*roushizhe* 肉食者], such as king and ministers, have to think about. The matter concerning the defense of the world is an obligation which even the people of low social status have to fulfil" (Gu 2011: 527). On this passage Liang comments:

> What he named as 'country' [*guo* 國] which ordinary people have no obligation to defend, obviously denoted the imperial government and royal house, not the country [*guojia* 國家]. Meanwhile, did the 'world' which we all have the duty to defend really denote the country? In all his writings, there existed no concept of modern country at all. On the contrary, what he strongly encouraged people to defend was neither a country, nor a race, but a culture. Instead of imbuing people with a notion of state, he actually advocated a doctrine transcending nationalism [*chao guojia zhuyi* 超國家主義]. (ZGWH: 189)

According to Liang's reading, the "world" here is the world of Chinese culture in which the entire Chinese nation lived. Dynasties and royal houses have changed frequently, while the world/culture has always been there. The investigation of its essence is the goal of Liang's ZGWH, and the exploration of its future development and improvement was the goal for his next major work.

5 Conclusion

In ZGWH, Liang claimed that he had never substantially changed his idea about "the premature birth of Chinese culture." He kept seeing it as the ultimate source for all the problems in China. At the same time, he introduced "reason" for its explanation, defining it as "the premature enlightenment of reason." Similar to the case in DXWH, this change was closely related to the inspiration of a western thinker. Now Bertrand Russell replaced Henri Bergson, and "reason" superseded "intuition." As a matter of fact, Liang's "reason" was synonymous to Russell's "spirit," designating "an impersonal feeling." Thinking about Liang's contribution to the movement of Contemporary Confucianism, we may assume that Russell indirectly participated in the formation of the movement through Liang's introduction of "spirit"/ "reason" into his sociological and philosophical agenda.

Based on his understanding of "reason," Liang investigated the cause for the absence of religion in the Confucian tradition. He argued that, thanks to the prevalence of the Ethical Teaching, the Chinese nation completed a process of replacing religion with morality in its early stage. The key for the completion existed in two social programs which Confucius promoted, namely "arranging the ethical standings to organize society" and "setting the ritual-music system to foster reason [among people]."

Liang was a serious student of Marx and Engels' materialist conception of history. He believed that this conception revealed the essence of Western culture and provided a great method for our investigation on human society and history. In the meanwhile, he disagreed with the mainstream Chinese interpreters of Marx and Engels on the issues of Chinese social structure and Chinese historical epochs. It was Liang's position that the applicability of Marx and Engels' view on class struggle and the classification of historical epochs could not be extended to China. For a long historical period, Chinese society had undertaken a cyclical movement with no substantial alteration in economy and politics. It became a "profession-differentiated society" with no division of class and an "ethic-based society" in which a warm relationship brought its members together.

References

DXWH *Dong-Xi wenhua ji qi zhexue* 東西文化及其哲學 [*Eastern and Western Cultures and Their Philosophies*; 1921], *LSMQJ*, 1989, vol. 1: 319–547.

LSMQJ *Liang Shuming quan*ji 梁漱溟全集 [*Complete Works of Liang Shuming*, vols. I–VIII]. Jinan: Shandong Remin Chubanshe, 1989–1993.

WNLD *Wo nuli de shi shenme?* 我努力的是什麼? ["What do I work for?"; 1941], *LSMQJ*, 1993, vol. 6: 160–262.

XCJS *Xiangcun jieshe lilun* 鄉村建設理論 [*Theory of Rural Reconstruction*; 1937]. Beijing: Shangwu Yinshuguan, 2017.

ZGWH *Zhonguo wenhua yaoyi* 中國文化要義 [*The Fundamentals of Chinese Culture*; 1949]. Shanghai: Shanghai Renmin Chubanshe, 2018.

Alitto, Guy. 1986. *The Last Confucian: Liang Shu-ming and the Chinese Dilemma of Modernity*. Berkeley: University of California Press.

Dirlik, Arif. 1978. *Revolution and History: Origins of Marxist Historiography in China, 1919–1937*. Berkeley: University of California Press.

Gu, Hongliang 顧紅亮. 2015. On the Confucianization of Russell's Philosophy in Liang Shuming 論梁漱溟對羅素哲學的儒化. *Academic Monthly* 學術月刊 47: 42–47.

Gu, Yanwu 顧炎武. 2011. *The Completed Works of Gu Yanwu* 顧炎武全集. Vol. 18. Shanghai: Shanghai Guji Chubanshe.

Lau, D.C., trans. 2003. *Mencius*. New York: Penguin Books.

Marx, Karl and Fredrich Engels. 1978. *The Marx-Engels Reader*. Edited by Robert C. Tucker. New York and London: W. W. Norton & Company.

Russell, Bertrand. 1971. *Principle of Social Reconstruction*. London and New York: Routledge.

Chapter 10
Liang the Political Philosopher: Contemplating Confucianism and Democracy in Republican China

Hung-Yok Ip

1 Introduction

Time flies. Confucianism, which was critiqued severely by iconoclastic intellectuals in early twentieth-century China, has now become an internationally vibrant philosophy. Since the early 1990s, the exploration of the relationships between Confucianism and democracy has made significant strides. Scholars have debated the relationships between the two. Samuel Huntington declared fundamental differences between them, as he drew attention to the collectivist, family-based, and hierarchy-oriented characteristics of Confucian culture, which, in his view, does not grant support to liberty, equality, and the individual (Huntington 1991: 24–30). To the contrary, Francis Fukuyama is skeptical of the linkage between Confucianism and authoritarian politics (Fukuyama 1995). In more recent decades, scholars have continued to compare and contrast the Confucian and democratic traditions (Elstein 2010).

In addition, an increasing number of thinkers have been dedicated to the various possibilities of blending Confucianism and democracy. According to Kɪᴍ Sungmoon (Kim 2018), two positions have emerged from works which ponder how the Confucian tradition and democracy could merge. The first position is fashioned by the Confucian meritocrats, who reject, critique, and/or carefully delimit the functions of democracy for their belief in the leadership of the virtuous and the wise. And the second position is held by the Confucian participatory democrats, who perceive participation in political decision-making processes as crucial for moral growth, and therefore attempt to include political involvement, equality, and popular sovereignty in their politics.

H. Y. Ip (✉)
Oregon State University, Corvallis, OR, USA
e-mail: hip@oregonstate.edu

T. Meynard, P. Major (eds.), *Dao Companion to Liang Shuming's Philosophy*, Dao Companions to Chinese Philosophy 17,
https://doi.org/10.1007/978-3-031-18002-6_10

The global emergence of Confucian philosophy is fashioned to a significant extent by authorial voices active in the English-speaking world. But the intellectual endeavor of thinkers who did not or do not publish in English must not be neglected. Some of them had or have contemplated democracy and Confucianism long before the currently ascendant interest in the Confucian tradition in the international community. Their significance is indicated in the expanding pool of English-written scholarship on them. For instance, Stephen Angle and David Elstein delve into the writings of a number of modern and contemporary Chinese Confucian thinkers, ranging from Mou Zongsan and Xu Fuguan to Jiang Qing and Bai Tongdong (Angle 2012; Elstein 2014). Some of them, such as Jiang Qing and Bai Tongdong, can be regarded as Confucian meritocrats (Bell 2015), and others—for instance, Xu Fuguan—share quite a bit with Confucian participatory democrats (Elstein 2014: 71–75). But much can still be done if we wish to deepen our understanding of non-English-speaking thinkers' participation in the construction of various Confucian democracy discourses.

Therefore, in this chapter, I would like to examine Liang Shuming (1893–1988), exploring how he can be regarded as a voice of modern and contemporary thinkers' collective enterprise of Confucian democracy. This chapter is divided into a few sections. To understand Liang's place in the international history of Confucian democracy, I will first describe that history itself ("The Contemporary Scene"). I will then discuss how Liang discussed democracy and Chinese culture at various stages in his pre-1949 career, when he was a young scholar catapulted to fame by his famous work, *Eastern and Western Cultures and Their Philosophies* (DXWH); when he committed himself to the project of rural reconstruction; and when he worked on *The Fundamentals of Chinese Culture* (ZGWH) as well as was active in the political arena ("Democracy in *Eastern and Western Cultures and Their Philosophies*," "Reconstructing Rural China," and "War, Politics, and Cultures"). By taking into consideration Liang's identities as a serious thinker and political activist, and by heeding China's cultural and political reality from the 1920s to the 1940s, I will describe the main characteristics of Liang's reflections on democracy and Confucianism at various phases of his career.

As I sketch the development of Liang's thought, I seek to show the following: By imagining possibilities of cross-fertilization between what he perceived as opposite cultures, by utilizing concepts like intuition (*zhijue* 直覺) and ethical rationality (*lixing* 理性), and by dissecting Chinese and Western cultures, philosophies, societies, and politics, Liang recognized—sometimes reluctantly—the value of democracy. He appreciated democracy by projecting that it would benefit the collective—be it the human race or the world, the West, or China (a collective-oriented instrumentalist perspective); he assumed democracy's contributions to the individual in terms of moral development or personal happiness (an individual-oriented instrumentalist perspective); and he believed in the intrinsic value of democracy (an autonomous-value perspective).[1]

[1]The conceptualization of these perspectives is based on Ip 1991. It is also to some extent inspired by Kim 2018.

On the basis of my analysis of Liang's career in the Republican period, I will then position Liang in relation to the Confucian meritocrats and the Confucian participatory democrats ("LIANG Shuming in a Comparative Perspective"). I argue that although Liang foreshadowed considerably these contemporary thinkers' ideas, he set himself apart from them for his appreciation of the significance of democracy for the individual's happiness, and for his belief in democracy's natural correctness.

2 The Contemporary Scene

2.1 Melding Confucianism and Democracy: The Confucian Meritocrats

To illustrate how Confucian meritocrats perceive Confucianism and democracy, I would like to give Daniel Bell as an example. In *The China Model: Political Meritocracy and the Limits of Democracy*, Bell presents what he calls an "ideal" based on his understanding of Confucianism, and on his assessments of the contemporary leadership of the People's Republic of China (PRC). He stresses that China's political elite—selected through a set of meritocratic mechanisms which let only individuals with superior intellect, social skills, and virtues enter the top echelon of the government hierarchy—have accomplished a great deal, especially in the sense that the government has been able to lift millions of people out of poverty in the time span of just a few decades. He argues that the one-person-one-vote system, which he treats as the most fundamental feature of democracy, is not necessarily superior to meritocracy, when both are measured by established standards of good government.

Aware of the significant imperfection of China's ruling elite, Bell makes it clear that what he tries to defend is not the reality of Chinese leadership, but the ideal behind the leadership—what he calls a vertical democratic meritocracy. According to him, it is defined by local democracy (such as village elections) and progressively meritocratic governance beyond the bottom level. Bell also believes that the sustainability of meritocracy depends on a number of democratic conditions: the rule of law, the prevention of prolonged political hierarchy, and freedom of speech—conditions that the Chinese state does not have currently—can check abuses of power, fight corruption, and allow the voices of peripheralized contingents to be heard. But at the same time, to refine China's meritocracy, which in his view is tainted by a selection process burdened with political connections and wealth, he also argues for a higher degree of meritocracy: his suggestion is that officials should be chosen for their ability and virtues. In Bell's analysis, not only has Confucianism played a part in the fashioning of the meritocracy ideal, but it also promises to help refine the existing, insufficiently meritocratic system. Officials should be educated in Confucian culture, in which political performances and moral accomplishments are linked. In addition to noting approvingly the Singaporean political elite's relatively recent advocacy of compassionate meritocracy, Bell also extends his appreciation to the PRC's bureaucrats' training process, in which the virtues of officials can be cultivated as they are assigned responsibilities in poor areas.

Developing his theory on democratic meritocracy, Bell on the one hand sounds explicitly China-oriented, as he dwells on the strengthening of the current Chinese meritocratic system. But on the other hand, he also believes that his work is oriented towards the humankind. He is confident that a refined meritocracy has something valuable to offer to the Western world, which has so far self-complacently clung to its one-person-one-vote system: electoral democracies can benefit by heeding the advantages of meritocracy, including a highly trained and effective civil service and, more importantly, an intellectually and morally superior leadership that can handle complex issues and conceive policies beneficial for their citizens, for the future generations, and for the human and natural worlds (Bell 2015).

2.2 *Melding Confucianism and Democracy: The Confucian Participatory Democrats*

To examine the position of the Confucian participatory democrats, I would focus on TAN Sor-Hoon. In *Confucian Democracy: A Deweyan Reconstruction of Confucianism*, Tan expresses her concern about the tension between Asia, which is dedicated to its own norms and values, and the West, which has tended to impose its own version of democracy and liberalism on the non-West. Such tension can, in her view, be resolved through both parties' efforts to build a common framework—one that is neither Eastern nor Western, but truly global—for communication and exchange. For her interest in this framework, she synthesizes Confucianism and Deweyan pragmatism, proposing a Confucian alternative to liberal democracy.[2]

In Tan's analysis, Asians, who are more committed to the community, do not necessarily appreciate the concept of individual autonomy, an essential ingredient of liberal democracy. But in the West, there are also thinkers who, for their disagreement with a single-minded, uncritical embrace of individual autonomy, stress that democracy should be reshaped with serious attention to communitarian concerns. Their critical positions on liberal democracy to a significant extent echo the Asians' search for the kind of democracy which can better balance the individual and the community. Tan believes, therefore, that the Western communitarian tradition and

[2] Just as Daniel Bell is only one among a considerable number of Confucian meritocrats, TAN Sor-Hoon is only one among an impressive number of Confucian participatory democrats. I focus on Bell because he can be regarded as one of the most high-profile, and most articulate, Confucian meritocrats on the international stage. I choose to discuss Tan because of her rich and influential examination of John Dewey (Tan 2004; Tan and Whalen-Bridge 2008), someone relevant to modern Chinese intellectuals, including LIANG Shuming.

Asian community-oriented political philosophy could join forces to reshape democracy.

Tan offers a detailed comparative analysis of Confucianism and Deweyan pragmatism. She argues that Confucius and John Dewey conceptualize the individual as a social being, as both situate a person's sense of self in his/her experiences that come from his/her interaction with others in webs of social relationships and with the natural environment. In addition, Tan also explains how Deweyan pragmatism and Confucianism resemble each other in defining the ideal community: both are characterized by tolerance to differences within the community and by receptivity to outsiders. Furthermore, both the Confucian tradition and the Deweyan pragmatic thought assume the undivorceable interconnection between politics and ethics. According to Confucianism, good politics helps establish socio-political harmony and order through proper social relationships, based on the individuals' ability to perform their moral duties in accordance with their roles. And whether one has a good life is determined by whether one can take part in politics properly, helping others to grow morally as well as elevating one's own moral caliber. As for Dewey, the inclusion of the good in the political realm is the essential condition that makes associated living fulfilling for humans. Last but not least, Dewey and Confucius have strong confidence in humans. Confucius believes that all humans could contribute to the socio-political order, and Dewey trusts humans' ability to make intelligent judgment.

But at the same time, Tan also calls attention to the differences between Confucian political philosophy and Deweyan pragmatism. Although both Confucius and Dewey think that the construction of a community necessitates efforts to work on all aspects of human interaction, and the non-separation of feeling and thinking, Confucianism stresses training in ritual practice, a process of learning and habitualization that allows individuals to undertake proper action. But Dewey stresses cooperative inquiry, which, as opposed to solitary thinking, would lead to intelligent outcomes and non-oppression through the sharing of views, constructive criticism, and the edifying of discourses. A community built through cooperative inquiry is non-oppressive. Moreover, if both Dewey and Confucius are committed to the people, Confucius desires a government for the people, whereas Dewey embraces both the concept of government for the people and that of government by the people. A comparative analysis of parallels and contrasts between Confucianism and Deweyan pragmatism will, Tan presumes, give rise to visions of how Confucianism could be reshaped, and how Dewey's democracy project could be pursued (Tan 2004; Sun 2005).

Now, let us turn to Liang Shuming.

3 Democracy in *Eastern and Western Cultures and Their Philosophies*

3.1 Creating a Space for the Fusion of Opposite Cultures

Liang authored *Eastern and Western Cultures and Their Philosophies* during an era when iconoclasm, associated with the New Culture movement, reached unprecedented heights. He was a conservative. But as Edmund Fung points out, being conservative in modern China could not be equated with an adamant opposition to change and to the West (Fung 2010: 62). Liang thought that China's hope rested on cultural transformation, as he defined culture as "a way of life in which people resolve the contradiction between the will's demands and the obstacles presented by the environment" (Alitto 1979: 83). In addition, he supported democracy, which he identified as an essential ingredient of Western culture. But he attempted to do so without abandoning Confucianism. In *Eastern and Western Cultures and Their Philosophies*, Liang summarized his position on cultural change as follows: the Chinese "should completely accept Western culture while fundamentally reforming its mistakes," and should also "critically reappraise and bring forth anew China's original attitude" (Alitto 1979: 121). This, according to Guy Alitto, reveals Liang's self-contradictory thinking: because Liang assumed that culture was a holistic expression of one unified underlying attitude, "he had denied himself the easy solution of advocating a blending of Chinese and Western cultures" (Alitto 1979: 121).

Alitto's criticism is not exactly wrong, because Liang did emphasize the fundamental differences between cultures. I would like to argue, however, that Liang had never conceptualized culture as static. Instead, he time and again stressed the fluidity of cultures, noting the role of human agency in propelling cultural transformation: in his view, humans rethink their needs in response to serious challenges in their evolving circumstance, and will reshape their cultures accordingly. Writing *Eastern and Western Cultures and Their Philosophies*, Liang exercised his own historical agency—and urged his fellow countrymen to do the same—by taking into consideration China's conditions. He also conjectured the direction Westerners would take as they reacted to their own culture's problems. In addition, Liang believed that fundamentally different cultures shared the simple fact that they were constructed by humans, who share certain human qualities. In so doing, he created a space of imagination for the amalgam of Eastern and Western cultures—hence the blending of Confucianism and democracy.[3]

To explain this further, I examine the ways in which Liang explained Western and Chinese cultures.

[3] In Liang *Shuming and the Populist Alternative in China*, Catherine Lynch offers her own interpretation to resolve the perceived tension between Liang's views on Chinese and Western cultures (Lynch 2018: 93–113). Philippe Major also offers an analysis of Liang's traditionalist, anti-traditionalist, and reconciliatory views on Chinese tradition and modern Western culture (Major 2018).

3.2 Democracy: Both Beneficial and Problematic for Westerners

Liang Shuming posited three cultural types—Western, Chinese, and Indian—which represented three distinct ways of life: Western culture, which was endowed with well-developed science and democracy, affirmed humans' will to the satisfaction of desires; Chinese culture, which was buttressed by Confucianism, regulated the will by moderating desires; and Indian culture, which was Buddhist in nature, rejected desires (Meynard 2011: 27).[4] He also asserted that these three distinct ways of life respectively characterize three successive historical stages along which, theoretically speaking, human beings should and would proceed (DXWH: 525–28). His discussion on democracy unfolded as he reflected on China and the West.

According to Liang, Western culture originated in the basic issue that humans had to confront at the first historical stage—the challenge of survival. Western culture is therefore driven by the attitude of struggle, of striving forward in order to obtain what one wants and satisfy one's primal desires (DXWH: 381). In Liang's account, the attitude of struggle, deliberately readopted by modern Westerners when they rejected the medieval, withdrawn way of life, was derived from the people's recognition of "self" (*wo* 我).[5] This recognition led to the struggle for, the striving forward of, self. The conquest of nature and the development of the scientific method were products of the application of the attitude of struggle with nature. But humans also used the same attitude vis-à-vis other humans and society. In order to survive, they did not hesitate to compete with one another. They even dared change a form of society which they found unsatisfactory—their aggressiveness led to the defeat of established authorities (DXWH: 362–67). Gradually, democracy emerged through the operation of this attitude of struggle in the human realm.

Liang presented this account of the historical origins of democracy:

> [Democracy] came from humans' awakening to their nature. They tried to liberate themselves from the church, the Pope, and the feudal lords. . . . Because of the awareness of human nature, they wanted to acquire the rights which ensure to them the expression of this nature. . . . Naturally, in order to obtain these rights, they resisted and rebelled against those existing elements and institutions which appeared to be obstructive. (DXWH: 389)

Liang emphasized that democracy was the antithesis of despotism: "In democracy there is the assertion of the individual will." For him, individual self-assertion meant the denial of the distinction between who occupied authoritative positions and who did not, a distinction marked by "the inequality of rights" (DXWH:

[4] See Chap. 5 of this volume by Zbigniew Wesołowski. It discusses Liang's views on culture.

[5] It may be useful to clarify what Liang meant by the recognition of self—an element that persisted in his democratic thought from the 1920s to the 1940s. Talking about the recognition of self in the framework of democracy, Liang referred to people's concerns for their nature as humans, mainly their different kinds of needs, desires, and emotions. It was according to such an understanding that Liang thought that the Chinese were not as concerned about their selves as Westerners (DXWH: 479–81; XCJSL: 240–59; ZGWH: 245–50).

51–52). According to Liang, inequality, from the standpoint of the individual, was a problem for individual liberty. He was keenly aware of the results of the inequality of rights in the public and social realms: if one person enjoys an overwhelming power of self-assertion with regard to public social issues, he observed, others' private lives will be controlled by him. But at the same time, he was also aware of the danger caused by individuals' uncoordinated self-assertiveness, which would undermine the fabric of a country or society (DXWH: 362). "The lack of any organizational structure could," he pointed out, "destroy the coherence of a community" (DXWH: 367).

For this reason, Liang appreciated the necessity of organization: he reflected on how society could be structured in a way that all of its members as individuals could assert themselves (*shenzhan gexing* 伸展個性) but at the same time could work together to move forward. In his analysis, the value of a republic lay not only in its recognition of all members' voices, but also in its ability to help them coordinate and reconcile with one another (*xietiao* 協調). In sum, Liang defined democracy as "the development of individuality and social organization" (DXWH: 367–69).

Liang thought that democracy contributed a great deal to the West. Germinating in and reflecting the Western attitude of struggle, democracy and science worked in tandem to create the power of the West: "Westerners … were able to transform nature when they deal with nature, and to change society when they deal with society. Therefore, [they] have conquered nature, defeated authorities, renovated technologies and all kinds of things on a daily basis, and reform their institutions constantly" (DXWH: 494).

However, he was also aware of democracy's inability to meet human needs in the evolution of history. Westerners were, as he saw it, destined to travel a historical trajectory through which they would part ways with the spirit of struggle. Once the preservation of life was no longer a problem, people's interests would naturally shift to enjoying life and tranquility of spirit. Chinese culture, unique for its stress on harmony and on modulating the hopes and desires of the self, would offer what they wanted (DXWH: 494–95). In addition, Liang surmised that after the challenge of survival had been basically solved, Westerners would have to address the issue of human relationships. "In the West," he observed, "people set a clear boundary between oneself and others. As soon as they start talking, they focus on rights and responsibilities, and legally defined relationships. Westerners feel it necessary to calculate [benefits, rights, and so forth], although the other side could be their father, son, husband, or wife" (DXWH: 479). Liang judged that this approach to human relationships must have caused much suffering. In response to the agonies caused by their own way of life, he projected, Westerners would feel drawn to Chinese culture. Examining the intellectual trend of post–World War I Europe, he believed that the West was beginning to understand the attractiveness of Confucianism, which, directed at managing human relationships, promised reconciliation and harmony (DXWH: 496–98).

3.3 Confucianism: Just What the West Needed

Explaining Confucianism, Liang Shuming appropriated the concept of intuition, which he thought was characteristic of Chinese metaphysics. He believed, ontologically, that all those schools which studied the basic nature of change pointed to the principle of the harmony of opposite forces. And epistemologically, to feel, or recognize, the state of harmony, one has only intuition on which to rely. Confucianism was one of such schools. Because of his belief in harmony, Confucius did not rigidly adhere to any so-called objective principles or absolute ethical standards. When he judged, behaved, or acted, he followed his intuition. In Liang's view, keenness of intuition is *ren* 仁 (DXWH: 453–54). If a person has *ren*, his performance will be congruent with Heavenly principles. Liang quoted Wang Gen 王艮, the Ming dynasty philosopher, when he defined Heavenly principles as natural principles (*tianli* 天理): "the principles that naturally or automatically exist" (DXWH: 454). Liang made it clear that natural principles were not well-defined ethical formulas to be understood and then implemented. Instead, they were virtues that would be naturally realized when action was guided by keen intuition (DXWH: 454). *Ren* is incompatible with self-centered, utilitarian calculation. While one acts in accordance with *ren*, one is not concerned about the consequences of one's actions. One acts because of a deep emotional commitment to what one understands as rightness or natural principles (DXWH: 454–62).

According to Liang, to lead humans to implement *ren*, Confucius focused on cultivating humans' commitment to family-based relationships, where deep feelings begin. Echoing the Confucian statement that "filial piety and fraternal respect are the foundation of *ren*" (DXWH: 467), Liang tended to give more weight to proper conduct of the subordinates. He explained: "If a person possesses filial piety and fraternal respect, he can naturally cope with society and other people in a proper way without any artificial instruction." He also assumed that filial and fraternal sentiments would be critically deepened by ritual practice and music (DXWH: 468).

In Liang's analysis, Westerners were predetermined by the progress of their own culture, which was marked by the spirit of struggle, science, and democracy, to choose the Confucian road. Moreover, he was confident that the West's nascent turn to Confucianism would eventually lead it out of the suffering caused by the kind of existence dictated by the recognition of self, and by a strong focus on struggling forward—to handle or struggle against nature or other humans for one's own sake. In *Eastern and Chinese Cultures and Their Philosophies*, Liang states that the West could travel to higher civilizations steadily because its history started in the right way: successfully overcoming the challenge of survival but suffering tremendously for their way of life, Westerners were willing to tread the Confucian path, and would eventually travel the Buddhist path, a road that the human race should take (DXWH: 498, 526–29).

However, Liang thought that if Confucianism promised to be beneficial to the West, the reality of Confucian culture was hurting China.

3.4 Chinese Culture as a Hindrance to China and Liang's China-Oriented Instrumentalist Appreciation of Democracy

China's essential challenge, said Liang, was the prematurity of her culture. Besides bringing about "a kind of half-baked attempt at fulfilling the underlying spirit, which neither succeeded nor failed, but rather stagnated in a vague state of limbo" (Alitto 1979: 104), such prematurity also constituted the cause of China's social, economic, political, and even diplomatic difficulties. He stated, "We stress harmony with nature before we have conquered nature. That is why until now we are still controlled by nature. We emphasize compromise and yielding to others before we have developed our individuality. That is why to this day we still cannot liberate ourselves from the control of different authorities" (DXWH: 529). The current unsatisfactory situation of China was, he pointed out, caused by Chinese culture (DXWH: 530).

Because of its underdeveloped, unpromising, and stagnant cultural shape, Liang observed, China lacked the ability to compete with the West, let alone the ability to realize the Confucian ideal. As far as China's survival was concerned, he stated that China must adopt the essence of Western culture—the recognition of self and the attitude of struggle—in a thoroughgoing fashion. With regard to science and democracy, two major products of the attitude of struggle, Liang regarded the latter as the more urgently needed. He thought that consolidation of individual rights and reestablishment of social order were the two most urgent tasks at this moment: without individual rights and social order, China "cannot become a real nation internationally and cannot develop any kind of construction domestically" (DXWH: 530). Accentuating that "the rule of the minority causes political instability and turbulence," Liang voiced this clarion call for the Chinese people to adopt an attitude of struggle:

> Our political system is Western but our people's attitudes remain unchanged. They are indifferent to politics and do not fight for their rights. As these attitudes do not fit in the Western system, the Western system has been appropriated and abused by the minority. The people must struggle against the minority in order to establish a genuine democratic system. (DXWH: 534)

It is obvious, therefore, that a China-centered instrumentalism underlay Liang's acceptance of democracy. However, Liang appreciated democracy by having in mind the individual as well.

3.5 Democracy as a Condition for Individual Happiness; Democracy as an Intrinsic Truth

Liang not only saw the value of democracy for the collective—for China or the West—but also noted the linkage between democracy and individual happiness. He admitted that history witnessed how Confucian culture was not favorable to the individual. To begin with, the second way of life, molded by the Duke of Zhou and Confucius, guided the Chinese to take a direction which would not induce them to build a democratic culture. In addition, the fate of Confucianism since Confucius was such that it was misunderstood, misinterpreted, and misrepresented. From ancient to modern China, many Chinese thinkers had failed to grasp the essence of Confucianism. If original Confucianism highlighted reciprocity between individuals who occupied different positions in hierarchical relationships, Chinese reality, which took shape in an underdeveloped Confucian culture, was marked by a different kind of Confucian philosophy, which emerged in ancient China, and ritual practices (DXWH: 477–79). Since the Song dynasty, Confucian culture had become increasingly extreme, rigid, and doctrinaire. The spread of such a culture resulted in the unfortunate fact that Chinese society and individuals were oppressed (DXWH: 477).

In addition to collective-oriented and individual-oriented instrumentalist ends which democracy served, also worthy for Liang was the autonomous value that he ascribed to democracy. His view that democracy was intrinsically right can be seen in how he perceived the relation between intellect and intuition within Western culture.

Writing his famous book, Liang contrasted the two cultures: whereas Chinese culture is driven by intuition, Western culture embraces intellect (*lizhi* 理智), which consists of reasoning and calculation propelled by self-related utilitarian goals. However, Liang did not perceive intuition as a quality monopolized by the Chinese. It was, in his view, a kind of human quality shared by members of Western culture as well: "Intellect is an instrument which cannot motivate itself to work. It is intuition which pushes the operation of intellect." Thus, the ultimate root of Western culture, which he identified as the recognition of self, "was also derived from intuition"—i.e., derived from what humans naturally accept as right. Because this intuition-based recognition has been so powerful, it had served as the dynamic motivating the individual to struggle by wielding their intellect. "In Western life," Liang said, "it was intuition which directed and used intellect" (DXWH: 485).

Given the intuitional roots of the recognition of self, the question arises as to why the operation of the Western attitude of struggle has created so many problems for humankind. Here, Liang differentiated between the Western attitude as such and its unrestrained use and extreme development: "Every kind of attitude, at the beginning, is good; its defects will only be seen as it is incessantly used and developed by humans; its uselessness will be shown when a new period has come" (DXWH: 525). Thus, despite the failings of modem Western culture, Liang regarded democracy and its root—the recognition of self—as having the kind of natural autonomous value that is appreciated through intuition. Against this background, Liang believed in the autonomous value of freedom. When he reflected on the death of Li Chao (李超), a young woman who committed suicide to defy a marriage arrangement imposed on her by her family, Liang represented freedom as something humans automatically embrace, "We pursue freedom … because we feel the intolerableness of the lack of freedom" (DXWH: 538).

3.6 *Whither China?*

It must be noted, nevertheless, that Liang could never be content with China's mere adoption of democracy. This looked unwise at a time when Western culture was about to make an "Eastern turn." What, then, should China do when the West began to transition to Confucian culture? Positing the malleability of culture, Liang proposed the following: the Chinese must adopt Western culture completely but also reshape it thoroughly, and at the same time assess Chinese culture critically to recover its original nature. He thought that Western culture could be renovated by infusing the genuine Chinese attitude into it—that is, the Chinese could create an amalgam of the Western attitude of struggle and the Confucian way of *gang* (剛). Liang defined *gang* as "a kind of dynamics supported not by desires but by one's deep, solid emotional commitment to what one intuitively perceives as right" (DXWH: 537). In his imagining, just as the spirit of struggle empowered Westerners, it would also enable the Chinese to act dynamically for their country, the individual, or simply what they knew was right. And *gang* would ensure that the Chinese attitude of struggle was not propelled by desire-dictated and self-centered calculation. This, he pointed out, was how the Chinese should pursue freedom: their quest for freedom should be generated by a profound commitment to—that is, by their inability to bear with the absence of—freedom, rather than by the advantages and benefits associated with it.

As a diligent thinker, in the following decades Liang continuously reshaped his own thought, as he reflected on China's conditions, Confucianism, democracy, and world cultures. However, he always did so by presuming the incompatibility between cultures as well as the transformability of cultures, and by believing in human agency and shared human qualities. In addition, Liang always believed in the world-oriented, West-oriented, China-oriented, individual-serving, and autonomous value of democracy.

4 Reconstructing Rural China

After publishing *Eastern and Western Cultures and Their Philosophies*, Liang became increasingly critical of the first way of life, as he expressed his concern that recognition of self and struggle for self, which he equated with individualism, would destroy Chinese culture (ZGMZ: 127). By the early 1930s, Liang had altered his recipe for merging Western and Eastern cultures. He criticized himself harshly: "[I once thought that] we must borrow the attitude that marked the first way of life—that is, the attitude of struggle—and integrate it into the second way of life... In hindsight, this is sheer stupidity! ... I failed to see the unchangeability of the Chinese attitude" (XCJSL: 243). In addition, identifying Chinese culture as one based on a more morally admirable vision of human life, he posited what he called an inviolable truth: "If it is permissible that we change to elevate ourselves to a higher existence, it is impermissible that we change to lower our existence" (XCJSL: 243). Therefore, Liang offered a program of rural reconstruction, which he characterized as a "move eastward."

It must be noted, however, that despite his self-criticism, Liang introduced a new combination of East and West.

4.1 A Different Approach to Blending Eastern and Western Cultures

Liang replaced intuition, formerly considered to be the basis of the Chinese attitude, with what he called ethical rationality (*lixing*). Whereas intuition was considered to be the human instinct to follow natural ethical principles, ethical rationality was understood by Liang as one's calm, proper, open-minded, non-self-centered, and kind attitude to others, and one's conformity with natural principles (XCJSL: 181–86). Liang also explicitly differentiated physical natural principles (*wuli* 物理), which he thought were objective, from human natural principles (*qingli* 情理), which he presented as being derived from human feelings and therefore were subjective. When Liang spoke of human natural principles, he meant something similar to his "natural principles" in the previous period (XCJSL: 181–86). In his view, while ethical rationality is the unique nature and value of being human (XCJSL: 186), Confucius "was the first man who recognized the meaning of being human" (ZGMZ: 62).

It is obvious, then, that as ethical rationality was the basis of the Chinese attitude, the Chinese attitude was much more noble than the Western attitude of struggle and its socio-political product, democracy. Instead of struggling with others, Liang contended, the Chinese people have preferred to seek peace and happiness through self-improvement and self-examination. In contrast to being boastful and competitive, the Chinese people have tended to be modest because of their dedication to self-examination and moral perfection. While Western democracy, a system of mutual surveillance, is derived from the distrust of others, the Chinese people, who have developed a commitment to human relationships (*lunli* 倫理) based on their love for the family, emphasize trust and respect, but not equality and rights. Instead of building a political system that acknowledges the equality between humans and protects the individual's rights, the Chinese handle human relationships with rituals

(XCJSL: 250–53). In addition, above all, Western democratic politics was created to support the Westerners' pursuit of desires; but, in contrast, the Chinese people preferred to seek the true meaning of being human—the realization of congruence between one's life and natural principles (XCJSL: 259).

Interestingly, however, Liang still incorporated democratic elements into his program of rural reconstruction, as he thought that a problem that plagued China was the Chinese people's underdeveloped organizational techniques. He was interested in making use of democracy, which he regarded as an effective approach to organization. He identified political participation and individual liberty, which he defined as the freedom to manage one's own life, as the two defining features of the democratic approach to organizing (XCJSL: 283–84).

How, then, did he explain the possibility of blending Western and Chinese cultures? Liang left open the space of cultural amalgamation in a couple ways. As he posited that although the spirits (*jingshen* 精神) of Chinese and Western cultures were different, both Westerners and Chinese, as humans, possess ethical rationality (XCJSL: 186). In addition, and perhaps more importantly, Liang imagined that the East-West blending that he proposed was something oriented towards Chinese culture, characterized by humans' pursuit of moral self-elevation. In his analysis, not only were the Chinese ingredients in his proposal of combining Chinese and Western cultures congruent with democracy, but they also heralded the characteristics to which Western democracy would turn—or was, indeed, turning.

First, advocating the adoption of the practice of political participation, Liang nevertheless noted the tension between the people's right of political participation, which in his view was associated with majority rule, and the Chinese emphasis on moral improvement, derived from ethical rationality. In his view, the study of (natural human) principles and the cultivation of character need the guidance of those who are morally and intellectually superior, but not a majority-based decision. Therefore, although he borrowed democracy as a powerful organizational principle, he also proposed the marriage of majority involvement and minority leadership of "the virtuous" and "the wise," a union which would not impede the Chinese efforts to travel to higher moral planes (XCJSL: 284–91). Observing the professionalization in state legislation and government administration in the West, he pointed out that Westerners began to respect experts, whose knowledge was not shared by everyone. And as he idealized the rise of totalitarianism in Europe, he argued that Westerners learned to appreciate the leadership of a superior minority. A high-quality minority leadership well-supported by the people should not be regarded as anti-democratic: regarding active political participation as democratic, he stressed that minority rule backed by the majority was a more advanced manifestation of democracy (XCJSL: 289–93).

Second, although Liang thought that liberty and rights should be part of the democratic organizational structure China would build, he made it clear that he only supported the kind of liberty and rights that matched the Chinese attitude, marked by the individual's respect for others. He said, "There is something we must heed:

Westerners compete with each other out of their concern about themselves. But the Chinese always take into account others. Therefore they exercise self-restraint, suppressing their own voices and, when they speak, focusing on their responsibilities" (XCJSL: 295). In his view, a Chinese person's commitment to the well-being of others was righteousness (*yi* 義), while a Western individual's conventional concern about his own well-being reflects something much inferior—his preoccupation with benefits (*li* 利). However, Liang approved of a recently minted version of liberty and rights in the West: realizing the socially destructive nature of their fixation on the individual, people in the West came to support the individual's rights as well as social duties (XCJSL: 298). Assuming that this recent version signified the beginning of the West's shift to Chinese culture, Liang expressed his hope that the West would further improve itself. He said, "When their support for the concept of rights is not driven by their concern for themselves, and when they do not view responsibilities and duties as others' matters, they will be like us" (XCJSL: 295).

4.2 The West, China, the Individual, and the Issue of Autonomous Value

Liang noted how democracy helped the West to get organized and gain strength (XCJSL: 193–95), but strove to build an organizational structure which was better by what he regarded as Chinese standards. Consequentially, he introduced a mode of organization that uncoupled the right of participation and majority rule, thereby weakening the independent historical agency and the self-determination of the non-elites in organizational hierarchies. Liang was confident about his new organizational mode: with a substantially ethicized organizational mode oriented to ethical rationality, he imagined, the Chinese would open a new path of progress not only for themselves, but also for the world. For this reason, he said he had hopes when he envisaged the future of the human race (XCJSL: 309–10). In sum, what Liang regarded as democratic—respect for the individual and active participation—would contribute to the moral elevation of the West and the world, as these practices would help enhance the organizational ability of a Confucian-inspired collective.

Liang also projected that with the organizational structure he invented, the Chinese could address two China-oriented tasks: economic-technological development and the establishment of social order. Mass participation could, he stated, enhance rural reconstruction workers' understanding of rural problems and elevate the people's enthusiasm for taking part in these two tasks (XCJSL: 318–20, 337–38). Furthermore, Liang's advocacy of ethical education reflected two interrelated motivations: nation-oriented instrumentalism and culturalism. For his belief in the lofty nature of Chinese culture, Liang assumed that ethical education would improve his country's overall moral condition and that, by constructing harmonious interpersonal and social relationships and by cultivating the people's will to undertake personal and social improvements, moral education would also contribute to China's economic-technological development and social order (XCJSL: 565–68).

By stressing that his democratized but essentially meritocratic organizational mode would guide humans morally, Liang assumed that respect for the individual and the right to participation would benefit the individual's self-refinement. But at this stage, Liang was quite critical of individual happiness as a criterion for justifying the value of democracy. He asserted, with some disapproval, that "modern European law which emphasizes the protection of human rights was drawn up only in order to grant support to individual desires" (ZGMZ: 136). Even so, Liang still had praise for the West's commitment to human rights. The modern European political system, he acknowledged, created a paradise in the human world. "It has enabled humans to achieve happiness in this life" (ZGMZ: 134). At the same time, recognizing that Confucius was a crucial figure in the creation of the Chinese system of human relationships, he continued to acknowledge explicitly that this system was the ultimate origin of "the ritual which ate people" (XCJSL: 201), even though it was the rigid ritual rather than the relationships per se which had the actual effect of stifling the development of individuality. He sympathized with the Chinese fascination with the modern West's celebration of the individual: they were bound to find their own culture suffocating and unacceptable when they had the chance to encounter modern Western culture (XCJSL: 202). Thus, Liang did not totally lose his appreciation of the individual-serving value of democracy.

Liang also remained committed to the autonomous value of democracy. "This," he wrote, "is an axiom: Each individual should enjoy his own liberty" (ZGMZ: 103), and "We are forced to worship democracy for … its congruence with natural principles" (ZGMZ: 102–3). And he included liberty and equality in the realm of ethical rationality (XCJSL: 186).

5 War, Politics, and Cultures

In the 1940s, LIANG Shuming continued to examine cultures and democracy and led an active political life. He cofounded the Democratic League, searching for a road for China, which went through two wars—the Sino-Japanese War and the Chinese Civil War. He also worked hard to mediate between the Guomindang (GMD) and the Chinese Communist Party (CCP). In this decade, he universalized democracy but stressed the culturally conditioned differences between Western and Chinese democracy.[6] Nevertheless, he also regarded both as closely intertwined with ethical rationality: while the Chinese emphasis on ethical rationality shaped the uniqueness of Chinese democracy, Western democracy was not only a specific manifestation of ethical rationality, but also a more effective basis for the further development of ethical rationality. Noteworthy is that with a firm belief in the universality of

[6]In the 1940s, Liang still identified the calm and proper handling of communication with others and one's conformity with natural principles as basic for ethical rationality (ZGWH: 123–30).

democracy, Liang expressed his admiration for Western democracy's world-oriented instrumentalist, West-oriented instrumentalist, individual-oriented instrumentalist, and autonomous values during a period when he found Western democracy increasingly problematic as a means to China's improvement.

5.1 Reflecting on China's Reality

In the 1940s, Liang still pledged loyalty to meritocratic minority leadership capable of leading followers to refine themselves morally (ZGWH: 256–57). He pointed out: "Since the Song dynasty, … we have increasingly focused on the contrasts between those who are virtuous and those who are ignorant. Majority rule is beyond our imagination and comprehension" (ZGWH: 253). But at the same time, he still assigned himself the historical mission of fighting for democracy: he argued that democracy served as the foundation for a people to get organized, thereby leading to the political power of the West (ZGWH: 70–71).

In addition, Liang did not equate appreciation of meritocracy with an acceptance of one-party dictatorship. Observing Chinese politics, he was gravely concerned about the tyranny—potential or real—of one-party dictatorship when he observed China's political reality. Contemplating how the Chinese could stand up against the Japanese, Liang identified national unity as the prerequisite of the struggle against foreign invasion. This, he thought, could not be achieved by the one-party monopoly of the GMD, which repressed the activities of other parties (Alitto 1979: 309–10).[7] As the Chinese Civil War was to end, Liang also reminded the CCP that one-party dictatorship would undermine the nation's peace and unity. In 1949, he pressed the Communists to tolerate dissidents (*yijizhe* 異己者). He readily admitted the power of the CCP, pointing out that its use of violence would lead to the unification of China soon. "However," he also stressed, "this kind of unification will be devoid of both genuine unity and democracy. Without unity and democracy … unification cannot be maintained in the long run" (JGZG: 822–23).

Interesting enough, if Liang criticized one-party dictatorship and had confidence in the organizational power of democracy, he also doubted, in the mid-1940s, that democracy would improve the Chinese economy. He recalled his words on the occasion of his second visit to Yan'an in 1946 as follows:

> What China urgently needs now is economic construction. But in order to rebuild the Chinese economy effectively, we must have a strong government which persistently plunges into this task with a definite, consistent plan. The competition and alternation between two parties would cause political instability …, and would make long-term economic construction impossible… . I am suspicious of the emulation of the Western political system. This system does not fit in with China's historical and cultural tradition. Moreover, it does not suit China's present situation and needs. (Wang 1988: 91)

[7] To learn more about Liang's complex attitudes towards democracy, one-party rule, and one-party dictatorship, readers can refer to Fung 2006: 208–10.

In terms of a political system, then, where should China go? Liang confessed his confusion: "I really do not know how to respond if you ask me what kind of government I want and what I plan to do in realizing my political opinion and design" (Wang 1988: 105).

In sum, Liang's thoughts on democracy were highly ambivalent. He did not abandon the concept of meritocratic minority leadership, but was pained by the political problems that plagued and would occur in China when one-party rule became a dictatorship. In addition, on the one hand, he posited that democracy, which served as the foundation for a people to get organized, could help foster China's national unity. But on the other hand, he was concerned that it could not conduce economic reconstruction effectively.

However, amid ambivalence, Liang universalized democracy as he compared and contrasted Chinese and Western cultures in his celebrated work, *The Fundamentals of Chinese Culture*.

5.2 Observing Cultures: Democracy as a Universal Phenomenon

In his book, Liang integrated the concepts of liberty, equality, rights, and related institutional and socio-political arrangements into a universalized framework of democracy. He listed five basic elements of the democratic spirit, explaining their connections among one another:

First, democracy means the generalization from one's recognition of one's self to other people's selves; "only caring about oneself but ignoring others" is anti-democratic.

Second, because of the recognition of others' selves, the commitment to equality between humans emerges.

Third, the commitment to equality leads to the view that the problems of society must be solved not by the forcible assertion of one's will, but by rationality, which depends on discussion among, and then the consensus of, the people.

Fourth, the emphasis on equality, discussion, and consensus implies the principle of majority rule. Regarding public and social matters, the majority's opinion should be respected.

Fifth, the respect for individual liberty and rights is derived from the first point. While public and social matters should be decided by all the members of a society, an individual should have freedom in managing his or her personal affairs. The public and society must not repress this kind of freedom (ZGWH: 240–41).

Liang then emphasized that democracy is a tendency, and that the realization of democracy will vary in degree. Moreover, in his view, there have been cultural and national differences in realizing democracy: China, whose culture was oriented towards a person's respect for others, developed a democratic tradition characterized by the realization of the first three basic democratic elements, whereas in the West, preoccupation with self was the basis for democracy.

5.3 *Observing Cultures: Western Democracy's Contribution to the Happiness of the Individual*

Liang retained his individual-oriented instrumentalist commitment to democracy. Approving democracy's contribution to individual happiness, he mainly perceived this contribution as the achievement of the West. To him, the pursuit of individual happiness was a major motivation that led the West to realize democracy: "When the Westerners determined to pursue their earthly happiness, they definitely believed that liberty is happiness and that happiness is created by liberty. Thus liberty was established" (ZGWH: 249).

In China, stated Liang, individuals' feelings and freedom of expression had never been discovered or recognized. Surely, he was proud of the Chinese mode of human relationships, and stressed the use of ritual and music for the fostering of ethical rationality—the basis for one's proper handling of others. But he also sympathized with the May Fourth iconoclasts' condemnation of rituals.

Liang explicitly depicted the cause-and-effect relationship between the Chinese system of human relationships and the repression of self. "In China," he wrote, "individual freedom could not be developed owing to the Chinese emphasis on enhancing one's moral consciousness." He continued: "In China, an individual does not exist for himself; he exists for others. . . . This [neglect or repression of individuals] is the biggest defect of Chinese culture" (ZGWH: 250–51). In his view, TAN Sitong's call for breaking through all kinds of nets "was a reaction to this condition" (ZGWH: 251). Chinese culture in which individuals were suppressed was bound to be rejected, when the Chinese were stimulated by the modern West (ZGWH: 285).

5.4 *Observing Cultures: Western Democracy, Its Contribution to Moral Growth, and Its Autonomous Value*

Though accentuating the relative moral shallowness of Western democracy, Liang also stressed the importance of the Western version of democracy as the foundation for the further development of ethical rationality.

Examining Western democracy, Liang pointed out the following: class-based competition, especially the bourgeoisie's struggle against feudalism, challenged hierarchical relationships and liberated humankind. If in the mid-1940s Liang cast doubt on the value of democracy to China's economic development, in *The Fundamentals of Chinese Culture* he thought that democracy brought about stunning economic growth in the West (ZGWH: 189–91). More importantly, Liang argued that because Western democracy led to economic growth and affluence and empowered all members of a society, it practically forged a historical situation where humans would turn to ethical rationality. He said:

> The improvement of economic development and material life successfully gratifies humans' physical desires and thus reduces the importance of these desires in their hearts. When everyone becomes powerful in socio-political terms, the use of sheer power will not be respected. In the future, the complete realization of socialism and democracy … will enable ethical rationality to become the ultimate force determining everything in the world. The Western path, due to its practicality, will finally reach this state. (ZGWH: 287)

In sum, Liang expressly stated his belief in Western democracy's contribution to the field of rationality.

If Liang trusted that Western democracy had the power to generate moral growth, he lamented Chinese democracy's lack of momentum for change. Liang pointed out that Chinese culture, which was plagued by a premature pursuit of rationality, smothered the development of individual liberty and rights because it perpetuated an increasingly inflexible relationship-based social structure, overemphasized one's respect for others, and failed to engender the historical context that called attention to ethical rationality (ZGWH: 252–62). As Chinese democracy was not built upon the people's eagerness for their individual liberty and rights, it was weak, albeit more noble for its focus on moral rightness (ZGWH: 287).

Moreover, not only does Western democracy facilitate moral growth individually and socially, but it also possesses autonomous value. Through class-based struggle, Liang projected, more and more people would evolve to be real humans, and become true equals with one another. This, he said, is congruent with ethical rationality (ZGWH: 186).

6 Liang Shuming in a Comparative Perspective

From the 1920s through the 1940s, Liang Shuming continuously contemplated the amalgamation of Confucianism and democracy. He did so by taking into account the concepts of liberty and rights, the relationships between meritocracy, majority rule and political participation, and culturally conditioned manifestations of democracy. Although he reassessed his views and sometimes employed new concepts to discuss the Confucian and democratic traditions, his thought was also marked by a significant degree of continuity. Throughout these decades, if he perceived China and the West as fundamentally different, he also assumed the transmutability of cultures. In addition, he believed that cultures—or rather humans—shared something deeper than their manifest and fundamental differences: it was intuition in the 1920s, and ethical rationality in the two decades that followed. And he by no means cast doubt on humans' interest or ability to reshape their cultures. On the surface, Liang's appreciation of democracy never ceased to fluctuate. For instance, he was critical of minority rule in the 1920s, supported the rule of the virtuous and the wise during the period of rural reconstruction, and in the 1940s expressed his serious concern about one-party dictatorship without giving up his belief in governance based on superior minority leadership. He appeared less enthusiastic about democracy's value for individual happiness in the 1930s, and questioned the benefits democracy could bring to the Chinese economy in the 1940s. But basically, during these decades, he maintained his assumption that democracy was good for various human collectives, including the world, the West, and China; was beneficial for individuals' moral growth and/or happiness; and last, but not least, was valuable in itself.

6.1 Confucian Meritocracy

To a certain extent, Liang can be regarded as a Confucian meritocrat. While it is beyond the scope of this chapter to compare and contrast Liang and Daniel Bell thoroughly, I would like to point out some major parallels between the two.

Liang made his distrust of majority rule clear when he was committed to the reconstruction of rural China, arguing that morally and intellectually superior minority leadership was better than majority rule. Bell is also concerned about the flaws of the rule of majority, especially the one-person-one-vote system. In his analysis, one of the flaws of majority rule is none other than the "tyranny of the majority." Bell points to the nineteenth-century origin of this concept: J. S. Mill, who popularized it, was worried that the majorities, who could be irrational and motivated by their self-interests, tend to use the power granted to them in the democratic process to oppress the minorities and enact problematic policies (Bell 2015: 21). But Bell also draws attention to a different interpretation of the tyranny of the majority: the source of the tyranny is the majority's lack of knowledge. "The basic problem," he writes, "is not that most voters seek to maximize their self-interest, but rather that most voters lack the knowledge necessary to make informed political judgments." As he sees it, even if the majority act to obtain what they want in the democratic process, they are not endowed with sufficient knowledge to fulfill their objective. In sum, they lack the competency to expand their self-interest (Bell 2015: 22–23).

However, observing how the Chinese leadership ran the state, Bell is aware of the imperfection of China's significantly meritocratic governance. He identifies the invocation of virtues as a key component in the Chinese leadership's self-improvement. The state should deselect those who do not care about the people, assess how much candidates for official positions are willing to sacrifice for the country, or choose the right persons on the basis of peer review. In addition, he also suggests reshaping the current civil service examination system. In this respect, Confucianism should be given a key role, because basic knowledge of the Confucian classics would be particularly helpful in the Chinese context. According to Bell, the classics form a rich pool of cultural knowledge about how to act well in politics and in society more generally (Bell 2015: 88). Furthermore, he thinks that compared to the Marxist classics, which do not focus on the moral caliber of political leaders, Confucian texts are more effective in fostering the elite's virtues.

Not unlike Bell, Liang supported the concept of meritocracy in a context where the Chinese leadership was far from perfect: he constructed his own vision of meritocratic organization when the GMD elite was fragmented, disordered, and corrupt, and the revolutionaries who challenged it were violent. However, if Bell invests hope in the Chinese elite's Confucian self-reform, Liang chose to imagine the bright future that meritocracy could potentially bring forth to his country. Meritocracy not only helps rescue China from poverty, backwardness, and weaknesses, but, more importantly to Liang, also guides the Chinese or even the world to move upward—to journey to moral progress. Therefore, Liang is different from Bell. While Bell certainly does not reject moral growth as an admirable goal that Confucian-inspired meritocracy could fulfill (Bell 2015: 143), he basically appreciates the China model—for individuals, for China, and for the world—in terms of its efficacy in economic growth, poverty alleviation, and other goals (like environmental degradation). This is not to deny that these goals that Bell cherishes lack moral implications. It is clear, however, that Liang focused much more on how his model of Confucian-inspired meritocracy will contribute to humans' individual moral progress in China, the West, and presumably the world.

Certainly, both Liang and Bell appreciate democracy to a certain extent. Even when he was most critical of democracy, Liang still thought that minority leadership of the virtuous and the wise, which was important for China, the West, and the future of humankind at the individual and collective levels, must be backed by the democratic practice of popular participation. Envisioning how current Chinese leadership could become more beneficial to China and Chinese citizens, Bell includes in his vertical model of meritocracy such democratic procedures as election and referendum, which help curb corruption, maintain order, or create legitimacy (Bell 2015: 168, 174–78).

In sum, by explaining how democracy could consolidate or reform meritocracy, Liang and Bell in a sense also acknowledge the collective-oriented and individual-oriented instrumental value of democracy.

6.2 *Confucian Participatory Democracy*

Liang also shares interesting parallels with TAN Sor-Hoon, in addition to differing from her.

Throughout his career in the Republican era, Liang recognized the individuals' rights and liberty but always insisted on contextualizing the formation of the individual in webs of human relationships. Self-assertion, self-expression, the pursuit of self-interests, and the defense of one's rights must not be done in a self-centered fashion—i.e., one must move beyond self-centeredness, honoring the presence of one's family, community, and society. This social, context-based conceptualization of the individual is shared by Tan, who is critical of the strong emphasis on rights and the individual's autonomy. In formulating her vision of Confucian democracy, Tan appreciates an important connection between Confucianism and the Western communitarian tradition, which refuses to endorse in totality the individualistic values of Western liberal democracy. Comparing Confucius and Dewey, she points out that both of them view the individual as a social being, and perceive the individual as a person who develops a sense of self by interacting with his or her environment, including especially its social aspect. It is unsurprising, therefore, that like Liang, Tan hopes to build a society which would nurture humans' moral growth, refining their character through their association with others.

Liang is also comparable to Tan in the sense that he noted how the modern West possessed "voices of dissent" which are critical of an overly strong commitment to the self and its interests and desires. For instance, in *Eastern and Chinese Cultures and Their Philosophies*, he cited Bertrand Russell and Peter Kropotkin, believing that their writings part ways with the self-centeredness of Western culture. Russell posited, Liang observed, that human behaviors are only partly driven by desires (DXWH: 497–99). He called attention to Kropotkin's theory of mutual aid, explaining how it questioned the Darwinist concept of evolution. Certainly, he did not miss Dewey's critical position on modern Western democracy. Theorizing on rural reconstruction, he referred to Dewey's critique of interests-based human relationships in the West (Gu 2015: 136).[8]

It should be noted, however, that Liang was bolder in explaining the role that Confucianism can play in the progress of human life, although obviously both he and Tan think that Confucianism would help improve the world. This is because, in Liang's envisioning, the Confucian path is destined to be the path Westerners, the most powerful group of people, would choose as they were forced to resolve the problems caused by the self-centeredness, competition, and conflicts of their own democratic culture. If Tan focuses on how, for his visible agreement with Confucianism, Dewey appears different from other Western thinkers (Sun 2005: 223), Liang assumed that Western ideas that mesh with Confucianism signify a predetermined turn that the West will take.

Certainly, Liang cannot be regarded as a Confucian participatory democrat, if we take into consideration how he sang praises of meritocracy in the 1930s and 1940s. He made it abundantly clear that the rule of majority is unfit not only for effective governance in a technologically advanced and knowledge-based society, but also for the lofty goal of elevating a society's moral caliber. To be sure, he did not reject the majority's right to participation, and in fact attempted to integrate this democratic feature into his theory on how to organize a collective. And Gu Hongliang is not wrong when he points out that Liang hoped to harmonize meritocratic and majority-based politics (Gu 2015: 139). The truth still is, however, that by prioritizing the leadership of the wise and the virtuous, and by regarding the majority's genuine support for the supposedly virtuous and wise leadership's cause as sufficient, he de-emphasized the value of self-determination in a meritocratic structure oriented towards moral progress.

---

[8] On Liang's appropriation of Deweyan thought, see Gu 2015.

In Liang's envisioning, democracy is beneficial to moral development at both individual and social levels. From the 1920s through the 1940s, he explained the value of democracy for moral growth in varied ways: for instance, the majority's participation and individual liberty promise to grant significant support to a meritocratic system in which the virtuous and the wise lead others to gallop on the path of moral self-refinement; Western democracy weakens humans' preoccupation with material and monetary profits by generating prosperity; and as the widespread acceptance of equality in the West empowered all, no one would be tamed by force and oppression. But Tan's perception of the value of political participation for the individual's moral improvement is much more straightforward: political participation, she says in no uncertain terms, is "part of personal growth" (Tan 2004: 121). She assumes that a person preoccupied with his needs and wishes can only be "ethically stunted" (Tan 2004: 121). But a person can refine himself if he learns to take ethical ends seriously. And in her view, political participation is an important step in a person's endeavor to interact with his environment, a process through which he learns to appreciate the social nature of humans.

I would also like to draw attention to how Liang differs from Tan by quickly comparing their views on the individual's freedom and rights. In developing Confucian democracy on the basis of Dewey's thought and Confucianism, Tan does not dwell deeply on the different contexts in which the American philosopher and Confucius operated respectively. As Sun Youzhong points out, Dewey's critical position on negative freedom—the individual's freedom from restrictions to act—was his response to American society, and such freedom has been underdeveloped in China (Sun 2005: 224). It must be noted that Tan is not entirely insensitive to how, despite its original humaneness, Confucianism—particularly, its ritual practices—became increasingly rigid and, as a result, denied the individual's negative freedom. For instance, she reflects on how, departing from the *Book of Rites*, which does not condemn remarriage, the Song Neo-Confucian scholar Cheng Yi 程頤 was against a widow's freedom to marry by stressing that the loss of chastity was a matter much more serious than starvation (Tan 2002: 87–88). In response, Tan recognizes the oppressive nature of a reified Confucianism, endorsing a reformist approach to tradition. For this reason, she recognizes how the concepts of individual freedom and rights could be relevant to a person's happiness. However, at the same time, she does pay more attention to the consequences—the social impact—of one's conduct than to one's freedom to express oneself (Sun 2005: 224).

To the contrary, Liang expressed a stronger appreciation of the instrumentalist significance of rights and freedom for the individual's happiness. From the 1920s through the 1940, Liang criticized Confucian scholars who caused human suffering by misinterpreting Confucianism. Moreover, by positing the prematurity of Confucian culture, he emphasized the following: as the Chinese did not travel far along the path leading to democracy (and science) because of the prematurity of their relationships-centered culture, they had upheld the virtue of respect for others before they developed a sense of self-recognition. The outcomes of their premature respect for others were, according to Liang, unfortunate: not only China but also the Chinese individuals suffered. In fact, this attention to individual happiness also makes LIANG Shuming different from Daniel Bell, who focuses on the practical value of meritocracy.

Finally, if KIM Sungmoon is correct that neither the Confucian meritocrats nor the Confucian participatory democrats embrace democracy for its intrinsic value (Kim 2018: 37–38), Liang further sets himself apart from Bell and Tan as a "strong democrat" in the sense that, unlike the other two, he, who expressed reservations and ambivalence about democracy, persistently assumed the natural rightness of democracy. Through his important works, Liang reveals his multilayered commitment to democracy—to its collective-oriented, individual-oriented, and, last but not least, autonomous values. In sum, Liang displays the broad intellectual compass that he was able to achieve in the capacity of a cultural conservative: he boldly asserted the fine qualities of Chinese culture when Chinese culture was under attack; and he seriously contemplated the worth of democracy when he was critical of democracy.

References

DXWH *Dongxi wenhua ji qi zhexue* 東西文化及其哲學 (*Eastern and Western Cultures and Their Philosophies*; 1922), *LSMQJ*, 2005, vol. 1: 319–547. (A comparative analysis of Chinese, Western, and Indian philosophies and cultures.)

JGZG Jinggao Zhongguo gongchantang 敬告中國共產黨 ("My advice to the CCP"; 1949). *LSMQJ*, 2005, vol. 6: 819–823.

LSMQJ *LIANG Shuming quanji* 梁漱溟全集 (*Complete Works of LIANG Shuming*, vols. I to VIII). Jinan: Shandong People Press, 1989–1993.

XCJSL *Xiangcun jianshe lilun* 鄉村建設理論 (*Theory of Rural Reconstruction*; 1937). *LSMQJ*, 2005, vol. 2: 141–586. (Discussion on how to reshape rural communities.)

ZGMZ 1971. *Zhongguo minzu zijiu yundong zhi zuihou juewu* 中國民族自救運動之最後覺悟 (*The Final Awakening of the Chinese People's Self-Salvation Movement*; 1932), 3rd ed. Shanghai. Reprint, Taibei. (Discussion on how the Chinese should save their nation and culture).

ZGWH *Zhonguo wenhua yaoyi* 中國文化要義 (*The Fundamentals of Chinese Culture*; 1949). *LSMQJ*, 2005, vol. 3, 1–316. (Discussion on basic features of Chinese culture.)

Alitto, Guy. 1979. *The Last Confucian: LIANG Shu-ming and the Chinese Dilemma of Modernity*. Berkeley: University of California Press.

———, ed. 2015. *Contemporary Confucianism in Thought and Action*. Berlin: Springer.

Angle, Stephen C. 2012. *Contemporary Confucian Political Philosophy*. Cambridge: Polity Books.

Bell, Daniel A. 2015. *The China Model: Political Democracy and the Limits of Democracy*. Princeton: Princeton University Press.

Elstein, David. 2010. Why Early Confucianism Cannot Generate Democracy. *Dao: A Journal of Comparative Philosophy* 9: 427–443.

———. 2014. *Democracy in Contemporary Confucian Philosophy*. New York: Routledge.

Fukuyama, Francis. 1995. Confucian and Democracy. *Journal of Democracy* 6 (2): 20–33.

Fung, Edmund S.K. 2006. *In Search of Chinese Democracy: Civil Opposition in Nationalist China 1929–1949*. New York: Cambridge University Press.

———. 2010. *The Intellectual Foundations of Chinese Modernity: Cultural and Political Thought in Republican China*. New York: Cambridge University Press.

Gu, Hongliang. 2015. LIANG Shuming's Conception of Democracy. In *Contemporary Confucianism in Thought and Action*, ed. Guy Alitto. Berlin: Springer.

Huntington, Samuel. 1991. Democracy's Third Wave. *Journal of Democracy* 2 (2): 12–34.
Ip, Hung-Yok. 1991. LIANG Shuming and the Idea of Democracy in Modern China. *Modern China* 17 (4): 469–508.
Kim, Sungmoon. 2018. *Democracy After Virtue: Toward Confucian Pragmatic Democracy*. Oxford: Oxford University Press.
Lynch, Catherine. 2018. *LIANG Shuming and the Populist Alternative in China*. Leiden: Brill.
Major, Philippe. 2018. Tradition and Modernity in LIANG Shuming's *Eastern and Western Cultures and Their Philosophies*. *Philosophy East and West* 68 (2): 460–476.
Meynard, Thierry. 2011. *The Religious Philosophy of LIANG Shuming: A Hidden Buddhist*. Leiden: Brill.
Sun, Youzhong. 2005. Review of *Confucian Democracy: A Deweyan Reconstruction*. *Charles P. Peirce Society: A Quarterly Journal in American Philosophy* 41 (1): 221–225.
Tan, Sor-Hoon. 2004. *Confucian Democracy: A Deweyan Reconstruction*. Albany: State University of New York Press.
Tan, Sor-Hoon, and John Whalen-Bridge, eds. 2008. *Democracy as Culture: Deweyan Pragmatism in a Globalizing World*. Albany: State University of New York Press.
Wang, Donglin 汪東林. 1988. *Interview with LIANG Shuming* 梁漱溟問答錄. Changsha: Hunan renmin chubanshe. (An interview with LIANG Shuming).

Chapter 11
Liang Under Mao: The Reconciliation of Confucianism and Buddhism with Marxist Ideology

Yim Fong Chan

1 Introduction

Whereas some New Confucian scholars such as MOU Zongsan 牟宗三 (1909–1995), TANG Junyi 唐君毅 (1909–1978), and ZHANG Junmai 張君勱 (1887–1969) found Marxist ideology incompatible with traditional Chinese culture, and especially Confucianism, urging others to leave mainland China before the Chinese Communist Party (henceforth: CCP) took control of it, LIANG Shuming 梁漱溟 (1893–1988) was one of the many intellectuals who chose to stay. In his article "Liang nian lai wo youle naxie gaibian" 兩年來我有了哪些改變 (What changes I have made in the past two years), Liang admitted that he found it difficult to accept the communist ideology in the past, but he changed his perception towards the CCP after a trip to Henan, Shandong, and six provinces in North-Eastern China he undertook in 1950 in view of inspecting different enterprises and agricultural cooperatives (LNL: 889). A brief examination of Liang's work after 1949—including *Zhongguo jianguo zhi lu* 中國建國之路 (*The Path to the Establishment of the Chinese Nation*, 1951; henceforth ZGJG), *Renlei chuangzaoli de da fahui da biaoxian* 人類創造力的大發揮大表現 (*The Great Expression and Great Manifestation of Human Creativity*, 1961; henceforth RLCZL), *Zhongguo—lixing zhi guo* 中國—理性之國 (*China: Nation of Reason*, 1970; henceforth ZGLX), and *Renxin yu rensheng* 人心與人生 (*Human Mind and Human Life*, 1984; henceforth RXYRS)—reveals Liang's use of a staggering number of Marxist terminologies and a strong sense of recognition of the legitimacy of the CCP. During the first few years after the establishment of the People's Republic of China (henceforth: PRC), he repeatedly claimed that the essence of traditional Chinese culture was crucial for the realization

Y. F. Chan (✉)
University of Basel, Basel, Switzerland
e-mail: yimfong.chan@unibas.ch

T. Meynard, P. Major (eds.), *Dao Companion to Liang Shuming's Philosophy*, Dao Companions to Chinese Philosophy 17,
https://doi.org/10.1007/978-3-031-18002-6_11

of socialism in China (YJWL: 850–853, ZGJG: 394–406), so that these two issues were not antagonistic in Liang's understanding. In what follows, I focus on analyzing RXYRS, which I regard as representative of Liang's philosophical thought in the twilight of his life, as this book discusses Confucianism and Buddhism more conspicuously than other works after 1949; besides, Liang also claimed the importance of this work as it aims to provide solutions to the problems of human life.

Liang repeatedly stated that the issues about China (*Zhongguo wenti* 中國問題) and human life (*rensheng wenti* 人生問題) were the two aspects that concerned him most in his life (ZGWH: 4–5, ZZYWG: 79, RXYRS: 526). According to his 1966 letter "Zhi Zhongyang wenge bing zhuan Mao zhuxi" 致中央文革並轉毛主席 (To the Central Cultural Revolution Committee and to Chairman Mao), Liang expressed his confidence that the CCP could resolve the problems of China and thus he could concentrate on studying the solution for the issues of human life (ZZYWG: 79–80). This implies Liang's acceptance of the leadership of the CCP, but he thought the latter was incomplete without a philosophy of life that he could provide. Therefore, in the preface to RXYRS, he clearly stated the purpose of the book was to deal with life problems (RXYRS: 526). In the first line of chapter one, he stated that his book aims at "helping human beings understand themselves; at the same time, it aims at introducing ancient Eastern learning to today's academics" (RXYRS: 537). His goal was to investigate the nature of the heart-mind (*xin* 心) by examining the daily lives of human beings, thereby attempting to predict the social, mental, and spiritual transformations that they would experience in the future. These transformations involve different attitudes to life and corresponding ways of living, so he called his study a "life philosophy" (RXYRS: 540).

Liang Shuming already had the intention to write RXYRS in the 1920s after publishing *Dong-Xi wenhua ji qi zhexue* 東西文化及其哲學 (*Eastern and Western Cultures and Their Philosophies*; henceforth DXWH). As he realized the application of certain psychological terms in the explanation of Confucianism in DXWH was inappropriate, and as he developed new ideas about the most significant aspect of the distinction between human beings and animals (RXYRS: 770), he wanted to write a book to correct the mistakes in DXWH and explain his latest understanding about the human heart-mind.[1] Therefore, this book could be regarded as a continuation of DXWH. Some 30 years later, Liang intended to write the book again and wrote a preface in 1955, but he did not formally start writing the work until 1960. The writing period was separated into two. During the first period, between 1960 and 1966, he finished chapters one to seven. He temporary stopped writing as the draft and books he referenced in it were confiscated by the Red Guards on August 24, 1966 during the Cultural Revolution (RXYRS: 618). On September 10, Liang wrote a letter to the Cultural Revolution Committee and Mao Zedong 毛澤東 (1893–1976) to ask for the return of the manuscript to him (ZZYWG: 79–80). After

[1] When Liang taught a course on Confucianism at Peking University in 1923–1924, he had already included his new understanding about the human heart-mind, which later became the main theme of RXYRS. In 1927, he also gave talks to university students on the same topic in Beijing. Please refer to RXYRS: 526.

receiving the manuscript,[2] he finished writing the remaining chapters in the second period between 1970 and 1975.

Between these two periods, it is worth noting that he turned to write ZGLX from 1967 to 1970. Apart from including a mostly positive evaluation toward the leadership of Mao Zedong and the Communist Party (ZGLX: 316–317), in this book, Liang argued that the successful realization of socialism in China was due to its subtle relationship with the essence of Chinese culture,[3] and specified this essence as moral reason (*lixing* 理性), which is one of the core concepts in RXYRS. Besides, he stated that the heart-mind and self-consciousness (*zijue* 自覺) would play important roles in the realization of communism in the future, and asked the reader to refer to RXYRS (ZGLX: 289). When Liang finished writing ZGLX in 1970, he decided not to publish it but rather presented it as a birthday gift to Mao in 1972.[4] He attached a note to the book, stating it was for internal reference only, which means the target readership of ZGLX was the core members of the Communist Party. While RXYRS focuses on examining the nature of the heart-mind with the function of self-consciousness, and on discussing the fundamental idea of moral reason, the two books are related to each other and thus RXYRS might be regarded as the philosophical basis for ZGLX.

In the existing research on RXYRS,[5] the relationship between Marxism, Confucianism, and Buddhism is rarely discussed, while the analysis of Buddhism is nearly absent. In this chapter, I argue that in RXYRS, Liang further elaborated his thought of the threefold model of cultural development suggested in his 1921

[2] To the best of my understanding, Liang did not mention the date that he received the returned manuscript in his complete works.

[3] In ZGLX, Liang quoted his previous work *Zhongguo wenhua yaoyi* 中國文化要義 (*Substance of Chinese Culture*, 1949) several times to explain the relation between the realization of socialism in China and the characteristics of traditional Chinese society. At the same time, he criticized the USSR severely for their revisionism. He believed that China was the cornerstone of anti-revisionism, which would lead the international proletarian revolution in the future. See ZGLX: 215, 289, 324.

[4] According to Li Yuanting, Liang presented ZGLX as a birthday gift to Mao on his 80th birthday. He brought the work to the reception of Xinhua Men 新華門 and asked the staff to send it to Mao directly (Li and Binghua 2009: 272). Please also refer to ZGLX: 201.

[5] Wang Zongyu 王宗昱 (1990) focuses on Liang's evaluation of Western psychological studies and his attempt at establishing a heart-mind theory. Wen-Shun Chi (1970) provides an analysis of Liang's thought about culture and Chinese society after 1949. He highlights the differences between the thought of Liang and the communist party, which made him became the target of criticism. Zheng Dahua 鄭大華 (2006) distinguishes three periods in Liang's perception of Marxism, including the May Fourth Movement, during the 1930s and 1940s, and after 1949. Zheng thinks that Liang borrowed some terms and ideas from Marxism for developing his thought after 1949, which is mainly represented by RXYRS. However, Zheng asserts that Liang's application of Marxist theory reflected his superficial understanding of this school of thought. In Catherine Lynch's study (2011), she mainly differentiates different forms of utopianism represented by Liang Shuming and Mao Zedong. As to Gong Pengcheng 龔鵬程 (1993a, b), he analyses how Liang's thought complied with the ideology of Marxism and Maoism. He claims that Liang's pragmatic mindset made him become a defender of the party and even deviate from his identity as a Confucian scholar.

publication DXWH, as he accommodated the three phases of cultural development in the two periods of socialism and communism, especially for the case of China. He claimed that the essence of "Western culture" was represented by the collective mode of production during the socialist stage; while Confucian and Buddhist teachings would be prevalent in the early and late periods of communism respectively. To explain the social transformation from socialism to communism, he suggested that self-consciousness was the driving force that propels individuals and the whole society to move forward. He explained that self-consciousness always complies with the nature of human life, and brings human beings to the final destination of Buddhist enlightenment.

In the following analysis, I first compare Liang's view of history in DXWH and RXYRS, and show how the latter is highly influenced by Marxism. Second, I clarify some of the core concepts of RXYRS, as Liang imposed peculiar interpretations onto them, which would easily cause misunderstanding if they were apprehended based on their literal meaning. Third, I analyze the significance of self-consciousness in the social transformation Liang promoted, as well as his challenge to historical materialism in the development of history. Besides, the importance of Confucianism and Buddhism in the book will be highlighted, which explains Liang's epistemological and ontological views. On the whole, I seek to show how Marxist ideology could be reconciled with Confucianism and Buddhism in Liang's interpretation, while also explaining the role self-consciousness plays in the context of socialism, Confucianism, and Buddhism. Given that my aim, in the following sections, is to get a better sense of Liang's complex project, I will not comment on the viability of Liang's design of human development and the accuracy of his perception of human nature.

2 The Views of History in DXWH and RXYRS

In DXWH, LIANG Shuming proposed his threefold model of cultural development,[6] involving "Western," "Chinese," and "Indian" cultures, which is conspicuously similar to his view of history in RXYRS. The model of cultural development advanced in DXWH can be illustrated by a pyramidal model with "Western cultural" at the base, "Chinese culture" in the middle, and "Indian culture" at the top. He asserted that all societies, regardless of their geographical locations, would undergo such a bottom-up cultural development process. The formulation of this model was based on his understanding of three types of obstacles that human beings need to tackle, which include obstacles from the physical world, other sentient beings, and the nature of the impermanence of the natural world. These obstacles can be construed as material, emotional, and spiritual needs respectively. Liang

[6]Please also refer to Zbigniew Wesołowski's chapter "Liang the Philosopher of Culture" in the present volume for the details of Liang's model of cultural development.

maintained that human thought and actions are propelled by an intangible "Great Will" (*da yiyu* 大意欲). Due to this Great Will, human beings continuously seek satisfaction and shift their attention to the next level of needs once those of the former level are satisfied. Based on Liang's understanding, each of the aforementioned "cultures" can help humanity satisfy one of the three types of needs. He regarded them as transcultural and transnational intellectual resources that provide appropriate remedies to human beings, as each of them carries irreplaceable value and function during one of the three cultural phases.

According to Liang's interpretation of the essence of "Western culture", its most significant feature is the application of reasoning (*lizhi* 理智) with the spirit of rationality, which facilitated the development of science and democracy in the West. With the extensive application of reasoning, Liang appreciated the accurate and efficient division of labor that flourished with the development of capitalism, which brought sufficient material enjoyment to people in the West, but he also severely criticized entrepreneurs for requiring the working class to work in deplorable conditions. As he understood "Western culture" as a manifestation of utilitarianism, he interpreted "reasoning" as selfish calculation, which results in a sense of alienation between people and finally urge them to seek social change. During the first phase of cultural development, Liang assumed basic material needs in society could be gradually fulfilled. People would then pay more attention to building close and harmonious relationships with others so as to satisfy their emotional needs. He predicted the competitive attitude of life that is driven by reasoning would be supplanted by a compromising attitude, which represents a shift of cultural development. During the second phase of history, he found Confucian teachings about interpersonal relationship and the understanding of the cosmos were particularly applicable. In particular, he suggested utilizing intuition (*zhijue* 直覺) to understand the cosmos as a ceaseless flux. Instead of merely following rigid rules, human beings would adapt themselves to changing circumstances, especially when it comes to interpersonal issues. Liang assumed both material and emotional needs could be gradually fulfilled during the second phase, but he thought the suffering caused by the nature of the impermanence of the natural world would be unbearable when human beings shift their attention to this issue. Liang thought Buddhist enlightenment would be the final resort, and this is what he meant by "Indian culture."

In RXYRS, although Liang preserved to a great extent his view of history as divided into three phases, he was also deeply influenced by Marxist understandings of history. The extensive application of Marxist and Maoist ideology and terminologies in RXYRS is noticeable, which is different from his previous works such as DXWH (1921) and *Zhongguo wenhua yaoyi* 中國文化要義 (*Substance of Chinese Culture*; henceforth ZGWH) (1949). Since the 1950s, Liang started explicitly expressing his support to the leadership of the communist party in ZGJG (1951) and RLCZL (1961). In RXYRS, Liang firmly expressed his approbation of Marxism. He claimed this school of thought had insisted to study the ideal of society and the interests of human life on the basis of the scientific spirit and historical facts. He basically accepted the Marxist theory of social evolution,[7] and believed communism would be realized universally in the future. However, he doubted if such sequence of development was applicable to all societies in the world (RXYRS: 687). In particular, he questioned whether China had slavery in the ancient past, but attributed to China the Asiatic mode of production (SLZG: 246–269, JTWM: 304). Hence, Liang avoided discussing primitive communism, slavery, and feudalism in the case of China, but focused on examining the current development after the founding of the PRC. He asserted that thanks to the essence of traditional Chinese culture and the leadership of the CCP, China had successfully attained socialism before capitalism was fully developed, and he anticipated communism would eventually be realized after this socialist phase.

Liang's view of history in RXYRS can be regarded as a further elaboration of the threefold model of cultural development in DXWH, as he expected China would experience three phases of development. In addition to the socialist phase, Liang divided communism into two phases in which Confucianism and Buddhism would be manifested respectively. Similar to DXWH, he insisted that the sufficient development of the previous phase would form the precondition for the next. Regarding the meaning of "Western culture," Liang had a significant change since the 1950s. In ZGJG (1951), Liang claimed that his understanding of Western culture focused more on group organization (*tuanti zuzhi* 團體組織) and the development of science and technology (*kexue keji* 科學科技) compared to his discussion of the West in DXWH (ZGJG: 344). In light of this claim, democracy and capitalism no longer represent "Western culture" in Liang's thought since the 1950s. In the 1970s, he reaffirmed this contention by claiming that "the philosophy of the communist party is the truth of mundane teaching. It can also be called the essence of the Western spirit." (YGDFR: 487) Hence, "Western culture" carries different meanings in DXWH and RXYRS: in the former it refers to the development of science, democracy, and material advancement, and in the later, it denotes the collective mode of production and socialist social systems that China had adopted.

Liang strongly believed socialism would be replaced by communism and regarded this transition as a natural trend. He kept on employing a threefold cultural model, but reinterpreted the three phases with socialist and communist elements. Based on Liang's understanding, the collective mode of production in China would fulfil the basic needs of daily life. He anticipated there would then be a social transformation to the early stage of communism, in which people would contribute to society according to their capacities and obtain what they need. However, people would be bothered by mental restlessness during this phase. Similar to DXWH, he thought Confucian teaching would be applicable to solve this problem. As to the latter stage of communism, Liang associated it with the realization of Buddhism:

[7] Liang generally accepted the Marxist theory of the five stages of social development, namely primitive communism, slave society, feudalism, capitalism, and communism. According to the discourse of the CCP, socialism is the transitional period between capitalism and communism.

> In the daily life [of this stage], there will be no suffering caused by the deficiency in terms of the objective conditions. People will begin to be bothered with and realize the fact that they are not liberated from the mundane world, so that they will seek to free themselves from the [mundane] life that is not free. On the one hand, they will subjectively have the realization of seeking to transcend the mundane world; on the other hand, the conditions of possibility of supramundane [religious] practice will be objectively satisfied. From then on, the time for the rise of genuine religion will have come.
>
> 正是在此生活中，客觀條件更無任何缺乏不足之苦，人們方始於苦惱在自身初不在外大有覺悟認識，而後乃求解脫此生來不自由之生命。一面主觀上有出世覺悟，一面客觀上亦備足了修出世法的可能條件，而後真宗教之興起，此其時矣。(RXYRS: 750)

Liang thought that the satisfaction of material needs would provide a favorable condition for people to think about the emancipation of the constraints of human life. He affirmed his belief and claimed that “the genuine religion was found only in the precocious [culture that is represented by] Buddhism in ancient Indian. It will become prevalent during the final stage of communist society. This is my prediction” (RXYRS: 744). This quote reveals Liang’s thought about the compatibility between communism and Buddhism, whereas the final destination of social development was the attainment of nirvana. Such anticipation should be highlighted as a unique and peculiar insight of this book, as it goes against the rejection of religion in orthodox Marxism.

3 Liang’s Understanding of the Heart-Mind

LIANG Shuming’s prediction of the future path of human development reflected his acceptance of the official CCP discourse about the current and future stages of history in China, while he also attempted to integrate Confucianism and Buddhism into the framework of communism. Against historical materialism, however, Liang attributed the driving force of history to the nature of the human heart-mind. In RXYRS, Liang attempted to give a philosophical explanation of how the human heart-mind propels the development of history rather than merely reflecting the material condition of societies. To examine Liang’s theory of the heart-mind, core concepts in RXYRS including *xinlixue* 心理學, *renxin* 人心, and *shengming benxing* 生命本性 (the nature of human life) will be clarified. Besides, Liang’s employment of a number of dichotomies, such as the contrast between *shen* 身 (body) and *xin* 心 (heart-mind), *gong* 公 (public) and *si* 私 (private), and *ju* 局 (narrowness) and *tong* 通 (openness), should be noted, as they play an important role in illuminating Liang’s understanding of the heart-mind.

The book title *Renxin yu rensheng* highlights the two central concepts of the work—concepts that are closely related to each other. *Renxin* refers to the human heart-mind, while *rensheng* 人生 (human life) refers to the political and social ideal that he regarded as a manifestation of the heart-mind. The heart-mind is the most fundamental concept that Liang wanted to articulate, and he named his study “*xinlixue*” (心理學), providing a particular interpretation of this term. “*Xinlixue*” literally refers to the scientific study of the mind and behavior, which was a neologism used to translate "psychology." Liang was not satisfied with the current boundary of this study, however; he claimed that most psychologists focused on the scientific analysis of consciousness, which only belongs to the shallow level of the human mind, and failed to provide a thorough examination of the human heart-mind (RXYRS: 632–633). He insisted that psychology should cover both the objective and subjective aspects of the mind; the former referring to the scientific examination of consciousness, while the latter denoting the inherent inclination and preference of human beings, which is related to ethics and the Neo-Confucian understanding of *xin* and *li* (principle). As the latter involves the behavior and moral judgement human beings make in daily lives, Liang regarded it as rather subjective. Owing to his peculiar interpretation of this discipline, he thought deeply about the positioning of *xinlixue*: "[It] should lie between philosophy and science, natural science and social science, pure science and applied science, and should form the core of all these" (RXYRS: 540–541). In the preface to RXYRS, Liang claimed that "all schools of ethics have their own '*xinlixue*' as basis; all of their views about ethics (or human life) are inseparable from their perception of human *xinli* and human life" (RXYRS: 525–526). Therefore, when Liang mentioned *xinli* or *xinlixue*, he did not merely refer to the study of the mind and behavior, but a combination of the scientific study of the human mind as well as the philosophical explanation of the general trend, inclination, and preference that human beings would have in daily life. Due to this involvement in value judgement, Liang also regarded RXYRS as an investigation of human nature (*renxinglun* 人性論) (RXYRS: 542).

In order to articulate the function of the heart-mind (*xin*), Liang highlighted how it differs from the body (*shen* 身). He categorized the study of the biological function of the brain as "*shen*," and called this study physiology (*shenglixue* 生理學). He identified the functions of the brain and heart-mind as follows: the brain is responsible for the mechanical function of the nervous system for the whole body, while the heart-mind is responsible for integrating different possibilities, so that human beings, as subjects, could achieve higher flexibility and enjoy more freedom in the face of different obstacles.[8] In Liang's study of the heart-mind, he hypothesized that there are similar inclinations between human beings, especially for people who share a similar living environment, life experience, and culture. Therefore, he tended to adopt a collective approach to observe the similar inclinations of the same group of people, and suggested that there is a correlative relationship between human heart-mind and society. While heart-mind is inevitably influenced and shaped by society, society develops according to the preference of the collective heart-mind during different historical phases (RXYRS: 540).

Xin, usually translated as "heart-mind" in studies of Chinese philosophy, is the core concept of the book. As Liang assumed that there is a reciprocal relationship between the collective power of the heart-mind and the development of society, the

[8] Liang explained this with the example of learning to ride a bicycle: while the brain is responsible for indicating the mechanical function and coordination of the body, the heart-mind is responsible for creating specific skills and patterns for cycling after sufficient practice. See RXYRS: 634.

way he understood the heart-mind would inevitably affect his study of future social development, and vice versa. For the sake of clarifying this core concept, the function and significance of heart-mind can be distinguished. First of all, Liang pointed out that the most important and fundamental feature of the heart-mind is the sense of *zijue* 自覺 (self-consciousness),[9] which is also considered to be the core of the subjective aspect of *xinlixue*. Liang asserted that self-consciousness is inherently possessed by all human beings (RXYRS: 593); it is omnipresent in consciousness, even though its condition may swing between strong, weak, subtle, and noticeable. To further explain this feature, Liang applied a theory of Yogācāra Buddhism and stated that self-consciousness originates from the self-witnessing aspect (*zizhengfen* 自證分),[10] the third of the four parts of cognition (*sifen* 四分).[11] In the Yogācāra theory of cognitive mental functioning, *zizhengfen* refers to the self-witnessing (or self-authentication) of the cognizing aspect (*jianfen* 見分) in the consciousness. Liang highlighted this self-witnessing characteristic and associated it with the concept of self-consciousness. He asserted that self-consciousness is situated in the depths of the heart-mind, which provides a pure and faint sense of awareness (*weiwei you jue* 微微有覺) and enables human beings to "witness" the movement of thought when they pay attention to it (RXYRS: 587–588). Owing to this perceivability of self-consciousness, he asserted this function of the mind should be rooted in the self-witnessing aspect (此自覺應是根於彼自證分而有者) (RXYRS: 587), but highlighted the differences between the two: human beings can realize and witness their self-consciousness, but they are unable to perceive the functioning of the self-witnessing aspect; they can only recognize and accept there is such functioning in the consciousness (RXYRS: 587). By associating the concept of self-consciousness

[9]According to a footnote in RXYRS, Liang mentioned his preference for "awareness" rather than "consciousness" as the English translation of *zijue* (RXYRS: 589). As "consciousness" has been extensively used as the translation of *yishi*, he wanted to clearly distinguish it from the meaning of *zijue*, so he adopted "awareness" as the translation. In this chapter, however, "self-consciousness" is adopted as the English translation of *zijue*. This is mainly because Liang's concept of *zijue* is associated with Mao Zedong's application of the same term in his 1937 article "Shijian lun" (On Practice) and 1938 article "Lun chijiu zhan" (On Protracted War), while "*zijue*" in Mao's works is usually translated as "conscious" or "self-conscious." Besides, Liang's concept is also related to the concept of "Bewusstsein" in Friedrich Engels's 1880 article "Die Entwicklung des Sozialismus von der Utopie zur Wissenschaft" (Socialism: Utopian and Scientific), which is also translated as "consciousness" in English. In order to maintain the consistency of the translations, the latter is adopted throughout the chapter whenever Liang's concept of *zijue* is mentioned.

[10]See Charles Muller, "Self-witnessing Aspect 自證分," *Digital Dictionary of Buddhism*, http://www.buddhism-dict.net/cgi-bin/xpr-ddb.pl?q=自證分.

[11]According to Yogācāra Buddhism, when the cognitive mental functioning is activated, the mind itself is divided into four aspects (*sifen*) with particular functions. Cognitive function is established based on these four aspects. The four aspects include: *xiangfen* 相分 (the object which is perceived), *jianfen* 見分 (cognizing aspect, the function of seeing the form of an object), *zizhengfen* 自證分 (self-aware part, self-witnessing aspect), and *zhengzizhengfen* 證自證分 (reconfirming self-aware part, re-witnessing aspect). See Charles Muller, "Four Parts 四分," *Digital Dictionary of Buddhism*, http://www.buddhism-dict.net/cgi-bin/xpr-ddb.pl?56.xml+id(%27b56db-5206%27). On the *sifen*, please also refer to Li Jingjing's chapter "Liang the Buddhist."

with the self-witnessing aspect, Liang attempted to provide an ontological explanation of the former by applying a Yogācāra system of cognition. Its correlation with the self-witnessing aspect emphasizes the feature of subjective knowing in consciousness, which is useful for Liang to argue that self-consciousness could attain certain subjective knowledge.

Regarding the cognitive function of the heart-mind, Liang designated consciousness (*yishi* 意識) and self-consciousness (*zijue* 自覺) as two sides of the same coin, which were mapped onto his two understandings of *xinlixue*. On the one hand, he categorized those mental activities that involve responses to the external world, such as perception and judgement, as the function of consciousness; on the other hand, he identified those involving the attainment of truth, benevolence, and beauty as the function of self-consciousness. Liang further explained the nature of self-consciousness as follows:

> It is this sense of selflessness [*wusi de ganqing* 無私的感情] that makes human beings great; the human heart-mind is equipped with self-consciousness which is the site where the sense of selflessness is situated. Human beings must transcend considerations of gains and losses so that then they can deal with them correctly.
>
> 具此無私的感情，是人類之所以偉大；而人心之有自覺，則為此無私的感情之所寄焉。人必超於利害得失之上來看利害得失，而後乃能正確地處理利害得失。(RXYRS: 593)

Based on this quote, Liang highlighted the features of selflessness in self-consciousness, which could lead human beings to transcend their personal interest and make appropriate decisions. Liang assumed self-consciousness as inherently present in all people, and thus supposed everyone at birth is fundamentally good in nature.

In addition to attributing the sense of selflessness to self-consciousness, Liang also called this sense "*lixing*" (理性)[12] in his theory of heart-mind. In the context of Liang's philosophy, Guy Alitto points out that the term is not translatable by the usual English equivalent "reason," as the concept denotes "the normative sense which directs moral action" and "the sense of right and wrong which makes man human" (Alitto 1976: 228). In light of this connotation, John Hanafin translates *lixing* as "ethical reason" (Hanafin 2003: 203), while Thierry Meynard thought it can be best translated as "moral reason" (Meynard 2011: 99). As a matter of fact, Liang's use of this term can be seen as a response to Bertrand Russell's (1872–1970) trichotomy of the most significant features of human beings suggested in his 1916 publication *Principle of Social Reconstruction*: instinct (*benneng* 本能), reasoning (*lizhi* 理智), and spirituality (*lingxing* 靈性) (RXYRS: 530). Liang did not agree with Russell when he wrote DXWH and claimed that the first two were enough to

[12]The term *lixing* was firstly introduced in his 1934 talk "jianshen taolian yaozhi" 精神陶煉要旨 (Essence of spiritual cultivation) (Liang 1934: 492–519). He further developed this concept in his 1949 publication ZGWH. In RXYRS, he asked the readers to refer to chapter 7 of ZGWH for reference. See RXYRS: 611. For the details of *lixing*, please also refer to An 1997.

distinguish human begins from animals.[13] When he wrote ZGWH in the 1940s, however, he changed his mind and added *lixing* as another critical feature, which is similar to the connotation of spirituality suggested by Russell. According to Liang's explanation, the aforementioned "spirituality" is based on an "impersonal feeling,"[14] which forms the basis of religion and ethics. *Lixing* possesses similar connotations as "spirituality," but Liang adopted the former term and regarded it as a critical feature of human beings, representing "the emotional aspect of human heart-mind that is liberated from animal instinct" (RXYRS: 611). Owing to the influence of the theory of evolution, Liang believed human beings still share two instincts with animals, which he characterized as the quests for survival and reproduction. While animals are entangled by these two quests, human beings are evolved and can liberate themselves from these entanglements due to their mental abilities, which Liang called "the operation of thinking of humanity" (*renlei xinsi zuoyong* 人類心思作用). He stated that mental abilities are separated into two types: reasoning (*lizhi*) and moral reason (*lixing*). The former refers to the intellectual aspect,[15] while the latter refers to the emotional one. Thus, Liang suggested a trichotomy of his own, which includes instinct (*benneng* 本能), reasoning (*lizhi* 理智), and moral reason (*lixing* 理性).

In Liang's analysis, impulse is concomitant with instinct so that originally, human beings inevitably acted according to an impulsive energy. However, human beings learned to control their impulses with reasoning along the process of evolution, as it enables human beings to think objectively and achieve reasonable solutions in the face of different problems. Liang claimed that moral reason was further developed based on the objective mindset of reasoning, so that human beings could transcend their personal interest, think impartially, and behave altruistically for the common good. Liang described the manifestation of moral reason as "*dagong wusi*" (大公無私), which refers to an all-encompassing, impartial, and selfless mind. Owing to the difference between reasoning and moral reason, Liang argued that judgements obtained from reasoning reveal *wuli* 物理 (the principle of things), while those derived from the use of moral reason express *qingli* 情理

[13] In DXWH, "instinct" refers to the natural instinct that humans share with animals (the quests for survival and reproduction) as well as their quest for moral perfection. See DXWH: 452–457.

[14] Liang used "impersonal feeling" as the English translation of "*wusi de ganqing*" (無私的感情) when he explained Bertrand Russell's concept of spirituality (see RXYRS: 533), which means human beings tend to think and act without considering their personal intertest and preferences. In this chapter, I prefer to use "sense of selflessness" as the translation of *wusi de ganqing*, because it is more compatible with the concept of "forgetting the self" in the following discussions.

[15] In RXYRS, "reasoning" mainly refers to logical thinking that is based on an objective and rational mindset, but not the selfish calculations that Liang discussed in DXWH.

(reasonableness).[16] Liang regarded reasoning and moral reason as the two mental abilities of the heart-mind, and attributed the superiority of human beings over animals to these two features, which he thought were opposed to instincts. According to Liang, the manifestations of reasoning and moral reason could contribute differently in the development of human society: the former could serve as the basis of science, while the latter was the basis of morality. Therefore, he summarized them as follows: "reasoning is the clever application of the heart-mind; moral reason is the virtue of the heart-mind" (理智者人心之妙用; 理性者人心之美德) (RXYRS: 614). Liang reiterated the importance of these two mental abilities in RXYRS, and he thought that they were particularly manifest in socialist society (RXYRS: 686).

In Liang's discussion of the heart-mind, he also contrasted the latter with the human body (*renshen* 人身). He claimed that human beings would not be satisfied by merely fulfilling the two instinctive needs, the quests for survival and reproduction, that are generated by the body. They would have a further need for breaking the barriers of the heart-mind so as to attain integration with others and even oneness with the cosmos. He stated that the body demarcated the natural boundary between human beings, but people can still stay connected with others thanks to their heart-minds, as they can share their thoughts and feelings, and even establish a sense of empathy with each other. Thus, building a harmonious relationship between people is possible. Furthermore, Liang took a further step and asserted that the heart-mind would eventually realize it is part of the great cosmos, which would lead it to attain a full integration with the cosmos and its infiniteness.[17] Based on this understanding, Liang suggested that human beings should not consider their personal interest, but remain conscientious of all other living beings and even non-living things: "All matters are related to my life; nothing is excluded" (RXYRS: 620). Such a realization of oneness is instigated by the sense of selflessness, which is used to illuminate the role of impartiality and inclusiveness in RXYRS.

To adapt his argument about the heart-mind to the times, Liang made use of terminologies he borrowed from Mao Zedong's 1938 article on military strategies and tactics called "Lun chijiu zhan" 論持久戰 (On Protracted War), including "initiative" (*zhudongxing* 主動性), "flexibility" (*linghuoxing* 靈活性), and "planning" (*jihuaxing* 計劃性) (Mao 1991: 439–518, RXYRS: 550–600). He thought that these military strategies were applicable to describe the functions of the heart-mind, as they share a common goal of gaining the initiative (RXYRS: 550). According to

[16] The translations of *wuli* and *qingli* are borrowed from Huang 2017: 354. While *qingli* can be literally translated as "principle of emotion," I prefer to adopt Huang Yong's translation of "reasonableness." According to Liang, human beings are able to make reasonable and appropriate moral judgements by employing moral reason that is embedded in self-consciousness. By comparison with *wuli*, *qingli* refers to adjustable moral principles that are reasonably made in different circumstances. In this sense, translating *qingli* as "reasonableness" is a more appropriate as it implies the meaning of evaluating different moral judgments before making the most reasonable and suitable one. Liang also explained the difference between *wuli* and *qingli* in ZGLX. He regarded righteousness, fairness, and honesty as the virtues that belong to *qingli*. See ZGLX: 366.

[17] Liang claimed that such integration with the cosmos could only be experienced by human beings, which highlights another difference between human beings and animals. See RXYRS: 615, 620.

Liang, "initiative" in the heart-mind is manifested by the realization of the subjectivity of the self, so that human beings can take the active role in creating something new. "Flexibility" is regarded as an auxiliary element that facilitates the attainment of initiative. He used the example of a battle, in which a detailed division of labor and centralized management by a leader are necessary; the troop could only attain higher flexibility under this circumstance. Likewise, he thought that impulses, represented by the body, should be controlled so that human life could achieve more without being controlled by it. Human beings would then be able to take the predominant role in mastering the external world, instead of being passively subjected to it. As to Liang's discussion of "planning," it covers his understanding of the developmental trend of human life: human beings can be liberated from the entanglement of the two instinctive needs, and eventually be able to connect with the great life of the cosmos. Such a developmental model, Liang thought, was a manifestation of the dominating role of the heart-mind over things or the physical world (*wu* 物) (RXYRS: 598).

In RXYRS, Liang also portrayed human life as the manifestation of the heart-mind. He claimed that human life bears an original nature (*shengming benxing* 生命本性) that indicates the inclination of the heart-mind. From Liang's point of view, the evolution of all living things develops from confinement to liberation. The evolution of human beings is driven by their self-consciousness, which can be conceptualized as a specific willpower. Such continuously ascending (*xiangshang de* 向上的) willpower is based on the self-reflective, all-encompassing, and impartial mind, which propels humanity's progressive breakthrough from existing conditions and gradually leads to the final liberation. Among all living things, only human beings are inherently endowed with this willpower, so that they can break through the confinements of the two instinctive needs that belong to the level of the body, and gradually strive for different levels of liberation by fully utilizing the function of the heart-mind. As mentioned above, Liang described the nature of self-consciousness by appealing to the sense of selflessness (*wusi de ganqing* 無私的感情), which espouses the elimination of "*si*" (selfish calculation and consideration), which should be replaced by "*gong*" (公 inclusiveness, impartiality). In short, two aspects of the original nature of life can be distinguished: first, it is equipped with ascending willpower that propels human beings to seek progress continuously; second, the internal will inclines to abandon selfishness and embrace inclusiveness. With these two features, Liang thought that the nature of life would lead human beings to become more flexible and freer (RXYRS: 617, 631).

"Liberation" and "freedom" in Liang's thought involve two levels: the basic level refers to the liberation of the heart-mind from its entanglement with the body, which is achieved by fulfilling the two basic human needs. Liang claimed that such needs could be fulfilled by the centralized mode of production in socialist society, which depends on the intensive cooperation between people. This implies that people should obey the collective and contribute to society with an altruistic attitude, while the self and selfish motives (*sixin* 私心) should be minimized. The higher level of "liberation" refers to the liberation from the considerations and prejudices of the self.[18] This level can be attained when self-consciousness is fully developed. Such liberation is manifested by the establishment of a great harmonious community (*Datong*大同) in which there is no national boundary. Liang anticipated that in such a society, all human beings would have a high sense of virtue and tend to put others first, and thus the whole human community would be fully integrated. Along with forgetting the self and eliminating the self, Liang expected human beings would be able to attain oneness with the cosmos, and eventually attain the ontological basis of human existence.

According to this understanding of human nature, however, there should be no conflict, hatred, and injustice in the world. How about the dark side of human nature? At this level, Liang adhered to the Marxist ideology and implicitly stated that evil is caused by the emergence of social hierarchies. Human beings originally acted according to the nature of life in the primitive stage of development, but such pure nature was later contaminated by the differentiation of classes. People held different social positions and thus tended to consider interest according to their class. Thereupon, selfishness is generated and brings forth conflict and antagonism between classes. Liang therefore thought that the original nature of human beings was covered by their dispositions specific to their social class (*jiejixing* 階級性). Liang believed that such hierarchical system was an inevitable stage of history for most societies,[19] but in the future both national borders and social classes would be abolished. Then, people would no longer consider their interest from the viewpoint of selfishness, and thus the goodness of human nature would be recovered. In this sense, I suggest that RXYRS is Liang's attempt to guide people to further eliminate their sense of selfishness, so that they could become selfless (*wusi* 無私) in the communist stage.

4 Liang's Anticipation of the Realization of Communism and Rejection of Historical Materialism

In RXYRS, Liang maintained that the realization of socialism in China was mainly reflected by the centralized mode of production which allowed for the rapid growth of industrial productivity. Owing to centralized management, human beings became more powerful due to their exploitation and consumption of natural resources. Within 20 years of the establishment of the PRC, Liang claimed that China had made remarkable accomplishments in terms of production, which were even greater

[18] In this context, "freedom" and "liberation" refers to the emancipation from desires. See RXYRS: 593.

[19] In RXYRS, Liang did not clearly state whether historically China had social classes or not. In ZGWH, Liang ascertains that Chinese society was not structured into different social classes but into professions. See ZGWH: 145–157 and chapter 9 of this volume.

than that of the USSR (RXYRS: 681–682).[20] He asserted that human beings would be able to conquer nature during the last stage of social transformation. Such transformation from socialism to communism would mark the transition of the heart-mind from the state of spontaneity (*zifa* 自發) to that of self-consciousness (*zijue* 自覺) (RXYRS: 681). Liang expected all societies in the world would experience such transformation (RXYRS: 761).

"Spontaneity" and "self-consciousness" were previously used by Friedrich Engels (1820–1895), Vladimir Lenin (1870–1924),[21] and MAO Zedong, so their adoption strengthened the Marxist and Maoist content in RXYRS. In the first chapter, Liang had already used these terms when stating his purpose behind the writing of the book: "If human beings are not going to understand themselves, how can we human beings evolve from the spontaneous historical transformation to the planned creation of the history with self-consciousness?" (RXYRS: 538). Liang made a footnote and asked his readers to refer to Engels's 1880 article "Die Entwicklung des Sozialismus von der Utopie zur Wissenschaft" (Socialism: Utopian and Scientific). In Engels's article, "spontaneous" and "consciousness" are not used as a contrast in terms of historical evolution.[22] According to the English translation, "spontaneous" refers to the form of division of labor that is devoid of any preconceived plan (Engels 1901: 68). As to "consciousness" and "consciously," they are used in the context of mastering nature, social organization, and even the goal of making history one's own (Engels 1901: 89). Engels did not compare these two terms, but Liang put them together and highlighted the contrast between the two.

Liang's application of the terms "spontaneity" and "self-consciousness" was also influenced by MAO Zedong. He employed "conscious activity" (*zijue de nengdongxing* 自覺的能動性) from Mao's "On Protracted War," which he found was resonant with his own understanding of self-consciousness. According to Mao, "conscious activity" refers to the capacity for action that is peculiar to human beings: it enables them to derive ideas, principles, and opinions from objective facts, and put forward plans, policies, strategies, and tactics. He thought that it is a characteristic that distinguishes human beings from things (Mao 1991: 477).[23] Liang subscribed to Mao's explanation and further suggested that the three functions of the heart-mind, including initiative, flexibility, and planning, could be reca-

[20] Please also refer to RLCZL, in which Liang expressed his appreciation for the centralized leadership of the CCP. It is worth noting that Liang's understanding of foreign affairs was limited by the sources he had access to. According to Liang's diary in the 1960s and 1970s, he read a newspaper called *Cankao xiaoxi* 參考消息 (The Reference News) regularly. This newspaper was published by Xinhua News Agency 新華社, an official news agency of the government, which was the only agency that translated and republished foreign news during Mao's period. Liang also quoted a piece of foreign news from this newspaper in RLCZL. Please refer to Liang 1961: 417.

[21] Regarding Lenin's application of the terms, please refer to Van den Stock 2020: 610–611.

[22] It is worth noting that the German term "Bewusstsein" is translated as "consciousness" in most of the English translations, including the version translated by Edward Aveling in 1901. The Chinese translation of the term is "*zijue*." Liang also used this Chinese term when he quoted Engels' article. See RXYRS: 538.

[23] Liang focused more on the differentiation between human beings and animals. See RXYRS: 770.

pitulated by the term "conscious activity" (RXYRS: 550). Hence, he borrowed and reinterpreted Mao's terms in a skillful manner, in order to integrate them to his own argument.

Another possible source of influence by Mao is related to his 1937 article "Shijian lun" 實踐論 (On Practice). In this article, Mao stated that when the proletariat started its social revolution against the bourgeoisie, it entered "a period of spontaneous struggle" (*zifa douzheng shiqi* 自發鬥爭時期). Later on, "a stage of conscious change" (*zijue de jieduan* 自覺的階段),[24] also known as communism, would arrive when all human beings consciously transform themselves and the world (Mao 1991: 288, 296). According to Mao, opponents of communism would also experience a transformation in the process, albeit by coercive means in their case. Liang also used the term "*zijue*" in RXYRS but he kept silent about the coercive means Mao believed to be necessary during political movements. Even though "Shijian lun" was not mentioned in RXYRS, there is a similar application of "spontaneity" and "consciousness" in it, referring to the socialist and communist phases respectively. Liang insisted such transformation was mainly represented by the change of the heart-mind from the manifestation of "spontaneity" to that of "self-consciousness" (RXYRS: 657, 662, 681, 694, 761, 766, 767).

Spontaneity and self-consciousness are frequently used by Liang when referring to the mode of thinking that people would have during the socialist and communist stages respectively. The meaning of the two terms can be further clarified by taking a closer look at ZGLX, which Liang wrote between 1967 and 1970 when he temporary stopped writing RXYRS. In this work, Liang claimed that all mental and physical activities instigated by spontaneity originate from the instincts and physical needs of the body, while self-consciousness relates to thought and actions that involve reflection and contemplation. In order to explain the difference between the two, he compared the reasons why both proletarians and intellectuals participate in social revolution. Proletarians, he asserted, mainly do so because of the economic oppression they face in their daily lives, while intellectuals do not experience such kind of oppression, but they nevertheless seek to improve the current situation. Liang designated the former reason as spontaneous and the latter as self-conscious (ZGLX: 234, 237). In this sense, he suggested the communist party should retain the leading role in enlightening the masses so that their sense of self-consciousness could be raised (ZGLX: 238–239). Furthermore, he asserted that society is not fully developed if self-consciousness is only possessed by individuals who do not consider society in a collective sense; as for an advanced society, all members should manifest self-consciousness conspicuously, which also means the whole society would move towards the same direction.

Liang basically accepted the communist discourse of social evolution and anticipated China would evolve from the stage of socialism to communism. However, his interpretation of the two representative spirits, spontaneity and self-consciousness,

[24]The English translation of "*zifa douzheng shiqi*" and "*zijue de jieduan*" are quoted from Mao 1966.

reflected his rejection of historical materialism to describe parts of the process of social development. This shows a conflict between his thought and the political ideology of the time. According to Karl Marx's (1818–1883) *Zur Kritik der politischen Ökonomie* (Contribution to the Critique of Political Economy), historical materialism designates material forces of production and relations of production as the two decisive factors that constitute the economic structure of society and the corresponding social consciousness. In the preface of the book, he states

> The mode of production in material life determines the general character of the social, political, and intellectual process of life. It is not the consciousness of men which determines their existence; it is on the contrary their social existence which determines their consciousness. (Marx 1904: 11–12)

In RXYRS, Liang expressed his disagreement, claiming that social evolution is ultimately propelled by the collective power of self-consciousness during the communist stage. According to Liang's understanding, the action of spontaneity during the socialist stage was related to the entanglements of the two instinctive needs of human beings, symbolized by the "body" (*shen* 身) in Liang, and self-consciousness was associated with the heart-mind that could think and make judgements impartially. The transformation from the former to the latter across the two stages of social evolution represents a leap whereby human beings escape from the confinement of the body in order to rise to the level of the heart-mind. Liang described this latter condition as "the body serving the purpose of the heart-mind" (*shen wei xin yong* 身為心用) (RXYRS: 767). In this sense, historical materialism is only valid for a period in the development of history when human beings are constrained by their material desires and material conditions of production. Upon the realization of communism, when the heart-mind takes the command, historical materialism will cease to offer a convincing account of human behavior and social organization.[25]

Liang anticipated the realization of communism would mean the abolition of old systems, which entailed the end of national borders and social classes. The whole world would become a Great community in which all people would cooperate and coordinate with each other as one single entity (*xietiao ruo yi* 協調若一). Also, owing to the power of self-consciousness in terms of participation in collective production, Liang thought that human beings would tend to cooperate rather than compete with each other, given that increase in production would satisfy the material needs of daily life. Liang believed that when human beings are no longer entangled with survival problems, the previously opaque heart-mind could be developed to its full capacity. He anticipated that the level of satisfaction in terms of material needs might be similar during both socialist and communist stages, but human beings would experience an unprecedented satisfaction with their emotional and spiritual needs in the later stage.

[25] I would like to thank one of the anonymous reviewers who suggested highlighting Liang's peculiar understanding of the limited validity of historical materialism. Please also refer to Van den Stock 2020: 606–612.

According to Liang, the socialist period saw the manifestation of the heart-mind in terms of initiative, flexibility, and planning. Liang explained these aspects highlighted the subjectivity of human beings, which help them become autonomous and proactive in order to "make history." He insisted such realization of subjectivity led socialist China to reach astonishing achievements in terms of production, so that this period would also provide the precondition for the development of the heart-mind in the next historical phase. Liang stated that the above three functions of the heart-mind only represented its clever application (妙用), which belongs to the level of reasoning, within which the virtues of righteousness and impartiality are not yet manifest (RXYRS: 613–614). He stated that "reasoning is the clever application of the heart-mind, while moral reason is the virtue of the heart-mind." (RXYRS: 614) As Liang claimed the communist stage would be a period of self-conscious change, in which the manifestation of moral reason—"the virtue of the heart-mind"—is based on self-consciousness, the first phase of communism that embraces Confucianism would involve the development of virtue in human life. In order to prepare China to transform from socialism to communism, Liang thought that the essence of traditional Chinese culture was crucial for the full development of self-consciousness.

5 The Implicit Confucian Teaching in Communist Society

This section discusses Liang's argument about the importance of traditional Chinese culture during the first phase of communism. In his letter "Zhi Zhou zongli bing zhuan Mao zhuxi" 致周總理並轉毛主席 (To Premier Zhou and to Chairman Mao) in 1968, Liang claimed that the essence of traditional culture was a crucial factor that facilitated the success of the proletarian revolution in China, allowing China, rather than Russia, to become the leader of the world revolution (*shijie geming* 世界革命) (ZZZL: 81–82). In this sense, he did not see any incompatibility between traditional Chinese culture and socialism or communism, but even claimed the embedded moral reason in traditional Chinese culture facilitated the realization of socialism before capitalism was fully developed in China. According to Liang, moral reason was a product of China's precocious development of self-consciousness, while he also interpreted the communist phase of social evolution as a grand manifestation of self-consciousness. Such peculiar understanding made him confident in believing China would play a leading and pivotal role in realizing the world revolution (ZGLX: 215). Liang predicted all human beings would experience a long transitional period during which people's heart-mind would transform from being spontaneous to self-conscious; he called this period "the growth of morality" (RXYRS: 744).

Liang stated the critical role of both reasoning and moral reason during the communist phase, which is that of facilitating the smooth functioning of society, thanks to a reasonable arrangement of daily life and the maintenance of social order. He reiterated that all human beings would belong to the same society without any national distinction. In the first phase of communism, Liang believed human beings would be equipped with a high standard of self-consciousness and self-discipline so that the legal system would be replaced by social etiquette (*lisu* 禮俗), based on the Confucian teachings of ritual propriety (*li* 禮) and music (*yue* 樂) (RXYRS: 753–763).[26] He attributed such future achievements to the full manifestation of the heart-mind (RXYRS: 686). As mentioned in the last section, reasoning is related to the intellectual faculty and the realization of the subjectivity of human beings, which allows for an important increase in production. Liang described moral reason as the fountainhead of all kinds of virtues so that people could cooperate in this global society with mutual trust, respect, and understanding (RXYRS: 693). Liang thought that such sense of empathy is possible because human beings have the inclination to emancipate from the barrier of the body and connect with their heart-mind during the communist period. Therefore, this period would see the combination of reasoning and moral reason, representing science and morality respectively. He insisted it was not his subjective assertion but the trend of future development that was based on "objective facts" (RXYRS: 689). As for the absence of discussion of morality in Marxist theory, Liang was aware of it and tried to give a peculiar explanation: "Marx and Engels developed their theory on the basis of science. [Although] they did not mention morality, morality was already embedded in it. Even though it [their theory] is said to be entirely unrelated to ethics [*lunli xue* 倫理學], [I found] it can still be considered as a better type of ethics." (RXYRS: 541–542, 733) Palpably, Liang's emphasis on "*lixing*" as morality was his own addition to Marxist theory.

Liang thought that the process of social transformation was accompanied by the rise of awareness of morality. To clarify his view, Liang employed the term "genuine morality" (*zhen daode* 真道德) in RXYRS. In the early stage of social development, only a small number of outstanding individuals could realize the meaning of genuine morality, while most people only follow the moral rules set by their society. In order to understand "genuine morality," one must rely on the function of self-consciousness of the heart-mind in a state of profound stillness (*shenjing de zijue* 深靜的自覺).[27] Liang set two criteria for discerning genuine morality. First, it is based on the ascending power of self-consciousness (RXYRS: 737), meaning that it is the reflection of self-motivated human nature. He thought that human beings should comply with this flow and always show earnest endeavor for improving themselves. Having this attitude and acting accordingly would be regarded as "moral." Liang also had an idiosyncratic understanding of *daode* 道德 (morality). He explained *dao* 道 as the nature of life in the cosmos, which is also represented in the original nature of human life (*shengming benxing*). Instead of apprehending *de* 德 as a noun with

---

[26] In DXWH, Liang had already asserted that the application of the reward or punishment system relies on people's mindset of selfish calculation. As he anticipated human beings would no longer focus on the issues of the body during the communist stage, he believed the mindset of selfish calculation would also be abandoned.

[27] Liang quoted Indian poet Rabindranath Tagore's terms "inner consciousness" and "our innermost being" to explain his term "*shenjing de zijue*." See RXYRS: 715.

the meaning of virtue, Liang explained *de* as a verb having the meaning of *de* 得 (to get, to obtain), which refers to the heart-mind's ability to obtain something (RXYRS: 731). "*Daode*" in this context means the knowledge obtained by oneself when one complies with the natural flow of the cosmos, which is always self-motivated to strive for the best. Examples of self-motivated behavior include "being diligent in learning, possessing the feeling of shame, putting things into practice, and being unsatisfied with moral degradation" (RXYRS: 633). In short, Liang asserted that a moral life should be vigorous in achieving higher goals. If a person does not comply with this nature of the cosmos, Liang defined such person as immoral (RXYRS: 731, 733, 735). To avoid degeneration toward immorality, Liang thought one had to rely on the power of self-consciousness.

As Liang stated that *dao* was the nature of life in the cosmos, which is in ceaseless flux, he saw flexibility as another criterion of genuine morality. He claimed that each society tends to have their own criteria to discern right from wrong, good from evil; their social norms and regulations would then be set up accordingly. But the so-called good habits resulting from this only represent the "morality" that is needed by that particular society, and not "genuine morality." According to Liang, genuine morality is generated by self-consciousness, which leads human beings to be self-disciplined and act appropriately (RXYRS: 715, 735, 742). Thus, genuine morality allows a large extent of flexibility. A moral person should be able to act properly in accordance with his current and specific circumstance. With the power of self-consciousness, human beings should have an independent and autonomous mind to judge which action to take, without having to follow rigid rules. Therefore, Liang explained *yi* 義 (righteousness), one of the core virtues in Confucianism, in terms of *yi* 宜 (appropriateness) (RXYRS: 741). He also criticized the popular teaching of the "Three Guiding Principles" (*sangang* 三綱) and the "Five Constant Regulations" (*wuchang* 五常),[28] and claimed those Confucian scholars who set such rules of conduct had misunderstood the teachings of Confucius and Mencius. In order to explain the concept of self-consciousness, he associated it with the concept of innate moral knowledge (*liangzhi* 良知) and briefly mentioned the thought of Mencius 孟子 (372–289 BC) and WANG Yangming 王陽明 (1472–1592) (RXYRS: 666). Hence, self-consciousness, the core concept of Liang's heart-mind theory, is directly related to Confucianism.[29] Liang affirmed the value of Confucianism, but he thought that it could only be fully realized in communist society, as he expected human beings would be equipped with a high sense of self-consciousness during that period.

Equipped with the high sense of moral reason inherent in self-consciousness, Liang anticipated the cultivation of "genuine morality" would be prevailing, which is mainly manifested in human relations. To clarify his understanding of human relations during the communist phase, he borrowed and reinterpreted the Confucian

[28] "Three Guiding Principles" refer to the obligations attached to three key relationships, including the ruler and his subjects, father and son, and husband and wife. "Five Constant Regulations" refer to five virtues: benevolence, righteousness, propriety, wisdom, and trust.

[29] Similar to DXWH, Liang associated Confucianism with the essence of traditional Chinese culture, but he mentioned "Confucianism" explicitly only a few times in RXYRS.

terms "*lun*" (倫; human relations) and "*lunli*" (倫理; ethics). According to Liang, human relations should include all kinds of relations in society, while ethics refers to the appropriate ways according to which human beings should treat each other. He interpreted ethics as reasonableness (*qingli* 情理), which is based on *qing* 情 (humaneness).[30] In short, Liang explained that both sides involved in a relationship should take the active role in putting the other first (*yi duifang weizhong* 以對方為重) and put aside their own interest (RXYRS: 738). As in DXWH and ZGWH, Liang still regarded *lun* (human relations) as the essence of Chinese culture, but he gave a new interpretation of it in RXYRS, putting greater emphasis on the parties involved in society rather than the five ethical relations (*wulun* 五倫)[31] in the Confucian tradition. Owing to the influence of Marxist and Maoist ideology, Liang paid more attention to society rather than merely individuals. As he had already assumed the heart-mind tends to eliminate barriers and become more inclusive with the sense of selflessness, he thought it was selfish for one to only have concerns for one's own family and country (RXYRS: 736). Thus, ethics in RXYRS no longer focuses on the five ethical relations but covers all kinds of relations in society. It includes the relations between individuals and the collective, between those in charge of the factory and the workers, and between countries, among others. Liang insisted that all actors should put others first, respect each other, and fulfil their obligations. As a result, he assumed both sides in the relationship would at the same time enjoy rights without fighting for them.[32]

Such predictions are related to Liang's understanding of the original nature of life: "the good is based on openness, while evil originates from narrowness. The original nature of life has the inclination to attain openness" (RXYRS: 736). When this understanding applies to human relations, "narrowness" means focusing on the self or family, while openness refers to the breaking down the barrier between the self and non-self with the sense of inclusiveness. Liang described such sense as "including the other as if a single entity" (RXYRS: 739), so that there is no differentiation between the self and the other. Based on this way of thinking, he thought that the sense of self-consciousness would lead human beings to attain a further step of inclusiveness—to attain harmony within the cosmos by breaking the differentiation between human beings and the physical world. Liang thought that the relation between human beings and nature could be interpreted in two ways: *youdui* 有對 (antagonistic) and *wudui* 無對 (non-antagonistic). The former refers to the antagonistic relation as nature is regarded as an object for exploration and exploitation; the latter refers to the emancipation of the above relationship and the attainment of oneness with the cosmos. In order to experience this integration with the cosmos, which

[30] It should be noted that "*qing*" in this context means the understanding and kindness towards other people, so translations that carry neutral connotations such as feeling, emotion, or disposition are inaccurate. As for the explanation of *qingli*, please also refer to note 16.

[31] The five ethical relations refer to those between the father and the son, the ruler and his subjects, husband and wife, the elder and younger brother, and friends.

[32] Liang used the term "*jinlun*" (盡倫) to refer to the fulfilment of obligations in a relationship. See RXYRS: 737.

Liang regarded as a sublimation of the heart-mind, he attributed to self-consciousness the key to "open the door to the cosmic life," while Confucianism was the study to realize self-consciousness (RXYRS: 662–663).

Comparing the essence of Western and Chinese cultures that Liang associated with the merits of reasoning and moral reason respectively, he thought that the essence of Chinese culture carried an irreplaceable value as it fulfils the emotional needs of human beings by emphasizing the connection and harmonious relationship between people. During the first phase of communism, Liang anticipated both material and emotional needs of human beings could be solved. Yet this would not yet represent the end of history. He expected there would be a final phase of social transformation, as human beings would realize that they remained confined within the endless cycle of death and rebirth (RXYRS: 722).

6 Nirvana: The Ultimate Liberation

In previous studies of RXYRS, the Buddhist perspective was rarely discussed. To leave the Buddhist dimension undiscussed, however, would not be a complete examination of RXYRS, as the text describes the ultimate destination of human development as nirvana (RXYRS: 744, 769). According to Liang, the transformation from the first to the second phase of communism was a quest from "genuine morality" to "genuine religion" (*zhen zongjiao* 真宗教) (RXYRS: 768).[33] Liang claimed both of them share the same root of self-consciousness (RXYRS: 715), so Confucianism and Buddhism are compatible with each other from the point of view of Liang. As in DXWH, Liang acknowledged Buddhism as the sole "genuine religion," because it is an atheist religion that pursuits emancipation from the mundane world. When Buddhism is mentioned in both DXWH and RXYRS, it particularly refers to Yogācāra Buddhism, as Liang regarded it as the most authoritative and representative school in Buddhism.

Based on the doctrine of Yogācāra Buddhism, Liang differentiated the mundane world from the supramundane. The former refers to the "transient world of phenomenal appearances," and the latter denotes the spiritual world, which Liang also regarded as the noumenal. The phenomenal world involves arising and ceasing (*shengmie* 生滅), such as birth and death, beginning and end, but the noumenal does not. He argued that if arising and ceasing in the phenomenal world is real, then the condition of "neither arising nor ceasing" (*bushing bumie* 不生不滅) in the

[33] Liang stated that "humankind has taken up its historical mission to strive for the realization of communist society, which represents the endeavour to advance towards the moral world. The future [of human beings] will finally pass from the realization of genuine morality to that of genuine religion" (RXYRS: 768). In this sense, Liang included religion in his discussion of Marxist social transformation, which was originally excluded in Marxism or Maoism.

supramundane realm should also be regarded as real.[34] He attributed Confucianism to the mundane world, as it could not lead human beings to emancipate from *saṃsāra*, the cycle of death and rebirth. Therefore, he expected human beings would move on and seek the way out through "genuine religion" to achieve ultimate liberation.

Liang's understanding of the ultimate liberation is rooted in his own reinterpretation of the Yogācāra theory of eight consciousnesses.[35] He divided the eight consciousnesses into three groups, designating the first six consciousnesses simply as "consciousness" (*shi* 識), and the seventh and the eighth as "will" (*yi* 意) and "heart-mind" (*xin* 心)[36] respectively (RXYRS: 720). Liang explained that the first six consciousnesses belong to the shallow level of the human mind, while the other two play relatively fundamental roles. The first five consciousnesses arise in connection with the five sense organs for sensory data collection.[37] The sixth consciousness, thinking,[38] conceptualizes the manifold phenomena with the help of its direct interaction with the senses. It is a form of conscious awareness that is subject to interruptions. The primary function of the seventh consciousness, *manas* (*monashi* 末那識), is to perceive the subjective position of the eighth consciousness and construe it as one's own self, thereby creating self-attachment.[39] Unlike the sixth consciousness, it constitutes the subconscious regions of the mind that function every moment without lapse. As for the eighth consciousness, Liang regarded it as the subjectivity of human perception and called it "*xin*" (heart-mind 心),[40] and claimed that all manifestations of the world are created by the heart-mind (RXYRS: 720). Besides, he asserted that the eighth consciousness could represent the whole of human life. On this basis, he interpreted the Buddhist quote "all things are created by the mind alone" (*yiqie weixin suo zao* 一切唯心所造) as meaning that "all things are created

[34] Regarding the condition of the supramundane world, he claimed that it is impossible to imagine, as imagination itself belongs to the phenomenal sphere. See RXYRS: 717.

[35] Please also refer to Li Jingjing's chapter "Liang the Buddhist" in the present volume for the details of the eight consciousnesses.

[36] Liang innovatively connects the Yogācāra *xin* with the Neo-Confucian heart-mind, which is not in accord with the orthodox Yogācāra doctrine of consciousness-only. (I would like to thank one of the anonymous reviewers who suggested highlighting this issue.)

[37] The first five consciousnesses include: visual, auditory, olfactory, gustatory, and tactile.

[38] In RXYRS, Liang interpreted the sixth consciousness with the function of thinking, but Charles Muller claims that the sixth consciousness is also understood to be the locus of perception, feelings and intention. See Charles Muller, "mano-vijñāna 意識" *Digital Dictionary of Buddhism*, http://www.buddhism-dict.net/cgi-bin/xpr-ddb.pl?61.xml+id(%27b610f-8b58%27).

[39] Charles Muller, "manas 末那識" *Digital Dictionary of Buddhism*, http://www.buddhism-dict.net/cgi-bin/xpr-ddb.pl?q=末那識.

[40] Liang's interpretation of the eighth consciousness is different from the commonly used metaphor in Yogācāra Buddhism, explaining this consciousness as "a repository consciousness that receives and stores the karmic seeds which thereafter serve as the cause of conscious experience." See Charles Muller, "ālayavijñāna 阿賴耶識" *Digital Dictionary of Buddhism*, http://www.buddhism-dict.net/cgi-bin/xpr-ddb.pl?96.xml+id(%27b963f-8cf4-8036-8b58%27).

by human life" (RXYRS: 720). Owing to such interpretation, Liang associated the eighth consciousness with his own theory of the heart-mind.

According to the Yogācāra theory of consciousness, the conceptualization of the external world involves two aspects of cognition, the perceived (*xiangfen* 相分) and the perceiving (*jianfen* 見分). When the subject attempts to perceive the object, the subject itself is limited by its unique condition, which involves "*zhengbao*" 正報 (direct retribution or reward resulting from activities in prior lifetimes) and "*yibao*" 依報 (circumstantial retribution or the circumstances we are born into). Based on this condition, the subjectivity of human perception is the basis for the transformation of consciousness and thus makes the whole process possible. As this process takes place within consciousness, Liang explained that the grasper (*nengqu* 能取) and that which is grasped (*suoqu* 所取) both belong to the same entity. The perception of the world then mainly depends on the transformation of our own consciousness. Liang claimed that the eighth consciousness in each sentient being forms the basis of this transformation; hence, each sentient being should be regarded as an independent entity in terms of the conceptualization of the external world. Liang used the term "universe" (*yuzhou* 宇宙) in DXWH (Liang 1921: 376) to denote this; however, in RXYRS, Liang employed the term "world" (*shijie* 世界) (RXYRS: 718–719) to refer to the unique conditions of each sentient being based on their *zhengbao* and *yibao*. In this sense, each sentient being has their own world, and the heart-mind form their ontological foundation.

With this ontological basis, Liang claimed that the fundamental reality of the "world" of each sentient being was originally self-contented. Owing to the mistaken pursuit of satisfaction in the external world, the dichotomy between exterior and interior is brought forth, which gives rise to the discrimination between the external world and the self. Liang thought that such misconception was generated by the attachment to the self involved in the sixth and the seventh consciousnesses (RXYRS: 720). The former attachment refers to the "attachment to a self by discrimination" (*fenbie wozhi* 分別我執), which is created during the process of conceptualization; the latter refers to a more profound, concealed, and stronger "inborn attachment to the self" (*jusheng wozhi* 俱生我執) that is generated by *manas*. As this "inborn attachment to the self" operates subliminally, it is one of the most difficult attachments to break. The "attachment to a self by discrimination," by comparison, is easier to eliminate, as this consciousness has interruptions. In order to attain ultimate liberation, Liang thought that it was necessary to "eradicate the two attachments (*er zhi* 二執), eliminate the two hindrances (*er zhang* 二障) and cut off the two kinds of grasping (*er qu* 二取),[41] so that [sentient beings] could be emancipated from the endless cycle of death and rebirth" (RXYRS: 723). With the abandonment of the above attachments, hindrances, and grasping, the false dichotomy of

[41] The two attachments refer to attachment to the reality of a self (我執) and attachment to the reality of phenomena (法執). The two hindrances mean afflictive hindrances (Skt. *kleśâvaraṇa* 煩惱障) and cognitive hindrances (Skt. *jñeyâvaraṇa* 所知障). The two kinds of grasping refer to the grasper (*nengqu* 能取) and that which is grasped (*suoqu* 所取).

exterior and interior can be corrected, which facilitates the attainment of ultimate liberation (RXYRS: 722).

However, these attachments are embedded in our consciousness, which implies human beings are inevitably entangled in mistaken and deluded thoughts in daily life. Owing to this inevitability, Liang tended to acknowledge the "reality" of both the phenomenal and the noumenal that was supported by the *Yogācārabhūmi-Śāstra* (*Yujiashi dilun* 瑜伽師地論; Discourse on the Stages of Yogic Practice) of Yogācāra Buddhism. He accepted the notion of "four realities"[42] (*si zhenshi* 四真實) expounded in this Buddhist treatise (RXYRS: 724–726). The first one is called "reality as formulated by mundane cognition" (*shijian ji cheng zhenshi* 世間極成真實), and refers to the knowledge obtained by sensation; the second one is "reality as formulated by accurate reasoning" (*daoli ji cheng zhenshi* 道理極成真實), which refers to the intellectual knowledge obtained by logical reasoning, including all scientific knowledge.[43] Liang claimed that the perception of these two "realities" are inseparable from one's "inborn attachment to the self," which is further consolidated by the "attachment to a self by discrimination" due to the sixth consciousness. Therefore, he identified the first two as mundane reality, which are different from the other two that are related to the attainment of the supramundane. The third one refers to "reality as formulated by the cognition purified of the afflictive hindrances" (*fannao zhang jing zhi suo xing zhenshi* 煩惱障淨智所行眞實), which entails the attachment to the self (*wozhi* 我執)[44] that creates afflictive hindrances (Skt. *kleśâvaraṇa* 煩惱障) is eradicated by Yogācāra practice. The contaminated consciousness could be transformed to pure cognition (*zhuan ranshi cheng jingzhi* 轉染識成淨智) for the attainment of the emptiness of self (RXYRS: 726). The fourth is "reality as formulated by the cognition purified of the cognitive hindrances" (*suozhi zhang jing zhi suo xing zhenshi* 所知障淨智所行眞實), which means the one can free oneself from cognitive hindrances (Skt. *jñeyâvaraṇa* 所知障) created by "the attachment to dharmas (phenomena)" (*fazhi* 法執).[45] Liang believed the elimination of this attachment would lead to the attainment of the ontological basis of the

[42] Please refer to Charles Muller, "four realities 四真實" *Digital Dictionary of Buddhism*, http://www.buddhism-dict.net/cgi-bin/xpr-ddb.pl?q=四眞實 and "reality 真實義" *Digital Dictionary of Buddhism*, http://www.buddhism-dict.net/cgi-bin/xpr-ddb.pl?77.xml+id(%27b771e-5be6-7fa9%27).

[43] Liang also regarded the knowledge obtained by the application of dialectical materialism and historical materialism in Marxism as scientific knowledge. See RXYRS: 724.

[44] Liang distinguished four afflictions, including self-delusion (我癡), self-view (我見), the conceit "I-am" (我慢), and the addiction to things that are pleasing to oneself (我愛). See Charles Muller, "Affliction 煩惱," *Digital Dictionary of Buddhism*, http://www.buddhism-dict.net/cgi-bin/xpr-ddb.pl?q=煩惱.

[45] "Attachment to dharmas (phenomena)" refers to the unconscious attachment to the reality of phenomena. According to Charles Muller, it is the belief that "although the self is an illusory conglomerate of the five aggregates, the compositional elements of existence are inherently real." See Charles Muller, "Attachment to (the reality of) dharmas 法執," *Digital Dictionary of Buddhism*, http://www.buddhism-dict.net/cgi-bin/xpr-ddb.pl?q=法執.

universe (*yuzhou benti* 宇宙本體), which he called "thusness" (*zhenru* 真如)[46] and "Dharma nature" (*faxing* 法性).[47]

How can human beings attain ultimate liberation by eradicating the two attachments, eliminating the two hindrances and cutting off the two kinds of grasping? As in DXWH, Liang insisted that the Yogācāra practice of meditation was the key to eliminate each level of consciousness gradually in order to transform consciousness into fundamental wisdom. During the practice of meditation, the profound stillness of self-consciousness would be awakened, so that human beings could eliminate the subjective perception of the self by *manas* as well as the thinking generated by the sixth consciousness, and eventually perceive the pure sensory data collected by the first five consciousnesses (RXYRS: 719). As for the final destination of human beings, Liang claimed twice that

> as long as human beings appear, [in the end] they will pass away. They will not passively vanish from the earth, but will take the active role to terminate their existence. This was called 'to revert to nothingness' [*huanmie* 還滅] by ancient Indians, while Buddhists called it 'accomplishing Buddhahood.'
> 人類出現即有消逝，卻是人類將不是被動地隨地球以俱盡者，人類將主動地自行消化以去。此在古印度人講之還滅，在佛家謂之成佛。(RXYRS: 769)[48]

According to Liang, the supreme enlightenment of everyone would bring about the end of mundane existence once and for all. The end of history thus refers to the end of *saṃsāra* and the entry into nirvana.

As to his discussion of the "four realities," it explains why Liang thought that serious endeavor in the mundane world should be made even though he held a Buddhist worldview. Instead of regarding the knowledge obtained by sensation and logical reasoning as delusion, Liang acknowledged their mundane facticity as they naturally appear in daily life under the "inborn attachment to the self." At the same time, the knowledge obtained by the first six consciousnesses are also useful for fulfilling the two major instinctive needs of human beings. In order to satisfy these basic needs universally, he asserted that the replacement of capitalism by socialism would lead to a fair distribution of economic resources, allowing citizens to contribute to the betterment of the country. After accomplishing sufficient and stable level of supplies necessary for basic needs, Liang anticipated human beings would aspire to build a harmonious relationship with others during the communist stage. He designated moral reason as the essence of traditional Chinese culture, which is featured by the sense of selflessness. When we consider this feature within Liang's Buddhist worldview, such inclination of "forgetting the self" would facilitate the elimination of the "attachment to the self" along the pathway towards Buddhist enlightenment. Finally, at the final stage of communism, Liang thought that human beings would

---

[46] "Thusness" means things as they are; the establishment of reality as empty. See Charles Muller, "Thusness 真如," *Digital Dictionary of Buddhism*, http://www.buddhism-dict.net/cgi-bin/xpr-ddb.pl?77.xml+id(%27b771e-5982%27).

[47] "Dharma nature" refers to the true nature of things. See Charles Muller, "Dharma nature 法性," *Digital Dictionary of Buddhism*, http://www.buddhism-dict.net/cgi-bin/xpr-ddb.pl?q=法性.

[48] Liang also expressed the same thoughts in RXYRS: 744.

pursue ultimate emancipation from *saṃsāra*, so Buddhist teaching and practice would become popular.

7 Concluding Remarks

To conclude, the views expressed in RXYRS are based on LIANG Shuming's understanding of the original nature of human life, which is embedded with ascending energy—manifested by the function of self-consciousness—that continuously seeks flexibility and liberty. In the course of pursuing ultimate liberation, Liang thought that self-consciousness, where the sense of selflessness is situated, played a critical role in propelling human beings to release themselves from their current confinement. Such pursuit of liberation had been emphasized in his discussion of the mode of production in socialist and communist societies, of the actualization of "genuine morality" in connection with Confucian teachings, and even of the attainment of Buddhist enlightenment. The transformation of the heart-mind along the social transformation can also be regarded as a process of self-discovery and self-actualization. The ascending energy of self-consciousness leads human beings to explore various potentials and possibilities in each of the historical stages, so that they could bring out the best in themselves. The infinite potential of the heart-mind is the main theme Liang wanted to articulate in RXYRS. He regarded writing the book as an important task (Liang & Alitto 2013: 83), which was expressed in the epilogue of RXYRS: "As the whole of humankind is in need of a vision for the future, I have no choice but to write this book" (RXYRS: 772). Liang was 83 years old when he finished writing the book in 1975, while the book was finally published in 1984,[49] only 4 years before his death. In this book, Liang endeavored to demonstrate the value of Confucianism and Buddhism by claiming their compatibility with Marxism[50] in such a way as to establish a close connection between his political, social, and spiritual ideals.

These ideals are closely related to his own observation of the sufferings that human beings encounter in the mundane world. Owing to his acceptance of Marxist ideology after 1949, he thought socialism would solve the problem of material need efficiently. Human beings would then seek "genuine morality" during the first phase of communism. Liang thought these two phases would provide a precondition for the actualization of the last Buddhist phase, so he did not see any incompatibility between the three schools of thought. This conclusion can be supported by Liang's 1958 letter "To the CPPCC Rectification Office" (*Zhi zhengxie zhengfeng bangongshi* 致政協整風辦公室), in which he states: "I don't think there is any conflict

[49] For the reason of such delay of publication, please refer to Alitto 1986: 346–347.

[50] Liang wrote the book under a specific political environment during Mao's period. In particular, Confucius was severely criticized during the "Criticize Lin, Criticize *Kong* Campaign," while religions were also denounced under Marxist ideology.

between the idea of the supramundane and communism. On the contrary, I think that the value of Buddhism can only be discovered in a communist society. As everyone knows, the supramundane [can only be attained] by eradicating the two attachments (attachment to the self and the dharmas), and communism can be of remarkable help to eradicate the attachments (especially the attachment to the self)" (ZZXZF: 85–86). In this sense, it is fair to assert that the phases of socialism and the early stage of communism in RXYRS, which Liang regarded as the manifestation of the essence of "Western" and "Chinese" cultures,[51] are the preparation for the ultimate enlightenment in Buddhism. They can be regarded as skillful means (*fang-bian* 方便)[52] deployed in order to reach the final destination.

Acknowledgement This work was supported by the Swiss National Science Foundation (SNSF) as part of the project "The Exterior of Philosophy: On the Practice of New Confucianism."

References

DXWH Dong-Xi wenhua ji qi zhexue 東西文化及其哲學 [Eastern and Western Cultures and Their Philosophies; 1921]. *LSMQJ*, 2005, vol. 1: 319–547.

JSTL Jingshen taolian yaozhi 精神陶煉要旨 ["Essence of Spiritual Cultivation"; 1934]. *LSMQJ*, 2005, vol. 5: 492–519.

JTWM Jintian women yingdang ruhe pingjia kongzi 今天我們應當如何評價孔子 ["How Should We Evaluate Confucius Today"; 1974]. *LSMQJ*, 2005, vol. 7: 270–315.

LNL Liang nian lai wo youle naxie gaibian 兩年來我有了哪些改變 ["What Changes I Have Made in the Past Two Years"; 1951]. *LSMQJ*, 2005, vol. 6: 873–890.

RLCZL Renlei chuangzaoli de da fahui da biaoxian 人類創造力的大發揮大表現 [The Great Expression and Great Manifestation of Human Creativity; 1961]. *LSMQJ*, 2005, vol. 3: 415–521.

RXYRS Renxin yu rensheng 人心與人生 [*Human Mind and Human Life*; 1984]. *LSMQJ*, 2005, vol. 3: 523–772.

SLZG Shilun zhongguo shehui de lishi fazhan shuyu makesi suowei yazhou shehui shengchan fangshi 試論中國社會的歷史發展屬於馬克思所謂亞洲社會生產方式 ["A Discussion on the Historical Development of Chinese Society as Marx's so-called Asiatic Mode of Production"; 1974]. *LSMQJ*, 2005, vol. 7: 246–269.

YGDFR Yige Dongfang ren de makesi zhuyi guan 一個東方人的馬克思主義觀 ["An Oriental's view of Marxism"; 1970s]. *LSMQJ*, 2005, vol. 7: 486–487.

YJWL Yijiu wuling nian xiang lingdao dang jianyi yanjiu zhongguo wenhua, shezhi zhongguo wenhua yanjiusuo zhi cao'an 一九五零年向領導黨建議研究中國文化, 設置中國文化研究所之草案 ["A Proposal to the Leading Party for Studying Chinese Culture and Establish an Institute for Chinese Studies in 1950"; 1950]. *LSMQJ*, 2005, vol. 6: 850–853.

ZGJG Zhongguo jianguo zhi lu 中國建國之路 [*The Path to the Establishment of the Chinese Nation*; 1951]. *LSMQJ*, 2005, vol. 3: 317–414.

[51] Interestingly, Liang regarded socialism and not communism as representative of "Western culture." He insisted that communism is a manifestation of "Chinese" and "Indian" cultures. This reflects his own interpretation of communism and his determination to preserve the spirits of Confucianism and Buddhism.

[52] Regarding the discussion of "skilful means" in DXWH, please refer to Meynard 2011: 68–71.

ZGLX *Zhongguo—Lixing zhi guo* 中國—理性之國 [*China: Nation of Reason*; 1970]. *LSMQJ*, 2005, vol. 3: 201–485.

ZGMZ *Zhongguo minzu zijiu yundong zhi zuihou juewu* 中國民族自救運動之最後覺悟 ["The Final Awakening of the Chinese People's Self-Salvation Movement"; 1931]. *LSMQ*J, 2005, vol. 5: 44–118.

ZGWH *Zhongguo wenhua yaoyi* 中國文化要義 [Substance of Chinese Culture; 1949]. *LSMQJ*, 2005, vol. 3: 1–316.

ZSZN *Zishu zaonian sixiang zhi zai zhuan zai bian* 自述早年思想之再轉再變 ["My Account of the Changes in Thinking during My Early Years"; 1969]. *LSMQJ*, 2005, vol. 7: 178–186.

ZZXZF *Zhi zhengxie zhengfeng bangongshi* 致政協整風辦公室 ["To the CPPCC Rectification Office"; 1958]. *LSMQJ*, 2005, vol. 8: 85–87.

ZZYWG *Zhi zhongyang wenge bing zhuan Mao zhuxi* 致中央文革並轉毛主席 ["To the Central Cultural Revolution Committee and to Chairman Mao"; 1966]. *LSMQJ*, 2005, vol. 8: 79–81.

ZZZL *Zhi zhou zongli bing zhuan Mao zhuxi* 致周總理並轉毛主席 ["To Premier Zhou and to Chairman Mao"; 1968]. *LSMQJ*, 2005, vol. 8: 81–83.

Alitto, Guy. 1976. The Conservative as Sage: LIANG Shu-ming. In *The Limits of Change: Essays on Conservative Alternatives in Republican China*, ed. Charlotte Furth. Cambridge, MA: Harvard University Press. (A study of LIANG Shuming's life and thought in the 1920s and 1930s).

———. 1986. *The Last Confucian: LIANG Shu-ming and the Chinese Dilemma of Modernity*. Berkeley: University of California Press. (A biographical study of LIANG Shuming's thought and life from the dimension of Confucianism).

An, Yanming. 1997. LIANG Shuming and Henri Bergson on Intuition: Cultural Context and the Evolution of Terms. *Philosophy East and West* 47 (3): 337–362. (An analysis of Liang's philosophical concepts and the evolution of these terms).

Chi, Wen-Shun. 1970. LIANG Shu-ming and Chinese Communism. *The China Quarterly* 41: 64–82. (A concise analysis of Liang's thought and its conflict with Maoist communism).

Engels, Frederick. 1901. *Socialism: Utopian and Scientific*. Translated by Edward Aveling. New York: New York Labor News Company.

Gong, Pengcheng 龔鵬程. 1993a. Deviating from Confucius' Land: LIANG Shuming and China (Part 1) 背離孔子的國度:梁漱溟的中國 (上). *Legein Monthly* 鵝湖月刊 219: 17–25. (An analysis on Liang's approbation of Marxism and Maoism after 1949)

——— 龔鵬程. 1993b. Deviating from Confucius' Land: LIANG Shuming and China (Part 2) 背離孔子的國度:梁漱溟的中國 (下). *Legein Monthly* 鵝湖月刊 220: 29–36.

Hanafin, John. 2003. The 'Last Buddhist': The Philosophy of LIANG Shuming. In *New Confucianism: A Critical Examination*, ed. John Makeham. New York: Palgrave Macmillan. (A study of Liang's Buddhist thought).

Huang, Yong. 2017. New Confucianism. In *A Concise Companion to Confucius*, ed. Paul R. Goldin. Hoboken: Wiley.

Li, Yuanting 李淵庭, and Yan Binghua 閻秉華. 2009. *A Chronological Biography of LIANG Shuming* 梁漱溟年譜. Beijing: Qunyan Press. (A detailed chronological record of LIANG Shuming's life).

Liang, Shuming, and Guy S. Alitto. 2013. *Has Man a Future? Dialogues with the Last Confucian*. Berlin: Springer. (An interview manuscript that records the dialogues between LIANG Shuming and Guy Alitto in 1980).

Lynch, Catherine. 2011. Radical Visions of Time in Modern China: The Utopianism of MAO Zedong and LIANG Shuming. In *Radicalism, Revolution, and Reform in Modern China*, ed. Catherine Lynch, Robert B. Marks, and Paul G. Pickowicz. Lexington: US.

Mao, Zedong 毛澤東. 1991. *Mao Zedong xuanji* 毛澤東選集 [The Selected Works of Mao Zedong]. Tianjin: Renmin chubanshe.

———. 1966. *MAO Tse-tung: Four Essays on Philosophy*. Peking: Foreign Languages Press.

Marx, Karl. 1904. *A Contribution to the Critique of Political Economy*. Chicago: Charles H. Kerr & Company.

Meynard, Thierry. 2011. *The Religious Philosophy of Liang Shuming: The Hidden Buddhist*. Leiden, Boston: Brill. (A detailed analysis of Liang's religious philosophy).

Van den Stock, Ady. 2020. Liang Shuming's *China: the Country of Reason* (1967–1970): Revolution, Religion, and Ethnicity in the Reinvention of the Confucian Tradition. *International Communication of Chinese Culture* 7 (4): 603–620.

Wang, Zongyu 王宗昱. 1990. Sou-ming Liang and Psychology 梁漱溟與心理學. *Monthly Review of Philosophy and Culture* 哲學與文化 17 (7): 826–837 (A discussion on Liang's evaluation of Western psychological studies and his attempt to establish a heart-mind theory).

Zheng, Dahua 鄭大華. 2006. Liang Shuming and Marxism 梁漱溟與馬克思主義. *Journal of Hunan University* 湖南大學學報 20 (5): 5–15. (An analysis of Liang's perception of Marxism in three different periods).

Chapter 12
Liang Shuming's Legacy in Hong Kong and Taiwan Since 1949: Liang's Philosophical Connection with Tang Junyi

James Zhixiang Yang

1 Introduction

LIANG Shuming 梁漱溟, who lived from 1893 to 1988 and was known as "the last Confucian"[1] in modern China, did not leave mainland China after 1949, when the Chinese Communist Party (CCP) founded the People's Republic of China (PRC). He therefore had no access to the intellectual communities in Hong Kong or Taiwan during the last 40 years of his life. However, despite Liang's physical isolation from these two territories, the New Confucian School that he and his colleagues had founded in the Republican period in the mainland migrated to Hong Kong and Taiwan after 1949 (Liu 2020: 367–382).[2] In other words, the establishment of the

[1] This title is derived from Alitto 1979. LIANG Peishu 梁培恕, the second son of LIANG Shuming, also used "The Last Confucian" as his book's title. See Liang 2012.

[2] According to Liu Shuxian's "A Reexamination of the Investigation of Contemporary New Confucianism," the contemporary New Confucian school consists of three generations. The first group of the first generation includes LIANG Shuming (1893–1988), XIONG Shili 熊十力 (1885–1968), MA Yifu 馬一浮 (1883–1967), and ZHANG Junmai 張君勱 (1887–1969). The second group in the same generation includes FENG Youlan 馮友蘭 (1895–1990), HE Lin 賀麟 (1902–1992), QIAN Mu 錢穆 (1895–1990), and FANG Dongmei 方東美 (1899–1977). The second generation includes TANG Junyi 唐君毅 (1909–1978), MOU Zongsan 牟宗三 (1909–1995), and XU Fuguan 徐復觀 (1903–1982). The third generation includes YU Yingshi 余英時 (1930–), LIU Shuxian 劉述先 (1934–), CHENG Zhongyin 成中英 (1935–), and DU Weiming 杜维明 (1940–). See Liu 2020. Of note, John Makeham (2003) argues that there was no self-conscious New Confucian school or movement until the 1970s.

J. Z. Yang (✉)
BNU-HKBU United International College, Zhuhai, China
e-mail: jameszhxyang@uic.edu.cn

T. Meynard, P. Major (eds.), *Dao Companion to Liang Shuming's Philosophy*, Dao Companions to Chinese Philosophy 17,
https://doi.org/10.1007/978-3-031-18002-6_12

communist regime in mainland China shifted the scholarship of Republican New Confucianism to a group of intellectuals from Hong Kong and Taiwan known as the Hong Kong-Taiwan Contemporary New Confucians (*gang tai xin rujia* 港台新儒家).

The study of Liang Shuming's legacy in Hong Kong and Taiwan since 1949 therefore requires us to analyze how the two territories' New Confucian scholars interpret and advance Liang's philosophy. One way to examine Liang's influence in Hong Kong and Taiwan is by exploring his intellectual connection with one of the most representative and significant New Confucian scholars, Tang Junyi 唐君毅 (1909–1978).

For at least two reasons, Tang is an exemplary choice for this study. First, Liang Shuming left a deep mark on Tang Junyi's early life. From 1917 to 1924, Liang was a teacher of Chinese and Indian philosophy at National Peking University, and Tang was one of his students. The two men also interacted socially outside the lecture room (Tang [1974] 2017: 141–142). After 1949, when Tang escaped to Hong Kong, he and Liang continued to correspond for a long time. Tang considered Liang to be his most reliable mentor and friend (Tang [1951] 2017: 888). In the days just before his own death, Tang recollected how generously and thoughtfully Liang had treated him at university (Sun 2019: 113). Second, as New Confucianism migrated from mainland China after 1949, Tang played a pivotal role in promoting the philosophical approach of New Confucianism in Hong Kong, Taiwan, and overseas. His influence was so widespread that his fellow New Confucian scholars awarded him the title "Giant in the Realm of Cultural Consciousness (文化意識宇宙之巨人)" (Hu 2008: 146).

Tang's close acquaintance with Liang and his preeminent role in the Hong Kong-Taiwan New Confucian School make him an ideal focus of study for shedding light on how Liang's New Confucianism was retained, transferred, and developed in Hong Kong and Taiwan.

In this paper, I illuminate Liang Shuming's legacy in Hong Kong and Taiwan since 1949 by exploring the philosophical dialogue between him and Tang Junyi. My inquiry begins by examining the family and historical factors that contributed to the New Confucian scholarship of both Liang Shuming and Tang Junyi. I also discuss Liang's *Eastern and Western Cultures and Their Philosophies* (*Dong-xi wenhua ji qi zhexue* 東西文化及其哲學; hereafter DXWH), which founded a philosophical framework for the development of New Confucian scholarship. Next, I turn to the question of how Tang and his colleagues inherited and developed some of Liang's important ideas, synthesizing them into their own philosophy. Last, I provide an overview of how Liang's legacy was received in Hong Kong and Taiwan under Tang's influence.

2 The Influence of Confucian Fathers[3]

During LIANG Shuming's formative years, his father, LIANG Ji 梁濟 (1858–1918), played a crucial role in shaping and strengthening his Confucian ideals. As a former Neo-Confucian official-scholar of the late imperial period, LIANG Ji advocated the pathway from "being the sage on the inside" (*neisheng* 內聖) to "being kingly on the outside" (*waiwang* 外王) in the face of China's unprecedented difficulties and challenges (Alitto 1979: 24; Xu 2012: 201–205; Liang 2012: 3–15). The Confucian notion of *waiwang* strongly emphasizes the Confucian scholars' commitment to achieving outstanding accomplishments in political affairs so as to bring order and prosperity to the entire empire. Following this conviction, LIANG Ji believed that all learning and teaching were futile unless they were beneficial to empowering the country (ZSZN, 177). Therefore, the Neo-Confucian father rejected the classical civil-service oriented examination and instead supported a new style of practical education (ZSZN, 181). In 1906, one year after the imperial civil service examination had ended, LIANG Ji sent his 13-year-old son to a new middle school in Beijing, the capital, where the teen could learn "practical knowledge" (*shixue* 實學) (WDZX: 668).

Compared with *waiwang*, the other half of the twin Neo-Confucian concept, *neisheng* had a greater impact on LIANG Ji. In fact, the discourse of Neo-Confucian philosophy since the Song-Ming period (960–1644) has thoroughly revolved around this idea. In contrast to *waiwang*, *neisheng* focuses mainly on the perfection of individual inner morality, which was regarded by Neo-Confucian scholars as the root of all things good. Consequently, when emphasizing the significance of the spread of "practical knowledge" in Chinese society, LIANG Ji asserted that "the purification of people's heart" (*zheng ren-xin* 正人心) should be the determinative factor for achieving the goal of national salvation (Alitto 1979: 24). From the Neo-Confucian father's perspective, the development of a Confucian scholar into being "sage inside" was required for the realization of being "kingly outside." The formula of *neisheng-waiwang*, which was advocated by LIANG Ji, became a framework within which LIANG Shuming could develop his own thinking.

The advent of the Republican period in 1912 did not bring about the economic prosperity and social stability that most Chinese intellectuals had hoped for. In November 1918, LIANG Ji, in the depths of despair, committed suicide by drowning in a lake in Beijing. Before his life came to an end, he wrote his last words, called "A Letter to the World" (敬告世人書), which revealed his anxiety about China's future but also his faith in Confucian ethics (Liang 2012: 11). LIANG Shuming understood that his father's life was a reflection of a moral principle in Confucianism: "scholar-apprentices (*shi*士) should never be ashamed of their unrefined clothing and coarse food. Instead, they should be ashamed of their incompetence in bringing

[3] In this section, my discussion on LIANG Ji's influence on LIANG Shuming to some extent draws reference from Yang 2019.

a happy life to common people" (士不耻惡衣惡食，而恥匹夫匹婦不被其澤) (WDZX: 664).

LIANG Ji's death was a key factor that caused LIANG Shuming to downplay his desire to become a Buddhist monk and instead to choose Confucianism as the foundational principle for his life.[4] What is more, inspired by the spirit of LIANG Ji's sacrifice for his Confucian belief, LIANG Shuming dedicated himself to exploring a pathway through which he could achieve national salvation through the rejuvenation of the Confucian tradition (ZS, 11).

TANG Junyi's lifelong dedication to Confucianism was also strongly influenced by his father, TANG Difeng 唐迪風 (1886–1931). As a faithful Confucian scholar of Sichuan Province, TANG Difeng led TANG Junyi to follow his path. However, like most young people of the May Fourth Period, influenced by the ideas of democracy and science, TANG Junyi was initially obsessed with pursuing Western learning (Hu 2008: 12). He demonstrated a scornful attitude toward his father's belief in Confucianism and, like other Chinese iconoclasts of the May Fourth Period, often castigated the role of the Confucian tradition in Chinese society (Hu 2008: 21).

Unfortunately, TANG Difeng died unexpectedly of an epidemic in 1931, leaving his son suffering unbearable regret. As the eldest son, TANG Junyi took full responsibility to support the family after his father's death. He made great efforts to serve as a father figure for his younger siblings, in keeping with the traditional Confucian principle that "the eldest son should behave like the father does" (*zhangxiong bi fu* 長兄比父). Moreover, the loss of his father caused TANG Junyi to rethink the meaning of Confucianism in his personal life and in Chinese society. Shortly after his father's death, Tang made a decision that echoed LIANG Shuming's: he would follow his father's example, devoting his life to studying Confucianism.[5]

The life resolutions made by both LIANG Shuming and TANG Junyi after their fathers' deaths observed the Confucian value of filial piety (*xiao* 孝). According to the *Analects* of Confucius: "While a person's father is still alive, observe what he intends; when his father dies, observe what he does. A person who for three years refrains from reforming the ways (*dao* 道) of his late father can be called a filial son" (*Analects* 1999: 188). Given the central place of the family in Confucian thought, appropriate family feelings based on filial engagement are the origin from which a pathway through life emerges. In a sense, the tradition of filial piety denotes a moral standard, a way of life, as well as a cultural norm in the school of Confucianism. More to the point, the implementation of Confucian filial piety is an indispensable precondition for a Confucian scholar-apprentice (*shi*) to achieve the horizon of "*ren*" (仁). As the Confucian scholar You Zi 有子 argued, "As for filial and fraternal responsibility, it is, I suspect, the root of authoritative conduct (*ren*)" (*Analects* 1999: 71).

[4] In *The Religious Philosophy of* Liang *Shuming: Hidden Buddhist*, Thierry Meynard argues that Liang cherished the religious belief as a Buddhist throughout his lifetime.

[5] See TANG Junyi's diary on June 23, 1961, in Wu 2014: vol.1, 252.

Thus, both LIANG Shuming's and TANG Junyi's lifelong commitment to Confucianism started with the practice of Confucian filial piety, an important way toward "the purification of people's heart" (*zheng ren-xin*) to achieve the status of "being the sage on the inside" (*neisheng*). By this measure, it is accurate to say that Liang and Tang had similar psychological, cultural, and life experiences with their fathers. As MOU Zongsan 牟宗三 (1909–1995): "Among the younger generation of scholars, my friend TANG Junyi perhaps can deeply understand him [Liang] because they have a shared outlook on life" (Mou 1988: 2). This shared outlook was to become a strong linkage that connected TANG Junyi and LIANG Shuming both emotionally and philosophically.

3 Reflections of LIANG Shuming and TANG Junyi on the May Fourth Movement

In addition to the profound paternal influence, the outbreak of the May Fourth New Culture Movement was a significant factor that contributed to Liang's and Tang's embrace of Confucian ideals. One of the most significant themes of the May Fourth New Culture Movement was the reevaluation of Confucianism's role in Chinese society. Chinese iconoclasts of the May Fourth era, such as LU Xun 魯迅 (1881–1936), CHEN Duxiu 陳獨秀 (1879–1942), LI Dazhao 李大釗 (1889–1927), WU Yu 吳虞 (1872–1949), and HU Shih 胡適 (1891–1962), saw Confucianism as a barrier that prevented China from transforming itself into a modern nation-state (Chow 1960: 300–313). Their critiques claimed that the traditional bonds of the family system, predicated on Confucian and Neo-Confucian morality and virtue, had psychologically poisoned Chinese people.

While advocating for the introduction of democracy and science, these scholars specifically castigated the destructive effect of the Confucian principle of Three Cardinal Bonds and Five Ethical Webs (*sangang wuchang* 三綱五常) on Chinese society. In a short fiction work, *The Diary of a Madman* (*Kuangren riji* 狂人日記), LU Xun used the phrase "eating people" (*chi ren* 吃人) to suggest that Confucian ethics was devouring the spirit of the Chinese people (Grieder 1983: 271). Likewise, CHEN Duxiu claimed that "if we want to embrace democracy, we definitely have to oppose Confucianism and its other socio-political derivatives, including Confucian ritualism, the cult of women's purity, and traditional ethics and politics" (Chen 1984: vol. 1, 317). Throughout the May Fourth New Culture period, the slogan "Down with Confucius and Sons" (*dadao kongjiadian* 打倒孔家店) was a significant theme, one that was shared by progressive Chinese intellectuals (Chow 1960: 300–313).

Although Confucianism had lost its prestigious status among the Chinese intellectual community during the early Republican period, its substantial influence in Chinese society and among intellectuals made it difficult to be expunged completely. The historian LIN Yusheng 林毓生 argued that Chinese intellectuals of the

May Fourth generation vividly embodied the utmost ideal of the Confucian scholar-apprentice (*shi*) model concerning national destiny (Lin 1979: 26–55). Scholars who defended Confucianism against the iconoclasts' attacks harbored mixed feelings, combining their awareness of cultural nostalgia with their ultimate concern for cultural and social order "under heaven" (*tianxia* 天下). In keeping with this concern, most New Confucian scholars shared what they considered a sacred responsibility to save China by retaining and realizing the ideal of Confucianism. For example, during the May Fourth period, in the face of Chinese social and economic crises, Liang wrote several weighty essays that expressed his aspiration to bring harmony and prosperity to Chinese society; these include "Without Us, What Will Happen to Chinese People?" (*Wucao buchu ru cang sheng he* 吾曹不出如蒼生何; 1917), "My View on Life" (*Wo zhi renshengguan rushi* 我之人生觀如是; 1923), and "What Should We Do?" (*Wuchai dang hewei* 吾儕當何為; 1924). These writings all reflect a Confucian moral principle that corresponded to his father's ideal. That is to say, as a Confucian exemplary person, who will enjoy the status of immortality in Chinese history, one's foremost concern must be the country and not to enjoy oneself.

The May Fourth New Cultural Movement posed a destructive threat to Confucianism, but it also provided New Confucian scholars like LIANG Shuming an unparalleled opportunity to reinterpret Confucianism. According to Liang, under the influence of Confucianism, the Chinese nation had been well integrated and cohesive and, unlike European countries of the medieval period, had avoided developing religious tyranny over scholarly thought (ZGWH: 86–92; JTWM: 312–313). Unfortunately, Liang posited, the sense of joy in life and dynamic thought had disappeared from the system of Confucianism since the Song dynasty, when the philosophical school was transformed into an official ideological dogma (*lixue* 理學) (JTWM: 312–313). The dogmatized Confucian value system thus had become merely "a spiritual opium" used by emperors of dynasties past to poison the minds of Chinese people (JTWM: 312–313). In response to Confucius' critics of the May Fourth era, Liang concluded:

> What Confucius' critics want to attack are the "Three Cardinal Bonds and Five Ethical Webs." They regard these things as the essence of Confucianism. In fact, none of them [Three Cardinal Bonds and Five Ethical Webs] have anything to do with the truth of Confucianism. (KZZMM: 770)

Accordingly, Liang contended that it was unreasonable for Chinese iconoclasts to blame Confucianism for all of China's failures since the late Qing period. Instead, in his view, searching for the truth in Confucianism should be the most urgent task for modern Chinese intellectuals (KZXS: 3).

In targeting the anti-traditionalism of the May Fourth period, New Confucian scholars opposed the cult of scientism embraced by most liberal intellectuals. Pro-scientism scholars regarded the scientific method, which had led to remarkable accomplishments in the material world, as the best guide for all pursuits in Chinese society (Xie and Li 2019: 3–4). These scholars even claimed that all Chinese classical learning was dead knowledge, dismissed as a "historical fossil" (Mao 1919:

731–745). Aligning himself with a group of cultural conservatives, including LIANG Qichao 梁啟超 (1873–1929) and ZHANG Junmai 張君勱 (1887–1969), LIANG Shuming argued against pro-scientism liberal intellectuals. As a professor of philosophy at National Peking University during the May Fourth period, Liang had a long debate with his colleague, HU Shih, who believed that China lagged behind the West because it had not adopted a scientific system of thought. Therefore, in Hu's view, Western civilization was superior to Chinese civilization in a general sense (Zhang 2014: 477). Lashing out at this notion, Liang defended the Confucian tradition:

> How ignorant and absurd we would be if we felt sorrow about the absence of science in Chinese society. There are some inherent reasons to explain why science could not grow out of China. How ignorant and absurd we would be if we felt sorrow about the absence of democracy in Chinese society. There are still some inherent reasons to explain why democracy could not grow out of China. By the same token, how absurd and ignorant we would be if we felt sorrow about the absence of capitalism in China. There are also some inherent reasons to explain why capitalism could not grow out of China. (ZGMZ: 418)

Stimulated by the May Fourth Movement, Liang continued to think about those "inherent reasons" stemming from the Confucianism-based Chinese cultural system, which fundamentally differentiated China from the West. "Since the May Fourth Movement, some scholars regard the New Culture Movement as the renaissance of Chinese civilization. In fact, this movement is only a result of the rise of Western culture in China. How can we think of it as the renaissance of Chinese civilization?" (DXWH: 539).

The Chinese intellectual community's anti-traditionalism and zeal for scientism during the May Fourth period became a catalyst for Liang's redefinition of Confucianism. Similarly, the May Fourth period presented an historical opportunity for TANG Junyi to reconsider the Confucian tradition. As pointed out earlier, during Tang's studies at National Peking University during the May Fourth New Culture period, he was fascinated by Western learning. Yet even though HU Shih enjoyed high popularity among the university students, his liberal ideas never interested TANG Junyi. He recalled:

> Then I attended HU Shih's other lecture titled "Our Attitude toward Western Culture." […In this speech] he held that Eastern culture is self-satisfied and conservative while Western culture is unsatisfied and progressive. I think that he drew such a conclusion only from the perspective of Western culture. At that time, I felt that his point of view was totally incorrect after listening to his speech. I did not know for sure what he meant by "progressive." […] Where should we see the "progressive"? (Tang [1974] 2017: 139)

From Tang's perspective, HU Shih's mind was so preoccupied with scientific thought that he had lost the feeling of joy in his life (Tang [1974] 2017: 139). In the 1950s, when Tang taught Chinese culture and philosophy in Hong Kong, he reflected on the negative effects of anti-traditionalism and the cult of scientism on Chinese society during the May Fourth period. In an essay titled "The Development of the Spirit of the Chinese Youth during the Last Sixty Years" (六十年來中國青年精神之發展), Tang argued:

> The shortcomings of the youth spirit of the May Fourth Movement demonstrate the aspect of negative destruction. At that time, it was indeed laudable that young people displayed the spirit of vigorousness. However, as a critical part of the May Fourth Period, the New Cultural Movement essentially focused on the development of skepticism and critical thinking, attacking Confucius and the Confucian ethical code, launching literary revolution, and so on. As a result, the youth's spirit of vigorousness had been transformed to be a destructive force. (Tang [1955] 2017b: 161)

Although Tang praised the patriotic feelings of the youth of the May Fourth period, he regretted the movement's effect on Chinese culture and tradition. He came to believe that blindly imitating Western ideas could never solve Chinese difficulties. Tang said:

> The rise of scientism generated some scientists and scholars from other disciplines… Most of them once studied in Western countries, and they admired Western civilization. Even though they lived in China… they only cared about their own academic freedom, freedom of thought, and social status. Besides, they thought that any concerns over the issues of country and nation, history and culture were empty. (Tang [1955] 2017b: 162)

Tang held that scholars of the May Fourth generation were obsessed with introducing Western individualism, so that they neglected the importance of cultural tradition to Chinese society. From his perspective, the individualism advocated by those scholars was at most an instrument for attacking Confucian norms and Chinese culture (Tang [1955] 2017b: 163). The May Fourth New Culture Movement was a significant historical force that inspired Tang, like Liang, to devote his life to Confucian scholarship. More specifically, as TANG Junyi recalled during his later years, a common thread binds his and Liang's New Confucian scholarship together: their philosophical thinking is founded on their own experience, and the vital force of dynamic life (*shengming* 生命) is a foundation of their own experience (Tang [1974] 2017: 150). It is clear that, for both Tang and Liang, historic events as well as family experiences were crucial factors in the development of their life journeys and their New Confucian philosophy.[6]

Although Tang and Liang shared a common perspective on the May Fourth period, they disagreed with each other about the communist regime under the CCP. In January of 1950, called on by MAO Zedong 毛澤東 (1893–1976) and ZHOU Enlai 周恩來 (1898–1976), Liang chose to settle in Beijing to support the new communist regime. In a 1951 letter to Tang, he described the founding of the People's Republic of China as "the birth of the Chinese nation's new life (*zhonghua minzu xinshengmin de kaiduan* 中華民族新生命的開端)" (ZTJY: 310) and strongly encouraged Tang to join him in contributing to the development of "New China." By contrast, Tang migrated to Hong Kong in 1949 and, from then on, was inclined to take on the role of a cultural loyalist (*wenhua yimin* 文化遺民) who strived to advance the Chinese cultural heritage amidst the transformation of dynasties and political turmoil (He 2015: 110–124).

Unlike Liang, Tang was concerned that the triumph of the communist revolution in China would require the destruction of Confucianism-based Chinese culture

---

[6] Readers interested in Liang's philosophy of life can refer to Chap. 7 in this volume.

(Chen 2005: 48). His worries proved correct with the advent of the Cultural Revolution of 1966–1976 (Chen 2005: 48). From 1949 until his death in 1978, TANG Junyi embraced his identity as a Confucian cultural loyalist by studying, interpreting, and spreading the Confucian heritage outside the mainland. In 1950, Tang Junyi worked closely with his colleagues, including influential New Confucian scholars QIAN Mu 錢穆 (1895–1990) and ZHANG Pijie 張丕介 (1905–1970), to found the New Asia College (*Xinya shuyuan* 新亞書院) in Hong Kong. The idea of a "New Asia" signified for them the rebirth of Asia in the context of a history of colonization by Western powers, and they envisioned a generation of New Asia graduates who would uphold the spirit of the Confucian-style academy begun during the Song-Yuan period and extending China's cultural heritage overseas (Hu 2008: 71).

4 The New Confucian Philosophical Framework Created by LIANG Shuming[7]

To defend Confucianism against the attack from the May Fourth Chinese iconoclasts, LIANG Shuming in 1921 published his famous book, DXWH. In this work, LIANG Shuming attempted to examine the unique value of Chinese culture in the context of world civilization. Liang's inquiry into the essence of Chinese culture relies on his theory of the reappearance of three cultural periods (*wenhua san qishuo* 文化三期說).[8] His discourse follows the path of culture-life-will. Liang defined culture as a "way of life," and "life" as the relationship between the individual and his or her environment (DXWH: 352). In his view, culture is shaped by will (DXWH: 352).

Liang categorized world civilization into three types: Western culture, Chinese culture, and Indian culture. Western culture, in LIANG Shuming's view, was the prototype of the first stage of the evolution of world civilization; it derived from the basic needs and material requirements of human survival (DXWH: 345–371). This culture's "will" is to seek the pleasure of satisfaction, emphasizing reason, utility, scientific knowledge, the conquest of nature, and a life of ceaseless struggle (DXWH: 345–371, 379–382). Chinese culture represents the second stage, which takes the middle path and accommodates the relationship between humans and the environment (DXWH: 382, 392–393). This cultural type is based on the will's self-adjustment and self-sufficiency and the cultivation of inner peace. Liang asserted that maintaining a balance between their desires and the environment could led the Chinese people to achieve great spiritual happiness while enduring material poverty (DXWH: 383). Indian culture represents Liang's third stage of cultural development, in which the "will" of the people is to turn backward for ultimate

[7] In this section, my analysis of Liang's DXWH partially draws reference from Yang 2019.

[8] This translation is derived from Lin 2009.

enlightenment (DXWH: 382–383). Liang pointed out that Indian people believe the world to be an illusion. Therefore, both self-denial and austerity play an important part in their religious practices (DXWH: 383).

Liang characterized Chinese culture as a "premature" culture. He claimed that China had developed the second stage, having the will to be in equilibrium with nature, before the first stage, which would allow the pursuit of material well-being and rationality (DXWH: 528). Liang proposed that, for the sake of national salvation, China should avoid taking the path of India, but instead borrow the ideas of democracy and science from the West (DXWH: 528).

Alongside the Neo-Confucian formula of *neisheng-waiwang*, DXWH implied that all accomplishments in the West related to the outer world—including science, democracy, capitalism, and rule of law—belong to the category of *waiwang* (being kingly outside) from the perspective of Hong Kong-Taiwan New Confucian scholars (Chen 2012: 4). In contrast, as some researchers mentioned, Liang's argument signified that Confucianism-based Chinese culture attached importance to the inner workings of the mind, which falls into the realm of *neisheng* (being the sage on the inside) (Grieder 1970: 145; Xu 2012: 201–210). As a result, moral and spiritual cultivation are the main themes running through a Confucian person's life; the Confucian person's life goal is to pursue a spirit of happiness and tranquility instead of outer material achievement (DXWH: 464–466).

In proposing to "vitalize" the school of Confucianism, DXWH borrowed the idea of "vitalism" from Henri Bergson (1859–1941), one of the most influential Western philosophers during the May Fourth period.

> Henri Bergson strongly criticized any fixed and measurable idea from the supremacy of science. He believed that metaphysical philosophy requires a soft and flowing idea, which was opposed to the thought of scientism. His philosophy opened a pathway for the development of the Chinese style of thought. (DXWH: 445)

In Liang's view, Confucius and Bergson both understood human life as a continuous flow during which only intuition can appear (Alitto 1979: 98–101).[9] In other words, both philosophical approaches emphasized the permanent flowing of free will and vital force in human life, as well as opposed the stance of scientism. Accordingly, Liang held that Confucian scholars always followed an intuition to live a moral life that rejected calculation and rationality (DXWH: 450). He asserted:

> Confucius got an idea from his metaphysical learning. He asked you to not to worry about [your life]. [However], your fundamental mistake is to find a resolution to calculate your life… Our life is a continuous flow, which will take the right and most appropriate way… Therefore, according to the school of Confucianism, "the will of heaven is our natural disposition, following our natural disposition is the Dao" (*Tianming zhi weixing, shuanxing zhi weidao* 天命之謂性, 率性之謂道). The only thing you need to do is to follow your natural disposition. Following natural disposition is the knowledge and ability that any common couple can understand and retain. This knowledge and ability should be called innate knowledge (*liangzhi* 良知) and innate ability (*liangneng* 良能) respectively in Mencius' words. Today we call either *liangzhi* or *liangneng* a human intuition. (DXWH: 452)

[9] On Liang and Bergson, see Chap. 4 in this volume.

Through citing Mencius' quote in his following writing, Liang went on to illuminate how *liangzhi* or *liangneng* as a human intuition could conduct someone to become a compassionate person:

> Everyone has such an intuition and instinct to pursue goodness and righteousness. Therefore, Mencius said: "All people have a heart which cannot stand to see the suffering of others (*ren jie you bu ren ren zhi xin* 人皆有不忍人之心)… Why do I say all human beings have a heart which cannot stand to see the suffering of others? If an infant were about to fall into a well, anyone would be upset and concerned. This concern would not be due to the fact that the person wanted to get on good terms with the baby's parents, or because he wanted to improve his reputation among the community or among his friends. Nor would it be because he was afraid of the criticism that might result from a show of non-concern." (DXWH: 452)

For Liang Shuming, Mencius' idea of "*ren jie you bu ren ren zhi xin*" denoted the aspect of *ren* in the school of Confucianism (DXWH: 452). In other words, taking Mencius' idea as an example, Liang affirmed that the core ethical idea of Confucianism, the character of *ren* (仁), is in fact a reflection of acute intuition. Likewise, for a Confucian scholar, *ren* becomes an inner state of being, peaceful yet full of vitality. Following this conviction, Liang concluded: "The thought of Confucianism completely follows intuition. The most important mission that Confucian scholars want to achieve is to sharpen their intuition…. Consequently, Confucius encouraged people to pursue '*ren*'" (DXWH: 454). In keeping with the intuition of *ren*, Liang viewed the essence of the universe from the perspective of vitalism. He remarked:

> The word "life" (*sheng* 生) is the most important idea in Confucianism… The essence of Confucius' thought is to follow a natural way, carrying out a spiritual and lively flow. He thought that the universe will be full of a natural life (*sheng* 生) and force flowing everlastingly throughout all things (DXWH: 448).

In Liang Shuming's philosophical thinking, the notion of vitalism is the key to understanding the concept of *ren* and the sum of all living beings in the universe. By "vitalizing" Confucianism, Liang Shuming in DXWH transformed this classical philosophical system from a "dead" ideology into a spirited philosophy of life. In light of the perceived spiritual destruction of Western civilization since World War I, Liang firmly believed that only "vitalized" Confucianism could become the teacher of the West. Taking the stance of a cultural nationalist, he made confident predictions in DXWH:

> Confucius wholeheartedly focused upon the emotional aspect of humanity…. The difference between Confucius and Westerners and their basic point of conflict lie precisely in this! Westerners never paid attention to this in the past. Now, they should start sidling up to the school of Confucianism. Therefore, I will not doubt that Westerners will take the path prescribed by Confucius. (DXWH: 498)

Liang's writings demonstrate his cultural pride in Confucianism. From this Confucianism-based standpoint, Liang proposed an idea called "new sprouts growing out of old roots" (*laogen fa xinya* 老根發新芽) during the rural reconstruction movement of the 1930s (JSTL: 504–508). Here, the New Confucian thinker compared the tradition of *neisheng* in Confucianism to an "old root." Likewise, "new sprout" was an analogue of a modern civilization consisting of science, democracy, and self-ruled association. Simply put, Liang's idea of "new sprouts growing out of old roots" defined a relationship between the Confucian tradition and Western learning. For New Confucian scholars like Liang, "the purification of people's heart" pertinent to the *neisheng* approach must be a philosophical foundation for introducing Western technology and systems to achieve the goal of strengthening China.

DXWH illuminated a pathway for the New Confucian scholars who fled to Hong Kong and Taiwan after 1949. Liang's ideas about "intuition" influenced TANG Junyi's thinking. The young New Confucian recalled:

> He [Liang] greatly enjoyed talking about Eastern and Western cultures, and his discourse on Chinese culture followed intuition.... *Eastern and Western Cultures and Their Philosophies* had been published in the tenth year of Republican China (1921), and I read it a couple of times.... I felt that rationality was very convictive. Instead, intuition for me was unreliable.... However, as I became older and older, "intuition" became more and more important in my mind. (Tang [1974] 2017: 142)

Liang's philosophy resonated with MOU Zongsan as well as with TANG Junyi. As an influential New Confucian scholar who knew LIANG Shuming before 1949,[10] MOU Zongsan praised Liang's accomplishment in 1988, following Liang's death.

> Mr. Liang was indeed a cultural revivalist of modern Chinese history. During the early part of the Republican period, on the one hand, ZHANG Taiyan 章太炎 and WU Zhihui 吳稚晖 advocated the approach of nihilism. They wanted to cancel everything by appealing to "Emptiness" and "Formlessness" in Buddhism. On the other hand, HU Shi and CHEN Duxiu proposed the idea of total Westernization. In face of these currents of thought, Liang is the only person who dared to hold the flag of traditional culture, counterweighting those anti-traditionalist thoughts. This is the most meaningful thing he has done during his lifetime. (Mou 1988: 4)

Furthermore, Mou claimed, "Mr. Liang opened a new path for the evolution of Chinese culture.... It is believed that Liang indeed became a symbol of Chinese culture" (Mou 1988: 4). Although Mou was occasionally very critical of Liang's scholarship,[11] he nevertheless implied that DXWH had founded a theoretical framework under which New Confucian scholars of Hong Kong and Taiwan could develop their own systems of thought. His view of LIANG Shuming was further echoed by ZENG Zhaoxu 曾昭旭, a Taiwanese follower of MOU Zongsan and TANG Junyi.

---

[10] Before 1949, Mou and Liang had an argument on the issue of whether the rural reconstruction could serve China or not. In the meantime, Mou disagreed with Liang on his point of view of the Communist Revolution. Despite some disparities between Mou and Liang, Mou still reaffirmed the irreplaceable role of Liang's works in New Confucian Scholarship. See Mou 1988.

[11] In his lecture "Objective Understanding and the Remaking of Chinese Culture," MOU Zongsan criticized Liang's understanding of Chinese culture in his *Essentials of Chinese Culture* (中國文化要義) as superficial. In particular, he disagreed with Liang's assertion of "Ethical principles are the common standard; the professional vocations are just distinct paths (倫理本位, 職業分途)." Mou pointed out that such an argument only mirrored the actual social situation in China, instead of the culture that shaped society. In addition, Mou believed that Liang's academic research on Confucianism, Buddhism, and Daoism was weak. See Mou 2014: 39–41.

Following Liang's death in 1988, ZENG Zhaoxu published an essay in *Legein Monthly* (*E'hu* 鵝湖) (July 1988) titled "The Recollection of LIANG Shuming as a Man Unifying Knowledge and Action: How to Understand Confucianism and its Scholars" (懷踐履篤實的梁漱溟先生——兼論何謂儒學與學者). In this work, Zeng recalled the influence of DXWH on his thought when he was 24 years old:

> Before reading Mr. LIANG Shuming's description of Confucius' view of life in DXWH… I really felt that the ideas from Confucian classical books, which I had studied, were like some scattered pearls… Fortunately, the book by Mr. Liang presented me with a main thread connecting each scattered pearl to become a beautiful necklace. Later on, I spent one year organizing and refreshing my thoughts. It was the first time that I found my aspiration, and had an incredibly authentic understanding of Confucius and Confucianism… Since then, I truly started my journey to pursue my scholarship. During my academic voyage, I have read the books by the masters like TANG Junyi, MOU Zongshan, and XIONG Shili, and went all the way back to the Song-Ming Neo-Confucian School… I believe Mr. Liang's DXWH is the first book which exerted an enormous impact on my thinking during my formative period. (Zeng 1988: 4–5)

Evidently, Liang's DXWH constructed a solid foundation, on which ZENG Zhaoxu could get access to the thoughts of New Confucians of Hong Kong and Taiwan.

In sum, Liang's philosophical framework embraced three implications. First, Liang raised a concern over how to save and preserve Confucian-based Chinese civilization in the face of challenges from anti-traditionalism and the zeal of scientism. Within such a context, an inquiry into the cultural and philosophical ontology of Confucianism became a focal point in Liang's research. Second, Liang redefined the school of Confucianism from the perspective of vitalism, simultaneously demonstrating the aspect of spirituality in Confucian thought. Third, Liang's thought presented a cultural-philosophical approach to the examination of Chinese, Indian, and Western cultures, based on his Theory of the Reappearance of Three Cultural Periods. Even though Liang never visited Hong Kong or Taiwan after 1949, his attempts to achieve the goal of "new sprouts growing out of old roots" inspired overseas New Confucian scholars to dedicate themselves to transferring, reinterpreting, and applying the Confucian heritage. This point is further evidenced by LIANG Shuming's Confucian intellectual connections with TANG Junyi.

5 Intellectual Connections Between LIANG Shuming and TANG Junyi

After escaping to Hong Kong in 1949, TANG Junyi continued to correspond with LIANG Shuming. Tang also included Liang's works in his reading lists during the early years of residence in Hong Kong.[12] In a letter to Liang, he wrote:

> Although the book *Substance of Chinese Culture* (*Zhongguo wenhua yaoyi* 中國文化要義; hereafter ZGWH) has not circulated widely here [in Hong Kong], those who are interested

[12] See TANG Junyi's diary on August 8 and 9, 1950, in Wu 2014: vol. 1, 36.

> in your works still strive to get the book. The Master [Liang] is truly knowledgeable and compassionate. Ordinary people are not able to judge your works only based on political view and secular standard. A peaceful feeling and calm mind between the lines in your writings indeed make the book easily accessible to the readers. (Tang [196?] 2017: 889)

In a letter addressed to Liang on January 28, 1971,[13] Tang expressed:

> [Very often] I see some of my friends and young people here [in Hong Kong] read your previous works.... The orientation of the Eastern and Western cultures, which had been predicted in your works [DXWH] fifty years ago, will have an everlasting impact on us. (Tang [1971] 2017: 891)

These letters show that LIANG Shuming made an indelible mark on TANG Junyi's intellectual life. During China's long lockdown from the outside world after 1949, TANG Junyi greatly contributed to boosting LIANG Shuming's image as one of the leading scholars of New Confucianism in overseas Chinese intellectual communities. As a result of Tang's enduring efforts, Liang's book, ZGWH, was published in both Hong Kong and Taiwan during the 1960s (Sun 2019: 117). For decades, this was one of Liang's most widely read works among overseas readers (Sun 2019: 117).

Furthermore, while exploring his own scholarly pathway in Hong Kong, Tang advanced and developed Liang's New Confucian thought. During the 1950s, Tang wrote several influential works on the uniqueness of Chinese culture and the Confucian tradition, such as *The Value of the Spirit of Chinese Culture* (*Zhongguo wenhua zhi jingshen jiazhi* 中國文化之精神價值; 1951), *Reconstruction of the Humanistic Spirit* (*Renwen jingshen zhi chongjian* 人文精神之重建; 1955), *The Development of the Chinese Humanistic Spirit* (*Zhongguo renwen jingshen zhi fazhan* 中國人文精神之發展; 1958), and *Cultural Consciousness and Moral Rationality* (*Wenhua yishi yu daode lixing* 文化意識與道德理性; 1958). Aligned with the cultural conservatism embraced by New Confucian scholars of the Republican period, most of Tang's works explored the truth of Confucianism and targeted the ideas of anti-traditionalism and scientism (Wu 1991: 111).

A careful reading of LIANG Shuming's and TANG Junyi's works reveals sophisticated connections between the two scholars' thoughts. First of all, both of the scholars viewed human culture in a very broad sense. In particular, their works paid substantial attention to the multiplicity of the world cultural system. In Liang's DXWH, in keeping with his Theory of Reappearance of Three Cultural Periods, the formula of culture-life-will accommodates a diversity of lifestyles and philosophical systems, thereby accounting for the orientations of Chinese, Western, and Indian civilizations.

In *Cultural Consciousness and Moral Rationality*, TANG Junyi likewise utilizes the approach of cultural philosophy to investigate the role of moral rationality in human cultural consciousness (Major 2022: 129). Both Liang and Tang agree on the fundamental belief that the school of Confucianism embraces cultural universals,

[13] In *The Collection of Letters from and to* Liang *Shuming*, the date of this letter is marked as "196?". However, Liang's DXWH was released in 1921, which in principle means that Tang should have written this letter around 1971.

which are applicable to all people (Major 2022: 131). However, compared to Liang, Tang seems to be mostly interested in human culture in general. That is to say, he displays a broader cultural perspective such that his definition of "culture" covers all walks of human life, including religion, politics, the economy, the military, society, law, arts, ethics, and so forth (Tang [1958] 2005b: 18–22).

Important to note, despite the fact that comparing Eastern and Western culture is not the main aim of this work, to some extents, TANG Junyi also borrows from LIANG Shuming a cultural-comparative method of reflecting on the essence of Confucian humanism. In *Reconstruction of the Humanistic Spirit*, Tang compares Chinese, Western, and Indian cultures and identifies the significant differences among them—an approach that recalls Liang's work in DXWH (Tang [1955] 2005: 221–328, 351–406). Similarly, Tang echoes Liang when using the pattern of "being the sage on the inside" to develop his arguments. In fact, as early as the 1940s, Tang revealed his inclination to embrace the Confucian School of Mind and Nature (*xinxing zhi xue* 心性之學) through studying mind or nature as an philosophical ontology (*xin zhi benti* 心之本體) in the two works of his early years, *Life Experience* (*rensheng zhi tiyan*人生之體驗) and *Establishment of Moral Self* (*daode ziwo zhi jianli* 道德自我之建立) (Hu 2008: 52).

In TANG Junyi's following years as a New Confucian scholar, the Confucian School of Mind and Nature, which was traced to the source from Mencius' system of thought, played a significant role in his investigation of morality, life, tradition, and culture. For instance, Tang regarded Mencius' teaching as a major part of his philosophical foundation. In *Cultural Consciousness and Moral Rationality*, Tang wrote:

> Since Confucius passed away, Mencius attached great importance to the relationship between "Justice" (*yi* 義) and "Fortune" (*li* 利)… His thought focused on human life. In contrast, Xunzi (荀子) concentrated on studying culture, such as the difference between "Civilization" (*wen*文) and "Wilderness" (*ye* 野) and the gap between "Civilization" (*wen* 文) and "Natural Disposition" (*zhi* 質)… However, Xunzi neglected the fact that the essence of human mind is relevant to *lixing* 理性 or *xingli* 性理 (the principle of human nature). Instead, it has nothing to do with the basic instinct of human beings. (Tang [1958] 2005b: 5)

After elaborating significant differences between Mencius and Xunzi, Tang announced in his following writings:

> Therefore, in this book, my argument on the foundation of humanism is not based on natural disposition… My work follows the spirit of Mencius, which emphasizes that the foundation of humanism, as the principle of *xingli* or *lixing*, should surpass and master the realm of nature. (Tang [1958] 2005b: 5)

Given this comment above, Tang's vision of humanism had been framed by his utilization of Mencius' idea of the principle of human nature. As discussed previously, for LIANG Shuming, Mencius' teaching clearly demonstrates the crucial role of intuition, which consists of "innate knowledge" or "innate ability," in the implementation of the character of *ren* in Confucianism. It is worth noting that "innate knowledge" or "innate ability" is identical with the principle of human nature in the philosophy of Mencius (Fu 2018: 256–257).

Hence, the passages from Tang quoted above show that his understanding of Mencius was similar to Liang's. Furthermore, echoing Liang's sense of cultural pride, Tang in *Reconstruction of the Humanistic Spirit* exhibited his recognition of what is distinctive and valuable within the Confucian tradition.

> The greatness of Confucian spirituality lies in the fact this system of thought is grounded in the life of the human being and the idea of humanism.… Therefore, from the point of view of Confucianism, politics, democracy, and the ideology relevant to any kind of political system are all secondary concepts. Instead, things such as the realm of humanity and personality, the secular world, and human nature, are the supreme ideas. (Tang [1955] 2005: 155)

Simply put, this passage shows that Confucianism from Tang's perspective refers to a vivid philosophy that included not simply the formal political apparatus, the ethical code, and social institutions, but a wide range of cultural products that were part of all spheres of human life. In characterizing the differences and similarities between Confucianism and Buddhism, Liang made a similar comment:

> The ultimate purpose of Confucian learning is to become aware of the unlimited possibilities of human life, then to achieve the status of "realization of its nature in practice." Therefore, the learning can meet Heaven's demands. (RFYTL: 155)

Clearly, Liang and Tang both believed that the school of Confucianism was a dynamic cultural tradition embracing the feature of vitality. For the two scholars, the ideal of humanism was centered on Confucianism as a living system of thought.

In line with TANG Junyi, MOU Zongsan addressed the importance of Liang's vitalization (*shengminghua* 生命化) of Confucianism to the development of New Confucian scholarship:

> Only he (Liang) was able to imbue the living spirit to Confucius, so that we have a chance to face the truth of Confucius' life and wisdom.… At the same time, it is fair to say that he opened a door for the revival of the Song-Ming School of Mind in Confucianism, and in doing so, we can connect ourselves to the life and wisdom of Song-Ming Confucian scholars. (Mou 1970: 112)

Simultaneously, inspired by LIANG Shuming, Mou interpreted the character of *ren* from the perspective of dynamic life relevant to Confucian cosmology:

> The creation of mind is identical with the creation of the character of *ren*. Correspondingly, the substance of Confucius' *ren* reflects the spirit of the life of the universe.… Therefore, through embracing the character of *ren*, a Confucian gentleman can go beyond the limitation of flesh and body, integrating his life into all living things from heaven and earth, as well as combining nations and the world into the oneness. (Mou 1955: 97–98)

In Liang's analysis, the character of *ren* usually means a vital force flowing in the universe, a sharp intuition to do the right thing, a lively spirit based on ritual and music, and a dynamic outlook on life (ZH: 94–96). Mou's argument in this paragraph closely matches Liang's definition of *ren*.

In short, following the Chinese Communist Revolution, a group of intellectuals in exile in Hong Kong and Taiwan propagated the voice of the New Confucian school, which had been founded during the Republican Period. Due to great efforts by TANG Junyi and his fellow scholars, the school of New Confucianism was advanced and developed beyond mainland China after 1949. As one of the pivotal branches of China's New Confucianism, LIANG Shuming's system of thought had an unparalleled opportunity to interact with overseas Chinese intellectual communities.

6 TANG Junyi, the 'New Confucian Manifesto,' and Going Beyond LIANG Shuming

In 1958, addressing the Western scholarly community's misconceptions about Chinese culture, TANG Junyi signed "A Manifesto on the Reappraisal of Chinese Culture: Our Joint Understanding of the Sinological Study Relating to World Cultural Outlook" (為中國文化敬告世界人士宣言) (Hu 2008: 107). Tang's fellow New Confucian scholars, including MOU Zongsan, XU Fuguan, and ZHANG Junmai, contributed to this historic document, but Tang is believed to have been its main drafter. To a great extent, therefore, this Manifesto reflects the development of TANG Junyi's intellectual thought (Hu 2008: 126). The Manifesto's release can be seen as the beginning of what has come to be called the New Confucian School of Hong Kong and Taiwan.

It is worth pointing out several sophisticated theoretical and philosophical connections between this Manifesto and LIANG Shuming's New Confucian philosophy. Connected to Liang's ultimate concern about the future of Chinese culture, the Manifesto demonstrates the endeavors of TANG Junyi and his fellow Confucian intellectuals to preserve and promulgate the school of Confucianism. Similarly, the Manifesto represents the reactions of Tang and other overseas New Confucian scholars to the anti-traditionalism and zeal of scientism that arose from the May Fourth New Culture period (Gan 2018: 5–6). The authors' foremost purpose in writing this document was to correct the faulty perceptions of Chinese culture held by Western sinologists and post-May Fourth scholars as a result of their idealizing scientific methods (Gan 2018: 5–7). Reflecting Liang's DXWH, the Manifesto also aims to create a space for the development of Confucianism in the face of serious challenges from Western culture. To this end, TANG Junyi and his fellow scholars viewed themselves as the bearers of the life of Confucian culture and unanimously treated the Chinese cultural tradition with "sympathy and respect" (Tang et al. [1958] 1974: 134). In the Manifesto, they addressed the key issues that LIANG Shuming had argued for in his works since the May Fourth period, including the vitality of Confucianism, the relation between China and the West, and the function of democracy and science in the Confucian tradition.

In the Manifesto, TANG Junyi generally followed the New Confucian pathway pioneered by LIANG Shuming, but adapted to his own philosophic thinking. When reading over the manuscript, it is relatively uncomplicated to detect the existence of significant connections between the thoughts of the two New Confucian thinkers, as well as instances in which Tang transformed some of Liang's key ideas. Both Liang and Tang paid attention to the cultural continuum in Chinese civilization. However, compared to Liang, Tang and his fellow Manifesto scholars were more inclined to understand cultural continuity in China from the perspective of cultural legitimacy. According to the Manifesto,

> The essence of Chinese culture is the disposition of "single rootedness" (*yi ben xing* 一本性), which means that Chinese culture in nature is an independent system.… There has been an orthodox idea connecting all periods of ancient Chinese culture thoroughly. Yin (殷) inherited the culture of Xia (夏) after the downfall of Xia dynasty, and Zhou (周) inherited the culture of Yin (殷) after the downfall of Yin dynasty. All the changes led to the fact that a unified orthodox culture penetrated the period of the three dynasties.… Politically, China experienced a variety of divisions and unifications.… Neither political division nor unification disrupted the continuity and stability of Chinese culture. This should be called the inheritance of Confucian Orthodoxy or *daotong* (道統). (Tang et al. [1958] 1974: 137)

Notably, for most Confucian cultural loyalists (*yimin* 遺民), *daotong* has to be intertwined with their political and cultural identity. In contrast to LIANG Shuming's enthusiastic support for "New China" after 1949, Tang and his New Confucian colleagues thought of the Chinese Communist Revolution as a grave threat to Chinese culture. In light of such a conviction, Tang chose to recognize the Republic of China (ROC) on Taiwan as a legitimate Chinese government although he held an ambivalent view of the Guomingdang regime, a position that suggests his cultural and political orthodoxy (He 2015: 113).[14] In this regard, as the key writer of the Manifesto, Tang adopted the stance of a Confucian cultural loyalist engaged in preserving Chinese culture among the overseas Chinese community.

In addition, TANG Junyi and his colleagues further developed LIANG Shuming's theory in terms of the relationship between Confucianism and religion.[15] As a New Confucianism pioneer, Liang wrote in DXWH: "Only the spiritual life embraced by Confucius, which played a somewhat religious and artistic role in Chinese people's lives, can match the Western School of Vitalism" (DXWH: 480). In ZGWH, Liang further emphasized that although Confucianism is different from religion, Confucian ritual and music sometimes assume a religious role (ZGWH: 210). In short, Liang treats Confucian ethics as a substitute for religion in Chinese society (ZGWH: 196–216).

By contrast, TANG Junyi and the Manifesto's other contributors endeavored to uncover a religious aspect embraced by the school of Confucianism itself. Tang pointed out in the Manifesto that Confucianism possessed a religious nature, even though it did not have a formal system like that of Western religion with regard to transcendence and eternity. In contemporary Western society, Tang claimed, religion is separate from politics and ethics, whereas in Chinese culture, it is historically common for culture, religion, ethics, and politics to be intertwined. Hence, Tang further explained in the Manifesto:

---

[14] As TANG Junyi's diary shows, he attended a ceremony in Hong Kong each year on October 10 to commemorate the founding day of the ROC. In Wu 2014: vol. 2, 111, 188, 207, 249.

[15] Readers interested in Liang's philosophy of religion can refer to Chap. 6 in this volume.

> From the dimension of Chinese moral teaching and practice, there must be a feeling of religious transcendence. In Chinese ethical theory, we must not downplay ideas such as the integration of heaven with man's morality (*tian ren he de* 天人合德), the harmony between heaven and man (*tian ren he yi* 天人合一), the sameness between heaven and man (*tian ren bu er* 天人不二), and the shared substance between heaven and man (*tian ren tong ti* 天人同體), which were emphasized by ancient Chinese scholars.… For the ancient Chinese, *tian* referred to the idea of a personal god. The concept of *tian* from Confucius, Mencius, Laozi, and Zhuangzi is different respectively. However, it is very difficult to ignore the fact that the implication of *tian* from their perspectives definitely exceeded the realm of individual personality and human relationships in the secular world (Tang et al. [1958] 1974: 143).

In fact, this important passage reflects TANG Junyi's idea of synthesizing religion with humanism, a conviction he elaborated in his works. In the preface to his book *The Value of the Spirit of Chinese Culture*, Tang argued:

> My view on the essence of Chinese culture is that it is not anti-religious. I believe that Chinese philosophy, ethics, and politics were all derived from the spirit of the worship of heaven. Therefore, it is inappropriate to say that there is no religion in Chinese culture. Conversely, I believe that in Chinese culture, religion had been synthesized with the realm of humanism. (Tang [1953] 2005: Preface)

Taking this line of argument further, he wrote:

> Since the Confucius-Mencius period, Confucian philosophy has emphasized a main theme: someone who knows his nature will understand Heaven, and to preserve his mind, and nourish his nature, is the way to serve Heaven. In the meantime, Confucius-Mencius' worship of ancestors and old sages, and their respect for the way of Heaven and cultural tradition, still accommodated a religious spirit. However, such a religious spirit must be synthesized with moral principle. (Tang [1955] 2005: 72)

In LIANG Shuming's view, religion and Confucianism belong to different realms, but these writings by Tang demonstrate that he explored the issue of religion within the body of Chinese culture. In Tang's analysis, the substance of Chinese culture actually absorbed certain parts of primitive religion, making it thereafter impossible for Confucianism-based Chinese society to exclude a spirit of religion. In this respect, Tang revised LIANG Shuming's notion that Confucian ethics was a substitute for religion in Chinese society.

A final point to mention about the Manifesto is the perspective of TANG Junyi and other New Confucian scholars about the relationship between the Confucian tradition and Western democracy. In this regard, Tang and his colleagues made significant revisions to LIANG Shuming's ideas. From Liang's perspective, in Western culture, the intellectual orientation toward the external world led to the development of science, while individual self-interest and desire for one's rights resulted in democracy. Despite Liang's positive view of Western democracy and science,[16] he believed that these two cultural assets were fundamentally incompatible with

[16] Readers interested in Liang's view of Western democracy can refer to Chap. 10 in this volume.

Chinese society, which was based on the cultural system of ethically oriented differentiation among roles.[17]

In light of this understanding, Liang firmly believed that neither Western democracy nor a Soviet-style class struggle was suitable for the Chinese nation's future (Gan 2019: 95–112). In the Manifesto, Tang worked closely with other leading scholars to demonstrate the compatibility of the Confucian tradition with Western democracy. "It cannot be said that in Chinese politics, there is no tendency to favor the establishment of democracy [or that] there is no seed for the growth of democratic thought in Chinese culture." (Tang et al. [1958] 1974: 162). For Tang Junyi, the School of Mind and Nature (*xin xing zhi xue*) in Confucianism became a strong linkage connecting the Confucian tradition with Western democracy. Following the vision of goodness of human nature (*xingshanlun* 性善論) stemming from the Confucian School of Mind and Nature, Tang asserted:

> What is the root of the principle of democracy in the spirit of traditional Chinese humanities? This is a respect for a holistic personality. Likewise, human personality should be regarded as a magnificent Confucian spirituality in harmony with the will of heaven.... Both Confucius and Mencius treated the preservation of classic culture as their indispensable responsibilities.... Confucian human nature is indeed a disposition which was able to appreciate the worth of all kinds of cultures in human life. This is the doctrine of Goodness of Human Nature in Confucianism. (Tang [1955] 2005: 340)

He further explained:

> According to such a vision, ordinary people and ancient sages share the same nature. The doctrine covers a whole realm of Chinese humanities. At the same time, this view on human nature grows out of everyone's mind. It embodies the spirit of equality in Confucianism...Today the ultimate foundation of Western democracy is located in human dignity and equality. So, isn't the spirit of Confucianism the same as the spirit of democracy? (Tang [1955] 2005: 340)

This significant passage shows that Tang interpreted the implications of democracy using the Confucian formula *neisheng-waiwang*, which was once utilized by Liang Shuming as a framework to conduct his own cultural philosophy and practice.[18] In line with this conviction, Tang repeatedly expressed that the essence of modern democracy is in conformity with Mencius' ideal. That is, if all people had the potential to become moral sages like Yao (堯) and Shun (舜), they could be educated to be democratic citizens, equally participating in social and political institutions (Tang [1958] 2005a: 464). For instance, in the Manifesto, Tang wrote:

[17] In DXWH, Liang thought that China could import and implement democracy and science on the Chinese soil. However, he changed his perception in the late 1920s.

[18] In his works titled *Intellectuals in a Big Time*, Xu Jiling (許紀霖) points out that the two significant concerns that Liang Shuming dedicated to pursuing during his life were respectively the question of life and the question of society. While the former belongs to the sphere of *neisheng*, the latter falls into the category of *waiwang*. Xu also thought that Liang should be treated as a symbolic figure embracing the ideal of *neisheng-waiwang* in modern Chinese history. See Xu 2012: 205.

> If everyone could be treated as an equal political subject, it would be natural that the establishment of the constitution, as a channel for the exercise of fundamental political rights, must follow public will. It is to say that the construction of the moral foundation in Chinese culture and history can be politically developed into a democratic system… (Tang et al. [1958] 1974: 165–166)

Tang's view on the relation between Confucianism and Western democracy was further bolstered by his colleague, Mou Zongsan. Mou strived to reform the formula *neisheng-waiwang* in order to make Confucianism compatible with Western democracy. In the context of classical Confucianism, *waiwang* normally concentrated on a political statecraft relevant to governing the country and bringing harmony to the world. By contrast, Mou redefined *waiwang* by infusing it with elements of science and democracy. He maintained:

> The most urgent mission for contemporary Confucian scholars is to connect democratic politics with the tradition of *waiwang*. …Democracy should be the form of a new *waiwang*. [S]cience should be integrated with another indispensable part [democracy] in the content of new *waiwang*.…[S]cience can become the material for new *waiwang*." (Mou 1955: 305–309, 312–313)

As a dedicated New Confucian scholar, Mou was confident in Chinese culture's competence to assimilate any foreign idea, including Buddhism and Western democracy and science (Mou 1991: 5). This led him to the formula "new *waiwang* emerging out of old *neisheng*" (*lao neisheng kaichu xin waiwang* 老内聖開出新外王)," which recalls Liang's proposal "new sprouts growing out of old roots."

Of note, both Tang and Mou believed that the May Fourth intellectuals had failed to establish a democratic system in China because they failed to see the Confucian tradition as a foundation upon which Western learning could take root. Based on this lesson, the New Confucian scholars of Hong Kong and Taiwan believed that the growth of democracy and science in Chinese society required the society to retain the core part of Confucianism, in particular the approach of *neisheng*. This, in turn, would require the Chinese people to adopt the goal of constitutional democracy as an indispensable element of *waiwang*. In this line of thinking, Tang Junyi and his fellow scholars significantly broadened the realm of *waiwang* beyond Liang Shuming's characterization of it. Underpinned by these thoughts, Tang Junyi and his Manifesto co-authors announced: "The [Confucian] ideal of 'all under heaven belonging to the people' (*tianxia wei gong* 天下為公), based on the idea of equality [in Confucianism], is the root of democratic political thought; at least, this ideal can become a seed for the growth of such political thinking" (Tang et al. [1958] 1974: 164).

Like Liang Shuming, the New Confucian scholars also expressed an optimistic view of the Chinese influence on Western culture. In the Manifesto, they summarized the five points they believed Western people could learn from Chinese culture: the spirit of "living in the moment"; "the insight of being adaptable and spirit-like"; "a feeling of compassion"; "the wisdom of retaining culture"; and the view that "the whole world is like one family" (Tang et al. [1958] 1974: 173–187). It is important to mention that neither Liang Shuming nor the Manifesto authors viewed democracy as the end of human history. On the contrary, they saw democracy merely as an instrument for achieving the Confucian ideal of bringing harmony to the world. Like LIANG Shuming, the Manifesto authors trusted that "the purification of people's heart" relevant to *neisheng* should be the determinative factor for modernizing China.

In short, the Manifesto, signed by TANG Junyi, MOU Zongsan, XU Fuguan, and ZHANG Junmai in 1958, surpassed the scope of LIANG Shuming's thinking in several aspects, including Confucianism as *daotong*, the Confucian tradition's connection with democracy and science, and its relationship with religion. Because of these developments in their thinking, the scholars of TANG Junyi's generation were more capable of improving the dialogue between the Confucian tradition and Western culture than the New Confucian scholars of the Republican period were.

7 Aftermath

Consistent with the feeling of "sympathy and respect" for Chinese culture that he expressed in the Manifesto, Tang in 1961 published a paper "The Dispersal and Drifting About of the Flowers and Fruit of the Chinese Nation" (*Zhonghua minzu hua guo piao ling* 中華民族之花果飄零). In this work, he described the rich cultural heritage of China as a fallen tree, with its flowers and fruits dispersed and drifting away with the wind, taking shelter under the trees of others for survival (Tang [1961] 2005: 3–25). In 1964, Tang published another paper titled "The Dispersal and Drifting About of the Flowers and Fruits and the Self-Replanting of Our Spiritual Roots (*Hua guo piao ling ji ling gen zi zhi* 花果飄零及靈根自植)," which argued that even though ethnic Chinese people might reside overseas, they could still preserve their Chinese cultural identity by "self-replant[ing] one's spiritual roots (*Lin gen zi zhi* 靈根自植)" (Tang [1964] 2005: 26–52). Both articles struck a chord with a great deal of Chinese people from Hong Kong, Taiwan, and overseas, sparking spirited debates on the future of Chinese culture. Likewise, both articles embraced Tang's identity as a Confucian loyalist bearing a feeling of cultural nostalgia extending from the first generation of New Confucian scholars like LIANG Shuming.

From 1966 to 1975, Tang made painstaking efforts to finish and publish his substantial book, *On the Origin of Chinese Philosophy* (*Zhongguo zhexue yuan lun* 中國哲學原論). Following the method of "discussing philosophy through the history of philosophy" (*yi zhexueshi lun zhexue* 即哲學史以言哲學) (Tang [1968] 2006: 3), Tang systematically traced the timeline of Chinese intellectual history to build his arguments about significant issues in Chinese philosophy, including nature (*xing* 性), principle (*li* 理), *dao* (道), and teaching (*jiao* 教). Although this work concentrated on classifying and interpreting classical works of Chinese philosophy, his research did not take the form of a rigorously scientific survey. Instead, the primary goal of this book was to demonstrate the importance of the Confucian tradition of "being the sage on the inside" (*neisheng*) in the development of Chinese philosophy, connecting his own life with the thought and the life of ancient sages (Jing 1989: Section 3).

In 1978, the last year of his life, Tang published his final great work, *The Existence of Life and the Horizon of Mind* (*Shengming cunzai yu xinling jingjie* 生命存在與心靈境界). This book synthesized the varied aspects of his intellectual thought, including the systems of Chinese, Western, and Indian philosophy. Like Liang's DXWH, Tang's *The Existence of Life and the Horizon of the Mind* uses the approach of cultural comparison. In Tang's final philosophical works, he posited that the existence of human mind was a precondition for understanding a diversity of spiritual dynamics, which could produce different types of human consciousness. Based on this assumption, Tang identifies a system of nine "horizons" (*jingjie* 境界), different levels of our perception of the world. In brief, for Tang, the system of nine "horizons" tied together all human life experiences, scientific knowledge, religious beliefs, and ethical norms (Hu 2008: 132–142). Compared with LIANG Shuming's formula of culture-life-will, TANG Junyi's horizon of mind infused the features of "universality" and "transcendence"[19] with his own Confucian philosophy.

8 Conclusion

In his entire lifetime, Liang made only one trip to Hong Kong, in 1941, at the eve of the Pacific War, and he never visited Taiwan. Therefore, his influence on Hong Kong and Taiwan could not be direct. In light of this situation, this paper has investigated LIANG Shuming's effect on Hong Kong and Taiwan since 1949 by studying his intellectual connections with TANG Junyi.

LIANG Shuming and TANG Junyi took leading roles in preserving and disseminating Confucianism before and after 1949,[20] respectively. Although they belonged to different age groups, they were in fundamental agreement in their ultimate concerns about the Confucian tradition. Both men saw themselves as saviors of Chinese culture in the face of unprecedented challenges from anti-traditionalism and Western civilization. For both scholars, an intertwined combination of family and historical factors contributed to their lifetime pursuit of New Confucian scholarship. However, in contrast with Liang's collaborative attitude toward the CCP, Tang chose to escape to Hong Kong in 1949 and retain the spirit of the Confucian tradition in exile.

As a trail-blazer in the New Confucian School, LIANG Shuming proposed "new sprouts growing out of old roots" by "vitalizing" Confucianism. The framework of *neisheng-waiwang* and the approach of cultural philosophy, which he used in DXWH, permeated into TANG Junyi's works after 1949. In particular, "A Manifesto

[19] In *The Existence of Life and the Horizon of Mind*, "transcendence" not only embraces the dimension of religious humanism originating from the veneration of Heaven and supernatural spirits, but also refers to the realm of the mind-heart in which the subject and object can be interconnected.

[20] Although Liang kept on writing after 1949, Communist China systematically outrooted social and cultural conditions for the growth of the New Confucian School during Mao's period.

on the Reappraisal of Chinese Culture," written by Tang and his colleagues in 1958, was a symbolic document of Hong Kong-Taiwan New Confucianism that advanced some of Liang's key ideas while surpassing the scope of Liang's discourse.

In Confucian intellectual genealogy, both TANG Junyi and MOU Zongsan have been deemed disciples of XIONG Shili (Wu 1991: 110). Nevertheless, in terms of philosophical concerns, some scholars categorize Liang and Tang in the same group (Wu 1991: 110). To align with Xiong, Mou paid substantial attention to Confucianism's metaphysical aspects. Tang, on the other hand, followed LIANG Shuming in placing more emphasis on the discovery of the originality of Chinese culture. Going beyond Liang's idea of culture-life-will, TANG Junyi generated a system of nine horizons of mind, which could accommodate all kinds of culture.

The intellectual connections between Liang and Tang were reciprocal in nature. Whereas TANG Junyi made efforts to continue, develop, and transfer LIANG Shuming's New Confucian philosophy in Hong Kong, LIANG Shuming simultaneously paid substantial attention to the development of Tang's scholarship. As soon as his books were published, Tang managed to mail them to Liang. Upon reading Tang's works, Liang frequently copied meaningful passages from them into his notebooks (ZTZZ:312). After Tang's death, Liang expressed his thoughts in a letter to his former student HU Yinghan (胡應漢):

> How sorrowful I feel about TANG Junyi's death. However, he truly understood the meaning of life and death. I used to extract some passages from his works. Now I would like to quote a small paragraph as follows: "the ontology of mind should not be confined in space and time, and it [the mind] will be eternally true. Therefore, it is not reasonable to say that everyone must die (our life will not end) only because of the perishing of his or her body. Since someone was born, his or her flesh shall experience a long process from birth to death thoroughly. This process must be accompanied by psychological transformation. Therefore, from birth to death the human body is but the manifestation of one stage of the mental exercise of the mind itself. As a result, it is unquestionable that people will have life after death or the next generation will renew one's psychological activities." I believe that TANG Junyi must come back to life! (ZHYH: 458)

Tang's theory of ontology of mind evidently resonated with LIANG Shuming. As a leading figure among overseas New Confucian scholars after 1949, Tang worked tirelessly to apply his Confucian ideals to the local cultural and educational field in a way that is reminiscent of how LIANG Shuming had dedicated himself to the cause of rural reconstruction in Shandong Province during the 1930s. As one of the founders of the well-known New Asia College, Tang was appointed professor of philosophy at the Chinese University of Hong Kong in the early 1960s. He remained at the university, as professor and later as dean, until his retirement. During this period, he was also invited by the University of Taiwan to serve as a visiting professor (Hu 2008: 73–85, 131–142). In addition, he traveled abroad on lecture tours to Japan, Korea, Europe, and the United States. It is fair to say that, working closely with his New Confucian fellows, Tang assigned to those in exile in Hong Kong and Taiwan the mission of keeping alive the consciousness of their community, the Chinese diaspora.

Even though Liang and Tang never visited each other after 1949, they maintained scholarly and intellectual ties in addition to the bond of friendship. Confucius once said in the *Analects*, "an exemplary person never leaves *ren* for even the time of a single meal. In moments of haste he acts according to it. In times of difficulty or confusion he acts according to it" (*Analects* 1999: 90). According to this description, both LIANG Shuming and TANG Junyi can certainly be counted among the group of exemplary people.

References

DXWH *Dong-Xi wenhua ji qi zhexue* 東西文化及其哲學 [Eastern and Western Cultures and Their Philosophies; 1921]. *LSMQJ*, 1989, vol. 1: 319–547.

JSTL *Jingshen taolian yaozhi* 精神陶煉要旨 ["Key to Spiritual Cultivation"; 1934]. *LSMQJ*, 1989, vol. 5: 493–519.

JTWM *Jintian women yingdang ruhe pingjia kongzi* 今天我們應當如何評價孔子 ["How to Understand Confucius Today"; 1974]. *LSMQJ*, 1989, vol. 7: 270–314.

KZXS *Kongzi xueshuo zhi chongguang* 孔子學說之重光 ["The Rejuvenation of the Doctrine of Confucius"; 1934]. *LSMXS*, 2004: 3–11.

KZZMM *Kongzi zhen mianmu jiang yu heqiu* 孔子真面目將於何求 ["How to Find out the Truth of Confucius"; 1923]. *LSMQJ*, 1989, vol. 4: 767–774.

LSMQJ *LIANG Shuming quanji* 梁漱溟全集 [*Complete Works of L IANG Shuming*, vols. I to VIII]. Jinan: Shandong Remin Chubanshe, 1989.

LSMWL *LIANG Shuming wanglai shuxin ji* 梁漱溟往來書信集 [*Collection of Letters from and to LIANG Shuming*], edited by LIANG Peikuan. Shanghai: Shanghai renmin chubanshe, 2017.

LSMXJ *LIANG Shuming xuanji* 梁漱溟選集 [*Selective Works of LIANG Shuming*], edited by CHEN Lai. Changchun: Jilin renmin chubanshe, 2006.

LSMXS *LIANG Shuming xiansheng lun RuShiDao*梁漱溟先生論儒佛道 [*LIANG Shuming's Lectures on Confucianism, Buddhism, and Taoism*]. Guiling: Guangxi shifan daxue chubanshe, 2014.

RFYT *RuFo yitong lun* 儒佛異同論 [*Treatise on Differences and Similarities;* 1916]. *LSMQJ*, 1989, vol. 7: 152–169.

WDZX *Wode zixue xiaoshi* 我的自學小史 ["A Short History of My Self-Learning"; 1942]. *LSMQJ*, 1989, vol. 2: 659–698.

ZGMZ *Zhongguo minzu zijiu yundong zhi zuihou juewu* 中國民族之自救運動之最後覺悟 ["The Last Enlightenment of Chinese Nation's Self-Strengthen"; 1932]. *LXMXJ*, 2006: 375–418.

ZGWH *Zhongguo wenhua yaoyi* 中國文化要義 [*Substance of Chinese Culture*; 1949]. *LSMQJ*, 1989, vol. 3: 1–316.

ZH *Zhaohua* 朝話 [*Morning Speeches*; 1932–1935]. *LSMQJ*, 1989, vol. 2: 35–132.

ZHYH *Zhi Hu Yinghan* 致胡應漢 ["Letter to Hu Yinghan"; 1978]. *LSMWL*, 2017, vol. 1: 458.

ZS *Zishu* 自述 ["Self-Introduction"; 1934]. *LSMQJ*, 1989, vol. 2:1–34.

ZSZN *Zishu zaonian sixiang zhi zaizhuan zaibian* 自述早年思想之再轉再變 ["Intellectual Transformations during My Early Years"; 1969]. *LSMQJ*, 1989, vol. 7: 177–184.

ZTJY *Zhi Tang Junyi* 致唐君毅 ["Letter to Tang Junyi"; 1951], *LSMWL*, 2017, vol. 1: 310.

ZTZZ Zhi Tang Zhizhong 致唐至中 ["Letter to Tang Zhizhong"; 1983], *LSMWL*, 2017, vol.1:312.

Alitto, Guy S. 1979. *The Last Confucian: L IANG Shu-ming and the Chinese Dilemma of Modernity*. Berkeley: University of California Press.

Ames, Roger T., and Henry Rosemont Jr., trans. 1999. *The Analects of Confucius*. New York: Ballantine Books.

Chen, Duxiu 陳獨秀. 1984. Statement of Defense for My Journal 本誌罪案之答辯書. In *The Selective Works of Chen Duxiu*, vol. 1 陳獨秀文章選編 上. Beijing: Shenghuo, Dushu. Xinzhi. Sanlian Press.

Chen, Qijuan 陳奇娟. 2012. Study of Liang Shuming's Thought of *neisheng-waiwang* 梁漱溟"內圣外王"思想研究. PhD Dissertation, Nanjing University of Science & Technology.

Chen, Xueran 陳學然. 2005. Tang Junyi's Reflection on the May Fourth 唐君毅對五四的詮釋. *Legein Monthly* 鵝湖 359: 44–57.

Chow, Tse-tsung. 1960. *The May Fourth Movement: Intellectual Revolution in Modern China*. Cambridge: Harvard University Press.

Fu, Pei-jung 傅佩榮. 2018. *Fu Pei-jung's Discourse on Pre-Qin Philosophy* 傅佩榮的哲學課: 先秦儒家哲學 Beijing: Beijing lianhe chuban gongsi.

Gan, Chunsong 幹春松. 2018. The Problem Consciousness of New Confucian Within the 'Manifesto' on Behalf of Chinese Culture 從1958年的《為中國文化敬告世界人士宣言》看港臺新儒家的問題意識. *Confucian Classroom* 孔學堂 4: 107–121.

——— 幹春松. 2019. *Ethics and Order: State and Society in Liang Shuming's Political Thought* 倫理與秩序:梁漱溟倫理與秩序. Beijing: The Commercial Press.

Grieder, Jerome B. 1970. *Hu Shih and the Chinese Renaissance: Liberalism in the Chinese Revolution, 1917–1937*. Cambridge: Harvard University Press.

———. 1983. *Intellectuals and the State in Modern China*. New York: Simon and Schuster.

He, Yi 何一. 2015. The Complex of Cultural Loyalism of Contemporary New Confucians and Its Value 現代新儒家的遺民情結及其價值. In Bao, Shaolin 鮑紹霖, Huang, Zhaoqiang 黃兆強, and Ou, Zhijian 區誌堅, eds., *Northern Scholars Moved South: The Origin of Literature, History, and Philosophy of Hong Kong and Taiwan*, vol. 1 北學南移:港臺文史哲溯源 學人卷. Taipei: Showwe Information Co., Ltd.

Hu, Zhihong 胡治洪. 2008. *Biography* of *Tang Junyi* 唐君毅. Kunming: Yun Nan Education Press.

Jing, Haifeng 景海峰. 1989. Brief Introduction of Mr. Tang Junyi's Life and Works 唐君毅先生之生平與著作述略. *Shen Zhen University Journal* 2深圳大學學報2. URL: http://www.guoxue.com/master/tangjunyi/ tangjunyi.htm. Accessed 4 December 2020

Liang, Peishu 梁培恕. 2012. *The Last Confucian Master in China: Remembering My Father Liang Shuming* 中國最後壹個大儒: 記父親梁漱溟. Nanjing: Jiang Su Wen Yi Press.

Lin, Anwu 林安梧. 2009. Liang Shuming and His Theory of the Reappearance of Three Cultural Periods. In Thierry Meynard, ed, *Contemporary Chinese Thought* 40 (3): 16–38.

Lin, Yusheng 林毓生. 1979. *The Crisis of Chinese Consciousness: Radical Anti-traditionalism in the May Fourth Era*. Madison: University of Wisconsin Press.

Liu, Shuxian 劉述先. 2020. A Reexamination of the Investigation of Contemporary New Confucianism 現代新儒學研究之省察. *Research Journal of Chinese Literature and Philosophy* 中國文哲研究集刊 20: 367–382.

Major, Philippe [Ma Feili] 馬斐力. 2022. The Culture that Can Transcend Culture: The Cultural Philosophies of Liang Shuming and Tang Junyi 超越文化之文化: 梁漱溟與唐君毅的文化哲學. In Ho Chien-hsing 何建興 and Yang Deli 楊德立, eds., *Cultural Interpretation and the Negotiation Between Traditions* 文化詮釋與諸傳統之交涉. Taipei: Institute of Chinese Literature and Philosophy, Academia Sinica.

Makeham, John. 2003. *New Confucianism: A Critical Examination. London: Palgrave Macmillan.*

Mao, Zishui 毛子水. 1919. National Heritage and the Spirit of Science 國故和科學精神. *New Tide* 新潮 1 (5): 731–745.

Mou, Zongsan 牟宗三. 1955. *Philosophy of History* 歷史哲學. Hong Kong: Keung Seng Press.

——— 牟宗三. 1970. *The Study of Life* 生命的學問. Taipei: San Ming Shu Ju Press.

——— 牟宗三. 1988. The Liang Shuming that I Knew 我所認識的梁漱溟. *Legein Monthly* 鵝湖157: 2–4.

——— 牟宗三. 1991. Chinese Culture's Past and Future 中國文化的過去與未來. In Huo Taohui 霍韜晦, ed., *International Conference Proceedings on Tang Junyi's Thought* I 唐君毅思想國際會議論文集 (1). Hong Kong: Fa Zhu Press.

——— 牟宗三. 2014. Objective Understanding and the Remaking of Chinese Culture. In Jason Clower, trans./ed., *Late Works of Mou Zongsan: Selected Essays of Chinese Philosophy*. Leiden: Brill.

Sun, Jiahong 孫家紅. 2019. Missing Old Friends with Nostalgia for the Distant Motherland: Reading the Only Five Correspondences between Liang Shuming & Tang Junyi and Commemoration of the 40th Anniversary of Tang Junyi's Death 遙對故人思故國: 讀梁漱溟、唐君毅兩先生五封往來書信並紀念唐君毅先生逝世四十週年. *Chinese Cultural Studies* 中國文化研究 Fall 2019: 112–132.

Tang, Junyi 唐君毅. [1951] 2017. Letter to Liang Shuming 致梁漱溟. In Liang Peikuan 梁培寬, ed., *The Collection of Correspondences of Liang Shuming*, vol. 2 梁漱溟往來書信集 第二冊. Shanghai: Shanghai People Press.

——— 唐君毅. [1953] 2005. *The Value of Spirit of Chinese Culture* 中國文化之精神價值. Guilin: Guanxi Normal University Press.

——— 唐君毅. [1955] 2005. *Reconstruction of the Humanistic Spirit* 人文精神之重建. Guilin: Guanxi Normal University Press.

——— 唐君毅. [1955] 2017b. The Development of the Spirit of the Chinese Youth during the Last Sixty Years 六十年來中國青年精神之發展." In Li Liming李黎明, ed., *Inspiration in Life: Early Years of Four Great Scholars* 生命的奮進:四大學問家的青少年時代. Beijing: Jiu Zhou Press.

——— 唐君毅. [1958] 2005a. The Realization of the Democratic Ideal and the Consciousness of Objective Value 民主理想之實現與客觀價值意識. In Tang Junyi, *Chinese Humanities and Contemporary World* 中華人文與當今世界. Guilin: Guanxi Normal University Press.

——— 唐君毅. [1958] 2005b. *Cultural Consciousness and Moral Rationality* 文化意識與道德理性. Guilin: Guanxi Normal University Press.

——— 唐君毅. [196?] 2017. Letter to Liang Shuming 致梁漱溟. In Liang Peikuan 梁培寬, ed., *The Collection of Correspondences of Liang Shuming*, vol. 2 梁漱溟往來書信集 第二冊. Shanghai: Shanghai People Press.

——— 唐君毅. [1961] 2005. The Dispersal and Drifting About of the Flowers and Fruit of the Chinese Nation 中華民族之花果飄零. In Tang Junyi, *Chinese Humanities and Contemporary World* 中華人文與當今世界. Guilin: Guanxi Normal University Press.

——— 唐君毅. [1964] 2005. The Dispersal and Drifting About of the Flowers and Fruits and the Self-Replanting of Our Spiritual Roots 花果飄零與靈根自植. In Tang Junyi, *Chinese Humanities and Contemporary World* 中華人文與當今世界. Guilin: Guanxi Normal University Press.

——— 唐君毅. [1968] 2006. *Fundamental Discourses on Chinese Philosophy: The Dao as Nature* 中國哲學原論:原性篇. Beijing: Zhongguo shehui kexue chubanshe.

——— 唐君毅. [1971] 2017. Letter to Liang Shuming 致梁漱溟" In Liang Peikuan 梁培寬, ed., *The Collection of Correspondences of Liang Shuming*, vol. 2 梁漱溟往來書信集 第二冊. Shanghai: Shanghai People Press.

——— 唐君毅. [1974] 2017. The Intellectual Atmosphere during the Early Republican Period and My Life Experience with Studying Philosophy 民國初年的學風及我學哲學的經過. In Li Liming李黎明, ed., *Inspiration in Life: Early Years of Four Great Scholars* 生命的奮進:四大學問家的青少年時代. Beijing: Jiu Zhou Press.

Tang, Junyi 唐君毅, Zongsan Mou 牟宗三, Junmai Zhang 張君勱, and Fuguan Xu 徐複觀. [1958] 1974. A Manifesto on the Reappraisal of Chinese Culture: Our Joint Understanding of the Sinological Study Relating to World Cultural Outlook 為中國文化敬告世界人士宣言. In Tang Junyi, *On the Dispersal and Drifting About of the Flowers and Fruit of the Chinese Nation* 說中華民族之花果飄零. Taipei: San Min Book Co., Ltd.

Wu, Rujun 吳汝鈞. 1991. Mr. Tang Junyi and Contemporary Confucianism 唐君毅先生與當代儒學. In Huo, Taohui 霍韜晦, ed., *International Conference Proceedings on Tang Junyi's Thought* IV 唐君毅思想國際會議論文集 (IV). Hong Kong: Fa Zhu Press.

Wu, Xingwen 吳興文, ed. 2014. *Diary of Tang Junyi* 唐君毅日記. Chang'chun: Jilin Press.

Xie, Xiaojuan 謝曉娟 and Junlin Li 李俊玲. 2019. On the Trend of Scientism in the May Fourth New Cultural Movement 論五四新文化時期的科學主義思潮. *Journal of China University of Mining & Technology (Social Sciences)* 中國礦業大學學報(社科) 3: 3–12.

Xu, Jiling 許紀霖. 2012. *Intellectuals in a Big Time* 大時代中的知識人. Beijing: Zhonghua Book Company.

Yang, James Zhixiang. 2019. New Confucian Liang Shuming's Transformation of John Dewey's Philosophy in Chinese Rural Education. *Beijing International Review of Education* 1 (4): 673–694.

Zeng, Zaoxu 曾昭旭. 1988. Remembrance of Liang Shuming: A Man Unifying Knowledge and Action 懷踐履篤實的梁漱溟: 兼論何謂儒學與儒者. *Legein Monthly* 鵝湖 157: 4–5.

Zhang, Rulun 張汝倫. 2014. *Study of Modern Chinese Thought* 現代中國思想研究. Shanghai: Shanghai People Press.

Chapter 13
Liang Shuming's Reception in Mainland China Since the 1980s

Huajun Zhang

1 Introduction

LIANG Shuming 梁漱溟 (1893–1988) is a significant but controversial figure in modern Chinese history. He initiated an intensive debate on Chinese culture with his early work *Eastern and Western Cultures and Their Philosophies* (*Dong-Xi Wenhua Ji Qi Zhexue,* 東西文化及其哲學, abbreviated as DXWH) published in 1921. He resigned from the lecturer position at Peking University in 1924 and led the rural reconstruction experiment in Shandong province started in 1931. After 1949, he stayed in the mainland but kept an independent attitude. His public defiance of MAO Zedong 毛澤東 (1893–1976) during a central meeting in 1953 has often been considered a demonstration of his independent character as a traditional and modern intellectual. He suffered persecution during the Cultural Revolution (1966–1976) but survived. Throughout his life, his thoughts on China's modernization experienced several changes, yet amid such changes some of his views remained unaltered.

During the Cultural Revolution, Liang was harshly criticized on ideological grounds. Since the 1980s, Liang's thought has been re-evaluated by academics. In the 1990s, several books on Liang's life and thought were published in the mainland. MA Yong 馬勇 and ZHENG Dahua 鄭大華published two books each on Liang (Ma 1991, 1992; Zheng 1994, 1999), WANG Donglin 汪東林 published his interviews with Liang (Wang 1992), and CAO Yueming 曹躍明 (Cao 1995) and GUO Qiyong 郭齊勇 and GONG Jianping 龔建平 (Guo and Gong 1996) authored studies dedicated to Liang's thought. Works published during this period significantly re-evaluated Liang's thought and moved away from the harsh criticism it had previously sustained. After Liang's death in 1988, his sons, students, and close followers

H. Zhang (✉)
Faculty of Education, Beijing Normal University, Beijing, China
e-mail: zhanghj@bnu.edu.cn

T. Meynard, P. Major (eds.), *Dao Companion to Liang Shuming's Philosophy*, Dao Companions to Chinese Philosophy 17,
https://doi.org/10.1007/978-3-031-18002-6_13

edited *The Complete Works of Liang Shuming*, published from 1989 to 1993 in 8 volumes and re-published in 2005 by Shandong Renmin Press.

From the late 1980s to 2000, studies re-evaluating Liang's thought for the most part moved from rejecting to accepting the value of his views on China's modern transformation. Studies of this period can be divided into two groups: those adopting a Confucian perspective and those opting for other kinds of perspective. The Confucian perspective also includes some scholars who are not Confucian themselves but have sympathy for Confucianism. As to scholars opting for a non-Confucian perspective, they often adopted a Marxism position and were inclined to classify Liang's work into the category of subjective idealism (e.g., Zheng 1987, 1988).[1] However, some scholars in the fields of Confucian philosophy and religious studies have shown a more sympathetic understanding of Liang's work. Guo Qiyong and Gong Jianping have on the one hand situated Liang's thought in the context of the development of Confucian thought in Chinese history, but they have also, on the other hand, put it in conversation with the work of modern Western philosophers such as Martin Heidegger (1889–1976) (Guo and Gong 1996). Wang Zongyu 王宗昱 also avoided the trap of political ideology by locating Liang's thought in the contexts of Buddhism and Confucianism as well as in relation to Western thinkers such as Henri Bergson (1859–1941) (Wang 1989a, b). Ma Dongyu 馬東玉 highlighted an important reason that explains why Liang's work was highly valued by scholars in the 1990s. During this decade, mainland China experienced widespread economic reforms toward marketization. The old questions of whether China needs to westernize and the extent to which it should westernize became urgent again. Also, as a rising power, the uncertain cultural identity of the nation came to be increasingly regarded as an issue. Liang was insightful on all these issues. His efforts to reconstruct an ethical society in a modern world became highly appealing (Ma 1993).

After the turn of the twenty-first century, the interest in Liang's thought persisted. Younger scholars joined the ranks of Liang Shuming specialists. Scholars in the disciplines of philosophy and religious studies began to share their interest in Liang's work with historians, sociologists, political scientists, educationists, and psychologists. In 2003, Guy Alitto's book *The Last Confucian* was published in Chinese (Alitto 艾愷 2003). One of the translators is Wang Zongyu, a religious studies expert and a good interpreter of Liang's early thought. During this period, Gu Hongliang 顧紅亮 also studied Liang from the perspective of the concept of "lifeworld" (Gu 2008).

In the last two decades, the study of Liang thrived. Thousands of articles on him were published in academic journals, many of which explored the possibility of drawing from Liang's thought in order to face the challenges of the twenty-first century. An important number of scholars in the field of philosophy, such as Chen Lai 陳來, Gao Ruiquan 高瑞泉, and Gu Hongliang, wrote extensively on Liang.

[1] Zheng Dahua is a prolific author writing about Liang's thought. It is interesting that Zheng's attitude to Liang's work gradually changed in the recent decades. In his recent work, Zheng (2006) made efforts to understand Liang's thought with a more open and dynamic framework of Marxism.

Historian Luo Zhitian 羅志田 published extensively on Liang by situating him in the landscape of China's transition to modernity in the early twentieth century. Sociologists, political scientists, and legal scholars, among others, also made significant contributions to the study of Liang. I discuss some of them in the following section, although I should note that it is impossible, in this short essay, to provide an *exhaustive* account of the profuse literature on Liang published in mainland China since the 1980s.

As China's economic development continued in the first twenty years of this century, the social crisis in many areas intensified. Many people harbored strong feelings of nihilism and experienced a loss of values and meanings in daily life. Scholars have found similarities between the contemporary challenges faced by Chinese society and the crisis experienced in the early twentieth century. Liang was deeply involved in attempting to find solutions to the crisis China faced in the early twentieth century, and he continued looking for solutions to the many issues that plagued Chinese society throughout his life (Gao 2019). For this reason, scholars have found it helpful to explore his approach toward the modern transformation of China, an approach which—despite is being targeted at China—could contribute to the democratic development of the world. This focus might also explain why Liang's rural reconstruction effort was extensively discussed by scholars in both the social sciences and the humanities (Wu 2005; Gan 2017; Pan et al. 2018).[2]

In the following sections, I divide the study in terms of the questions raised by scholars, as this can better highlight how scholars have sought to answer contemporary issues by studying Liang. Moreover, to study the reception of Liang's thought in Liang's way, it is better to classify the works by the questions they attempt to answer. Liang once said that he was not a scholar or an expert, but a person who dealt with questions.

The key question in the contemporary study on Liang is an old one, but interpreted through the lens of a new time: What is the best approach to modernization for China? For Liang, the question could be divided in two: (1) how can China become a modern nation in the world, and (2) how can Chinese people feel peaceful living in this modernized nation? The questions do not imply that Liang was a nationalist. To some extent, he was, because he always held the project of building a modern Chinese nation as a priority. But he also held a cosmopolitan perspective, since he considered the future of the Chinese tied to the future of human beings as a whole (Gu 2010a: 60).

Today, China is an economic superpower. This differs from a hundred years ago, when China had fallen behind economically and the existence of the nation was seriously challenged. But what does economic development mean? Does it mean that China has also become a cultural superpower and could lead the future development of the world? And what does Chinese culture mean today? It is definitely not identical to traditional Chinese culture, nor does it resemble Western cultures.

[2] It should be noted that Liang's rural reconstruction efforts were not only studied by scholars but also by many social workers in rural communities.

Intellectuals today share the same worries Liang and many other intellectuals had about the loss of cultural identity a hundred years ago (Luo 2016a).

Based on the key question of China's modern transformation, I review three issues addressed by contemporary mainland studies of Liang since the late 1980s. It should be noted that most of the literature reviewed, however, was published since the turn of the twenty-first century.

The first issue relates to Liang's idea of culture. Did Liang propose a multicultural approach or a singular cultural approach? Following this question, is Liang a cultural conservative or reformist? How does Liang deal with the relationship between westernization and the renovation of Chinese traditional culture? Since the modernization of Chinese culture remains an unfinished project, these questions were hotly debated by scholars in the recent decades.

To understand these issues, however, we need a better comprehension of the philosophical ideas of Liang. Therefore, the second issue dealt with by this review is that of Liang's philosophy of life. How did Liang develop his philosophy of life by creatively mixing ideas from Buddhism, Confucianism, and Western philosophies? How did his self-identification as a Buddhist influence his modern interpretation of Confucianism? A narrower question is: How can we understand Liang's replacement of the concept of "intuition" (*zhijue* 直覺) by that of "ethical rationality" (*lixing* 理性)?

Finally, to understand Liang properly, we cannot avoid an important episode of his life: the rural reconstruction in Zouping County, Shandong Province. Therefore, the third issue addressed by the literature reviewed in what follows is Liang's theory and practice of rural reconstruction. In the practice of rural reconstruction, Liang gradually developed his confidence in the modern transformation of Chinese culture. Though the rural reconstruction movement failed in the historical context of the 1930s, many contemporary scholars realize its significance for today's society.

2 Liang's Approach to China's Cultural Modernization

Liang was deeply involved in the cultural debates of the New Cultural Movement in the 1910s and the 1920s. He received great attention thanks to his book DXWH, which was first published in 1921. In the radical atmosphere of the time, in which traditional culture was considered a barrier to the establishment of a modern nation, Liang's proposition to consider Chinese culture more advanced than Western culture was easily misunderstood as conservative and was harshly criticized by the radical intellectuals who advocated complete modernization. Interestingly, Liang denied he was a cultural conservative and claimed he fully accepted the value of science (*sai xiansheng* 賽先生) and democracy (*de xiansheng* 德先生). This positioned him as the opponent of traditionalists (Luo 2016b). How can we understand Liang's seemingly paradoxical position on culture and its evolution during his lifetime? He himself admitted his thought both changed and remained consistent from his early works until his death.[3]

According to one group of scholars, Liang held that culture should evolve toward singularity. This group considers that Liang's cultural position was mainly influenced by the social evolutionism introduced to China by YAN Fu 嚴復 (1854–1921). LI Xianghai 李翔海 (1998, 2009) argues that Liang proposed a singular cultural approach to evolution from Western culture to Chinese culture and then to Indian culture. According to Li, that Chinese culture represents the future direction of world culture in Liang's view betrays a tendency toward a China-centric worldview that remains limited and even dangerous in today's world. WANG Zongyu (1990: 58) also suggests that Liang mistakenly held a singular and evolutionist view of culture in his early works and ignored the uniqueness of each local culture. The main differences between Li and Wang is that the latter limits his discussion to Liang's early works and highlights that the influence of social evolutionism in China's contemporary social sciences is still pertinent and relevant. GAO Like 高力克 (1990: 100) and LI Weiwu 李維武 (2001: 33) also suggest that Liang's singular approach to cultural evolution was misleading for China's modernization.

But is this view a misinterpretation of Liang? Some authors clearly regard Liang as an advocate for the development of a plurality of cultures. JING Haifeng 景海峰 (1994) characterizes Liang's position as a cultural relativism that differs from the once popular approach of "Chinese essence and Western utility" (*zhongti xiyong* 中體西用) in that it is a dynamic new approach to respond to the challenge of westernization in China's modern transition. CAO Yueming (1994: 70) shares similar views. Based on an analysis of Liang's *Essence of Chinese Culture* (*Zhongguo wenhua yaoyi* 中國文化要義, 1949; abbreviated to ZGWH), OUYANG Zhesheng 歐陽哲生 (2018: 175) argues that Liang actually held a critical perspective toward traditional culture. Therefore, Liang opposed cultural universalism and had a positive view of cultural pluralism. Following this logic, Liang proposed that China could not follow the developmental path of the West and had to create its own.

How can we understand such paradoxical interpretations of Liang's cultural position? In their monograph on Liang's philosophy, Guo and Gong (1996: 97) suggest that Liang emphasized the uniqueness of particular cultures but also admitted the universality of culture. That is, the value of a particular culture lays in its ability to overcome the limitations of locality and be included in the universal culture of humanity. Thus, Liang implied that Chinese culture had the significant value of potentially contributing to world culture. This interpretation avoids the contradiction between the singular and plural approaches to cultural development.

CHEN Lai (2000: 3–4; 2001: 265) argues that Liang was not opposed to Western culture and recognized the benefits of science and democracy for modern society. Also, Liang was not the advocate of a romanticized ancient society. He was deeply

[3]This review uses GU Hongliang's periodization of Liang's works into three periods: Liang's analysis of culture in the 1920s being classified as "early works," Liang's theory of rural reconstruction in the 1930s forming his "middle works," and Liang's development of his philosophy of life after the 1940s counting as his "later works." (Gu 2010b).

involved in the complicated challenges related to the modern transformation of China, but this did not refrain him from holding a cosmopolitan position. Liang therefore realized the progressiveness of modern Western culture while also being alert to its weaknesses. Moreover, although he had full confidence in traditional Chinese culture, he also sharply understood what of pre-modern Chinese culture needed to be reformed. In Liang's own words, "this old tree did not die and could have new buds" (JYYRS: 67).

To respond to the contradictory interpretations of Liang's cultural position, the contemporary historian Luo Zhitian wrote a series of articles from 2016 to 2018. In them, Luo contextualizes Liang's position in relation to various debates between Liang and intellectuals of his time such as Hu Shi 胡適 (1891–1962) during the early twentieth century. Though Luo focuses on the early works of Liang, mainly DXWH, his analysis demonstrates the dynamic and dialectical character of Liang's philosophy of culture, which shows insights relevant beyond the socio-historical context in which it emerged. It is the consensus of contemporary scholars (e.g., Zheng 1988; Wang 1990; Luo 2016a) that Liang accepted "complete westernization" (*quanpan xihua* 全盤西化) in his early works—a position that did not change until the period of rural reconstruction in the 1930s. But Liang was dissatisfied with intellectuals who proposed radical westernization, such as Hu Shi and Chen Duxiu 陳獨秀 (1879–1942). He did not believe modern Western culture could be the future direction of Chinese modernization. In other words, Liang accepted the value of Western culture only for the particular time period in which China was at the time, but China needed to return to its own tradition in the future. Luo (2016a) calls this process a "cultural turnabout" (*wenhua fanshen* 文化翻身). Luo recognizes a paradox in Liang's cultural reconstruction project, however. If Chinese culture had to be completely westernized, who would be responsible to lead the next stage of return to Chinese culture? China would lose its cultural identity in the first stage of westernization. Luo concludes that Liang could not solve this contradiction and had to give up the path of westernization. Interestingly, Luo (2017a: 156) argues Hu Shi was aware of the risk of Liang's proposal of radical westernization from the very beginning. Luo further suggests that in ZGWH, Liang corrected his cultural view and made his position more dialectical. Liang agreed that cultures had their unique characteristics and values. Even though they might share many commonalities or universal values, small differences between them might be crucial (Luo 2017b: 98). In this way, Liang rejected both the approach of "Chinese essence and Western utility" and that of "complete westernization." He implied that although Chinese traditional culture shared universal values with Western culture, it had to be treated as an organic whole and could thus not be reconciled with, or transplanted in, Western culture. Thus, it was clear that China's modernization had to be initiated from within, and motivated by, its own culture.

This does not entail, however, that Liang was a cultural conservative (Chen 2000; Ouyang 2018: 180). Or we could say that Liang was a rebellious conservatist (Zhou 2005). Gao Ruiquan (2019: 49) suggests that to understand Liang's philosophy of culture, it is crucial to read his middle and later works, such as *Theory of Rural Construction* (*Xiangcun jianshe lilun* 鄉村建設理論, 1937) and ZGWH (1949), which focus on the reconstruction of the social order through the elaboration of what Wu Fei (2005) calls "new etiquette and custom" (*xin lisu* 新禮俗) for people living in the countryside. In Gao's view, although it is possible to call Liang a cultural conservative, his conservatism does not have the negative connotations of backwardness or old-fashionedness. Instead, Liang explored a promising new approach to modernization for China, which differed both from radical liberalism and cultural conservatism.

Ouyang (2018: 174) reminds his readers that it would be misleading to interpret Liang's work in the framework of historical materialism or social Darwinism, since both assume a unilinear development of society. He suggests that Liang deliberately separated culture from economic development. This distinction represents a crucial difference between Liang and his opponents. It was the basis upon which Liang could adopt a Chinese approach to modernization which avoided the above contradiction highlighted by Luo (2016a). In other words, even though China was economically backward, this did not entail that Chinese culture was similarly backward. This point of view is very thought-provoking for China today, given how economic success has not resolved the anxiety experienced by many over China's cultural identity.

Chen Lai's interpretation of Liang's philosophy of culture contributes to further clarifying the meaning of culture in Liang's works (Chen 2000). Chen (2000: 2) suggests that Liang distinguishes between culture as a reflection of the local habits of a specific nation and culture as a spiritual disposition cultivated in history. The latter conception of culture does not indicate the unique ways of life of a people but represents an approach to human living that emphasizes collaboration, equality, and humanness. This conception refers to universal values shared by all human beings. For Liang, that Chinese culture had value for the future of world development did not mean that people all around the world would speak Chinese or would adopt the Chinese way of daily life. It meant that people could adopt an attitude of living together peacefully centered on "ethical rationality" (*lixing*).

Both Ouyang and Chen explicitly make the point that culture as an attitude toward life should be separated from socio-economic development. This interpretation of Liang's philosophy of culture creates a new space for the possibility of the modern transformation of Chinese culture. It indicates that cultural modernization is not be necessarily consistent with economic development. It also implies a critique of the May Fourth enlightenment movement, during which the value of Chinese culture was first seriously challenged and later completely denied. By reinterpreting Liang's philosophy of culture, contemporary scholars can reaffirm the potential value of Chinese culture as an attitude toward life which could lead China to a modern state.

Adopting this conception of culture, Gan Chunsong 幹春鬆 (2017: 2) argues that in his early works, Liang tried to correct the unilinear conception of historical development which was popular in the New Culture Movement. Liang was alert that materialism might overemphasize economic development at the expense of spiritual elements in social development. Also following this conception of culture, Wei Wenyi 魏文一 (2016) emphasizes the idea of "*gang*" (resoluteness, 剛) put forth in DXWH as a key concept to understand Liang's conception of Chinese culture as an attitude toward life. He proposes that *gang* could consistently explain Liang's integration of Buddhism, Confucianism, and Western ideas. This effort of integration also implied the possibility of modernizing the Chinese attitude of *gang*. Although *gang* was a notion primarily developed in the *Analects*, Liang creatively connected it with Buddhism. The life attitude of *gang* indicated the possibility of transcendental experience beyond the various existing boundaries and limitations of this-worldly life. Wei (2016) suggests that we need to take Liang's effort of integrating Buddhism and Confucianism as the intellectual foundation for his further inclusion of the Western attitude toward life which was exemplified by the scientific and democratic ways of life. In Wei's interpretation, Liang's philosophy of culture could thus move beyond the debate on the singular versus plural approaches to cultural development discussed above. It is also inappropriate, Wei argues, to identify Liang as an evolutionist or a conservative.

In Liang's view, the preservation of Chinese culture, as an attitude toward life, did not entail going back to the living style and customs of ancient times. It simply meant reviving the tradition of "learning about the self" by keeping the sensitivity and motivation to improve one's understanding in relation with others and with the world, so that one's life could be enriched with evolving wisdom (KZXS: 552). Zheng Dahua (2006: 96) considers that this emphasis on learning about the self as (*ziji xue* 自己學) was a significant effort of Liang toward the modern transformation of Confucianism. Guo and Gong (1996), Ren Jiantao 任劍濤 (2015), and other scholars also echo this view, which might become a promising direction for cultural development in the future. I return to this point of view in the next section. Here, suffice it to quote a paragraph of Zheng (2006: 96) as an example:

> Liang Shuming considered that the "true Confucianism" established by Confucius was not systematic norms and models of ritual, nor was it a systematic school of thought. Instead, the discipline could be called a "*ziji xue*" (a discipline of learning about the self)… According to Liang, "*ziji xue*" is a discipline that "focuses on reflecting of one's own life, rather than focusing on things not connected to one's life … and thus makes one's life progress." Therefore, the key of Confucianism is to turn one's attention to the progress of one's own life so that knowledge works for one's life, instead of life working for knowledge.

Here we can see that Liang's idea of "*ziji xue*" emphasizes the practice of self-cultivation central to the Confucian tradition. This relates to Liang's faith in the creativity of the individual mind. Pointing out this idea of Liang reflects efforts, by contemporary Chinese scholars, to take a more plural and open position to understand the value of Confucianism in the contemporary context.

3 Liang's Philosophy of Life

Liang's philosophy of culture is closely related to, or even determined by, his philosophy of life. More and more Chinese contemporary scholars have come to realize the significance of Liang's philosophy of life for modern society, especially his emphasis on ethical relationships and the tranquility of mind in a chaotic society

(Zhao 2007; Xu 2008). In this section, I review studies that address how Liang integrates his understanding of Buddhism, Confucianism, and Western philosophy into his own philosophy of life. Although his ontology of cosmic life (*yuzhou shengming* 宇宙生命) was clearly influenced by Bergson and Buddhism—especially Yogācāra epistemology (*weishi xue* 唯識學)—most contemporary scholars suggest Liang's philosophy of life mainly represents his effort to transform Confucianism into a modern school of thought.[4] They base their assertion on the fact that Liang developed the Neo-Confucian idea of the mind and developed the concept of *ren* (humanness, 仁). He also creatively interpreted the concept of "intuition" (*zhijue* 直覺) in his early works and replaced it with the concept of "ethical rationality" (*lixing* 理性) in his later works. The last two concepts became keys to understand the evolution of Liang's philosophy of life. Therefore, in the second part of this section, I discuss how contemporary scholars have interpreted these two concepts as they relate to Liang's philosophy of life. I also consider the argument that Liang's idea of *ziji xue* is closely connected to his philosophy of life.

3.1 Liang's Philosophy of Life and Its Position in Confucianism and Buddhism

Liang's philosophy of life was embedded in a deep life crisis he experienced in his early years. How to live a free life in an unfree world was the fundamental question for Liang. Being fully engaged in the social issues of the early Republican years and having a very independent personality, Liang encountered a serious personal crisis and attempted suicide twice. He then realized that it might be impossible for the individual to gain complete freedom in the world. He tried to solve the crisis by converting to Buddhism.

LIU Yuebing 劉岳兵 (1993) has provided us with a study of Liang's first important work on Buddhism, his *Treatise on Finding the Foundation and Resolving Doubt* (*Jiuyuan Jueyilun* 究元決疑論, 1916). He argues that the basic ideas Liang upheld throughout his life were already present in this work. This means that Liang's thought started from Buddhism and never abandoned the Buddhist position. In this work, Liang found that Buddhist wisdom was the way to overcome the illusion of reality and reach the radical transcendence of freedom. Liang's early works drew a sharp contrast between Buddhism and Confucianism. While Buddhism aspires to the supramundane world (*chushijian* 出世間), Confucianism calls for self-cultivation in daily life. Buddhism promotes the idea of no-self (*wuwo* 無我) and

[4] In *The Religious Philosophy of* Liang *Shuming*, Thierry Meynard (2011) takes a different position and considers Liang as a Buddhist who took Confucianism as a bridge in the mundane world to achieve radical transcendence. Some contemporary scholars of mainland China also emphasize the Buddhist dimension of Liang's thought, e.g., CHENG Gongrang 程恭讓 (1998) and ZHANG Wenru 張文儒 (2001). Quite a few mainland scholars, e.g., TANG Wenming 唐文明 (2010), hold that the Buddhist perspective is not necessary to understand Liang's original thought.

no-life (*wusheng* 無生) while Confucianism advocates for self-cultivation (*xiushen* 修身) and generating life (*sheng-sheng* 生生).[5] Given such sharp differences, Liang's intellectual identity as a Confucian or a Buddhist remains debated.[6] In the last two decades, more Chinese scholars have come to realize that both Confucianism and Buddhism are crucial to understand Liang's thought. Liang was engaged in an effort to connect Buddhism and Confucianism to make living free possible in the modern world.

Li Xin 李昕 (2013a: 50) has analyzed Liang's attitude toward Confucianism and Buddhism by focusing on the creativity of the mind (*shixin chuanghua* 識心創化) in Yogācāra epistemology and how this creativity could be put to the task of establishing a relationship with Confucianism. In Yogācāra, the creativity of the mind can transform the basic mode of cognition from "consciousness" (*shi* 識) into "direct knowing" (*zhi* 智). This is a process called "transforming consciousness into direct knowing" (*zhuanshi chengzhi* 轉識成智). "Direct knowing" refers to an "affirmative moment [that] set up a mode of experience beyond cognition and consciousness" (Meynard 2011: 113). Liang later developed the concept of intuition (*zhijue*) as a Confucian concept similar to the Buddhist notion of "direct knowing." Meynard considers that Liang regarded Confucian intuition as the "first step in direct perception," while Buddhist direct perception was the "next step" (Meynard 2011: 100). Thus, Confucianism and Buddhism formed a continuum (*huitong* 會通).

Wang Ruoxi 王若曦 (2016) has studied the Buddhist concept of suchness (*zhenru* 真如)[7] and the Confucian concept of *sheng-sheng* to reflect on how Liang creatively built a connection between Buddhism and Confucianism in his later works and thus solved the tension between the two schools of thought present in his early works. By admitting Liang's dual identities as a Confucian and a Buddhist, some scholars (e.g., Chen 2009: 38; Zhao 2007: 59–60) suggest that we cannot simply consider Liang a Confucian or Buddhist, or someone who displays both identities independently of one another, but we need to understand how Liang creatively integrated the two schools of thought into the development of his own thought.

As an active participant of the New Cultural Movement, Liang was also influenced by the Western ideas introduced by Chinese intellectuals. French philosopher Henri Bergson was one of the most influential Western thinkers for Liang. Liang discussed Bergson's philosophy of life and borrowed the notion of intuition from

---

[5]The idea of "*sheng-sheng*" is a concept of Chinese philosophy originating from *The Book of Change* (*Zhouyi* 周易). The translation of this concept into English is debatable. Some translate it as "generating life," e.g., Wu Fei 吳飛 (2018), while others translate it as "continuous life and growth," e.g., Ding Yun 丁耘 (2020). Here, I use Wu's translation to highlight the continuous and dynamic process of life.

[6]For example, Guy Alitto's work *The Last Confucian:* Liang *Shu-ming and the Chinese Dilemma of Modernity* (1979) focuses on Liang's Confucian thought, while Thierry Meynard's work *The Religious Philosophy of* Liang *Shuming: A Hidden Buddhist* (2011) approaches Liang from a religious perspective, emphasizing the Buddhist dimension of his thought.

[7]The direct translation of "*zhenru*" (真如) is: "truth" (*zhen* 真) and "such as this," or "suchness" (*ru* 如). It is a basic concept of Buddhism used to indicate the essence of the cosmos.

Bergson. Wang Zongyu (1989a, b) has provided a detailed analysis of how Liang understood Bergson. Wang argues that in his early works, Liang mainly relied on Chinese translations of Bergson's work and did not understand Bergson correctly. Being fully engaged in Buddhism at the time, Liang interpreted major concepts of Bergson's, such as "life" and "intuition," through the prism of Buddhism. This echoes how Liang's later discussion of Dewey (Gu 2010b) was inserted in a Confucian framework. Therefore, the contemporary mainland Chinese literature on Liang suggests that the major resources of Liang's philosophy of life originate from his creative interpretation of Buddhism and Confucianism.

One of the main issues regarding Liang's philosophy of life relates to the idea of "the essence of the cosmos" (*yuzhou bentilun* 宇宙本體論). Li Xin (2013a) suggests that Liang took a dual position on the essence of the cosmos. According to Li Xin, on one hand, Liang considered the cosmos the unchanged *zhenru* (suchness) which was not created and could not be destroyed (*busheng bumie* 不生不滅). On the other hand, the cosmos never stopped changing. The cosmos here is not a physics concept but a philosophical one. It indicates the unlimited wholeness which includes both levels of reality: the realized and the potential reality. The second perspective on the cosmos outlined above is mainly derived from the Confucian notion of *sheng-sheng*, which originates from *The Book of Change* (*Zhouyi* 周易). Li interprets that Liang considers the cosmos is life, because it indicates the liveliest and the most sensitive energies which creatively generate new lives. The human mind is in the center of this cosmic life because it is the human will (*yiyu* 意欲) that generates the endless continuum of life (*xiangxu* 相續) (Wei 2016: 177). Therefore, the cosmos is not a singular reality, as the creativity of the human will can generate new and multiple realities in the changing flow of the cosmos.

In his later works, including *Human Mind and Human Life* (*renxin yu rensheng* 人心與人生, 1984; abbreviated to RXYRS), Liang abandoned the word "will" but continued to consider the human mind (*renxin* 人心) the key of cosmic life. This is because, in Liang's view, the main characteristics of the human mind are that it is the most active, the most sensitive, and the most creative thing in the cosmos. Therefore, it is the human mind that makes the connection (*tong* 通) between lives and things in the cosmos possible (Chen 2016: 96–97). Also, it is the human mind that can understand and coordinate the changing flow of the cosmos, and deal with the endless conflicts and tensions generated in the cosmos when different lives and things interact with each other (Zhao 1993: 23). The connections established by the mind are not intellectual but rely on the feeling of the moment; on an intuition devoid of the thinking process of reasoning or calculation. This feeling is the moral intuition thanks to which the human mind can build ethical connections with others. In Confucianism, it is called *ren* (humanness), and in Buddhism, *bei* (empathy, 悲). By connecting the feelings of the individual mind/heart with others in the cosmos, *ren* or *bei* breaks the dualism of the self and others (Li 2013b). Guo and Gong (1996: 193) consider that Liang's cosmic life echoes the Confucian notion of the "Unity of Human and Universe" (*tianren heyi* 天人合一).

Liang was heavily influenced by the Confucian school of mind (*xinxue* 心學) of the Ming dynasty, especially the Neo-Confucianist Wang Gen (王艮, 1483–1541),

the leader of the Taizhou School (*Taizhou xuepai* 泰州學派). This school of thought holds a naturalist understanding of mind. That is, the practice of mind is considered a natural activity that should follow the discipline of nature. By drawing from such an understanding of the mind, Liang could reaffirm the crucial role of intuition, the most natural of feelings. However, as Guo and Gong (1996: 275–276) suggest, Liang later realized that although the intuitive ability of the human mind is granted by nature, it should be developed. The human mind is not innately endowed by nature; it represents a potentiality waiting for its realization. Therefore, it is crucial to make efforts so that the potentiality of the human mind for creativity and connecting with the cosmos can be fully realized. Such an emphasis on the practice and deliberate efforts of the individual took Liang away from the experience of mystical awakening and brought Confucianism back to the ethical practice of daily life.

Because the human mind is not innately endowed but requires efforts to realize its potential and connect with other lives and things in the cosmos, cosmic life can be regarded as the outcome of the moral practice of self-cultivation. By explicitly introducing this philosophy of life in DXWH, Liang confirmed that modern Confucianism should go back to the tradition of Confucius to focus on practice (*jianlü zhi xue* 踐履之學) rather than the "study of moral principles" (*yili zhi xue* 義理之學). In other words, Liang's philosophy of life is about how to live in the world and strive to become a good person, and as such can be regarded as an answer to the question he asked in his early life regarding the possibility of living a free life in an unfree world. Li Zhengang 李振綱 (1992) recognizes this point in Liang's RXYRS, which Liang considered his most important work. According to Li (1992: 75–76),

> The major idea of Liang Shuming's *Human Mind and Human Life* on moral practice is that "morality means not losing one's mind for a second"... The difference between the noble man and the vulgar man depends on every second of daily life, on whether one keeps one's mind for every moment of one's life. Therefore, the improvement of one's moral character is a lifelong effort of self-cultivation in every moment of daily life.

This is an important reminder for the contemporary understanding and practice of the Confucian tradition. We need to go back to the tradition established by Confucius on the moral practice of being a good person, rather than exclusively focus on the reading of the classical texts. The Confucian tradition was first and foremost a daily practice for common people; a practice of self-cultivation toward the realization of life, transformed from the life of the self to the life of cosmos, as Liang elaborated in his philosophy of life.

3.2 From Intuition to Ethical Rationality: What Changed and What Remained Unchanged in Liang's Thought

As a thinker who had a long intellectual life, Liang's thought remained strikingly consistent. But it is also easy to recognize a number of changes his thought underwent throughout his lifetime. One of the most obvious and well-discussed change is his replacement of the concept of "intuition" (*zhijue*) in his early works with the concept of "ethical rationality" (*lixing*) in his later works. The fact that contemporary Chinese scholars have highlighted this change in Liang's thought has to do with the socio-historical context (studied in Luo Zhitian 2018). In the context of the rapid economic and technological development of Chinese society, evaluating the side-effects of the worship of technology and capital is a serious issue. In academia, it is necessary to examine the limitations of the scientific method as the only legitimate approach to knowledge.

As Wang Zongyu (1989a, b) argues, in Liang's early works, and DXWH in particular, "intuition" has two levels of meaning. At one level, it refers to a way of knowing opposed to scientific reasoning. As Wang (1989b: 50) notes, this understanding of "intuition" draws from Henri Bergson and Yogācāra Epistemology. At a more fundamental level, however, "intuition" is a way of living (Wang 1989a: 71) embedded in the Confucian idea of humanness (*ren*). It is the natural feeling that allows the individual to build connections with other lives and things in the cosmos. "Intuition" implies a state of the human mind that is at its most active, its most creative, and its most sensitive to the life of others (Li 2005: 10; Li 2013a: 51). Xu Guxiang 徐古祥 (2018) considers Liang's concept of "intuition" a crucial part of his philosophy of life. He suggests that if "life" (*sheng* 生) is the essence (*ti* 體), then "intuition" is the utility (*yong* 用). Humanness (*ren*) entails the realization of life, the cosmic life transformed from individual life. Intuition, in this generating process of life, is a way of living that makes humanness (*ren*) possible. It is also through "intuition" that the individual can cultivate his or her spiritual life, and then transform into the cosmic life (Dong 1993: 64).

While reflecting on the concept of "intuition" in his early works, Liang gradually realized that it could be misleading. During the period of rural reconstruction in the 1930s, he started using the concept of "ethical rationality" (*lixing*) to replace "intuition." However, according to both Li Jinglin (2005) and Li Xin (2013a), the meaning of "ethical rationality" remained consistent with "intuition," insofar as it indicated the humanness and ethical conscience (*liangzhi* 良知) of the individual. Both concepts were opposed to non-reflective feelings (or instincts, *benneng* 本能) and calculative reasoning (*lizhi* 理智). In Liang's view, the replacement of "intuition" with "ethical rationality" preserved the connotation of selfless feelings toward others (*wusi de ganqing* 無私的感情) but avoided the risk of being interpreted as an instinct. The use of "ethical rationality" also indicated Liang's departure from Western philosophers of life such as Henri Bergson.

Quite a few contemporary scholars recognize the significance of this conceptual change, and on this basis have come to lay a greater emphasis on Liang's later works, such as ZGWH and RXYRS. Guo and Gong (1996: 8) consider the concept of "ethical rationality" as the key idea to understand Liang's thought and his lifelong efforts to put it in practice. Gan Chunsong (2018) also emphasizes the importance of the concept of "ethical rationality" to understand Liang's thought from the early to the later works and its application to social and political theoretical discussions. Compared to "intuition," the concept of "ethical rationality" lays greater emphasis on the cultivation of the mind, which has for goal the transformation of the mind from attachment (*youdui* 有對) to non-attachment (*wudui* 無對), as well as the creative establishment of connections with others. It is only when having established a connection with others that the individual can have ethical feelings toward them (*wusi de ganqing*). In Liang's words, ethical rationality involves "having a strong mind that seeks self-perfection" and "a depth of feelings toward others" (*xiangshang zhi xin qiang, xiangyu zhi xin hou*, 向上之心強, 相與之情厚) (JYYRS: 192). It includes personal feelings based on the individual's evolving understanding of relations with others and his or her effort to reach meaningful connections with others, nature, and the cosmos. On this basis, Chen Lai (2005) summarizes Liang's Confucian ethics as "caring for others" (*yi taren weizhong* 以他人為重).

3.3 The Practice of Self-Cultivation as a Promising Direction for the Future of Modern Education

One reason that Confucianism was harshly criticized by liberal intellectuals during the New Culture Movement was its focus on ethical relations rather than individual rights and freedom. Confucianism was equated to "a cannibalistic code of ethics" (*chiren de lijiao* 吃人的禮教) which was hostile to the development of individuality. Liang agreed that Chinese modernization had to rely on a new culture which would respect and encourage the development of individuality. However, he did not agree that Confucianism was "a cannibalistic code of ethics." Instead, he highlighted the Confucian tradition of "self-cultivation" of Confucianism, which he called "learning about the self" (*ziji xue*). This practice of "learning about the self" or "self-cultivation" was not a science; it belonged in neither the social sciences nor the humanities. It could not be included in any discipline of the modern academy. Instead, it referred to the cultivation of the moral character of the person, with the aim of "becoming a person" (*chengren* 成人) (Guo and Gong 1996: 122; Liu 2001: 95; Ren 2015: 23; Gu 2018: 39). Liang considered that "to become a person" by learning or cultivation was the foundation for an ideal society which was ritually ordered (Gao 2019: 52).

Liang's idea of "self-cultivation" is based on his notion of "ethical rationality." As discussed above, "ethical rationality" overcomes calculative reasoning insofar as it allows people to deeply care about others. Though ethical rationality represents a natural feeling that everyone may potentially have, it requires lifelong efforts to break the barrier that separates the self from others. Chen Chang 陳暢 (2019: 130) suggests that Liang's concept of "ethical rationality" is related to the fundamental relations of individuals connected to each others by feelings, an idea that can be traced back to Wang Yangming's (王陽明, 1472–1529) discussion of "the moment of stimulus-response" (*ganying zhiji* 感應之幾), with *gan* (感) having its origin in *The Book of Change*. The system of "stimulus-response" is meant as a description of the natural order of the universe, viewed as an open system which influences all life and which can receive response from life. Individuals with a very sensitive mind can build emotional connections with other lives and things in the universe thanks to ethical conscience (*liangzhi*). However, the human mind easily finds itself trapped in calculating and reasoning, which leads it to ignore its own feelings as well as those of others. This is why the practice of "self-cultivation" is so important as a lifelong effort of the individual to build his/her moral character and "become a person." Liang's contribution is that he used a modern concept, "ethical rationality," which could be relatively easily understood in modern China and avoid the inclination of mysticism.

Liang's efforts to continue the Confucian tradition of "self-cultivation" relied on his confidence in the contribution of Confucianism to modern society. His focus on caring for life has the potential to establish a dialogue with modern Western philosophy of life as well. For a better future, he insisted on the importance of the practice of self-cultivation, through which the individual could connect his/her personal life to that of the universe. The key was to break the barrier of the individual mind and open one's feelings to the lives of others. In this sense, the practice of self-cultivation is the cultivation of life, not only of human life but also of all life in the universe. In the context of today's ecological crisis, Liang's ideas are still valuable.

4 The Asset of Liang's Theory and Practice of Rural Reconstruction

The theme of Liang's theory and practice of rural reconstruction became an attractive issue for social scientists after 2000. The resurgence of interest in this topic is surely related to the Chinese social context. After a decade of economic reform since the early 1990s, the gap between the urban and rural areas was seriously enlarged. The issue of rural development became an urgent one. Some scholars in the humanities also noticed the significance of Liang's theoretical and practical innovations in terms of rural reconstruction.

Liang's practice of rural reconstruction mainly took place in Zouping County, Shandong Province, in the 1930s, when China was in danger of losing its sovereignty. Liang considered the nation needed reconstruction, and that it should start from the countryside. The idea of reconstruction was opposed to that of revolution. Liang did not agree that China's nation-building could be realized through a violent revolution. The price of a violent revolution would be too high, since it could easily lead to violence within society (Yang 2015: 29). On the basis of his analysis of the reality of China's social classes, Liang considered that the peasants should be the main body of social reconstruction. Therefore, if intellectuals desired to participate to national salvation, they needed to unify the peasants. This was the motivation behind Liang's decision to resign from the lecturer position at Peking University and lead the rural reconstruction movement in Shandong Province.

Some scholars consider—mistakenly, I believe—the failure of Liang's rural reconstruction movement as inevitable because of weaknesses in Liang's theory itself. For example, Feng Shusheng 馮書生 (2018: 61) argues that the failure of Liang's rural reconstruction was due to his being too optimistic regarding the individual's ethical rationality. It was impossible to make the masses reach the virtue of a noble human being. However, it might be possible that Liang did not fully understand the revolutionary changes in China's social structure at the time. Lü Xinyu (2012: 112) suggests that we need to study the victory of the Communist Party in the 1940s based on class revolution, with the uniting of the working class and the peasant class.

Other scholars have praised Liang's theory and practice of rural reconstruction, considering it as the most original and innovative idea of Liang on China's modernization. Li Shanfeng 李善峰 (2016) points out that the special contribution of Liang's rural reconstruction was that he expanded Confucian practice from the field of moral practice to the broader field of social practice, including economic development. In other words, Liang believed that the value of Confucianism in modern society could not be exclusively located at the level of the moral development of the individual. However, Li (2018) further points out that the significant value of Liang's design of rural reconstruction was that the cultivation of the individual mind was the key to the economic and political reconstruction of society. Therefore, Liang emphasized the importance of helping rural dwellers develop new life habits and improve their moral character and spiritual status. According to He Zhaotian 賀照田 (2012: 91), rural reconstruction entailed the reconstruction of the life habits and ethics of society, "to awaken the people's inner desire for goodness," the most important means to bring about national salvation.

As discussed earlier in this chapter, Liang was obviously not a conservative who would like to go back to the old times. He sharply criticized the backwardness of the old system of ethics, and the degenerated spirit of a closed, dogmatic, and depressed culture thanks to which the active and creative human mind deadened. Liang considered that the major mission of rural reconstruction, as Wang Yue 王悅 (2013: 83) notes, was to awaken the lively spirit of rural dwellers through what he called "the cultivation of spirit" (*jingshen taolian* 精神陶煉). It was also during this period of rural reconstruction that Liang gradually replaced "intuition" by the concept of "ethical rationality" (Gan 2018), and that he argued that the sharpening of one's ethical rationality was the key to build a new ethics (Wang 2013: 81).

Wu Fei 吳飛 (2005: 232–233) commends Liang for his effort to build a new ethics and explains this effort from a sociological perspective. He agrees with Liang that at the time, China needed social reconstruction on the basis of a new ethics, a mission that political revolution could not fulfill. Wu suggests that even though Liang's proposal was too idealistic for the social reality at the time, it was a very modern one that was still valuable today. Wu (2009: 68) further points out that the reason Liang proposed the practice of a new ethics was to explore a modern model of national development. China could not become a modern state without the cultivation of the individual's ethical rationality. Therefore, political, economic, and social reconstruction was rooted in educational and ethical development. Wu (2009: 68) suggests that Liang's objective was to realize a kind of modern politics centered on education.

Gan Chunsong (2017) has explicitly discussed Liang's proposal for a modern politics centered on education, which Liang called "the unity of politics and education" (*zhengjiao heyi* 政教合一). The customary meaning of *zhengjiao heyi* in Chinese is "the unity of politics and *religion*," given that "*jiao*" (教) can refer to both religion (*zongjiao* 宗教) and education (*jiaoyu* 教育). Gao explains that Liang's idea of "*jiao*" referred to neither religion nor education, but rather to cultivation (*jiaohua* 教化), which focuses on the development of one's moral character. Because of his dissatisfaction with the Kuomintang's use of this concept of *zhengjiao heyi* in its propaganda, however, Liang later came to describe his idea of rural reconstruction as "the unity of construction and cultivation" (*jianjiao heyi* 建教合一). Liang believed that by awakening the spirit of goodness of the individual mind, this model of rural reconstruction could help rural dwellers and all Chinese people establish a new ethics.

How did Liang practice "the unity of construction and cultivation" in his rural reconstruction efforts? According to the study of Wei Wenyi (2017: 108–109), in Zouping County, he established a system in which rural dwellers were the main body and the village schools (*cunxue* 村學) and county schools (*xiangxue* 鄉學) were the main institutes. Generally speaking, he transformed the administrative system into an educational system. Through this schooling community, Liang expected that peasants could cultivate their individual mind with the continued support of the intellectuals. In this way, Liang suggested that rural dwellers could gain new perspectives to guide their daily life, and new customs and new cultures could then be developed. In other words, peasants could awaken their natural feelings of caring for others and get rid of the tendency to calculate and compete for personal interests in this schooling community. They could also learn about new technologies for farming, but spiritual cultivation was always the priority in the community.

Though Liang's rural reconstruction efforts failed due to the invasion of the Japanese army, it is interesting to witness the resurgence of scholarly interest in Liang's rural reconstruction in the 2000s. In the new era of peace and prosperity, China is facing a problem of modernization similar to that Liang faced almost a century ago: How can people find peace inside their minds rather than feel that they lag behind in the context of fast social changes? How can people practice the goodness of their mind and care for the feelings of others in a suitable way? That is the challenge of the establishment of a new ethics in the contemporary context.

5 Conclusion: Will the World Be Better?

What is the right direction for China's modern development? This is the question Liang and many of his contemporaries of the early twentieth century asked. Chinese society experienced the ups and downs of various movements and revolutions in the last century. Even though China has to some extent achieved economic success today, it is still experiencing cultural anxiety. Does China need to further westernize or does it need to turn to its own cultural tradition? Or, as Liang proposed in his early works, could China be modernized without giving up its cultural tradition?

These unsolved questions make Liang's thought still highly relevant and attract scholars to reinterpret his thought from different perspectives.

In this review, I mainly focused on three interrelated issues in Liang's philosophy. First, his philosophy of culture; second, his philosophy of life; and third, his theory and practice of rural reconstruction. It is not appropriate to categorize Liang as merely a Buddhist or a modern Confucian, even though he considered himself both. He might also have accepted the labels of Marxist or conservative, or even that of liberal. This is because he was always open to new ideas which might help him solve the central questions he identified. His openness of mind was grounded in his faith in the potential goodness of the human mind. He was confident that the human mind had the potential to correct previous mistakes and lead an ethical life which was centered on caring for others. This spiritual but areligious faith made Liang's original thought and his noble personal character a spiritual monument in the history of China's modernization. Is Liang an exceptional figure in a century full of crisis and suffering? Did Liang's lifelong efforts embody the key to the spirit of Chinese culture in the past thousands of years of history? If so, the aim of today's study of Liang's thought should be to make this spiritual key explicit and pass it on to the next generations.

References

DXWH *Dong-Xi wenhua ji qi zhexue* 東西文化及其哲學 [*Eastern and Western Cultures and Their Philosophies*; 1921], *LSMQJ*, 1989, vol. 1: 319–547.

JYYRS *Jiaoyu yu rensheng: Liang Shuming jiaoyu wenji* 教育與人生:梁漱溟教育文集 [*Education and Human Life: The Collection of Liang Shuming on Education*]. Beijing: Contemporary China Press, 2012.

KZXS *Kongzi xueshuo zhi chongguang* 孔子學說之重光 ["The Recovery of Confucius' Doctrine"; 1934], *LSMQJ*, vol. 5: 548–556.

LSMQJ *Liang Shuming quanji* 梁漱溟全集 [*Complete Works of Liang Shuming*, vols. I to VIII]. Jinan: Shandong People Press, 1989–1993.

RXYRS *Renxin yu rensheng* 人心與人生 [*Human Mind and Human Life*; 1984], *LSMQJ*, 2005, vol. 3: 523–772.

ZGWH *Zhongguo wenhua yaoyi* 中國文化要義 [*Essence of Chinese Culture*; 1949], LSMQJ, 2005, vol. 3: 1–316.

Alitto, Guy. 1979. *The Last Confucian: Liang Shu-ming and the Chinese Dilemma of Modernity*. Berkeley: University of California Press.

——— 艾愷. 2003. *The Last Confucian: Liang Shu-ming and the Chinese Dilemma of Modernity* 最後的儒家:梁漱溟與中國現代化的兩難. Trans. Wang Zongyu 王宗昱 and Ji Jianzhong冀建中, Nanjing: Jiangsu Renmin Press.

Cao, Yueming 曹躍明. 1994. The Issue of Modern Chinese and Western Cultures and Liang Shuming's View of Culture 近代中西文化問題與梁漱溟的文化觀. *Journal of Tianjin Social Sciences* 天津社會科學 1: 64–70.

——— 曹躍明. 1995. *Study on Liang Shuming's Thought* 梁漱溟思想研究. Tianjin: Tianjin Renmin Press.

Chen, Lai 陳來. 2000. Rethinking the New Culture Movement: On Liang Shuming in the Late Period of the May Fourth Movement 對新文化運動的再思考—從"五四"後期的梁漱溟說

起. *Journal of Nanchang University (Humanities and Social Sciences)* 南昌大學學報(人社版). No. 1: 1–5.

——— 陳來. 2001. Liang Shuming and His Early View of Chinese and Western Cultures 論梁漱溟早期的中西文化觀. *Journal of Wuhan University (Humanity Sciences)* 武漢大學學報(人文科學版) 54.3: 261–269.

——— 陳來. 2005. Caring for the Other: Liang Shuming's Confucian Ethics '以對方為重':梁漱溟的儒家倫理觀. *Academic Journal of Zhejiang* 浙江學刊 1: 5–14.

——— 陳來. 2009. Liang Shuming and Tantric Buddhism 梁漱溟與密宗. *Hebei Academic Journal* 河北學刊 29.6: 30–38.

——— 陳來. 2016. The Idea of Mind as Being in China's Modern Philosophy 中國近現代哲學的心本實體論. *Chuanshan Journal* 船山學刊 3: 90–99.

Chen, Chang 陳暢. 2019. Liang Shuming's New Idealism Theory: Research on the Theory of Ethical Society from the Perspective of Idealist Metaphysics 梁漱溟的新心學——心學形上學視野中的'倫理社會'學說研究. *Social Sciences* 社會科學 9: 127–134.

Cheng, Gongrang 程恭讓. 1998. Review of the Buddhist Thought of Liang Shuming 梁漱溟的佛教思想評述. *Confucius Studies* 孔子研究 2: 66–75.

Ding, Yun 丁耘. 2020. On the Classification of Teachings and the Foundations of Continuous Life and Growth: An Explanation on Dao 判攝與生生之本——對道體學的一種闡釋. *Philosophical Trends* 哲學動態 12: 37–50.

Dong, Defu 董德福. 1993. A Comparison Between Liang Shuming's and Feng Youlan's Philosophies of Life and their Methods 梁漱溟與馮友蘭人生哲學及其方法之比較. *Academic Journal of Zhongzhou* 中州學刊 5: 64–68.

Feng, Shusheng 馮書生. 2018. A Comparative Study on Liang Shuming's Moral Philosophy and Its Historical Value 比較視域下梁漱溟的道德哲學及其時代價值. *Journal of Humanities* 人文雜誌 11: 55–62.

Gan, Chunsong 幹春鬆. 2017. Rural Reconstruction and the Establishment of Modern Political Conventions: A Research on Liang Shuming's *Theory of Rural Reconstruction* 鄉村建設與現代政治習慣的建立——梁漱溟'鄉村建設理論'探究. *Journal of Hunan University (Social Sciences)* 湖南大學學報(社會科學版) 31.4: 1–9.

——— 幹春鬆. 2018. Liang Shuming's Concept of '*lixing*' and His Political and Social Theories 梁漱溟的'理性'概念與其政治社會理論. *Literature, History and Philosophy* 文史哲 1: 117–134.

Gao, Like 高力克. 1990. Modernization and Confucian Life: The Dilemma of Liang Shuming's Philosophy of Culture 現代化與儒家人生——梁漱溟文化哲學的困境. *Journal of Beijing Normal University* 北京師範大學學報 6: 96–102.

Gao, Ruiquan 高瑞泉. 2019. The Modern Reconstruction of the Confucian Concept of Order: A Discussion Centered on Liang Shuming 儒家秩序觀念的現代重勘:以梁漱溟為中心的討論. *Jianghai Academic Journal* 江海學刊 3: 47–53.

Gu, Hongliang 顧紅亮. 2008. *The Confucian's Lifeworld* 儒家生活世界. Shanghai: Shanghai Renmin Press.

——— 顧紅亮. 2010a. Liang Shuming's Conception of Education and Its Significance 梁漱溟的教育觀念及其意義. *Journal of Nanjing Social Sciences* 南京社會科學 1: 56–61.

——— 顧紅亮. 2010b. Liang Shuming's and John Dewey's Philosophy of Life 梁漱溟與杜威的生命哲學. *Xue Hai* 學海 5: 74–80.

——— 顧紅亮. 2018. The Discourse of Liang Shuming's Confucian Self-Cultivation 梁漱溟的儒家修養話語體系. *Confucius Studies* 孔子研究 4: 38–43.

Guo, Qiyong 郭齊勇, and Jianping Gong 龔建平. 1996. *Liang Shuming's Philosophical Thought* 梁漱溟哲學思想. Wuhan: Hubei Renmin Press. (This book has a comprehensive and reflective introduction on Liang's thought in the context of Chinese intellectual history as well as a comparative perspective with some Western modern thinkers.)

He, Zhaotian 賀照田. 2012. When the Confident Liang Shuming Facing the Victory of Revolution …: Understanding Again Liang Shuming's Questions and the Modern Chinese

Revolution, I. 當自信的梁漱溟面對革命順利.......——梁漱溟的問題與現代中國革命的再理解之一. *Open Times* 開放時代 12: 74–96.

Jing, Haifeng 景海峰. 1994. Liang Shuming's Understanding and Acceptance of Western Culture 梁漱溟對西方文化的理解與容受. *Journal of Shenzhen University (Humanities and Social Sciences)* 深圳大學學報(人文社會科學版) 11.4: 33–40.

Li, Jinglin 李景林. 2005. Intuition and Ethical Rationality: The New Interpretation of Liang Shuming on Confucian Rationality 直覺與理性——梁漱溟對儒家理性概念的新詮. *Journal of Humanities* 人文雜誌 2: 9–13.

Li, Shanfeng 李善峰. 2016. The Modern Transformation of Confucianism and the Reconstruction of the Traditional Social Structure: The Discussion Based on Liang Shuming's Rural Reconstruction Experiment 儒學的現代轉型與傳統社會結構的重建——以梁漱溟的鄉村建設實驗為核心的討論. *Shandong Social Sciences* 山東社會科學 10: 57–63.

——— 李善峰. 2018. The Localization Experiment of The Reconstruction of the Rural Community: The Example of Liang Shuming's Zouping Rural Reconstruction Experiment District 鄉村團體組織重建的'本土化'嘗試——以梁漱溟的鄒平鄉村建設實驗區為例. *Shandong Social Sciences* 山東社會科學 11: 50–57.

Li, Xianghai 李翔海. 1998. Reflection on the Turn of the Century: Liang Shuming's View on Chinese and Western Cultures in the Perspective of Postmodernism 世紀之交的回觀——後現代視野下的梁漱溟中西文化觀. *Journal of Beijing Social Sciences* 北京社會科學 3: 60–66.

——— 李翔海. 2009. The Significance and Theoretical Limitation of the View of Cultural Returning: The Example of Liang Shuming's View on Chinese and Western Cultures '復歸'論的文化意蘊與理論局限——以梁漱溟中西文化觀為例. *Exploration and Free Views* 探索與爭鳴 3: 58–62.

Li, Xin 李昕. 2013a. The Duality of Confucianism and Buddhism in Liang Shuming's Thought: An Interpretation in the Perspective of Mind Creating Theory 從識心創化的角度看梁漱溟思想中的儒佛二重關係. *Academic Research Journal* 學術研究 12: 48–52.

——— 李昕. 2013b. From the Happiness of No-Attachment to the Heart of No-Attachment: The Thinking Process of Liang Shuming on the True Spirit of Confucian Humanities 從'無對之樂'到'無對之心'——梁漱溟探索儒家'仁愛'真精神的思想歷程. *Journal of Jiangnan University (Humanities and Social Sciences)* 江南大學學報(人文社會科學版) 12.3: 39–45.

Li, Weiwu 李維武. 2001. Globalization and the Cultural Conservatism of the Contemporary New Confucianists 全球化與現代新儒家的文化保守主義. *Academic Monthly* 學術月刊 9: 30–40.

Li, Zhengang 李振綱. 1992. A Modern Confucian's Exploration on Goodness and Beauty: A Review of Liang Shuming's Philosophy of Ethics and Aesthetics 一位現代儒家對'善'與'美'的探究——梁漱溟道德哲學與藝術哲學評述. *Journal of Hebei University* 河北大學學報 3: 74–79; 136.

Liu, Changlin 劉長林. 2001. Liang Shuming's Modern Reconstruction of the Character of the Confucian Sage 梁漱溟對儒家聖賢人格說的現代重構. *Confucius Studies* 孔子研究 5: 86–96.

Liu, Yuebing 劉岳兵. 1993. The Growth of the Embryo of Liang Shuming's Thought and Its Influence: A Discussion from *Jiuyuan Jueyilun* 梁漱溟思想胚胎之發育及其影響——從《究元決疑論》說起. *The Journal of Humanities* 人文雜誌 5: 62–65.

Luo, Zhitian 羅志田. 2016a. A Cultural Emancipation: Liang Shuming's Longing and Embracement 文化翻身:梁漱溟的憧憬與困窘. *Journal of Modern Chinese History* 近代史研究 6: 49–68.

——— 羅志田. 2016b. A Conservative New-Trend Seeker: Liang Shuming and the Complex of Old-and-New, East-and-West in the Early Republican Period 守舊的趨新者:梁漱溟與民初新舊東西的纏結. *Academic Monthly* 學術月刊 12: 136–148.

——— 羅志田. 2017a. The Dialectical Evolution: The Debates on World Culture Between Liang Shuming and Hu Shi After the May Fourth Movement 辯證的進化:后五四時代關於世界文化的辯論——側重梁漱溟與胡適. *Journal of Tianjin Social Sciences* 天津社會科學 3: 144–156.

——— 羅志田. 2017b. Totality vs. Particularity: LIANG Shuming's Thinking on Culture 整體與個別:梁漱溟對文化的思辨. *Journal of Nanjing University (Philosophy, Humanities and Social Sciences)* 南京大學學報(哲學.人文科學.社會科學) 4: 88–99.

——— 羅志田. 2018. Intuition and Analysis: The Tension Between Two Epistemologies, The Examples of LIANG Shuming and TU Xiaoshi 直覺與分析:民初兩種認識取向的緊張——側重梁漱溟和屠孝實. *Journal of Tianjin Social Sciences* 天津社會科學 1: 139–149; 160.

Lü, Xinyu 呂新雨. 2012. The Foundation of Constitutionalism: LIANG Shuming's Thought and Practice Before and After the War of Resistance Against Japan 憲政的根基——抗戰前後梁漱溟的思想與實踐. *Beijing Cultural Review* 文化縱橫 6: 106–112.

Ma, Dongyu 馬東玉. 1993. On the Newness of the Contemporary New Confucianism 論當代新儒家的'新.' *Journal of Liaoning Normal University (Social Sciences)* 遼寧師範大學學報(社科版) 3: 67–71.

Ma, Yong 馬勇. 1991. *A Study on LIANG Shuming's Cultural Theory* 梁漱溟文化理論研究. Shanghai: Shanghai Renmin Press.

——— 馬勇. 1992. *Biography of LIANG Shuming* 梁漱溟評傳. Hefei: Anhui Renmin Press.

Meynard, Thierry. 2011. *The Religious Philosophy of LIANG Shuming: The Hidden Buddhist*. Boston: Brill.

Ouyang, Zhesheng 歐陽哲生. 2018. Cultural Identity, Cultural Reflection, Cultural Self-Consciousness: An Inquiry Based on LIANG Shuming's *Essence of Chinese Culture* 文化認同·文化反省·文化自覺——以梁漱溟著《中國文化要義》為本的探討. *Journal of Tsinghua University (Philosophy and Social Sciences)* 清華大學學報(哲學社會科學版) 1: 172–182.

Pan, Jia'en 潘家恩, Zhen Zhang 張振, and Tiejun Wen 溫鐵軍. 2018. The Dialectic Between 'Iron Hook' and 'Tofu': A Perspective on the Tensions in LIANG Shuming's Thought in the 1950s '鐵鉤'與'豆腐'的辯證——對梁漱溟20世紀50年代思想張力的一個考察視角. *Open Times* 開放時代 2: 99–117.

Ren, Jiantao 任劍濤. 2015. Two Approaches for Discussing the History of Chinese Political Thought: The Examples of LIANG Shuming and MOU Zongsan 中國政治思想史'接著講'的兩種路向——以梁漱溟、牟宗三為例. *Tian Fu Xin Lun*天府新論 4: 20–29.

Tang, Wenming 唐文明. 2010. *A Modern Concern: Cultural Politics and The Future of China* 近憂:文化政治與中國的未來. Shanghai: East China Normal University.

Xu, Fulai 徐福來. 2008. The Theory and Practice of Ethical Life: LIANG Shuming's Role in and Contribution to the New Confucian Group 倫理人生的義理與實踐——梁漱溟在現代新儒家陣營中的特色與貢獻. *Journal of Anhui University (Philosophy and Social Sciences)* 安徽大學學報(哲學社會科學版) 32.2: 28–32.

Xu, Guxiang 徐古祥. 2018. The Logical Structure of LIANG Shuming's Discussion of Confucius' Philosophy of Life in His Early Works 梁漱溟早期論孔子人生哲學的邏輯結構. *Academic Exchange* 學術交流 8: 33–38.

Wang, Donglin 汪東林. 1992. *Interview with LIANG Shuming* 梁漱溟問答錄. Changsha: Hunan Press.

Wang, Ruoxi 王若曦. 2016. *Zhenru* and *Sheng-sheng*: A Study on the Evolution of LIANG Shuming's Ontology '真如'與'生生'——梁漱溟本體思想的演進軌跡及其思考. *Confucius Studies* 孔子研究 6: 148–153.

Wang, Yue 王悅. 2013. From the Philosophy of Culture to Rural Reconstruction: The Changed and the Unchanged in LIANG Shuming 從文化哲學走向鄉村建設——梁漱溟的變與不變. *Confucius Studies* 孔子研究 6: 77–86.

Wang, Zongyu 王宗昱. 1989a. LIANG Shuming and Henri Bergson's Philosophy, I 梁漱溟與柏格森哲學(上) *Social Scientist* 社會科學家 3: 69–74.

——— 王宗昱. 1989b. LIANG Shuming and Henry Berson's Philosophy, II 梁漱溟與柏格森哲學(下). *Social Scientist* 社會科學家 4: 50–56.

——— 王宗昱. 1990. On LIANG Shuming's Cultural View in His Early Works 論梁漱溟早期的文化觀. *Donyue Tribune* 東岳論叢 5: 55–58; 19.

Wei, Wenyi 魏文一. 2016. 'Resoluteness' as the Attitude toward Life and the New Intelligentsia: Liang Shuming's Early Discussion on the Path of Chinese Culture '剛'的人生態度與新知識分子——梁漱溟早期論中國文化的路向. *Sociological Studies* 社會學研究 4: 169–192.

——— 魏文一. 2017. The County School and Village School in Liang Shuming's Theory of Rural Reconstruction 梁漱溟鄉村建設理論中的鄉學和村學. *Xue Hai* 學海 5: 103–111.

Wu, Fei 吳飛. 2005. Liang Shuming's 'New Etiquette and Custom': Reading Liang Shuming's *Theory of Constructing the Country* 梁漱溟的'新禮俗'——讀梁漱溟的《鄉村建設理論》. *Sociological Studies* 社會學研究 5:228–233.

——— 吳飛. 2009. Rural Reconstruction and Modern Chinese Civilization 鄉村建設與現代中國文明. *Peking University Education Review* 北京大學教育評論 7.3: 65–75.

——— 吳飛. 2018. On *Sheng sheng* (generating life): A Response to Prof. Ding Yun 論'生生'——兼與丁耘教授商榷. *Journal of Study of Chinese Culture* 中國文化研究 Spring: 1–24.

Yang, Qingmei 楊清媚. 2015. System and Human Mind: A Review of Fei Xiaotong and Liang Shuming's Thoughts on Rural Reconstruction 制度與人心——重溫費孝通與梁漱溟的鄉村建設思想. *Popular Tribune* 群言 3: 27–30.

Zhang, Wenru 張文儒. 2001. Liang Shuming and the Buddhist Thoughts 梁漱溟與佛學. *Journal of Xiangtan Normal University (Social Science Edition)* 湘潭師範學院學報(社會科學版) 23.2: 5–11.

Zhao, Xingliang 趙行良. 2007. Liang Shuming's Discussion of the Common Grounds and Dissimilarities Between Confucianism and Buddhism梁漱溟論儒佛異同與會通. *Journal of Hunan University of Science and Technology (Social Sciences Edition)* 湖南科技大學學報(社會科學版) 10.4: 56–61.

Zhao, Dezhi 趙德志. 1993. Liang Shuming and the Philosohy of Life 梁漱溟與生命哲學. *Journal of Social Sciences* 社會科學輯刊 3: 20–24.

Zheng, Dahua 鄭大華. 1987. Liang Shuming and Cultural Conservatism in the May Fourth Period 梁漱溟與五四時期的文化保守主義. *Seeker* 求索 4: 111–118.

——— 鄭大華. 1988. Liang Shuming's Understanding and Exploration on Chinese Culture 梁漱溟對中國文化的認識與探索. *Journal of Beijing Normal University* 北京師範大學學報 12: 58–67.

——— 鄭大華. 1994. *Liang Shuming and Hu Shi: A Comparative Study on Cultural Conservatism and Westernization* 梁漱溟與胡適——文化保守主義與西化思潮的比較. Beijing: Zhonghua Shuju.

——— 鄭大華. 1999. *A Review on Liang Shuming's Academic Thought* 梁漱溟學術思想評傳. Beijing: Beijing Library Press.

——— 鄭大華. 2006. Seeking the Modern Transformation of Confucianism: Liang Shuming and Modern Chinese Scholarship 謀求儒學的現代轉化——梁漱溟與現代中國學術. *Confucius Studies* 孔子研究 3: 94–103.

Zhou, Ding 周鼎. 2005. Liang Shuming and Liu Xianxin: The Center and Periphery of Modern Chinese Cultural Conservatism 梁漱溟與劉咸炘:現代中國文化保守主義思潮的中心與邊緣. *Social Science Journal* 社會科學輯刊 6: 156–159.

Chapter 14
The Many Faces of Liang Shuming: One Hundred Years in the Reception of Liang's Thought in European Languages (1922–2022)

Philippe Major and Milan Matthiesen

1 Introduction

LIANG Shuming 梁漱溟 (1893–1988) is a complex, multifaceted, and elusive historical figure. The chapters included in this volume certainly testify to this, but this is also the impression one gets from reviewing the reception of Liang's thought in European languages, from the first mention of his name in a book review by FENG Youlan 馮友蘭 (1895–1990) in 1922 to the publication of the book in which the present chapter is inscribed. Through the years, Liang has been described in sharply contrasting ways. He has been introduced as a philosopher, a social reformer or activist, a religious thinker, an educator, a legal thinker, and a political figure. His thought has been studied in local and global contexts, and has been approached from the perspectives of philosophy, sinology, history, religious studies, sociology, and political science. Described as a conservative, a restorationist, a fundamentalist, and a modern thinker, Liang has also been labeled a Confucian, a Buddhist, and a populist.

At times the dissonance between these various interpretations of a single man's ideas gives the impression that perhaps Liang has served as a mirror reflecting the interpreter's gaze. At other times it seems that the historical evolution of the academic field in the Euro-American region accounts for the changing views Liang's thought elicited through time. But overall, the many faces of LIANG Shuming laid bare by this short history of the reception of his thought in European languages are also revealing of the complexity and tensions of the man and his thought; tensions which in turn manifest the historical context in which he evolved, this long century

P. Major (✉) · M. Matthiesen
University of Basel, Basel, Switzerland
e-mail: philippe.major@unibas.ch; milan.matthiesen@unibas.ch

T. Meynard, P. Major (eds.), *Dao Companion to Liang Shuming's Philosophy*, Dao Companions to Chinese Philosophy 17,
https://doi.org/10.1007/978-3-031-18002-6_14

that marks China's slow and arduous passage from the First Sino-Japanese War to the reform and opening-up period.

In what follows, we provide an overview of the different faces of LIANG Shuming that emerge from the pool of monographs, edited volumes, and articles published in academic or missionary journals in English, French, and German from the 1920s onwards.[1] Our goal is not to give an exhaustive overview of the field (we in no way purport to have included all the literature discussing or mentioning Liang in the one hundred years covered). Rather, we aim to provide a historical typology of the many roles ascribed to Liang through time. The end result is a genealogy of sort—one that challenges some deep-seated assumptions about Liang by tracing them back to a particular and contingent historical moment and by situating them within a broad spectrum of alternative positions vying for attention in the small but diverse discursive space allotted to the thought of LIANG Shuming in European-language scholarship.

Our discussion is essentially organized in a chronological manner. We first provide an overview of the reception of Liang's thought in the limited number of books and articles that mention and discuss him during the Republican period and the Mao years. We then take a closer look at the many ways in which Liang's thought has been interpreted since 1976. Given that the number of scholars studying Liang drastically increases after 1976, we categorize the reception of Liang's thought for this period under six sub-headings: Liang the last Confucian, building on Alitto's work,[2] Liang the modern populist, Liang the New Confucian, Liang the Buddhist, and finally the more miscellaneous category of "new approaches."

[1] We could not find any publication specifically dedicated to the study of LIANG Shuming in Italian. Further research would be needed to assess the extent of the reception of Liang's thought in other European languages. We exclude from our study works published in European languages that were translated from non-European languages (most often Chinese). It is also worth noting that the translation of Liang's works in English has only recently begun with the publication by Amsterdam University Press of *Fundamentals of Chinese Culture* (*Zhongguo wenhua yaoyi* 中國文化要義; 1949; hereafter ZGWH) (Liang 2021), translated by LI Ming (Guangdong University of Foreign Studies). A short section of *Eastern and Western Cultures and Their Philosophies* (*Dongxi wenhua jiqi zhexue* 東西文化及其哲學; 1921; hereafter: DXWH) and Alitto's 1980 interviews with Liang are also available in English (Liang 2001; Liang and Alitto 2013). Two of Liang's books have also been translated in French: ZGWH was translated by Michel Masson (Liang 2010) and DXWH by LUO Shenyi 羅慎儀 (Liang 2000), the daughter of linguist LUO Changpei 羅常培 (1899–1958), whose notes taken during the 1921 lectures given by Liang in Jinan 濟南 formed the basis of the text of DXWH we now have. German translations of long excerpts from DXWH are also available in Wesołowski 1997.

[2] Since Alitto's work had a lasting impact in the field, this category includes articles that build on Alitto's scholarship and provide new interpretations of Liang's work on themes as diverse as Liang's relation to Mao, his rural reconstruction movement, his views on democracy, his redefinition of *zhijue* (直覺) and *lixing* (理性), and his conservative outlook.

2 The Republican Period

The first mention of LIANG Shuming in European languages we could find dates back to 1922, during which year FENG Youlan, who would soon become one of the central figures of Chinese philosophy, published a review of DXWH in the *Journal of Philosophy* (Fung 1922). Feng's review positions Liang's work in two contexts. First is the New Culture Movement, still ongoing at the time, which Feng construes as "an evolution rather than a revolution of the Chinese culture" (611). Liang's work, Feng maintains, "is the first conscious and serious attempt to grasp the central idea [of the New Culture Movement, i.e., the "self-consciousness and self-examination of the old," according to Feng] and to show the excellences and the defects of the old Chinese culture in comparison with the European and the Indian" (611–612). While more recent scholarship has tended to see Liang's work as a conservative reaction *against* the New Culture Movement, Feng rather sees it as an integral part of it.

The second context in which Liang's magnus opus is projected remains, unlike the first, rather implicit through the piece until the very last sentence, in which Feng qualifies DXWH as "a philosophical work." Overall, Feng's references to famous Euro-American philosophical figures such as Bertrand Russell (1872–1970), William James (1842–1910) (to which Liang is compared), Leonard Hobhouse (1864–1929), and John Dewey (1859–1952) give the reader a sense that Liang belongs to this group of illustrious thinkers. As such, Feng reads Liang's book as a philosophical answer to the New Culture Movement, thus situating it at the confluence of the local (the New Culture Movement) and the global (philosophy).

After summarizing Liang's distinction between the European, Chinese, and Indian "moods of life," which lingers at greater length on the Confucian mood, Feng criticizes Liang for failing to see that his own version of Confucianism, stressing intuition as it is, remains incompatible with the scientific outlook present at the core of the European mood.[3] Mentioning in passing that Liang remains "always a student of Buddhism" (614), Feng does not further comment on the question of whether the work is Confucian or Buddhist in nature, perhaps since he is more interested in presenting it to the readers of the *Journal of Philosophy* as the product of a philosopher, rather than the representative of a particular school of thought.

Apart from FENG Youlan's book review, missionary periodicals were the main source of knowledge on Liang's thought in European languages before the establishment of the People's Republic of China (hereafter: PRC). While most articles mentioning Liang's name in such periodicals do so in passing, some introduce his thought at greater length. This is the case of a 1926 article by missionary Frank R. Millican (1883–1961).

Printed in *The Chinese Recorder*, a monthly journal published in Shanghai from 1867 until its closure by Japanese forces in 1941, the article presents Liang's 1921

[3] Feng remains open, however, to the idea that another type of Confucianism could be compatible with it; which opens up a window into Feng's later elaboration of his own *xin lixue* 新理學.

book as proof that "the Chinese have reached the reflective stage in their contact with western civilization" (Millican 1926: 698), after passing through the stages of rejecting and accepting western civilization wholesale. Despite its early date, the article places Liang's work in a context that is rather familiar: the debate on the (in) compatibility of Eastern and Western cultures during the late 1910s and early 1920s, represented in Millican by Dewey, Russell, LIANG Qichao 梁啟超 (1873–1929), and HU Shi 胡適 (1891–1962) (without mention of CHEN Duxiu 陳獨秀 [1879–1942], LI Dazhao 李大釗 [1889–1927], or DU Yaquan 杜亞泉 [1873–1933]).

Moving on, the article provides a rather lengthy summary of DXWH, paying attention to Liang's views on the philosophies of the three cultures but focusing particularly on his comparative observations on religion. In contrast to FENG Youlan's book review, this gives the reader the overall impression that Liang is ultimately a religious thinker more than a philosopher—an approach to Liang that remains for the most part unexplored in European-language scholarship until the work of Thierry Meynard more than 80 years later. Particularly emphasized in Millican's summary is the role of Buddhism in Liang's thought, which provides humanity with the only true religion of other-worldliness, understood as "a state in which the individual becomes oblivious to the phenomenal universe and has a direct sense of ultimate Reality (i.e., Chen Ru 真如)" (704). Yet Millican also notes that Liang, despite "holding to his own belief in Buddhism," does not "see any possibility of it gripping the popular mind" and "so he turns to Confucianism" (702). Unlike Buddhism, Confucianism focuses on this-worldliness, which "is what China needs to-day" (702).

An earlier but shorter mention of Liang's DXWH also appeared in the same journal in a 1923 article by John Leighton Stuart (1876–1962), the first president of Yenching University and a prominent missionary educator in China. Discussing missionary work and the future of religion and Christianity in China, he introduces Liang as an "open-minded, fine-spirited and widely-read scholar" (Stuart 1923: 74), whose writings Stuart situates, not unlike Feng, under the umbrella of the Chinese "literature of Intellectual Awakening" and the New Culture Movement (72). In a brief manner, Stuart reiterates the main theses of Liang's DXWH, acknowledging its philosophical importance even though Liang argued that the existing religions of his day would most likely decay in the future. Like Millican, Stuart thus emphasizes the text's engagement with religious issues, while also mentioning that although Liang's "own predilections are still" those of an "ardent Buddhist," he nevertheless renounced the Buddhist attitude in order to ensure the survival of China (75).

In an article entirely devoted to Liang as an educator, published by Bingham P.H. Tai (1925) in 1925 in the small-scale Shanghai-based journal *The China Weekly Review*, Liang is introduced as the savior of the Chinese educational crisis meandering between the abolishment of the old system and the newly introduced Western institutions of learning. Tai further presents Liang as an important Chinese scholar and philosopher who recently turned Confucian after formerly pursuing the way of Buddhism. The focus of the author nevertheless lies on Liang's ideas on education, which he summarizes in four points following Liang's work at the Sixth Middle School of Shandong in Caozhou. Liang's education program, Tai maintains, (1) offers a general emphasis on life as a whole, compared to a specialized teaching of differentiated subjects, (2) it seeks the cultivation of friendship between teachers and students, and among the students themselves, criticizing the lifeless and indifferent atmosphere in regular schools, (3) it maintains discipline not through an overbearing apparatus of rules, but through an appeal to the students' honor, and finally, (4) it focuses on the teacher's self-fulfillment by granting them enough free time to freely pursuit their own studies and engage with their students during meals and after classes. Interestingly, Tai's article remains to this day the only European-language article, with the exception of Zhang 2013a, 2015, which is entirely dedicated to the introduction of Liang's ideas on education and his work in Caozhou.

Besides the aforementioned articles that include extensive passages on Liang, we were also able to find many brief mentions of Liang's name—oftentimes merely a single sentence or a paragraph—in China-based English-language journals from the early 1920s up to the 1940s. These present him as a political figure (*The North-China Herald* 1932), as the leader of the Democratic League (*The China Weekly Review* 1947), as a political activist promoting his socialist views on the economy and the civil war (*The China Weekly Review* 1933, 1949), and as a representative and forerunner of the movement for rural reconstruction and mass education in the countryside (*The North-China Herald* 1934; *The Chinese Recorder* 1936; *The China Critic* 1940).

Finally, Alfred Forke (1867–1944), a renowned German sinologist specialized in Chinese philosophy, dedicated a few passages to the work of LIANG Shuming in a 1942 article published in *Zeitschrift der Deutschen Morgenländischen Gesellschaft* (*Journal of the German Oriental Society*). Along with the other thinkers discussed in the article (such as HU Shi, CHEN Duxiu, LI Dazhao, etc.), Liang is denied the title of an "actual philosopher," a term Forke reserves for figures such as KANG Youwei 康有為 (1858–1927), WANG Guowei 王國維 (1877–1927), and LIANG Qichao. The article stresses Liang's commitment to find a solution for China's problems at the time by focusing on its own traditions, instead of blindly following Indian or European strands of thought such as Buddhism or Democracy, which Liang deemed unfit for China's current political state. On this basis, Forke describes Liang as one of the few thinkers in modern China who goes against "the reform efforts of his contemporaries and advocates for old Chinese culture" (Forke 1942: 236). Although rather novel at the time of publication of Forke's article, this interpretation would soon become commonplace during the Mao period and thereafter.

3 The Mao Years

The Mao period saw a growing diversification of the scholarship on LIANG Shuming. Philosophical approaches building on the reception of Liang during the Republican period were supplemented by a growing attention to Liang's rural reconstruction movement and his participation in politics. Finally, some scholars also reassessed Liang's work from the perspective of its relation to communism, the CCP, and Mao.

3.1 Philosophical Approaches

We saw that FENG Youlan and Millican both present Liang as a philosopher (and a religious thinker, in the latter's case) and situate him in the context of the New Culture Movement. Two articles published during the Mao years (but written during the Republican period) can be viewed as indebted to such views, although both also significantly redefine the nature of Liang's philosophical enterprise and its relation with the New Culture Movement.

The first article, by O. Brière (1949), reviews the evolution of Chinese philosophy during the first half of the twentieth century. O. Brière was a Jesuit who taught at Université l'Aurore in the French concession of Shanghai. Originally published in French in the *Bulletin de l'Université l'Aurore* in the very month of the establishment of the PRC, this lengthy article was then translated in English and published as a monograph 7 years later.[4] The second article, by author of *On Asia's Rim* (1963) Andrew T. Roy (1903–2004), who spent 42 years as a Presbyterian missionary in China and Hong Kong, introduces Liang's interpretation of Confucius' (*Kongzi* 孔子) way of life as presented in DXWH. Although published in the Hong Kongese *Chung Chi Journal* in 1962, it is based on a chapter of his doctoral dissertation submitted in 1949 in the Philosophy department of Princeton.[5] As such, both articles were probably written around the same period of time, before the establishment of the PRC.

Like Feng and Millican, Brière and Roy both locate Liang and his DXWH (the main object of their analysis) within the context of the New Culture Movement, although unlike them (but similarly to Forke), they view him as defending Confucianism *against* May Fourth iconoclasm. Brière describes Liang as a "defender of tradition" who "arose to protest against the iconoclasts" (Brière 1956: 27), while Roy mainly sees Liang as an opponent of the New Culture group, which is here represented by HU Shi's views.

Also like Feng and Millican, both Brière and Roy understand Liang to be a philosopher, although they both tend to lay a stronger emphasis on Liang's commitment to Confucianism and downplay the Buddhist dimension of his thought that was particularly highlighted in Millican. Roy in fact positions Liang in the context of the longue durée of the history of Confucian philosophy. Bypassing altogether the question of Liang's acceptance of science and democracy in DXWH, he presents the work as seeking the reactivation of the way of Confucius. It is also of interest that despite Roy's philosophical training, his approach remains for the most part exegetical. After a long summary of Liang's interpretation of the way of life of Confucius, Roy closes his article by asking whether Liang's interpretation of the Confucian way of life is in accord with the classics. His conclusion is that Liang provides one of many possible interpretations of Confucianism, although one

[4] All references are to the English translation, as we could not find the original French article.

[5] This might explain why Roy does not reference Brière's article or its English translation.

ultimately influenced by Taoism, Buddhism, and "modern Western philosophies of evolution" (Roy 1962: 154).

In a short subsection on Liang, the first one to introduce Liang's "philosophy" to francophone readers (to our knowledge), Brière provides an idiosyncratic interpretation of Liang's distinction between the three paths opened up by Western, Chinese, and Indian cultures, postulating that "since Chinese civilization adopts the happy medium, it is preferable, the other two being manifestly exaggerated" (Brière 1956: 28). In Brière's view, therefore, the reason Liang discouraged the practice of Buddhism is not that it was too precocious, but rather that it was one of two possible extremes against which Confucianism represented the middle path.[6] In doing so, Brière played a significant role in introducing Liang *as a Confucian philosopher*, and as one defending tradition *against* the iconoclasm of May Fourth, a paradigm that would remain for the most part unchallenged for more than 50 years.

The idea that Liang valued Confucianism for its ability to forge a middle path between Indian and Western cultures is also expressed by CHAN Wing-tsit 陳榮捷 (1901–1994) (Dartmouth College) in his 1953 monograph *Religious Trends in Modern China* (Chan 1953: 23).[7] Like Brière and Roy, Chan introduces Liang as "the first strong advocate [of Confucianism] after the Intellectual Renaissance" (32). Liang defended Confucianism—to which he converted after a Buddhist phase (22)—against the anti-Confucianism that reached its climax in 1918 (21). His mention that Liang's Confucianism centers on a "philosophy of life" (22) also suggests that Chan views Liang, again like Brière and Roy, as a philosopher rather than a religious thinker. However, while reviewing the debates on the fate of religion in modern times later on in the book, Chan seems to contradict his previous assessment by describing Liang during the early 1920s as a Buddhist (221) or a Buddhist layman (226). This tension between the Buddhist and Confucian readings of Liang's philosophy reveals one of the most important fault lines along which the reception of his thought would be divided in the post-Mao period.

3.2 Rural Reconstruction

The Mao years also saw the emergence of a growing interest in Liang's involvement in the rural reconstruction movement. This is exemplified by two articles: one by historian Lyman P. van Slyke (1929–) of Stanford University and the other by Harry J. Lamley (1928–), historian at the University of Hawaii. Their articles were published in the *Journal of Asian Studies* and the *Chung Chi Journal* in 1959 and 1969 respectively.

[6] Intriguingly, although this interpretation is contradicted by a number of statements made in DXWH, it adequately depicts the rationale Liang appeals to in explaining his own "conversion" to Confucianism.

[7] Chan seems to have read Brière's article as he references the original French-language version twice (32, 93).

Van Slyke's article, based on an M.A. thesis submitted to Berkeley in 1958, is presented as an attempt to diversify and deepen our knowledge of Liang by going beyond the focus on DXWH that he sees as characteristic of the previous scholarship devoted to him. Against the view that Liang is but a philosopher, van Slyke describes him as "a man for whom theory was nothing aside from practice" (van Slyke 1959: 472). This is the first mention of what became a central component of the reception of Liang's thought in the aftermath of Mao's death: the idea that Liang's thought and life can be interpreted by appealing to his attempt at bridging the gap between theoria and praxis. In van Slyke, this interpretative framework leads him to carefully balance his outline of Liang's views on rural reconstruction with a discussion of the main institutional features of the Shandong Rural Reconstruction Research Institute (*Shandong xiangcun jianshe yanjiuyuan* 山東鄉村建設研究院).

Van Slyke stresses the political dimension of Liang's rural reconstruction writings, which he maintains aimed at striking a balance between the Chinese Communist Party (hereafter: CCP) and the Guomindang (hereafter: GMD). This put the movement at risk, however, as Liang could not tap the resources of either political camp and had to rely on "semi-independent provincial leaders" (473). The movement's dependence "upon continued provincial support and upon continued provincial autonomy" (473), allied with other historical exigencies—the Great Depression, Japanese imperialism, etc.—meant that Liang's rural reconstruction program could not but fail.

In contrast to Brière and Roy, van Slyke does not portray Liang as a Confucian. Rather, he emphasizes Liang's commitment to "China's racial spirit," which he describes as revolving around its discovery of "human reason" (*lixing* 理性).[8] Van Slyke is in fact more interested in the plurality of the resources from which Liang's thought draws, be they Buddhist of the "'Mind Only' variety," Confucian, or Western (Bergson, Russell, and Dewey). But overall, the general picture that emerges from van Slyke's account is that of a practically-minded intellectual who was concerned with putting into practice a rural reconstruction program that could save China from the threat of imperialism while also avoiding the trap of adopting Western solutions that did not conform to Chinese problems.

In his article, Lamley follows van Slyke in opposing the portrayal of Liang as a philosopher "or merely a polemicist" (Lamley 1969: 50). Rather, he sees him as a rural reconstructionist first and foremost, and as "one of modern China's better known conservative reformers" (50). Lamley puts forth the view that Liang remained a rural reformist through his life, so that his "activities as a reconstructionist" cannot be reduced to his Zouping 鄒平 years in the 1930s (52). Lamley particularly focuses on Liang's participation in the Rural Work Discussion Society (*Xiangcun gongzuo taolunhui* 鄉村工作討論會) from 1933 to 1935, and on his relationship with other members, such as Yan Yangchu 晏陽初 (1893–1990). He argues that Yan and

[8] It should be noted that van Slyke did not have access to ZGWH at the time of publication of his article (see 462n22).

Liang, representatives of the modernist/westernized and traditionalist orientations of the rural reconstruction movement respectively, were the most important leaders at the annual meetings. Both fought to retain a certain autonomy from the GMD and politics in general (as van Slyke had noted with regard to Liang), and both presented rural reconstruction as an alternative to the rural administrative reforms advocated by members of the Society who were more directly involved with the Nanjing government.

3.3 Participation in Politics

Apart from Liang's rural reconstruction effort, his participation in politics during the 1940s also drew greater attention from scholars during the Mao years, although to our knowledge no study entirely devoted to it was produced during this period. In his 1952 book *The Third Force in China*, fellow Democratic League (*Minzhu tongmeng* 民主同盟) member ZHANG Junmai 張君勱 (1887–1969), also known as Carsun Chang, briefly introduces Liang's involvement in the League's effort to propose a resolution to the civil war, which led to his clash with ZHOU Enlai 周恩來 (1898–1976) in 1946, who called Liang a "hypocrite" (Chang 1952: 182) despite the two having been "close friend[s] of many years' standing" (184).[9] The following year, Melville T. Kennedy Jr. (Bryn Mawr College) published an article on the Democratic League, in which he introduces Liang as "a gentle scholar who foresaw the salvation of the country in transformed village life and agriculture" (Kennedy Jr. 1953: 144). Although "by temperament he was hardly suited for the rough business of national politics" (144), Kennedy Jr. nevertheless stresses Liang's leading role in the establishment of the United National Construction League (*Tongyi jianguo tongzhihui* 統一建國同志會), "the first organized forerunner of the Democratic League" (140).[10] In the German language, sinologist Thomas Scharping also briefly discusses Liang's activities as a political activist vehemently fighting for the future of China in a 1972 monograph devoted to "the Democratic League and its precursors" (Scharping 1972). However, it should be noted that Zhang, Kennedy Jr., and Scharping do not discuss Liang's thought—the subject of the present study—at any length.[11]

During this period, the bulk of European-language scholarship on Liang's political activities is devoted to Liang's relationship with the CCP and MAO Zedong 毛澤

[9] On this episode, see also Lynch 2018: 202–203.

[10] Liang's role in the formation and activities of the United National Construction League is also discussed in van Slyke 1967: 170–177.

[11] The first article written on the Democratic League in European languages (to our knowledge) does not mention LIANG Shuming's involvement (see Tseng 1946). In his 1950 monograph *The Government and Politics of China*, CH'IEN Tuan-sheng mentions Liang in passing, describing him as "a Chinese scholar of ascetic habits and mystic temperament" (Ch'ien 1950: 358). Ch'ien however maintains that Liang was not interested in politics "as the term is commonly understood" (358).

東 (1893–1976). This topic did not draw much attention until the 1970s, however. One reason is that the events surrounding the falling out between Liang and Mao in 1953 remained unknown to the Euro-American public until the publication of *Ten Years of Storm* by CHOU Ching-wen 周鯨文 (1908–1985) in 1960. The lack of available sources undeniably also made it difficult to deal with this topic before the 1980s. Yet CHI Wen-Shun (University of California, Berkeley) devotes a 1970 article to the topic of "Liang Shu-ming and Chinese Communism."

Despite the scarcity of sources available, Chi argues that the reason why Liang, along with HU Shi, was a recurrent source of criticism in the PRC is due to his continued "intellectual influence," which Chi regards as "a latent factor in ideological trends of the Mainland" (Chi 1970: 64). Reviewing Liang's work from the 1920s to the 1940s, while stressing that Liang never fitted "the mould of a scholar, philosopher or social reformer" (64), Chi points out various aspects of Liang's thought that *might* explain the communist attack on him years later, such as its idealism and its opposition to the application of Marxist class analysis to Chinese society. Although now that we have access to far greater sources, we know that most attacks on Liang had more to do with political and ideological exigencies than with the Marxist evaluation of his work, Chi's article represents a first attempt at making sense of Liang's experiences under Mao's regime.[12]

3.4 Re-evaluating Liang's Relation with the CCP

Finally, another trend in the Mao-period reception of Liang consists in a re-evaluation of his thought from the perspective of the victory of communism and the CCP. Two articles represent this trend, which is closely tied to the Western impact—Chinese response paradigm and the rise of modernization theory in the American academic setting.

Such an ex-post approach is explicit in a 1953 article by Albert H. O'Bryant (Oneonta State University Teachers College). From a historical perspective, O'Bryant situates Liang's political thought within the context of "China's later day 'response to the West'" (2) in order to better understand the "failure of Chinese liberalism" (1). Within this context, O'Bryant seems to inscribe Liang in a group of "Chinese liberals" defined rather broadly as non-communist intellectuals who "advocated progressivism, democracy, and reform in the Nationalist Government, and who tried to make their voices heard amidst the thunder from the extreme Right and extreme Left" (O'Bryant 1953: 28n1).

O'Bryant differs from his predecessors on two counts: first, his analysis focuses on *The Final Awakening of the Chinese People's Self-Salvation Movement* (*Zhongguo minzu zijiu yundong zhi zuihou juewu* 中國民族自救運動之最後覺悟; hereafter ZGMZ) instead of the more usual DXWH, and second, he does not

[12] Chi would later revisit the same topic in his monograph (Chi 1986).

particularly emphasize the Confucian character of Liang's thinking (he calls his Confucianism "very limited" (25)). Under O'Bryant's pen, Liang appears as a political thinker or philosopher who must be situated less in traditional categories (Buddhist, Confucian) than in modern ones. This might be due to his adoption of the "Western impact—Chinese response" model, but overall O'Bryant is careful to point out the complexity of Liang's thought, which he contends cannot be easily pigeonholed as left or right, and cannot be assigned "such over-simplified and implication-laden terms as 'traditionalist'" (27).

Another example of an ex-post reading is provided by a review of ZGWH (here translated as *The Essence of Chinese Civilization*) written by Harry J. Lamley. Published the year before Mao's death, the review presents Liang as "one of modern China's most resolute and outspoken conservative thinkers," who "stubbornly refused to renounce completely his past mode of thought and social outlook" under communist rule (Lamley 1975: 682). The establishment of the PRC thus offers Lamley the key framework within which Liang's 1949 work can be retrospectively understood. Although Liang "failed" to acknowledge the rapid advance of the CCP in this work, his rejection of Marxism even after 1949 made him a celebrated figure outside of China, and notably in Hong Kong, where ZGWH was republished by the anti-communist Chi Sheng Book Co. (*Jicheng tushu gongsi* 集成圖書公司).

Despite this, Lamley highlights that Liang did not write the work as a direct attack against Marxism. Rather, westernization served as his "real nemesis" (683). This is revealing of what Lamley calls "Liang's ethnocentrism," according to which "Chinese civilization is superior to the Western tradition" (683) due to its ability to develop *lixing*, understood as "moral intuition." In a tone indebted to modernization theory and Joseph Levenson's *Confucian China and Its Modern Fate*, Lamley concludes that Liang's "vague assertions concerning a '[*lixing*] essence' which epitomizes the spirit of Chinese civilization are of historical interest, for they number among the dying embers of the traditionalistic, though not essentially traditional, fire that ethnocentric Chinese intellectuals had kept alive for over a century in mainland China to ward off foreign incursions into the very substance of an alleged indigenous Chinese spirit and mode of life" (684).

Greatly indebted to modernization theory, this interpretation cannot but make Liang appear out of touch with the reality of his days. This is also the impression one gets from reading CHOW Tse-tsung's (University of Wisconsin) monograph on the May Fourth Movement (Chow 1960), in which Liang is presented as a conservative who ultimately rejected modernization. "In his defense of Confucianism and traditional civilization," Chow comments, Liang "actually deprecated Western learning and advocated in effect a sort of 'Eastward Ho!'" (330). It is against such depictions of Liang as a conservative defending the "indefensible" that the first monograph written about Liang in European languages situates itself.

4 Liang the Last Confucian

Published in 1979 and based on his doctoral dissertation of 1975, Guy Alitto's (University of Chicago) intellectual biography *The Last Confucian: Liang Shuming and the Dilemma of Modernity*[13] set the direction of the European-language reception of Liang's thought in the post-Mao period. Few scholars can, to this day, write about Liang without referring back to this monograph.

Alitto's work can be regarded as a response to interpretations, such as CHOW Tse-tsung's, which make of Liang a conservative estranged from the trends of his time and representing the last bastion in the Chinese defense of their past. Against scholars who relegate him to the dustbin of history, Alitto presents Liang as a man of his time who was engaged, both at the international and national levels, in the main debates of his day. At the international level, he sees Liang as taking part in a "world-wide response to a common universal 'nonconservative,' nontraditional phenomenon—modernization" (Alitto 1986: 9).[14] This world-wide conservative response includes the "romantic philosophies of Vitalism and Intuitionism in France and Germany" (x), with whom Liang shared a criticism of rationalism and "'the brave new world' of unlimited technological salvation" (9). By linking Liang to figures more familiar to the Euro-American public, Alitto is able to argue, against Joseph Levenson's thesis, that Liang's defense of tradition was part of a modern, cosmopolitan trend and did not represent the last amber left burning amidst the ashes of tradition.

At the national level, Alitto stresses Liang's intellectual affinities not with the conservatives of his day, but rather with progressive members of the modernizing avant-garde: HU Shi, CHEN Duxiu, LI Dazhao, and most of all MAO Zedong. Liang shared with these thinkers, but also with the worldwide conservative intellectuals, a strong concern for "the crisis of modernity" (134). His thought can in fact be regarded as an answer to what Alitto calls "the dilemma of modernity," by which he refers to China's need to "reap the material benefits of modernization without its inevitable attendant evils" (223), such as alienation, industrialization, and capitalism. Liang's answer to this dilemma, Alitto suggests, is "Confucian modernization," which involves the revival not of historical Confucianism but of the original spirit of Confucius (*gang* 剛), which could be used by China to modernize along Western lines while avoiding the dark side of modernity. In this way, "China could preserve the heritage of the sages [...] and still acquire 'wealth and power'" (122). In Alitto's view, Confucian modernization also forms the core of Liang's rural reconstruction movement, which represents Liang's attempt at bridging the theoria/praxis gap by putting in practice the ideas he had presented in DXWH.

---

[13] All references are to the second edition (Alitto 1986), which includes an epilogue describing Alitto's interviews with Liang in 1980 and 1984.

[14] Alitto understands modernization along the lines of Max Weber's notion of rationalization. He had previously presented this view in Alitto 1976.

Apart from the international conservative and the national progressive milieux, Alitto also situates Liang, like Roy before him, in the longue durée of Confucian history. For him, Liang suffered from "a delusion of sagehood" (59) which instilled in him the messianic need to defend Chinese culture and save China and the world in the process. Describing Liang as "the saintlike champion of tradition" (20) and "this century's foremost Confucian traditionalist" (3), Alitto often compares him with ancient sages such as Confucius or Mencius (Mengzi 孟子) (274). Alitto in fact depicts the mission of Liang's life—after what Alitto sees as Liang's conversion from Buddhism to Confucianism—as that of ensuring the transmission of the Confucian *dao* 道 in the modern age, given that "he and he alone had fully comprehended" it (7). But as Frederic Wakeman Jr. mentions in a foreword to the monograph, Liang's "attachment to Confucian values" did not "solely" represent, pace Levenson, "a Chinese patriot's search for emotional gratification [...]: it was also a cosmopolitan thinker's quest for intellectual moorings in a society troubled by the anomie and alienation of modern times" (x).

Central to Alitto's research is the question of how an ardent defender of tradition such as Liang could uphold views also shared by the most progressive figures of his day such as Mao. His contention is that "the Confucian sage" and "the Marxist Revolutionary" both "shared a bone-deep Chineseness, which, in the end, made them closer to each other than to many Westernized Chinese liberals and members of either the [GMD] or CCP" (286). Common to both men was their anti-urbanism and anti-consumerism, as well as their stress on rural development, local self-initiative, and self-sufficiency (196). Both also professed an aversion to bureaucracy and a suspicion of "civil routinization and even institutionalization" (205). And both hoped to form a "new humanity" (206) by relying on "moral and intellectual improvement" through "intimate group contact" (273). Where they differed is on the question of class struggle and violence, both of which Liang rejected (217). Yet Alitto concludes "it was the communists who realized Liang's ultimate goal: the revival and reintegration of China based upon an impassioned mass commitment to a common ethic—a 'religion that was not a religion,' as Liang often described Confucianism" (273). After 1949, Alitto states provokingly, "it was Mao, not Liang, who had become the sage of a revitalized China" (332).[15]

Like many before him, Alitto thus portrays Liang as a defender of tradition, but he also highlights how this defense was meant to answer *the* dilemma of his day, centered on the global issue of modernization. This view inherits the modernization theorists' tendency to put Liang in the context of tensions between global modernity and local traditions, although unlike them, Alitto stresses the fact that Liang's

[15]Alitto also suggests that Mao's sinicization of Marxism might have been the result of his 1938 Yan'an talks with Liang (290–291).

solution to the modern dilemma amounts not to a return to the past, but to what we would now call an "alternative modernity."[16]

Alitto's emphasis on the "dilemma of modernity," as the monograph's subtitle puts it, is however somewhat complexified by the main title of the monograph, which characterizes Liang as the *last* Confucian—a position that seems to presume, on par with modernization theorists, that the Confucian tradition is indeed dying out in China's process of modernizing, despite Liang's conviction that Confucianism represented the culture of the future. Although the monograph does not provide an explanation as to what Alitto ultimately meant by calling Liang the *last* Confucian, in subsequent publications he clarifies that his title refers to Liang's ability, in contrast to thinkers like XIONG Shili, to bridge the gap between theory and practice, a trait Alitto seems to regard as a necessary component of the Confucian persuasion.[17] This also seems to be the interpretation of Frederic Wakeman Jr., who, in his preface to the book, points out that Liang might indeed deserve "the title of China's last Confucian *political activist*" (xiv; our emphasis). This suggests that Alitto, working both against and within the framework of modernization theory, sees in Liang at one and the same time a modern and historically relevant conservative *and* the last representative of praxis-oriented Confucianism.

5 Building on Alitto's Work

As can be expected, Alitto's intellectual biography elicited a number of responses from LIANG Shuming scholars and opened up new avenues that led to the diversification of perspectives on Liang's thought. In what follows we categorize the work of scholars who have built on Alitto's work to provide new interpretations of Liang's thought under five themes: (1) Liang's relation with Mao, (2) his rural reconstruction movement, (3) his views on democracy, (4) his reasons for replacing the term *zhijue* 直覺 with that of *lixing* from the 1930s onwards, and finally (5) his role as a modern Chinese conservative.

[16] Dilip Parameshwar Gaonkar understands "alternative modernities" as site-based. This entails that although similar "cultural forms, social practices, and institutional arrangements do surface in most places in the wake of modernity," "at each national and cultural site, those elements are put together (reticulated) in a unique and contingent formation in response to local culture and politics" (Gaonkar 2001: 16).

[17] Alitto emphasizes this point in his introduction to the Chinese translation of his monograph (Ai 1995: 4). In a 2015 article, in which he argues Liang was first and foremost an activist, Alitto also makes the point that "alone among the twentieth-century New Confucians, Liang seems to have seamlessly joined his thought and his life, his theory with his practice. This one integrating aspect [...] is based upon a decidedly 'Confucian" conscience and conscientiousness in performing the role of the Confucian intellectual as moral leader and example" (Alitto 2015: 111).

5.1 Liang and Mao

On the topic of Liang's relation with Mao, two French-language articles can be highlighted. First, in a 1981 article (Masson 1981b), French sinologist and Jesuit Michel Masson (Chinese University of Hong Kong) explicitly follows Alitto in highlighting his contemporaneity and rejecting the conventional view according to which Liang was an "old-fashioned conservative" (580). Like Alitto, Masson positions Liang within the context of Chinese modernity, the dilemmas of which Masson hopes to uncover by studying "Liang the Confucian," and by putting him in parallel with "Mao the Marxist" (580). Masson agrees with Alitto that the two men have much in common intellectually, a phenomenon he also attributes to the "deep Chineseness" ("*sinicité profonde*"; 591)—or "Chinese anthropology"—that underscores the thought of both men.

Despite the many differences between the two, "we find in Liang," Masson says of the Chinese anthropology at the basis of his educational program, "a perception of human nature and its perfectibility, a moralizing tonality, and a tendency toward indoctrination that are also important characteristics of Mao" (585). Both men also share views on Chinese politics that are structured around the traditional, Confucian ideal of the virtuous elite. Yet despite the "deep Chineseness" of the ideas Liang and Mao have in common, Masson anticipates Catherine Lynch in concluding that such ideas are nevertheless also "found in most populist movements worldwide during the nineteenth and twentieth centuries" (591).[18]

The topic of Liang's relation to Mao is also at the center of an article by sinologist and anthropologist Joël Thoraval (1989). Highlighting, like Alitto, how Liang saw himself as a sage waiting to make manifest the ideal order imagined by Confucius in ancient times (26), Thoraval translates at length Liang's recollections, expressed in his interviews with Wang Donglin 汪東林, of his 1953 falling out with Mao. He points out that on the one hand, Liang—a "philosopher, educator, political figure" and "more than that" (22)—shared with Maoist ideology the ideal of moral transformation, while on the other, he objected the application of Marxist class analysis to Chinese society and rejected class struggle. As such, Thoraval argues Liang cannot be simply regarded as a Confucian sage opposed to an illegitimate rule by the CCP, even if he "never ceased to consider himself as invested with the duty of denunciation in the face of the new power, whenever his advice was solicited by it" (27).

---

[18] Twenty-nine years later, Masson's translation of *Zhongguo wenhua yaoyi* into French was published by Institut Ricci – Cerf (Liang 2010). In his introduction (Masson 2010), Masson presents the work as particularly relevant in the context of a China that no longer sees modernity and tradition as antithetical, and is looking for new ways to reconcile the two. Of interest is that Masson distances Liang from the New Confucians who left the mainland in 1949, arguing that unlike them, in the ZGWH, "Liang does not attempt to philosophically salvage Confucianism" (20). See also Masson 1981a for a comparison of Liang's take on Chinese culture and modernity with those of Feng Youlan, Tang Junyi 唐君毅 (1909–1978), and Yin Haiguang 殷海光 (1919–1969).

5.2 Rural Reconstruction

Two articles published in the 1990s directly address Alitto's portrayal of Liang's rural reconstruction movement, the first in opposition to it, and the second mostly in accord with it. In a 1990 article, historian Alfred H. Y. Lin (University of Hong Kong) follows van Slyke and Lamley in introducing Liang as "a theoretician and a political and social activist" (Lin 1990: 21) first and foremost, and "not simply a philosopher" (38). Lin's main target is Alitto's description of Liang's rural reconstruction movement as "revolutionary conservative" (Alitto 1986: 274). Against this view, Lin goes so far as to describe Liang as a "fundamentalist" and "restorationist" (32) who essentially promoted a form of "Confucianism in action" in the hope to reinstate the "'original' Confucian culture as distinct from the vulgarized 'historical' Confucian culture of the past several centuries" (31).[19] To be sure, Liang also incorporated cultural ideas borrowed from the West in his rural agenda, but this is far from meaning that Liang "wanted China to achieve modernity through 'rural reconstruction'" (35) as Alitto had suggested. In fact, Lin concludes, Liang's restoration efforts amounted to a revival of the formula of "Chinese learning for substance, Western learning for practical use" (*Zhongti Xiyong* 中體西用) of the late Qing period, and took place in the general context of his "struggle against the ideologies of modernism" (38).

In German, the topic of Liang's rural reconstruction movement is also taken up in a 1994 article by Bettina Gransow (FU Berlin). Like Alitto, Gransow characterizes Liang as a representative of "Confucian modernization" whose cultural philosophy found its practical expression in the rural reconstruction movement of the 1930s. Going through primary and secondary sources concerning Liang's efforts to establish village communities based on Confucian teaching and learning, Gransow provides a detailed picture of the years during which the project was running. She reads Liang's theoretical and political writings as a challenge toward the May Fourth Movement, arguing for the "self-salvation of the Chinese people" instead of going the way of Democracy (represented by the GMD and Europe) or Communism (represented by the CCP and Russia). China would only be able to find rejuvenation if she was able to focus on her own legacy, which Liang identified as the rural village structure.

Gransow also interprets Liang's philosophical and practical work as a forerunner of the 1980s debates in mainland China that explored the revaluation of Confucianism and the possibility of achieving economic modernization without the need to relinquish Chinese cultural values. Due to Liang's political engagement and his lasting disagreement with Mao on China's development during the 1950s, Gransow argues that evoking Liang's name in the political discourse of the 1980s symbolized the proposition of a stronger emphasis on rural development as opposed to the urban

[19] This was in fact precisely the point of Alitto in calling him a revolutionary: because *his* Confucianism had not been manifested in history, to implement it in practice amounted to a revolutionary break from the past.

development advocated by the party line. Liang is thus presented as receiving new attention and importance in Mainland China, making him one of the pioneers of alternative developmental strategies.

It is also worth mentioning that some scholars have built on the interest with broadening the scholarly understanding of Liang outside the confines of his philosophical thought that we saw at work in van Slyke and Lamley, although not necessarily in direct response to Alitto's monograph.[20] One case in point is the work of sinologist Stig Thøgersen (Aarhus University). In a 1998 article, Thøgersen emphasizes, like van Slyke and Lamley before him, the importance of going beyond the study of Liang's thought in understanding his rural reconstruction movement. Thøgersen warns against the tendency to see the movement "as a manifestation of LIANG Shuming's ideas" (Thøgersen 1998: 139), and focuses his attention instead on a number of tensions between the theory and practice of the movement. One of the tensions highlighted by Thøgersen is that while Liang emphasized the need for local self-government against the top-down approach favored by the state, his movement retained significantly paternalist elements. As such, it remained a rather top-down affair, although this time the top was represented by the intellectual elite, and not the state. Thøgersen points out how the intellectuals engaged in the movement saw themselves as fulfilling the role of enlighteners of the villagers, and as such "showed little curiosity about their world" (159).[21]

A second tension Thøgersen emphasizes is that between the expectations of the villagers on the one hand and that of Liang and other intellectual leaders of the movement on the other. It is to Thøgersen's benefit that he attempts to reconstruct the villagers' reaction to the movement, despite the difficulty to do so with the sources available. He comes to the conclusion that villagers tended to be more responsive to "those features that pointed up the social ladder and out from the narrow village world." In other words, "they responded positively to the access to modernity offered to them, rather than to Liang's visions of a re-traditionalized 'rural' social order" (158). Despite Liang's idiosyncratic ideas, Thøgersen concludes that in practice, his rural reconstruction movement did not differ in important ways from other movements of the sort. "Face to face with rural realities, Liang became more of a prototype modernizer and less of the anti-state protector of village China whom we meet in his writings" (158).[22]

---

[20] The Rural reconstruction movement, and Liang's role in it, is also approached in other sources such as, for example, Merkel-Hess 2016.

[21] A similar critique of the elitism and paternalism of Liang's rural reconstruction model is made in Lin 1990: 36–37.

[22] Thøgersen expands on these ideas in Chap. 6 of his monograph on the village schools of Zouping (Thøgersen 2002). He also revisits the topic of the relationship between state, intellectual, and peasants in Liang's thought in Thøgersen 2009. See also Thøgersen 1995 for an interesting discussion of the importance for Liang of the Danish folk high school model, which in its self-conception "coincided almost exactly with what LIANG Shuming was looking for: a Third Way to modernity born out of rural society and delivered by a spiritual genius rooted in traditional culture" (283).

5.3 Democracy

Moving on to the topic of democracy, intellectual historian Ip Hung-yok (Oregon State University) studies, in a 1991 article, Liang's views on democracy in parallel to those of May Fourth iconoclasts. Ip challenges Alitto's claim that Liang was a *reluctant* supporter of democracy whose position presumed an incompatibility between Western and Chinese cultures. She stresses that in his writings from the 1920s to the 1940s, Liang supplemented his utilitarian commitment to democracy—whether nation-oriented or individual-oriented—with an autonomous value commitment to it, meaning that democracy was an end onto itself for Liang. Moreover, Liang did not conceive of democracy and Chinese culture as incompatible, but instead continuously reconceptualized the best ways in which the two could be reconciled, around the notion of *gang* 剛 in the 1920s, that of one-party rule in the 1930s,[23] and that of ethical rationality (*lixing*) in the 1940s.

Given that Ip sees in Liang a continued commitment to the intrinsic, autonomous value of democracy throughout the Republican period, she concludes that Liang provides a counter-example to the narrow, nation-oriented utilitarian take on democracy Andrew Nathan regards as the "central tradition" of Chinese democracy (Nathan 1986). On this basis, she also challenges Benjamin Schwartz's highly influential thesis according to which modern Chinese intellectuals' interest in democracy merely rested on a desire to achieve national wealth and power. Although not unconcerned with the fate of the nation, Liang "was definitely not a reluctant advocate of what he perceived as the Western essence [as she sees Alitto arguing], driven solely by a nationalistic concern for wealth and power" (Ip 1991: 505).

5.4 Zhijue *and* Lixing

Also explicitly challenging Alitto's portrayal of Liang is a 1997 article by AN Yanming (Clemson University), who approaches the thought of LIANG Shuming—a "prominent philosopher and social reformer in contemporary China" (An 1997: 337)—from the perspective of cultural history in order to get a sense of the Gadamerian prejudices that might explain the process of translation that took place between Bergson's notion of intuition and Liang's *zhijue*. An's main thesis is that Liang took an epistemological notion and made it an ethical one, due to the "inherited presuppositions of Chinese culture" according to which priority is ascribed to ethics over epistemology (337).[24]

[23] Ip highlights the undemocratic dimension of Liang's one-party rule, but she also shows how Liang retained his commitment to both "democracy's individual-oriented utilitarian and autonomous values" (Ip 1991: 491) during this period.

[24] Joseph Ciaudo extends this argument to the reception of Bergson's notion of intuition in early Republican China in general in Ciaudo 2016.

An's article also challenges Alitto's interpretation according to which Liang abandoned the concept of *zhijue* for that of *lixing* simply not to go out of fashion. Rather, An suggests this terminological shift underscores an important development in Liang's thought. By adopting *lixing*, Liang wished to discard the earlier connotations of *zhijue* as instinct and as a method of knowledge, while retaining the Confucian meaning of *liangzhi* 良知. Although An also highlights the Buddhist and Bergsonian imports of Liang's thought, he nevertheless tends, not unlike Alitto, to emphasize the extent to which Liang inherited from the Confucian tradition. He in fact argues that by making *lixing* an aspect of the human "operation of thinking" superior to *lizhi* 理智 (reason), and by associating the former with China and the latter with the West, Liang essentially followed ZHANG Zhidong's 張之洞 (1837–1909) *Zhongti Xiyong* model. "This proves once again," An concludes, "that Confucianism is still a fundamental element in Liang's later thought" (357).[25]

5.5 *Liang as a Conservative*

Finally, two articles further address the topic of Liang's conservatism. While many scholars have described Liang as a conservative over the years, few have taken the time to define what they meant by "conservatism" and to locate Liang's conservatism within the historical context of its emergence. Breaking new ground on this front is a 2009 article by intellectual historian Edmund S. K. Fung (Western Sydney University). Challenging Benjamin Schwartz's strict distinction between political and cultural conservatisms (Schwartz 1976), Fung studies the cases of LIANG Shuming—"leader of the Rural Reconstruction Group" (Fung 2009: 788)—and ZHANG Junmai, among others, to highlight the political dimension of cultural conservatism during the Republican period, which he sees as closely intertwined with war and nationalism. Fung labels Liang and Zhang "politico-cultural" conservatives to stress the fact that they "did not pit the nation against the state, or tradition against modernity; rather, they stood for both" (788).

Focusing on Liang's rural reconstruction period, Fung portrays both Liang and Zhang as "'moral innovators' spreading the message of national rebirth and renewal as a way of saving the nation and achieving modernity" (789). This position, Fung suggests, can be viewed as conservative only given the historical context of Republican China, where "to be conservative was to be nationalistic, but not necessarily vice versa" (789). As to Liang's rural reconstruction movement, Fung characterizes it, against Alitto's claim that it was a "non-political solution to China's modern crisis" (Alitto 1986: 205), as "a national self-salvation movement involving the political awakening of the peasants" and seeking an "alternative modernity

[25] An builds on this interpretation in an article that introduces Liang's thought from 1921 to 1949 in An 2002.

reflecting the country's conditions in the 1930s" (Fung 2009: 792).[26] Liang's alternative modernity *avant la lettre* differs from the progressive, anticolonial one that has been under discussion since the beginning of this century (e.g., Gaonkar 2001), however, insofar as it remains culturally conservative in essence.

In a 2008 article, Adam K. Webb (Johns Hopkins University) follows Alitto in portraying Liang as part of a "world-wide conservative response" to modernity, locating him in the context of an Asian-wide countermodern wave following the First World War. Liang is made to represent the Confucian response to modernity, while Rabindranath Tagore and Muhammad Iqbal do the same for Hinduism and Islam respectively. Webb attributes the failure of the wave against "liberal democracy," of which he sees the three men as representatives, to their disconnectedness "from the European core and from one another in any relevant sense" (Webb 2008: 210). This failure, in short, was not due to the superiority of "liberal modernity," but to "power imbalances and networks" (211). Webb is one of the few scholars to adopt a global perspective in approaching Liang's thought, although he is not the only one, as we will see.

6 Liang the Modern Populist

Another perspective on Liang's thought is provided by Catherine Lynch's monograph *Liang Shuming and the Populist Alternative in Modern China*. Although only published in 2018, after Lynch's passing in 2015, the monograph is the result of Lynch's doctoral dissertation, completed in 1989 at the University of Wisconsin-Madison. Her work is a direct product of the opening of China to foreign researchers, as much of Lynch's research comes from direct interviews she conducted with Liang Shuming and people close to him, mostly during the years of 1980–1981.

Although for reasons undisclosed Lynch's work scarcely mentions or references Alitto's biography, it can nevertheless be seen as both in continuity and in rupture with it. In continuity because Lynch also adopts an intellectual history approach, and she provides an international context within which Liang's thought can be situated—in this case the Narodnik populist movement. Not unlike Alitto, Lynch also portrays Liang as a "modern, cosmopolitan thinker" who was much more concerned, like Mao—whose relation to Liang is discussed at length in the last

[26] Fung also discusses Liang's thought in his 2000 book *In Search of Chinese Democracy*, in which he suggests (independently of Lynch, it appears) that the ideas underpinning Liang's rural reconstruction movement share "a striking resemblance to Mao Zedong's populism" (152).

chapter[27]—with the future of China than with its past (Lynch 2018: 39, 214). From this perspective, Lynch downplays Liang's "conversion" from Buddhism to Confucianism, and emphasizes another conversion, an "awakening" taking place in late 1926 and early 1927, following a period of intense doubt that began after the publication of DXWH. It is at this level that Lynch's interpretation departs in important ways from that of Alitto (who emphasizes the continuity between Liang's thought before and after 1927).

Faithful to her rejection of the conservative reading of Liang's oeuvre, Lynch characterizes the 1927 awakening as rooted not in a changed perspective on the Chinese past, but a change of heart regarding the application of Western solutions to Chinese problems. The beginning of the dissolution of the first united front, in 1926, plays an important role in Lynch's narrative. Following this event, Liang finally allowed himself to admit—against his 1921 views that Chinese culture could be revived only after China had adopted Western models—that "both the capitalist and the Communist Wests […] were predicated on a class structure which did not apply in China" (152). This realization opened the way to Liang's "conversion" to populism and his emphasis on the need of local solutions to local problems. Liang's rural reconstruction efforts, and his involvement in politics during and after the Second Sino-Japanese War, thus represent the direct result of Liang's awakening to populism in 1927.

Borrowing theoretical resources from the scholarship on Russian populism, Lynch draws a number of parallels between the Narodniks and Liang—and, through Liang, modern Chinese populism broadly conceived. She particularly highlights two commonalities between Liang and his Russian populist counterparts. First, both emphasized the importance of establishing close ties between the peasants and the intellectual elite. History could no progress on its own; it required the direction of "self aware, awakened individuals" (215).[28] Second, both upheld a "nonlinear concept of progress," in the sense that they believed the economic and industrial "backwardness" of their nations provided them with an opportunity to skip the capitalist phase and directly move on to the next phase: some form of socialism adapted to local needs. This particular stance is characteristic of the intellectuals of "modern changing societies," who are prone to exhibit what Lynch, following Andrzej Walicki, calls "populist asynchronism" due to their position between the "industrialized, capitalist West and agrarian, traditional Russian" or China (183).

---

[27] On the topic, see also Lynch 2011, in which Lynch argues that both Liang's and Mao's thought were "utopian" in the sense decried by Marx, meaning that they downplayed the significance of historical materialism. It is their rejection of historical materialism that enabled them to argue capitalism was not a necessary step in their respective quest to reach the end of history, while at the same time relocating the social foundations of history's drive in the peasantry, pace Marx. This allowed them both to turn China's "backwardness" into an advantage rather than a deficit.

[28] It is important to note that Russian populism differs in important ways from the received meaning of populism in the American setting, where anti-elitism and anti-intellectualism remain central components of the populist stance. Lynch links Liang's populism to its Russian, and not American, counterpart.

Unfortunately, Lynch's novel interpretation did not affect in important ways the reception of Liang's thought in European languages, as it remained unpublished for nearly 30 years. Instead, two competing visions of Liang, along with Alitto's, were to take the central stage from the 1990s onwards: one that regards Liang as a member of "New Confucianism," and another that redefines Liang as a Buddhist thinker.

7 Liang the New Confucian

By describing Liang as the *last* Confucian, Alitto situates him at the end point of a tradition going back to the pre-Qin period. In contrast to this view, one of the many interpretative frameworks to emerge after 1976 positions Liang at the *starting point* of a modern school of thought retrospectively called "New Confucianism."[29] The first mention of New Confucianism in European languages dates back to an article published the year of Mao's death by intellectual historian CHANG Hao 張灝 (Ohio State University). While much can be said of this influential article, what matters for our purpose is that Chang traces the birth of "New Confucianism," which he takes the New Confucian Manifesto of 1958 to be its main expression, to "the development of a major trend of Chinese conservatism which had its origin in the early 1920s" (Chang 1976: 288).

Within this context, Chang presents Liang as "a leader of cultural conservatism" (276–77) and one of the "seminal New Confucians" (281), along with XIONG Shili 熊十力 (1885–1968) and the cosignatories of the Manifesto (MOU Zongsan 牟宗三 [1909–1995], TANG Junyi, XU Fuguan 徐復觀 [1904–1982], and ZHANG Junmai). Liang's important role in this narrative is explained by the fact that Chang takes "New Confucianism" to be a reaction against scientism. While he lays great emphasis on ZHANG Junmai's role in attacking scientism in the 1923 debate on science and the view of life, he regards DXWH as a precursor leading the charge against it. Although Chang's article mostly focuses on the 1958 Manifesto and has comparatively little to say on Liang's thought, it nevertheless influenced or presaged in important ways the later reception of Liang's thought. This can be shown by taking a closer look at a number of studies that position Liang's thought in what can be called the "New Confucian paradigm."

In a 1991 article introducing New Confucianism to the French public, sinologist Léon Vandermeersch (École pratique des hautes études) situates Liang at the forefront of the first generation of New Confucians (along with XIONG Shili and FENG Youlan). He emphasizes the importance of DXWH, which he describes as proposing a Confucian alternative to the capitalist, dehumanized society that resulted from the Industrial Revolution in Europe. Later on, in his preface to the French translation of DXWH, published in 2000, he provides a more comprehensive analysis of the work of "philosophy of history of the cultures of humanity," which for him

[29] On the retrospective creation of New Confucianism, see Makeham 2003b.

represents "the first serious effort of the modern re-establishment of Confucianism" (Léon Vandermeersch 2000: xiv). However, this does not entail that the work should be understood as conservative, since Liang's Confucianism, Vandermeersch stresses, is compatible with modernization and democratization. As such, DXWH is for him "in favour of a progressivism finding new roots in the values of the Chinese tradition; in favour of what would later be called *New Confucianism*" (xii).

In English, the first academic presentation of Liang within the New Confucian paradigm after CHANG Hao's article we could find dates back to an essay published in the journal *Chinese Historians* by JIANG Jin (Stanford University) in 1993. Jiang situates Liang within the general framework of China's response to the West following the Opium Wars. "One of the few outspoken defenders of Chinese culture" in the context of May Fourth iconoclasm (Jiang 1993: 2), Liang developed a "philosophy and socio-political practice [that] represented a rare attempt of reviving classical Confucianism" (4). For this reason, Jiang compares Liang to XIONG Shili, portraying both as "*forerunners* of twentieth-century New Confucianism" (11; our emphasis).

Liang and Xiong in fact represent two alternatives within the general framework of New Confucianism: "Xiong's modern Confucianism had the potential to develop into a pure academic metaphysics or an ethico-religious belief for its followers, whereas Liang's reflects his effort to restore a classical Confucianism following the line from Confucius and Mencius to Wang Yangming" (12). Although also laying a significant emphasis on the Buddhist import of Liang's thought, Jiang nevertheless concludes that because Liang embodies a calling to transform the world Jiang sees, against Max Weber (1864–1920), as the result of a tension inherent in Confucianism, he "was perhaps the greatest Confucian *in the classical sense* in the twentieth century" (26; our emphasis). Although clearly inheriting the New Confucian paradigm initiated by CHANG Hao,[30] Jiang also comes close to Alitto's view according to which Liang's desire to fulfil the traditional goal of uniting thought and action accounts for his being the last Confucian.

Following Chang and Jiang's articles, the New Confucian paradigm found its first systematic expression in European languages in Umberto Bresciani's (Centro Internazionale Arte Cultura Societa) 2001 book *Reinventing Confucianism: The New Confucian Movement*.[31] Bresciani's monograph devotes a chapter to each of the main figures of the "New Confucian movement," including LIANG Shuming. While a number of scholars had previously associated Liang with what they saw as a Confucian revival following the May Fourth Movement (Brière, Roy), and while CHANG Hao does present Liang as a member of the New Confucian school, Bresciani goes further in describing Liang not only as the "forerunner"—as JIANG Jin had done before him—but also as the "initiator" of a modern school or movement known as "New Confucianism." Although it had not yet penetrated the

[30] Jiang in fact adopts CHANG Hao's terminology of "crisis of meaning" (5), although without referencing Chang's article.

[31] The monograph was subsequently published in Italian (Bresciani 2009).

Euro-American reception of Liang's thought, this view and the genealogical framework (heavily influenced by the work of MOU Zongsan) that made sense of it were by then quite widespread in Taiwan, where Bresciani obtained his PhD and where he lived for 30 years.[32]

In his chapter on Liang, Bresciani introduces his life, work, and *philosophical* thought. While this is not the place to summarize the chapter, it is worth noting that Bresciani qualifies the publication of DXWH "as the milestone indicating the *beginning* of the New Confucian Movement" (Bresciani 2001: 59; our emphasis), following Liang's "conversion" to Confucianism (72–73). Although Bresciani acknowledges that Liang considered himself a Buddhist "throughout his life" (82), he nevertheless argues that in his emphasis "on moral concerns above everything else" and in his "stress upon union of knowledge and action," Liang "is typically and genuinely Confucian in his attitude" (78). Moreover, he maintains that Liang "launched the ideas which became important, if not the dominating, themes of the New Confucians' doctrines" (82). As such, Bresciani's monograph plays a central role in the gradual tendency to view Liang as a founding member of "New Confucianism." This view, however, was soon to be challenged by scholars paying closer attention to the Buddhist dimension of Liang's thought.

8 Liang the Buddhist

As we saw above, apart from Catherine Lynch, most scholars writing after the death of Mao have emphasized the Confucian character of Liang's thought. This paradigm was severely challenged at the beginning of the twenty-first century by John J. Hanafin (University of Melbourne) and Thierry Meynard (Sun Yat-sen University), but was already put in question in the 1990s in the work of Zbigniew Wesołowski (Monumenta Serica), the author of the only German-language monograph on Liang (1997).

In his monograph, based on his doctoral dissertation of 1996, Wesołowski describes his approach toward the work of Liang as "pragmatic," in the sense that it follows the spirit of the unity of knowledge and praxis (*zhixing heyi* 知行合一) also emphasized in Alitto. On this basis, Wesołowski apprehends Liang through his self-definition as a "thinker" (not a philosopher) and further as a man of action, exemplified by his engagement in the rural reconstruction movement and his deep concern with the future of China. Wesołowski also characterizes his approach as "immanent," meaning that he relies almost entirely on Liang's texts themselves, and particularly, as the title of his monograph suggests, on DXWH. While he offers

[32] The influence of Taiwanese scholarship on Bresciani is explicit when he claims that "LIANG Shuming is *unanimously* considered the forerunner, the initiator of the New Confucian Movement" (56). While this was certainly true of Taiwan, his Euro-American readers might not have unanimously agreed on this point. On the role played by MOU Zongsan on the formation of the New Confucian genealogy of the way, see Makeham 2003a.

occasional remarks on Western philosophy (such as Kant, Dilthey, the Frankfurt School, etc.), other Chinese philosophers, as well as other texts published by Liang, DXWH remains the central focus of his analysis.

Like Meynard would do 10 years later, Wesołowski answers the question of whether Liang was a Buddhist or a Confucian by highlighting Liang's indebtedness to Buddhist thought, referring to him as a "Buddhist in Confucian disguise." However, he understands Liang's view of historical development as the core of his thought, symbolizing the threefold problems of human life: the material (represented by the pragmatic West), the social (represented by Confucian China) and the individual-spiritual (represented by Indo-Buddhism). This leads Liang to affirm the universal value of Confucianism and Buddhism as higher stages of human development vis-à-vis the then dominant Western influence represented by the May Fourth Movement, which in Liang constitutes merely the first stage of history.

The first chapter focuses on elucidating the genealogy of Liang's thought, identifying Confucianism, Buddhism and Henri Bergson's philosophy of life as the three pillars of his "radically life-oriented" thought. The second chapter then dissects Liang's notion of life, showing its interconnectedness to the three world cultures representing three different modes of life. The final chapter expounds Liang's notion of culture and identifies three general cultural theorems in Liang's thought. First, individual "geniuses" (Confucius, Buddha, Mozi), who represent the ideal manifestation of a certain doctrine, induce the rise of a culture. Second, the "premature" cultural trends started by Confucius and the Buddha that vanished during most of history will re-emerge in future stages of humanity. Third, each culture has its point of culmination marking the true fulfilment of its doctrine in a sequential order. The final part of the third chapter then examines the relation between Liang's notion of culture and the three universal characteristics of human culture: religion, philosophy and science, and democracy.

In another article published in 1996, Wesołowski builds on the missionary reception of Liang's thought during the Republican period, in that he draws greater attention, as Meynard would also soon do, to the religious dimension of Liang's thought. Wesołowski almost exclusively bases his analysis on Liang's DXWH, opting once again for an "immanent" approach. Wesołowski starts out by illustrating the historical and individual contexts of Liang's concept of religion, locating it in the colonial intrusion of the West since the Opium Wars and in debates among intellectuals concerning Buddhism and the aspired establishment of a Chinese religion by prominent thinkers such as KANG Youwei, with whom Liang strongly disagreed. According to Wesołowski, Liang characterizes religion as a phenomenon of human history generally containing two essential parts: transcendence (*chaojue* 超絕)—i.e. any form of knowledge that goes beyond reason and the sensual perception of the world, manifested in totems, animism, a personal god, or Buddhist emptiness—and mysticism (*shenmi* 神秘), which derives from the human disposition, expressed in religious awe and obedience, granting the believer solace and encouragement. Wesołowski then situates Liang's discussion of religion in the framework of his views on historical progress, according to which theistic religions such as Christianity and Islam, which solely rest on humanity's disposition and want for solace and encouragement, will be superseded by the "atheistic religions" of Confucianism and Buddhism.

While Wesołowski's prior studies on Liang's cultural and religious thought were mainly based on a close exegesis of DXWH, in a 2005 English-language article, he expands his analysis to the development of Liang's cultural thought between 1921 and 1949. Presenting Liang's work against the backdrop of the historical context, of his individual experiences, and of the challenges raised by Western philosophy, he argues Liang's cultural thought constitutes a theory of justification of Chinese culture, or "sinodicy." As he had argued previously, Wesołowski shows how Liang accomplishes this task by constructing a teleological model of historical development, in which Confucianism and Buddhism represent more advanced stages of development than the pragmatist or utilitarian West. Precisely through the comparison with the West, Wesołowski states, was Liang able to regain his cultural identity, affirming the validity of Confucianism and Buddhism by relegating them to a future stage of history.[33]

The "Confucian paradigm" was further challenged by a 2003 article published in *New Confucianism: A Critical Examination*, in which John J. Hanafin draws on Chinese-language scholarship produced after 1976—including interviews Liang gave in the 1980s, in which he announced he had remained a Buddhist throughout his whole life—to put forth the argument that Liang's "spirit, views, and philosophy" (Hanafin 2003: 187) are Buddhist in nature. Hanafin situates Liang's thought within the context of the reemergence of interest in Yogācāra following the reintroduction of a number of Yogācāra works, in the 1890s, that had been lost in China since the Yuan 元 dynasty. Liang, according to Hanafin, continuously upheld "the superiority of Buddhist philosophy and its worldview over that of Confucian philosophy" (189), so much so that his interest in Confucianism (and later Marxism) can be viewed as ultimately grounded in his commitment to Buddhism. This was made possible by the fact that Liang saw Buddhism as providing answers to ultimate, other-worldly issues, while he understood Confucianism, under the guise of WANG Gen 王艮 (1483–1541), as a this-worldly, social philosophy (193, 207).

Hanafin supports these assertions not only with comments that Liang himself made regarding his relation to Buddhism and Confucianism, but also with an analysis of Liang's epistemology and metaphysics. On this last point, Hanafin maintains that Liang's interest in Bergson and the *Book of Changes* (*Yijing* 易經) was rooted in his Yogācāra conception of the world as constantly in flux, while the appeal WANG Yangming's 王陽明 (1472–1529) construal of the heart-mind (*xin* 心) held for him is to be explained by its "parallel to the *Weishi* [唯識; i.e.: Yogācāra] notion of *citta* (mind) and *cittamātra* (mind only)" (195). Hanafin concludes that Liang was always a Buddhist and "never an authentic Confucian" (206).

Soon after the publication of Hanafin's article, the topic of Liang's ultimate allegiances was further elaborated upon by Thierry Meynard, first in two articles

[33] In Chinese, see also Wesołowski's monograph on Liang's conception of culture in DXWH and ZGWH (Wei [Wesołowski] 2003).

published in 2007 and 2008, and then in a 2011 monograph based on his Chinese-language doctoral dissertation of 2003. In the monograph, at the time only the second one in English to be entirely devoted to Liang, Meynard adopts a multidisciplinary approach that borrows from the fields of interreligious dialogue, sinology, and philosophy. Unlike other specialists of Liang, who have portrayed him as a philosopher, intellectual, social reformer, or political figure, Meynard situates Liang in the longue durée of Sino-Western religious dialogues dating back to the Jesuit missions of the sixteenth century, painting a portrait of Liang as first and foremost a *religious* thinker (as Millican had implied in his 1926 review of DXWH). Indeed, Meynard recognizes that DXWH adopts an approach he qualifies as "anthropological and cultural philosophy" (Meynard 2011: 21), but Liang nevertheless makes of religion the central component of culture, given that it informs the attitude each of the three cultures he studies adopted from the very start.[34]

Notably on the basis of the interviews Liang gave in the 1980s, Meynard argues that Alitto's classification of Buddhism and Confucianism as different *phases* in the evolution of Liang's thought should be thoroughly rethought, as should the "New Confucian" paradigm that posits Liang as one of the founding figures of the movement. Challenging the binary logic these views assume—Liang can be *either* Buddhist *or* Confucian—Meynard follows Hanafin in proposing in their spite to construe Liang's allegiance to Confucianism as an integral part of his overall Buddhist commitment.

This idiosyncratic approach to both Confucianism and Buddhism, Meynard contends, is made possible by the fact that Liang's religious views rely on a strict distinction between the this-worldly and the other-worldly (as Millican had pointed out in 1926). Buddhism's value lies in its ability to transcend the world (*chushi* 出世). Although Liang makes of this form of transcendence the norm around which his understanding of religion revolves—Buddhism, for Liang, is the only "true religion" (47)—it also entails that Buddhism has no practical value for this-worldly issues. As such, Buddhism could provide the resources to solve China's problems only at the cost of distorting the original message of the school—a cost Liang was not ready to pay.

Instead, Meynard proposes, Liang advocates the preservation of a pure form of Buddhism, which could not be truly realized until eschatological times. Until then, what China needed, to solve its issues which were definitely this-worldly, was Confucianism, whose metaphysically grounded morality could avoid the trap of attachment to the world and to the subject-object divide, since Confucianism's was

[34] In a 2012 article, Meynard reflects further on Liang's relation with philosophy. He compares Liang's attempt at inserting Buddhism within the framework of the newly emerged field of philosophy with similar attempts made by XIONG Shili and TANG Yongtong 湯用彤 (1893–1964). His conclusion is that Liang adopted a cultural stance which made of Buddhism "a foreign culture and philosophy" (Meynard 2012: 210). Yet Meynard also emphasizes that Liang was "given the label of 'philosopher' by an academic institution [Peking University] eager to attract bright minds. Without Cai [Yuanpei]'s [蔡元培] [intervention], Liang would most probably never have started his career as a 'philosopher' and would likely have become a Buddhist monk" (189).

a morality of selflessness which could bring about a fusion between humans and the universe. As such, while Liang concedes that Confucianism is a form of morality and "not quite a true religion," he nevertheless believes "it performed many of a religion's functions" (147).

Meynard also highlights that Confucianism's quasi-religious morality is placed by Liang "at the mid-point between a Christian engagement with the world and the Buddhist drive to escape from it" (147); as a bridge connecting the social religion of Christianity with the religion of transcendence of Buddhism. This entails that only once this-worldly problems would be met with Confucian solutions could Buddhist enlightenment be within humanity's reach. This discourse, which against Auguste Comte sees in religion not the past but the future of humanity (48), amounts to making of Confucianism a skilful means (*fangbian* 方便) employed for Buddhist ends.[35] Despite his endorsement of Confucianism, however, Liang was ultimately "dedicated to the bodhisattva path, which he pursued using the unorthodox means of promoting Confucianism" (139). Liang, in other words, was a hidden bodhisattva dressed in Confucian robes.[36]

Meynard's interpretation not only challenges Alitto's paradigm and that of New Confucianism—Meynard reserves the term "New Confucian" for thinkers like XIONG Shili and MOU Zongsan (124)[37]—it also questions Lynch's understanding of Liang as a modern thinker interested in social reforms. Under Meynard's gaze, Liang should rather be viewed as a religious figure; not just a Buddhist disguised in the robes of a Confucian, but also a bodhisattva disguised in the clothes of a modern thinker and social activist. This becomes clear when Meynard addresses Liang's rural reform movement. Like Lynch, he emphasizes the importance of Liang's 1927 "awakening" in his decision to involve himself in rural reconstruction, but unlike her, he emphasizes the religious nature of this awakening and the rural reconstruction program devised by Liang.[38]

[35] Meynard had previously made this argument in Meynard 2007a.

[36] In Meynard 2014, Meynard further comments that in DXWH, Liang reworked Yogācāra theories to make room for Confucianism. He did so first by introducing a third mode of knowledge, intuition, which allowed for the possibility of morality, contrasted to the immorality of Western reasoning (*biliang* 比量)—based on its being "stained with selfishness" (Meynard 2014: 231)—and the amorality of Buddhism's direct perception (*xianliang* 現量). Second, Liang also deployed an evolutionary scheme in which intuition functioned as a mediating stage between reasoning and direct perception. Meynard concludes that Liang's DXWH does not amount to intellectual syncretism, however, as "it can be rightly claimed that his thought is ultimately not syncretic but Buddhist" (241).

[37] See Meynard 2015 for a further discussion of how Liang's thought differs both from mainland New Confucians and from New Confucians who left the mainland in 1949.

[38] Meynard had made the argument that Liang's rural reconstruction movement was aimed at bringing about a harmonious form of society that could make the religious fusion between human beings and universe more readily accessible in Meynard 2007b. This article is partially reproduced in Chap. 10 of the monograph. Meynard also edited a volume of *Contemporary Chinese Thought* on Liang, for which he wrote an introduction (Meynard 2009).

9 New Approaches

Since at least the 2010s, new approaches to LIANG Shuming's thought have been proposed by a variety of scholars. Three are discussed in this section. The first provides a discursive perspective on DXWH, the second approaches Liang as a philosophical or socio-historical resource, and the third tends to treat Liang as a modern sage whose writings provide a source of wisdom from which to draw.

9.1 Discursive Approach

First is an approach that pays attention to the issue of authority that underscores the way in which "Confucianism" is constructed by Liang, without committing to whether Liang should be categorized as a Confucian or Buddhist thinker. This approach is exemplified by the work of Philippe Major (one of the authors of this chapter). In two articles published in 2017, Major (University of Basel) follows the tradition initiated by Brière and Roy in portraying DXWH as written in reaction against May Fourth iconoclasm, although he also highlights that Liang's approach remains very close to that of May Fourth—notably in its emphasis on culture as the main locale where solutions to China's problems can and should be found.

Like modernization theorists, Major (2017a) reads DXWH (his main object of analysis) as the product of historical tensions between tradition and modernity, but unlike them, he does not situate these tensions in a historical metanarrative which presumes the disappearance of tradition. Rather, he investigates the discursive tools that were at the disposal of Liang in his attempt at presenting his own take on "tradition" and "Confucianism" as valuable within a discursive framework saturated with May Fourth iconoclasm. One of his points is that DXWH's construal of "Confucianism" is to a great extent negatively predetermined by the discursive field, in the sense that only a Confucianism made to appear as the reversed image of the May Fourth portrayal of modernity could be presented as valuable within DXWH's historical metanarrative. Moreover, by adopting and modifying the metanarrative of modernity in a way that peripheralized the role of Western culture in it, "Confucian culture" could be reauthorized by being projected onto the next phase of History, but it could be so "only at the cost of being de-complexified, homogenized, and de-historicized; only at the cost of being no longer Chinese" (Major 2017a: 182).

Another point made by Major (2017b) is that issues related to the authority of tradition remain central to the discourse of DXWH. Liang's goal, in this text, is not only to reauthorize "Confucianism" as he construed it, but also to present DXWH and himself as the sole legitimate representatives of the tradition in modern China. By claiming that Confucius' philosophy of life was misunderstood throughout Chinese history, Liang manages to present himself as the first Confucian able to understand what Confucius ultimately meant. Liang's rejection of Confucian history is thus closely related to an effort to build what Major calls a "genealogical mode of textual authorization" whereby the text and its author are shown to be in direct spiritual simultaneity with the ancient sage. Moreover, by presenting the philosophy of life said to be directly passed down from Confucius to Liang as a *natural* way of life, DXWH avails itself of what Major calls a "rhetoric of naturalization" that is meant to immunize Liang's Confucianism from critique while also distinguishing it from historical manifestations of Confucianism said to be unnatural and inauthentic.[39] Confucianism can thus be purified from what was precisely the object of the criticisms of the May Fourth iconoclasts: its enmeshment in state power as well as the oppressive nature of its social hierarchies.

The overall picture that emerges from Major's take on Liang is that of an intellectual concerned not only with the fate of tradition in modernity, but also with his own ability to ascribe to himself the authority of tradition. By redefining "Confucianism" in a manner that could be recognized as legitimate within the May Fourth discursive framework, Liang's "Confucianism" ended up to a great extent shaped by this discursive framework. From this perspective, Liang's thought cannot be regarded as entirely his own, given how much it was shaped and defined by the discursive milieu of the time. This can be read as a rethinking of previous approaches to Liang's thought, especially philosophical ones, that tend to lay a rather strong emphasis on Liang's agency in developing his ideas. Instead, in partial continuity with Alitto and Lynch, Major sees in Liang a medium through which the discursive field of the time can be rethought.

9.2 Liang as a Philosophical or Socio-Historical Resource

The second approach we would like to mention is that of treating Liang as a philosophical or socio-historical resource from which to draw. In *John Dewey, Liang Shuming, and China's Education Reform* (2013), Zhang Huajun 張華軍 (Beijing Normal University) proposes a philosophy of education that seeks to develop a "continued sense of self in the radically changing Chinese society" (Zhang 2013b: 2). Given the philosophical approach she adopts, Zhang's goal is not that of providing an overview of the thought of John Dewey and Liang Shuming. Rather, the pragmatist philosopher and the "Confucian scholar" (1) provide Zhang with

[39] In a 2018 article, Major develops on this point to argue that the fact Liang has been perceived as a modern and a conservative thinker can be related to the tension between the manifestations of Confucianism in history—which he rejects—and the spirit of Confucianism which he adheres to. Liang is modern in rejecting the historical traditions of China, but traditionalist or more properly "revivalist" in attempting to salvage a pure spirit from the dustbin of history.

resources from which she draws in order to propose her own conceptualization of individuality.[40]

This approach, while not uncommon in Chinese-language scholarship, is rather novel in European languages, in which Liang tends to be treated as an object of research rather than a philosophic resource from which one can borrow. By "initiating a dialogue" between Liang and Dewey, while clearly pointing out the importance of her own role in the process (she also calls it a "trilogue"), Zhang positions Dewey and Liang on a common ground: as philosophers of individuality. On this front, she continues the tradition of situating Liang in a global community of philosophers—a tradition initiated 90 years previously by FENG Youlan.[41]

A similar approach to Liang is offered in the only other piece written in European languages comparing Liang's thought to that of Dewey. In "LIANG Shuming's Conception of Democracy" (2015), GU Hongliang 顧紅亮 (East China Normal University) first makes the historical argument that Liang's conception of democracy—especially during the rural reconstruction period—was significantly influenced by that of Dewey, both directly and indirectly, through the medium of fellow reformer TAO Xingzhi 陶行知 (1891–1946). But Gu goes further in making the philosophical argument that Liang—a "representative of the modern Neo-Confucianism" who was "labeled as Conservative by some scholars" (Gu 2015: 132)—developed a new type of "Confucian democracy"—a term he explicitly borrows from Roger T. Ames and TAN Sor-hoon, but which in Liang denotes "the union of the ethical 'feeling' [Liang's *lixing*] and democracy" (143). Gu regards Liang's Confucian democracy as an alternative form of modernity grounded in the Confucian tradition and thus better adapted to the Chinese milieu. Although Gu points out important shortcomings in Liang's Confucian democracy—such as the potential danger of his emphasis on responsibility over rights (139)—he nevertheless also conceives it, not unlike Zhang, as a philosophical resource, one that "does not mark the end of the topic" but "provides room for us to think more deeply about another version of democracy" (143).

In contrast with Zhang and Gu's philosophical approach, Bernardo Poetzelberger takes a historical approach toward the work of LIANG Shuming in his 1993 German-language doctoral dissertation. Focusing on ZGWH, to which he adds a few references to DXWH and Liang's texts on rural reconstruction, Poetzelberger primarily treats Liang as a historian and sociologist. His work is therefore not examined through the philosophical lens, but is rather construed as a valuable contribution to the conceptual history of the "state" in the global and Chinese contexts. The

---

[40] Zhang borrows from two aspects of Liang's thought in particular. First, she builds on Liang's discussion of the "inner self" (*shenxin* 深心) to supplement Dewey's emphasis on self-transformation as the product of interaction with the external realm. Second, she stresses the importance of Liang's selfless self—the self that "moves beyond [its] own unique feelings" (Zhang 2013b: 106) and avoids both the extremes of individualism and collectivism.

[41] Zhang revisits these issues in Zhang 2013a, in which she draws from Liang in order to provide a critique of the small-self/big-self dichotomy—exemplified by HU Shi—that has dominated the instrumentalized field of education. On this, see also Zhang 2015.

dissertation carefully analyses the meaning of the concepts "*tianxia*" 天下 (All Under Heaven) and "*guo*" 國 (state) throughout Chinese history and presents the complex patterns of their semantic changes through time, taking LIANG Shuming's explanations as one of the important sources on this topic. Liang's texts are therefore set on an equal footing with other important Western and Chinese texts, as a resource informing us on the theory and history of the state.[42]

9.3 Liang the Modern Sage

Finally, it is also worth mentioning a third approach to Liang's thought, which can be traced back to before the advent of the twenty-first century. In a 1996 article, LEE Zangzhou (Chinese name unknown) and GAO Lin (高琳) (South China Normal University), two former students of Liang, set themselves the goal to "introduce to the people the abstruse but originally creative theoretical system" (Gao and Lee 1996: 59) of *Mind, Heart, and Life* (*Renxin yu rensheng* 人心與人生; hereafter RXYRS), which Liang had directly taught them in early 1986. The authors produce a number of charts that synthesize Liang's "glorious thinking" (65) so that readers can use them to "come straight to the quintessence of Oriental culture" (60). Overall, the piece reads like a proselytic attempt at conveying Liang's message to a broader public outside China, notably by conveying it in a language, appealing to "modern cerebral science," that makes it appear more scientifically grounded.

This seems to be the first example, in European languages, of scholars treating Liang as a modern sage who can guide humanity along the path of an awakening whereby the human mind becomes "identical with cosmic mind" (63). This can be done by developing the "spirit of rational introspection and thorough comprehension of life" present in "the three representatives of Oriental culture": Confucianism, Taoism, and Buddhism (61–62). Liang, in this framework, is no longer the representative of a single school, but becomes a spokesman of, if not a metonym for, the "quintessence of Oriental culture."[43]

Another interesting case in which Liang is treated as a modern sage is XU Zhangrun's 許章潤 (Tsinghua University) 2017 monograph on Liang's "narrative about law," which is based on Xu's doctoral dissertation submitted at Melbourne

[42] Liang is also approached as a philosophical source of inspiration by Liu Lulu in her German-language doctoral dissertation of 2015. She analyzes Liang's notion of culture and his involvement in the rural reconstruction movement as resources from which to draw in order to work toward an ideal modern Chinese culture.

[43] An article written by Liang's son LIANG Peishu 梁培恕 (2015) shares a similar goal of introducing RXYRS to the Euro-American public. It is less religious than humanistic in approach, however.

University in 1999.[44] In this monograph, Xu introduces Liang as an "oracular spokesman of Chinese culture and a figure of great spiritual significance in Chinese legal thinking" (Xu 2017: xvii). Liang, Xu continues, "is one of the most powerful and original Confucian minds this century" (xvii) and is "the pioneer of the New-Confucianism movement in modern Chinese history" (xviii).

While accepting the New Confucian paradigm and rejecting Alitto's (xxviii), Xu goes further in presenting Liang's view on law as nothing short of the "incarnation of the modern Chinese soul in the realm of law" (xviii); as the "jurisconsult of the Chinese people" (xxiii). While he associates Liang with New Confucianism more explicitly than GAO Lin and LEE Zangzhou, he, like them, nevertheless depicts him as the spokesman of the Chinese soul, insofar as his thought manages to incorporate Taoism and Buddhism as well. It is based on his interpretation of Liang as the representative of authentic Chinese culture that Xu can then proceed with his attack on the representatives of iconoclasm and wholesale westernization, and particularly those in the ranks of the CCP. Xu admits that Liang enables him to "focus upon those aspects of modern Confucian legal culture which helps [sic] to unveil the mask of legitimacy afforded [sic] the Communist Party in China" (xxx).

10 Conclusion

We began this essay by pointing out how the many faces revealed by our short overview of the reception of Liang's thought in European languages might have been caused by a variety of factors: some historical, some of an academic nature, some more narrowly related to the interpreter's gaze, and some actually rooted in the diversity and complexity of Liang's thought itself. Owing to the fact that these causal factors are not exclusive in nature, however, it is often difficult to single out which might be at play in any particular instance. Despite such difficulties, we would nevertheless like to point out some of the dominant and interrelated factors that account for the wealth of divergent views on Liang highlighted in this survey of the European-language reception of his thought.

First, the reception of Liang's thought has been far from immune from the tide of history. The establishment of the PRC, for example, has prompted scholars to reassess Liang's work in view of its relation to Mao and the CCP. It is in fact by putting Liang's work in parallel with the thought of Mao that many scholars have been able to challenge interpretations of his thought inscribed within the framework of modernization theory. Within this context, scholars have also been able to highlight significant elements in Liang's thought that share populist sentiments with Mao and other intellectual figures in China and beyond.

---

[44] Xu is more known for his trenchant critique of the abolition of term limits by Xi Jinping 習近平 and later of the CCP's handling of the COVID-19 crisis, which led to his detention in 2020 and his losing his post at Tsinghua University. On these topics, see Geremie R. Barmé's discussion at http://chinaheritage.net/xu-zhangrun-許章潤/.

After Mao's death, the opening of the mainland to foreign scholars and the relative relaxation of censorship allowing Liang to be interviewed by both Chinese and foreign scholars have also played major roles in the reception of Liang's thought in European languages. Such trends have notably allowed scholars to challenge deep-seated assumptions and complexify their interpretative frameworks by confronting them with the man's rather syncretic self-perception as both a Buddhist and a Confucian, but also as a modern thinker who rejected the anti-May Fourth characterization of his thought that had been central since the establishment of the PRC. From the 1980s onwards, we see a rift emerging between a Taiwan-influenced reading of Liang as the founder of New Confucianism on the one hand and an interpretation that finds resources in the interviews Liang conducted during the 1980s. The geopolitical stakes at work in Taiwan-PRC relations can in fact be regarded as directly affecting the scholarly reception of Liang, regarded either as a New Confucian standing firm and tall in the face of Mao and the CCP or as a syncretic thinker close to Mao on several points, including the latter's populist tendencies.

Other trends in the reception of Liang's thought can be directly related to the evolution of the academic field. Changes in the field of sinology, for example, are rather straightforwardly reflected in the reception history presented above. The significant role played by missionaries in the field prior to the establishment of the PRC meant that a greater emphasis was placed on Liang's participation in a cross-religious dialogue during that period. Also, while the Confucian classics play a significant role in the interpretation of early sinologists such as Andrew T. Roy, the establishment of Area Studies after World War II shifts in important ways the kind of questions scholars ask about Liang. From then onwards, scholars tend to pay less attention to Liang's relation to the past (whether religious or philosophical) and emphasize topics such as that of modernity. Modernization theory also bore its mark on the tendency to view Liang as a historical figure alienated from the time, a view that was particularly prevalent during the Mao period. We can also see the multiplication of alternative readings of Liang's oeuvre after 1976 as the direct effect of the growing emphasis on plurality of perspectives, diversity, and interdisciplinarity in the Euro-American academic milieu during that period.

Finally, in some cases it appears that the reception of Liang's thought also allows us unique views into the interpreters themselves. On this front, one would be tempted to point out the work of Jesuits and missionaries who have tended to emphasize the religious dimension of Liang's thought. While this is certainly the case, we should also bear in mind that the reverse is also true: scholars without outspoken religious affiliations have tended to discard, for the most part, the religious dimensions of his thought. It might also be of interest to investigate how the political commitments upheld by Liang's interpreters might have colored their reading of the man: one can perhaps assume that conservatives might tend to find more value in Liang's thought, while progressives might either retain a critical attitude toward it or alternatively point out its modern and progressive elements.

Ironically, the growing interest in classifying Liang's thought in strict categories from the Mao period onwards has in fact been matched with a growing diversity of interpretations which has rendered such classification increasingly arduous. This phenomenon might be related to the intensification of competitiveness in the academic field—itself related to the commodification of knowledge—whereby scholars must seek real estate in their discursive field by positioning themselves in opposition to one another. Perhaps the fact that Liang's thought affords plenty of room for diverse interpretations played a role in the relative interest Euro-American scholars have found in the thought of Liang.

In the end, however, we must also return to the elusiveness of Liang's thought itself, which has provided the raw material without which the diversity and at times contradictory interpretations it has elicited would not have been possible in the first place. The diversity of these interpretations can certainly be viewed as the result of a number of historical, academic, and personal factors, but factors that were ultimately *enabled* by the complexity and multifaceted nature of Liang's thought itself. While the interpreter's gaze is certainly reflected in the reception of Liang's thought, it is also the various facets of Liang's thought that find themselves reflected in the diversity of its reception. It is precisely these many faces of Liang, reflected as through a broken glass in the reception of his thought, that we hope the present chapter has brought to the fore.

Acknowledgement This publication was supported by funding from the Swiss National Science Foundation for the project "The Exterior of Philosophy: On the Practice of New Confucianism."

References

Ai, Kai 艾愷 [Guy Alitto]. 1995. *The Last Confucian: Liang Shuming and the Dilemma of Chinese Modernization* 最後的儒家:梁漱溟與中國現代化的兩難. Trans. Wang Zongyu 王宗昱 and Ji Jianzhong 冀建中. Nanjing: Jiangsu remin chubanshe.

Alitto, Guy. 1976. The Conservative as Sage: Liang Shu-ming. In *The Limits of Change: Essays on Conservative Alternatives in Republican China*, ed. Charlotte Furth. Cambridge: Harvard University Press.

———. 1986. *The Last Confucian: Liang Shu-ming and the Chinese Dilemma of Modernity*. 2nd ed. Berkeley: University of California Press.

———. 2015. Liang Shuming: A Lifelong Activist. In *Contemporary Confucianism in Thought and Action*, ed. Guy Alitto. Heidelberg: Springer.

An, Yanming. 1997. Liang Shuming and Henri Bergson on Intuition: Cultural Context and the Evolution of Terms. *Philosophy East & West* 47 (3): 337–362.

———. 2002. Liang Shuming: Eastern and Western Cultures and Confucianism. In *Contemporary Chinese Philosophy*, ed. Chung-Ying Cheng. Boston: Blackwell Publishers.

Bresciani, Umberto. 2001. *Reinventing Confucianism: The New Confucian Movement*. Taipei: Ricci Institute.

———. 2009. *La filosofia cinese nel ventesimo secolo: I nuovi confuciani*. Rome: Urbaniana University Press.

Brière, O. S. J. 1949. Les courants philosophiques en Chine depuis 50 ans (1898–1950). *Bulletin de L'Université L'Aurore* 3.X.50.

———. 1956. *Fifty Years of Chinese Philosophy, 1898–1950*. Trans. Lawrence G. Thompson. New York: Macmillan.

Ch'ien, Tuan-sheng. 1950. *The Government and Politics of China*. Cambridge: Harvard University Press.

Chan, Wing-tsit. 1953. *Religious Trends in Modern China*. New York: Columbia University Press.

Chang, Hao. 1976. New Confucianism and the Intellectual Crisis of Contemporary China. In *The Limits of Change: Essays on Conservative Alternatives in Republican China*, ed. Charlotte Furth. Cambridge: Harvard University Press.

Chang, Carsun [Zhang Junmai]. 1952. *The Third Force in China*. New York: Bookman Associates.

Chi, Wen-Shun. 1970. LIANG Shu-ming and Chinese Communism. *The China Quarterly* 41: 64–82.

———. 1986. *Ideological Conflicts in Modern China: Democracy and Authoritarianism*. New Brunswick: Transaction.

Chou, Ching-wen. 1960. *Ten Years of Storm: The True Story of the Communist Regime in China*. New York: Holt, Rinehart and Winston.

Chow, Tse-tsung. 1960. *The May Fourth Movement: Intellectual Revolution in Modern China*. Cambridge: Harvard University Press.

Ciaudo, Joseph. 2016. Bergson's 'Intuition' in China and Its Confucian Fate (1915–1923): Some Remarks on *Zhijue* in Modern Chinese Philosophy. *Problemos* 2016: 35–50.

Forke, Alfred. 1942. Moderne chinesische Denker. *Zeitschrift der Deutschen Morgenländischen Gesellschaft* 96 (2): 208–260.

Fung, Edmund S.K. 2000. *In Search of Chinese Democracy: Civil Opposition in Nationalist China, 1929–1949*. Cambridge: Cambridge University Press.

———. 2009. Nationalism and Modernity: The Politics of Cultural Conservatism in Republican China. *Modern Asian Studies* 43 (3): 777–813.

Fung, Yu-lan [Feng Youlan]. 1922. Review of *Eastern and Western Cultures and Their Philosophies*. *Journal of Philosophy* 19 (22): 611–614.

Gao, Lin, and Zangzhou Lee. 1996. *Mind, Heart and Life*: Some Reflections from LIANG Shuming's Thoughts. *Journal of Human Values* 2 (1): 59–66.

Gaonkar, Dilip Parameshwar. 2001. On Alternative Modernities. In *Aternative Modernities*, ed. Dilip Parameshwar Gaonkar. Durham and London: Duke University Press.

Gransow, Bettina. 1994. Ein Wegbereiter 'Konfuzianischer Modernisierung.' LIANG Shuming und die ländliche Aufbaubewegung der dreißiger Jahre. *Bochumer Jahrbuch zur Ostasienforschung* 18: 1–20.

Gu, Hongliang. 2015. LIANG Shuming's Conception of Democracy. In *Contemporary Confucianism in Thought and Action*, ed. Guy Alitto. Heidelberg: Springer.

Hanafin, John J. 2003. The 'Last Buddhist': The Philosophy of LIANG Shuming. In *New Confucianism: A Critical Examination*, ed. John Makeham. New York: Palgrave.

Ip, Hung-Yok. 1991. LIANG Shuming and the Idea of Democracy in Modern China. *Modern China* 17 (4): 469–508.

Jiang, Jin. 1993. LIANG Shuming and the Emergence of 20th-Century New Confucianism. *Chinese Historians* 6 (2): 1–26.

Kennedy, M., Jr. 1953. The Chinese Democratic League. *Papers on China* 7: 136–175.

Lamley, Harry J. 1969. LIANG Shu-ming, Rural Reconstruction and the Rural Work Discussion Society, 1933–1935. *Chung Chi Journal* 8 (2): 50–61.

———. 1975. Review of *Chung-kuo wen-hua yao-i*. *Journal of Asian Studies* 24 (4): 682–684.

Liang, Shuming. 2000. *Les cultures d'Orient et d'Occident et leurs philosophies*. Trans. LUO Shenyi. Paris: Presses Universitaires de France.

———. 2001. The Cultures of the East and West and Their Philosophies. Trans. Andrew Covlin and YUAN Jinmei. *Dao: A Journal of Comparative Philosophy* 1(1): 107–127.

———. 2010. *Les idées maîtresses de la culture chinoise*. Trans. Michel Masson. Paris: Institut Ricci – Cerf.

Liang, Peishu. 2015. Humankind Must Know Itself. In *Contemporary Confucianism in Thought and Action*, ed. Guy Alitto. Heidelberg: Springer.

Liang, Shuming. 2021. *Fundamentals of Chinese Culture*. Trans. LI Ming. Amsterdam: Amsterdam University Press.

Liang, Shu Ming, and Guy S. Alitto. 2013. *Has Man a Future? Dialogues with the Last Confucian*. Heidelberg: Springer.

Lin, Alfred H.Y. 1990. Confucianism in Action: A Study of LIANG Shuming's Theory and Practice of Rural Reconstruction in the 1930s. *Journal of Oriental Studies* 28 (1): 21–43.

Liu, Lulu. 2015. *Die Konstruktion der modernen nationalen Gesellschaft Chinas am Beispiel des nationalen Ordnungsverständnisses der kulturkonservativen Intellektuellen Chinas*. Doct. diss. from Gottfried Wilhelm Leibniz Universität Hannover.

Lynch, Catherine. 2011. Radical visions of time in modern China: The utopianism of MAO Zedong and LIANG Shuming. In *Radicalism, Revolution and Reform in modern China*, ed. Catherine Lynch, Robert B. Marks, and Paul G. Pickowicz. Lanham: Rowman & Littlefield.

———. 2018. *LIANG Shuming and the Populist Alternative in China*. Leiden, Boston: Brill.

Major, Philippe. 2017a. Rethinking the Temporalization of Space in Early Republican China: LIANG Shuming's *Eastern and Western Cultures and Their Philosophies*. *International Communication of Chinese Culture* 4 (2): 171–185.

———. 2017b. Textual Authority and Its Naturalization in LIANG Shuming's *Dong-Xi wenhua ji qi zhexue*. *Monumenta Serica: Journal of Oriental Studies* 65 (1): 127–149.

———. 2018. Tradition and Modernity in LIANG Shuming's *Eastern and Western Cultures and Their Philosophies*. *Philosophy East & West* 68 (2): 460–476.

Makeham, John. 2003a. The New *Daotong*. In *New Confucianism: A Critical Examination*, ed. John Makeham. New York: Palgrave.

———. 2003b. The Retrospective Creation of New Confucianism. In *New Confucianism: A Critical Examination*, ed. John Makeham. New York: Palgrave.

Masson, Michel. 1981a. Culture chinoise et modernité: quatre témoins. *Études* 354 (1): 33–49.

———. 1981b. Dilemmes de la modernisation en Chine : les pensées de LIANG Shuming. *Project* 155: 579–592.

———. 2010. Avant-propos du traducteur. In *Les idées maîtresses de la culture chinoise*. Ed. LIANG Shuming. Trans. Michel Masson. Paris: Institut Ricci – Cerf.

Merkel-Hess, Kate. 2016. *The Rural Modern: Reconstructing the Self and State in Republican China*. Chicago: University of Chicago Press.

Meynard, Thierry. 2007a. Is LIANG Shuming Ultimately a Confucian or Buddhist? *Dao* 6: 131–147.

———. 2007b. Intellectuels chinois contemporains en débat avec les esprits : Le cas de LIANG Shuming (1893–1988). *Extrême-Orient, Extrême-Occident* 29: 55–69.

———. 2009. LIANG Shuming's Thought and Its Reception. *Contemporary Chinese Thought* 40 (3): 3–15.

———. 2011. *The Religious Philosophy of LIANG Shuming: The Hidden Buddhist*. Leiden, Boston: Brill.

———. 2012. Introducing Buddhism as Philosophy: The cases of LIANG Shuming, XIONG Shili and TANG Yongtong. In *Learning to Emulate the Wise: The Genesis of Chinese Philosophy as an Academic discipline in Twentieth-century China*, ed. John Makeham. Hong Kong: Chinese University Press.

———. 2014. LIANG Shuming and his Confucianized Version of Yogācāra. In *Transforming Consciousness: Yogacara Thought in Modern China*, ed. John Makeham. Oxford: Oxford University Press.

———. 2015. Confucianism as the Religion for Our Present Time: The Religious Dimension of Confucianism in LIANG Shuming's Thought. In *Contemporary Confucianism in Thought and Action*, ed. Guy Alitto. Heidelberg: Springer.

Millican, Frank R. 1926. LIANG Shou Ming (梁漱溟) Sees It Though. *The Chinese Recorder*: 698–705.

Nathan, Andrew J. 1986. *Chinese Democracy*. Berkeley: University of California Press.

O'Bryant, A.H. 1953. LIANG Sou-ming: His Response to the West. *Harvard Papers on China* 7: 1–33.

Poetzelberger, Bernardo. 1993. *Tianxia und guojia bei LIANG Shuming (1893–1988): Konsens und Konflikt im chinesischen Beitrag zur traditionellen Ordnungsvorstellung*. Doct. diss. from Rheinische Friedrich-Wilhelms-Universität, Bonn.

Roy, A.T. 1962. LIANG Shu-ming and HU Shih on the Intuitional Interpretation of Confucianism. *Chung Chi Journal* 1 (2): 139–157.

Scharping, Thomas. 1972. *Der Demokratische Bund und seine Vorläufer 1939–1949: chinesische Intelligenz zwischen Kuomintang und kommunistischer Partei*. Hamburg: Institut für Asienkunde.

Schwartz, Benjamin I. 1976. Notes on Conservatism in General and in China in Particular. In *The Limits of Change: Essays on Conservative Alternatives in Republican China*, ed. Charlotte Furth. Cambridge: Harvard University Press.

Stuart, John Leighton. 1923. The Christian Dynamics for China. *The Chinese Recorder*: 71–77.

Tai, Bingham P.H. 1925. A New Educational Enterprise. *The China Weekly Review*: 219–221.

The China Critic. 1940. Chungking Rural School. October 24, 1940.

The China Weekly Review. 1933. Three Research Conferences Hold Meetings in North China. September 2, 1933.

———. 1947. Gov. Reorganization Held Up by Differences of Viewpoint. April 5, 1947.

———. 1949. Masses Weekly. March 12, 1949.

The Chinese Recorder. 1936. Peasant Schools. March 1, 1936.

The North-China Herald and Supreme Court & Consular Gazette. 1932. Local Autonomy in Three Provinces. September 28, 1932.

———. 1934. Reform Movements in Shantung. February 13, 1934.

Thøgersen, Stig. 1995. LIANG Shuming and the Danish Model. In *Cultural Encounters: China, Japan and the West: Essays Commemorating 25 Years of East Asian Studies at the University of Aarhus*, ed. Søren Clausen, Roy Starrs, and Anne Wedell-Wedellsborg. Aarhus: Aarhus University Press.

———. 1998. Reconstructing Society: LIANG Shuming and the Rural Reconstruction Movement in Shandong. In *Reconstructing Twentieth-Century China: State Control, Civil Society, and National Identity*, ed. Kjeld Erik Brodsgaard and David Strand. Oxford: Clarendon Press.

———. 2002. *A County of Culture: Twentieth Century China Seen from the Village Schools of Zouping, Shandong*. Ann Arbor: University of Michigan Press.

———. 2009. Revisiting a Dramatic Triangle: The State, Villagers, and Social Activists in Chinese Rural Reconstruction Projects. *Journal of Current Chinese Affairs* 38 (4): 9–33.

Thoraval, Joël. 1989. LIANG Shu Ming: Qu'était devenu le 'dernier Confucéen' sous le régime communiste? *Bulletin de Sinologie* 52: 22–26 and 53: 22–29.

Tseng, Chao-lun. 1946. The Chinese Democratic League. *Current History* 11 (59): 31–37.

Van Slyke, Lyman P. 1959. LIANG Sou-ming and the Rural Reconstruction Movement. *The Journal of Asian Studies* 18 (4): 457–474.

———. 1967. *Enemies and Friends: The United Front in Chinese Communist History*. Stanford: Stanford University Press.

Vandermeersch, Léon. 1991. Le nouveau confucianisme. *Le Débat* 66: 5–15.

———. 2000. Préface. In *Les cultures d'Orient et d'Occident et leurs philosophies*. Ed. LIANG Shuming. Trans. LUO Shenyi. Paris: Presses Universitaires de France.

Webb, Adam K. 2008. The Countermodern Moment: A World-Historical Perspective on the Thought of Rabindranath Tagore, Muhammad Iqbal, and LIANG Shuming. *Journal of World History* 19 (2): 189–212.

Wei, Siqi 魏思齊 [Zbigniew Wesołowski]. 2003. *LIANG Shuming's (1893–1988) Conception of Culture: An Explanation Based on* Eastern and Western Cultures and Their Philosophies *and* Fundamentals of Chinese Culture 梁漱溟(1893–1988)的文化觀:根據《東西文化及其哲學》與《中國文化要義》解說. Xinzhuang: Fu Jen Catholic University Press.

Wesołowski, Zbigniew. 1996. LIANG Shumings (1893–1988) Religionsbegriff. In *'Fallbeispiel' China – Ökumenische Beiträge zu Religion, Theologie und Kirche im chinesischen Kontext*, ed. Roman Malek. Steyler Verlag: Nettetal.

———. 1997. *Lebens und Kulturbegriff von LIANG Shuming (1893–1988): dargestellt anhand seines Werkes "Dong-Xi wenhua ji qi zhexue."* Sankt Augustin: Institut Monumenta Serica.

———. 2005. Understanding the Foreign (the West) as a Remedy for Regaining One's Own Cultural Identity (China): LIANG Shuming's (1893–1988) Cultural Thought. *Monumenta Serica* 53: 361–399.

Xu, Zhangrun. 2017. *The Confucian Misgivings: LIANG Shu-ming's Narrative About Law*. Singapore: Springer.

Zhang, Huajun. 2013a. Individuality Beyond the Dichotomy of 'Small Self and Big Self' in Contemporary Chinese Education: Lessons from HU Shi and LIANG Shuming. *Frontiers of Education in China* 8 (4): 540–558.

———. 2013b. *John Dewey, LIANG Shuming, and China's Education Reform: Cultivating Individuality*. Lanham: Lexington Books.

———. 2015. A Vision for One's Own Life: Lessons from HU Shi and LIANG Shuming on Education in China. In *Re-envisioning Chinese Education: The Meaning of Person-Making in a New Age*, ed. Zhao Guoping and Zongyi Deng. New York: Routledge.

Index

T. Meynard, P. Major (eds.), *Dao Companion to Liang Shuming's Philosophy*, Dao Companions to Chinese Philosophy 17,
https://doi.org/10.1007/978-3-031-18002-6

M